JOSEPH M. GOEDERTIER, C.I.C.M., M.A.
(Columbia), is a scholar of long standing
in both Chinese and Japanese studies. A
native of Belgium, he began his career as
both scholar and missionary in the Orient
with a long period of residence in China.
For almost eighteen years now, he has lived
in Japan, where he is a Research Fellow of
the Oriens Institute for Religious Research, Tokyo, under whose auspices the
dictionary was compiled. The Oriens Institute is affiliated with the Immaculate
Heart of Mary Mission Society (C.I.C.M.),
with headquarters in Brussels. Father
Goedertier's published work includes
three volumes in Dutch on the cultural
history of Japan, Dutch translations of
Chinese fiction, and a Japanese-English
exposition of the Catholic catechism.

A DICTIONARY OF JAPANESE HISTORY

A DICTIONARY OF
JAPANESE HISTORY

JOSEPH M. GOEDERTIER, C.I.C.M.
Research Fellow, Oriens Institute for Religious Research, Tokyo

WALKER/WEATHERHILL
New York & Tokyo

This dictionary was compiled under the auspices of the ORIENS INSTITUTE FOR RELIGIOUS RESEARCH, 2-28-5 Matsubara, Setagaya-ku, Tokyo. The institute is dedicated to the scientific study of those factors that influence Japan's meeting with Christianity and operates under the Japan Province of the Immaculate Heart of Mary Mission Society.

FIRST EDITION, MAY, 1968

LCC CARD No. 68-15703

TABLE OF CONTENTS

PREFACE   7

A DICTIONARY OF JAPANESE HISTORY   11

APPENDIX 1. PRE-MEIJI PROVINCES AND MODERN
            PREFECTURES   318
APPENDIX 2. JAPANESE ERA NAMES AND DATES   319
SUBJECT INDEX   325
CHARACTER INDEX   371

9-12-68

PREFACE

This book is the first in a series of three volumes designed both for Western students of Japanese civilization and for general readers of Japanese literature. In a total of more than 1,100 entries, this first volume offers concise explanations of such subjects as significant political events, major wars and battles, important feudal clans, features of government and social structure, styles of architecture and painting, outstanding works of literature, and major religious and social developments. The range is from prehistoric to modern times. The two other volumes, now in preparation, cover the fields of biography and geography, and for this reason only a few personal and place names appear as entries in the present volume.

For purposes of conciseness, this work follows the selection of entries made for *Nihonshi Shōjiten,* a historical dictionary compiled under the supervision of Dr. Atsushi Kobata, of Kyoto University, and published by the Fukuinkan Shoten, Tokyo, 1957. Dr. Kobata is recognized as one of the most outstanding authorities on Japanese history, and his guiding principle in the compilation of *Nihonshi Shōjiten* was to provide a basic knowledge of historical facts in concise form: the knowledge, in a word, that an educated Japanese is likely to require. The selection of entries for *Nihonshi Shōjiten* therefore represents the historical facts commonly treated in authorized textbooks for higher education in Japan.

In addition to *Nihonshi Shōjiten,* the Japanese sources used for the present work include the following: the one-volume *Nihonshi Jiten,* compiled and published in 1962 by the National History Research Seminar, Department of Literature, Kyoto University; the revised and enlarged edition of *Daijiten,* published in thirteen volumes by Heibonsha, Tokyo, 1954; *Dai Nihon Jimmei Jisho,* compiled and published in five volumes by the Dai Nihon Jimmei Jisho Kankō-kai, Tokyo, 1951–52; and other works. Western sources which have been consulted include G. B. Sansom's three-volume work, *A History of Japan;* Edwin O. Reischauer and John K. Fairbank's *East Asia: The Great Tradition;* and John K. Fairbank, Edwin O. Reischauer, and Albert M. Craig's *East Asia: The Modern Transformation.* Again, for purposes of conciseness, no reference to the foregoing sources or to primary Japanese sources is made in the dictionary entries. Primary Japanese sources, however, can easily be found in the above-mentioned *Nihonshi Jiten.*

A few notes on typographical arrangements will assist the reader in making efficient use of the dictionary. The Hepburn system is used throughout for the transliteration of Japanese terms; modifications of the Wade-Giles and the McCune-Reischauer systems are used for Chinese and Korean terms respectively. All Japanese, Chinese, and Korean personal names are given in the order of surname first, given name last. The entries are in dictionary order— that is, strictly according to the English alphabet, irrespective of the number of words involved—and appear in boldface type, followed by their Japanese writings. Small capitals are used in the text to indicate cross references—that is, terms which are in themselves entries. If a cross-referenced term appears more than once in any given entry, however, it is in small capitals on its first appearance only. Japanese characters for terms other than main entries will be found in the Subject Index. The Character Index lists all important terms in the dictionary by their *kanji* (Japanese characters).

Two appendices are provided, one giving the pre-Meiji provinces with the corresponding modern prefectures and the other giving the names of Japanese emperors and eras with their corresponding dates according to the Western calendar.

I am much indebted to my confrere, Father Francis Uyttendaele, who generously helped me in the compilation of the indexes.

JOSEPH M. GOEDERTIER

A DICTIONARY OF JAPANESE HISTORY

A

agata-nushi 県主 (the estate master). The name of a local official of the pre-Taika period. The *agata-nushi* was an estate master, and his rank was only one degree below that of the provincial magnate known as KUNI NO MIYATSUKO. The heads of the powerful clans of the various territories were appointed *agata-nushi*, and this post was often transmitted by inheritance. The *agata-nushi* had various titles or KABANE, such as *kimi*, MURAJI (leader of a group), *atae*, OBITO, and others. *Obito* was the title most frequently used. The office of *agata-nushi* was abolished after the Taika Reform.

agemai 上米 (rice tax). One of the financial policies introduced in 1722 by Shōgun Yoshimune (1684–1751) of the Tokugawa government. Every daimyō had to contribute one hundred *koku* (one *koku* equals 4.96 bushels) per 10,000 *koku* of rice harvested or the equivalent in money. In return, the period of the daimyō's alternate attendance (SANKIN KŌTAI) at the shōgun's court was shortened by six months. By collecting this tax, the government was able to pay the salaries of the retainers and the direct vassals of the shōgun. The daimyō were satisfied because the reduction of the period of attendance meant a substantial saving. However, as the alternate attendance of the important daimyō at the shōgun's court was an old law aimed at maintaining the court's prestige, the *agemai* was abolished in 1731.

Agura-nabe 安愚楽鍋. The name of a literary work of the early Meiji era. The work was written in 1871 by the humorist Kanagaki Robun (1828–92). *Agura-nabe* 趺坐鍋 means "sukiyaki." The work belongs to the class of light literature; in it the author satirized the new civilization as reflected in various aspects of life.

Aikoku Kōtō 愛国公党 (the Patriotic Public Party). First political association of the Meiji era. Four cabinet members presented a memorial to the government and asked for the establishment of a parliamentary government. The councilors were among those who had retired from public service following the parliamentary decision not to wage war with Korea in 1873. The four were Itagaki Taisuke, Gotō Shōjirō, Etō Shimpei, and Soejima Taneomi. They were joined by Yuri Kimimasa and others and organized this political association to stimulate public opinion. The association was first called Kō-fuku-anzen-sha, and in January 1874 it made a start under the name Aikoku Kōtō. However, it failed to develop sufficient political strength and was consequently dissolved. This party was different from the Old Liberal Party, which was established by Itagaki Taisuke in the middle of the Meiji era.

Aikoku-sha 愛国社 (the Patriotic Association). A political association of the early Meiji era. In 1875, followers of the AIKOKU KŌTŌ party held a convention in Ōsaka and, centering around the RISSHI-SHA (a private school organized by Itagaki Taisuke for the purpose of teaching democratic principles), organized a political society aimed at the actualization of a constitutional parliamentary government. Because the leader of the movement, Itagaki Taisuke, joined the government as minister of public works, the movement was temporarily dissolved. In 1878, a revival of the movement was planned, and the following year Kōno Hironaka, of the northeastern provinces, joined the movement, now spreading on a national scale. In 1880, two metropolises, twenty-two prefectures, and 87,000 petitioners participated in the Ōsaka convention, and a committee for the introduction of a parliamentary system was formed. The Aikoku-sha was absorbed into this new organization. The movement for democratic rights aimed at the establishment of a national assembly. It had popular support and succeeded in bringing about the issuing of an imperial edict (1881) which announced the inauguration of a national assembly (Diet).

Aka-Ezo Fūsetsu-kō 赤蝦夷風説考 (Report on Kamchatka). A book in two volumes written by Kudō Heisuke (1734–1800) and printed in 1783. It was a forerunner in its field, as it proposed an open-door policy for the country and the development of Hokkaidō. "Aka-Ezo" means Kamchatka. The book describes the circumstances that led to the contact of the Japanese with the Russians in the Kurile Islands and Karafuto as a result of Russian expansionism toward the south. It explains the necessity of developing Ezo—that is, Hokkaidō. Upon the publication of this book, the government conducted a survey of Ezo and Karafuto. The book was followed by the publication of Hayashi Shihei's (1738–93) treatise on coastal defense and Honda Toshiaki's (1744–1821) treatise concerning the opening of the country.

amimoto-amiko 網本・網子. Term indicating the feudal relationship between the head of a fishing industry and those who worked under him. The *amimoto* was the owner of the nets; the *amiko* were his workers. This relationship was similar to the one that existed between the landowner and his laborers. The *amimoto* provided the *amiko* with a building lot, a field, and even food, but the whole catch of fish was his. When the system gradually declined, it was generally determined that the *amimoto* would acquire about one-third of the total haul. With the development of the fishing industry, *amiko* had to be invited from faraway areas, and a contract-employment system was used.

Ankoku-ji 安国寺 (Ankoku-ji temples). Zen temples built all over the country by Ashikaga Takauji (1305–58). On the recommendation of the Buddhist priest Musō Soseki (1275–1351), Takauji began in 1339 to build a temple

(Ankoku-ji) and a pagoda (Rishōtō) to commemorate those killed in action during the destruction of the Kamakura shogunate.

Anna no hen 安和の変 (the civil strife of the Anna era). A political change that occurred in 969 (second year of the Anna era), during the middle Heian period. With the accession to the throne of Emperor Reizei (950–1011), Fujiwara no Saneyori (900–970), the chief adviser to the emperor, overthrew Minamoto no Takaakira (914–82), who was in power politically. As a result of this strife, the Fujiwara family swept away all political opposition, and members of this family exclusively held the positions of regent (SESSHŌ) and of chief adviser to the emperor (KAMPAKU).

Ansei no kari-jōyaku 安政の仮条約 (the provisional treaties of the Ansei era). Provisional commercial treaties concluded in 1858 with the United States and European countries. The treaties were concluded without imperial sanction by Ii Naosuke (1815–60), the chief minister of the shōgun. The first treaty was concluded with the United States, but similar treaties with Holland, Russia, England, and France followed. Many points, such as the granting of extraterritorial rights to foreigners and the lack of Japanese tariff autonomy, were disadvantageous to Japan. Amendment of the provisional treaties was an important diplomatic issue throughout the Meiji period.

Ansei no taigoku 安政の大獄 (mass imprisonment during the Ansei era). The great oppression of the antiforeign party in 1858 by Ii Naosuke (1815–60), the chief minister of the shōgun. Two important pending problems—the conclusion of commercial treaties with the United States and the succession to the shogunate—were tentatively solved by Ii, who, on his own authority, concluded the treaties with the United States and decided to make Tokugawa Yoshitomi of Kii successor to the shogunate. The loyalists and antiforeigners (their movement is known as *sonnō-jōi*) were violently opposed to these decisions, and the Mito clan received an imperial secret order to revamp the shogunate. Ii took drastic steps. He confined the court nobles and the feudal lords and arrested the loyalists, whom he punished by death and imprisonment. These measures inflamed the anger of the loyalists, who assassinated Ii at the Sakurada-mon in 1860.

Anzan seitetsu-jo 鞍山製鉄所 (the Anshan iron factory). Industrial establishment in South Manchuria during the Taishō and Shōwa eras. Before and after World War I, Japanese industry made great strides, and investments in iron and steel were made in Korea and Manchuria. The Manchurian Railroad Company secured the iron mines of Anshan in South Manchuria and, in 1918, established an iron foundry. When Manchurian business developed, Anshan, together with Fushun, became the center of the special interests of South Manchurian heavy industry.

Araragi-ha アララギ派 (the Araragi school). A modern school of *tanka* poetry. Itō Sachio (1864–1913) and other poets, who joined the school of the poet Masaoka Shiki (1867–1902), launched the poetry magazine *Araragi*. The school, which stresses realism in the Man'yō style, is named after the magazine. The school still exists.

Arimatsu-shibori 有松絞 (Arimatsu cloth). White-spotted cotton cloth manufactured in the neighborhood of Arimatsu, Aichi Prefecture. It is believed that it was first produced during the Keichō era (1596–1615) and that its production was protected and encouraged by the law of Owari. Arimatsu was a teahouse stop on the Tōkaidō highway, and the neighboring Narumi was a relay station. The production of Arimatsu-shibori was restricted to these two localities, and the cloth was sold to travelers. The raw material was cotton from Chita Peninsula (Aichi Prefecture) which was dyed in a sober color. As a subsidiary industry, it was much appreciated by the people of the neighboring villages and towns. However, the privilege of the two localities was abolished after the Meiji Restoration, and Nagoya's industry is now more prominent in the field.

Arita-yaki 有田焼 (Arita pottery). Ceramic ware produced in the neighborhood of the town of Arita in Saga Prefecture. The manufacture of this pottery started as early as 1598 (the year after the second Korean expedition), when the Korean ceramist Yi Sam-p'yong (in Japanese, Ri Sam-pei) was brought to Japan by Nabeshima Naoshige (1538–1618), the lord of Saga. Ri Sam-pei discovered a potter's clay of superior quality (quartz trachyte) not far from Arita. The manufacturing of this ceramic ware became centered around this place but spread to other localities as well. Arita-yaki is also called Imari-yaki, because it was exported from the port of Imari.

ashigaru 足軽 (light foot soldiers). The light foot soldier originated in the Kamakura period. In the fourteenth and fifteenth centuries, when greater battles were fought, the *ashigaru* became active, and during the Ōnin Civil War (ŌNIN NO RAN) even outlaws joined them. They were valued during the civil wars, when the daimyō organized them in groups. During the Edo period, they formed the lowest grade of soldiers. After the introduction of the rifle, the foot soldiers carried firearms and played an important role on the battlefield. They took a decisive part in the Nagashino battle (in Aichi Prefecture), when Nobunaga crushed Takeda Katsuyori (1546–82). Foot soldiers were called *zōhyō,* and in peacetime they rendered sundry services.

Ashikaga Gakkō 足利学校 (Ashikaga College). A school founded during the Kamakura period and established in Ashikaga, Shimotsuke Province (Tochigi Prefecture). After a period of decline, the school grew in importance after it was restored in 1439 by the warrior Uesugi Norizane (?–1466). During the

Sengoku era, or the period of civil war (from the close of the fifteenth to the close of the sixteenth century), the school was patronized by the Hōjō family and gathered a large number of students from various parts of the country. By 1550, this number was about three thousand. It was the only center of Chinese classical learning in the Kantō district. The college was closed after the Meiji Restoration.

Ashikaga uji 足利氏 (the Ashikaga clan). A family of shōguns of the Ashikaga shogunate. Descendants of Minamoto no Yoshiie (1039–1106), they lived in Shimotsuke Province (Tochigi Prefecture). The Nitta belonged to the same family, and from the Kamakura period on, they were the influential direct retainers of the shōgun. An Ashikaga became shōgun at the time of Takauji (1305–58), and the clan inaugurated the Muromachi shogunate, reaching the zenith of its power under the rule of the third shōgun, Yoshimitsu (1358–1408). Powerful branches of the family were the Hosokawa, the Shiba, the Hatakeyama, and the Imagawa. However, the increase in power of the military provincial governors and the deterioration of the manor system led to the weakening of the shōgun's authority. Yoshinori (1394–1441) was able to temporarily check the usurpation of authority, but the rule of the eighth shōgun, Yoshimasa (1435–90), witnessed the Ōnin revolt (ŌNIN NO RAN), which developed into a civil war, and the shōgun's power all but vanished. In 1573, when Yoshiaki (1537–97) was banished by Nobunaga, the Muromachi shogunate, which had given the country fifteen shōguns, came to an end.

Ashio dōzan 足尾銅山 (the Ashio copper mine). A copper mine in Ashio, Tochigi Prefecture. The mine dates from the Edo period. It is believed to have been discovered in 1609. In 1647, it was put under the control of the BAKUFU. It flourished particularly between the years 1684 and 1688, when yearly production exceeded 1,500 tons. Its copper made up a major part of Nagasaki exports. However, from about 1736, production decreased and the government gave up controlling the mine. In 1876, it became the possession of the mining industrialist Furukawa Ichibei (1832–1903). Financed by the Shibusawa concern, Furukawa enlarged the mine, perfected the equipment, and made the Ashio copper mine into one of the greatest copper mines of the country.

Asuka Kiyomigahara Ryō 飛鳥浄御原令 (the Temmu Code). Laws and ordinances compiled in twenty-two volumes by the Temmu court and promulgated in 689. They were also called Temmu Ryō and were an addition and correction of the Ōmi Code (ŌMI RYŌ). They formed the substance of the Taihō Code (TAIHŌ RITSURYŌ), which was promulgated in 702.

ayabito 漢人. In ancient times, *ayabito* was the general name of the Chinese and their descendants who had become naturalized Japanese. After the destruction of the Chinese colony Lo-lang (in Korean, Nangnang; in Japanese, Rakurō) in North Korea (near P'yongyang), many Chinese became natural- ized nationals of Kudara (in Korean, Paekche) and Kōkuri (in Korean, Ko- guryo), and some became naturalized Japanese. Distinguished among them are Wani, Achiki, and Achi no Omi, who lived in the fourth century during the reign of Emperor Ōjin. The descendants of Achi no Omi were called *Yamato no aya uji* and also *Yamato no fubito-be* (YAMATO NO AYA NO ATAE); those of Wani were called KAWACHI NO AYA UJI and also *Kawachi no fubito-be*. The advanced techniques of the *ayabito* played an important role in the de- velopment of handicrafts, and their literary ability and talent for writing chronicles were equally important to administrative affairs in ancient Japan. According to the chronicle *Shinsen Shōji-roku*, written in 815, 324 naturalized families lived in the central provinces. Among these families, 162 were of Chinese origin.

Azuchi 安土. The castle town of Oda Nobunaga situated in Ōmi Province (Shiga Prefecture). In 1576, Nobunaga moved from Gifu to Azuchi and made Azuchi his stronghold. Here he favored freedom of trade and of guild organiza- tion (RAKUICHI-RAKUZA) and abolished all forms of monopoly. Here also he permitted the building of a Christian church and seminary. The castle, Azu- chi-jō, was completed in 1579. It was the first to have a castle tower, and, though it was built on a hill, it greatly differed from the traditional mountain type. This gorgeous stronghold also included mansions for the daimyō. The walls of every castle room were decorated by the imaginative brush of Kanō Eitoku (1543–90), and the castle itself first introduced the Azuchi-Momoyama style of art.

Azuchi-Momoyama bunka 安土桃山文化 (Azuchi-Momoyama culture). A cultural period which lasted about half a century (1573–1614) and which was centered around Nobunaga's Azuchi Castle and Hideyoshi's Momoyama Castle. The age of Nobunaga and Hideyoshi is commonly called the Azuchi- Momoyama period, after their respective headquarters. The period reflected the taste of the warlords and wealthy merchants. In the cultural field, the period was one of splendor and magnificence and found expression in the architecture of the Azuchi and Momoyama castles as well as in their gor- geous wall paintings done by such masters as Kanō Eitoku (1543–90) and Kanō Sanraku (1559–1635). Buddhist art was declining, and profane art con- cerned with human life flourished. The traditional rigid tea ceremony was now conducted with more freedom. Not only the court nobles but also the common people and the merchants took part in the great tea parties at Kitano. Popularization of culture was also expressed in the KABUKI (viz., the OKUNI KABUKI, a sort of Kabuki in which the female dancers of IZUMO TAISHA performed the *nembutsu* dance in Kyōto; the origin of today's Kabuki), JŌRURI (a kind of ballad-drama), and RYŪTATSU-BUSHI (a sort of ballad originated by the Nichiren priest Ryūtatsu which formed the origin of the Tokugawa ballad). All these forms of art were intimately connected with the life of the merchants and were very popular. Consequently, this period exerted a profound cultural influence.

Overseas culture was absorbed as a result of the trade of the red-seal ships (SHUIN-SEN), of the introduction of *namban* ("southern barbarian") culture, and of the Korean expeditions during the Bunroku-Keichō eras (in 1592 and 1597). New foreign elements therefore appeared in the Azuchi-Momoyama culture, particularly in art and architecture.

azukari-dokoro 預所. An office set up by manor lords in order to enable them to directly control their feudal domains. At the close of the Heian period, some private warriors had seized land rights, the actual owners being unable to control or administer their manors. Therefore, these owners established the *azukari-dokoro*. The *azukari-dokoro* had no relation to the men attached to the manor but was organized by the right-hand men of the feudal lord and was especially concerned with the levying of land taxes. However, the organization declined during the Kamakura period, when the stewards (JITŌ) controlled immense estates. By the end of this period, powerful stewards took over the rights of the *azukari-dokoro* and used the privileges of the manor lords for their own purposes.

Azuma Kagami 吾妻鏡. A chronicle in fifty-two volumes, which describes the events of the Kamakura period. The historical facts from 1180 to 1266 are chronologically described and are mainly based on the official records of the Kamakura shogunate. The style is Chinese but has a Japanese flavor. The work was written during the latter half of the Kamakura period. Social life of the warriors is vividly depicted, and, as far as the society of the Kamakura warriors is concerned, the book offers valuable historical material. Tokugawa Ieyasu admired the book because it dealt with the shogunate, and for this reason he had it published.

B

bakufu 幕府 (military government). Military government under a shōgun. In 1192, Minamoto no Yoritomo (1148–99) was appointed "barbarian-subduing generalissimo" *(seii-taishōgun)* and established the KAMAKURA BAKUFU. In 1338, Ashikaga Takauji (1305–58), who was named to the office of generalissimo, inaugurated the MUROMACHI BAKUFU at Kyōto. In 1603, Tokugawa Ieyasu (1542–1616), being appointed generalissimo, inaugurated the EDO BAKUFU, which lasted until the Meiji Restoration.

bakuhan taisei 幕藩体制 (structure of the EDO BAKUFU). Economic structure of the Edo government based on the principle that the military government itself was the greatest daimyō and that it directly controlled the land of the whole country. The revenue of Japan was estimated at about twenty million *koku* (one *koku* equals 4.96 bushels). Seven million *koku* belonged to the shō-gun. Three million *koku* were the revenue from the estates of the direct feudatories of the shōgun. The remainder belonged to the 260 daimyō whose feudal domains were granted to them by a shogunate license.

bansha no goku 蕃社の獄 (oppression of scholars of Dutch learning). Op-pressive measures against the scholars of Dutch (Western) learning (1839). Already in 1830 Watanabe Kazan (1793–1841), Takano Chōei (1804–50), and Ozeki San'ei (1788–1840) had organized a study group for Dutch learn-ing called SHŌSHI-KAI. Learning about the government's intention to enforce the expulsion edict against the American vessel *Morrison,* which was expected to arrive snortly, Watanabe and his friends were much disturbed. Watanabe wrote *Shinki-ron,* and Chōei published his pamphlet *Yume Monogatari.* Both advocated Western learning and criticized the shogunate's exclusion policy. They supposed that the authorities had mistaken the name of an English missionary in China, Dr. Morrison, for the name of a ship and warned the BAKUFU against its antiforeign policy. But the magistrate Torii Yōzō, who hated the scholars of Dutch learning, accused them of being in communica-tion with the Westerners and of plotting the exploitation of Ogasawara (the Bōnin Islands) for the purpose of making a base of operations against the government. Watanabe and Ozeki committed suicide, and Takano was con-demned to life imprisonment.

Bansho Torishirabesho 蕃書取調所 (Office for the Study of Barbarian Writings). A research institute or school for Western sciences established in 1856 by the shogunate in Edo. The office was first called Yōgakusho but changed its name when it was organized in 1856. The study of the Dutch language was of prime importance, but courses in other languages were sub-sequently added. In the early stages, only the shōgun's retainers were ad-mitted to the school, but from 1861, clansmen were also admitted. In 1862, the school was transferred to Hitotsubashi and was called Yōsho Shirabesho. In 1863, the name was changed to KAISEIJO, and admittance was no longer restricted. Bansho Torishirabesho was the forerunner of Tōkyō University.

bantō 番頭. 1) Kamakura and Muromachi periods. A considerable number of influential farmers, especially in the Kinki district, were called *bantō.* They were village headmen. Some village headmen of the Edo period were also called *bantō.* 2) Edo period. Merchant employees who succeeded in securing social position after having been apprentices and substitute merchants were called *bantō.* They were invested with authority in their master's house.

bashaku 馬借 (teamsters). The traffic workers, especially in the Kinki district, during the Kamakura and Muromachi periods. The *bashaku* were powerful between Sakamoto and Ōtsu in Ōmi Province (Shiga Prefecture) and in Kizu in Yamashiro Province (Kyōto Prefecture). They held a monopoly over the transportation of merchandise. They were so influential that, in 1428, they requested from the government a general cancellation of peasant debts and lighted the fuse which set ablaze the first large-scale agrarian uprising in the whole Kinki territory. This uprising is referred to as the uprising of the *bashaku (bashaku-ikki)*. (See also DO-IKKI.)

be 部 (guilds). Pre-Taika guilds hereditarily attached to clans. Various tasks and duties were imposed upon the guilds. The members of the guilds, or "guild people" *(be no tami)*, were directly engaged in agricultural and industrial work. There were three classes of guilds according to the three classes of clans to which they belonged. Some guilds were under the direct control of the court. To these belonged guilds with a special occupation, such as the guild of court ritualists *(nakatomi-be)*, the guild of scribes *(fubito-be)*, the guild of mirror-makers *(kagami-tsukuri-be)*, the guild of military men *(saeki-be)*, the guilds engaged in compulsory agricultural service, such as the namesake guild (MINA-SHIRO, established by emperors or court nobles in the name of a princess or a deceased member of the family, but actually to increase their own wealth), and the succession guild (MIKOSHIRO, established by an emperor to perpetuate his memory or to leave something to posterity). The rice-field guilds of farm laborers *(ta-be)* also belonged to this group. Other guilds were privately owned by powerful families and were given a clan name, such as Ōtomo-be, Soga-be, etc. And still other guilds, though engaged in the direct service of the court, were controlled by powerful clans.

The first of these three categories clearly illustrates the origin and meaning of the guilds. After the Taika Reform the whole system was abolished, but part of the guilds directly engaged in court service remained, and it was included in the new penal and administrative code. This part included the TOMO-BE and the *zakko,* or corporations engaged in making industrial products and artifacts, and now belonged to government departments.

Besshi dōzan 別子銅山 (the Besshi copper mine). A copper mine in Ehime Prefecture operated from 1691. This mine is where the wealth of the Sumitomo concern originated. It was discovered in 1690 by Izumiya (SUMITOMO), a copper dealer of Ōsaka, who opened it the following year. Production rights in perpetuity were granted by the shogunate, and the mine was recognized as an official copper mine. The name "Besshi" was adopted in 1749, when the Tachikawa copper mine on the northern side of Izumiya's mine joined it. The mine flourished during the Meiji period, when Western techniques and equipment were introduced. As a result, the port of Niihama at the foot of the hill developed rapidly.

biwa hōshi 琵琶法師. Buddhist priests who, during the middle ages (Kamakura and Muromachi periods), recited stories while playing the lute. These minstrels composed many songs based on the HEIKE MONOGATARI and sang these historical sagas to the accompaniment of the lute. During the Muromachi period, the songs were called *heikyoku* and *Heike biwa* and were popular among the warriors as well as among the common people.

bōko 房戸 (a unit of families). The family system in ancient Japan according to which one to three single families formed one unit. Only single families were registered, and officially the *bōko* was not well defined, but some believe that at the end of the Nara period, when the group system of villages collapsed, the *bōko* became the social unit. However, another view holds that the *bōko* were gradually absorbed by the village groups.

Bon odori 盆踊 (the Bon festival dance). Dances performed yearly from the thirteenth to the sixteenth of July around the festival time called *urabon*. There are various theories about the dance's origin, but records show that it dates from the beginning of the Muromachi period.

Boshin Sen'eki 戊辰戦役 (the Boshin Civil War). Armed conflict in 1868 between shogunate supporters and loyalists. The conflict is named after the cyclic characters for that year, Boshin. It began with the battle of Toba-Fushimi and was followed by a battle east of Edo fought by Tokugawa Yoshinobu (1827–1913), a battle of the shogunate fighting squad SHŌGITAI, a battle against the Aizu clan in Fukushima Prefecture, and finally the battle of Hakodate in May 1869. The fall of Hakodate is not included in the Boshin conflict.

Buke Sho-Hatto 武家諸法度 (Laws for the Military Houses). Laws promulgated for the warriors and the daimyō by the Edo shogunate. Originally, they were the Genna Ryō (laws of the Genna era) or laws in thirteen articles promulgated in 1615 by the second shōgun, Hidetada (1579–1632), but these were followed by additional enactments by each new shōgun. The content changed according to the circumstances, but it never differed greatly from that of the original laws of the Genna era. They all dealt with the conduct of the military class and the daimyō, the maintenance of peace and order in the feudal domains, the residential castles, marriage, and alternate attendance, and they were aimed at controlling warriors and daimyō. Up to the time of Shōgun Iemitsu (1604–51), many daimyō violated the law and were punished.

buke-zukuri 武家造 (style of dwellings of warriors). The style of the houses of the Muromachi and, more particularly, the Kamakura warriors. It was a simplification and adaptation of the style called SHINDEN-ZUKURI that was characteristic of the mansions of court nobles in ancient times. The building site was surrounded by a moat and an enclosure, the house being suggestive of a castle. In the center was the main structure, the *omoya*. There were also the donjon *(yagura)*, the watchmen's lodge *(tōzamurai)*, the stables *(umaya)*, and other installations required by a samurai. In Muromachi days, a taste for Zen simplicity became prominent, and the military developed a new style of living apartments referred to as SHOIN-ZUKURI.

bummei kaika 文明開化 (Western civilization). Introduction of Western civilization in the early Meiji period. Most intellectuals of the day were awake to the fact that life had to be emancipated from the fetters of feudalism, that the formation of individual character was all-important, that people had to associate as equals, and that general social conditions had to be improved. The nation as a whole, however, made more of imported articles and of daily necessities. Accordingly, Western dress and social customs were introduced. A song of the day went: "If you knock on a cropped head, you hear the sound of civilization" (*Zangiri atama o tataite mireba, bummei kaika no oto ga suru*). The rickshaw and sukiyaki made their appearance. The post office, omnibus, train, steamer, the cutting off of topknots, abolition of sword wearing, the prohibition of tattooing, the solar calendar, photography, Western dress, brick buildings, the lamp, exhibitions or fairs—all were well received. The sudden modernization of the country is explained by the fact that the Meiji government wanted to follow the path of the great powers of Europe and of the United States. It also wanted to revise the unequal treaties and increase its wealth and military power.

Bummeiron no Gairyaku 文明論の概略. A book written by the founder of Keiō University, Fukuzawa Yukichi (1834–1901), and published in 1875. The author insists upon freedom and independence for the modern citizen and upon a liberal standard of politics based on harmony between the government and the people.

bunchi-seigen rei 分地制限令 (law on limitation of parceled land). A law of the Edo shogunate limiting the parceling of the farmer's lot. In 1673, the law prescribed that a village headman with an income of less than twenty *koku* (one *koku* equals 4.96 bushels) and an ordinary farmer with an income of less than ten *koku* were not allowed to parcel their lots. In 1713, the law prescribed that the allotted plot as well as the parceled one should be large enough to yield at least ten *koku* and that the plot should cover an area of at least one *chō* (2.45 acres). The law was intended to prevent the impoverishment of the farmers resulting from an endless parceling of tracts of land.

Bungakukai 文学界. A literary magazine of the Meiji period. Launched in 1893 by Kitamura Tōkoku (1868–94), it flourished under Shimazaki Tōson (1872–1943), Hirata Tokuboku (1873–1943), Baba Kochō (1869–1940), and others. Contributions were also made by Tayama Katai (1871–1930) and Higuchi Ichiyō (1872–96). In 1898, publication of the magazine was discontinued.

Bungei Kyōkai 文芸協会. A group of dramatists established in 1906 by Shimamura Hōgetsu (1871–1918), with Ōkuma Shigenobu (1838–1922) as chairman and Tsubouchi Shōyō (1859–1935) as adviser. The group performed dramas of Shakespeare. Upon the withdrawal in 1913 of Hōgetsu and Matsui Sumako (1886–1919), the Bungei Kyōkai was dissolved.

Bunka-Bunsei jidai 文化·文政時代 (Bunka-Bunsei period). Forty years of rule of the eleventh shōgun, Tokugawa Ienari (1773–1841), at the beginning of the nineteenth century. Taking advantage of Matsudaira Sadanobu's (1758–1829) Kansei Reform (KANSEI NO KAIKAKU), the shōgun inaugurated what is styled "the overmature period of the Edo culture." Ienari himself lived in extravagance, and the warriors and merchants sought only pleasure. The nation was called a paradise. This period also witnessed the rooting of the national market in the production of commodities by rural communities. This production constituted the economic foundation of the Tempō era (1830–43) and of the transition period at the close of the feudal age.

Bunka Shūreishū 文華秀麗集. Anthology of poetry written in Chinese and published in three volumes in 818. On the order of Emperor Saga (786–842), the compilation was made by Fujiwara no Fuyutsugu (775–826) and others. Along with the anthology KEIKOKUSHŪ (published in 827), it is a representative work of the Chinese literature which flourished at that time.

bunkoku 分国 (domains of warriors). The term for the provinces which were the domains of daimyō during the Sengoku period—that is, during the period of civil war from the close of the fifteenth to the close of the sixteenth century. As a result of the Ōnin Civil War (ŌNIN NO RAN), most constables (SHUGO) lost their power. Some who were still living in the Sengoku period and also new warriors who had been in the service of constables rejected the manor system and established firm authority over one or more provinces. Regional lords became autonomous, and their domains—one or more provinces—were called *bunkoku*. These lords promulgated their own strict laws known as BUNKOKU-HŌ, military autocracy being enforced. The daimyō of this period relied on the cooperation of the villages, whose autonomy they partially recognized. Strengthening the partnership system of the villages, they also fortified the rural spirit of solidarity. This was the origin of the Edo rural administrative system. The retainers of the daimyō not only were given a share in the domain but also were enfeoffed by the lord of the whole domain. The administration of a *bunkoku* had a strong individual character and differed in various provinces according to the way of living, the different currency, and the different weights and measures. Along with the development of trade and the expansion of the financial sphere, Nobunaga and Hideyoshi established their political power. A uniform national economy which was the foundation of the Edo feudal system came into being.

bunkoku-hō 分国法 (the laws of the warriors' domains). Administrative laws within the domains of the daimyō during the Sengoku period, or the period of civil war from the close of the fifteenth to the close of the sixteenth century. They were also called "house laws" *(kahō)*. At the close of the middle ages (the end of the Muromachi period), the daimyō rejected the Muromachi regulations and enforced their own laws in their respective domains called BUNKOKU. The most famous of these laws were the Asakura Toshikage Jūshichi Kajō, the Imagawa-ke Kana-mokuroku, the Ōuchi-uji Hekisho, the Jinkai-shū of the Date clan, the Shingen Kahō of the Takeda clan, the Sōunji-dono Nijūichi Kajō of the Hōjō clan, the Chōsokabe Motochika Hyakkajō, the Yūki-ke Hatto, and the Yoshiharu Shikimoku of the Rokkaku clan. All these laws resembled the code of law known as the JŌEI SHIKIMOKU (promulgated in 1232) but were adapted to the circumstances of each *bunkoku*. The common feature of all these laws was a strict control of the corporation of vassals as well as of the farmers. In case of disputes or of implication in any affair on account of kinship *(enza)*, responsibility was collective. Independent inheritance of a domain as well as independent buying or selling of a domain was prohibited, and severe punishment was inflicted. Even everyday life was controlled.

Bunroku-Keichō no eki 文禄・慶長の役 (expeditions of the Bunroku-Keichō eras). Hideyoshi's expeditions to Korea in 1592 and 1597. Hideyoshi had destroyed the Hōjō clan and united the country. He then planned to subjugate Ming China and expected Korea to be instrumental in asking tribute from China. Korea, however, fearing the powerful Ming dynasty, refused to mediate. Hideyoshi then decided to conquer Korea and in 1592 (the first year of the Bunroku era) sent an amphibious force of 150,000 men to Korea. They reached P'yongyang, where they ran into Ming forces. Hideyoshi had to conclude peace and to withdraw his troops. This expedition is referred to as *Bunroku no eki*.

As the peace treaty of Ming China had used abusive language, Hideyoshi decided to send a second expedition to Korea in 1597 (second year of the Keichō era). But he died before the expedition could fulfill its mission, and, following his last injunctions, the expeditionary forces were withdrawn. This expedition is known as *Keichō no eki*.

The two expeditions ended with a great loss of men and materials. However, one result was good—the Japanese had brought home thousands of Korean artisans and scholars, and the arts of printing, dyeing, weaving, and ceramics were studied in a new light.

buntsuke 分付 (BUNZUKE)

bunzuke 分付 (dependent farmers). This is an abbreviation of *bunzuke hyaku-shō* and means "dependent farmers." During the Edo shogunate, two or three sons of a farmer, instead of independently establishing a family, could receive a small plot of land from the eldest son or from the master, in whose name they cultivated it. They could cultivate the plot, keeping a household of their own, but the land tax was collected by the head family or by the master, upon whom the employees were always highly dependent.

bushidan 武士団 (corporations of warriors). Corporations of warriors or military clan groups during the Kamakura and Muromachi periods. At the close of the Heian period, when the system of residential feudal lords developed, the warriors organized military groups throughout the country, the members of these groups belonging to the same clan. In the center of the group was the head (SŌRYŌ). The vassals of warriors (IE NO KO and RŌTŌ) were united on the basis of a master-servant relationship. During the Kamakura period, usually a direct vassal of the shōgun or a constable (JITŌ) headed the military corporation and assumed control over father and sons, brothers, nephews, and nieces. Then the master-servant relationship became the basis on which rested the unity of the corporation. In Muromachi times, the warriors' corporations strengthened the territorial community spirit in the frontier districts and the remote mountainous districts, relying on the clan god. These corporations were also called "one family" *(ichizoku)* and "a party" (TŌ).

bussan-kata 物産方 (KOKUSAN KAISHO)

Byōdō-in 平等院. A temple built during the Heian period by Fujiwara no Yorimichi (992–1074). The temple was located in Uji City, Kyōto Prefecture. Originally the building was the villa of Minamoto no Tōru (822–95) and later became the villa of Fujiwara no Michinaga (966–1027). In 1052, Yorimichi transformed it into a temple called Byōdō-in. When the Fujiwara clan reached the zenith of its power, the buildings were magnificent, but later they were laid waste by fires caused by warfare. Rebuilt, the new construction gradually deteriorated. Today, besides the Hōōdō (Phoenix Hall), only two or three buildings remain. One masterpiece of art is kept in the Hōōdō: a statue of Amida made in 1053 by Jōchō (?–1057), a representative sculptor of the Fujiwara period. The Byōdō-in was first a temple belonging to the Tendai sect of Buddhism. Today it belongs to both the Tendai and the Jōdo sects.

C

Cairo Sengen カイロ宣言 (the Cairo Declaration). An international declaration made during World War II. In November 1943, President Roosevelt of the United States, Generalissimo Chiang Kai-shek of China, and Prime Minister Churchill of England concluded an agreement in Cairo regarding Japanese aggression. To check Japanese aggression it was decided to strengthen the allied offensive. Japan would have to return the territories she annexed after World War I, and Korea must be free and independent. The decisions concerning Japan were reaffirmed in the Potsdam Declaration (POTSDAM SENGEN) and were the foundation of postwar Japan.

Cambodia (KAMBOJA)

cha-no-yu 茶の湯 (the tea cult). China adopted the tea-drinking habit in the T'ang age (618–906). Introduced into Japan during the Heian period, it fell into disuse. Eisai (1141–1215), of the Kamakura period, and other Zen priests imported tea from Sung China (960–1279). In the beginning, Zen temples and the nobility used it as a medicine, but it gradually became popular as a beverage. The fashionable society of the Namboku period (1336–92) held sumptuous tea parties which were also gambling milieux, while the common people and the secluded bonzes began to enjoy the "quiet taste of drinking tea" *(wabi-cha)*. The Buddhist priest Shukō (1422–1502), who was patronized by Shōgun Ashikaga Yoshimasa (1434–90), refined the tea cult and introduced the four-and-a-half-mat room for *wabi-cha*. This was adopted by the tea-ceremony master Takeno Jōō (1504–55). At the close of the Sengoku era (end of the sixteenth century), the tea cult became popular in Sakai, near Ōsaka, especially among the daimyō. Under the patronage of Hideyoshi, the tea-ceremony master Sen no Rikyū (1521–91), who was born in Sakai, laid down for later generations definitive rules for the tea cult. The ideals were summarized in "tranquil respect and serenity" *(wakei-seijaku)*.

Chian-iji Hō 治安維持法 (Law for Maintenance of Public Peace). Law for the control of socialism at the close of the Taishō and during the Shōwa era. After World War I, the government, in its effort to suppress the socialist movement, proposed to the Diet a law for the control of radical socialism (1922). The proposal met with strong opposition from both houses and was rejected. There also developed a movement for universal suffrage which had begun in early Taishō and which had gained momentum with the growth of the working class. In 1925, the Wakatsuki (Reijirō) cabinet, which had included the proconstitutional parties, established a law for universal suffrage but at the same time promulgated the Law for the Maintenance of Public Peace. The cabinet acted in fear that universal suffrage, which originally was a demand of the bourgeois class, would become a communist demand. The peace-maintenance law was first applied in the case of the Dairen communist incident in 1927, then in the case of the March 3, 1928, incident, which occurred on the occasion of the first election employing universal suffrage. An amendment by Prime Minister Tanaka (Giichi) to the effect that the death penalty should be enforced was rejected by the Diet, but Tanaka promulgated the amendment as an emergency imperial ordinance. The amended bill was aimed at those who organized, joined, or supported organizations established for the purpose of revolutionizing the national and private property systems. Liberals as well fell under the application of the law. Throughout the Pacific War, the law suppressed the socialist movement and freedom of thought.

Chichibu jiken 秩父事件 (the incident at Chichibu). An incident of which one cause was the aggravation of the movement for democratic rights in Meiji days. In 1884, farmers of the Chichibu district in Saitama Prefecture started a riot. Shouting "reduction of taxes" and "away with the conscription law," more than 10,000 farmers raided the houses of the wealthy and burned the debt certificates held there. The government mistook the riot for a socialist demonstration and dispatched troops because the riot took place not far from Tōkyō. But the movement grew in intensity as the government took more oppressive measures.

chigai hōken 治外法権 (extraterritorial rights). Consular jurisdiction in international law. Consular jurisdiction was recognized in 1858 (the fifth year of the Ansei era) by the Five Powers Treaty, or *Ansei Gokakoku Jōyaku* (ANSEI NO KARI-JŌYAKU). Consulates with extraterritorial rights for their respective nationals were established in the treaty ports, but violence committed by foreigners who relied on their extraterritorial rights, and the pride of a sovereign nation, resulted in the abolition of the treaty's unequal extraterritorial rights in 1897.

chigyō 知行 (management of a domain). The possession and management of a domain or the domain itself. The *chigyō* system was introduced during the Heian period when the penal and administrative code *(ritsuryō)* had weakened. It aimed at economic returns and gave to the court and the nobility special administrative and tax-collecting powers. Under the manor system, the management of a fief was called *chigyō,* and the management of both the domain and its profits was called a "complete *chigyō*" (ICHIEN CHIGYŌ). However, in the Edo period, a *chigyō* indicated the management of a plot given as salary by the shogunate or a feudal lord. A daimyō was the manager of a fief with a yield of at least 10,000 *koku* (one *koku* equals 4.96 bushels). A smaller fief was a *chigyō,* and the feoffee was a *chigyō-tori.* The allowance of a stipend of rice instead of a plot was called *kirimai-tori* (KIRIMAI) or *kuramai-tori.*

chigyōkoku-sei 知行国制 (system of administration of provinces). A feudal system originated in the Fujiwara period. The purpose was to compensate for the proceeds derived from the private residences given to the court and the nobility. The proceeds, however, were reduced to nothing. They were already lacking during Nara times, and it seems that the collapse of the allowance system of the penal and administrative code was responsible for the deficiency.

According to this system, emperors, powerful vassals, and influential shrines and temples became the possessors of specific provinces. The management of these fiefs was called the "administration of provincial affairs." The system developed during the period of cloister government (INSEI), when cloistered emperors governed. The Taira clan, for instance, possessed a fief of more than thirty provinces. Similarly, the Kamakura shogunate, when it established itself, possessed nine provinces as *chigyōkoku,* which were called the Kantō Go-bunkoku.

chihanji 知藩事 (land administrators). The name of the new territorial heads after the return of the land and the people to the emperor in the early Meiji era. In 1869, after the return of all the fiefs, the government gave the name of *chihanji* to the former landlords and entrusted them with the management of their former domains. With the situation in each domain the same as before, the government effected the abolition of clans and the establishment of prefectures (1871), bringing the feudal system legally to a close.

chimbata 賃機 (leased weaving looms). A form of home industry related to the manufacturing of fabric. It is also called *debata.* The textile manufacturer would put a weaving loom at the disposal of people who wanted to utilize it in their own homes. These people worked for the manufacturer and received wages from him. This form of home industry originated in the early Edo period and flourished until the middle of the Meiji era, but it declined when the factory system gained ground. Today it is still in operation for the manufacturing of some silk fabrics and hemp cloth.

chinso 賃租 (tenancy rent). Farmland tenancy in the penal and administrative code system (RITSURYŌ-SEI). The tenancy rent paid to the owners in the spring was called *chin;* that paid in the fall was called *so.* This kind of tenancy of private farmlands flourished in pre-Taika times. Because the farmers, however, were unable to live on only partitioned farmland (KUBUNDEN) under the allotted farmland system (HANDEN NŌMIN), more public farmland fell under the *chinso* tenancy system. This was especially true from the second half of the Nara period, when the allotted-farmland system collapsed.

Chinzei bugyō 鎮西奉行 (the administrator of Kyūshū). An official title of the administration of Kyūshū during the Kamakura period. After the destruction of the Taira clan, Minamoto no Yoritomo (1148–99) established in 1186 the office of administration of Kyūshū. This office was called *Chinzei bugyō.* After the invasion by the Mongols, when the office of commissioner of Kyūshū (KYŪSHŪ TANDAI) was established, the administration of Kyūshū fell under the commissioner's control. Likewise, during the subsequent Muromachi period, the administration of Kyūshū was controlled by the commissioner of Kyūshū.

Chion-in 知恩院. The headquarters and main temple of the Jōdo sect (JŌDO-SHŪ) of Buddhism. It is situated in Kyōto and is built on the site where the founder of Jōdo, Hōnen (1133–1212), explained his *nembutsu* (salvation by the invocation of the name Amida) and where Hōnen died and was entombed. His disciple Genchi (1183–1238) built the temple, which he dedicated to his master. The present edifice, however, was built in 1639.

chishi 地子 (land rent). Land rent or farm rent in ancient times and during the Kamakura and Muromachi periods. According to the penal and administrative code *(ritsuryō),* the rent of public farmland was one-fifth of the harvest. In the manor system, a land rent was also to be paid. It was sometimes levied for special expenditures, or a powerful landowner would unscrupulously levy additional rents on the farmers.

chishisen 地子銭 (farm rent paid in money). CHISHI was farm rent paid in rice by the farmer. When the currency system was introduced, this rent was to be paid in money and was called *chishisen.* Later, taxes, which were more like surtaxes, also had to be paid on streets and on building ground.

chiso kaisei 地租改正 (land-tax reform). A modern reform of the land-tax system made in the early Meiji era. It was introduced in 1873 and was brought to completion after seven years of effort. The result was that the feudal stipend in rice as a tax basis was abolished and that land was valued on the basis of its proceeds. The tax rates fixed at three percent of the land value were also abolished, and the system of the addition or reduction of taxes according to a rich or a poor harvest was adopted. Taxes levied by way of produce, etc. were changed into monetary taxes, and the taxpayer became the owner of the farmland. This was a consolidation of the private-property system and at the same time a decisive step toward the spread of the monetary system. Aiming at stabilizing finances, the government levied taxes which differed little from the former land taxes paid in rice. The landowner, who was the taxpayer, shifted the tax burden to the shoulders of the tenant farmer, from whom he requested a high tenancy rent which amounted to half the total tax. With prices rising, the landowners amassed profits while the owner farmer or the tenant farmer became destitute. Wealthy landowners also amassed more land property. The self-supporting economy of the farming villages collapsed when the land which they had formerly owned in common became the property of the government.

chitsuroku shobun 秩禄処分 (hereditary-stipend measure). A financial policy in the early Meiji period. As a result of the Meiji Restoration, the ex-military class lost its privileges, but, after the abolition of the clans and the establishment of prefectures, the hereditary stipend or *chitsuroku* was granted as before. However, when the total stipend amounted to more than half the government expenses, the government, which had granted the hereditary stipends from 1873 to 1875, abolished them in 1876 in order to stabilize finances. On the basis of the number of *koku* of rice (one *koku* equals 4.96 bushels) calculated in terms of the rice price, the government issued pension bonds redeemable every year, to begin with the year 1882. This measure signaled the end of the lower military class.

chō 調 (produce tax). In ancient times, the tax payable in commodities other than rice. A paragraph in the *Chronicle of Emperor Sujin (Sujin-gi)* mentions the tax to be paid by the male *(yuhazu no mitsugi)* and by the female *(tanasue no mitsugi)*. The Taika Reform established in 646 the *denchō* and the *komaichō*. Taxes were payable in raw silk, cotton, or other articles from local production. Then the Taihō and Yōrō slave-labor codes *(fueki-ryō)* imposed taxes directly on the person in the form of labor. Only the males were taxable, and by categories: 1) those from twenty-one to sixty years of age *(shōchō)*, 2) old men (i.e., those over sixty) and partly incapacitated men *(jichō)*, and 3) those from sixteen to twenty years of age *(chūnan)*.

chōgin 丁銀 (silver coins). A kind of silver coin of the Edo period. The coin was pure currency by weight, its weight being about 43 *momme* (one *momme* equals 3.75 grams). The *chōgin* was a bullion of uneven quality on which a mark was stamped. A supplementary silver coin called MAMEITA-GIN was also used. The earliest coins of this category were those of the Keichō era (1596–1614). They were often recoined from the Genroku era (1688–1703) on, but, excepting the recoinage of the Kyōhō era (1716–35), the other recoinages worsened the quality, and the market dropped. An effort was made to regulate the market by yearly recoining the same *chōgin* and *mameita-gin,* but with the appearance of numerical currency such as *gomomme-gin* (from 1765 to 1772) and *nishu-gin* the coins as currency lost their value.

chōhei rei 徴兵令 (conscription law). A law promulgated in 1872 aimed at establishing the basis of a modern army by universal conscription. After the restoration, Ōmura Masujirō (1824–69), following the examples of Europe and the United States, planned the adoption of the conscription system. After Ōmura's assassination, Yamagata Aritomo (1838–1922), who rejected Saigō Takamori's (1827–77) theory of reshaping the former military class into a regular army, established military conscription after Saigō's retirement. In an early stage, exemption from military service and enrollment by proxy were allowed, but this situation made the peasants' burden intolerable. Farmers rioted, urging a reform of the conscription law, and at the same time demanded a tax reduction.

Chōjū Giga 鳥獣戯画 (picture scrolls of birds and animals). Four picture scrolls of the Heian period. They are ascribed to Toba Sōjō Kakuyū (1053–

1140) and are owned by the Kōzan-ji temple of Kyōto. Frogs, rabbits, monkeys, etc. take on human roles and satirize the society of the day.

Chōkohō jiken 張鼓峰事件 (incident at Changkufeng). A clash between Japanese and Soviet troops in 1938 on the border of Manchuria and Russia. The Japanese army, after having established an independent Manchuria, wanted to sound the military strength of its potential enemy Soviet Russia. It attacked at Changkufeng but was unsuccessful, and hostilities were suspended.

chokushi-den 勅旨田 (imperial land). Land owned by the emperor during the Heian period. It is believed that the grant of property was conferred at the end of the Nara period in order to deal with the financial difficulties resulting from the structure of the penal and administrative code *(ritsuryō)* and to strengthen the economic foundation of the imperial household. Large tracts of taxless wasteland (FUYUSO-DEN) were to be cultivated, and the compulsory service of the peasants with allotted farmland (HANDEN NŌMIN) was demanded. This, however, harmed production, and the manor-adjustment law (SHŌEN-SEIRI REI) of 902 repealed the grant. All the land owned by the imperial household from 897 was included in the revocation and was given to the people for cultivation.

Chōsen (kindai) 朝鮮 (近代) (modern Korea). After the Sino-Japanese War (1894–95), Korea became temporarily an independent country, known to the Japanese as Dai Kankoku. The political and economic oppression by Japan which had ousted the Chinese from Korea, along with the military oppression by Russia (after the North China incident, Russia had invaded Manchuria), caused the instability of the Korean government. Furthermore, uprisings of peasants who were opposed to the feudal system of the Yi dynasty (1392–1910) occurred frequently. Meanwhile, Japan tried to patronize the Korean ruler Taewongun (in Japanese, Daiinkun; 1821-89), carried out a coup d'état in the Korean court, and placed Taewongun under Japanese influence. With the outbreak of the Russo-Japanese War in 1904, Japan exacted from Korea the Japan-Korea Offensive and Defensive Alliance and, taking advantage of her victory over Russia, tried to impose her authority over Korea by means of diplomatic activities. Soon the acting resident general Itō Hirobumi (1841–1909) was appointed to Korea (1905–9) in order to gain complete control over the country. Resenting the Japanese oppression, Korean separatists assassinated Itō at Harbin Railway Station. But the following year (1910), Japan annexed Korea and appointed a governor general, strengthening the colonial rule.

After World War I, Korea awakened to democracy and socialism. Son Byong-hui (in Japanese, Son Hei-ki), leader of the Ch'ondogyo (in Japanese, Tendō-kyō) religion (a religion founded in 1860, based on Confucian, Buddhist, Taoist, and Christian elements and with political affiliations), made a demand for Korean independence at the peace conference of Versailles (1919). The movement for independence spread in Korea, and on March 1, 1919, civilians started a peaceful demonstration. The demonstration, however, was drowned in blood as 2,000 civilians were killed in what is known as the "March 1 incident," or the *banzai* riot incident *(banzai sōjō jiken)*. The nationalist movement went underground, but the struggle of Kim Il-sung (in Japanese, Kin Jissei), as well as the provisional government of the Republic of Korea, organized in Shanghai by Dr. Syngman Rhee (Lee Sung-man), received international support.

Upon the collapse of Japan after World War II, independence was promised to Korea, but an American-Soviet agreement divided the country at the thirty-eighth parallel. Friction between North and South followed upon this partitioning and led to an international war. Though a cease-fire agreement has been reached, the division between North and South remains unchanged.

Chōsen (kodai) 朝鮮 (古代) (ancient Korea). Ancient Korea included the following states:

Kudara (Paekche), kingdom in southwest Korea, 18 B.C.–A.D. 663
Kōkuri (Koguryo), kingdom in northern half of Korea, 37 B.C.–A.D. 668
Kōrai (Koryo) dynasty, 918–1392
Shiragi (Silla) kingdom in southeast Korea: Old Silla, 57 B.C.–A.D. 668; United Silla, 668–935
Mimana (Imna or Kaya; also Karak), southern tip of Korea, founded A.D. 42

However, the dates for the founding of the various Korean states are unreliable.

Chōsen (Ri-shi) 朝鮮 (李氏) (Korean monarchy, the Yi dynasty). The dynasty which ruled the Korean peninsula from the last years of the fourteenth century to the early twentieth century, or from 1392 to 1910. General Yi Song-gye (in Japanese, Ri Sei-kei), of Kōrai kingdom, received from Kōrai's King Kong Yang (in Japanese, Kyōjō) —a puppet king whom Yi had put on the throne—the authority to rule the country. Yi, who usurped the throne, was enthroned in 1392 and called the country Choson (in Japanese, Chōsen). He thus brought the Koryo dynasty to an end after 474 years of rule. The new dynasty lasted for 518 years, and there were twenty-seven reigns. Though a bulwark of China, the Yi monarchy was also a tributary nation to China. It entertained good relations with neighboring countries, especially with Japan. But Korea suffered a calamity at the hands of Hideyoshi, who waged the Jinshin wars (BUNROKU-KEICHŌ NO EKI). In the first half of the seventeenth century, Korea was invaded by China. In the nineteenth century, it became the scene of the Sino-Japanese War and the subsequent encroachment of Japanese influence. After the Sino-Japanese War, the Japanese name for the country became Dai Kankoku (Great Korea). In 1905, Korea was made a Japanese protectorate, and in 1910 it was annexed by Japan. The dynasty then ceased to exist.

Chōsen sōtoku-fu 朝鮮総督府 (government general of Korea). Government general of Korea and colonial rule established by Japan after the annexation of Korea in 1910. This dictatorial control over Korea exercised for thirty-five years by Japanese overlords came to a sudden end on V-J Day, August 14, 1945.

chōshi 徴士 (government officials). Officials elected to the government for a period of four years, early Meiji era. SEITAISHO, the Statement of the Forms of Government, drafted in 1868, effected the separation of the three powers, administrative, legislative, and judiciary. The government, which presided over the legislation, had an upper and a lower board. The upper board was composed of *chōshi* or officials who were elected from members of the imperial family, court nobles, lords and samurai, and the common people.

Chōshū seibatsu 長州征伐 (subjugation of the Chōshū clan). The name of the two battles fought at the end of the Edo period by the shogunate against the Chōshū clan. After the battle of Hamaguri-gomon in 1864 (HAMAGURI-GOMON NO HEN), the shogunate, having procured an imperial mandate to chastise the rebels, sent a punitive force against Chōshū. The expedition ended without fighting because the Chōshū antiforeign influence had weakened as a result of the Shimonoseki incident in 1864 (SHIMONOSEKI JIKEN) and because the conservative elements of the clan had punished the antiforeign vassals, thus showing their submission. However, the radical elements of the Chōshū clan allied with the Satsuma clan, which purchased war material from an English firm in Nagasaki. Furthermore, the loyalist Takasugi Shinsaku (1839–67) had fully equipped and modernized his military corps called KIHEITAI and also opposed the shogunate. In 1865, the shogunate again dispatched a punitive expedition which, however, was unsuccessful everywhere. Furthermore, several peasant uprisings occurred in the rear. Shōgun Iemochi (1846–66) died in Ōsaka in 1866, and his successor, Shōgun Yoshinobu (1827–1913), ordered the cessation of hostilities, thus exposing the weakness of the shogunate.

Chōsokabe uji 長曾我部氏 (the Chōsokabe clan). A clan of daimyō who ruled Tosa Province (Kōchi Prefecture) during the Sengoku era (close of the fifteenth to close of the sixteenth century). Motochika (1539–99) controlled the whole of Shikoku, but in 1585, when he surrendered to Hideyoshi, his possessions were reduced to Tosa Province only. The Hundred Articles of Chōsokabe Motochika (Chōsokabe Motochika Hyakkajō) are a model of provincial law. Motochika's son, Morichika (1575–1615), sided with the

Toyotomi in the battle of Ōsaka and perished together with the Toyotomi clan.

Chūson-ji 中尊寺. A temple of the Tendai sect of Buddhism, built in the northeastern district during the Fujiwara period. The temple is located in HIRAIZUMI in Nishiiwai County, Iwate Prefecture. In 1105, Fujiwara no Kiyohira (?–1126) began the construction of the temple, which reflected the wealth, gorgeousness, and power of the Fujiwara family, then at the climax of its influence. Subsequent wars and fires destroyed all the buildings except the Konjikidō and the Kyōzō. It seems that the Mutsu branch of the Fujiwara family intended to spread the Kyōto culture to the northeastern district and consequently constructed this temple. The buildings, images of Buddha, art objects, and industrial products which are preserved faithfully reflect the characteristics of the Fujiwara culture.

D

Daidō Danketsu undō 大同団結運動. Political agitation in the early Meiji era. About the year 1887, nongovernment politicians, though at odds about some matters, formed a federation known as the Daidō Danketsu, rallied around their leader Gotō Shōjirō (1838–97), and were unanimous in opposing the government. They protested against certain "humiliating" foreign-treaty revisions proposed by Inoue Kaoru (1835–1915) and obtained the support of the former Progressive Party, the Liberal Party, and the ultra-nationalists. Consequently, the government ordered an end to the treaty revision, and Inoue resigned. But the antigovernment movement aimed at nothing less than a reduction of land taxes, freedom of speech and assembly, and treaties on equal terms. The movement spread throughout the country when the former liberalists held round-table conferences and when a general meeting of the members of the Daidō Danketsu was held in Ōsaka. As a countermeasure, the cabinet of Itō Hirobumi (1841–1909) issued a peace-preservation ordinance (HOAN JŌREI) at the end of 1887. This ordinance banished the so-called unofficial politicians from within twelve kilometers of Tōkyō. Finally, the leading factions of the Daidō Danketsu were won over to the government's side, and the movement was dissolved.

Daigaku 大学. State school of higher learning for the education of government officials under the penal and administrative code of 710 (ritsuryō). It was under the administration of the Department of Ceremonial. The curricula of the Daigaku or University Bureau (Daigaku-ryō) included Confucian classics (myōgyō), law (myōbō), history (kiden), literature (monjō), mathematics (san), and writing (sho). The professors were either doctors of Chinese classics, of reading (on hakase—that is, teachers of Chinese pronunciation), of writing, or of mathematics. In addition, there were two assistant professors. Later the titles of doctor of law and of literature were also created, and lecturers were added. There were 400 students. Admission was confined to the sons of princes and nobles of the fifth rank and upwards, to the sons of naturalized Japanese of Chinese origin (AYABITO), or to the sons of families of the eighth rank and upwards upon petition. Studies were completed in nine years. The Daigaku was located to the south of the present Nijō Castle of Kyōto but was destroyed by fire in 1177.

daigaku rei 大学令 (law concerning universities). A law promulgated in 1918 concerning the educational system during the Taishō era. It provided for a university education based on liberalism. Private universities were also recognized. This was the outcome of the economic development and spread of democratic ideas after World War I.

Daigo-ji 醍醐寺. Headquarters of the Daigo-ji branch of the Shingon sect of Buddhism. The temple is located in Fushimi, Kyōto City. It was founded by the priest Shōbō (832–909), who built a hermitage in the mountains for his ascetic practices. Many buildings were added by the emperors Daigo (885–930), Suzaku (923–52), Murakami (926–67), and later by the Muromachi shogunate. During the Bummei era (1469–87), the temple was partly destroyed in the Ōnin Civil War but was rebuilt by Hideyoshi. Many buildings such as the five-storied pagoda built in 951, the Kondō and the Sambō-in (both erected during the Momoyama period), and considerable sculpture, pictures, and handwriting specimens, dating from the Fujiwara period (894–1185) and after, are preserved.

daigyaku jiken 大逆事件 (high treason incident). The oppression of socialism at the end of the Meiji era. In 1907, the Socialist Party was ordered to dissolve. The following year, a demonstration welcoming the socialists who were released from prison led to the so-called red-flag incident *(akahata jiken)*. Premier Saionji was replaced by Katsura. However, as the Katsura cabinet opposed the socialist movement, four syndicated workmen of Aichi Prefecture, emulating men of action such as Kōtoku Shūsui (1871–1911), plotted to assassinate Emperor Meiji. The plot was detected in 1910, and the conspirators were arrested. Though Kōtoku was not directly involved in the plot, the government, which intended to eradicate socialism, accused him of being the main conspirator. Together with twelve others, Kōtoku was condemned to death following a private trial. Other repressive measures were taken. This incident was also a pretext for the government to oppress the democrats. All writings about socialism were prohibited. It was a dark age for socialism, and it lasted until the so-called rice riots (KOME SŌDŌ) in 1918.

Daiichi Ginkō 第一銀行 (The First National Bank). A modern bank established according to the state-banks regulations which raised funds by public subscription. Its pivot was the Mitsui and Ono companies. The founder of the bank was Shibusawa Eiichi (1840–1931). In 1878, a branch office was established in Pusan, Korea. It contributed to the development of the Korean market.

Daikakuji-tō 大覚寺統 (the Daikakuji imperial line). The imperial line which begins with Emperor Kameyama (1249–1305). The name derives from the monastery Daikaku-ji, in which Kameyama and his descendants lived from 1276. This line conflicted with the JIMYŌIN-TŌ, the imperial line which begins with Emperor Gofukakusa (1243–1304) and ends with Emperor Gokomatsu (1377–1433). The Jimyō-in was a monastery to which Emperor Gofukakusa retired in 1259. Through the intervention of the KAMAKURA BAKUFU, it was arranged that the succession was to alternate between the two lines. But this measure caused the anger of Emperor Godaigo (1288–1339) of the Daikakuji line and led to civil war and to the Kemmu Restoration (KEMMU NO CHŪKŌ), or the temporary restoration of the imperial rule. However, the revolt of Ashikaga Takauji (1305–58), who seized Kyōto, forced the emperor to flee to Yoshino (1336), where he established the Southern dynasty as opposed to the Northern dynasty established in Kyōto by the Jimyōin line. The Daikakuji line was discontinued in 1392 after peace was restored between the two dynasties.

daikan 代官 (deputies). During the Kamakura and Muromachi periods, the deputy who performed duties in place of an official or of the shōgun himself. At the end of this period, the constable's deputies (shugo-dai) were called the "great deputies" (dai-daikan) or district deputies (GUNDAI), and they took part in administrative affairs. The land stewards' deputies (jitō-dai) were also called daikan. They collected land taxes. Likewise, the Toyotomi clan appointed deputies for the collecting of land taxes from direct vassals.

During the Edo period, deputies were called gundai and daikan. They directly administered the land and took part in civil administration, collecting land taxes and attending to police matters, lawsuits, etc. Furthermore, each feudal domain also appointed deputies. The levying of taxes was often the only duty of these deputies.

daimyō 大名. The lord of a manor or a feudal lord. Originally, the daimyō was the possessor of many name fields or MYŌDEN (the name of the original occupant serving as a title of ownership). But when the power of the warriors increased and became dominant, a powerful warrior or samurai was called "daimyō." From the Namboku period to the end of the Muromachi period, the constable daimyō (SHUGO DAIMYŌ) strengthened and increased their provincial territory. However, from the time of the Ōnin Civil War, many of these constable daimyō were ruined, and in their place the newly risen families received the title instead. Another type of daimyō was the *sengoku daimyō* or civil-war baron. During the Edo period, a daimyō was a vassal with a holding of land assessed at over 10,000 *koku*. According to the degree of relationship or intimacy with the Tokugawa clan, the daimyō were divided into "related clans" (SHIMPAN), hereditary-vassalage daimyō *(fudai)*, and outside lords (TOZAMA DAIMYŌ), who were not hereditary feudatories of the Tokugawa. The *fudai* were, in general, insignificant daimyō who took part in administrative affairs of the shogunate, but there were many powerful daimyō among the *tozama*. The BAKUFU made great efforts to control the *tozama* and, by promulgating the Laws for the Military Houses (BUKE SHO-HATTO) and demanding alternate attendance (SANKIN KŌTAI), succeeded in controlling them.

Dai Nihonshi 大日本史. A work on Japanese history begun during the Edo period by Tokugawa Mitsukuni (1628–1700), the lord of Mito from 1661 to 1700. The work, which includes 397 volumes, relates events from the time of Jimmu Tennō to the time of Emperor Gokomatsu (1377–1433). It somewhat resembles the Chinese work *Shih Chi,* as it is divided into a historical part or basic annals of the emperors *(hongi),* biographies *(retsuden),* classified history *(shi),* and tables *(hyō).* The work was begun in 1657, and a compilation office called *shōkō-kan* was established on the feudal lord's estate in Edo. Confucianists such as Asaka Tampaku (1656–1737), who was appointed president of the office, were asked to assist. *Dai Nihonshi* was meant to continue the official history *Sandai Jitsuroku,* which describes events of the reigns of the emperors Seiwa (850–80), Yōzei (868–944), and Kōkō (830–87). However, *Dai Nihonshi* is a history of feudal moralism, and its backbone is the Confucian theory of the legitimacy of the ruler and of duty toward the sovereign. Worthy of special mention are the facts that Empress Jingū was inserted in the biographies of the imperial consorts, that Prince Ōtomo (Emperor Tenchi) was inserted in the basic annals of the emperors, and that the Southern dynasty was considered to be the only legitimate one. The work deeply influenced national history at the beginning of the Meiji era. It is attributed to the whole Mito clan, as successive generations assisted in the collaboration, and it was brought to completion in 1906.

Dai Nippon Sangyō Hōkoku-kai 大日本産業報国会 (Association for Service to the State Through Industry). An association of wartime workmen during the Shōwa era. In 1938, the government, in order to obtain cooperation for the war machine, dissolved the former labor unions and organized all workmen on a fascist basis, putting them under the direct control of the state. The government attained its ultimate aim of increasing and strengthening war production in 1940 when the Federation of Labor was dissolved. The wartime service association itself was dissolved when the country surrendered at the end of World War II.

Dai Nippon Teikoku Kempō 大日本帝国憲法 (Imperial Constitution). Constitution promulgated in 1889. It is also known as the Meiji Constitution. From early Meiji times, the necessity of promulgating a constitution was felt by such politicians as Iwakura, Kido, Ōkubo, and others. Consequently, a draft was made. The movement for democratic rights had made itself felt, and the government could not ignore the demand for the establishment of a national Diet. Accordingly, in 1881, imperial instructions concerning both the promulgation of a constitution and the establishment of a national Diet were published. However, the clan government's purpose was to establish an emperor system, and it ignored popular claims.

A model for the constitution was found in the Prussian constitution. Through the efforts of Itō Hirobumi, Inoue Kowashi, Itō Miyoji, Kaneko Kentarō, and the German jurist Karl Roesler, the constitution, which centered around the monarch, was completed and promulgated on February 11, 1889. There was very little guarantee of civil rights, and even that little was restricted. Likewise, the parliament had very little authority. Undemocratic institutions such as the House of Peers and the Privy Council remained. The will of the people was not reflected in the government, and the affairs of state were conducted by absolute bureaucrats. Later, on the basis of the supreme command's prerogative of independence, military absolutism tended to ignore the constitution and established a fascist government. The Imperial Constitution was abolished in 1947 when the new constitution became effective.

Dai Tō-A Kyōeiken 大東亜共栄圏 (Greater East Asia Co-Prosperity Sphere). A Japanese instrument of aggression during World War II. After the worldwide economic panic of 1929, England, the United States, France, and other countries set up an economic bloc, thus widening the split between the haves and the have-nots. As a countermeasure, Japan set up the Japan-Manchuria bloc, to which China was added upon the opening of the Sino-Japanese hostilities. Later, Inner Mongolia, French Indo-China, the Philippines, Thailand, Burma, Indonesia, and Malaya were included. This bloc developed into a military, financial, and cultural corporation aimed at strengthening the economic bloc by means of joint defense and mutual assistance. There followed, however, a fierce clash of interests with the United States and England, two countries which had exerted control in the Far East for a long period. This situation in turn led to the Pacific War. Japan, elated by her first victories, established in 1942 the Ministry of Greater East Asia Affairs, and Premier Tōjō concurrently served as its head. In the following year, the Greater East Asia Conference was held in Tōkyō, and a joint declaration was issued. In actuality, the Co-Prosperity Sphere was nothing but a scheme for aggression and a means of carrying out the war. The so-called independent countries were invested with mere puppet political powers. The Co-Prosperity Sphere never succeeded in influencing the popular movements of the various countries involved.

Daizōkyō 大蔵経 (the complete Buddhist scriptures). Compilation of the complete Buddhist scriptures. The first compilation was made in China in the sixth century. In Japan, the copying of the complete scriptures began after Buddhism was introduced. The complete Buddhist scriptures were also called *Issaikyō*. Other copies were brought to Japan from China and Korea. The *Daizōkyō* were published through the efforts of Tenkai (1536–1643), this edition being known as *Tenkai-ban,* and of Tetsugen (1630–82), this edition being called *Tetsugen-ban* or the Tetsugen edition.

Dajōkan 太政官 (Council of State). The supreme organ of government under the penal and administrative code system (RITSURYŌ-SEI). Of equal rank was the Department of Religion or Jingikan. The machinery of administration was set up by the Taihō Code promulgated in 702. The Council of State was presided over by the chancellor or *dajō-daijin,* supported by the minister of the left *(sadaijin)* and the minister of the right *(udaijin).* Under their direction were placed the great councilors *(dainagon),* the minor councilors *(shōnagon),* the controller of the left *(sadaiben),* the controller of the right *(udaiben),* the vice-controller of the left *(sachūben)* and of the right *(uchūben),* the minor controller of the left *(sashōben)* and of the right *(ushōben),* secretaries and junior secretaries of the left and the right *(sau-daishōgeki),* and the recorders and junior recorders of the left and of the right *(sau-daishōshi).* Everyone had a special duty to perform in one of the eight departments or ministries. The eight departments were the Department of Central Affairs (Nakatsukasa-shō), the Department of Ceremonial (Shikibu-shō), the Department of Civil Administration (Jibu-shō), the Department of Popular Affairs (Mimbu-shō), the Department of War (Hyōbu-shō), the Department of Justice (GYŌBU-SHŌ), the Department of the Treasury (Ōkura-shō), and the Department of the Imperial Household (KUNAI-SHŌ). During the Heian period new organs were created such as the Bureau of Archivists (KUROUDO-DOKORO) and the Regency (KAMPAKU). The *kampaku* became particularly powerful when the official Council of State as established by the penal and administrative code lost much of its real function. Formally, at least, the Dajōkan system lasted until 1885, when it was replaced by the cabinet system.

dajōkan-satsu 太政官札 (paper money). Inconvertible paper money of the early Meiji era. By a decree of the central government in 1868, this first national paper currency was issued for a period of thirteen years. It was also called *kinsatsu.* The paper money of the Edo period was merely clan currency (HANSATSU). After the Meiji Restoration, the new government was without resources and issued this money, which circulated only in places where government forces were located. However, the issuing of these unguaranteed notes after the establishment of the government did not win the confidence of the people. The paper money gradually depreciated and finally disappeared from the market.

Dannoura 壇の浦. The northern coast at the eastern entrance of the Strait of Shimonoseki, Nagato Province (Yamaguchi Prefecture). Here the Taira clan was exterminated by the Minamoto in a great naval battle in 1185.

Danrin-fū 談林風 (Danrin style). A school of haiku (HAIKAI) poetry started by Nishiyama Sōin (1605–82). It was opposed to the formalism, traditionalism, and classical style of the Matsunaga Teitoku (1571–1653) school (TEIMON-HA), the style of which was known as *Teimon-fū*. Sōrin inaugurated a free haiku style, the wording, subject matter, and form of which were liberated from rules. The Danrin school derives its name from a compilation of this kind of haiku called *Danrin Toppyaku-in* made in 1675 by Tashiro Shōi. The new style was temporarily popular and included Ihara Saikaku (1642–93) among its followers, but it declined when it became overextravagant.

Dazaifu 太宰府. Administrative headquarters of the governor general of the eleven provinces of the Western Circuit, or Saikaidō, under the penal and administrative code system of 710. The governor general was responsible for the administration, diplomatic relations, and defense of the area under his jurisdiction. The remains of this administrative center can still be seen in the town of Daizaifu in Fukuoka Prefecture. From ancient times, the Western Circuit was of special importance as far as diplomatic relations and national defense were concerned. It was important that the central government should impress this part of the country with its prestige, and therefore it established this headquarters, which was like a replica of the government on a small scale. The origin of Dazaifu is old, but the place was particularly active from the sixth and seventh centuries and throughout the time of the penal and administrative code system. The governor general was called *sotsu*. He assumed the leadership over all the provincial governors of Kyūshū. The place was important enough to have an office of conscripted men, called *sakimori no tsukasa,* for safeguarding the posts of the Western Circuit. When the sending of envoys to T'ang China was discontinued, Dazaifu became the center of private trade with China. From the second half of the twelfth century, when the warrior class became powerful, Dazaifu declined.

dembata eidai baibai kinshi rei 田畑永代売買禁止令 (law prohibiting transactions in rice fields). A law of the EDO BAKUFU prohibiting the buying and selling of rice fields. It was first promulgated in 1643. The penal clauses included imprisonment and expulsion of the seller and imprisonment of buyers and attestors. The purpose was to prevent accumulation of rice fields in the hands of wealthy farmers and consequent destitution of the poor. Taking into account, however, the high rate of land taxes and the spread of a currency economy, it is doubtful whether this law was strictly complied with. We know that transactions in rice fields were performed in the form of redeemed pawns, etc. The same happened in various clans. The Kaga clan, for instance, though it strictly prohibited pawning of rice fields, permitted transactions. Consequently, the punitive provisions were gradually relaxed.

Dengaku 田楽 (rustic music). A dance ritual of ancient times. It was also performed in the middle ages (Kamakura and Muromachi periods). Originally, it was related to the religious ceremony of thanksgiving to the god of the harvest. Its popularity increased in Kyōto, especially during the middle and late Heian period. In Namboku times, the so-called Kanjin Dengaku (ritual dances for the promotion of virtues) were performed to obtain funds for the restoration of shrines and temples. These dances became a sightseeing spectacle, and, for open-air performances, special stages were constructed. The Dengaku Nō added dramatic elements to Dengaku and, together with Sarugaku Nō, forms the origin of NŌGAKU or Nō drama.

Deshima 出島. A small island at the head of Nagasaki Bay and residence of the Dutch merchants during the Edo period. It was reclaimed from the sea in 1634 when the Portuguese moved in. After the expulsion of the Portuguese, the Dutch who were in Hirado moved to Deshima and were allowed to trade under very strict conditions (1641). Their trading houses, or factories, included sixty-five buildings. For this leased land and for the buildings, the Netherlands East India Company paid to the townspeople of Nagasaki a yearly amount of 55 *kan* (about 206 kilograms) of silver. Deshima was the only channel of communication with foreign countries up to the end of the Edo period and the only place from which Western knowledge infiltrated into Japan.

dogū 土偶 (clay figurines). A kind of clay figurine of the Jōmon type (JŌMON-SHIKI DOKI). These small statues represent anthropomorphic beings (mostly women) and, in a later period, also animals. The expression is not realistic, and the statuettes look mysterious rather than symbolic. Though their use is uncertain, they probably had some religious or superstitious significance. The techniques used in making the *dogū* were the same as those used for other earthenware of the Jōmon type, though there was a local difference between the figurines of the northeastern district, the Kantō district, and the central district.

dōhoko, dōken 銅鉾・銅剣 (copper halberds, copper swords). Copper halberds and copper swords of the Yayoi type. They are believed to have been imported from the continent in the first or second century. These sharp-edged tools were later imitated and manufactured in Japan, but it is thought that from the way they were buried they were treated as treasured articles with some religious or superstitious significance. They were mostly unearthed in northern Kyūshū and in districts west of the Inland Sea, whereas the bronze bells called DŌTAKU were found in the Kinki district.

doi 土居 (warrior's mansion). The mansion of a warrior during the middle ages (Kamakura and Muromachi periods), also known as *hori no uchi*. In defense against invaders, the mansion was surrounded with an earthwork construction, or with a moat, and was located on an elevated spot or else in an accessible place. The *doi* controlled the surrounding villages. These mansions disappeared, however, at the close of the Muromachi period, when warriors and farmers separated and warriors and their families went to live in the castle towns.

do-ikki 土一揆 (agrarian uprisings). Agrarian uprisings, or uprisings of the "soil people" *(domin)* during the Muromachi period. The growth of the agrarian population after the Namboku period was conspicuous. When the villages formed leagues for their mutual defense, the farmers were determined to oppose the lending of money at high interest by constables, landlords, sakè brewers, and money-lending agencies (DOSŌ), which all practiced usury. The first large-scale uprising of the rural population is thought to be the one which took place in 1428 in Ōmi Province (Shiga Prefecture). It started as an uprising of teamsters (BASHAKU), but spread to such provinces as Yamashiro, Yamato, Kii, and Kawachi. The group attacked the *dosō* (a type of pawnbroker) and requested from the MUROMACHI BAKUFU the promulgation of an "act of virtuous government" or "act of grace" (TOKUSEI-REI). The *tokusei* was a kind of moratorium by which the payment of debts and similar obligations were reduced or suspended. The uprising of 1428 is known as *Shōchō no do-ikki* or the uprising of the Shōchō era (1428–29). This sort of agrarian uprising was invariably opposed to usury and called for favorable edicts. The targets were sakè brewers, moneylenders, and pawnbrokers. Sometimes the uprisings were also called TOKUSEI-IKKI. When they became more violent, they were led by influential peasants who farmed their own land and who were known as name masters (MYŌSHU), and by the local gentry *(jisamurai)* who were bound by no loyalty to a great master but were men with a strong feeling of independence. These leaders, taking advantage of the farmers' uprisings, strengthened their own positions. During the Yamashiro uprising of 1485, which occurred in southern Yamashiro (Kyōto Prefecture), the power of the peasants was so strong that they forced the Hatakeyama partisans to withdraw. Here again, resistance was particularly strong on the part of the local gentry and of the name masters, who, at the same time, served their own private purposes. In general, the uprisings were organized by poor farmers, local gentry, and name masters. But as a result of the uprisings, the local gentry and name masters often became vassals of the great houses.

With the establishment of the "system of independent rulers of a whole province or more" *(daimyō ryōgoku-sei)*, rulers known as civil-war barons *(sengoku daimyō)* repressed the agrarian uprisings. The uprisings of the Edo period were called peasants' uprisings or HYAKUSHŌ-IKKI.

Dōjima kome ichiba 堂島米市場 (the Dōjima rice market). A rice market in Ōsaka established in the early Edo period. It seems to have originated in Yodoya, where various clans sold the rice surplus of their storerooms. During the Genroku era (1688–1704), Yodoya became the so-called *kessho* (a place where confiscated goods were kept or sold), and the rice market was established at Dōjima. During the Kyōhō era (1716–36), shareholders united, and the place became a speculative market. During Meiji days, however, under Western influence, Dōjima was transformed to a stock-exchange market, and in 1893 it officially became the Dōjima Rice Joint Stock Corporation.

dōken 銅剣 (DŌHOKO).

Dōshisha 同志社. A private college established in 1875 by Niijima Jō (1845–90). Niijima returned from the United States in 1874 and considered it his mission to give his people a spiritual education based on Christianity. The college was founded in Kyōto and greatly contributed to the Meiji cultural development.

dosō 土倉 (money markets). Money markets during the middle ages (Kamakura and Muromachi periods). Kamakura vassals operated money markets, but from the Muromachi period, when cities prospered, the institutions flourished. They took articles in pawn and made an advance of money at a usurious rate of interest. These pawnshops, together with the sakè breweries, became the target of the agrarian uprisings. They were, however, an important source of revenue for the Muromachi government, which, in return for the taxes collected, protected them. Consequently, the social and financial position of the *dosō* rose, and it is believed that in Kyōto there were several hundred. Some of the institutions invested money in Sino-Japanese trade. The *dosō* were also called *tsuchi-kura* and *to-kura*.

dōtaku 銅鐸 (bronze bells). A bell-shaped bronze of the Yayoi type. Its height varies from about 20 centimeters to about 1.5 meters. It has the shape of a hanging bell. In the earliest period, it had a design of running water, but later vertical and horizontal lines, called *kesa-dasuki*, were more frequent. Sometimes between these patterns were added clever ornamental portrayals of contemporary life. It was first thought that the *dōtaku* served as a musical instrument, but it was buried in such a way as to imply that it was a religious instrument used in the community. The cultural center of the *dōtaku* was the Kinki district, whereas the cultural center of the copper swords, *dōken* (see DŌHOKO), and of copper halberds, *dōhoko,* was northern Kyūshū.

dōza 銅座 (copper guilds). Public offices in the Edo period which controlled the refining and the trade of copper. In an early stage, the offices were in the hands of the merchants of Ōsaka, but when copper became an important export article in Nagasaki, the control of it was tightened, and in 1738 a copper guild was established as an additional office to Ōsaka's silver guild. It became independent in 1766 as a result of the financial policy of the shogunate minister Tanuma Okitsugu (1719–88). The copper guilds were under the control of the commissioner of finance (KANJŌ BUGYŌ), the magistrate of Nagasaki, and the town commissioner of Ōsaka. They were organized by officials of Nagasaki trading houses and by the merchants of Ōsaka. Their main duties consisted of buying, through the Ōsaka wholesale dealers, the copper mined from the various provinces, refining it, and forwarding it to Nagasaki.

E

eboshi 烏帽子. A kind of headgear. From the Heian period it was universally used with the ordinary dress. The use was inaugurated by the warrior class at the ceremony of the coming of age. Those who assisted the young person coming of age put the *eboshi* on him. Between both parties arose a relation similar to that of parent and child. The persons thus related were called *eboshi-oya* and *eboshi-ko*.

Echigoya 越後屋. The predecessor of the Mitsukoshi Department Store. In 1673, Mitsui Takatoshi (Mitsui Hachirōemon, 1622–94) set up in Edo a chain of dry-goods stores under the name of Echigoya. Mitsui was a merchant of Ise, the descendant of a warrior with the title of lord of Echigo. He adopted the name Echigo as the name of the house. Later he moved his stores to Suruga. His motto was "cash payment and no discounts" (*gengin, kakene nashi* 現銀掛け値なし), and he sold his dry goods by the piece. His reputation rose, and it is said that at one time he sold as much as a thousand *ryō* worth in a day. Mitsui also founded a money-exchange business and made huge profits buying dry goods in Ōsaka. In 1896, the enterprise became Mitsui Dry Goods Stores. In 1904, however, the enterprise separated from Mitsui and established itself as a joint-stock corporation with a capital of 500,000 yen, changing its name to Mitsukoshi Dry Goods Stores.

Edo bakufu 江戸幕府. Military government established in 1603 in Edo by Tokugawa Ieyasu (1542–1616); also known as the Tokugawa BAKUFU. The Edo *bakufu* was organized after the model of the Kamakura and Muromachi *bakufu*, but it was more powerful politically and economically. Consequently, it was able to enforce alternate attendance (SANKIN KŌTAI) and to maintain its seclusion policy. The land was either under direct control of the shōgun or of one of his retainers and was divided into about 260 feudal domains controlled by daimyō. Authority was granted to the daimyō but only by a special license to which the official red seal had to be attached. In this way the daimyō were brought under control. The *bakufu*, based on a system of feudal domains, perfected a detailed administrative organization and established a pyramid-like feudal rule, the apex being the shōgun. Japanese feudal society had now reached the highest degree of development. Along with the growth of a floating economy, the townspeople became influential, inaugurating the golden age of the plebs. At the end, restlessness with the feudal society caused by financial troubles and by the opposition of farmers and townspeople as well as pressure from abroad brought about the downfall of the *bakufu* and the start of a new era, the Meiji Restoration.

Edo-machi bugyō 江戸町奉行 (the Edo magistrate). The name of an office of the EDO BAKUFU. The Edo magistrate took charge of the executive, judicial, and police administration. He was attended by 25 law officers and by 120 constables. He also attended the Supreme Court or Hyōjōsho. The number of these officials was usually limited to two, one for the northern and one for the southern part of the city, but the service was alternated monthly. Ōoka Echizen no Kami Tadasuke (1675–1751), the magistrate who was in office during the Kyōhō era (1716–36), is still famous for his wisdom and perspicacity.

efu 衛府 (guard headquarters). The guard headquarters for the defense of the imperial palace and for the escort of imperial carriages. The Taihō Code, TAIHŌ RITSURYŌ (702), established five such offices, the *emon* or gate guards, the left palace guards *(saeji)*, the right palace guards *(ueji)*, the left military guards *(sahyōe)*, and the right military guards *(uhyōe)*. The organization underwent several changes, but in 811 six guard headquarters were established, viz., the right and left military guards, the right and left palace guards, and the right and left imperial bodyguard *(sau-konoe)*. During the ninth century, when peace in the capital (Kyōto) was disturbed, the authority of the guard headquarters was strengthened, and, in due time, the police known as KEBIISHI made their appearance. When the authority of the police became more powerful, the *efu* disappeared.

egōshū 会合衆 (autonomous bodies). Autocratic organizations in the towns at the end of the Muromachi period. When the towns flourished, they broke away from the influence of the civil-war barons *(sengoku daimyō)* and became autonomous. Wealthy merchants such as the wholesale dealers organized themselves in almost despotic bodies. Most famous of these *egōshū* was that of SAKAI.

eidaka 永高. A kind of KANDAKA (the amount of revenue of land represented in currency) which came into use in the middle of the sixteenth century. During the Muromachi period, the land tax formerly paid in rice had to be paid in money, and the *kandaka* system was inaugurated, especially in the Kantō district, which was the domain of the Hōjō family. Among the coins in circulation in the eastern provinces many were called *eiraku-sen* (EIRAKU TSŪHŌ) because they were cast in 1412, the ninth year of the Chinese era Yung-lo, or Eiraku (1403–24). These coins became the standard currency. Land taxes were also calculated on the *eiraku-sen* basis, and the name *eidaka* (amount of money paid in *eiraku-sen* currency) came into general use.

Eiga Monogatari 栄華物語. Historical tale in forty volumes of the late Heian period. The author as well as the year of compilation is unknown. One opinion holds that the work was written between the years 1028 and 1037; another opinion prefers the years 1069–74. The work relates in chronological order the historical events from the last year of the reign of Emperor Uda (888–97) to the year 1092 and stresses the glory *(eiga)* of Fujiwara no Michinaga (966–1027). It is a first attempt to relate historical events in *monogatari* literary style. The work may be considered as a continuation of the *Six National Histories* or RIKKOKUSHI. As far as history is concerned, many passages describe court customs, but in general the accounts fall short, as no national events are mentioned. In its literary style, composition, and expression, there are many points of similarity to GENJI MONOGATARI.

Eihei-ji 永平寺. The head temple of the Sōtō branch of Zen Buddhism in Fukui Prefecture. It was built against a steep hill in 1243 by Dōgen (1200–53), who was oppressed by the bonzes of Hiei-zan. Dōgen was assisted financially by Hatano Yoshishige, a wealthy landowner of Echizen. Dōgen himself renounced wealth and honor and by practicing the religious meditation called *zazen* became a faithful adept of the law of Buddha.

Eikyō no ran 永享の乱 (the revolt of the Eikyō era). The dispute between the governor general of the Kantō district, Ashikaga Mochiuji (1398–1439), and his chief retainer, Uesugi Norizane (?–1466), who was backed by the MUROMACHI BAKUFU. Mochiuji, as governor general of Kantō, wielded power and despised the Muromachi *bakufu*. But after the death of Shōgun Ashikaga Yoshimochi (1386–1428), his younger brother Yoshinori (1394–1441) became shōgun. Mochiuji was hunted down by Yoshinori. Uesugi rebuked Mochiuji but incurred his wrath, and Mochiuji sent a force to attack Uesugi. Uesugi retired to Kōzuke (Gumma Prefecture), asking for help from the *bakufu*. In 1438 (tenth year of the Eikyō era), Yoshinori sent a large army to attack Mochiuji, who committed suicide (1439). This marked the end of the power of the governors of the Kantō district.

Eiraku tsūhō 永楽通宝 (the Eiraku currency). Copper coins cast during the Eiraku (in Chinese, Yung-lo) era (1403–24) of the Chinese Ming dynasty. They are also called *eiraku-sen*. Shōgun Ashikaga Yoshimitsu (1358–1408), in order to strengthen the BAKUFU's financial policy, engaged in trade with Ming China and imported Ming coins. Most of the imported coins were Eiraku currency. After the middle of the Heian period, coins were no longer cast in Japan. However, with the growth of a floating economy, the need for coins was felt, and the Eiraku currency spread rapidly. It was most appreciated in the eastern provinces. The circulation of Eiraku currency was prohibited by the Edo *bakufu* in 1608.

eji 衛士 (military guards). Military guards of the imperial household, established after the Taika Reform of 646. These guards were enrolled from the army corps of the various provinces and had to serve in Kyōto alternately for one year. They were attached to the gate guards' headquarters or *emon-fu* (EFU) and to the right and left palace guards' headquarters *(sau-eji-fu)*. According to the Taihō Code, they had to serve for at least one year, but actually this term was considerably extended, causing a heavy burden to the farmers. In 722, a reform was carried out, and the term of service of the *eji* was limited to three years. Following the development of the warrior class, the *eji* lost their importance.

ekiba-temma 駅馬・伝馬 (station horses). Horses placed at various stations at the disposition of officials. At the time of the Taika Reform (646), they made their appearance in the KINAI (the five home provinces). Under the penal and administrative code system (RITSURYŌ-SEI), a stable *(umaya)* was set up in the various provinces at intervals of about twenty kilometers. *Ekiba* were provided. In every county *(gun)*, *temma* were put at the disposition of officials. The *ekiba* were kept ready for rapid service, while the *temma* were used for non-urgent purposes. However, with the collapse of the penal and administrative code system, the number of horses was reduced and the organization fell into decay. The pack horses kept ready in every official post station during the Edo period were also called *temma*.

eki-sei 駅制 (communication system). System of communication in ancient Japan. According to the Taihō Code of 702, a stable *(umaya)* had to be set up in every province at intervals of about twenty kilometers. Horses, horse equipment, and equipment for protection against rain were kept ready. They were used by officials. A family *(ekiko)* was in charge of all the duties connected with the station. This family had to cultivate the rice field of the station as well as its own and had to cover all the expenses of the station. As far as communication in the central and local territories was concerned, this *eki-sei* was of great importance, but the heavy burden imposed on the *ekiko* and the corruption of local administration in the late Heian period brought about the collapse of the system.

emakimono 絵巻物 (picture scrolls). Scrolls with paintings representing a narrative. Between the paintings writing is often added to explain the narrative. It is a form of art proper to Japan, and it integrates literature and script as well as painting. There are picture scrolls from the Nara period such as *Kako Genzai Inga-kyō,* but the art flourished especially at the end of the Heian and the beginning of the Kamakura period. Such works as GENJI MONOGATARI EMAKI, *Shigisan Engi Emaki,* and CHŌJŪ GIGA belong to the late Heian period. Famous also are the following works belonging to the Kamakura period: *Kitano Tenjin Engi, Kasuga Gongen Reigenki, Ishiyama-dera Engi, Ippen Shōnin Eden, Hōnen Shōnin Gyōjō Ekotoba, Boki Ekotoba, Ban Dainagon Ekotoba, Heiji Monogatari Ekotoba, Nenjū Gyōji Emaki.* The post-Kamakura style lost its vigor because of a tendency toward rigidity.

empon 円本 (one-yen books). Publications of the early Shōwa era. As a result of the depression caused by the 1923 Kantō earthquake, complete works were published by subscription, and the *empon* era was inaugurated. *Empon* means "one yen per book."

endenhō 塩田法 (salt-farm techniques). Methods of obtaining salt from the sea. Salty soil along the seacoast is used for the manufacture of salt. In ancient times, salt was obtained by the boiling of sea water. This was known as the "direct boiling method" or *chokushahō,* but from the early middle ages salt farms were used. A natural dry beach was utilized, and salt-containing sand was accumulated. This method of accumulating salty sand was called *agehama-shiki.* Concentrated salt water from the sea was sprinkled on the sandy beach where sunshine or wind evaporated it. The salt was then taken out. This method was improved upon in early modern times. Making use of the phenomenon called capillarity, sea water is elevated to the surface of the salt farms. This is known as *irihama* and was already practiced in Akō during the Kan'ei era (1624–44). The Inland Sea region has always been rich in salt farms. Owing to the topography of this region, the *irihama* method is widely used. Favorable conditions such as weather and a direct communication link with Ōsaka make the Inland Sea region an ideal one for salt farms. It accounts for eighty percent of the total output of the whole country. This region was known as Jisshū Enden because it mainly included the following ten provinces *(jisshū):* Harima (Hyōgo), Bizen and Bitchū (Okayama), Bingo and Aki (Hiroshima), Suō and Nagato (Yamaguchi), Awa (Tokushima), Sanuki (Kagawa), and Iyo (Ehime).

Engaku-ji 円覚寺 (ENKAKU-JI)

Engi-shiki 延喜式 (code of the Engi era). Compilation in fifty volumes of detailed rules and forms supplementing the codes. Upon the order of Emperor Daigo (885–930), Fujiwara no Tokihira (871–909) began the work in 905. It was enlarged by Tokihira's younger brother, Tadahira (880–949), and completed in 927. The annual ceremonies of the court, the etiquette of the various officials, and the duties of provincial government offices were included. It superseded part of the Kōnin-shiki (820) and the Jōgan-shiki (871) and added official commands. Because both the Kōnin-shiki and the Jōgan-shiki have been lost, the Engi-shiki is a precious source of information about the evolution of juridical ideas and practices in ninth-century Japan.

Enkaku-ji 円覚寺. Main temple in Kamakura of the Enkaku-ji branch of the Rinzai sect of Buddhism. Hōjō Tokimune (1215–84) requested the Yüan-dynasty government to send a Chinese Zen priest to Japan. Mugaku Sogen (1226–86) was sent and arrived in Japan in 1280. He founded the temple in 1282. Both centers of Rinzai Buddhism, the KENCHŌ-JI and the Enkaku-ji flourished, and in the Muromachi period Enkaku-ji became one of the Kamakura GOZAN (the Five Zen Monasteries, celebrated for their literary achievements). The Shariden in the compound of Enkaku-ji is a famous construction. It is built in Chinese Sung style—that is, in KARA-YŌ, which was introduced during the Kamakura period.

Enryaku-ji 延暦寺. Headquarters of Tendai Buddhism on Mount Hiei founded in 788 by Saichō (767–822). Many members of the imperial household and the nobility were converted to Tendai, and from the Heian period through the middle ages Enryaku-ji's influence grew. From the late Heian period, Enryaku-ji presented the spectacle of a mighty kingdom or a stronghold with some 3,000 buildings, numerous monks, and monk-soldiers. Education included the Four Doctrines called En-Mitsu-Zen-Kai. The first doctrine is *engyō* and teaches the harmonious or *emman* and the exquisite or *zetsumyō;* the second doctrine is esoterism or MIKKYŌ; the third teaches Zen religion or ZEN-SHŪ; the fourth teaches the Buddhist precepts or the *kairitsu*. As far as faith is concerned, the *nembutsu* (invocation of the name of Buddha with faith) is stressed. Tendai further holds that all living beings possess the Buddha nature. Founders of religions such as Ryōnin (1072–1132), the founder of Yūzū Nembutsu or interpenetrating *nembutsu;* Genkū or Hōnen (1132–1212), the founder of JŌDO-SHŪ or Amidism; Eisai (1141–1215), the founder of RIN-ZAI-SHŪ; Shinran (1173–1262), the founder of Shin-shū; Dōgen (1200–53), the founder of SŌTŌ-SHŪ; and Nichiren (1222–82), the founder of Nichiren-shū, were all disciples of the Tendai school. In 1571, all the Tendai temples on Mount Hiei were burned down by Nobunaga, but they were partly restored by Hideyoshi.

erizeni 撰銭 (selected coins). From the Kamakura period, copper coins were largely used. This hard currency was imported from T'ang, Sung, and Yüan China, and, during the Muromachi period, also from Ming China. There was a rich variety of coins, but some of them were badly damaged during the long wars and by fire; others were counterfeit coins. For business transactions, etc., the custom was inaugurated of choosing the good coins *(erizeni)* and discarding the bad ones. The Muromachi government issued an *erizeni* prohibition edict *(erizeni rei)*. Excluding counterfeit currency, the government circulated various other coins equally. It prohibited the practice of *erizeni* because it harmed currency circulation. However, the prohibition was mostly ignored.

Ezo 蝦夷. A race which, in ancient times, lived in the northeastern territories. The theory that the Ezo were the ancestors of the Ainu has weakened considerably. In ancient Japan the Ezo were also called Emishi. The invasion of the Ezo territories was begun in the fifth century by the Yamato court and continued after the Taika Reform (646). Tales about Yamato Takeru no Mikoto reflect these expeditions. Large-scale expeditions were carried out in the seventh century by Abe no Hirafu and in the ninth century by Sakanoue no Tamuramaro (758–811). At strategic places palisades called *ki* were built. The Ezo who surrendered were assimilated and were allowed to live peacefully in an enclosed area, or they could move to the interior of the country. Though these large-scale expeditions ended in early Heian times, still later some Ezo were from time to time assimilated by the inlanders. Among the powerful clans of the northeastern districts at the end of the Heian period, there were many descended from the Ezo. Hokkaidō was called Ezo until the end of the Edo period.

F

fubito 史 (FUHITO)

fudasashi 札差 (financial agent). A financial agent for the bannermen (HATAMOTO) and household retainers (GO-KENIN). Originally *fudasashi* meant a receipt *(fuda)* with the name of the recipient of stored rice. The receipt was attached to a bamboo pole which was inserted *(sasu)* in the straw packages of the rice office. The bannermen and household retainers received from the BAKUFU a rice allowance from the official granary at Asakusa. Merchants then sold the rice on commission. But gradually the merchants advanced money to the needy bannermen and household retainers on the security of their rice stipends and, asking exorbitant interest, amassed a fortune. They organized corporations (KABU-NAKAMA) and monopolized transactions. They led extravagant lives. The *fudasashi's* luxurious way of living was known as *Kuramae-fū*—that is, the style of Kuramae, where the *bakufu's* Asakusa rice granary was.

fudoki 風土記. Geographical descriptions and local histories written during the Nara period. In compliance with an imperial edict issued in May 713, the works were written and offered to the emperor. They record the products, conditions of the soil, old stories, and exceptional circumstances of the various provinces. The most important descriptions are those of Harima (Hyōgo Prefecture), Hitachi (Ibaraki Prefecture), Izumo (Shimane Prefecture), Bungo (Ōita Prefecture), and Hizen (Nagasaki Prefecture). The customs of the local people in ancient times, as well as their legends, are recorded in detail.

fuhito 史 (recorders and archivists). One of the titles (KABANE) which existed before Emperor Temmu (622–86) brought about changes in the eight titles (YAKUSA NO KABANE) and in the ranks of the dignitaries. The title *fuhito (fumi-hito)*, or *fubito*, was given to those who held the records and archives, to the shipping controllers, and to those who were in charge of the granaries and domains under direct control of the court (MIYAKE). Many of the *fuhito* were naturalized Japanese of Korean descent (AYABITO). Instances of such titles are *achiki no fuhito*, title of the recorders and archivists; *fune no fuhito*, a title conferred by Emperor Kimmei (509–71) upon the Korean Ō Shin-ji, who was a shipping control officer *(fune no osa* or *fune no tsukasa)* holding the records of the shipping taxes; and *shirai no fuhito*, the title conferred on those in charge of the *miyake* or imperial granaries and domains.

fujin-sansei ken 婦人参政権 (suffrage for women). The women's suffrage movement began to take shape in 1916. In 1924, an association was formed for the realization of suffrage for women. The organization asked for a motion in its favor in the Lower House but was unsuccessful. Woman suffrage was recognized after the Pacific War when the election law was amended (1945).

Fujiwara-kyō 藤原京 (the capital of Fujiwara). The capital during the reign of Empress Jitō (645–702) and Emperor Mommu (683–707). It corresponded to the territory surrounded by the three mountains, Unebi, Miminashi, and Kagu in the northeast of Yagi, in Takaichi (ancient reading "Takechi") County, Nara Prefecture. With the completion of the penal and administrative law structure and the increase of communications with the Asian mainland, the former capital Asuka became too small. Consequently, Empress Jitō built the new capital Fujiwara and moved there in 694. The plan of the city was much like the one of the following capital, HEIJŌ-KYŌ. Fujiwara was the capital until 710, when it was moved to Heijō. The culture referred to as Hakuhō flowered with the imperial capital Fujiwara-kyō.

Fukuhara 福原. The name of an old locality in the vicinity of Kōbe City, Hyōgo Prefecture. When the antipathy of court nobles and shrines and temples towards the Taira clan grew, and in order to cope with the revolt of Minamoto no Yorimasa (1104–80), Taira no Kiyomori (1118–81) sent for the infant emperor Antoku (1178–85), the cloistered emperor Goshirakawa (1127–92), and the ex-emperor Takakura (1161–81), and moved the capital to Fukuhara in 1180. But for various reasons such as the smallness of the place and the petition of the bonzes of Hiei-zan's ENRYAKU-JI, who wanted to restore the former capital, Kiyomori, after five months, moved the capital back to Kyōto. In those days, Fukuhara was an important port, and it is believed that Kiyomori, in moving the capital to Fukuhara, had an eye to profits deriving from trade with Sung China.

Fukūkenjaku Kannon Zō 不空羂索観音像. A Buddhist statue made in dry lacquer *(kanshitsu-zukuri)* and preserved in the Sangatsudō (or Hokkedō) of Nara's Tōdai-ji. Together with the clay statues of the Bodhisattvas Nikkō and Gakkō on its left and right side, respectively, and the two hollow dry-lacquer *(dakkatsu kanshitsu)* statues of Kongō Rikishi, the Fukūkenjaku Kannon is a representative work of Tempyō (710–94) sculpture. The statue, with its three eyes and eight arms *(sammoku-hachibi)*, gives a feeling of sternness. It is a national treasure.

Fukushima jiken 福島事件 (the incident at Fukushima). The first incident in connection with the introduction of the parliamentary system. The Liberal Party of Kōno Hironaka (1849–1923) in Fukushima was the center of the democratic movement in the northeastern districts. Mishima Michitsune (1835–88) was appointed governor of Fukushima Prefecture with unofficial orders to eradicate the Liberal Party and open new roads. In 1882, he disregarded the opposition of the farmers, who were unable to bear the burden of opening roads, and imprisoned Kōno, who was charged with plotting the overthrow of the government. Taking advantage of this incident, the government suspended the prefectural assemblies throughout the country and intensified the suppression of the democratic movement. The result, however, was the movement's growing more violent.

fumie 踏絵 (treading picture). An image of Christ or of the Virgin on which people during the Edo period were made to tread to prove that they were not Christians. Some of the images were made of copper, others of wood, and they were rectangular or oval. The practice was enforced in the Edo Christian stockade *(Kirishitan yashiki)* and in parts of Kyūshū. It was abolished in 1875 in view of world opinion.

Funai 府内. Present-day Ōita City. From the early Kamakura period, members of the Ōtomo clan wielded power as administrators of Bungo (Ōita Prefecture). Their castle city began to flourish from about the sixteenth century. Of particular fame was the powerful daimyō Ōtomo Sōrin (1530–87), lord of Bungo, who adopted the Catholic doctrine, though he became a Christian only twenty-seven years later, and made his territory into a center for Christianity. This territory was the safest refuge for the early missionaries when they were harassed.

furōnin 浮浪人 (vagrants). Persons who left their own domiciles (places of registration) and moved to other provinces. Originally, the word was used to distinguish between those who moved but paid their entire taxes (CHŌ and YŌ) and those who had taken flight, paying no taxes. With the breakdown of the penal and administrative code system (RITSURYŌ-SEI), only a few people paid the *chō* and *yō* taxes, and in the Heian period the word *furōnin* came to mean "fugitives." The occasion which led to this vagrancy *(furō)* was the oppression and destitution resulting from the tax collections of the *ritsuryō* government. After the middle of the Nara period, when more land became private property, the *furōnin* gathered around the wealthy landowners and the feudal lords. The increase of the number of *furōnin* was one of the reasons for the collapse of the *ritsuryō* system.

Fusen Jōyaku 不戦条約 (Antiwar Pact or Kellogg-Briand Pact). An international pact. In 1927, the French Foreign Minister Briand proposed a pact outlawing war. The American Secretary of State Kellogg asked the cooperation of all countries for world peace. The pact, in which fifty-nine countries participated, was concluded in 1928. At the time of the ratification of the pact, the Privy Council was opposed to the text because of the words "in the name of the people." This opposition resulted in considerable difficulties, with which the democratic cabinet of Hamaguchi had to cope.

Fushimi-jō 伏見城 (Fushimi Castle). The castle is also known as Momoyama-jō and Fushimi-Momoyama-jō. In 1594, Hideyoshi transferred the regency (KAMPAKU) to his adopted son Hidetsugu (1568–95) and built a castle, contemplating a life of retirement. The castle was magnificent and a model of castle architecture. The Karamon and the Shoin of Nishi Hongan-ji in Kyōto are remains of Fushimi-jō.

futomani 太占 (divination). A kind of divination practiced in ancient times. It was used as a means of knowing the divine will when important affairs of state were conducted. It was also called *shika-ura* because the shoulder bone of a deer was burnt by charcoal. The charcoal was obtained from the bark of the kind of cherry tree known as *uwamizu-zakura.* (In ancient times *uwamizu-zakura* was called *habaka* and included various sorts of *sakura* such as *kani-zakura, kaba-zakura,* and *inu-zakura.*) The fortune was told according to the patterns produced by the cracks which appeared following the burning. It seems that this method was widely practiced in the primitive period and until the introduction from China of divination by tortoise shells *(kame-ura* or *kiboku).*

futsū-senkyo undō 普通選挙運動 (movement for universal suffrage). A political movement originating in the early Meiji era when a popular vote was demanded during National Assembly debates by those who advocated democratic rights. But in 1890, during the first voting for the Imperial Diet's Lower House, a mere 460,000 people (who had paid a direct national tax of fifteen yen or more) were given the right to vote. In 1900, an amendment provided for the tax's reduction to ten yen as the property qualification limit, and the number of eligible voters increased threefold. At the dawn of the twentieth century, an association for the realization of popular suffrage began to spread its ideas among the working class. With the growth of bourgeois influence, and in order to cope with the clan government, the political parties continued their opposition to a restricted election. Then, in the early Taishō era, along with the movement for the safeguarding of the constitutional government, the popular-suffrage movement spread throughout the country. As a result, the popular-vote law was promulgated in 1925. However, at the same time, the peace-preservation ordinance (HOAN JŌREI) was also established, and association with politics by the working class was again thwarted.

fuyufunyū-ken 不輸不入権. Fiscal immunity rights in the manor system were called *fuyu-ken,* and the privilege of preventing government officials from entering a manor for harvest inspection was known as *funyū-ken.* These rights were not always restricted to land property but developed far enough to include police authority and jurisdiction. From the middle of the Heian period, these privileges fostered the tendency to make private property of public domains. The manor that recognized the *fuyufunyū* privilege was called KANSHŌFU-SHŌ.

fuyuso-den 不輸租田 (tax-free land). Tax-exempt land under the penal and administrative code system (RITSURYŌ-SEI). This tax-free land included the imperial household land *(kanden),* shrine land *(shinden),* temple land *(jiden),* government land *(kugaiden),* the land of government officials (SHIKIDEN), or the land of official post stations *(ekiden),* and the land of low-class people and of slaves who served government officials *(kanko-kannuhi kubunden).* From about the middle of the Nara period, the *ritsuryō* system declined greatly in prestige, and the system of attributing authority to the head of the family (KAFUCHŌ-SEI) was inaugurated. Furthermore, mighty clans made their appearance, and powerful shrines and temples as well as influential families became great landowners. This resulted in the development of the private manors. More and more land became exempt from taxes, and by the middle of the Heian period the amount of tax-free land had increased beyond reason. (See also CHOKUSHI-DEN.)

G

gaikokusen uchiharai rei 外国船打払令 (the order to expel foreign ships). Edict issued in 1825 by the BAKUFU to the effect that any foreign ship coming close to shore should be destroyed. The edict is also known as *mu-ninen uchiharai rei* or "no second thought expulsion order." From the close of the eighteenth century, acts of violence were committed by the crews of Russian and English vessels which intruded in home waters. Consequently, in February 1825, the government issued an order to the local authorities to destroy any foreign ship and to arrest or kill any members of its crew who might land. However, the edict was not strictly enforced, owing to the weakness of the *bakufu* and the clans as well as to some criticism within Japan. In 1842, the Japanese government heard details of the defeat of China in the Opium War and moderated its policy. The local authorities were instructed to supply foreign ships with food and fuel. In 1863, the Jōi, or antiforeign party, issued the "important order to carry out the expulsion of foreigners" *(jōi kekkō no dai-gōrei),* but it was no longer possible for the *bakufu* to enforce the order.

Gakkan-in 学館院 (the private school of the Tachibana clan). A private school of the Tachibana clan, established in 850 in Kyōto by Tachibana no Kachiko (786–850), the empress-consort of Emperor Saga (786–842), with the help of her younger brother Ujigimi. The purpose was to educate the members of the Tachibana family. Later the Gakkan-in became an annex of the University, or Daigaku-ryō, and, with the decline of the Tachibana family, ceased to exist.

gakkō rei 学校令 (edict on education). Educational system of the early Meiji period. In 1886, the statesman Mori Arinori (1847–89), who was minister of education, promulgated the new system of education. The educational reform was based on nationalism.

Gakumon no Susume 学問のすすめ *(Encouragement of Learning).* The name of a book written in the early Meiji era by the pioneer of modern education, Fukuzawa Yukichi (1834–1901), and published in installments between 1872 and 1876. The work contributed toward general education. It is based on Western thought and advocates academic freedom, independence, and self-respect.

gakusei happu 学制発布 (issuance of act on education). The first modern system of school education. After the abolition of clans and establishment of prefectures, the government established a Ministry of Education and proceeded to devise and enforce a complete national system of education. In 1872, modeled upon French state-controlled education and in line with the American education system, the new education act was promulgated. The proclamation included the words, "From now on, education is for all citizens. There will be no illiterate family in any village, nor an illiterate person in any family." The act aimed at the equality of all citizens through equality of opportunity and established general compulsory education. The plan provided for universities, middle schools, elementary schools, normal schools, and technical schools on a large scale. However, the financial resources of the government, as well as the level of understanding of the common citizen, were too limited, and the act was abolished in 1879 when a new ordinance called *kyōiku rei* was issued.

Garakuta Bunko 我楽多文庫. A literary magazine of the Meiji era. In 1885, a society of writers called Ken'yū-sha, which promoted realism and a colloquial style, was founded. Its leading figure was the novelist Ozaki Kōyō (1867–1903), who started the magazine *Garakuta Bunko*.

geba shōgun 下馬将軍. A nickname given to the shogunate minister Sakai Tadakiyo (1624–81), who wielded power under the weak-minded fourth shōgun, Tokugawa Ietsuna (1641–80). Because Sakai's residence was located near the notice board *(geba-fuda)* at the entrance of the shogunate castle, beyond which samurai were not allowed to go on horseback, Sakai was nicknamed *geba shōgun*.

Geijutsu-za 芸術座. A theatrical troupe of the New Drama School, Taishō era. In 1913, the writer Shimamura Hōgetsu (1871–1918) left the dramatic group called Bungei Kyōkai and, in cooperation with the actress Matsui Sumako (1886–1919), organized the Geijutsu-za association. Tolstoi's *Resurrection* was performed in various places. The early Taishō era marked the climax of the New Drama School.

gekokujō 下剋上. A social tendency during the Muromachi period. During the Kemmu Restoration (KEMMU NO CHŪKŌ) of 1334–36, scribblings on the walls at Nijō-kawara read, *"Gekokujō suru nariagarimono"* 下剋上する成出者. The meaning was "the low oppress the high," implying that the lower classes were rising and seizing power from the upper classes. From the Nambokuchō to the Muromachi period, the manor system began to disintegrate, and constables who had become great landlords (SHUGO DAIMYŌ) extended their influence. The upper classes were robbed of their land by the lower classes. The court nobles were dispossessed by the warriors, the shōgun by the governors—that is, by the high administrative officers called KANREI—and the constables (SHUGO) by their deputies. Instances of the confiscation of real power are the Muromachi shōgun Ashikaga Yoshitane (1446–1523), who was deposed by his prime minister, Hosokawa Masamoto (1466–1507); the Hosokawa, who were defeated by Miyoshi Chōkei (1523–64); and the Miyoshi, who were defeated by Matsunaga Hisahide (1510–77). Furthermore, agrarian uprisings (DO-IKKI) became more frequent, and the ruling class felt strong opposition. Likewise, the period of civil war (SENGOKU JIDAI) intensified the *gekokujō* movement and witnessed the rise of the *sengoku daimyō* or civil-war barons (DAIMYŌ).

Gempei Seisuiki 源平盛衰記. The name of a great war romance, written in the middle of the Kamakura period. The author is unknown. There are indications that the work was inspired by the commentaries on HEIKE MONO-GATARI, but its literary value is inferior. It influenced later literature. The central figure is Taira no Kiyomori (1118–81), and the work describes the rise and decline *(seisui)* of the Minamoto (Gen) and Taira (Hei) clans.

genin 下人 (serfs). Slave farmers during the middle ages (Kamakura and Muromachi periods). These serfs took care of the land and the house of a MYŌSHU (an owner of manor land in his own name) or, living in the house of a *myōshu*, provided the labor. The advantage was always with the master. The serf was an inherited article and was sometimes transferred to another proprietor or sold. However, the *genin* succeeded in establishing farming rights.

Genji Monogatari 源氏物語. A representative work of *monogatari* literature, middle Heian period. The authoress is Murasaki Shikibu (978–1015), and the work, comprising fifty-four chapters, was written between the years 1000 and 1010. Murasaki was influenced by the poetical ISE MONOGATARI, the romantic and realistic literature from the time of the publication of TAKETORI MONOGATARI, and the delicate psychological analyses found in the diaries of women. The work has been rendered into modern Japanese by Yosano Akiko and Tanizaki Jun'ichirō and translated into English by Arthur Waley.

The first forty-one chapters are devoted to the romantic life of numerous women who vie with one another for the favor of Hikaru Genji and his son Kaoru Kimi. There is also a tinge of loneliness in the life of Hikaru Genji. The next three chapters deal with the growth of Kaoru Kimi. The last ten chapters describe Kaoru's wavering between religion and earthly love. They are called *Uji jūjō,* the scene being Uji, near Kyōto. The Buddhist ideology of predestination underlies the whole work. The style is superb, and the literary doctrine of *aware* (sadness) as found in Heian literature here reaches its climax. There is no doubt that later works were influenced by *Genji Monogatari's* romantic world.

Genji Monogatari Emaki 源氏物語絵巻. A picture scroll illustrating selections from the GENJI MONOGATARI. The work probably belongs to the late Fujiwara period (894–1185). The four sections of which it is composed form a representative work of the YAMATO-E style of painting. The painter used deep colors, and the expression is graceful and delicate. It is supposed to be the work of a painter of nobility, perhaps of Fujiwara no Takayoshi (about 1150). The texts are written on paper embellished with colorful patterns, in the fluent and elegant cursive *kana* used during the late Fujiwara period. It is believed that these texts were written by the calligrapher Fujiwara no Korefusa (1030–96) in collaboration with five other calligraphers. Both the scroll *Shigisan Engi Emaki,* made in the same period, and the *Genji Monogatari Emaki* are representative picture scrolls or EMAKIMONO.

Genkō 元寇 (the Yüan or Mongol invasions). The Mongol invasions during the Kamakura period. After the Mongol conqueror Genghis Khan (1162–1227) had founded his Euro-Asiatic empire, his grandson Khubilai (1216–94) conquered Kōrai (Korea). Starting in 1266, Khubilai sent repeated envoys to demand that the Japanese enter into a tributary relationship with him. The shogunal regent Hōjō Tokimune (1215–84) refused to bow to the Mongols. Finally, in 1274, Mongol forces invaded Tsushima and Iki and landed in North Kyūshū. A storm destroyed the invading forces. This battle is known as *Bun'ei no eki* or the battle of the Bun'ei (1264–75) era. In 1281, the Mongols dispatched a second great force and attacked Hakata Bay. The invasions failed because of a typhoon and the resistance of the local vassals. This campaign is known as *Kōan no eki* or the battle of the Kōan (1278–88) era. A third invasion was planned by Khubilai, but it did not materialize because of internal troubles in the Yüan empire. The KAMAKURA BAKUFU, which had succeeded in repulsing the invaders, and the direct vassals, who had shouldered the burden of expenses, were economically hard pressed. Some of the vassals became disaffected, and this state of affairs undermined the *bakufu,* which was founded upon the vassalage system.

Genkō no hen 元弘の変 (the civil strife of the Genkō era). Civil strife of 1331 which resulted in the Kemmu Restoration (KEMMU NO CHŪKŌ) and in the destruction of the KAMAKURA BAKUFU. At the end of the Kamakura period, the direct vassals rebelled and undermined the foundation of the Kamakura regime. Previously, Emperor Godaigo (1288–1339) of the Daikakuji line (DAIKAKUJI-TŌ) had given his support to the courtiers Hino Suketomo (?–1332) and Hino Toshimoto (?–1332), who plotted to overthrow the Kamakura shogunate. The plot, which is known as SHŌCHŪ NO HEN, had failed. In 1331, the emperor himself recruited soldiers from the neighboring provinces, fled from Kyōto, and took refuge at Mount Kasagi, in Yamashiro Province. To defend the cause of the emperor, the warlord Kusunoki Masashige (1294–1336) fought the *bakufu* forces at the fortresses of Akasaka and Chihaya (near Nara). Meanwhile, the emperor was captured (1332) and exiled to Oki Island, but his son Prince Morinaga (1308–35) created an army at Yoshino and obtained the help of other loyalists such as Akamatsu Norimura (1287–1350). Finally, Ashikaga Takauji (1305–58) attacked Rokuhara in Kyōto, and Nitta Yoshisada (1301–38) marched on Kamakura. The Hōjō were destroyed, and the emperor, returning to Kyōto, inaugurated the Kemmu Restoration.

Genkō Shakusho 元亨釈書. A historical work on Buddhism, completed during the Kamakura period. It describes in thirty volumes the history of Buddhism from its origin in Japan to the second year of the Genkō era (1322). The author is the Buddhist priest Koken Shiren (1278–1346) of Tōfuku-ji temple. He completed the work in 1322. It is the first comprehensive Japanese work on the history of Buddhism and includes biographies of Buddhist priests, comments, and historical events.

gen-Nihonjin 原日本人 (Japanese prototype). The prototype of the Japanese race. From the study of the human bones found among the remains of the "rope pattern" *(jōmon-shiki)* culture, it is believed that the Jōmon man was the prototype of the Japanese race. The Jōmon culture was the first major Japanese culture and spread over the islands about the third millennium B.C.

Genrōin 元老院 (Senate). A legislative body of the early Meiji era. Unlike the American and European separation of the three powers, administrative, legislative, and judicial, a Council of State called DAJŌKAN was reorganized in 1875, and a senate (Upper House) and an assembly of provincial officials known as Chihōkan-kaigi (Lower House) were created. However, neither the Senate nor the Provincial Assembly had any representative or elective character, and both were dissolved in 1890 when the Imperial Constitution was promulgated and the House of Peers established.

Genroku bunka 元禄文化 (the Genroku culture). A culture which flourished under the influence of the newly risen townspeople during the Genroku (1688–1703) era. The center of the culture was Kyōto and Ōsaka, the so-called Kamigata. Confucianism and national literature flourished. Haiku poetry (HAIKAI), "floating-world booklets" (UKIYO-ZŌSHI), Kabuki, *jōruri* or puppet theaters, and "pictures of the floating world" or UKIYO-E were popular with the townspeople and flourished according to their taste. A very bright and showy period was inaugurated. In contrast to the later Edo culture and the Bunsei (1818–30) culture under the reign of Emperor Ninkō (1800–46), the Genroku culture was very youthful and vigorous.

Genroku jidai 元禄時代 (Genroku period). Genroku is the era name of a short period (1688–1703) under the thirty years of rule of the fifth shōgun, Tokugawa Tsunayoshi (1646–1709). When the BAKUFU authority was firmly established, commerce and industry began to flourish. Currency found its way into the rural communities, and the prosperous cities increased the wealth of the townspeople. Learning and the arts flourished. But the feudal lords and warriors as well as the farmers were financially pressed, and the political structure of the feudal system began to weaken.

gesu 下司 (manor official). The official in charge of the general supervision of a manor. Originally the characters were read *shita-zukasa* and meant the public servant with lower duties or "lower personnel" serving in the manor. Landowners would combine their property and make it into a manor, and the lord of the manor was appointed general supervisor. But sometimes the feudal lord appointed a general supervisor whom he accredited to the manor.

In both cases, the function of general supervisor was hereditary. The duties of a *gesu* were to control the yearly taxes, official affairs, and servants of a manor. In return, the *gesu* received a reward from the lord. In due time, the *gesu* themselves became landowners and name masters (MYŌSHU). By the end of the Heian period, many of these *gesu* joined the military class, and, when the KAMAKURA BAKUFU was established, they became direct vassals of the shō-gun and were appointed land stewards (JITŌ).

Gijō 議定 (Senior Council of State). A government office during the early Meiji era. In 1867, when the imperial rule was restored, the previous offices were abolished and three new offices created. They were the office of the President of the Council or SŌSAI, the Senior Council of State (the Upper House of the Deliberative Chamber) or Gijō, and the Junior Council of State (the Lower House of the Deliberative Chamber) or SAN'YO. All three were abolished in 1869 when the State Council or Sangi was established.

Gijō-kan 議政官 (Deliberative Chamber). Legislative body established in the early Meiji era. The policy of "referring all state affairs to public opinion" (*banki kōron ni kessuru* 万機公論に決する), as described in the Five-Point Charter Oath (GO-KAJŌ NO SEIMON), took concrete form, and on April 6, 1868, an Up-per and a Lower House were established. They were abolished in September of the same year.

Gikeiki 義経記. A military chronicle of the Muromachi period in eight parts. The author and the date of publication are unknown. The work describes the life of Minamoto no Yoshitsune (1159–89). It differs from previous war chronicles (GUNKIMONO), which described contemporary wars, and concen-trates on personal chivalry. It greatly influenced Nō songs and later litera-ture.

gimu-kyōiku seido 義務教育制度 (compulsory education system). Modern general education system. In 1872, a detailed education act was issued, which laid the foundation for compulsory education. Later, school attendance be-came compulsory, and the number of years of compulsory education was extended. General education was enforced.

Ginkaku 銀閣. A villa built by Shōgun Ashikaga Yoshimasa (1434–90) during the Muromachi period. It is located in the precincts of the Jishō-ji temple, in Kyōto. Ginkaku is an imitation of KINKAKU, erected by Ashi-kaga Yoshimitsu (1358–1408), but, whereas Kinkaku is built in the style called SHINDEN-ZUKURI, which is the style of mansions of court nobles, Gin-kaku is built in the style of SHOIN-ZUKURI or style of residential architecture. Kinkaku is a gorgeous building typical of the Kitayama culture, while Gin-kaku is rather representative of the tranquil Higashiyama culture, which strove for simple elegance. The painstaking construction of the landscape garden by Sōami (?–1525) is in beautiful harmony with the natural scenery of neighboring Higashiyama. The Tōgudō Dōjinsai of Jishō-ji is a representative structure in *shoin* style and constitutes the origin of tea-ceremony-room construction.

ginza, kinza 銀座・金座 (monopoly for silver and gold coins). Silver and gold mints during the Edo period. Gold mints were first established in Edo, Kyōto, and Sado, but later gold was minted only in Edo. Gotō Mitsutsugu (1571–1625) was known as a goldsmith and as headman of the gold coin foundry in Edo, this office being referred to as *kin-aratame yaku*. The office belonged hereditarily to the Gotō family until the exposure of fraud in the Bunka era (1804–18), when Gotō Kichigorō was ousted. The gold coin called "obang" (ŌBAN) was made in the *ōban-za*. In the *kinza* of Edo only the gold coin known as "kobang" *(koban)* was minted. The first *ginza* was established in Fushimi in 1601; it later moved to Kyōto. There were also *ginza* in Edo, Ōsaka, Nagasaki, etc. The chief silver-coin founder was called *ginfukinin,* and the office belonged hereditarily to the Daikoku Jōze family. The various *ginza* held the monopoly, in the form of a contract, for the mintage. Because from the later part of the Edo period the clans were not allowed to mint, the *ginza* were a source of revenue for the BAKUFU.

Gishi Wajin Den 魏志・倭人伝. Part of the Chinese historical work *San-kuo Chih* (in Japanese, *Sangokushi*). It bears the title *Wei Chih* (in Japanese, *Gishi*). Both this account and the historical work *Hou Han Shu* (GOKANJO), in its chapter "Tung I Chuan" or "Commentary on the Eastern Barbarians," deal with the *wajin,* who are the Japanese people. At the close of the third century (the early Chin dynasty), Ch'en Shou compiled *San-kuo Chih* or *Memoir of the Three Kingdoms,* which includes the *Wei Chih* (Wei Record). The author accurately describes the political situation of the Japanese islands in the middle of the third century, the condition of life of the people, and the relations of the Wei state with the land of Wa, called YAMATAI-KOKU. For the study of the history of ancient Japan, these records constitute valuable material. As for the identification of Yamatai, opinions differ. One holds that it was part of Kyūshū, while another favors Yamato.

gisō 義倉 (welfare granaries). A kind of social security system in the form of granaries during the Nara, Heian, and Edo periods. The *gisō* was under government control and took in deposits of grain. The purpose was to be able to distribute the deposits among the destitute in time of crisis or bad harvests. The families were divided into nine classes according to wealth or poverty, and taxes were collected in the form of millet. In this way the wealthy helped the poor, but since many people were unable to bear the burden of the taxes for the *gisō,* those who were too destitute were exempted from 706. With the collapse of the penal and administrative code system (RITSURYŌ-SEI) during the Heian period, the *gisō* were abolished, but the clans during the Edo period revived the system to provide against emergencies.

Gobō no Keiji 五榜の掲示 (the Five-Provision Notice). Laws and ordinances of the early Meiji era. They were promulgated in 1868 together with the Five-Point Charter Oath (GO-KAJŌ NO SEIMON) and included five provisions made public on the notice board of the Council of State or DAJŌKAN. The form of the bulletin and the contents of the ordinances did not differ from those of the BAKUFU. The proclamation made it clear that it was prohibited to form factions, to present direct petitions, and to desert the farm in order to escape taxes. These prohibitions were a mere continuation of the control of the feudal farmers.

go-bugyō 五奉行 (the five administrators). Government officers during the Momoyama period. The five administrators or commissioners who served Hideyoshi and his son Hideyori formed a sort of cabinet and took charge of various aspects of the administration. All five were warlords and trustworthy henchmen. Usually two or three of them acted jointly on important matters. The five administrators were Asano Nagamasa (1546–1610) for legal questions, Ishida Mitsunari (1563–1600) for public works, Maeda Gen'i (1539–1602) for the police and temples, Masuda Nagamori (1545–1615) for judicial affairs, and Nagatsuka Masaie (?–1600) for finance. The five administrators continued their duties after the death of Hideyoshi, but Mitsunari plotted against Ieyasu. His plot failed, however, and he was beheaded.

go-ichigo jiken 五・一五事件 (the incident of May 15, 1932). Fascist terrorism of May 15, 1932. Ōkawa Shūmei, Tachibana Kōzaburō, Homma Ken'ichirō, and other ultranationalists, with the help of forty-two young military officers, planned a military reform. They attacked the privileged classes, the big concerns (ZAIBATSU), and the political parties. They also attacked the offices of the prime minister, the minister of home affairs, the metropolitan police, the Nippon Bank, the Mitsubishi Bank, and the headquarters of the SEIYŪ-KAI political association and assassinated Prime Minister Inukai Tsuyoshi (1855–1932). Trying to black out Tōkyō, some attacked the electric transformer station. This incident was preceded by the assassination in February of Inoue Junnosuke (1866–1932), who was finance minister in 1923, and the assassination in March of the businessman Dan Takuma (1858–1932) by ultranationalists. The rebellion, which aimed at strengthening fascism, resulted in the defeat of the political parties and the formation of a coalition government.

go-kaidō 五街道 (five highways). The five highways during the Edo period, which linked the eastern and western provinces with Edo. They were the

Tōkaidō, Nakasendō, Ōshūkaidō, Kōshūkaidō, and Nikkōkaidō. The BAKUFU, which directly controlled the highways, aimed at maintaining central authority. Post horses *(temma)* were provided and relay stations *(shukueki)* set up, and, to control the thoroughfares, the office of *dōchū bugyō* or administration of the highways, was established.

Go-kajō no Seimon 五ヶ条の誓文 (the Five-Point Imperial Charter Oath). A charter oath in which the aims of the new government were laid down by Emperor Meiji for the restoration of imperial rule. On March 14, 1868, Emperor Meiji summoned the court nobles and feudal lords and took the Five-Point Charter Oath. He ordered that the oath be considered national policy and that it be obeyed. The text of the oath is:
1) Deliberative assemblies shall be established on an extensive scale, and all measures of government shall be decided by public opinion.
2) All classes, high and low, shall unite in vigorously carrying out the plan of government.
3) All classes of the people shall be allowed to fulfill their just aspirations so that there may be no discontent.
4) Uncivilized customs of former times shall be discontinued, and all new customs shall be based upon just and equitable principles of nature.
5) Knowledge shall be sought throughout the world in order that the welfare of the empire may be promoted.

The first draft was made by Yuri Kimimasa and Fukuoka Kōtei. The first words of the first article "deliberative assemblies... on an extensive scale" *(hiroku kaigi* 広会議) differ from those of the preliminary draft, which were "a council of feudal lords" *(rekkō kaigi* 列侯会議). This proves that the first article contemplated a course of action for which the cooperation of the feudal lords with the court was asked. The words "high and low shall unite" *(jōge kokoro o ichi ni shite* 上下心を一にして) aimed at controlling the oppression of the lower classes of warriors by the feudal lords, and the words "all classes of the people shall be allowed to fulfill their just aspirations" *(shomin kokorozashi o toge* 庶民志を遂げ) expressed the hope that the wealthy merchants and farmers would give their support to the new policy to strengthen its foundation. The words "uncivilized customs of former times" *(kyūrai no rōshū* 旧来の陋習) refer to the national isolation policy of the EDO BAKUFU and stress a policy of friendly relations with foreign countries. The Charter Oath may be considered the first constitution of modern Japan, though it was rather a reversion to prefeudal institutions.

Gokanjo 後漢書. History of the Later Han, or Hou Han, in 120 volumes by Fan Yeh (397–445) during the fifth century. Commentaries on the Eastern Barbarians, called "Tung I Chuan," are to be found in the 115th volume. This chapter deals with the *wajin* or Japanese and is known as *Gokanjo Waden* 後漢書倭伝. It offers valuable material for the study of conditions in Japan during the first and second centuries. Much of the material was taken from the GISHI WAJIN DEN of the previously compiled *Sangokushi* or *San-kuo Chih*, but there are also unique accounts such as the one of the tribute paid by the *wajin* in 57 to the first emperor of the Later Han dynasty, Kuang Wu Ti (who accorded the official seal to the Japanese envoys), and in 107 to Emperor An Ti.

go-kenin 御家人 (honorable house men). 1) Kamakura period. Warriors who were in a master-servant relationship with the shōgun and who considered themselves to be the shōgun's retainers. They were distinguished from the other warriors, who were called *hi go-kenin*. The BAKUFU confirmed the fiefs of the *go-kenin* from their ancestors down (HONRYŌ-ANDO) or granted them new farms *(shin'on)* or also appointed them constables (SHUGO) and stewards (JITŌ). In return, the *go-kenin* had the duty in peacetime of serving as guards *(ōban* or great watch) in Kyōto and Kamakura and in wartime of going on active duty *(hōkō* or service to the country). Thus the master-servant relationship between the shōgun and the *go-kenin* was based on favors and services. At the end of the Kamakura period, however, financial difficulties on the part of the *go-kenin* resulted in the loss of their domains, and the system existed only in name. 2) Edo period. Personal retainers of the shōgun with an income of 10,000 *koku* or less. They were inferior in rank to the HATAMOTO or bannermen, for, unlike the *hatamoto,* the *go-kenin* were never granted an audience with the shōgun. In the later part of the Edo period, financial troubles forced some *go-kenin* to sell their rank to the townspeople, and the system collapsed.

gōko 郷戸 (village family). The family system in ancient Japan was based on the *gōko.* According to the penal and administrative code system (RITSURYŌ-SEI), a local administrative section included one village with fifty families. The village was then called *ri,* and the unit which made up the village was called *ko* or family. Later the *ri* became a *gō,* which, in the Nara period, was an administrative area comprising several villages and, in the Muromachi period, a large self-governing village or group of villages. The family was also the unit which had to pay the taxes known as SO, YŌ, and CHŌ. The family was registered in the family census register, and farmland was allotted to it. The unit which made up the village family was called BŌKO. In a *gōko* lived many relatives, dependents such as sick people and small children (dependents were known as *kikō*), and servants. Most families were composed of about twenty members. The family of Inode, a wealthy land proprietor of Shima County in Chikuzen Province (Fukuoka Prefecture), was an exception and included 124 members.

It is believed that the *gōko* system collapsed, making room for the *bōko,* which strengthened its self-reliance, but another opinion holds that the *gōko* dissolved the *bōko,* made the *bōko* dependents into servants, and grew into large families which centered around the family head.

gokyō hakase 五経博士 (doctor of Confucian Classics). From the beginning to the middle of the sixth century, many officials of Kudara called "doctors of Confucian Classics" came to Japan, where they sojourned. According to an account in NIHON SHOKI, Tan Yō-ji sojourned in Japan in 516, Kankō Ammō in 516, and Ō Ryū-ki in 554. They were influenced by the culture of the Chinese Southern dynasty (420–589) and probably propagated the Five Confucian Classics in Japan. The Five Classics are known in Japanese as *Ekikyō, Shikyō, Shokyō, Shunjū,* and *Raiki.*

gonin-gumi 五人組 (five-man units). System of neighborhood associations of farmers and townspeople during the Edo period. Five or more neighboring families were made into a group, a head presiding over each group. The purpose was to make the group assume collective responsibility for the taxes to be paid and for the crimes committed within the group, and to enforce mutual inspection. Conversely, the group enjoyed mutual aid and joint security. Each neighborhood association was in the possession of a register in the preface of which were noted various regulations. When a meeting was held, an officer would read the regulations so that the attendants were fully informed. In the early Meiji era, the neighborhood associations were still in force, but they gradually disappeared, though vestiges are still to be found today. Besides the *gonin-gumi,* there were also *jūnin-gumi* or neighborhood associations of ten families, but their meaning and function were the same as those of the *gonin-gumi.*

Go-sannen no Eki 後三年の役 (the Later Three Years War). The civil war fought between Kiyohara no Iehira (?–1087) and Takehira (?–1087) on one side and Sanehira (circa 1080) of the same family on the other. Minamoto no Yoshiie (1039–1106), who was appointed governor of Mutsu in 1083, destroyed Iehira and Takehira at the Kanezawa stockade and restored peace. The war lasted, with periods of truce, from 1083 to 1089.

go-sekke 五摂家 (the five regency houses). The five chief branches of the Fujiwara family qualified by tradition for the office of regent (SESSHŌ) and of chief councilor to the emperor (KAMPAKU). They were the Konoe, Kujō, Nijō, Ichijō, and Takatsukasa. The Fujiwara family did not entrust local people with the power of regent or of chief councilor to the emperor, but Minamoto no Yoritomo (1148–99), trying to reduce the power of the Fujiwara house, sided with Kujō Kanezane (1149–1207) and assured Kanezane's appointment as regent. Thus were formed the two branch families descended from Fujiwara no Tadamichi (1097–1164), viz., the Konoe branch of Tadamichi's son Motozane (1143–66) and the Kujō branch of Tadamichi's third son, Kanezane. The two branches were further divided during the middle of the Kamakura period—the Konoe branch into the Takatsukasa and Konoe branches, the Kujō branch into the Ichijō, Nijō, and Kujō branches. It is to be noted that this division into five families occurred about the time of the division of the lineage of emperors into the Daikakuji (DAIKAKUJI-TŌ) and the Jimyōin (JIMYŌIN-TŌ).

gōshi 郷士 (village samurai). Samurai living in rural areas during the Edo period. There were various types of rural warriors—those who lived in the country following the recruiting of agrarian soldiers from the clans, the clansmen who were sent back to the country following the financial difficulties in the castle towns, and those who previously were wealthy farmers but who were raised to the status of samurai. The *gōshi* system of the Satsuma, Chōshū, and Tosa clans is well known. Most of these rural warriors were landowners and contributed toward the management of the villages. They lived as self-supporting farmers in peacetime, and some were responsible for the industrial development of the villages. Many loyalists of the restoration period belonged to this class of village samurai.

gōso 強訴 (appeal by force). Direct petitioning coupled with force. Instances of this method of appeal are the following:

1) After the middle of the Heian period, the monk-soldiers of the ENRYAKU-JI and Kōfuku-ji temples made direct petitions to the court using force. Invested with divine power because they carried a portable shrine of the Hie Shrine (HIE-JINJA) and the sacred tree *(shimboku)* of the Kasuga Shrine (KASUGA-JINJA), they plagued the court nobles, pushing through their demands.

2) During the Kamakura and Muromachi periods, the farmers used force to push through their petitions, demanding a reduction of, or exemption from, the exorbitant land taxes.

3) During the Edo period, many farmers banding together made petitions to the BAKUFU or to the clan administration or sacrificed one representative for the same purpose. When, from the middle of the Edo period, feudal control became weaker, the opposition of the farmers grew in intensity and the violent petitions ended in open rebellions.

gōson-sei 郷村制 (rural system). Rural system during the Edo period. The origin of the *gōson-sei* is to be found in the self-governing system of the villages after the latter part of the Muromachi period. About this time, serfs, attendants, and slaves (NAGO) became more independent, the number of self-supporting small farmers also increased, and not a few people, especially the smaller name masters (MYŌSHU), banded together to strengthen their position. From among this body were chosen the *satabito* (officials of a manor), the *otona* (those who officiated as name masters), etc. They held periodic meetings at the village shrine or at other places. The *gōson-sei* is also the origin of the *sengoku daimyō* (DAIMYŌ). However, Nobunaga, Hideyoshi, and Ieyasu held the *gōson* under their rigid control, and after the land was surveyed the villages played the role of a subordinate structure in the feudal system. The farmers were the core of the *gōson,* for they kept the farms and operated them in a self-supporting way. The village strengthened its solidarity by means of ceremonial observances in connection with the common interests of the inhabitants, such as planting, irrigation, and drainage or the use of anything in common, and also by means of the community religious ceremonies in honor of the clan god. On the other hand, the farmers had to pay the yearly land taxes, and the *gōson* was the unit of the payment. For the management of territories under direct jurisdiction of the shōgun, the offices of deputy constable (GUNDAI) and of the deputies called DAIKAN, who were lower in the administrative scale, were created. In addition, three local officials were chosen from among the farmers. Neighborhood associations (GONIN-GUMI) were established, and the members were made responsible for each other's conduct. In short, until the end of the Edo period, the *gōson-sei* was the foundation of the feudal regime.

go-tairō 五大老 (the five supreme councilors of Hideyoshi). An office established by Hideyoshi. Before his death, Hideyoshi, thinking of the future, appointed five men to the post of *tairō* (great elder). They were Tokugawa Ieyasu (1542–1616), Maeda Toshiie (1538–99), Mōri Terumoto (1553–1625), Uesugi Kagekatsu (1555–1623), and Ukita Hideie (1573–1655). But soon Toshiie died, and, when Ieyasu's influence grew, his office of supreme councilor became a mere name. With the battle of Sekigahara in 1600 (SEKIGAHARA NO TATAKAI), this particular office ceased to exist.

Gozan 五山 (the Five Zen Monasteries). A status of priority for certain Zen monasteries during the Kamakura and Muromachi periods. The name "Gozan" existed already in the Kamakura period, but the Five Monasteries were not yet determined. Ashikaga Yoshimitsu (1358–1408), in imitation of the system of temples under official administration *(kanji)* in Sung China, determined the Kyōto Five Zen Monasteries and the Kamakura Five Zen Monasteries. NANZEN-JI temple was the presiding foundation. The Five Zen Monasteries of Kyōto were TENRYŪ-JI, Shōkoku-ji, KENNIN-JI, TŌFUKU-JI, and MANJU-JI. Those of Kamakura were KENCHŌ-JI, ENKAKU-JI, Jufuku-ji, JŌCHI-JI, and JŌMYŌ-JI. Particularly the Kyōto Gozan enjoyed the protection of the MUROMACHI BAKUFU, and some bonzes took part in the *bakufu's* politics and diplomacy. The Gozan formed a cultural center, since Zen monks produced a distinctive and creative part of Ashikaga culture. The literature of the Five Monasteries was famous. It was known as GOZAN-BUNGAKU. Publications of sutras and literary works by the Five Monasteries were referred to as GOZAN-BAN.

Gozan-ban 五山版 (Gozan editions). The publishing which developed under the direction of the Zen monks of the Five Monasteries (GOZAN). Zen Buddhism flourished from the end of the Kamakura to the end of the Muromachi period. Buddhist priests of Sung China came to Japan, and Japanese priests went to Sung and Yüan China. Many outstanding books were brought to Japan. This cultural intercourse brought about the publication of books by the Five Monasteries. Most of the books dealt with Zen Buddhism, but there were also works on poetry and learning in general. Higher learning during the Muromachi period was almost entirely monopolized by Zen monks.

Gozan-bungaku 五山文学 (Gozan literature). Chinese literature which flourished in the Five Monasteries (GOZAN) during the Kamakura and Muromachi periods. From the end of the Kamakura to the end of the Muromachi period, Zen Buddhism flourished, as many Zen monks from Sung and Yüan China came to Japan, and many Japanese Zen monks went to China. When Ashikaga Yoshimitsu (1358–1408) sponsored trade with Ming China, he used Zen priests as envoys. Under Chinese influence Gozan literature came into being. The most distinguished scholars were Koken (or Kogen) Shiren (1278–1346), Zekkai Chūshin (1336–1405), and Gidō Shūshin (1325–88). These scholars not only wrote Chinese poetry and Chinese works on Zen Buddhism but also introduced Chinese literature as well as Sung learning to Japan. They were also instrumental in the rise of Confucianism and of Chinese literature in Japan.

Gukanshō 愚管抄. Great historical work of the Kamakura period, written in 1221, just prior to the civil war of the Jōkyū (1219–22) era, by the *waka* poet and first great Japanese historian, Jien (1145–1225). Jien was a Tendai abbot. The work comprises seven volumes and was the first critical and analytical work on Japanese history. It relates the events of each period from early times to the Jōkyū era. The work incorporates the Buddhist philosophy of life.

gumbi shukushō 軍備縮小 (disarmament). Political problem during the Taishō and early Shōwa eras. After World War I international tension grew as the powers pursued a rearmament policy. Japan's militarist policy toward China developed, the army was reinforced, and the building of a huge fleet was planned. The citizens, who had to shoulder excessive taxation, were opposed to the expansion of armaments, thus bringing dissension in the political parties. Japan took part in the Washington Conference for Naval Reduction (1921), the Geneva Conference (1927), and the Kellogg-Briand Pact (1928). In spite of the violent opposition of army circles to the London Conference of 1930, Prime Minister Hamaguchi, backing public opinion, effected a disarmament plan. Antagonism between the militarists thus facing disarmament and the political parties heralded the rise of fascism.

Gumma jiken 群馬事件 (the incident in Gumma Prefecture). An incident which occurred in the early Meiji era, following the intensification of the movement for democratic rights. In 1884, the Liberal Party of Gumma Prefecture took direct action, attacking usurers, wealthy companies, and the police. The attack ended in failure.

gundai 郡代 (deputy constables). The name of officials in charge of the civil and judicial administration of the feudal domains of 10,000 *koku* or more under direct jurisdiction of the EDO BAKUFU. The officials were under the control of the commissioner of finance or KANJŌ BUGYŌ. The *gundai* differed from the DAIKAN, as the *daikan* administered territory of less than 10,000 *koku* and as the territory was of a different nature. However, the service of both was the same. The *daikan* of the Kantō district was placed under the jurisdiction of the *gundai* Ina Tadatsugu (1550–1610). Ina was the official in charge of land belonging to the shogunate in the Kantō district. The *gundai* of Mino, Saikoku, Kawachi, Amagasaki, etc. were well known.

gundan 軍団 (military detachments). Detachments of men enlisted for military service during the penal and administrative code system (RITSURYŌ-SEI). In order to be prepared militarily, soldiers were recruited from various provinces. There were about 140 *gundan* in the whole country, and they were under the jurisdiction of their respective provincial governors, under whose direction commanders called *taigi* and *shōgi* were appointed. In wartime, many *gundan* made up an army corps or *gun,* and each army corps was commanded by a general or *shōgun* and an "assistant general" or *fuku-shōgun*. A "great general" or *taishōgun* commanded three army corps. The soldiers were exempted from corvée but had to pay miscellaneous taxes such as YŌ and the produce tax called CHŌ. They had to supply their own weapons and food, and they had to travel to their posts at their own expense. When requisitioned as gate guards (EJI) and frontier guards (SAKIMORI), many soldiers deserted, and the *gundan* system gradually collapsed. Furthermore, because the provincial governors owned their own weapons and soldiers, the central government changed its conscription method. Finally, the *gundan,* having changed substantially, were abolished by Emperor Kammu (737–806) in 792.

gunji 郡司 (rural district administrators). Local officers who, after the Taika Reform in 646, administered the rural districts or *gun*. These districts fell within the limits of the provinces ruled by local chieftains called KUNI NO MIYATSUKO. The *gunji,* whose character and ability were also judged, were chosen from among the local chieftains. They became *tairyō* or *shōryō*. Clerks with a good knowledge of writing and arithmetic were appointed *shusei* and *shuchō,* and their office was for life. Their duties roughly corresponded to those of the provincial administrators or KOKUSHI. A plot of land of 14.70 acres was allotted to them as salary (SHIKIDEN), and their function was financially more profitable than that of the *kokushi*. When the ancient national institutions began to collapse and peasant riots in the provinces became more frequent, the *gunji* joined the peasants and opposed the provincial administrators *(kokushi)*. During the eleventh century, the manor system developed, and the *gunji* disappeared, as they joined the warriors or the administrators of tax-free manors known as SHŌKAN and *shōji*.

gunkimono 軍記物 (military romances). The generic name of literary works dealing with battles fought in definite periods. They are also called *senkimono*. They belong to legendary literature and are typical products of the Japanese middle ages (Kamakura and Muromachi periods). The early Kamakura period produced HŌGEN MONOGATARI, HEIJI MONOGATARI, and HEIKE MONOGATARI. *Heike Monogatari* recounts the rise and decline of Taira no Kiyomori (1118–81) and has a different version in GEMPEI SEISUIKI. It is a masterpiece which became very popular owing to the minstrels called BIWA HŌSHI, who sang the tales to the accompaniment of the lute. From the early Muromachi period comes TAIHEIKI, which describes the upheavals of the Northern and Southern dynasties and which enjoyed great popularity. Later GIKEIKI and SOGA MONOGATARI appeared. The former describes the personal life of Minamoto no Yoshitsune (1159–89), the latter the vendetta of the Soga brothers, Sukenari (1172–93) and Tokimune (1174–93). Dates and authors of many of these romances are unknown, but it is believed that many were written by joint authors. The style, which is lucid, fluent, and vigorous, is the then new, mixed Japanese-Chinese style—that is, literary Japanese style embellished with Chinese words. It is a harmonious blending of the style of the declining aristocracy and that of the rising warrior class, as it combines elegance and virility. War romances were very popular. The finest among them are *Heike Monogatari* and *Taiheiki*.

Gunsho-ruijū 群書類従. Huge collection of Japanese literary and historical texts, completed during the Edo period by the blind scholar of classical literature Hanawa Hokinoichi (1746–1821). The work is divided into twenty-five sections, the main part including 1,271 documents and the sequel 2,103 documents. The sequel is known as *Zoku Gunsho-ruijū*. With the help of his pupils Yashiro Hirokata and Nakayama Shin, Hanawa collected the precious documents from ancient times up to the Edo period. As the author was highly critical in selecting his material, the work is very valuable. It was begun in 1779 and completed in 1822. It was published some time after the author's death.

Guze Kannon 救世観音. Another reading is "Kuze Kannon." This is a Kanzeon Bodhisattva which is also called Shō Kannon. The Kannon was the object of worship of Prince Shōtoku Taishi (573–621) and is still honored in many temples related to the prince. The wooden statue of Guze Kannon enshrined in Hōryū-ji's YUMEDONO in 739 is a typical work of Asuka (552–645) sculpture.

Gyōbu-shō 刑部省 (Department of Justice). 1) One of the eight departments under the penal and administrative code system or RITSURYŌ-SEI (646–1184). It was the Department of Justice and was called Utaetadasu-tsu-kasa. It was in charge of lawsuits, punishments, and prisons. With the establishment of the police commissioners (KEBIISHI), almost all the functions of the Gyōbu-shō passed into the hands of the *kebiishi,* and the Gyōbu-shō itself existed only in name. 2) Name of one of the ministries in the early years of the Meiji era. It was the Department of Justice established in 1869, which replaced the former Keihō-kan. It was abolished in 1871 and replaced by the Ministry of Justice, called Shihō-shō.

H

Hagi no ran 萩の乱 (rebellion at Hagi). Rebellion of politicians in the early Meiji years. In 1876, dissatisfied with the government's attitude, Maebara Issei (1834–76) and others, in concert with the revolt at Kumamoto, rebelled in Hagi, Yamaguchi Prefecture. The revolt was quickly quelled, Maebara was executed, and many of his followers committed suicide.

haibutsu kishaku 排仏毀釈 (anti-Buddhist iconoclasm). A movement aimed at separating Shintoism from Buddhism (SHIMBUTSU-BUNRI) and at rejecting Buddhism, early Meiji period. The national scholars who had contributed to the downfall of the shogunate and who advocated the restoration of Shintō as a state religion resented the syncretic Shinto-Buddhist system. In 1868, the new policy of uniting church and state known as *saisei-itchi* destroyed the feudal form of belief, which was a "combination of Shintoism and Buddhism" *(shimbutsu-konkō).* Two years later, this movement achieved its goal with the proclamation of imperial rule and the inauguration of ultranationalism. The opposition against Buddhism weakened, but the temples were no longer protected by the throne and political authorities, and their activities were limited to the propagation of their faith among the masses.

haihan-chiken 廃藩置県 (abolition of clans and establishment of prefectures). In 1871, the feudal domains became units of local administration under the central government, and prefectures were established. This reorganization was to be the foundation of a centralized monarchy. Upon the "return of the land and the people to the emperor" (HANSEKI-HŌKAN) in 1869, the clan system officially came to an end. However, metropolises, prefectures, and clans meddled in local administration, and the relations between the local administrators and the clan people were the same as before. Those who contributed toward the centralization of power were Kido Takayoshi (1833–77), Ōkubo Toshimichi (1831–78), and others. They also united the soldiers of the Satsuma, Chōshū, and Tosa clans, organized bodyguards, and brought opposition parties to bay. The clans had enormous debts but were saved by the government, which assumed financial responsibility. Finally, the system of clan administrators was abolished, administrative sections were united, and three metropolises and seventy-two prefectures were established. In 1889, the territorial division was reorganized following the establishment of three metropolises and forty-two prefectures.

haikai 俳諧 (seventeen-syllable verse). One of the shorter Japanese verse forms. The original meaning of *haikai* is "joke." *Haikai* was a sort of *renga,* or a *waka* poem in dialogue form, which was in vogue during the Muromachi period. With the popularization of arts and letters and under the stimulus of Yamazaki Sōkan (1465–1553), Arakida Moritake (1473–1549), and others, it developed into a special form. Matsunaga Teitoku (1571–1653) and Nishiyama Sōin (1605–82) influenced the development of *haikai* in another way. It was Matsuo Bashō (1644–94) who brought it to perfection. This poetical genius was responsible for the invention of the *haikai* in its present form. Yosa Buson (1716–83) and Kobayashi Issa (1763–1827) continued the art. During the Meiji era, Masaoka Shiki (1867–1902) originated a new style of *haikai* or haiku poetry by freeing it from formalism.

hai-Nichi undō 排日運動 (anti-Japanese movement in America). American movement which was opposed to the immigration of Japanese nationals. During the early Meiji years, many Japanese, as a result of the inequality of economic expansion, emigrated to Hawaii and the United States. With the Sino-Japanese War, the emigration suddenly increased, and, following the Russo-Japanese War, the total number of emigrants reached 30,000. Disturbed by this large immigration, the United States launched an anti-immigration movement. In 1906, an incident against Japanese students occurred in San Francisco. In 1907, following the Gentlemen's Agreement, the Japanese themselves limited the number of emigrants. In 1913, in California, Japanese ownership of land was restricted. Other states followed suit, and before long racial antipathy was felt. Meanwhile, steps were taken between the two countries to regulate the possession of land. In 1924, the Exclusion Act came into effect, prohibiting the immigration and naturalization of Japanese nationals. It was not equally enforced in all the states, but it inflamed antagonism between the two nations and was a remote cause of the Pacific War. (See also the following entry.)

hai-Nichi undō 排日運動 (anti-Japanese movement in China). A movement launched by the Chinese people against the inroads of Japanese capitalism. The inequality of Japanese economic expansion reduced the development of the national market. Therefore, from the time of Meiji, an expansionist policy was adopted in Korea and China. Japan tried to take advantage of the feudal situation in China, but the Chinese had already planned the modernization of the country and the administration. They resisted vigorously. During World War I, Japan forced the Twenty-one Demands (NIJŪIKKAJŌ YŌKYŪ) upon China. They were as much as an open invasion, and the Chinese promptly reacted. The movement of May 4, 1919, was only the beginning. The students of Peking University demanded the so-called Twenty-one Abolitions, which included a boycott of Japanese articles, the recapture of lost territory, etc. The students were also opposed to the pro-Japanese attitude of their government. The government itself tried to stop the movement, but students throughout the nation went on strike, and merchants as well as capitalists and workmen walked out in sympathy. The movement of May 30, 1924, which began with a strike at the Japanese spinning factories in Shanghai, placed the leading authority in the hands of the workmen, but the financiers, who feared this state of affairs, were opposed. All this resulted in violent anti-Japanese demonstrations by laborers and farmers in Mukden in 1927. With the Manchurian incident (MANSHŪ JIHEN), all Japanese commercial articles were boycotted in Shanghai and Tientsin. The movement even defied the resistance of the economic world, cultural circles, and the government and put up a struggle against the invasion of the Japanese army. This racial-emancipation movement was linked up with similar movements in other parts of the world and aimed at destroying every feudal vestige after the Ch'ing dynasty. (See also the preceding entry.)

Hakata 博多. Important port of Kyūshū and part of present-day Fukuoka City. As a port for DAZAIFU it was, from ancient times, an important locality for traffic with China, diplomatic relations with the continent, and national defense. As a port of trade with Ming China, it flourished during the Muromachi and Sengoku periods. Later, the center of commerce moved to Hirado and Bōnotsu. Hakata also became the battlefield of the struggle between the Ōtomo and Ryūzōji clans and was laid waste. In 1587, after the subjugation of Kyūshū, Hideyoshi ordered the restoration of Hakata, and during the Tokugawa period it again flourished as the castle town of the Kuroda clan.

Hakodate 函館. A port city in southern Hokkaidō. The ancient name was Usukeshi. The name "Hakodate" was first written 箱館. The city was formerly an island close to the mainland and later became connected to it by a sand bar. It was already well developed by the middle of the fifteenth century. During the Edo period, the castle town of Fukuyama (or Matsumae-machi), which belonged to the Matsumae clan, became the center of the administration of the Ezo territory, but Hakodate did not fall under its jurisdiction. By the Treaty of Kanagawa (KANAGAWA JŌYAKU) of 1854, the port of Hakodate (as well as that of Shimoda) was opened to foreign trade, and the commercial treaty of 1858 made it into a commercial port. The BAKUFU now controlled the whole Ezo territory, and the administrator's office *(bugyōsho)* was established on the site of the fort called Goryōkaku and secured a central position. The resistance of Enomoto Takeaki (1836–1908), who occupied the fort against the imperial expedition in the first year of the restoration (1868), has remained famous. After the Meiji era, Sapporo became the center of development and is also now an important center of communication and economic relations with Honshū.

Hakuba-kai 白馬会. The name of an association of painters in Western style, Meiji era. In 1896, Kuroda Kiyoteru (1866–1924), Kume Keiichirō (1866–1934), and others founded this art society. They were influenced by French impressionism. Painting in a bright and free style, they laid the foundation for the development of Western-style painting. The society was dissolved in 1911.

Hakusonkō (Hakusukinoe) no tatakai 白村江の戦 (the battle at Hakusonkō). The naval battle waged in 663 at the mouth of the Kum River (Kinkō) between Japan (which controlled part of Korea), allied with Kudara (Paekche), and Shiragi (Silla), allied with the Chinese T'ang forces. Hakuson is in the vicinity of present-day Gunzan (Kunsan). In 660, Kudara was destroyed by a Chinese naval expedition with the aid of Silla, but before long a wealthy clan of Kudara, known in Japanese as Kishitsu Fukushin, the bonze Dōshin, and others summoned King Pung Chang (in Japanese, Hōshō), who was in Japan, and, planning the restoration of the home country, asked Japan for aid. However, because of the internal troubles of Kudara and the weak-mindedness of King Pung Chang, the combined forces were decisively defeated by T'ang China and Silla despite liberal reinforcement from Japan. Japan lost her foothold in Korea (until the invasion by Hideyoshi) and had to withdraw from the peninsula.

Hamaguri-gomon no hen 蛤御門の変 (the uprising at Hamaguri Gate). A battle fought on July 18 and 19, 1864, near the Imperial Palace in Kyōto. It is also referred to as *Kimmon no hen* and *Genji no hen*. As a result of the Bunkyū political change and because of its reckless antiforeign policy, the Chōshū clan lost its influence in the capital. But in 1864, trying to restore its authority, the clan sent its troops to Kyōto, pressing the throne to acquit seven court nobles and the Mōri (father and son) and to subjugate the military commissioner of Kyōto, Matsudaira Katamori (1836–93). The petition was not heeded, and the Chōshū clan fought at Hamaguri-gomon against the Satsuma, Aizu, Kuwana, and other clans. The battle ended in the victory of the shogunate forces.

hambatsu 藩閥 (clanship). A league of the strong southwestern clans in the Meiji government. During the late Edo and early Meiji years, the four clans of Satsuma, Chōshū, Tosa, and Hizen became the central force for the overthrow of the shogunate and the establishment of a new government. Consequently, the main functions of the Meiji government were exclusively exercised by these four clans, especially by the Satsuma clan. The leaders were Saigō Takamori (1827–77) and Ōkubo Toshimichi (1831–78) of the Satsuma clan, Kido Takayoshi (1833–77) of the Chōshū clan, Itagaki Taisuke (1837–1919) and Gotō Shōjirō (1838–97) of the Tosa clan, and Soejima Taneomi (1828–1905) of the Hizen clan. After the argument for war with Korea, the government officials of the Satsuma and Chōshū clans strengthened their despotism. The navy was composed of men of Satsuma, the army of men of Chōshū. Even when the whole country was organized, the political power was transferred to the Satsuma and Chōshū clans, or else they wielded power as elder statesmen *(genrō)* in the Privy Council. When the supreme command became independent, the *hambatsu* exercised its influence in army circles. In 1918, when Prime Minister Hara Takashi (1856–1921) organized his cabinet on the basis of political parties, the power of the *hambatsu* began to decline.

handen nōmin 班田農民 (allotment-land farmers). The name for farmers under the system of the penal and administrative code (RITSURYŌ-SEI). The area of rice land allotted to a household amounted to two *tan* for each male over five years of age and two-thirds of that amount for each female over five years of age (a *tan* is about 0.245 acres). The holders of allotment land were liable to various taxes. As compared with the produce tax or *kōso,* the labor tax or *yōeki* was more dreaded. Those under the restrictions of the labor tax were a type of slave peculiar to Japan. Japan was a despotic country and stripped these people of all their belongings, making them into items of property. There were different grades of allotment-land farmers, depending on the size of the family and on whether the people were local officials or not. According to contemporary records, there were powerful families such as one of a rural district administrator (GUNJI) in Kyūshū which consisted of 124 members. An ordinary family (GŌKO) is thought to have had ten to twenty members, though there were also larger families. From the middle of the eighth century, the allotment-land system began to disintegrate, and consequently the farmers themselves developed into various grades. There were the wealthy farmers called *tomeru hyakushō* who later were related to the *dento* and the MYŌSHU. (The *dento* were cultivators who commended their own plots to landlords to obtain the landlord's protection, while keeping the land in their own possession; the *myōshu* were owners of land in their own name.) There were also the deserters or tax evaders. They were known as FURŌNIN.

hangaku, hankō 藩学・藩校 (clan schools). The clan schools during the Edo period. They were under the management of the daimyō and were operated for the retainers of his clan. It was the educational policy of the BAKUFU to establish schools for the education of the clan people. Studies included Confucianism, national literature, medicine, military arts, etc. In the late years of the Edo regime, Western sciences were added. From the middle of the eighteenth century, the number of these schools increased considerably because the political administration, as well as economic conditions, was in a critical state, and graduates from the clan schools were expected to improve the state of affairs.

Representative schools were the Meirin-dō in Nagoya and Kanazawa, the Kōdō-kan in Mito and Saga, the Gakushū-kan in Wakayama, the Meirin-kan in Yamaguchi, the Kōjō-kan in Yonezawa, the Shūyū-kan in Fukuoka, the Nisshin-kan in Aizu, the Denshū-kan in Karatsu, the Nitchi-kan in Akita, the Kōdō-kan in Takamatsu, the Jishū-kan in Kumamoto, and the Zōshi-kan in Kagoshima.

haniwa 埴輪 (clay figures). Clay figures placed outside burial mounds during the age of shell mounds. In the period prior to the shell mounds *haniwa* in the form of cylinders were used. Those of the later sepulchral mounds represent animals, human beings, various utensils, houses, storehouses, and also weapons. They accurately portray the life of the people. Tradition ascribes the origin of *haniwa* to Emperor Suinin, who banned the practice of self-immolation of attendants on the death of a master and ordered clay figures to be substituted for human beings. Another view holds that the courtier Nomi no Sukune recommended that the emperor abolish the custom of subjects killing themselves to follow their deceased masters. Sukune invited potters from Izumo to make *haniwa*. In recognition of his merit, Emperor Suinin gave him the title *hanishi no muraji* or "chief of potters."

hansatsu 藩札 (clan paper money). Clan paper money during the Edo period. There was a rich variety of *hansatsu* such as *kinsatsu, ginsatsu, zenisatsu,* and *beisatsu*. Much of this money was intended to re-establish financial stability. Temporarily at least, the *hansatsu* were efficient, but they also caused a rise in prices, restless social conditions, and even peasant riots. At the end of the Edo period, 244 clans used *hansatsu,* of which there were more than 1,600 kinds. In 1871, following the abolition of the clans and the establishment of prefectures, the new government took charge of the monetary system and the *hansatsu* were abolished.

hanseki-hōkan 版籍奉還 (return of the land and people to the emperor). A reform in the early Meiji era. In 1869, the clans voluntarily offered their fiefs to the throne. In 1867, the BAKUFU had lost its authority. The restoration of imperial rule and the Boshin Civil War (BOSHIN SEN'EKI) brought an end to the feudal regime, but the various clans remained as before. The new administration was unable to centralize the power, especially in the fields of internal affairs and economy. Kido Takayoshi (1835–77) conferred with Ōkubo Toshimichi (1831–78), Ōkuma Shigenobu (1838–1922), and Inoue Kowashi (1843–95) and persuaded the clan lords to return to the throne the land (*han* 版) and the people (*seki* 籍). In 1869, the most powerful groups, viz., the great western clans of Satsuma, Chōshū, Tosa, and Hizen, offered their fiefs to the throne. Later, the other clans followed suit. The former feudal rulers were appointed administrators of the domains surrendered, with the title of governor (CHIHANJI). Finally, in 1871, the feudal domains became units of local administration (prefectures) under the central government.

hanzei 半済 (half payment). A tax-collecting system during the Namboku and Muromachi periods. It is also referred to as *hansai*. Half of the yearly tax paid by the manorial lord was remitted to the warriors to meet military expenditures. The system was introduced by Ashikaga Takauji (1305–58). Though it was meant to be only a wartime emergency measure, it was never discontinued, and it extended to most provinces. The measure bore very hard upon the owners of estates and precipitated the collapse of the manorial system.

Haruma Wage ハルマ和解 (Japanese translation of Halma). An incomplete translation into Japanese of François Halma's Dutch-French dictionary. The work was begun in 1796 by Ōtsuki Gentaku's (1757–1827) disciple, Inamura Sampaku (1758–1811). It was the first Western dictionary to be published in Japan. It is also known as *Edo Haruma*.

Hatakeyama uji 畠山氏 (the Hatakeyama clan). 1) A family of powerful household retainers during the early Kamakura period. Among them, Hatakeyama Shigetada (1165–1205), who served Minamoto no Yoritomo (1148–99), was remarkable for both his wisdom and his valor. He was killed by Hōjō Tokimasa's (1138–1215) forces. 2) After Shigetada's death, Ashikaga Yoshizumi married Shigetada's widow. Yoshizumi received Shigetada's estate and continued the Hatakeyama line. (Another view holds that Yoshizumi married the widow of Hōjō Tokimasa.) Later the Hatakeyama served Ashikaga Takauji (1305–58) and wielded power. During the Muromachi period, a Hatakeyama became one of the three governors general or shōgun's deputies (KANREI). Violent succession quarrels between Yoshinari (?–1490) and Masanaga (?–1493), along with the feud between Hosokawa Katsumoto (1430–73) and Yamana Mochitoyo (1404–73), led to the civil war of the Ōnin (1467–69) era (ŌNIN NO RAN).

hatamoto 旗本 (bannermen). Direct retainers of the Tokugawa shōgun. Formerly the *hatamoto* were bodyguard soldiers in a general's camp. The fief of a *hatamoto* did not exceed 10,000 *koku*. Among the *hatamoto* were also personal retainers of the shōgun (GO-KENIN), but the bannermen had the right of audience with the shōgun. Being direct vassals of the shōgun, the *hatamoto* were proud of their rank, but in a long period of tranquility and peace they became impoverished, and their habits became corrupt. Some even sold their rank. The BAKUFU's reforms always tried to help the *hatamoto* (KANSEI NO KAIKAKU).

Hata uji 秦氏 (秦人) (the Hata clan). A group of immigrants from China. They were, like the AYABITO, Chinese who had emigrated to Taihō-gun (a place including present-day Keikidō, or Kyonggi-do, and Kōkaidō, or Hwang-hae-do, and other places in Korea. According to the tradition related in NIHON SHOKI, the leader, Yuzuki no Kimi, with other Chinese from 120 prefectures, came to Japan during the reign of Emperor Ōjin and became naturalized Japanese. They then organized themselves into the Hata guild, or Hata-be, and settled down in the northern part of Yamashiro Province, where they engaged in sericulture. Later the Hata clan spread to various parts of the country. In the latter part of the sixth century, they built a storehouse in the vicinity of the imperial palace. The leader was Hata no Sakenokimi. With his resources he built up his power. The main branch of the clan spread its authority to the southern part of Yamashiro Province, and the temple KŌRYŪ-JI (or Hachioka-dera) in Uzumasa, Kyōto, was erected in 604 by Hata no Kawakatsu on the orders of Shōtoku Taishi. When the capital moved to HEIAN-KYŌ, the Hata again played an important role owing to their financial power. The Hata are said to have been descendants of Emperor Shih Huang Ti (259–210 B.C.), the founder of the Ch'in dynasty.

Heian-kyō 平安京. The capital during the Heian period. On the recommendation of the courtier Wake no Kiyomaro (733–99), Emperor Kammu (737–806) in 794 moved the capital from Nagaoka-kyō to Uda in Otokuni County and called it Heian-kyō. The Hata clan (HATA UJI), which was powerful in the southern part of Yamashiro Province, greatly contributed to the removal of the capital. The city followed closely the plan of the Chinese capital Ch'ang-an. In the north, at center, was the Great Enclosure or Daidairi, which contained the imperial palace and the government offices. The Suzaku-ōji divided the city into two parts—the Sakyō or East City and the Ukyō or West City. Running east and west there were nine avenues or *jō*, and many wide streets ran north and south. Excepting the short transfer of the capital to FUKUHARA, Heian-kyō (the modern city of Kyōto) remained the site of the imperial palace until the Meiji era.

Heiji Monogatari 平治物語. A war tale in three volumes, early Kamakura period. Neither the author nor the date of publication is known. Judging from the composition and the style, the author is probably the same person who wrote HōGEN MONOGATARI. The tale describes, in a simple but animated style, the Heiji war (HEIJI NO RAN).

Heiji no ran 平治の乱 (the Heiji War). The rebellion of Fujiwara no Nobuyori (1133–59) and Minamoto no Yoshitomo (1123–60). This war (1159–60) was induced by the rivalry between Fujiwara no Michinori (?–1159) and Nobuyori and between Yoshitomo and Taira no Kiyomori (1118–81). The Minamoto being defeated by the Taira, Nobuyori was beheaded at Rokujō-gawara. Yoshitomo tried to escape to the eastern provinces but was assassinated by Osada Tadamune (circa 1160). This marked the climax of the Taira ascendancy, when power was taken away from the court nobles and transmitted to the warriors.

Heijō-kyō 平城京. The capital city during the Nara period. It corresponds to the western outskirts of present-day Nara. It was the capital from 710 to 784. In the north, at center, was the Daidairi or Great Enclosure, which included the Imperial Palace and the government offices. The Suzaku-ōji, running from north to south, divided the city into two parts, the eastern and the western city. Nine avenues, called *jō,* ran east and west; other avenues ran north and south, dividing the city into square blocks. Such a grand-scale capital had become necessary because the authority of the emperor and the court nobles had considerably increased and because the system of the penal and administrative code, known as RITSURYŌ-SEI, had been inaugurated.

Heike Monogatari 平家物語. A war romance in twelve volumes, early Kamakura period. The author is not known. The work relates the rise and fall of the Taira house. The downfall of the ancient nobility and the rise of the warrior class that made new history are faithfully described. The Buddhist concept of evanescence pervades the whole work. The style, which is elegant and powerful, transforms the tale into a long epic poem. Later, minstrels (BIWA HŌSHI) chanted the narratives to the accompaniment of the lute, spreading the tale throughout the country. The work greatly influenced later literature. It is a representative war tale or *gunki-monogatari* (GUNKIMONO).

Heimin-sha 平民社. A socialist organization of the Meiji era. In 1903, Kōtoku Shūsui (1871–1911), with Sakai Toshihiko (1870–1933) and others, launched a pacifist movement. They left the newspaper *Manchōhō,* organized the Heimin-sha Social Democratic Party, and published their own weekly HEIMIN SHIMBUN. They were imprisoned for their antiwar articles.

Heimin Shimbun 平民新聞. A socialist weekly published during the Meiji and Taishō eras and launched in November 1903. Opposing war, Kōtoku Shūsui (1871–1911), Sakai Toshihiko (1870–1933), and others organized themselves (HEIMIN-SHA), left the newspaper *Manchōhō,* and published the *Heimin Shimbun.* They took a firm stand against war and advocated democracy and a peaceful society based on liberty, equality, and humanity. The paper was very influential during the Russo-Japanese War, when it published editorials on Russian socialism and articles by the Russian Socialist Party and also carried communist propaganda. The government took drastic measures and in January 1905 abolished the paper. The subsequent paper titled *Chokugen* was also suppressed, and the Heimin-sha was liquidated in October 1905. After the dissolution of the Heimin-sha, two papers, *Hikari* and *Shin-kigen,* merged in 1906, when the Socialist Party was established, and became the daily *Heimin Shimbun,* but this paper also was abolished when the party was dissolved. In 1914, the socialists again published the *Heimin Shimbun.*

Hie-jinja 日吉神社 (Hie Shrine). A shrine in Ōtsu City which from ancient times was the shrine of the tutelary deity of the temple ENRYAKU-JI. The shrine flourished from Heian times along with the rise of Enryaku-ji. When the monk-soldiers of Enryaku-ji appealed by force to the court, they entered Kyōto carrying the portable shrine of Hie-jinja (GŌSO).

higaki-kaisen 菱垣回船 (cargo vessels). Vessels which operated a regular service between Ōsaka and Edo during the Edo period. *Higaki* is also written 檜垣. In order not to lose the cargo, both sides of the vessels were furnished with a lattice fencework (*kaki* 垣) of thin slats of cypress (*hinoki* 檜) in a lozenge-shaped pattern (*hishi* 菱)—hence the two writings of the word *higaki.* Usually the vessels carried a cargo of from 200 to 400 *koku,* but later cargoes of 1,000 *koku* were also transported. During the Kan'ei era (1624–44), the forwarding agents of Ōsaka made a fortune by means of these vessels. The so-called twenty-four shipping agencies (NIJŪSHI-KUMI DON'YA, also known as *nijūshi-kumi Edo-zumi-doiya*) secured a monopoly over the cargo vessels, transporting to Edo cotton cloth, cotton wool, vegetable oil, rice wine, etc. Later, backed by the rice-wine packers *(sakani-nushi)* of Nishinomiya and other places, the vessels known as "barrel vessels" (TARU-KAISEN) organized a regular service in competition with the *higaki-kaisen.*

Higashiyama bunka 東山文化 (Higashiyama culture). Culture which flourished under Shōgun Ashikaga Yoshimasa (1434–90) in the middle of the Muromachi period. The central figure of this culture was Yoshimasa, who lived a life of extravagance in his hillside villa GINKAKU in Higashiyama, a hill on the northeastern fringe of Kyōto, and who kept aloof from social turmoil. In this time of social and political disintegration, traditional culture came to an end. There were alternating currents of culture—that of the warriors, the court, and the Zen monks; the new culture from China and Japanese traditional culture; the culture of the nobility and that of the common people. All these forms merged to constitute Higashiyama culture. The main features of this culture were subjectivity and symbolism, quietude, and profundity. Its most remarkable artistic achievements were the paintings in India ink in Sung and Yüan style of Sesshū (1420–1506), the Nō plays and Nō songs of Komparu Zenchiku (1405–68), the style of residential architecture called SHOIN-ZUKURI, the landscape gardens in Zen style, the laying down of the ceremonial rules for tea drinking by Shukō (1422–1502), and the art of flower arrangement by Ikenobō Senkei (fifteenth century). Many of the cultural achievements of this time have been transmitted to the present generation. However, in the face of agrarian uprisings, and at a time when the "low oppressed the high" (GEKOKUJŌ), it would seem that this culture was one of warriors who, raised to nobility, tried to escape from the realities of life through extravagance.

hikan 被官 (farm workers). The farm workers as opposed to the landlord or to the landowner known as name master (MYŌSHU). They did farm work for larger proprietors. The Muromachi period witnessed an increase in power of the farmers who had centered around the name master. The name masters, as well as the farmers who served a great landlord or daimyō, strengthened their position. During the Edo period, the farmers who were forced into compulsory service *(buyaku)* were also called *hikan.* They had almost no independence, and their living, unlike that of the serfs called NAGO, was not guaranteed by their master.

hikitsuke-shū 引付衆 (assistant members of the Council of State). The name of an office during the Kamakura and Muromachi periods. The office consisted of assisting the Council of State or Deliberative Assembly called HYŌJŌ-SHŪ and of passing judgment on suits and appeals. During the Kamakura period, the suits concerning farmland were so numerous that, in 1249, Regent Hōjō Tokiyori (1227–63) formed a special standing committee designed to promote investigation by the Council of State of suits and appeals brought to it for judgment. The MUROMACHI BAKUFU likewise established a *hikitsuke-shū.*

hikyaku 飛脚 (postmen). Postmen whose origin is to be found in the Kamakura period but who were fully organized during the Edo period. The Edo regime established postmen with official duties. They were called *tsugibikyaku.* Postmen connecting various clans with Edo were known as *daimyō-hikyaku,* and postmen for the use of the common people were referred to as *machibikyaku.* Because the *machibikyaku* made three return trips a month from Edo to Ōsaka, they were also called *sando-hikyaku,* and since it took six days to make a single trip they were further known as *jōroku.*

Hinkyū-mondō Ka 貧窮問答歌. A poem composed by Yamanoue no Okura (660–733) and contained in MAN'YŌSHŪ. On a cold, wintry night, two destitute men have a dialogue *(mondō)* on poverty *(hinkyū).* The line "the growling of the village headman with rod in hand" *(shimoto toru sato-osa ga koe* 楚取る里長 が声), which describes the cruelty of the government under the penal and administrative code system, was often quoted to express the destitution of the people.

Hirado 平戸. An island off the northwest coast of Kyūshū and a commercial port of Hizen (Nagasaki Prefecture). From ancient times it was a port for trade with China. In 1550, after Portuguese ships entered the port, Hirado became the center of trade with Europe as well as one for spreading Christianity. From 1584, Spanish ships also entered the port of Hirado, but they were outrivaled by the Dutch. The Dutch and later the English established regular trading missions in Hirado and vied with each other for trade. Outdone by the Dutch, the English abandoned their trade missions in 1623. Finally, in line with the national isolation policy of the BAKUFU, the Dutch firm was ordered to dissolve in 1641. When it had moved to DESHIMA, a small artificial island in the harbor of Nagasaki, Hirado declined, and its only importance lay in its being the castle town of the Matsuura family.

Hiraizumi 平泉. The name of a town in Nishiiwai County, Iwate Prefecture, some fifty miles north of Sendai. From the end of the eleventh century to the beginning of the twelfth century, it was the stronghold of the Fujiwara family of Ōu (Mutsu and Dewa, or Aomori, Yamagata, Akita, and Iwate prefectures). The leading Fujiwara were Kiyohira (?–1126), Motohira (?–1154), and Hidehira (?–1187). Because of Kiyohira's merits during the civil war known as GO-SANNEN NO EKI, he and his descendants until the third generation were appointed police commissioners (ŌRYŌSHI) of Mutsu Province (Aomori Prefecture) and commanders in chief of the local government office *(chinjufu-shō-gun)*. Kiyohira built Hiraizumi systematically with regular streets and blocks. He also erected a monastery rivaling the most beautiful edifices of the capital city in its rich decoration and gorgeousness. This was the CHŪSON-JI, which can be compared with the BYŌDŌ-IN of Uji. The Golden Hall, erected in 1124 as part of the Chūson-ji, is one of the most beautiful examples of the sumptuously decorated architecture of the Fujiwara period. In 1189, Yasuhira (1155–89), the son of Hidehira, was destroyed by the forces of Minamoto no Yoritomo (1148–99) on the grounds that he had given refuge to Minamoto no Yoshitsune (1159–89) in Hiraizumi. Yoritomo's real purpose, however, was to destroy the Fujiwara stronghold, and this he succeeded in doing.

hitogaeshi 人返 (sending the people back). A policy of the EDO BAKUFU consisting of sending back to the countryside people who were concentrated in the cities. The increase of population in Edo, Kyōto, and Ōsaka and the decrease of population in rural districts caused a reduction in farm products and an increase of idle people in the cities. The *bakufu* feared social disturbance and tried to force the people to return to their land. The policy of *hitogaeshi* was part of the sweeping reforms attempted by Minister Mizuno Tadakuni (1794–1851) known as the Tempō reforms (TEMPŌ NO KAIKAKU), but the reforms were too drastic and ended in failure.

Hiunkaku 飛雲閣. A specimen of Azuchi-Momoyama architecture. It is an elegant small pavilion at the Nishi Hongan-ji, Kyōto. It was formerly part of

JURAKUDAI, which was Hideyoshi's residence from 1587, but was later moved to Nishi Hongan-ji. Most castles had many annexes which served as living quarters or as studies for the castle lord. Hiunkaku was one of these annexes. It is a three-storied building in residential style (SHOIN-ZUKURI), cheerful and free and rich in variety. It reflects the spirit of extravagance of the times.

hoan jōrei 保安条例 (peace-preservation ordinance). Disciplinary regulations promulgated in 1887 and intended to quell the antigovernment movement. The movement for democratic rights became more violent as the establishment of a constitution and the inauguration of the National Assembly became more urgent. This coalition movement, which involved all popular parties, delivered an attack against the government. In December 1887, Premier Itō Hirobumi (1841–1909) promulgated the peace-preservation ordinance. First, 570 demonstrators for democratic rights had to withdraw and to remain at a distance of three *ri* or 7.32 miles from the Imperial Palace. Then antigovernment associations, meetings, and dangerous documents were prohibited, as well as the carrying of weapons. Traveling was also limited, and inspection was enforced.

Hōgen Monogatari 保元物語. A war tale in three volumes of the early Kamakura period. The author is unknown. The main subject of the work is the exciting feats of Minamoto no Tametomo (1139–70) and the Hōgen insurrection (HŌGEN NO RAN) of 1156. This romance greatly influenced later literature.

Hōgen no ran 保元の乱 (the insurrection of the Hōgen era). A war which was fought in July 1156 and which was caused by the discord between Emperor Goshirakawa (1127–92) and ex-Emperor Sutoku (1119–64). Fujiwara no Yorinaga (1120–56), Minamoto no Tameyoshi (1096–1156) and his son Tametomo (1139–70), and Taira no Tadamasa (?–1156) defended the ex-emperor but were defeated by such supporters of Emperor Goshirakawa as Fujiwara no Tadamichi (1097–1164), Minamoto no Yoshitomo (1123–60), and Taira no Kiyomori (1118–81). The ex-emperor was exiled to Sanuki in Shikoku, Tameyoshi and Tadamasa were put to death, and Tametomo was exiled to Izu Ōshima. This event marked the decline of the imperial court and of the Fujiwara family, gave rise to the ascendancy of both the Minamoto and the Taira clans, and led to the first stages in the evolution of a feudal state.

Hōjōki 方丈記. Stray notes in one volume written by Kamo no Chōmei (1151–1213) in early Kamakura times. They describe Chōmei's life as a recluse after he retired in disappointment from court society. The book also describes the social chaos of the late Heian and early Kamakura periods and the dreadful natural calamities such as storms, earthquakes, plagues, and starvation. The whole work is pervaded with the Buddhist concept of evanescence.

Hōjō uji 北条氏 (the Hōjō clan). 1) Kamakura period. The Hōjō clan wielded the real power in the BAKUFU. Hōjō Tokimasa (1138–1215) helped Minamoto no Yoritomo (1148–99) raise troops and was instrumental in establishing the KAMAKURA BAKUFU. Consequently, he became the first regent, but later the office of regency became hereditary, and the Hōjō clan held the power. In 1333, Hōjō Takatoki (1303–33) was attacked in Kamakura by Nitta Yoshisada (1301–38). The Hōjō were annihilated, and the Kemmu Restoration was inaugurated. 2) The name of a *sengoku daimyō* (DAIMYŌ) of Odawara in Sagami Province (Kanagawa Prefecture). As this family has no connection with the Kamakura Hōjō, it is sometimes called Gohōjō. The founder of this powerful family was Hōjō Sōun (1432–1519), also called Ise Nagauji, who paved the way for complete control of the area. This family was exterminated by Hideyoshi in 1590.

hōken shakai seido 封建社会制度 (feudal society and system). The social system following the Heian period and preceding the advent of the capitalistic period—that is, from the Kamakura period to the Edo period, inclusive. The Kamakura and Muromachi periods are together called the middle ages or the earlier feudal society; the Edo or modern period is called the later feudal society. The middle ages may be considered the formative period of feudalism. Ancient elements such as the manor system were maintained, but there was marked progress toward a more genuine feudal system. Modern Japan witnessed the maturity of feudalism but also its collapse. In feudal society, farmland was the main source of revenue. The farmers were forced to till their land and to pay their taxes to the lord. A master-servant relationship between the warrior class and its subjects came into being. The vassals received farmland from their master, employed farmers, and paid their taxes, but in wartime they followed their master. Actually, the term "feudal system" means the whole national structure, but its use is sometimes limited to denote the master-servant relationship. "Feudal society" rather indicates the relationship between landlord and farmer. Another feature of Japanese feudal society was its inability to maintain either strict distinction between the social classes or a rigid rule to unite the country.

Hokkaidō kaitaku-shi 北海道開拓使 (Hokkaidō development commissioner). A government office for the administration of Hokkaidō in the early Meiji period. In 1869, a development commissioner was appointed, and the name Ezo was changed to Hokkaidō. The government invested a huge capital of fifteen million yen to foster the industrialization of Hokkaidō. For the purpose of helping the natives and for the defense of the territory, colonial troops (TONDENHEI-SEIDO) were organized. The main figure of the development board of Hokkaidō was Kuroda Kiyotaka (1840–1900), who became involved in the incident of the sale of government property (HOKKAIDŌ KAITAKU-SHI KAMBUTSU-HARAISAGE JIKEN). The office was abolished in 1882, when the three prefectures of Sapporo, Hakodate, and Nemuro were established. In 1886, the island was united under the Hokkaidō Board.

Hokkaidō kaitaku-shi kambutsu-haraisage jiken 北海道開拓使官物払下事件. In 1881, Godai Tomoatsu (1834–85), a businessman with political affiliations, proposed to sell government property of the Hokkaidō Development Office at a low price to friends of the administration. This caused an outbreak of protests in the press and opposition in the government by Ōkuma Shigenobu (1838–1922). Ōkuma, who advocated democracy in opposition to the Satsuma and Nagato clique in the government, was suspected of conniving with others against the government and was consequently dismissed from office in what is known as the "crisis of 1881." The public outcry subsided when the proposed sale was canceled and an imperial rescript promising a national assembly was issued.

Hokke-ikki 法華一揆 (Hokke uprisings). Uprisings of the Hokke sect of Buddhism, or Nichiren Buddhism, which occurred in Kyōto and Ōsaka at the end of the Muromachi period. At the end of the Kamakura period, the Hokke religion had spread in Kyōto and had converted many wealthy merchants and warriors. But in 1532, when fanatical uprisings (IKKŌ-IKKI) occurred in Yamashiro and Yamato, Hatakeyama Yoshinobu, in order to break the power of the Ikkō sect derived from Shinran's Amidist teachings, asked for help from the Hokke followers. This resulted in fighting between the two sects. The Hokke followers were victorious and ruled Kyōto for a time, but before long they were expelled from the city by the Hiei-zan monk-soldiers and by the BAKUFU. The Hokke uprisings occurred mainly among city merchants, pawnbrokers, etc., whereas the Amidist uprisings were more common in rural communities. But the Ikkō (Amidist) uprisings, centering around the temple Hongan-ji, succeeded in securing the authority of the feudal landlords, whereas the Hokke (Nichiren) uprisings were less successful owing to the disunity in the religious communities.

Hokke-shū 法華宗 (Nichiren sect of Buddhism). A sect of Buddhism founded in the middle of the Kamakura period by Nichiren (1222–82). It is also called Nichiren-shū. Nichiren believed that the Lotus Sutra *(Hokke-kyō)* transmitted most faithfully the will of Shaka, that a *mandara* of this sutra should be the main object of worship, and that by the recitation of "homage to the scripture of the lotus of the good law" *(namu myōhō renge-kyō)* every human being would attain Buddhahood. He boldly attacked all the other religions, which he thought were perverse. Though always in danger, he continued to make converts. He built his headquarters on Mount Minobu in Kai Province (Yamanashi Prefecture) and spread his religion among the Kantō warriors and merchants. During the Namboku period (1336–92), the religion spread to Kyōto, coming into open conflict with the Amidists or IKKŌ-SHŪ, and became still more popular when the monk Nisshin (1407–88) was persecuted. It further spread among the townspeople of Kyōto during the Ōnin Civil War, but from 1536, when Hokke temples in Kyōto were burned by the monk-soldiers of Hiei-zan, its influence began to wane.

Hōkō-ji 法興寺. A temple erected in 588 during the Asuka period (552–645) in Asuka, Takechi no Agata, in Yamato. The temple, which is also known as Asuka-dera, was built by Soga no Umako (?–626). By an edict of Empress Regnant Genshō (680–748), the temple was moved in 716 to the ninth avenue of the eastern part of HEIJŌ-KYŌ (Nara), where its name was changed to Gan-gō-ji or Gankō-ji. It was one of the seven major temples of Nara (NANTO SHICHI-DAIJI) and professed the Kegon religious tenets.

Hoku-Shin jihen 北清事変 (the Boxer Rebellion). The Boxer (I Ho T'uan or Giwa-dan) uprising in Ch'ing China during the middle of the Meiji era and the suppression of the uprising by other powers. Following the Sino-Japanese War, China lost most of her prestige. Other powers obtained leased territory and various kinds of concessions which endangered the unity of the empire. In the Chinese government, opposition was strongly felt between the constitutional monarchists, who advocated "self-strengthening through legislative reform" (*hempōjikyō* 変法自彊), and those who persistently advocated the ousting of foreigners. Following the coup d'état known as *Bojutsu seihen,* the antiforeign party took over. (*Bojutsu seihen* was the coup d'état of September 22, 1898. Empress Dowager Tz'u Hsi, with reactionary factions, confined Emperor Kuang Hsü, who had adopted the policy of K'ang Yu-wei). The Giwa-dan was a secret society deriving from the ancient Pai Lien Chiao (Byakuren-kyō), or White Lotus Sect, founded in 1351 by Han Shan-t'ung. The members of this society trained themselves in boxing. They intended to oust Christianity and the aliens. In 1900, the antiforeign upheaval broke out, and the northeast was the scene of most of the violence. Great Britain, France, Russia, Japan, and Germany all feared further conflagration and, to protect the life and property of their nationals, assembled an allied relief expedition in Tientsin and quelled the insurrection. The Boxer Rebellion induced the signing of an Anglo-Japanese alliance (NICHI-EI DŌMEI). Also, during the uprising, the Russians had taken possession of Manchuria, and this was a remote cause of the Russo-Japanese War (1904–5).

hombyakushō 本百姓 (independent farmers). Independent farmers during the Edo period. Possessing farmland, they were responsible for the taxes. In the land-surveying registers of Hideyoshi and those of the early Edo period, private farmland and the names of owners are registered. The owners possessed the right of cultivation and were distinguished from the farmers who possessed no land and who were called *mizunomi-byakushō* (MIZUNOMI). The *hombyakushō* were the basis of the rural community. They had the right of speaking in the meetings and the privileges of using water for irrigation and of commonage. They also had the right of directing the apportionment *(wari-chi)* of farmland. Consequently, the top-ranking farmers known as village headmen *(shōya)* or those who helped the *nanushi* administer the village (KU-MI-GASHIRA; see also MURA YAKUNIN), as well as assistant GUNDAI called *hyakushō-dai,* were all chosen from among the *hombyakushō.* The BAKUFU structure was based on the *hombyakushō,* who were strictly controlled by the *bakufu* and the clans, even as far as their food, clothing, and housing were concerned. They also shouldered the burden of 50–60 percent of the yield of the property owned and of various labor taxes known as *buyaku.* The *bakufu* and the clans which administered the farmer villages tried to sustain the *hombyakushō.* However, the fortunes of the landowner farmers fluctuated greatly with the develop-ment of commercial products and the infiltration of commercial capital into the villages. Some *hombyakushō* landed in the rank of *mizunomi-byakushō* and vice versa. The load of producing commercial commodities was added to the already heavy burden of the *hombyakushō,* and this situation induced peasant uprisings. Under the *bakufu* system, there were times when the rural com-munities were gravely perturbed.

hompa-shiki chōhō 翻波式彫法 (carving in rolling-wave style). A style used in the carving of the drapery of Heian images. The folds of the drapery of the wooden statues resemble the tops of breaking waves. This style consists of alternate parallel curves of broad, high, round-topped folds and narrow, low, ridged folds. It looks like the alternate high and low waves that beat on the beach. This technique was already known in the pre-Heian period, but only in later Heian times did it reach perfection.

honchi-suijaku (**honji-suijaku**) 本地垂迹. The ideology according to which the real entity *(honchi)* of the absolute Buddha, in order to bestow his favors on men and to save all living beings, left (垂) vestiges (迹) of himself every-where and, becoming god, presented himself under various manifestations. Already in the eighth century, it was assumed that the Shintō gods revered the Buddhist law and that it was a good practice to have both forms of wor-ship, Shintoist and Buddhist, in the same building. Such buildings were known as *jingū-ji.* In the ninth century, Buddhist sutras were recited before Shintō gods. Most conspicuous was the syncretism as expressed in *shimbutsu-shūgō* or *shūgō-Shintō.* In the tenth century there was a tendency to turn to Bodhisatt-vas for the origin of the Shintō gods. But it is the Kamakura period which produced the ideology of *honchi-suijaku.* The real entity behind the god Hachi-man (Hachimanjin) was considered to be Amida Nyorai; that of the great shrine of Ise was Dainichi Nyorai, as well as GUZE KANNON. From the four-teenth century, an original Buddha or Bodhisattva was even determined for Shintō deities which had no relation to any shrine. Izanami and Izanagi be-came mere Buddhist gods. A reaction against such theories and practices was to be expected. It was provoked by the scholar Yoshida Kanetomo (1435–1511). He advocated the "true theory that the roots as well as the leaves and flowers" were Shintō and that Shintō was the basis of Buddhism and Confucianism (YOSHIDA SHINTŌ).

Honchō Tsugan 本朝通鑑. A history of Japan, Edo period. It was begun in 1644 by Hayashi Razan (1583–1657) at Iemitsu's command and taken over in 1664 by Hayashi Shunsai (1618–80) by command of Ietsuna. It was then called *Honchō Hennen-roku*. A historiographic library was built in Shinobugaoka (in Edo), and materials from all over the country were brought together. Hayashi Baidō (1643–66) and Hayashi Hōkō (1644–1732), both sons of Shunsai, and others helped Shunsai compile the work, which was, by that time, called *Honchō Tsugan*. Brought to completion around 1670, it contains the history of Japan from the time of Emperor Jimmu to that of Emperor Goyōzei (1571–1617). The main part, in 310 chapters, has a compendium of thirty chapters. Five chapters covering an appendix and two chapters of explanatory notes with a list of works consulted complete the work. It follows a chronological order in imitation of the Chinese *Tzu-chih T'ung-chien* (in Japanese, *Shiji Tsugan*), completed in 1084. It also contains a wealth of historical materials and detailed articles. However, it lacks a consistent historical view. In line with the BAKUFU policy, the whole work is written from the standpoint of Confucian rationalism.

Hongan-ji 本願寺. The main temple of the JŌDO SHIN-SHŪ sect of Buddhism. In 1272, Shinran's daughter Kakushin-ni (1222–81) built the Ōtani Hongan-ji temple in Ōtani, Kyōto, where the remains of her father were interred. The Hongan-ji was founded during the time of Kakunyo (1270–1351) and flourished under the leadership of Rennyo (1415–99), its eighth chief abbot. Rennyo built a temple in Yoshizaki, Echizen Province (Fukui Prefecture), spreading his faith in the Hokuriku district. He built another Hongan-ji in Yamashina, near Kyōto, and the ISHIYAMA HONGAN-JI in Ōsaka. With Ishiyama Hongan-ji as its center, the surrounding area greatly developed and became powerful enough to resist the forces of Nobunaga at the time when Kennyo (1543–92) was the eleventh chief abbot. In 1591, the temple was moved to its present place in Kyōto and became Nishi Hongan-ji. It is the headquarters of the Shinshū Hongan-ji branch. Kennyo's son Kyōnyo (1558–1614) left the main branch and, according to Ieyasu's wishes, established Higashi Hongan-ji, which is the main temple of the Ōtani branch of Shinshū. Hongan-ji, being split in two, lost its political power.

Honnō-ji no hen 本能寺の変 (the insurrection in the Honnō-ji temple). In 1582, Oda Nobunaga, leaving Azuchi to help Hideyoshi in his struggle with Mōri Terumoto (1553–1625), took up his quarters in the Honnō-ji temple, Kyōto. At that time, one of Nobunaga's warlords, Akechi Mitsuhide (1528–

82), revolted. He attacked the temple Honnō-ji and killed Nobunaga. Mitsuhide now tried to assume supreme military power, but Hideyoshi, after being reconciled with Mōri, attacked and destroyed Mitsuhide in the battle of Yamasaki and succeeded Nobunaga. This victory established Hideyoshi's military position as well as his political authority.

honryō-ando 本領安堵 (recognition of vested rights to farmland). The recognition by the Kamakura and Muromachi BAKUFU of vested rights to farmland. The rights to farmland of the Kamakura vassals had grown under the penal and administrative code system (RITSURYŌ-SEI) and under the manor system. The *bakufu* recognized these vested rights and established a feudal master-servant (lord-retainer) relationship with the vassals. The *honryō-ando* was instrumental in bringing about this same relationship with the owners of reward fields (ONCHI) received from the lord.

honsō-gaku 本草学 (pharmacology). Chinese pharmacology. The name derives from the many plants used as medicinal herbs. *Honsō-gaku* (or *honzō-gaku*) was introduced in Japan in ancient times, but during the Edo period it was greatly improved along with other sciences. Kaibara Ekiken (1650–1714), the botanist Inō Jakusui (1655–1715), and others laid the foundation of Japanese *honsō-gaku*.

Hōryū-ji 法隆寺. A monastery founded during the Asuka period (552–645) and said to have been constructed by Shōtoku Taishi. It is situated in Ikaruga, Ikoma County, Nara Prefecture. It was one of the seven main temples of Nara (NANTO SHICHI-DAIJI) and belonged to the Hossō sect (HOSSŌ-SHŪ) of Buddhism. It has now become independent from the Hossō religion. There are many art treasures of inestimable value in the Hōryū-ji. Some of the famous buildings are the Kondō, Gojūnotō, Chūmon, Kairō, YUMEDONO, and Dempōdō. There are also such sculptural masterpieces as the Shaka Sanzon, Kudara Kannon, and GUZE KANNON and such craft objects as the TAMAMUSHI NO ZUSHI, Shishigari Monkin, etc.

Hosokawa uji 細川氏 (the Hosokawa clan). A family whose leading members held the position of deputy of the shōgun (KANREI) during the Muromachi period. The family was a side branch of the Ashikaga family of Mikawa Province (Aichi Prefecture) which, serving Ashikaga Takauji (1305–58), made itself meritorious in battle. One of the Hosokawa became a constable daimyō (SHUGO DAIMYŌ). He was the shōgun's deputy and became powerful as the administrator of ten provinces. Hosokawa 'Katsumoto (1430–73) wielded political power. Inducing the Ōnin Civil War (ŌNIN NO RAN), he led the eastern forces (east of Muromachi) to defend Ashikaga Yoshimi (1439–91). His descendants, Yūsai (or Fujitaka, 1534–1610) and Yūsai's son Tadaoki (1563–1645), served Nobunaga and Hideyoshi. After Hideyoshi's death, they sided with Ieyasu in the battle of Sekigahara. Tadaoki's son Tadatoshi (1586–1641) was promoted to the lordship of Kumamoto in Hizen (Nagasaki Prefecture) with a fief of 540,000 *koku* (1632).

Hossō-shū 法相宗 (the Hossō sect of Buddhism). One of the six Nara sects (NANTO ROKUSHŪ). It was spread in 661 by Dōshō (629–700), who had studied the doctrine under the Chinese Hsüan-tsang for eight years. Like Kusha-shū, Hossō-shū teaches that every being is but a manifestation of the human mind. The distinguished Buddhist priest and politician of the Nara period, Gembō (?–746), was a priest of the Hossō religion.

hyakushō-ikki 百姓一揆 (peasant uprisings). Concerted action by peasants who revolted against the authorities, Edo period. The uprisings were accompanied by desertion and destruction and by disorderly, direct, and forced appeals. The nature of the uprisings differed according to the time and locality. In an earlier stage, there were many irregular and direct appeals to the landlord or the deputies, but in the middle of the Edo period the peasants protested against the rural officials and the wealthy merchants. Their scope was larger and they were better organized. At the end of the Edo period, the uprisings aimed at a large-scale reform of society. Usually a bad crop caused accidental and scattered uprisings, but some of them shook feudal policy and exhibited such energy that they disorganized the BAKUFU. There were more than 1,200 uprisings during the Edo period, but there were also earlier uprisings the records of which have been lost.

hyakushō-uke 百姓請 (the allotment of manor management). The system according to which the management of a manor was given out to the name masters (MYŌSHU) by the real landlords *(ryōke)* or the nominal landlords *(honsho)*. The name masters had to pay a fixed annual tax. The system was already in use during the Kamakura period but became widespread during the Muromachi period, and it brought about the autonomy of the rural communities.

Hyōgo 兵庫. Commercial port facing Ōsaka Bay in western Kōbe. In ancient times it was called Muko, and the envoys of Silla (Shiragi) had their quarters there. It was an important port for overseas communications. Later the name was changed to Ōwada no Tomari. When Taira no Kiyomori (1118–81) developed FUKUHARA, he rebuilt Ōwada no Tomari in view of the trade with Sung China. The place was called Hyōgo in the middle ages. Especially during the Muromachi period, it became the key port for trade with Ming China. Hyōgo was also an important port on the Inland Sea line, and it thrived, having Kyōto in the background. It had a checking station and special facilities for transportation (TOIMARU) for lords. From the time of Hideyoshi, it further prospered as a port for Ōsaka, and it was of great service to the daimyō of the western provinces who traveled to Edo for alternate attendance. At the same time, it organized sea transportation to the west. At the end of the Edo period, it became one of the open ports (the others being Kanagawa, Nagasaki, and Niigata) following the signing of the provisional friendship treaties with foreign countries (ANSEI NO KARI-JŌYAKU). Hyōgo became a treaty port in 1867 when foreigners began to enter the country and when trade with foreign countries was opened. It may further be considered as the foundation of present-day Kōbe.

Hyōjō-shū 評定衆 (the Council of State). The name of an office during the Kamakura and Muromachi periods. In 1225, Regent Hōjō Yasutoki (1183–1242) established a Council of State or Deliberative Assembly including eleven members who were appointed advisers to the regent. It was the chief administrative and advisory organ of the government. The members of this deliberative assembly were to handle important administrative affairs of the BAKUFU and to pass judgment on suits. Imitating the Kamakura *bakufu,* the Muromachi *bakufu* also established a Hyōjō-shū, but its authority was weaker. The office was abolished with the downfall of the Ashikaga house.

hyōrō-mai 兵糧米 (commissariat tax). A tax on rice imposed by the BAKUFU of the Kamakura and Muromachi periods. The tax was laid on the various provinces for the foundation of a military society. Taira no Kiyomori (1118–81) had also levied this rice tax, but the most important taxes were imposed by Minamoto no Yoritomo (1148–99). In 1185, Yoritomo appointed one land steward (JITŌ) in each court domain *(kōryō)* and each provincial manor to levy a contribution of rice fixed at five *shō* (about two gallons) for each *tan* (0.245 acres) of rice land. The tax was equivalent to about two percent of the average yield. The land stewards were assessed the same amount, and this supplementary tax was also considered to be *hyōrō-mai*. Yoritomo, in levying this tax, aimed at furnishing the cost of his campaigns against Yoshitsune (1159–89).

I

iaku jōsō-ken 帷幄上奏権 (right of direct appeal to the throne by military authorities). A right of militarists in modern times. As opposed to state affairs, which were conducted by the government, military matters were controlled by military authorities. Besides, these military authorities had the right of direct appeal to the throne. From the Meiji era, when the militarists strengthened their position, this prerogative led to early Shōwa fascism and played an important role in what is known as the prerogative of the supreme command (TŌSUI-KEN).

ichien chigyō 一円知行 (complete management of domains). The management of the fief and its profits (CHIGYŌ), or the cumulative rights of the administrator of a manor during the Kamakura and Muromachi periods. These rights included the levying of yearly taxes, the administration of rural communities, and the appointment or dismissal of the administrator of the miscellaneous affairs of a manor known as SHŌKAN or *shōji*. The manor system established various interrelated rights such as those of the nominal landlord *(honsho)*, who often had more political power than the real landlord; those of the real landlord *(ryōke)*; those of the deputy who controlled the manor farmland (AZUKARI-DOKORO, who had control over the manor people, the yearly taxes, and the *shōkan*); and those of the GESU, who was the official in charge of the general supervision of the affairs of a manor. As the warriors became more powerful, the revenue of a manor was divided between the landlord and the steward (SHITAJI-CHŪBUN), and the rights of manorial management were divided between the steward, the provincial governor, and the farmers. At the same time, the system of tax collection by which a constable or deputy retained half of the tax for his own military use and remitted the remainder to the manorial lord (HANZEI) was in use. The authority of the manorial lord was thus eliminated, rights and control of the manor were simplified, and the constables who had become great landlords (SHUGO DAIMYŌ) made their appearance.

iden 位田 (rank fields). Farmland granted, according to their rank, to the *ritsuryō* officials of the fifth rank or higher. From 729, Buddhist monks and nuns were also treated as persons with rank, and *iden* was granted to them. Taxes for this land were duly collected by the proper officials, but in the case of monasteries, the taxes were remitted to the monastery in question. During the Heian period, *iden* could become manors. The size of the land granted was as follows. For imperial princes of the first grade *(ippon)*, 80 *chō* (one *chō* is the equivalent of 2.45 acres); of the second grade *(nihon)*, 60 *chō;* of the third grade *(sambon)*, 50 *chō;* of the fourth grade *(shihon)*, 40 *chō*. For the senior first rank *(shō-ichii)*, 80 *chō;* for the senior second rank, 60 *chō;* for the senior third rank, 40 *chō;* for the senior fourth rank, 24 *chō;* for the senior fifth rank, 12 *chō*. For the junior first rank *(jū-ichii)*, 74 *chō;* for the junior second rank, 54 *chō;* for the junior third rank, 34 *chō;* for the junior fourth rank, 20 *chō;* for the junior fifth rank, 8 *chō*.

ie no ko 家の子 (vassals of warriors). The vassals of warriors during the Heian and Kamakura periods. As opposed to vassals without blood relationship with the warriors (RŌTŌ), the *ie no ko* were relatives of the heads of the warrior association and cumulatively controlled many land stewards.

Iida jiken 飯田事件 (the incident at Iida). An incident of early Meiji times, caused by the intensification of the movement for democratic rights. In 1885, the members of the Democratic Party of Aichi Prefecture distributed secret documents for the reform of the government and planned a revolt in Iida,

Nagano Prefecture. The rebellion which started with the incident at Fukushima (FUKUSHIMA JIKEN) resulted in similar rebellions in various places.

Ikaiei 威海衛 (Weihaiwei). A seaport and district on the Shantung Peninsula,
northeast China, where in 1895, during the Sino-Japanese War, the Japanese
military and naval forces annihilated the Peiyang squadron, causing the
suicide of Admiral Ting Ju-ch'ang.

Ikaruga no Miya 斑鳩宮. A palace built by Shōtoku Taishi (573–621) during
the Asuka period (552–645). The palace was located in Ikaruga, Ikoma
County, Nara Prefecture. It was built in 601 but was destroyed by fire when
Shōtoku's son Yamashiro no Ōe no Ō (?–643) was suddenly attacked by Soga
no Iruka (?–645) and committed suicide in a temple called Ikaruga-dera
(former name of Hōryū-ji temple). In 739, the Buddhist priest Gyōshin (?–
758) built a Buddhist monastery on the site of the palace's remains. The center
of this monastery is the present-day YUMEDONO of HŌRYŪ-JI.

Ikkō-ikki 一向一揆 (the Ikkō uprisings). The frequent uprisings of the followers of the Ikkō sect of Buddhism (JŌDO SHIN-SHŪ) during the fifteenth and sixteenth centuries. From the early fifteenth century, when Rennyo (1415–99)
spread the doctrine of the sect in the Hokuriku district (HONGAN-JI), the revolts
became more violent in the provinces around the capital and in the Tōkai
and Hokuriku districts and were particularly directed against the constables
who had become great landowners (SHUGO DAIMYŌ). In Kaga (Ishikawa
Prefecture), the Ikkō believers drove out the hereditary constable and castle
lord Togashi Masachika (circa 1470) and ruled Kaga until 1576. Because most
of the believers were farmers, in actuality "the province was ruled by farmers"
(*hyakushō no motaru kuni* 百姓の持たる国). The stronghold of the sect was the
ISHIYAMA HONGAN-JI temple in Ōsaka. It was a large, fortified place and looked
like an unconquerable fortress. The defenders of the place put up a fierce
fight with Nobunaga but reached a compromise, and the Hongan-ji was
transferred to another district. Other uprisings at different places were also
quelled.

Ikkō-shū 一向宗 (the Ikkō religion). Another name for JŌDO SHIN-SHŪ. The
name also denoted part of the JI-SHŪ sect of Buddhism. The Jōdo Shin-shū
sect of Buddhism stressed the intense (*hitasura* 一向) belief in Amida Buddha
and was therefore called Ikkō-shū. But the founder Shinran (1173–1262) gave
it the name of Shin-shū, and the believers disliked the term Ikkō-shū. The
frequent uprisings of the followers of the sect were called IKKŌ-IKKI. After
the restoration the term Ikkō-shū was abandoned, and the sect is now known
as Jōdo Shin-shū.

ikoku keigo-ban 異国警固番 (guard against foreign countries). One of the duties of the warriors who were direct retainers (GO-KENIN) of the Kamakura shōguns. From 1268, in order to defend the western provinces, the BAKUFU assigned the warriors who possessed a fief in Kyūshū to the defense of their territory. The defense for a specified period of a determined territory in each province was carried out by the provincial governor or by the commissioners known as *bugyōnin* (the later KYŪSHŪ TANDAI or high commissioners of Kyūshū). Those who were assigned to this duty were released from the obligation of guarding Kamakura *(Kamakura ōban-yaku)*, protecting the provinces around the capital, and safeguarding the throne *(Kyōto ōban-yaku)*.

Ikuno ginzan 生野銀山 (silver mine of Ikuno). A silver mine in Ikuno, Hyōgo Prefecture, opened in the sixteenth century. The mine was discovered in 1542. Nobunaga, Hideyoshi, and Ieyasu directly controlled the mine, which prospered in the first half of the seventeenth century. The Meiji government also directly controlled the mine, but later the management was taken over by the Mitsubishi Company.

Ikuno no hen 生野の変 (rebellion at Ikuno). Ikuno is a silver-mining town in Hyōgo Prefecture. In 1863, taking advantage of the announced trip of Emperor Kōmei (1831–66) to Yamato, and in concert with the rebellion in Yamato Province (TENCHŪ-GUMI), the leader Hirano Kuniomi (1828–64) and his followers staged an armed riot against the Tokugawa regime. The rebellion, which was quelled within three days, is noteworthy because it heralded the general uprising against the shogunate and because wealthy farmers and leading farmer-soldiers took part in it.

Imagawa uji 今川氏 (the Imagawa clan). A powerful clan of the latter part of the middle ages. The clan, which became prominent among the gentry of the eastern provinces, is said to have been an offshoot of the Ashikaga clan. It gained strength during the Namboku period and became famous during the lifetime of the warrior and poet Sadayo (1325–1420). Later, Yoshimoto (1519–60) tried to unite the three provinces of Suruga, Tōtōmi (both Shizuoka Prefecture), and Mikawa (Aichi Prefecture) and experienced the climax of the Imagawa power. However, he was defeated and killed by the forces of Nobunaga in the battle of Okehazama. From this time, the Imagawa were threatened by the Takeda and Tokugawa families, and their influence declined.

Imakagami 今鏡. Historical tale in ten volumes of the late Heian period. The author is not known. Another historical work, the ŌKAGAMI, relates events to 1025, while the *Imakagami* describes events from 1025 to 1170, but there are few political accounts in the work since the stress is on describing the lives of the nobility. As far as the literary value is concerned, the *Ōkagami* is far superior.

imayō 今様. A kind of poetical song which was in vogue during the latter part of the Heian period. The word means "contemporary style," as opposed to the ancient style. The song became independent from the earlier Buddhist hymns, in which the virtues of Buddha and of eminent monks were praised in vocal music. Usually the verse form consisted of four lines, each divided into two parts of seven and five syllables. It was sung by female dancers in white robes wearing swords and men's headgear *(shirabyōshi)* or by women who performed the music and dance and who were known as *yūjo*. The *imayō* became popular among the nobility, and *imayō* contests *(imayō-awase)* were held. The literary work *Ryōjinhishō,* compiled by the cloistered Emperor Goshirakawa (1127–92), is a compilation of *imayō* songs. Whereas contemporary poems had a fixed form, the *imayō* form was free. *Imayō* poems are noteworthy because they vividly describe the feelings of the contemporary people.

imikura 斎蔵 (palace storehouse). A warehouse of the Yamato court where supplies were stored. The *imikura,* the *uchitsukura* (for personal property and furnishings of the sovereign and his household), and the ōKURA or national treasury were collectively called the "three storehouses" or *sanzō.* The oldest was the *imikura,* which was administered by the Imibe (Imbe) clan. In the latter part of the fifth century, the Hata clan was in charge of the accounts of the *sanzō.* The *Yamato no aya* and *Kawachi no aya* (AYABITO) were in charge of the chronicles and records of the *sanzō.*

imoji 鋳物師 (casters). Metal casters. Under the penal and administrative code system (Nara and Heian periods), the casters were under the rule of the court. Under the manor system, they belonged to the manorial lord and made farming implements and articles of daily use. During the middle ages, they established guilds, relying on the court and influential shrines and temples, and they secured exclusive rights for their business. They also manufactured pots and cauldrons and articles of daily use and thereby mitigated the severity of the farmers' lives.

inagi 稲置. Officers in charge of the levying of produce taxes in pre-Taika times. The office was next to that of the estate master or AGATA-NUSHI. Very often wealthy farmers inherited this office, so that the office itself became a title. It became the custom to describe the more important members of a clan or a corporation by the name of their hereditary office. In the "eight titles" (YAKUSA NO KABANE) established during the reign of Emperor Temmu (622–86), the title of *inagi* is described as being the lowest.

Innai ginzan 院内銀山 (the silver mine of Innai). A mine in Innai, Ogachi County, Akita Prefecture. According to *Innai Ginzanki* (Records of the Innai Silver Mine), compiled in 1636, the mine was discovered in 1596 by Usui Shichirōzaemon and was first operated in 1606 by the *rōnin* Murayama Sōbei.

In the beginning, production was very high, and a mining town of several thousand houses was built. Later the mine had periods of prosperity and decline. In 1817, it was directed by the Satake family, and it was most prosperous during the Tempō era (1830–44). After the restoration, it belonged to the Ono corporation, then to the Akita prefectural government, and finally to the Department of Industry (KŌBU-SHŌ). In 1885, the mine became the property of the mining industrialist Furukawa Ichibei (1832–1903). It is now abandoned.

in no chō 院庁 (government of the cloistered emperor). Executive body of the rule of the cloistered emperors. The word was first applied to the form of government with actual power invested in an ex-emperor, but gradually it came to mean the executive body of the cloister government. The executive staff was called *in no tsukasa* (INSHI), *in* meaning an ex-emperor's court.

insei 院政 (cloister government). A form of government exercised at the end of the Heian period by an ex-emperor who continued to administer state affairs. The practice was established by ex-Emperor Shirakawa (1053–1129) in 1086. In order to check the political domination of the Fujiwara clan, Emperor Gosanjō (1034–73) conceived the plan of a cloister government, and ex-Emperor Shirakawa put it into practice. Probably the landowners, in line with the movement for the adjustment of the manors and in order to secure the domains of the provincial governors, relied on the cloister of the ex-emperor to achieve their political ends. In the early period of the cloister government of the ex-emperors Shirakawa and Toba (1103–56), the opposition between the actual emperor with his regent and first adviser on the one hand, and the cloister government with its ministers on the other, was fierce. Shrines and temples were also opposed to cloister government. To strengthen its influence, the cloister government placed warriors to guard the palace of the cloistered ex-emperor *(hokumen no bushi)*. Later, when the warriors established their political authority, and during the last period of the cloister government of Goshirakawa (1127–92) and Gotoba (1180–1239), the cloister government became the stronghold of the old nobility, which violently opposed the warrior-politicians. Cloister government came to an end in 1221, after the civil war of the Jōkyū era (JŌKYŪ NO HEN), which was an unsuccessful attempt by the imperial court to regain administrative power.

inshi (in no tsukasa) 院司 (the executive staff of the ex-emperor's court). The executive staff of the *in* or the ex-emperor's court (IN NO CHŌ). The staff included the chief secretary of the cabinet, called *bettō,* the assistant secretaries known as *nennyo,* the judicial officers or *hankandai,* and the accounting officers or *shutendai.* The office of chief secretary was all-inclusive and concerned all the affairs of the court as well as the administration of the *in's* great estates.

Inu Kubō 犬公方 (the "Dog Shōgun"). Nickname given to the fifth shōgun,

Tokugawa Tsunayoshi (1646–1709). Tsunayoshi issued a decree saying that no living being should be killed. The decree is known as SHŌRUI AWAREMI NO REI. The shōgun particularly took pity upon dogs because of his own birth in the zodiac year of the dog, and this earned him the sobriquet of the "Dog Shōgun."

inu-ou-mono 犬追物 (chasing dogs). A martial art in vogue especially during the Kamakura period. Riding on horseback, one chased and killed dogs with an arrow. This sport, which is mentioned in records as early as 1222, was intended to drill the warriors in archery. It declined after the Muromachi period.

inzen 院宣 (an order of an ex-emperor's court). An order from the *in's* office. The *in* was the court of an ex-emperor. *Inzen* has the same meaning as the imperial order known as *rinshi*.

iriai 入会 (commonage). The common use by certain people of determined fields and mountains, rivers, and sea. Much forest land not yet being exploited, the neighboring people used it freely. But, along with the development of manors, quarrels broke out as soon as forest land was reclaimed, and the practice of commonage had to be limited and regulated. Similarly, during the Edo period, those clans which were urged to develop industry had to regulate commonage by law. Sometimes the *iriai* was limited to the people of one village community *(sonchū-iriai)*, sometimes people of other villages also took part in the commonage *(tason-iriai)*, and sometimes government land and land privately used by a person were worked in common by other people *(kan'yūchi-iriai, shiyūchi-iriai)*. The purpose of commonage was the common stocking of manure, fodder, fuel, construction material, fish, seaweed, etc. Many of these articles were determined at the opening gathering of the *iriai*. In certain places, land was used in common for the maintenance of irrigation waterways. The fee for joining the commonage was payment of a tax on fields and mountains in the case of clan property and payment to the village of a yearly land tax in the case of land owned by another village. Commonage exerted a great influence on the life of farmers and fishermen but gave rise to countless disputes. When the social classes became more strictly defined and as more influential people made their authority felt, many cases of the unjust use of land were recorded, and the commonage system collapsed. With the revision of the land tax in the early Meiji years, much common land was confiscated and became government property. This measure, however, resulted in the destitution of many farmers.

Ise Heishi 伊勢平氏 (the Ise branch of the Taira clan). The great grandson of Emperor Kammu (737–806), Prince Takamochi, was deprived of his princely rank in 824 and was granted the surname of Taira. His descendants were called Kammu Heishi. They were warriors who made themselves meritorious in battle. First they had their stronghold in the eastern provinces, but because of internal discord they lost their stronghold and were temporarily dispersed. The Koremori (1160–?) family joined the prosperous Ise branch or Ise Heishi. The descendants made a stronghold in Ise and Iga provinces (Mie Prefecture), where they settled and increased their prestige and power. The Ise Heishi influence even reached Kyōto and the western provinces.

Ise Monogatari 伊勢物語. A biographical tale of the early Heian period. It is also called *Zaigo-ga-Monogatari, Zaichūshō no Nikki,* and *Zaigo-chūshō Nikki.* The author is not known. The work, which is a classic, contains 125 chapters, and the main part includes the poetical biography of the hero, Arihara no Narihira (825–80). There are many notes in narrative style embellishing the *waka* poems. Together with TAKETORI MONOGATARI, it is a work of the early *monogatari* literature and inspired GENJI MONOGATARI as well as other literary works.

Ise Shintō 伊勢神道. A sect of Shintoism which originated in the Outer Shrine of Ise during the later part of the Kamakura period. It is also known as Watarai Shintō. In contrast to the ideology of HONCHI-SUIJAKU, which holds that Shintō gods are but manifestations of Buddhist gods, Ise Shintō advocates the theory that the original gods were the Shintō gods. The book which contains this theory is called *Shintō Gobu-sho.*

Ishii-Lansing Kyōtei 石井・ランシング協定 (the Ishii-Lansing Treaty). A treaty concluded in 1917 between Japan and the United States concerning Japan's rights in China. The treaty was concluded between the diplomat Ishii Kikujirō (1865–1945) and Secretary of State Robert Lansing (1864–1928). Following the Russo-Japanese War, relations between Japan and the United States became tense. Though Japan had concluded an entente with the United States in 1908, during World War I the conclusion of a new treaty concerning Chinese problems was urgent. This treaty included recognition by the United States of Japan's special interests in China, the Japanese promise not to interfere with the trade of foreign countries with China, and the Japanese promise not to violate China's independence and territorial integrity, to support the open-door policy, and to respect the principle of equal opportunity.

Ishiyama Hongan-ji 石山本願寺. The main temple of the Ikkō sect (IKKŌ-SHŪ) which flourished at the end of the Muromachi period. In 1496, Rennyo (1415–99) founded the Yamashina Hongan-ji temple in Kyōto (HONGAN-JI), but this temple was reduced to ashes by the followers of the Hokke (Nichiren or HOKKE-SHŪ) religion, and Rennyo moved to Ishiyama. It was a place of strategic importance, and a town was built around the temple (JINAI-MACHI) mostly for the Ikkō followers. It was a fortress, and it even resisted Nobunaga's policy of uniting the country. Hideyoshi built Ōsaka Castle on the spot where Ishiyama Hongan-ji was. The development of Ōsaka during the Edo period was partially due to the temple town of Ishiyama Hongan-ji.

Isoho Monogatari 伊曾保物語 *(Aesop's Fables)*. A translation from Latin into Japanese of *Aesop's Fables* by a Japanese Jesuit, printed in 1593. It is one of the oldest translations in colloquial Japanese. A popular work, it was appreciated for its tales.

isse-ichigen 一世一元 (one era name for one reign). A term meaning to determine and not to change the name of an era during the reign of the same emperor. From Emperor Mommu (683–707) on, each emperor determined the name of his era, changing that of the previous era. In the early Heian period, there was only one name for the era of each emperor—Kammu, Heizei, Saga, and Junna. Later the name of the era changed, even several times, during the reign of the same emperor. This was the result of a belief in good and bad omens known as *shōzui-saii*. During the Meiji Restoration, the *isse-ichigen* system was prescribed by an imperial edict.

Iwafune no ki 磐舟の柵 (the palisade of Iwafune). A palisade erected in Echigo Province (Niigata Prefecture) after the Taika Reform (646). The palisade was built in the neighborhood of present-day Iwafune in Niigata Prefecture against the inroads of the EZO (Ainu). It was a stronghold of long pales planted in a row. Officers and soldiers, who in peacetime cultivated farmland, lived inside the stronghold. The palisade was of strategic importance and facilitated communications.

Iwai no hanran 磐井の反乱 (the revolt of Iwai). A rebellion in 527 by Iwai, the governor of Tsukushi (Kyūshū). When the Japanese enclave of Mimana in Korea was threatened, Emperor Keitai (450–531) planned to send a reinforcement of 60,000 soldiers with Ōmi no Kenu (?–530) as their commander. However, Iwai, who was in league with the kingdom of Silla, held the expedition up for more than a year. The Yamato court sent Mononobe no Arakabi (?–536) to subdue Iwai. After a fierce battle, Arakabi succeeded the following year in destroying Iwai.

Iwami ginzan 石見銀山 (the silver mine of Iwami). A mine in Ōmori, Ōda city, Shimane Prefecture, operated from the Kamakura period. It is said to have been discovered in the fourteenth century. It prospered from 1533, when the Hakata merchant Kamiya Jutei operated it. During the Sengoku period, the great warlords Ōuchi, Amako, and Mōri competed with each other for the exploitation of the mine. After the battle of Sekigahara, the BAKUFU directly controlled the mine and established a shōgun's deputy office *(daikan-sho)* in Ōmori. In the early seventeenth century there was an increase in silver production, but later business slackened. In the middle of the Meiji era, the mine, which was under the management of the Fujita corporation, produced some copper and silver, but it was abandoned in 1923.

Izawa-jō 胆沢城 (the fortress of Izawa). A frontier fortress built in Iwate Prefecture during the Heian period in order to protect Ōu (Mutsu and Dewa provinces) against the encroachment of the EZO (Ainu). The subjugation of the Ezo had been carried out from ancient times, but it was intensified after the Taika Reform (646). In 802, Commander in Chief Sakanoue no Tamura-maro (758–811) built a fortress in Izawa in northern Japan and moved his headquarters *(chinjufu)* from TAGA-JŌ (in Miyagi Prefecture) to Izawa. After this stronghold against the Ezo was built, the subjugation of the Ezo tenta-tively came to an end.

Izayoi Nikki 十六夜日記. A short travel diary written by the poetess Abutsu Ni (1209–83) during the Kamakura period. The work, which is a classic, is in only one volume. After the death of her husband, inheritance quarrels broke out between Abutsu's real son and her stepchild. To put her case before the court, she made a journey to Kamakura in 1277. The work is an account of this journey. It is filled with feelings of motherly love and feminine senti-mentality.

Izumo no Okuni 出雲の阿国. Actress of the Azuchi-Momoyama period (1573–1614). Originally she was a maiden in the service of the great shrine of Izumo, but, in order to obtain funds to restore the main building of the Shintō shrine, she traveled to the provinces, where she performed *nembutsu* dances (NEMBUTSU ODORI). Later, these religious dances were staged, and around 1600 they became popular in Kyōto, where they were known as OKUNI KABUKI. They influenced the Edo KABUKI.

Izumo Taisha 出雲大社 (the Great Shrine of Izumo). A shrine dedicated to the mythical deity Ōkuninushi no Mikoto. The shrine is also called Kizuki Taisha. According to legend, the descendants of Amenohobi no Mikoto worshiped Ōkuninushi no Mikoto as the local chieftain (KUNI NO MIYATSUKO) of Izumo. The architectural style of the main shrine is called *taisha-zukuri*.

J

Jagatara-bumi じゃがたら文 (Jakarta correspondence). Letters sent to the homeland by Japanese nationals living in Batavia who were not allowed to return to Japan when the seclusion policy was enforced. Several of these letters have been preserved. The authors again and again implored the administrator of Nagasaki to grant them permission to re-enter the country. Permission was finally granted. The letters of the famous young girl Oharu were probably forged.

Jidai-tō 事大党. A Korean political party during the Meiji era. It is also called Shukyū-tō (Conservative Party) and Shina-tō (Pro-Chinese Party). This party was influential from 1882 to the Sino-Japanese War (1894–95). It was opposed to the Korean Independence Party (Dokuritsu-tō), which relied on Japan, and tried to maintain its traditional power, which it derived from the protection of China. The contention between the two parties gained momentum after the Jingo incident *(Jingo no hen)* of 1882. As a result of the Kōshin rebellion *(Kōshin no ran)* of 1884, the power of the Conservative Party was destroyed, but it was restored when the Chinese forces crushed the Independence Party together with the Japanese forces.

Jidō-fukushi Hō 児童福祉法 (Juvenile Welfare Law). A postwar law for the welfare of children, promulgated in 1947 and amended in 1949. It is also called *Jidō Kenshō* or the Children's Charter.

jieitai 自衛隊 (the self-defense corps). Postwar national police. Established in 1947, this police force replaced the former security patrol *(hoantai)* and the guards *(keibitai)*. The *jieitai* are divided into the land police, maritime police, and air police. Their main duty is self-defense against aggression but they are also called upon for assistance when natural calamities occur. They are equipped in modern military fashion.

jiin hatto 寺院法度 (laws for the temples). Laws and ordinances of the EDO BAKUFU for the control of temples. Issued during the Keichō era (1596–1615) and completed in 1615, they were gradually and individually applied to each religion and to each great temple. Sūden (1569–1633), the founder of the Konji-in temple, was well posted on the internal affairs of temples and was instrumental in the drafting of these laws. There was a rich variety of regulations, but the main purpose was to check the previous militant and secular conduct of monks and to establish shogunate control. At the same time, the shogunate encouraged the study of each religious sect and stressed interdependency of main and branch temples. Many stipulations reduced the competence of the court in dealing with the affairs of temples.

jikata 地方 (rural localities). Rural localities in the Edo period as opposed to towns or *machi-kata*. The *shōya* (or MYŌSHU, KIMOIRI), the KUMI-GASHIRA (or *kumiai-gashira*), and the *hyakushō-dai* were the officials in charge of the self-government of rural communities and were therefore called *jikata yakunin* or *jikata san'yaku*.

jikifu 食封 (rights to taxes). The right of members of the imperial family, of ministers and of government officials of the Nara and Heian periods to obtain all or part of the three kinds of taxes: so (land tax paid in rice), yō (labor tax paid in produce), and chō (produce tax paid in commodities other than rice). The privileges thus granted were called *fuko (fugo)* and included *ifu* (granted according to the rank of the official), *shikifu* (according to the official post), and *kōfu* (according to merit). An imperial decree at times provided special grants or an increase of the usual grants. However, these grants violated public ownership of land during the penal and administrative code system (RITSURYŌ-SEI) and led to the rise of the manorial estates.

jikiso 直訴 (direct appeals). (HYAKUSHŌ-IKKI)

Jikkinshō 十訓抄. A collection of narratives comprising three volumes, Kamakura period. The author is not known. The work was completed in 1252. Moral lessons for youth are woven into the tales. They cannot be considered as purely Buddhist narratives, as some Confucian influence is also evident.

Jimyōin-tō 持明院統 (Jimyōin line). The Gofukakusa (1243–1304) line of succession to the throne as opposed to the Daikakuji line (DAIKAKUJI-TŌ) of Kameyama (1249–1305). After Emperor Gofukakusa abdicated in 1259, he went to live in the Jimyō-in monastery. Kameyama and his descendants lived in the Daikaku-ji from 1276. There was a series of disputes between the two lines, and the KAMAKURA BAKUFU intervened. For a time the succession alternated between the two lines and led to perennial quarrels. When the Kemmu Restoration of Emperor Godaigo (1288–1339) ended in failure, Ashikaga Takauji (1305–58) forced Kōmyō (1321–80) to become emperor (1336) of the Northern dynasty, which for fifty years was antagonistic to the Southern dynasty headed by Emperor Godaigo of the Daikakuji line. When, in 1392, peace between the two dynasties was restored, only the Jimyōin line was continued.

jinai-machi 寺内町 (temple towns). Agglomeration of houses in the precincts of some temples in the late Muromachi period. The *jinai-machi* of the Ikkō sect were numerous. Commercial and industrial communities also settled in the precincts of castles, but the temple communities were well organized and powerful. The Ikkō uprisings which resisted Nobunaga's oppression were the result of the powerfully organized *jinai-machi* of ISHIYAMA HONGAN-JI. As opposed to communities formed outside the gates of temples and known as MONZEN-MACHI, the *jinai-machi* were instrumental in establishing the political and secular power of the IKKŌ-SHŪ.

Jingo-ji 神護寺. Temple of the Shingon sect of Buddhism, Kyōto. Built in the early Heian period (about 800), it was the abode of Kūkai (774–835). It deteriorated and was restored in the early Kamakura period by the monk Mongaku (1120–?). Among the many art objects preserved in the Jingo-ji are the wooden images of Yakushi Nyorai and the Godai Kokūzō. They are masterpieces of early Heian sculpture. Another possession is the portrait in the YAMATO-E style of painting of Minamoto no Yoritomo (1148–99), which is attributed to Fujiwara no Takanobu (1142–1205).

jinnin 神人 (shrine officers). A lower officer in the service of a shrine. From the Heian period, these officers joined the monk-soldiers of the great temples and, carrying a portable shrine, made petitions by force (GŌSO). The *jinnin* performed various duties in the shrines and attended to the religious services. Those of Kyōto's Hachiman-gū and Gion-sha formed a guild and secured a monopoly over the sale of the shrines' commercial articles. They were also exempted from taxation. During the late Edo period, when the influence of the temples and shrines declined, the *jinnin* became obsolete.

Jinnō Shōtōki 神皇正統記. Historical work in six volumes of the Namboku period (1336–92), completed in 1339 by Kitabatake Chikafusa (1292–1354). As a scholar, Chikafusa was the central figure of the Southern dynasty. He finished his book in the castle of Oda in Hitachi Province (Ibaraki Prefecture) while the castle was besieged by the forces of the Northern dynasty. His book was written for the people as well as to instruct Emperor Gomurakami (1328–68). It relates the history of Japan from its foundation to the reign of Emperor Gomurakami and holds strong views on the legitimacy of succession of the emperors of the Southern dynasty. Together with GUKANSHŌ it makes an outstanding historical treatise of the middle ages and is highly rated. But Chikafusa's historical view is one-sided, since he overemphasizes the supremacy of the imperial court.

Jinshin no ran 壬申の乱 (the civil war of 672). A civil war fought after the Taika Reform (646) over the succession to the throne. After the death of Emperor Tenchi (626–71), the emperor's son Ōama no Ōji (the later Emperor Temmu, 622–86), who went into seclusion at Mount Yoshino, attacked and destroyed Prince Ōtomo no Ōji, who, under the name of Emperor Kōbun (648–72), had ascended the throne in his palace of Ōtsu in Ōmi Province. Prince Ōama was enthroned as Emperor Temmu in the palace called Asuka no Kiyomihara no Miya in Yamato Province. As a result of this war, powerful clans such as Nakatomi, Soga, and others, which had sided with the Ōmi court, were overthrown, and the authority of the imperial court was firmly established.

jinushi tezukuri 地主手作 (landowner's manpower). The cultivation of a field by manpower engaged by the landowner. Though it was an old form of cultivation, the system became widespread during the Edo period, and management relied on the compulsory service of dependent farmers. This sort of administration was in force until the middle of the Meiji era. The area of land under cultivation varied from one or two *chōbu* (one *chōbu* equals 2.45 acres) to several *chōbu*. Later some farms turned unprofitable for the landowners because of the expenses for private serfs (GENIN) and employees, the cost of fertilizer, etc. Such farms were then tenanted.

jisha bugyō 寺社奉行 (commissioners of temples and shrines). The name of an office during the Edo period. The officials handled all matters involving temples and shrines and the clergy as well as the lawsuits of persons under direct jurisdiction of religious institutions. The same office existed during the Kamakura and Muromachi periods, but it was officially established in 1635 after Itakura Katsushige (1545–1624) and Sūden (1569–1633) of the Konji-in temple had been the first administrators of the affairs of temples and shrines. The *jisha bugyō* was one of the three kinds of commissioners *(san bugyō)* and from 1658 the office was usually held in addition to that of *sōshaban* (in charge of introducing the daimyō to the shōgun for an audience). The jurisdiction of the *jisha bugyō* was far-reaching.

Ji-shū 時宗. A branch of the Jōdo sect (JŌDO-SHŪ) of Buddhism, founded in 1275 by Ippen (1239–89). The priests of this sect traveled extensively, emphasizing the need to call on the name of Buddha *(nembutsu)*. They were called the "traveling saints" *(yugyō no hijiri)*. They were very active from the end of the Kamakura to the beginning of the Muromachi period. There is but a slight difference between the tenets of Ji-shū and those of Jōdo.

jitō 地頭 (land stewards). An office set up in the middle ages for the administration of manorial estates. Taira no Kiyomori (1118–81) had already made his own vassals land stewards. It was their duty to manage the manor and to levy taxes. The duty became more official when, in 1185, Minamoto no Yoritomo (1148–99), under the pretext of chastising Minamoto no Yoshitsune (1159–89) and of maintaining peace, demanded that the imperial court establish the office of *jitō* in the manors of all the provinces. His request was granted, and stewards were appointed in all provinces. The opposition of landowners, nobility, and religious foundations was violent, and Yoritomo made some changes in the system of estate managers, but the concession was more apparent than real, and he gradually enforced the system. After the civil war of the Jōkyū era in 1221, when the imperial estates of the cloistered ex-emperor Gotoba (1180–1239) were confiscated, the BAKUFU, in order to administer these confiscated imperial estates, appointed *jitō* from among the warriors (SHIMPO-JITŌ). The main duties of a *jitō* were the levying of taxes and the maintenance of peace, but gradually the *jitō* disregarded these duties and invaded the estates through such processes as UKEDOKORO, by which the stewards actually controlled the whole estate, and SHITAJI-CHŪBUN, whereby the estate was divided into two independent parts, one of which belonged to the estate master and the other to the steward. Finally, the *jitō* became either owners in their own name (MYŌSHU) or great landowners (DAIMYŌ).

Jitsugokyō 実語教. Elementary school textbook used from the early Heian period to the beginning of the Meiji era. Along with the development of children's education during the Muromachi period, the book came into wide use. It taught the value of knowledge and encouraged learning and filial piety.

Jiyū Gekijō 自由劇場 (Free School of Drama). Theatrical association of the late Meiji era. After the Russo-Japanese War (1904–5), drama entered a new ideological field. In 1909, Osanai Kaoru (1881–1928) organized the Free School of Drama, and Ichikawa Sadanji (1880–1940) acted in the plays of the Norwegian dramatist Ibsen.

jiyū minken undō 自由民権運動 (movement for democratic rights). A political movement demanding democratic rights from a despotic government in the early Meiji years. After the Seinan War (SEINAN SENSŌ, 1877) against Saigō Takamori (1827–77), the government strengthened its absolutism. Capitalists and farmers were opposed to this form of government and demanded their democratic rights. The demands became more clamorous in 1880 when the leaders of the movement formed an organization for the realization of their plans. The center of the organization was the Self-Help Society in Tosa (RISSHI-SHA) and the Sekiyō-sha in the northeastern districts. A rally was held in Ōsaka, and 87,000 men attended. They represented two metropolises and twenty-two prefectures. Kōno Hironaka (1849–1923), Kataoka Kenkichi (1843–1909), and others drew up plans for the introduction of a parliamentary system (1880). The government opposed these plans and issued public-meeting regulations, keeping control over all antigovernment activities. But the movement gained momentum and spread along with the advanced ideas of such men as Fukuzawa Yukichi (1834–1901), Nakamura Keiu (1832–91), and Nakae Chōmin (1847–1901). In 1881, corruption of the government and of businessmen with political affiliations was exposed in the incident of the commissioner for the development of Hokkaidō, Godai Tomoatsu (1834–85), who tried to dispose of government properties (HOKKAIDŌ KAITAKU-SHI KAMBUTSU-HARAISAGE JIKEN). Even within the government such men as Ōkuma Shigenobu (1838–1922) and others condemned Godai's action. Itagaki Taisuke (1837–1919) of the Risshi-sha and Kōno Hironaka of the Sekiyō-sha were leaders of the movement for a parliamentary system and delivered speeches all over the country. The movement reached a peak, and, pressed from all sides, the government fixed the year 1890 as the time for the inauguration of the National Assembly. Consequently, the democratic movement organized political parties such as Itagaki's Liberal Party (JIYŪ-TŌ) and

Ōkuma's Progressive Party (KAISHIN-TŌ), and a draft of a constitution was framed. However, from this time the repressive action of the bureaucrats in power was carried to an extreme. The government intended to maintain its oligarchic power and to build up imperial absolutism. It established a constitution and, strengthening its position, tried in every way to eradicate the democratic movement, which was now centered around the Liberal Party. It attempted the appeasement of Itagaki and other leaders, and coercive measures were enforced all over the country. Furthermore, the landowners were put at rest. All this resulted in the breaking up of the democratic movement, which had become independent from political activities. Meanwhile, riots such as those at Fukushima (FUKUSHIMA JIKEN), Kabayama (KABAYAMA JIKEN), and Chichibu (CHICHIBU JIKEN) broke out. The political activities of Ueki Emori (1856–92), one of the founders of the Liberal Party, Ōi Kentarō (1843–1922), a leading member of the Liberal Party, and others never reached maturity.

Jiyū no Ri 自由の理. The name of a book published during the early years of the Meiji era. The book is a translation by Nakamura Keiu (1832–91) of John Stuart Mill's *On Liberty* and was published in 1870. It deeply influenced the movement for democratic rights.

Jiyū-tō 自由党 (the Liberal Party). 1) A political party of early Meiji times. It was organized in 1881 and became the nucleus of the modern middle-class democratic movement. The origin of the party was the movement for the establishment of a parliamentary system launched by Itagaki Taisuke (1837–1919). This movement developed into a rally of 87,000 people representing two metropolises and twenty-two prefectures. The rally, centering around the Self-Help Society (RISSHI-SHA) in Tosa, aimed at setting up plans for the realization of a parliamentary system. Finally, the party was established, and a meeting commemorating the event was held by Ueki Emori (1856–92) and his followers. Itagaki was the president. Brewers and middle-class people, landowners, tenant farmers, discontented members of the ex-military class, and organized masses from all over the country, who demanded political rights and reduction of land taxes, obtained, in spite of oppression by those in power, the government's pledge to establish a National Assembly. The temperate Progressive Party (KAISHIN-TŌ) contended with the Imperialist Party (TEISEI-TŌ), which was the government party. Needy peasants who favored the leftists caused the Fukushima incident (FUKUSHIMA JIKEN) and, advocating the overthrow of the government, held demonstrations in Gumma (GUMMA JIKEN), in Kabayama (KABAYAMA JIKEN), in Chichibu (CHICHIBU JIKEN), and in Iida (IIDA JIKEN). As a result, the executive leaders of the Jiyū-tō reached a compromise with the government (1884). Landowners as well as tenant farmers obtained a raise in income and tempered their attitude. Finally, the Liberal Party was dissolved in 1884.

2) In 1890, when the first Deliberative Council was assembled, Ōi Kentarō

(1843–1922) again organized the Liberal Party. This party was linked with parasitic landowners, people of the middle class, and official bureaucrats. It was a reactionary political party, and its attitude completely differed from the antigovernment attitude of the former Liberal Party. It was dissolved in 1898.

3) After the Pacific War, a Liberal Party was formed in 1945 by Hatoyama Ichirō (1883–1959) and his old political friends. It was later called the Democratic Liberal Party (Minshu Jiyū-tō), but in 1949 the name was changed back to the Liberal Party. Its leader, Yoshida Shigeru (1878–1967), for a long time assumed the helm of state affairs, representing the interests of monopolistic capitalists, the bureaucracy, and landowners. Yoshida adopted a one-sided attitude of dependency upon the United States. In November 1955, with the fusion of liberals and conservatives, the Liberal Party came to an end.

Jōchi-ji 浄智寺. A monastery of the ENKAKU-JI branch of the Rinzai sect of Buddhism. Jōchi-ji is the fourth of the Five Monasteries (GOZAN) of Kamakura. It was built in 1283 by Hōjō Munemasa and his son Morotoki (1274–1311), but the founder of the monastery was the Chinese monk Gottan Funei (1197–1276). The monastery is now in disrepair.

Jōdo-kyō 浄土教 (the Jōdo faith). The belief in the rebirth of the Pure Land (Jōdo) of Amida Buddha. The Jōdo belief goes back to the time of Shōtoku Taishi (573–621), but it is generally admitted that the origin of Jōdo as a loosely organized religion is Tendai's *Jōgyō-zammai* as interpreted by Saichō (767–822) and Ennin (794–864). Genshin (or Eshin Sōzu, 942–1017) firmly established the Jōdo religion. In his ōJŌYŌSHŪ, he defends the opinion that only by the invocation of the name Amida Buddha *(nembutsu)* can rebirth in the Pure Land or paradise be attained. He thereby touches upon the current idea of the "latter degenerate days" *(mappō-jokuse)*. The society of those days was deeply convinced that the "latter degenerate days" were near, but Genshin offered a means to salvation. In the initial stage, the nobility's religious fervor was no more than a desire for worldly advantages. Prayers were offered to Buddha so that he might protect the nobles against all kinds of calamities *(kaji-kitō)*. For the same purpose, temples were built and Buddhist masses *(hōe)* offered. But when the Fujiwara family began to decline, grief and sadness filled the society of nobles, the current world presented the aspect of the "latter degenerate days," and a pessimistic view of life *(onri-edo)* prevailed. When Kūya (903–72) spread the practice of *nembutsu* among the masses, the Jōdo tenets reached the common people. The belief was further spread by numerous *"nembutsu* saints" *(nembutsu hijiri)* who followed in Kūya's steps. Thus the Jōdo religion penetrated deeply into the hearts of the people. Finally, at the end of the twelfth century, Hōnen (1133–1212) founded the Jōdo sect of Buddhism (JŌDO-SHŪ).

Jōdo Shin-shū 浄土真宗. A sect of Buddhism founded during the Kamakura period by Shinran (1173–1262). It is also known as Shin-shū and Ikkō-shū. It further developed the tenets of Jōdo and preached vicarious *(tariki)* salvation. The "opportunity of salvation was offered to evil men, too" *(akunin shōki)*. It was the time of the decline of the nobility and of the rise of warriors and great landowners. In particular, oppressed farmers were converted to Shin-shū. In Kamakura days, the sect was not yet powerful, but in the Muromachi period it made great strides under the influence of Rennyo (1415–99), reaching the rural communities of the provinces around the capital and of the Tōkai and Hokuriku districts. It turned to fanaticism with the famous Ikkō uprisings (IKKŌ-IKKI).

Jōdo-shū 浄土宗 (the Jōdo sect of Buddhism). A new sect of Buddhism founded during the late Heian period by Hōnen (1133–1212). Hōnen developed the Jōdo faith, which had already reached the masses, and held that by the invocation of "Homage to Amida Buddha" *(Namu Amida Butsu)* everybody could be reborn in the Pure Land or paradise (Jōdo). This doctrine, being easy to understand, fulfilled the hopes of the times. Consequently, it rapidly spread among the warriors and the common people. Though severely oppressed by traditional Buddhism, its influence grew steadily. The headquarters of Jōdo-shū is the CHION-IN temple in Kyōto.

Jōei Shikimoku 貞永式目 (the Jōei Formulary). A code of law adopted in 1232 by the Kamakura Council of State. It is also known as Goseibai Shikimoku. Formerly, the rights, duties, and lawsuits of direct vassals were regulated according to the customs of the warrior class, but after the civil war of the Jōkyū era (JŌKYŪ NO HEN) disputes arose among land stewards and owners of manorial estates and also among the vassals themselves. The BAKU-FU, in order to be able to make judgments, promulgated the Jōei Formulary. The formulary was the work of Hōjō Yasutoki (1183–1242) and contains fifty-one regulations. It is considered to be the oldest code for the military class. Based on the ethical principles of the warriors, the contents of the formulary are practical and direct. The formulary was only effective for feudal domains under the jurisdiction of the *bakufu,* and no attempt was made to apply it outside these domains. The landed proprietors who were not Kamakura vassals, the civilian officials, and the great monasteries were still subject to the Taihō Code. The Jōei Formulary grew in importance when the warriors succeeded in increasing their power. The laws of the MUROMACHI BAKUFU, the Sengoku era, and the EDO BAKUFU exerted a great influence on the legislation concerning the warriors.

jōgō 成功 (granting of offices). The granting of offices during the Heian period. In late Heian times, religious fervor drove the imperial family to hold many memorial services and to erect temples. The necessary funds were offered by the people. To indemnify the people, official ranks and offices were granted. This was called *jōgō*. However, the system harmed the national revenue and is thought to have been one of the causes of the collapse of the penal and administrative code system (RITSURYŌ-SEI).

jōi-ron 攘夷論 (policy to expel barbarians). A policy that spread in the late Edo period and that aimed at the expulsion of foreigners. It was opposed to the opening of ports. Narrow-minded ultranationalism, unreasonable fear of Christianity, and information gathered from the Dutch concerning aggression by Western powers caused an antiforeign attitude. In 1825, the BAKUFU had issued the order to destroy all foreign ships (GAIKOKUSEN-UCHIHARAI REI) but moderated its policy in 1842. Clan loyalists favored imperialism (SONNŌ-RON) as the only means to solve internal dissensions, and they allied with the anti-foreigners. Their claim, endorsed by the teaching of the Mito school (MITO-GAKU), became the main political current of the late Edo period. Even after the opening of the country, the court did not immediately reject the anti-foreign principle. Furthermore, antiforeign feeling was strengthened by the financial instability which threatened the life of the warriors. From about the Bunkyū era (1861–64), a turning point was noticeable. Realizing the impossibility of enforcing their antiforeign policy, the loyalists now turned their efforts toward the overthrow of the *bakufu*.

jōka-machi 城下町 (castle towns). Towns which developed around the residential castles of the daimyō. The Sengoku era produced many of these towns. As strategy and the military arts changed, castles were built on hills instead of on the plains. Warriors and merchants were forced to move to castle towns. By abolishing the monopolies of markets and guilds (RAKUICHI-RAKU-ZA), Nobunaga and Hideyoshi forced the merchants to flock together. In a previous period, castle towns acted as supply units, as they had to provide the necessary articles for combat personnel and military supplies. However, after Edo feudal society was firmly established, these towns became political as well as cultural centers, and they were economically successful. Defense had always been the main purpose of the *jōka-machi,* and, as the residential castle was invariably in the center, access to it was made difficult by a labyrinth of many roads and streets. Usually all the temples were concentrated in one section of the town, and other sections were reserved for each of the four social classes (warrior, farmer, artisan, and merchant). Even after the restoration, the castle towns of Ōsaka, Nagoya, Kanazawa, Fukuoka, Hiroshima, Shizuoka, etc. continued to be administrative, economic, and cultural centers.

Jōkyō koyomi 貞享暦 (the Jōkyō calendar). A calendar made in 1684 (Jōkyō era, 1684–88). Japan had been using the Semmyō calendar (SEMMYŌ REKI) for 823 years. Because this calendar had many mistakes, it was corrected by the astronomer Shibukawa Shunkai (Yasui Santetsu, 1639–1715), who, with his teacher, worked for more than ten years to prepare the Jōkyō calendar. The calendar was further corrected in 1754, 1798, and 1842. Finally, in 1872, the solar calendar was adopted.

Jōkyū no hen 承久の変 (the civil war of the Jōkyū era). Following the establishment of the Kamakura government, many court nobles lost their power and soon became eager to regain it. This discontent was the cause of the civil war of 1221, for which ex-Emperor Gotoba (1180–1239) raised troops to fight the BAKUFU but was defeated. The emperor was deposed, three ex-emperors including Gotoba were exiled, court nobles and warriors who had sided with Gotoba were punished, and about 3,000 manors were confiscated. The *bakufu* then appointed stewards from among the warriors (SHIMPO JITŌ) and placed an inspector general *(tandai)* in Rokuhara for the safeguarding of Kyōto. This marked the strengthening of the *bakufu* and the foundation of a military government.

jōmen hō 定免法 (law concerning land taxes). An Edo law for the levying of land taxes. *Men* 免 means the rate of taxation according to the yield in *koku* (one *koku* equals 4.96 bushels). This rate was one-tenth of the yield. *Jōmen* 定免 was the fixation of a rate of taxation on the average yield of several years or even more than ten years. This rate of taxation did not change even in times of bad harvests. In some districts the law was enforced very early, but when the BAKUFU tried to enforce the law after the Kyōhō era (1716–36), the farmers resisted, claiming that the Kemi law (KEMI HŌ) was still in force. In fixing taxation, the Kemi law took into account bad harvests.

Jōmon-shiki doki 縄文式土器 (rope-pattern earthen vessels). Earthen pottery used in the Stone Age. According to the period, the *doki* display different forms and patterns. Conventionally, the periods represent five stages: the initial, former, middle, latter, and final stages. The vessels were made by coiling, but not all of them had rope patterns. In the initial and final stages many vessels had shell patterns, spatula patterns, and others. Though the pottery is found all over the country, it differs on the two sides of a border running between Kuwana and Sekigahara. Most traces of this neolithic culture are found in the Kantō and northeastern districts, though there are also a few to the west of the home provinces. Jōmon vessels eminently represent Japan's neolithic culture. They are unusual in that they present a rich variety in shape as well as size.

Jōmyō-ji 浄妙寺. A temple of the Kenchō-ji branch of the Rinzai sect of Buddhism. It is the fifth of the Kamakura Five Monasteries (GOZAN). The temple was erected in 1188 by Ashikaga Yoshikane (?–1199). Among the faithful who worshiped in the temple were Minamoto no Sanetomo (1192–

1219), Taira no Masako (1157–1225), and Ashikaga Takauji (1305–58). Jōmyō-ji was made one of the Kamakura Five Monasteries in 1386.

jōruri 浄瑠璃 (ballad-drama). Originally, a kind of Japanese music. It originated in the middle of the Muromachi period and developed in the middle of the sixteenth century when it was accompanied by the newly introduced three-stringed SHAMISEN. In the early seventeenth century, when manipulated marionettes were added, the ballad-drama was born. It further developed and provided the main music for puppet dramas. Various schools of *jōruri* were created, but around the Genroku era (1688–1703) the famous musician Takemoto Gidayū (1651–1714) of Ōsaka developed the ballad-drama *gidayū-bushi,* which is the most celebrated variety of *jōruri.* He built the theater Take-moto-za, collaborated with the dramatist Chikamatsu Monzaemon (1653–1724), and brought the new *jōruri* to perfection.

Jōwa no hen 承和の変 (SHŌWA NO HEN)

jōyaku kaisei 条約改正 (treaty revision). Revision of unequal treaties was the main issue of Meiji diplomacy. The treaties concluded by Japan with the United States and European countries were unequal, as they bore the mark of colonialism. From the early Meiji era, Japan wanted complete independence and demanded the revision of unequal treaties. The inspection tour to Europe and the United States in 1871 by Iwakura and his suite had the same purpose but ended in failure. The government attributed this failure to lack of national prestige and adopted Western techniques calculated to enrich and strengthen the country. However, the democratic movement demanded expansion of democratic rights, on which the revision of treaties should be based. In 1878, Foreign Minister Terajima Munenori (1833–93) advocated diplomatic relations as a means to obtain equal treaties. But this tactic also failed. In 1887, through the efforts of the statesman Inoue Kowashi (1843–95), a conference with foreign representatives was held in Tōkyō. The problems dealt with the residence in Japan of foreigners and the trial of suits involving foreign nationals. When the foreign minister was prepared to sign an agreement abolishing extraterritorial rights but providing for the trial of suits involving foreign nationals in mixed courts in which foreign judges were to sit with Japanese, public anger obliged the government to repudiate the negotiations and to accept the resignation of Foreign Minister Inoue Kaoru (1835–1915). In 1889, Foreign Minister Ōkuma Shigenobu (1838–1922), who was even more outspoken than Inoue, failed in his efforts because of the opposition of ultranationalists. Neither did the efforts of Foreign Minister Aoki Shūzō (1844–1914) bear fruit. By now a national antiforeign feeling was strongly aroused. Finally, Japan's rights were recognized by England, which had adopted a different Far Eastern policy. In 1893, when Mutsu Munemitsu (1844–1897) was foreign minister, concrete plans were prepared for the revision of unequal treaties. The following year, England abolished extraterritorial rights, and other European countries as well as the United States followed suit. In 1897, the revision of treaties was completed. Tariff autonomy was restored in 1911 after the Russo-Japanese War, when Komura Jutarō (1855–1911) was foreign minister. The revision of treaties was brought about by the influence of Japan's growing capitalism, financial strength, and military prestige.

jukō (jugō) 准后. *Jukō* means "to correspond to the rank of an empress" and "to correspond to the three imperial ranks." The word is also an abbreviation of *jusangō* and *jusangū*. This rank or title had been established from ancient times in order to treat with marked distinction the imperial family, imperial consorts, relatives of the emperor on the maternal side, and illustrious vassals. In an early stage, all these people were granted an income according to their rank, but later *jukō* became a mere title. The first to be thus honored was Fujiwara no Yoshifusa (804–72). Others were the distinguished scholar Kitabatake Chikafusa (1292–1354) of the Namboku period (1336–92) and Mansai (1368–1435), the chief priest of DAIGO-JI temple during the Muromachi period.

Jukyō 儒教 (Confucianism). The moral teaching of Confucius, which mainly stresses the duties of the ruler and the ruled. If these moral principles were observed, it was believed, citizens would be well ruled and the country would be at peace. Confucianism reached Japan when writing was introduced. As an educational and moral system, it played an important role, especially after the Edo rulers had firmly established the feudal regime. In this period the Confucianism of Chu Hsi (in Japanese, Shu Ki; 1130–1200) as well as that Wang Yang-ming (in Japanese, Ō Yō-mei; 1472–1529) flourished together with the study of Chinese classics. Confucianism was the spiritual support of the clanship national structure. Even after the restoration, its influence was profound, since it was the moral foundation of nationalist absolutism.

junsatsu-shi 巡察使 (inspectors). Inspectors under the penal and administrative code system (RITSURYŌ-SEI). It was the duty of the *junsatsu-shi* to inspect the administration of the provincial and district authorities and to inquire about the hardships of the people. It was an extralegal *(ryōge)* office—that is, it was not mentioned in the Taihō Code. The *junsatsu-shi* were chosen from among men of stern integrity, with or without official occupation. They were only temporarily appointed. Together with the official inspectors known as *azechi,* the *junsatsu-shi* had great authority in matters of local administration.

Jurakudai 聚楽第. Hideyoshi's mansion in Kyōto. In 1585, Hideyoshi was made KAMPAKU or chief councilor to the emperor. When his relations with the imperial court improved, Hideyoshi started building his mansion in Kyōto and completed it in 1587. The following year he invited Emperor Goyōzei (1571–1617) to be his guest at a feast at Jurakudai, attended by several daimyō. Hideyoshi paid his respects to the emperor, and the daimyō pledged fidelity to Hideyoshi. The Jurakudai was a structure representative of the Momoyama style, but today only parts of it remain, such as the HIUNKAKU in the Nishi Hongan-ji temple compound and the Karamon in the Daitoku-ji temple compound, both in Kyōto.

Jūshichijō no Kempō 十七条憲法 (Constitution in Seventeen Articles). The first constitution of Japan, issued in 604 by Shōtoku Taishi (573–621). It was actually a code or collection of moral injunctions to the ruling classes. These injunctions were a turning point in the ideals of government and were inspired by Confucian and Buddhist principles. The central idea is the divine origin of the authority of the sovereign and respect for the value of the individual. This code became the core of the ideal government as expressed in the Taika Reform of 646.

K

kabane 姓 (titles). Titles conferred on clans in ancient times in order to indicate the degree of social standing within the aristocratic society. Originally the titles indicated the position within a corporation or an official function in the imperial court, but later, when upper and lower classes came into existence, the title served to describe social rank. Most important were the titles *omi* (clan chieftain) and MURAJI (group chieftain). The senior of the *omi* was the ō-OMI (leader of all clan chieftains), and the leader of the group chiefs was called ō-MURAJI (grand group chief). All these titles were abolished at the time of the Taika Reform in 646, but in 685 eight titles (YAKUSA NO KABANE) were re-established. They gradually underwent changes.

Kabayama jiken 加波山事件 (the incident at Kabayama). An incident resulting from the intensification of the movement for democratic rights in the early Meiji years. In 1884, the accomplices of the Fukushima affair (FUKUSHIMA JIKEN) failed in their attempt to assassinate Mishima Michitsune (1835–88), the governor of Fukushima Prefecture, and other high government officials. They entrenched themselves at Kabayama and put up strong resistance to the oppression by a despotic administration.

Kabuki 歌舞伎 (Kabuki drama). Popular drama of the Edo period, composed of songs, dances, and plays. The word "Kabuki" derives from *kabuku,* which means to perform an original play. Kabuki seems to have originated from the OKUNI KABUKI, which developed into Onna Kabuki and Wakashu Kabuki. All these forms of drama were subject to stringent BAKUFU regulations. When Wakashu Kabuki was prohibited, it was replaced by Yarō Kabuki. The performance also changed, as it was first based on the dance but later on dramatic situations. The foundation of Kabuki was firmly established during the Genroku era (1688–1703), when experts in drama, acting, and musical performance appeared. Dramas, music, stage equipment, and construction of theaters were successively brought to perfection. Around the Kansei era (1789–1801) Kabuki reached its climax. It became fashionable and represented the culture of wealthy merchants at a time when a currency economy was developing. As a result of ultranationalism during the early Meiji years, Kabuki went through many vicissitudes. Today Kabuki is representative of classical drama.

kabu-nakama 株仲間 (trade corporations). Trade bodies approved by the Edo government or by the clans. *Kabu* means the right of trading. Each year money was collected by the associates (MYŌGA-KIN), and trading by nonassociates was not recognized. The corporation fixed market prices and made many other arrangements. Some trade bodies were organized very early, but most of them were set up after 1781 following Tanuma Okitsugu's (1719–88) incitement to increase production. Local merchants, who relied on rural communities, were opposed to trade corporations, and in 1841 the corporations, following the sweeping reforms of Mizuno Tadakuni (1794–1851), were temporarily prohibited. Mizuno intended to check the rise of prices but failed owing to the general confusion. In 1851, the trade corporations were reestablished. When foreign trade began to expand, the corporations were threatened. They gradually lost their significance, and by 1872 they were ordered to dissolve.

kachōmai 加徴米 (additional rice tax). An additional rice tax levied on the manorial estates. Regular taxes were the annual ones and the farm rent paid in rice (CHISHI). However, in the Kamakura period, land stewards often collected *kachōmai,* which was officially recognized after the civil war of the Jōkyū era in 1221, when the warrior stewards (SHIMPO JITŌ) secured the right to collect an additional tax of five *shō* (one *shō* equals 3.18 pints) per *tan* (one *tan* equals 0.245 acres).

Kadensho 花伝書. A book on Nō (NŌGAKU) published during the Muromachi period. The book was written by Zeami (1363–1443) in order to transmit to his descendants the mysteries of the art of Nō, which he himself had received from his father Kan'ami (1334–85). The work is valuable not only as a book on Nōgaku but also as a treatise on art. It is favorably commented upon in the history of Japanese arts.

kadō 花道 (the art of flower arrangement). The art of arranging flowers is an ancient one dating from the custom of arranging flowers before the statues of Buddha when Buddhism was introduced. After the Kamakura period, it became an independent art which flourished during the Muromachi period. When the architectural style known as SHOIN-ZUKURI spread, the art known as *rikka (tatebana)* came into being. It developed into small-size *ikebana* for the decoration of the tokonoma of the living apartments *(shoin)*. A master of flower arrangement was Ikenobō Senkei (fifteenth century) of the Rokkaku-dō temple in Kyōto. His school has continued from generation to generation until the present day. During the Azuchi-Momoyama period, when the tea ceremony became popular, it became the custom to adorn the tea-ceremony room with simple, natural flowers, and the art of *nageire* (free-style flower arrangement) was inaugurated. In the Edo period, the art was transmitted secretly, and various rules were laid down.

kaezeni, kaemai 替銭・替米 (payment in currency or in rice). System of money circulation which corresponds to the later KAWASE and RYŌGAE or money exchange. The system was in use during the Kamakura and Muromachi periods. When the yearly land taxes of the manorial estates were paid at remote places, in order to bring many coins into circulation a bill of exchange (SAIFU) was used and converted into money at the place of taxation. This was called *kaezeni*. The payment in rice was called *kaemai*. During the Muromachi period, as industrial economy developed and currency circulation increased, this method of collecting taxes was used extensively. Exchange shops *(kaezeni-ya)* and exchange brokers *(saifu-ya)* for use in business transactions came into being.

kafuchō-sei 家父長制 (system of the family head). A system according to which everything in a household was under the control of the head of the family, who was invested with full authority. When production capacity in primitive society began to increase, it was felt that the authority of the male, who was burdened with many tasks, should grow and be recognized. The family head controlled men and beasts as well as the property. Because the system was general, it contributed to the growth of a slave society. In ancient times, the system was the foundation of the country and profoundly influenced the structure of society. It remained strong even in feudal society, as can be seen from the succession of family property.

Kagerō Nikki 蜻蛉日記. The first diary published by a woman, written in the middle Heian period. The writer was the mother of Fujiwara no Michitsuna. The book was written after 974. It is autobiographical and describes the writer's unfortunate family life with her husband Fujiwara no Kaneie (929–90). It gives a vivid picture of the position and the emotions of women of that aristocratic society, of the intense disappointment of the authoress with her husband, and of her fervent affection for her child. The diary has been translated into English by Edward Seidensticker as *The Gossamer Years*.

kageyushi 勘解由使 (audit officers). Functionaries during the Heian period who audited the accounts of provincial governors and local administrators at the end of their term of office. It was an extralegal *(ryōge)* office. The function itself was probably established in 797. It was the *kageyushi's* duty to regulate local administration. The functionaries examined the official documents which testified that there were no misappropriations by the former local governor such as embezzlement of taxes and loss of official property. The function was abolished in 806 but re-established in 824.

Kaichōon 海潮音. Anthology of translated poems by English, German, French, and Italian authors. The translations were made by Ueda Bin (1874–1916) and published in 1905. The work was greatly influential because of its elegant translations and because it expressed the essence of symbolism. Ueda Bin was a strong supporter of the school of symbolism.

Kaidōki 海道記. A travel account in two volumes, early Kamakura period. Like TŌKAN KIKŌ and IZAYOI NIKKI, it is a distinguished work. It describes the journey from Kyōto to Kamakura in the Kantō district. The author is not known. The book relates the events of the journey, which began in 1223 in Kyōto.

Kaifūsō 懐風藻. Anthology of poems written in Chinese, Nara period. The work was compiled in 791. It is the first collection of poems written in Chinese and is classed with MAN'YŌSHŪ. The opinion favoring Ōmi no Mifune (722–785) as the author has the strongest support, but other opinions exist. The anthology includes 120 poems by sixty-four poets and covers a period of eighty years. The poets are either court nobles or monks. The influence of Confucianism, of Lao Tzu, and of Chuang Tzu is evident. As compared with works of the early Heian period, *Kaifūsō* is rather artless and stiff.

kaikoku, kaikō 開国・開港 (opening of the country, opening of ports). (KANA-GAWA JŌYAKU and ANSEI NO KARI-JŌYAKU)

Kaikoku Heidan 海国兵談. A work in sixteen volumes written by Hayashi Shihei (1738–93) and published in 1791. The author tries to inform the people of the urgent necessity of coastal defense and describes the art of war on land and water, giving an account of weapons. He also criticizes the BAKUFU's politics and economy. The following year Shihei was punished by the authorities, and the publication of his work was prohibited.

Kaisei Gakkō 開成学校 (Kaisei College). A government college of the early Meiji years. The college was first known as KAISEIJO (1863) and was established for the study of foreign sciences, but in 1869 the name was changed to Kaisei Gakkō. Later it was temporarily called Daigaku Nankō and Daigaku Tōkō, but in 1877, being attached to the medical school, it became the Imperial University of Tōkyō.

Kaiseijo 開成所. A school for the study of Western sciences, established by the BAKUFU at the end of the Edo period. As forerunner of the Imperial University of Tōkyō, the Yōgakusho was established in Edo in 1855. The following year, it became the BANSHO TORISHIRABESHO, which was an office for the study of foreign documents. This was succeeded by the government college which was opened in 1857 and named Kaiseijo in 1863. Foreign languages, mathematics, and the sciences were studied.

kaisen 回船 (freight ships). Transportation vessels or freight ships *(kaisōsen)*. From the end of the middle ages, maritime regulations had been formulated in what is known as the Kaisen Shikimoku. During the Edo period, shipping developed rapidly along with the consolidation of navigation routes. The HIGAKI-KAISEN and the TARU-KAISEN which voyaged between Ōsaka and Edo were well known.

Kaishin-tō 改進党 (the Progressive Party). Political party of the early Meiji era, organized in 1882 by Ōkuma Shigenobu (1838–1922). It advocated the British two-chamber system of government. With the Liberal Party as a detached force, it obtained the support of the moderately propertied class and of the intellectuals. Key members of the party were Ōkuma Shigenobu, Maejima Hisoka, Inukai Tsuyoshi, Ozaki Yukio, Ono Azusa, Takada Sanae, and Shimada Saburō. All had resigned from office in 1881, following the disposal of government properties (HOKKAIDŌ KAITAKU-SHI KAMBUTSU-HARAISAGE JIKEN), for which they assumed responsibility. Fukuzawa Yukichi's (1834–1901) Keiō Gijuku joined the progressive movement, and so did Iwasaki of the Mitsubishi concern. In 1896, the party changed its name to Shimpo-tō and later was linked with the Constitutional Society (KENSEI-KAI) and with the Democratic Party (MINSEI-TŌ).

Kaitai Shinsho 解体新書. The first translation into Japanese of a book on anatomy. The original work is the Dutch *Tabulae Anatomicae,* and the translators were Maeno Ryōtaku (1723–1803), Sugita Gempaku (1733–1817), Katsuragawa Hoshū (1751–1809), Nakagawa Jun'an (1739–86), and others. The work was published in 1774. It was of great importance because it fostered the study of Western sciences, especially of medicine. Later Ōtsuki Gentaku (1757–1827), fulfilling the wish of Sugita Gempaku, revised and enlarged the book and published it under the title *Jūtei Kaitai Shinsho.*

Kaitoku-dō 懐徳堂. A Confucian school built in 1719 in Ōsaka by the disciples of the Confucian scholar Miyake Sekian (1665–1730) for the instruction of the townspeople. There was a revival of Western and other learning under the stimulus of Shōgun Yoshimune (1684–1751), and the school was officially recognized. It was later re-established by the Confucian scholar Nakai Chikuzan (1730–1804), under whose influence it became the center of learning in the Kansai district. The learning centered around the Confucianism of Chu Hsi, though that of Wang Yang-ming was not neglected. The characteristic feature of the school was that its education was always directed toward the townspeople.

Kai-tsūshō Kō 華夷通商考. A book on the situation in countries outside Japan, middle Edo period. The author is Nishikawa Joken (1648–1724), a Dutch interpreter of Nagasaki. The book was published in two volumes in 1695. The first volume deals with China, the second with Korea, the Ryūkyū Islands, the South Sea Islands, and India. The products of the various lands as well as their intercourse with Japan are described. A revised and enlarged edition in five volumes was published in 1780. It was the first work of its kind in Japan.

kaizuka 貝塚 (shell mounds). Deposits of refuse such as pottery fragments, bone and horn implements, stone implements, discarded utensils, animal bones, earthenware, and vast quantities of shells tossed aside after meals of shellfish. These shell heaps are the chief repositories of neolithic remains. Sometimes human bones are also found in them. They are valuable for their evidence of neolithic man and his life. About two thousand shell mounds have been found all over the country. Many belong to the Jōmon culture (3000–350 B.C.) (JŌMON-SHIKI DOKI). Those belonging to the Yayoi period (350 B.C.–A.D. 250) (YAYOI-SHIKI DOKI) are extremely rare. Most of the remains have been found along the Pacific coast, a very few along the Japan Sea coast. Sometimes they reveal the conditions of sea water and of the seacoast in ancient times.

kaji 鍛冶 (smithery). Refining of metals and manufacture of implements. The metalcraft of the Chinese mainland was introduced from the time of the sepulchral mounds, and swords began to be produced. During the middle ages, technique improved, and swords of excellent quality were manufactured. The art also resulted in the manufacture of agricultural implements.

Kajin no Kigū 佳人の奇遇. Political novel in sixteen volumes, published from 1885 to 1897 by Shiba Shirō (1858–1922), whose pseudonym was Tōkai Sanshi. Shiba wrote the book upon his return from the United States, where he studied economics. Like the book KEIKOKU BIDAN by Yano Ryūkei (1850–1931), this book also described the vicissitudes of foreign countries, encouraged national pride, and helped to create the ideological background of the movement for democratic rights.

kakeya 掛屋 (monetary agents). A kind of monetary agent for the use of the daimyō during the Edo period. The daimyō used to give to the custody of qualified tradesmen of Ōsaka the money they obtained from the sale of produce through the KURA-YASHIKI. They entrusted the tradesmen, who were called *kakeya,* with all receipts and disbursements. The daimyō could obtain money from the *kakeya* at any time, but when they met with financial difficulties they had to borrow money, so that the *kakeya* often controlled the clan's finances. The money-transaction business of wealthy businessmen such as Kōnoike Zen'emon (1667–1736) is well known.

kakibe 部曲 (serfs). Guild people *(be no tami)* privately owned by families in ancient times. They included soldiers defeated in war and people financially ruined. As opposed to house slaves, they were self-supporting farmers who tilled their own land. They paid various taxes to their master and were subject to corvée *(yōeki)* both in general and for the imperial court. The *kakibe* of the powerful Soga, Ōtomo, and other clans were scattered all over the several clan provinces and at times over more than ten provinces. From the time of the Taika Reform (646), the system was abolished, and serfs were accepted as free persons *(ryōmin)*.

Kakitsu no hen 嘉吉の変 (the Kakitsu incident). In 1441, the first year of the Kakitsu era (1441–44), the military commissioner of Harima, Akamatsu Mitsusuke (?–1441), assassinated Shōgun Ashikaga Yoshinori (1394–1441). Yoshinori had tried to curb the power of the constable daimyō and to restore the authority of the BAKUFU. He had also planned to deprive Akamatsu of portions of his fief and to give them the Akamatsu Sadamura family. Aware of this plan, Mitsusuke invited Yoshinori to a banquet in Kyōto and assassinated him. Yamana Mochitoyo (1404–73) annexed Mitsusuke's territory, and Ashikaga Yoshikatsu (1434–43), the son of Yoshinori, who had revenged himself by murdering Akamatsu, was made shōgun (1442).

Kamakura 鎌倉. The site of the BAKUFU during the Kamakura period (1185–1333). Like Kyōto during the middle ages, Kamakura flourished. Topographically, the city was a stronghold. It was also a business center of merchants, and vassals built their mansions there. These vassals worshiped at Tsurugaoka Hachiman-gū and at KENCHŌ-JI temple and, in general, at the Five Zen Monasteries (Kamakura GOZAN). Culture also developed. The MUROMACHI BAKUFU established in Kamakura a governor of the Kantō district (KANTŌ KANREI) and made Kamakura into the administrative center of the eastern provinces. However, when Ashikaga Shigeuji (1434–97), who governed the Kantō, established himself in a small place called Koga (KOGA KUBŌ) in Shimōsa Province (Ibaraki Prefecture), Kamakura began to decline.

Kamakura bakufu 鎌倉幕府. Military government established in Kamakura from 1185 to 1333. In 1180, Minamoto no Yoritomo (1148–99) made

Kamakura into his stronghold, established the Disciplinary Board (SAMURAI-DOKORO) for the affairs of the military class, and appointed Wada Yoshimori 1147–1213) chief of the Samurai-dokoro, or *bettō*. As the military government grew, two boards were added: the Secretariat for the Conduct of Official Affairs (KUMONJO) and the Judicial Board to inquire into disputes among vassals (MONCHŪJO). In 1192, Yoritomo was made generalissimo *(seii-taishō-gun)*. This rank was equivalent to that of commander in chief and gave him the authority to rule the country. Local administrators were the constables (SHUGO) and the stewards (JITŌ). The local government administration included also the office to safeguard Kyōto (KYŌTO SHUGO-SHOKU), the office of administration of Kyūshū (CHINZEI BUGYŌ), and the office of administration of Mutsu Province in the absence of the magistrate *(Mutsu rusu-shoku)*. After the civil war of the Jōkyū era (JŌKYŪ NO HEN), a commissioner of Rokuhara (ROKUHARA TANDAI) was appointed for the general administrative control of the provinces around the capital and of the district west of Mikawa Province. After the Mongol invasions a commissioner of Kyūshū *(Chinzei tandai)* was appointed for the defense of Kyūshū *(Chinzei bugyō)*. The master-servant relation between shōgun and vassals was the foundation of the regime. The vassals were granted the offices of constable and steward, or their vested rights were recognized. After Yoritomo's death, Yoriie (1182–1204) and Sanetomo (1192–1219) were made shōguns. When the Minamoto line of shōguns became extinct, the regent-shōguns *(sekke-shōgun)* and prince-shōguns *(shinnō-shōgun)* took over the office. Finally, the Hōjō clan held the real power and eventually managed to eliminate the meritorious vassals from the time of Yoritomo. As a result of their victory during the civil war of the Jōkyū era, the Hōjō strengthened their position still more and reached the climax of their power during the regency of Yasutoki (1183–1242) and Tokimune (1215–1384). They established the offices of assistant regent, who dealt with routine administration (RENSHO), members of the Council of State (HYŌJŌ-SHŪ), and assistant members of the Council of State (HIKITSUKE-SHŪ). They also promulgated the Jōei Formulary (JŌEI SHIKIMOKU). However, from the time of the Mongol invasions, vassals as well as the *bakufu* were in financial trouble. The political administration was corrupt, and finally, in 1333, the Kamakura regime was overthrown by the loyalists who supported Emperor Godaigo (1288–1339).

Kamboja カンボジャ (Cambodia). A kingdom in Indochina. From about the sixteenth century, Japanese vessels sailed to Cambodia. These vessels were known as red-seal vessels (SHUIN-SEN), which means that they were officially licensed vessels. Traffic was relatively heavy. The most important commercial center was Pnom-Penh, the capital of Cambodia, where a Japanese settlement (NIHON-MACHI) existed until the end of the seventeenth century.

kamekan 甕棺 (earthenware coffins). Coffins of the primitive period, in the form of Yayoi-type earthen jars. Many of these coffins existed during the Yayoi period (approximately 350 B.C. to A.D. 250), especially in northern Kyūshū. There were single coffins consisting of one earthen vessel, the opening of which was covered with a stone. Double coffins also existed, two earthen vessels being utilized with their openings facing each other. Adults were buried in big vessels, children in ordinary vessels. This method of burying perhaps reveals something of the primitive social structure with its strong community spirit.

kampaku 関白 (chief councilor to the emperor). An office the duties of which consisted of assisting the emperor and administering state affairs. The office was assumed for the first time by Fujiwara no Mototsune (836–91), who served Emperor Kōkō (830–87). It was the prerogative of the Fujiwara family. During the Kamakura period, the Fujiwara family split into five main branches. To the end of the Edo period, the office of *kampaku* was alternately assumed by a member of one of these branches. Exceptions were Hideyoshi and Hidetsugu (1568–95). A retired *kampaku* was called TAIKŌ, and a tonsured *taikō* was known as *zenkō*.

kampō igaku 漢方医学 (Chinese medicine). It is believed that the Buddhist monk Enichi introduced Chinese medicine in 623, after he had studied in T'ang China. In ancient times and during the middle ages, bonzes who had studied in T'ang and Sung China propagated Chinese medicine in Japan. During the Muromachi period, the physicians Manase Dōzan (1507–94) and Tashiro Sanki (1465–1537) introduced the so-called Li-Chu medicinal art (the medicinal art of Li Tung-t'an and Chu Tan-ch'i), which was based on the physiology explained in Sung Confucianism. Entering the Edo period, the old school of medicine was revived. Rejecting the abstract theories of the recent physicians, stress was put on experimentation. From the middle Edo period, the newly introduced Dutch medicine found many adherents, but Chinese medicine was still extensively practiced. Even in the early Meiji years, the two schools of medicine were opposed to each other, but, from 1875, Chinese medicine declined, as it was unable to comply with the rules which regulated the examinations for medical practitioners.

Kanadehon Chūshingura 仮名手本忠臣蔵. The name of a *jōruri* or puppet drama. It is a historical play in eleven acts and was jointly written by the dramatists Takeda Izumo (1691–1756), Miyoshi Shōraku (1706–72), and Namiki Senryū (Namiki Sōsuke, 1695–1751). The play was performed for the first time in 1748. It is a drama about the loyal retainers of Akō, but the story is placed in the Muromachi period. This change of time was manipulated with much skill, and the play was a great success from the very beginning. Today different forms of the drama appear in JŌRURI and KABUKI and even in motion pictures.

Kanagawa 神奈川. The name of a district in Yokohama City. The name of this locality appears in the middle of the Kamakura period. In the Edo period it was known as a relay station. In 1854, the Japan–United States friendship treaty (KANAGAWA JŌYAKU) was signed there, and a Kanagawa administrator was appointed, but the open port was in Yokohama. When Yokohama began to prosper, Kanagawa was incorporated into the city.

Kanagawa Jōyaku 神奈川条約 (Treaty of Kanagawa). A treaty of friendship concluded at KANAGAWA on March 3, 1854, between Japan and the United States. In July 1853, Commodore Perry of the United States had come to Uraga, pressing the authorities to sign a treaty. He then left and returned in 1854, and a treaty was signed. The ports of Shimoda and Hakodate were opened to American vessels. American ships obtained needed supplies; good treatment of shipwrecked seamen was ensured; an area where American nationals could freely walk was decided upon; an American consulate was to be set up; and a most-favored-nation clause was added. The American treaty was followed by similar agreements between Japan and Russia, Great Britain, and Holland. This marked the beginning of the opening of the country.

Kanazawa 金沢. 1) Prefectural capital of Ishikawa Prefecture and the center of the Kaga fanatic uprisings (IKKŌ-IKKI). Oyama Castle was built there. In 1580, after the annihilation of the Ikkō sect, Sakuma Morimasa (1554–83) was appointed governor of Kaga Province (Ishikawa Prefecture) by Nobunaga and lived in Oyama Castle. In 1583, Maeda Toshiie (1538–99), who received Kaga Province from Hideyoshi, secured a fief of one million *koku* and a residence in Oyama Castle. After the restoration, Kanazawa became the center of the prefectural administration. 2) A locality at the southern end of Yokohama City. In the middle Kamakura period, Hōjō Sanetoki (1224–76) built the SHŌMYŌ-JI temple in Kanazawa and founded the famous Kanazawa Library (KANAZAWA BUNKO).

Kanazawa Bunko 金沢文庫 (Kanazawa Library). A library founded during the middle of the Kamakura period by Hōjō Sanetoki (1224–76). Sanetoki built the SHŌMYŌ-JI temple in Kanazawa, Musashi Province, and collected many Chinese and Japanese books and documents and preserved them in the temple. Kanazawa became a great center of learning in the Kantō district. Today Kanazawa is part of Yokohama City.

kandaka 貫高. During the Kamakura and Muromachi periods, the amount of revenue of land of a daimyō or a functionary, evaluated in money, was called *kandaka*. After the Kamakura period, coin came to be used, and the yearly taxes were paid in currency. The custom spread rapidly, and during the Muromachi period it was a general practice. Taxes paid in currency came to be known as *bunsen,* and the fixed amount of *bunsen* for a determined plot of land was referred to as *kandaka*. When the currency known as EIRAKU TSŪHŌ was generally used for the payment of taxes, the amount of money paid in *eiraku-sen* currency was called EIDAKA. From the early Edo period, the value of a plot of land was computed according to the amount of production in rice and the system known as KOKUDAKA, or amount of production measured in *koku* (bushels), was adopted.

Kan'ei tsūhō 寛永通宝 (Kan'ei currency). Copper coins of the Edo period. In 1636 (the thirteenth year of the Kan'ei era), the BAKUFU established a currency guild. Coins were cast in Edo and in Sakamoto (Ōmi Province). These copper coins, which were sometimes recoined, were called *Kan'ei tsūhō* and were in use until the Ansei era (1854–60). There were coins of one *mon* and of four *mon*. Because all brass coins of four *mon* had a wave pattern, they were known as *nami-sen*.

Kangakuin 勧学院 (Fujiwara college). Private school of the Fujiwara family, Heian period. It was built in 821 in HEIAN-KYŌ by Fujiwara no Fuyutsugu (775–826) for the education of young men of the Fujiwara clan. During the tenth and eleventh centuries the Fujiwara were at the height of their prosperity, and the school flourished as a residential college in which the young men lived while attending the school.

Kanginshū 閑吟集. A collection of "little songs" (KOUTA) of the Muromachi period. It was completed in 1518, and the compiler is believed to have been the RENGA poet Sōchō (1448–1532). The work includes children's songs, boating songs, rice-planters' songs, etc. and describes the feelings of the common people in their daily life.

kangōfu 勘合符 (tallies). An identification mark issued by the Chinese authorities for the use of Japanese ships which traded with Ming China. China used the system in order to defend herself against smuggling by pirate vessels and delivered an attestation to official trading vessels. It provided for only one tribute-bearing voyage every ten years, and three ships were allowed each time, but no attention was paid to this rule. The main export articles of the *kangō* ships were swords, sulfur, copper, gold, folding fans, folding screens, gold lacquer, etc. Import commodities were copper coins, raw silk, silk fabrics, books, etc.

kan'i jūnikai no sei 冠位十二階の制 (system of twelve ranks). The first rank system in Japan. *Kan* means a cap, and *i* means rank. The system was one of the reforms of Shōtoku Taishi in 603. The six ranks of *toku* (moral excellence), *jin* (benevolence), *rei* (decorum), *shin* (fidelity), *gi* (righteousness), and *chi* (wisdom) were each divided into "great" *(tai)* and "small" *(shō)*—*taitoku, shōtoku,* etc.—to make twelve. Corresponding to these ranks, which were based on Confucian virtues, were colored caps in tones of purple, green, red, yellow, white, and black. The ranks were granted according to personal merit. The highest rank was represented by a cap of deep purple known as the "great virtue cap" *(taitokukan)*. Precedence at the imperial court was expressed by the color of the cap. Thus Shōtoku Taishi abolished the former system of titles (KABANE) accorded to clans often by heredity and inaugurated a new system of bureaucracy. Later the twelve ranks were further subdivided until they were abolished in 701.

kanjō bugyō 勘定奉行 (finance administrator). A high officer of the EDO BAKUFU who administered the finances and controlled the fiefs under direct jurisdiction of the *bakufu*. The *kanjō bugyō* also handled lawsuits in the eight provinces of the Kantō district. He was subordinate to the Council of Elders (RŌJŪ) and was chosen from among the bannermen (HATAMOTO). The number of finance administrators was limited to four. From about the Kyōhō era (1716–36), these finance officers were divided into two groups of two each, the accountants *(katte-kata)* and the police and lawsuit officers *(kuji-kata)*. They changed places on monthly shifts, and their remuneration was 300 *ryō*. There were three kinds of administrators: finance administrators, the administrator of Edo (EDO-MACHI BUGYŌ), and the administrator of temples and shrines (JISHA BUGYŌ).

kanko 官戸 (official serfs). A class of "base people" *(semmin)*—that is, unfree people—during the Nara and Heian periods. They were official serfs chiefly engaged in cultivating imperial lands. They included free people *(ryōmin)* who, as punishment for criminal offenses, were deprived of their hereditary civil rights. They included also children born to parents of whom one was a slave, and disabled servants or servants of more than sixty-six years of age. They were allowed to have their own families, and they received an allotment of land (KUBUNDEN), but all its produce went to the state. They received only a food ration. When a *kanko* reached the age of seventy-six, he became free.

Kankoku heigō 韓国併合 (the annexation of Korea). Political issue of the late Meiji era. Following the Korean-Japanese annexation treaty of 1910, Korea became Japanese territory. Authority over Korea exercised by Japan was strengthened as a result of the revolt of the Tōgaku-tō Party (TŌGAKU-TŌ NO RAN) in 1894 and of the Sino-Japanese and Russo-Japanese wars. After the Russo-Japanese War, a firm policy toward Korea was adopted. In 1907, the emperor of Korea had unexpectedly sent a secret messenger to the International Peace Conference of the Hague in Holland, with the purpose of presenting the Korea problem. This intensified oppression by Japan, forcing the Korean emperor to abdicate in favor of the crown prince. A Korean-Japanese agreement was concluded, and Japan seized authority over all military and economic matters. Korea became a protectorate. Japan's policy included taking over the leadership, administration, and protection of the country. But this policy meant the total loss of Korea's independence and resulted in her annexation. The Korean people suffered for thirty-five years under Japanese rule. Japan's domination came to an end after the Pacific War in 1945.

Kan no Wa no Na no kokuō no kin'in 漢委奴国王の金印. A gold seal found in 1784 on Shiganoshima in Hakata Bay. The inscription on the seal reads *Kan no Wa no Na no kokuō*. A less correct reading is *Ido-kokuō no in*. A passage in *Hou Han Shu* (GOKANJO) reads: "In 57, the king of the land of Wa no Na offered congratulations to the emperor and presented his tribute. Consequently, he was given the official seal." The gold seal found in 1784 is thought to be the seal mentioned in *Hou Han Shu,* though it is regarded as spurious by some scholars. Wa no Na is believed to have been a small independent community in North Kyūshū (second half of the first century), and the "king" was a local chieftain.

Kanō-ha 狩野派 (the Kanō school of painting). A school of painting which lasted from the middle Muromachi period to the Meiji era and which was most prominent during the Azuchi-Momoyama and the Edo periods. The founder of the school was Masanobu (1454–90). His son Motonobu (1476–1559) added the techniques of YAMATO-E to those of the Sung and Yüan art of painting *(kanga)* and gave a Japanese flavor to the *kanga*. He developed the typical trends of the Kanō school. During the Azuchi-Momoyama period (1573–1600), Eitoku (1543–90) and his adopted son Sanraku (1558–1635) served Nobunaga and Hideyoshi. They made gorgeous paintings symbolizing the splendor of the Momoyama culture. Eitoku's grandson Tan'yū (1602–74) dominated the other branches of the Kanō school and, as official painter of the BAKUFU, held a firm social position. However, after Tan'yū there were no great Kanō painters, although the school continued. The art became formal. The Kanō school lost originality, which is the life of every art, and declined.

kanrei 管領 (shōgun's deputy). An office of the Muromachi government. It was the highest office, with the duty of assisting the shōgun. The *kanrei* was the shōgun's deputy or governor general. The Shiba, Hosokawa, and Hatake-yama successively held the office of shōgun's deputy and were therefore called *sankan*. After the Ōnin Civil War (1467–77), the office declined.

Kansei igaku no kin 寛政異学の禁 (prohibition of heterodox learning). In 1790, second year of the Kansei era, Matsudaira Sadanobu (1758–1829), chief adviser to the shōgun, issued an ordinance controlling heterodox learning. He decided that only Chu Hsi Confucianism was orthodox and that un-orthodox teachers should not be appointed by the government. Chu Hsi Confucianism being the official learning, it had to be encouraged. It is thought that this ordinance was drafted according to a proposal by the Confucianist Shibano Ritsuzan (1736–1807). There were many opponents, but most clans conformed to the ordinance. Furthermore, as Chu Hsi Confucianism was already widely accepted, Sadanobu was temporarily successful. However, as Confucianism became formalized, it fell into decay.

Kansei no Kaikaku 寛政の改革 (the Kansei Reform). A series of restrictive edicts issued by Matsudaira Sadanobu (1758–1829), the chief adviser to the shōgun, middle Edo period. Sadanobu, castle lord of Shirakawa in Fukushima Prefecture, hoped to repair the effects of the misrule of Minister Tanuma Okitsugu (1719–88) and of the ravages of natural calamities and famine. He took as his models the shōguns Ieyasu and Yoshimune and forbade almost every form of expenditure. He kept prices down by uniting the trade corporations and by means of a monetary policy. He saved the bannermen (HATAMOTO) from poverty by contributing money to them. He gathered the outlaws by providing them a meeting place in Ishikawajima in Edo. He curbed the migration of farmers and tried to re-establish rural communities. He fostered increased production and carried out numerous remarkable reforms. He encouraged both cultural achievements and the military arts, prohibited unorthodox learning, and promoted Chu Hsi Confucianism (KANSEI IGAKU NO KIN). He exercised control over publications and suppressed loose morals and manners as well as dangerous thought. He punished Hayashi Shihei (1738–93) because Shihei's ideas about coastal defense caused unrest among the masses (KAIKOKU HEIDAN), though he was forced to turn his attention to coastal defense and to the use of Western strategy in order to be able to cope with Russian approaches in the north. These reforms, it is true, promoted good harvests and accounted for other temporary successes, but they met with great opposition and finally collapsed, partially because of the resistance of the ladies of the palace of the shōgun's consort (the Inner Palace, or Ō-oku).

kanshōfu-shō 官省符荘 (manors with official immunity). A manorial estate organized by obtaining a testimony of tax immunity from the Council of State (DAJŌKAN) and from the Ministry of Popular Affairs (Mimbu-shō). When the manorial estates were established, temples and shrines as well as wealthy families, after having fabricated a reason for obtaining fiscal immunity rights, made a petition to the government. When the government granted a permit, the Council of State and the Ministry of Popular Affairs made an investigation and ordered tax immunity. This sort of estate possessed powerful rights and was distinguished from ordinary estates.

Kantō dai-shinsai 関東大震災 (the Kantō earthquake). The great earthquake in the Kantō district on September 1, 1923. The earthquake caused fires in Tōkyō, Yokohama, and other cities. Half of Tōkyō was destroyed by fire.

The damage amounted to 5,500,000,000 yen, and the number of casualties reached 100,000. The financial situation, already weakened by World War I, became critical, and the horrors of the disaster agitated the masses, especially in the capital.

Kantō kanrei 関東管領 (shōgun's deputy in the eastern provinces). A government office established in Kamakura by the MUROMACHI BAKUFU for the administration of the eastern provinces. Ashikaga Takauji (1305–58) appointed his second son, Motouji (1340–67), *Kantō kanrei* or governor general of the eastern provinces. Uesugi Noriaki (1306–68) was appointed to assist Motouji, who was a child, as deputy or *shitsuji*. The deputies of the eastern provinces, relying on their extensive power, gradually opposed the *bakufu*. The fourth deputy, Mochiuji (1398–1439), was hunted down by the *bakufu* forces (EIKYŌ NO RAN). From this time, the *kanrei* was sent from Kyōto, and the office was taken over by the Uesugi family. But internal discord continued, and the office of *kanrei* declined until only the name remained. Uesugi Norimasa (1523–79) was deposed by Hōjō Ujiyasu (1515–71), but Uesugi Kenshin (1530–78) was appointed *kanrei* of the eastern provinces by Shōgun Ashikaga Yoshiteru (1536–65). After Kenshin, the office of *Kantō kanrei* was discontinued.

kanzei jishuken 関税自主権 (tariff autonomy). International treaties were concluded in 1858. A tariff rate was stipulated, but Japan's tariff autonomy was not recognized. The disadvantage of this harmed Japan's economic development until 1911. The demand for abolition of the unequal treaties by the movement for democratic rights aimed at the gaining of tariff autonomy, but this autonomy was not obtained until the year 1911, when extraterritorial rights were abolished.

Karafuto 樺太 (Sakhalin). Under the provisions of the Yalta Agreement in 1945, the southern part of Sakhalin became Soviet territory. From 1905 to 1945, it was Japanese territory. In 1485, the aborigines of Karafuto began to have relations with the Matsumae clan. Later, Hideyoshi appointed the daimyō of Matsumae to administer the Ezo territory. In the early Edo period a map of the island was drawn, and in the late Edo period Mogami Tokunai (1754–1836), Mamiya Rinzō (1780–1841), and others explored Karafuto. In 1869, the commissioner of colonization encouraged immigration but was unsuccessful. The southern inroads of the Russians in 1875 resulted in the exchange of Karafuto for the Russian Kurile Islands. After the Russo-Japanese War, the territory south of the 50th parallel became Japanese territory, and Japan secured the right to drill oil wells in North Sakhalin.

Karafuto-Chishima Kōkan Jōyaku 樺太千島交換条約 (Sakhalin–Kurile Islands Exchange Treaty). In 1875, the Meiji government, failing in its effort to colonize Sakhalin, ceded this island to Russia in exchange for the Russian

Kurile Islands. This solution settled the dispute with Russia which had begun at the end of the Tokugawa period. (See also entry above.)

Kara-yō 唐様 (Chinese style). A style of architecture imported from Sung China under the influence of Zen Buddhism, Kamakura period. The name *Kara-yō* (Chinese style) is used in contrast to the traditional *Wa-yō* (Japanese style). The *Kara-yō* was used in building monasteries belonging to the Zen religion. Remains of the style can be seen in the Shariden of Kamakura's ENKAKU-JI, in the Butsuden of Tōkyō's Shōfuku-ji, etc.

karō 家老 (chief retainers of manorial lords). Chief retainers or ministers of feudal lords. The *karō* were charged with the management of the affairs of a clan and were called elders *(toshiyori)*. They were also known as *shukurō* and as *otona*. During the Muromachi period, *karō* became the name of a government office. The official was called RŌJŪ and was a member of the shōgun's Council of Elders. During the Edo period, the officials were first called *karō* and were members of the Council of State, but later there were senior ministers (TAIRŌ), members of the shōgun's Council of Elders *(rōjū)*, and junior elders (WAKA-DOSHIYORI). The name *karō* was usually used during the Edo period to designate a feudal lord.

karoku 家禄 (hereditary stipend). A fixed allowance received by the warriors from their master. This stipend was hereditary. The system was introduced during the late Heian period but developed in the Edo period when the *karoku* became the bond that tied master and servant. However, after the restoration, the system deteriorated with the discontinuing of this feudal relationship and the need to consolidate public finance. In 1876, the *karoku* was abolished.

kasagake 笠懸 (hitting the bamboo hat). A kind of shooting on horseback, Kamakura period. To practice military arts, this kind of shooting, as well as the similar YABUSAME and INU-OU-MONO, was popular among the warriors. *Kasagake* was a military art consisting of hitting a bamboo hat, or any other target, with an arrow while riding on horseback.

kashiage 借上 (usury). Usury practiced during the Kamakura period. In those days, a currency economy developed, and many name masters (MYŌSHU) became usurers. Direct vassals ran into debt, and some had to sell or mortgage their estates. In 1297, the government promulgated what came to be known as an act of "virtuous administration" (TOKUSEI REI), which not only forbade the sale or mortgage of vassals' estates but also ordered the return without compensation of sold estates. However, this measure worsened the situation of the debtors because the law was easy to evade. During the Muromachi period, instead of *kashiage,* the pawnshops known as DOSŌ flourished.

Kasuga-jinja 春日神社 (Kasuga Shrine). The great Shintō shrine, erected in 710, in which from ancient times the clan god of the Fujiwara family was worshiped. The shrine is located in Kasugano, Nara City. The deities enshrined are Takemikazuchi no Mikoto, Iwainushi no Mikoto, Amenokoyane no Mikoto, and Himegami. Being the gods of wealthy clans, these deities were first worshiped in the districts where the clans lived. In 768, when the capital was HEIJŌ-KYŌ, national religious services in Kasugano were customary. During the Heian period, the shrine flourished together with Kōfuku-ji, which was the Fujiwara family temple, and the Kasuga festival was one of the three great festivals determined by imperial decree *(sandaichokusai)*. During the late Heian period, the monk-soldiers of the Kōfuku-ji temple appealed by force (GŌSO) to the imperial court and, to impress the authorities and the people, went to Kyōto holding up a sacred tree *(shimboku)* of Kasuga. During the Kamakura and Muromachi periods, the lower shrine officers organized trade guilds and were often active as tradesmen (JINNIN). The architecture of the main building *(shaden)* of Kasuga is representative of the style called *Kasuga-zukuri* (Kasuga style), and the building serves as a storehouse for many precious documents.

Kasuga no agata-nushi 春日県主. Wealthy clans or estate masters (AGATA-NUSHI) who, before the Taika Reform (646), lived together in the neighborhood of present-day Kasuga, Nara Prefecture.

katana-gari 刀狩 (the sword hunt). From the end of the Muromachi period through the Edo period, weapons were confiscated, and common people were not allowed to carry them. Some *sengoku daimyō* such as Asakura Yoshikage (1533–73) and Shibata Katsuie (1530–85) confiscated weapons, but the sword hunt of 1588 by Hideyoshi was of great significance. Hideyoshi proclaimed that all farmers were to hand in their weapons and that these confiscated arms would be melted down and turned into material for use in building a hall to house a huge image of the Buddha. The real purpose was to stop the agrarian uprisings. This *katana-gari* resulted in the emphasis of class distinction between soldiers and farmers and in the establishment of a system of social ranks. It deeply influenced the Edo feudal structure.

katana-kaji 刀鍛冶 (swordsmiths). The technique of swordmaking developed during the Kamakura period. Famous swordsmiths included Awataguchi Yoshimitsu (1227–91) of Kyōto, Fukuoka Sukemune and Osafune Nagamitsu (thirteenth century) of Bizen, and Okazaki Masamune (1264–1344) of Kamakura. They all displayed an exquisite skill. Records of exports during the Muromachi period reveal that swords were produced in great quantity.

katoku 家督 (house leadership). Control of the head of the family over its members in warrior society from medieval times on. Originally, either the eldest son or the second son could become the house leader, provided he was competent. He inherited the property and conducted the religious services. In the Edo period, the civil code, following the Edo warriors' legislation, provided that only the eldest son would become the family head and succeed to the family estate. After the Pacific War, civil law was changed, and traditional rights were denied.

Katsura Rikyū 桂離宮 (Katsura Detached Palace). An estate in the western outskirts of Kyōto, erected in the early Edo period. Originally it was the villa of the family of Prince Katsura, but in 1883 it was designated a detached palace. In ancient times, the site of Katsura Rikyū was the site of the mansion of Fujiwara no Michinaga (966–1027). The buildings erected by Prince Hachijō Toshihito and his son Toshitada during the Genna (1615–24) and Kan'ei (1624–44) eras, and during the Keian (1648–52) and Meireki (1655–58) eras, are still extant. The living apartment *(shoin)*, the tea-ceremony house, the landscape garden, through which flows a branch of the Katsura River, etc. are of elegant classical taste blended with the sober charm of the tea-ceremony cult. Katsura Rikyū is prized as a construction in pure Japanese style. A theory holds that the architect Kobori Enshū (1574–1647) designed it, but the assertion is groundless.

Kawachi no aya uji 西文氏. The descendants of Wani, a scholar from Kudara (a Korean kingdom), who became a naturalized Japanese about the end of the fourth century during the reign of Emperor Ōjin. According to tradition, Wani brought with him to Japan two Chinese works: ten volumes of the *Lun Yü* (in Japanese, *Rongo*) and one volume of the *Ch'ien-tzu-wen* (in Japanese, *Senjimon*). The *Kawachi no aya uji* served the imperial court with their literary art. They lived in Furuichi County, Kawachi Province (Ōsaka Prefecture). As they were granted the title OBITO, they were called *fumi no obito*. During the reign of Emperor Temmu (622–86), they were called *fumi no imiki*. They are known as *Kawachi no aya uji* as distinguished from the *Yamato no aya uji,* who lived in Yamato Province (AYABITO).

kawase 為替 (money order). A means of settling accounts with distant places, middle ages and Edo period. In the middle ages it was called *kawashi*. It was also called KAEZENI, and, when rice was paid instead of currency, it was referred to as KAEMAI. At the place where the yearly taxes were levied, a money order was drawn and handed to the man in charge of the exchange business, who arranged that an equal amount was paid to the tax bureau. He therefore used a bill of exchange (SAIFU). During the Edo period, when commercial transactions developed, money orders were frequently used. For this purpose messengers (HIKYAKU) made a round trip from Edo to Ōsaka three times a month. There were also remittance drafts from Ōsaka to Kyōto and from Ōsaka to markets in various places. Agencies for money-order exchange were the exchange shops *(ryōgae-ya)* of Edo and Ōsaka, as well as the exchange shops and similar banking organs in various places.

kazoku 華族 (peerage). From 1869, court nobles and feudal lords were given the title *kazoku*. Their rank followed upon that of the imperial family *(kōzoku)* and preceded that of the ex-military class. In 1884, an ordinance establishing a peerage was enacted, but in 1946 the peerage was abolished when the new constitution proclaimed: "Nobility or any other peerage system shall not be recognized."

kazoku seido 家族制度 (the family system). Customs, morals, legislation, etc. concerning family life, in particular the specific things which, during the feudal age, added importance to the family. During the Edo period, following the establishment of a feudal regime, the authority of the family head (KAFU-CHŌ-SEI) was absolute. The family existed for the continuance of the house, and individual liberty was denied. The family head conducted the family religious ceremonies and required absolute submission of the family members. He also assumed full responsibility for the education of the members of the family. He avoided involvement with the law because of collective responsibility of relatives *(enza)*. Even the severing of relations known as *kyūri* and disinheritance *(kandō)* had no other purpose than to continue the family line. The house leadership was the inheritance of the eldest son. From the second son on, the family members were treated coldly. When a younger son married, his wife was merely a subordinate member of the family. Under the feudal system, the rank of all females was low, and submission as expressed in ONNA DAIGAKU was accepted as a matter of fact. Even after the restoration, this old-fashioned tradition was cherished, as may be witnessed in the educational system and the civil code. After Japan's surrender, a democratic family system was introduced, but old-time traditions still linger.

kebiishi 検非違使 (police commissioners). An extralegal organ established in the early Heian period for tracking down offenders. It is believed that this office was established in 820 by Emperor Saga (786–842), but this date is uncertain. Originally the office was attached to the gate guards' headquarters *(emon-fu)* but became independent in 824 when the right and left *kebiishi-chō (sau-kebiishi-chō)* were established. The *kebiishi* performed not only police duties, which formerly belonged to the military guards, but also judicial functions, which formerly belonged to the board of censors *(danjōdai)*, the municipal office of the capital (KYŌSHIKI), and the Ministry of Justice (GYŌBU-SHŌ). With this twofold power, the *kebiishi*, together with the treasury officers *(kurando)* were the backbone of the administration throughout the Heian period. With the rise of the warriors, the office of *kebiishi* declined.

Kegon-shū 華厳宗 (Kegon sect of Buddhism). One of the six Nara sects

(NANTO ROKUSHŪ). It was introduced to Japan in 740 by a priest called Shinshō (?–742) of Silla (a kingdom in Korea). He reformed the doctrines of the SANRON-SHŪ and the HOSSŌ-SHŪ and preached that all beings were manifestations of the one essential truth. The headquarters of the sect is Tōdai-ji, and Rōben (689–773) was the second head of the sect. During the Heian period, the Kegon sect did not thrive, as it was oppressed by TENDAI and SHIN-SHŪ, but during the Kamakura period, the distinguished priests Kōben (or Myōe, 1173–1232) and Gyōnen (1240–1321) made many disciples in spite of the newly risen JŌDO-SHŪ and ZEN-SHŪ.

Keian no o-furegaki 慶安の御触書 (ordinance of the Keian era). A notorious ordinance concerning the farmers, issued in 1649 (second year of the Keian era) by the government during the reign of the third shōgun, Iemitsu (1604–51). It is made up of thirty-two articles embodying detailed regulations on farming, food, clothing, housing, and even family life. The ordinance is typical, as it includes regulations not related to economy.

keichō 計帳 (tax registers). Annual tax registers in ancient times for the purpose of introducing a uniform system of taxation. The register appeared along with the census registration at the time of the Taika Reform (646). According to article three of the reform, registers of population had to be drawn up. Before the thirtieth of the sixth month, the head of each household had to return each year a register called *shujitsu,* giving in detail the number of persons in the family, their ages, family relationship, and physical characteristics, and adding whether they were taxable or exempt. Using this information, the provincial office made up registers to be transmitted to the Council of State (DAJŌ-KAN). The household registers (KOSEKI), to be compiled every six years, and the *keichō* were the basis for the payment of taxes. Sixteen fragmentary documents of these registers are still extant, such as the one of Atago County in Yamashiro Province (733) and that of the *hayabito* (gate guards of the imperial palace, who also escorted imperial carriages, etc.) of the same province. Some are preserved in the SHŌSŌ-IN repository. From about the ninth century, the *keichō* system fell into disuse.

Keikoku Bidan 経国美談. Political novel of the early Meiji era. The work was published in 1883. The author is Yano Ryūkei (1850–1931), who was the executive leader of the Progressive Party. The movement for democratic rights underlies the work.

Keikokushū 経国集. Anthology of poems in Chinese in twenty volumes (only six are extant), compiled in 827 during the reign of Emperor Junna (786–840) by Yoshimine no Yasuyo (785–830) and Shigeno Sadanushi (785–852). The work also includes prose. Together with the earlier RYŌUNSHŪ and BUNKA SHŪREISHŪ, this work is a product of the golden age of Chinese-style literature in Japan. One hundred and seventy-eight authors are represented, including Emperor Saga (786–842), Kūkai (774–835), and others.

Keiō Gijuku 慶応義塾. A most influential private school. In 1858, Fukuzawa Yukichi (1834–1901) founded a private school for Dutch learning called Rangaku-juku. In 1868 (the fourth year of the Keiō era), he called the school Keiō Gijuku. It developed into Keiō University, which was the first private university in Japan. The teaching, which was an interpretation of Western ideals, was based on realism and practical knowledge, and many of the graduates joined the democratic movement or were active in the industrial world and other fields.

keishi 家司. *Keishi* were those who, in the Heian period, administered the family affairs of imperial princes, court nobles, regents and chief councilors to the emperor, and eminent ministers. *Keishi* was the generic term for the personnel belonging to the administrative and disciplinary boards and the treasury of each great family. The origin is to be found in the so-called *karei* or men responsible for the family affairs of princes and persons of the third rank or higher. In corresponding manner, during the Kamakura and Muromachi periods, the men in charge *(yoryūdo)* of the family affairs of members and assistant members of the Supreme Court, the Administrative Board, and the Judicial Board were called *keishi*.

keizai-antei kyū-gensoku 経済安定九原則 (nine-point economic stabilization program). Postwar administrative policy. In 1948, the United States Department of State, the Army, and the Supreme Commander for the Allied Powers (SCAP), General MacArthur, formulated a policy for achieving economic stability in Japan. SCAP was directed to order the Japanese government to "carry out an effective economic stabilization program calculated to achieve fiscal, monetary, price, and wage stability in Japan as rapidly as possible." In 1948, a nine-point economic stabilization program was adopted, and in 1949 Joseph M. Dodge, former president of the American Bankers Association, was sent to Japan, with the rank of minister, to see that the financial rehabilitation program was developed effectively. Dodge aimed at a balanced budget obtained through austerity and an increase in exports.

kemi hō 検見法 (law for levying taxes by inspection). A method of levying taxes, Edo period. *Kemi* means "to inspect (the yield)." The word was also written 毛見. The inspection was made every year, and taxes were imposed accordingly. It was a progressive way of collecting taxes, as both rich and poor harvests were taken into account. However, there were such defects as failure to determine the landowner's actual proceeds, making appropriations at the time of the harvest inspection, waste of time, and unfair practices of officials. Finally, around the middle of the Edo period, the law known as JŌMEN HŌ, calling for the payment of taxes equivalent to one-tenth of the yield calculated in *koku* (KOKUDAKA), came into force.

kemminshi 遣明使 (envoys to Ming China). Envoys sent to Ming China (1368–1644) by the MUROMACHI BAKUFU. Most of the envoys were Zen priests. From the Namboku period (1336–92), some warriors of the western provinces became pirates and raided the Chinese and Korean coasts. The Chinese rulers demanded that Prince Kanenaga (?–1383), commander in chief of an expeditionary force to the west, and the Muromachi military government control the Japanese pirates. In 1401, Shōgun Ashikaga Yoshimitsu (1358–1408) sent the Buddhist priest Soa and other envoys to China. Later, he sent seven more embassies to Ming China. The Ming court sent a special ambassador carrying a letter addressed erroneously to "Minamoto Michiyoshi, King of Japan" (日本国王臣源道義). With the purpose of expanding trade with China, Yoshimitsu, in his reply, made use of the name of the Chinese chronological era and adopted a subservient attitude. His son Yoshimochi (1386–1428) temporarily interrupted the intercourse between the two countries, but during the rule of Yoshinori (1394–1441) and Yoshimasa (1443–90) relations were resumed. In 1404, the Japanese envoys were granted tallies or identification marks (KANGŌFU) which permitted only one voyage of at most three vessels every ten years. But this limitation was often transgressed, and there were convoys of as many as thirteen ships. Daimyō of the western provinces, temples and shrines, merchants of Sakai and Hakata, and others engaged in the licensed trade and made huge profits, but from the middle of the sixteenth century trade declined.

Kemmu no Chūkō 建武中興 (Kemmu Restoration). Imperial rule of Emperor Godaigo (1288–1339). Emperor Godaigo, who had failed in the Shōchū (1324–26) and Genkō (1331–34) uprisings (SHŌCHŪ NO HEN and GENKŌ NO HEN), was banished to Oki, but, while Prince Morinaga (1308–35) and Kusunoki Masashige (1294–1336) were resisting the BAKUFU forces, warriors throughout the country sided with the emperor. Finally, Ashikaga Takauji (1305–58) took Rokuhara, a garrison in Kyōto, and Nitta Yoshisada (1301–38) entered Kamakura, destroying the Hōjō. In 1333, the emperor returned to Kyōto for the purpose of establishing direct imperial rule. He attended to government affairs through the office for lawsuits of the provinces (KIROKUSHO). He also established a tribunal for various claims (ZASSO KETSUDANSHO), which dealt with minor suits, and an office of awards (ONSHŌ-KATA) for the determination of rewards for good service to the royalist cause. He set up a new office for the control of warriors in Kyōto (MUSHA-DOKORO). Under this imperial regime, the warriors who had sided with the loyalists in the hope of enlarging their domains could not fulfill their dreams. They became dissatisfied, and discord arose between them and the imperial court. Furthermore, the new government, lacking a firm policy, lost the nation's confidence. Ashikaga Takauji, pretending to subdue the remnants of the ancient regime, carried the war to Kyōto, forcing Emperor Godaigo to flee to Mount Hiei. This marked the end of the Kemmu Restoration and the beginning of the civil strife of the Nambokuchō or the period of the Northern and Southern dynasties (1336–92).

kenchi 検地 (land surveying). The surveying of land in feudal times. The area of land and its quality were determined, and the amount of yield in *koku* was investigated. The taxes to be paid were determined accordingly, and the persons responsible for the payment of taxes were indicated. Land surveying was also performed for the territories belonging to the *sengoku daimyō,* but each estate and each provincial estate was different, so that the amount of revenue of land was calculated in various ways—for instance, by means of money (KANDAKA) or according to the amount of production in rice (KOKU-DAKA). Nobunaga, in order to organize land surveying, asked for a report on the conditions of each estate. Hideyoshi adopted this method and, from 1582, resumed land surveying in what is known as *taikō-kenchi* or Hideyoshi's survey. Hideyoshi also standardized weights and measures, adopted the *kokudaka* as a method of computing the value of land, and decided that the farmer himself was the person responsible for the payment of taxes. As a result, a land-surveying register was extant in each rural community, and complicated matters were simplified on the principle that one tract of land was to be cultivated by one farmer. The right of cultivation was recognized, and at the same time migration and buying or selling of land were prohibited, thus establishing a system of solidarity among the villages. Conjointly with the policy of sword hunting (KATANA-GARI), the separation of soldiers and farmers was effected, and the castle towns (JŌKA-MACHI) were consolidated. The whole system strengthened the structure of the feudal clans.

kenchi-chō 検地帳 (land-survey registers). Registers containing the results of land surveying—that is, the name of the farmer, the area and quality of arable land, and the amount of yield (KOKUDAKA). These registers were also called *mizu-chō.* In principle the register was based on the system of one tract of land for one farmer, but the farmers without cultivation rights were often registered as dependent farmers cultivating a plot for the master (BUNZUKE). Some farmers were not even mentioned in the registers. The registers established the right of cultivation, and at the same time the farmers were bound to their plot of land. The *kenchi-chō* were of great importance for the maintenance of the clan structure.

Kenchō-ji 建長寺. Headquarters in Kamakura of the Kenchō-ji branch of the Rinzai sect of Buddhism. Regent Hōjō Tokiyori (1227–63) of the KAMA-KURA BAKUFU was converted to Zen Buddhism and invited the priest Rankei Dōryū (1213–78) from Sung China. In 1253, Tokiyori built the Kenchō-ji for Dōryū and made him the first abbot. The Kenchō-ji flourished under the protection of the *bakufu* and was a school of learning for many distinguished Buddhist priests. During the Muromachi period, when Shōgun Ashikaga Yoshimitsu (1358–1408) established the Five Zen Monasteries (GOZAN), he made Kenchō-ji the first of the five Kamakura monasteries. Kenchō-ji and ENKAKU-JI were the center of the Rinzai religion in the Kantō district.

kenin 家人. Another reading of 家人 is *yakahito*. This was a class of unfree people *(semmin)* of the Nara and Heian periods. As guild people *(be no tami)* they already existed prior to the system of the penal and administrative code and did not become free people even when the *be no tami* were abolished at the time of the Taika Reform in 646. The Taihō Code (702) stipulated that they be *semmin* owned by private families. Like the slaves working for the government (NUHI), the *kenin* also received one-third of the land allotment of free people, but they had more freedom than the *nuhi* and were allowed to have their own families. The master could not employ all of the family members of the *kenin* simultaneously. Neither could a *kenin* be bought or sold. The *kenin* could become free people *(ryōmin)* at the will of the master. In that case the freed man received the surname of the master suffixed by *be*. From the end of the Nara to the early Heian period, the *kenin* as well as other "unfree people" were gradually set free. Though the word *kenin* survived, it came to mean a different thing.

Kennin-ji 建仁寺. Headquarters in Kyōto of the Kennin-ji branch of the Rinzai sect of Buddhism. Eisai (1141–1215) tried to build a Zen monastery in Kyōto but was prevented from doing so because of the opposition of the traditional Buddhist sects. He then moved to Kamakura, where his converts included the shōgun. With the help of the shōgun, Eisai built Kennin-ji in Kyōto. During the Muromachi period, Kennin-ji was ranked among the Five Zen Monasteries (GOZAN).

Kensei-kai 憲政会 (the Constitutional Association). A political party of the Taishō era. In 1916, after the death of the soldier-statesman Katsura Tarō (1847–1913), Katō Takaaki (1860–1926) continued the work of organizing the Constitutional Friends Association (Rikken Dōshi-kai), for which Katsura had laid the foundation and obtained the support of the Mitsubishi concern. In 1923, Katō was elected prime minister of the coalition cabinet of three parties, which he welded into one solid group known as the Kensei-kai Party. Later this party became the Democratic Party (MINSEI-TŌ).

Kensei-tō 憲政党 (the Constitutional Party). A political party of the middle Meiji era. In 1898, opposing the tax-increase bill of the third Itō cabinet, the Liberal Party and the Progressive Party, dissolving the Diet, merged and organized themselves to avoid the disadvantage of a separation of nongovernmental parties. The leaders were Itagaki and Ōkuma, who aimed at the defense of constitutionalism, the establishment of a party cabinet, and the development of a self-governing system of economic politics. The same year, the Ōkuma-Itagaki cabinet, which was the first party cabinet, was formed. However, the cabinet experienced difficulties occasioned by army circles, factional strife within the party, and Education Minister Ozaki's "slip of the tongue" (republican speech). Furthermore, the Liberals split into liberal and constitutional factions, and the Progressives split into progressive and constitutional factions. Finally, the cabinet collapsed. Later the Constitutional Party temporarily joined hands with the clan cabinet of Yamagata Aritomo (1838–1922), then broke off relations, and in 1900 participated in the formation of Itō Hirobumi's Political Friends Association (SEIYŪ-KAI). Before long the party was dissolved, and Itagaki retired from the political arena.

kensei-yōgo undō 憲政擁護運動 (movement for safeguarding constitutionalism). Political movement for safeguarding constitutional government, Taishō era. The political parties and the people, fighting against the militarists and a bureaucratic government, twice launched a movement for establishing a constitutional government. 1) In 1912, the liberalist Saionji cabinet, which was backed by the Political Friends Association (SEIYŪ-KAI), refused to create two additional army divisions. The army offered firm opposition, and the cabinet collapsed. The people, resenting the despotism of the militarists, demanded the overthrow of clannish factions and held a mass meeting for the safeguarding of constitutionalism. The newspapers supported the movement, and Inukai Tsuyoshi (1855–1932) and Ozaki Yukio (1858–1954) took the lead. Because Katsura had opposed the Diet, several thousand people surrounded the Diet in support of the Diet members belonging to the constitutional faction. The people, who were ordered to disperse, set fire to police quarters and raided the newspaper companies which supported the government. Fearing civil strife, Katsura resigned. 2) In 1924, when Kiyoura Keigo (1850–1942), who was an influential member of the House of Peers, formed a cabinet, the Constitutional Party and the Nationalist Party (KOKUMIN-TŌ) launched a proconstitutional and anti-Kiyoura movement. The Political Friends Association joined the movement, which gained public support, aiming at universal suffrage and a reform of the House of Peers. The dissolution of the Diet resulted in victory, through a general election, for the three constitutional factions. After the general resignation of the cabinet, a constitutional cabinet was formed with Katō Takaaki (1860–1926) of the KENSEI-KAI as prime minister. A government of political parties continued to govern until the incident of May 15, 1932 (GO-ICHIGO-JIKEN).

kentōshi 遣唐使 (envoys to T'ang China). Envoys sent to T'ang China (618–906) during the Nara and Heian periods. They were also called *saikaishi*. The sending of envoys began in 630, and the purpose was the introduction into Japan of Chinese culture and the fostering of trade. The envoy Awata no Mahito (?–719) and those who accompanied the envoys, such as Abe no Nakamaro (701–70), Kibi no Mabi (693–775), and many others, commanded admiration in T'ang China. Men like Kibi no Mabi, Gembō (?–746), Saichō (767–822), and Kūkai (774–835) were very meritorious in the field of politics, learning, and religion. But in 894 Sugawara no Michizane (845–902) declined the appointment of envoy to T'ang China because of the unrest in the country toward the end of the T'ang dynasty and because of the dangers of crossing the sea and meeting pirates. Thus the sending of envoys was discontinued until the establishment of the Sung dynasty (960–1279), but this interruption of relations with China at the end of the Heian period caused the flourishing of an indigenous culture.

Ken'yū-sha 硯友社. A literary association of the Meiji era. The leader was Ozaki Kōyō (1867–1903), and Ken'yū-sha was the first literary society in modern Japan. In 1885, Ozaki launched the literary magazine GARAKUTA BUNKO. The magazine advocated elegant prose and an art-for-art's-sake attitude. As it appeared at a time when political novels and light literature of the feudal-romance type dominated the stage, it appealed to the people and occupied a central place in the literary arena. Its period of greatest influence extended from the time of the Sino-Japanese War (1894–95) to about 1900.

kenzuishi 遣隋使 (envoys to Sui China). Envoys sent to Sui China (589–618) during the Asuka period. Japan had had intercourse with the Southern dynasty, and when the Sui dynasty built up its power Shōtoku Taishi (573–621), in order to introduce Chinese culture, entered into diplomatic relations with China and in 607 sent the courtier Ono no Imoko as the first envoy. The following year the Sui envoy Hai Sei-sei (in Chinese, P'ei Shih-ch'ing) reached Japan. Two other Japanese embassies, one in 608 and another in 614, left Japan for China. These diplomatic relations resulted in Japanese administrative reform and rendered remarkable services. In particular, the students, including Buddhist priests, who accompanied the envoys profoundly influenced Japanese culture at the time of the Taika Reform (646).

Ketsumei-dan jiken 血盟団事件 (incident of the Blood Brotherhood). Fascist terrorism in 1932. The right-wing ultranationalists, resenting the results of the London Naval Conference of 1930 (LONDON KAIGI) and determined to reform the nation, organized the Blood Brotherhood, the leader of which was Inoue Nisshō (1886–). Inoue plotted the assassination of the leaders of the political and economic world and engineered the murder of Inoue Junnosuke (1866–1932), the executive leader of the Democratic Party (MINSEI-TŌ), and Dan Takuma (1858–1932), the leader of the Mitsui concern. This incident marked the first step to fascism.

kibyōshi 黄表紙 (yellow-cover books). A kind of *kusazōshi* or illustrated story book, Edo period. They were written for adults, whereas the *kurohon, aohon,* and *akahon* were designed for children. The first *kibyōshi* was Koikawa Harumachi's (1744–89) *Kinkin Sensei Eiga no Yume.* These books had yellow covers and were therefore called *kibyōshi.* They were most popular during the An'ei (1772–81) and Bunka (1804–18) eras. Each page of the book was illustrated, and the text was of a comical nature. During the Kansei era (1789–1801), regulations concerning *kibyōshi* were rigidly enforced, and publication was temporarily discontinued. Some of the books changed to didactic novels. Many of the *kibyōshi* satirized the society of the time. Representative authors were Santō Kyōden (1761–1816), Jippensha Ikku (1765–1831), and Shikitei Samba (1776–1822). UKIYO-E masters illustrated the books.

kien-rei 棄捐令. An ordinance of the Edo period which annulled credits to be claimed from bannermen (HATAMOTO) and direct vassals. The ordinance aimed at saving the debtors from destitution. The order resembled the act of virtuous administration (TOKUSEI-REI) of the middle ages. The BAKUFU issued this ordinance twice: once in 1789 through Matsudaira Sadanobu (1758–1829) and once in 1843 after the Tempō reforms (1841–43). Sometimes the clans themselves issued similar ordinances. Temporarily, at least, the ordinances obtained their goal, but the merchants, suffering great losses, refused to lend money, and the distress of the warriors gradually worsened.

kiheitai 奇兵隊. The army of the Chōshū clan at the end of the Edo period. In 1863, the Chōshū clan fired upon an American vessel anchored in the Straits of Shimonoseki, but an American warship retaliated. Takasugi Shinsaku (1839–67), under sponsorship of the clan, created a corps of ruthless soldiers called *kiheitai. Kiheitai* soldiers were enrolled regardless of any social status, ability alone bringing promotion. The soldiers were trained in a modern way and showed their strength many times—in firing at American, Dutch, French, and English vessels; in defense against shogunate attacks (CHŌSHŪ SEIBATSU); in the battle of Toba and Fushimi (TOBA-FUSHIMI NO TATAKAI); and in the Boshin Civil War in 1868 (BOSHIN SEN'EKI). They also defeated, by military strength, the pro-shogunate higher warriors' class of the clan, while the lower warriors' class assumed the leadership of the clan government. The *kiheitai* corps was dissolved in 1869 when the clan's military system was reformed.

Kikuchi uji 菊池氏 (the Kikuchi clan). Powerful clan of Higo (Kumamoto Prefecture) in Kyūshū. As royalists, the Kikuchi attacked the pro-shogunate commissioner of Kyūshū (KYŪSHŪ TANDAI) during the civil strife of the Genkō era in 1331 (GENKŌ NO HEN). After the establishment of the Northern and Southern dynasties, Kikuchi Takemitsu (?–1373) sided with the Southern dynasty and was loyal to Prince Kanenaga (?–1383), the son of Emperor

Godaigo. Kanenaga was commander in chief of an expeditionary force to the west.

kimoiri 肝煎 (agents). Agents for the management of various affairs within a corporation. The word was in use during the middle ages (Kamakura and Muromachi periods). In the Edo period it became the name of an occupation of warriors. In addition to this, there are many instances of the use of the word *kimoiri* for designating the head of the MACHI YAKUNIN or of the MURA YAKU-NIN. Agents for the trade bodies known as KABU-NAKAMA and managers of forestry and irrigation were also styled *kimoiri*.

Kinai 畿内 (the five home provinces). From ancient times the local administrative districts included the "five home provinces and the seven circuits" *(goki-shichidō)*. The five home provinces were Yamashiro, Yamato, Kawachi, Settsu, and Izumi. They were in the neighborhood of the capital (Kyōto). Together with the seven circuits, the five home provinces were vaguely marked off during the period prior to the Taika Reform (646), but a definite line of demarcation was drawn after the Taika Reform. The imperial household resided in the capital. Many influential families and direct vassals lived in the neighboring provinces.

Kinchū narabi-ni Kuge Sho-Hatto 禁中並公家諸法度. Laws and regulations issued in 1615 by Tokugawa Ieyasu for the control of the imperial court. The shogunate drew up regulations governing the functions and behavior of the emperor and the imperial court. The regulations included seventeen articles which defined the pursuit of learning of the emperor; the precedence of princes, ministers, and priest-princes *(monzeki)*; the change of the chronological era; dress; the bestowing and receiving of official ranks; etc. In this way the BAKUFU deprived the imperial court of all administrative functions and at the same time assured itself a hand in all important court matters.

kinhon'i-sei 金本位制 (the gold standard). A modern monetary system. According to the new monetary regulations of 1871, the gold standard with the yen denomination was established. But, as there was an outflow of gold from the country, in 1878 a bimetallic (gold and silver) standard was adopted. In 1897, the gold standard was again adopted, using the indemnity of the Sino-Japanese War as a reserve fund. During World War I, an embargo was laid on gold export (1917). This embargo was lifted in 1930, but, pressed by the world crisis and by the expenses of the Manchurian incident of 1931 (MANSHŪ JIHEN), the government reimposed it. An economy of inconvertible paper notes continues in force at present.

kin-kaikin 金解禁 (the lifting of the gold embargo). In 1930, the embargo on the export of gold was lifted. The economic chaos caused by World War

I resulted in an embargo on the export of gold in various countries, but postwar industrial rehabilitation lifted this embargo. Only Japan, fearing that her financial capital would be affected, and in spite of the demand of the spinning industries and of other trading circles, did not lift the embargo. As a result, exchange rates dropped, and trade came to a standstill. Finally, the government contemplated a relaxation of the embargo. Following the financial panic of 1927, the great banks, which possessed unemployed capital, eagerly awaited this action. The lifting of the embargo was executed by Prime Minister Hamaguchi, but under pressure caused by the world crisis. Although the exchange rate recovered, there was a fall in prices and an outflow of specie. The national situation became worse, and in 1931 the gold embargo was reimposed.

Kinkaishū 金槐集. A one-volume collection of poetical works, early Kamakura period. The author is Minamoto no Sanetomo (1192–1219), who cherished the epic style of the MAN'YŌSHŪ and left these gems of poetry in *Man'yō* style.

Kinkaku 金閣. A Zen monastery built in 1397 as a mountain villa by Ashikaga Yoshimitsu (1358–1408). It is also called Rokuon-ji. The structure, a reproduction of the original, which was destroyed by fire in 1950, is in traditional SHINDEN-ZUKURI or mansion style. This style is characterized by elegant simplicity, but elements of Zen architecture and of Chinese style (KARA-YŌ) were also incorporated. These various elements were blended into a graceful whole and were in harmony with the beauty of the surrounding landscape gardens. The building eminently symbolizes the refined early Muromachi culture (KITAYAMA BUNKA).

kinseki-heiyō bunka 金石併用文化 (bronze-stone culture). The cultural level of the transition period between the Stone Age and the Bronze Age. In this period, which corresponds to the Yayoi period (about 350 B.C. to A.D. 250), stone and metal (usually bronze) were used conjointly. Stone axes, stone knives, flint arrowheads, etc. existed together with bronze swords, bronze halberds, and bronze bells. Toward the end of the period iron sharp-edged tools appeared. They eventually replaced stone sharp-edged tools but are believed to have been used simultaneously with them. According to another view, though bronze tools existed together with stone objects, they were of no practical use, as they were employed only in religious rites. The same view further holds that because it is admitted that iron tools rapidly replaced stone implements it would be inconsistent to argue the existence of a specific metal-stone culture.

kin'yū kinkyū-sochi rei 金融緊急措置令 (emergency financial measures ordinance). A measure to counter postwar inflation. In 1946, in order to prevent the catastrophe of a spiraling inflation, and to check the outflow of deposits, individuals were encouraged to live on an amount of 500 yen a month, and a currency-conversion program was formulated. The currency-conversion plan carried out in March 1946 temporarily reduced the currency in circulation from 62 billion yen in late February 1946 to 15.2 billion yen on March 12, 1946, but it had no lasting influence. By September the volume of new notes issued had reached 60 billion yen.

kin'yū kyōkō 金融恐慌 (banking crises). Financial crises in the early Shōwa era. A severe crisis followed the **Kantō** earthquake of September 1, 1923. The intervention of the Bank of Japan and the government held the number of bank failures to a minimum. The Bank of Japan discounted large amounts of what were called "earthquake bills" *(shinsai-tegata)*. The most severe crisis came in April 1927. A special session of the Diet revealed that the Bank of Formosa (Taiwan Ginkō) and many city banks had failed. Tanaka Giichi (1863–1929), who replaced Wakatsuki as prime minister, issued a monetary ordinance, but this measure resulted in the closing of stock markets and in the worsening of the financial chaos. The intervention of the government stabilized the situation for about one year. Then the depression resumed. This situation fostered monopolization by financial circles.

kinza 金座 (GINZA)

Kiri Hitoha 桐一葉. A literary work of the middle Meiji era. Tsubouchi Shōyō (1859–1935), dissatisfied with the historical dramas which tried to reform KABUKI, wrote new dramas with the purpose of Westernizing traditional drama. *Kiri Hitoha* is a representative work of these new dramas. It was written between 1894 and 1895.

kirimai 切米 (rice allowance). Rice allowance given to bannermen (HATA-MOTO) and household retainers (GO-KENIN) during the Edo period. Those who received rice were called *kuramai-tori*. The rice was delivered in spring, summer, and winter. Sometimes the rice was delivered ahead of time and was then called *torikoshi-mai*. It was the custom to deliver part of the allowance in cash. The part delivered in cash was not determined. The rice was supplied at the official rice store of Asakusa, and the administrator of the BAKUFU rice granary *(kura bugyō)* controlled the allowances. But the financial agents or brokers known as FUDASASHI, who lived in the neighborhood of Kuramae, took care of the receipt and selling of the rice and became usurers. As a result the bannermen and retainers were often reduced to destitution.

Kirishitan-ban キリシタン版 (Christian editions). Books published by the Society of Jesus during the sixteenth and seventeenth centuries. The missionaries of the Society of Jesus, as a means of spreading their faith, published books on the Catholic doctrine. The publications also included books on Japanese grammar and novels. The books were called *Kirishitan-ban*. About thirty of these books are extant, many of which are Amakusa editions or Nagasaki editions. Well known are *Amakusa-bon Heike Monogatari* and *Isoppu Monogatari* (ISOHO MONOGATARI), which are both published in romanized Japanese.

Kirishitan-shū キリシタン宗 (Christianity). The Catholic religion spread in Japan during the sixteenth century. In 1549, Francis Xavier, a member of the Society of Jesus, arrived in Kagoshima to spread the Catholic faith. It was the period of civil war (SENGOKU JIDAI). The daimyō wanted to trade with the West in order to enrich and strengthen their territory. Many of them were converted to the Catholic religion, which spread rapidly. From Kyūshū the new religion reached the Ōsaka-Kyōto district. Nobunaga, in order to oppose the strength of the Ikkō religion (IKKŌ-SHŪ), protected the missionaries and cooperated with the propagation of the new faith. He permitted the building of churches and schools. Hideyoshi was also in favor of the new faith but feared its growing influence and, in 1587, prohibited it. Ieyasu, seeking trade with the West, tolerated the religion. The number of adherents still grew. But the Christian ideology came into conflict with the feudal social order, and Ieyasu banned the religion and punished its followers. Iemitsu adopted a drastic anti-Christian policy. He closed the country and forbade the Japanese to leave the country. The Shimabara revolt (SHIMABARA NO RAN), in which Christians took part, was directed against this official oppression, but after the revolt anti-Christian policy became even more cruel. By means of picture treading (FUMIE), written pledges (KISHŌMON), the keeping of census registers of Christians, and temple certificates (TERAUKE-SEIDO), a very strict investigation was carried out. This policy lasted until the end of the Edo period.

kiroku 季禄 (seasonal stipends). Stipends paid according to rank to civil and military officials of the capital and to the officials of DAZAIFU, Iki, and Tsushima under the Taihō Code system. The spring and summer stipend was given to officials who were on duty at the imperial court for at least 120 days, or from the eighth lunar month to the first lunar month of the following year. The autumn and winter stipend was given to those who were on duty at the imperial court from the second to the seventh lunar month. The stipend consisted of coarse silk (or yarn for the spring and summer stipend), cloth, hoes (or iron for the autumn and winter stipend), etc. But from 711 (in 708 copper was found), money was also given. The custom declined when, at the end of the Heian period, the official treasury ran out of funds.

kirokusho 記録所 (record office). 1) Abbreviation of KIROKU SHŌEN KENKEISHO. 2) An office revived by Emperor Godaigo (1288–1339) during the Kemmu Restoration (KEMMU NO CHŪKŌ). Together with the tribunal for various claims (ZASSO KETSUDANSHO), the *kirokusho* was the central office of the new administration. Like the tribunal for various claims, the *kirokusho* was an office for lawsuits, but important matters were handled only by the *kirokusho*. Members *(yoryūdo)* of the *kirokusho* included Gojō Yorimoto (1290–1367), Nawa Nagatoshi (?–1336), and Kusunoki Masashige (1294–1336). The new administration, however, failed to solve the numerous problems concerning land tenure.

kiroku shōen kenkeisho 記録荘園券契所. An office set up in 1069 by Emperor Gosanjō (1034–73) for the management of manorial estates. It is also abbreviated KIROKUSHO. The management of a manor was no longer the duty of the local governor (KOKUSHI), but each landlord had to show his landlord certificate *(kenkei)*. This title deed was examined and its validity or invalidity ascertained. The emperor intended to confiscate all manors for which valid charters could not be produced. The system lasted only four years, until 1072, and all invalid manors were confiscated. The measure shook the economic foundation of the nobility, temples and shrines, and, especially, the regents.

Kiryū 桐生. A city in Gumma Prefecture and a distributing center for silk fabrics. During the middle ages (Kamakura and Muromachi periods), it was for a long time the stronghold of the Kiryū clan. Later the Yura clan took over the stronghold, but in 1590, when Hideyoshi subjugated Odawara, the Yura were exterminated. From earlier times, Kiryū was a center for the production of silk fabrics and developed into a market town. From about the Kyōhō era (1716–36), the merchants of Edo, Kyōto, and Ōsaka traveled to the town, which was very active. Manufacture of Kiryū fabrics was first a subsidiary business of farmers, but in time production of fabrics became an independent occupation. In 1738, a kind of Jacquard loom known as *takabata* (for making twill and brocade), in use in Nishijin (Kyōto), was introduced, and Kiryū succeeded in producing high-grade goods. During the Bunka (1804–18) and Bunsei (1818–30) eras, Kiryū reached a peak of activity and became a powerful rival to Nishijin, and by 1846 it had some 267 small weaving establishments, which together operated more than 5,000 looms. Nishijin even filed a petition in order to restrain Kiryū. At the end of the Edo period, a large-scale enterprise was attempted, but, as a result of the Tempō reforms and the shortage of raw silk after the opening of the country, as well as the pressure of the newly-risen Ashikaga market, Kiryū suffered a setback. In more recent times, Kiryū is known for its popular manufactured goods such as floss mixed weave, rayon sash material, etc.

kishinchi-kei shōen 寄進地系荘園 (commended land estates). Great estates which came into being because name masters (MYŌSHU) and small cultivators called TATO, as well as middling cultivators, commended their land to great territorial lords and to politically influential families. To the commendation was added "To curb the unlawful practices of the provincial government."

Land was commended to evade both the burden of taxation imposed by the codes and the pressure of provincial authorities. The practice became generalized about the middle of the Heian period. The politically influential persons or institutions were considered to be the real owners *(ryōke)*, or the nominal owners *(honsho)*, and the consignors were appointed manor officials (SHŌKAN), such as general supervisors of the manor (GESU) or controllers of the miscellaneous affairs of the manor *(shōji)*. Those to whom the land was commended were only concerned with receiving taxes, but the estate management was in the hands of the *shōkan*. Around the KINAI (the provinces around the capital) many consignors owned from one to five *chō* (one *chō* is 2.45 acres). Such consignors were scattered over the territory. But in the eastern provinces and in underdeveloped areas, many estates were as large as a whole district, and the *shōkan* managed to form powerful clans which owned the territory. In spite of this considerable difference between the land-tenure conditions in the Kinai and in the eastern provinces, as a rule the struggle for private property on the part of mighty landowners and feudal magnates against public ownership under the administrative code system resulted in the formation of estates composed of commended land. Later, the privileges of immunity or tax exemption and enclosure (provincial officials not being allowed to enter the manors)—that is, FUYUFUNYŪ-KEN—were secured, and the manors were passed to the Fujiwara, who were officials of the highest rank. This situation brought about the economic foundation of the golden age of the Fujiwara regents and of the Fujiwara chief advisers to the emperor.

kishōmon 起請文 (written pledge). A written document containing a pledge made to gods and Buddhas. There were many such pledges at the end of the ancient period (late Heian period) and especially during the middle ages (Kamakura and Muromachi periods). In the document was added that, if the pledge was not fulfilled, punishment by gods and Buddhas would follow. Usually the oath was taken in front of the clan god or any other worshiped deity. Later, only the intention was expressed without being in the presence of the image of the deity.

Kishū mikan 紀州密柑 (Wakayama tangerines). Tangerines grown in Kishū (Wakayama Prefecture), the center of production being Arida County (Arida-gun). They are also called Arida tangerines. The hills along the Arida River are suitable for the production of tangerines, and Minoshima is a convenient port for shipment. Cultivation began early. In the early Edo period, Wakayama tangerines were already sold in other provinces. During the period 1624–44, families of Kishū enjoyed protection for the transportation of tangerines to Edo. They made huge profits. About the middle of the Edo period, every year from 350,000 to 500,000 baskets of tangerines were shipped to Edo. Kyōto, Ōsaka, and Nagoya were also important buying centers. For the merchant clans of Kishū, this trade was an important source of revenue. A semi-government controller, a deputy shipper, and other officials in charge of the business were appointed. An office was established in Kitaminato, and selling was strictly controlled. The system remained unchanged until the early Meiji era, when independent shippers made their appearance. As government control loosened, trade associations were organized. This procedure is still in use today.

Kitayama bunka 北山文化 (Kitayama culture). The culture of the early Muromachi period, in particular of Ashikaga Yoshimitsu (1358–1408). It is called Kitayama culture because Yoshimitsu built his villa in Kitayama, Kyōto. It is compared with the Higashiyama culture (HIGASHIYAMA BUNKA) of Yoshimasa (1434–90). The main elements of this particular culture are the literature of the Five Zen Monasteries (GOZAN BUNGAKU), which flourished under the scholars Shun'oku Myōha (1311–88), Zekkai Chūshin (1336–1405), and Gidō Shūshin (1325–88); the perfection of Nō drama (NŌGAKU) under Kan'ami (1334–85) and his son Zeami (1363–1443); the popularity of linked verse (RENGA) under Nijō Yoshimoto's influence (1320–88); and the rise of India-ink painting (SUIBOKU-GA) in Sung and Yüan style under Minchō (1352–1431), Josetsu, Shūbun, and others. After the unification of the Northern and Southern dynasties, the MUROMACHI BAKUFU strengthened its authority. Kitayama culture, becoming the new culture of the warriors, merged with the traditional culture of the court nobles. Furthermore, following trade with Ming China, Chinese influence was also strongly felt.

Kiyohara uji 清原氏 (Kiyohara clan). A clan formed by the descendants of Prince Toneri (Toneri Shinnō, ?–735), the son of Emperor Temmu (622–86). The clan is also known as Seike and was respected as a family of scholars who made themselves meritorious during several generations. Historical personalities are Kiyohara no Natsuno (782–837); Kiyohara no Yorinori (1122–89), who, as a Confucian scholar, was secretary *(daigeki)* of the Council of State and doctor of literature *(monjō hakase);* Sei Shōnagon (circa 1000); Kiyohara no Takenori (circa 1060); and others.

Kizoku-in 貴族院 (House of Peers). A legislative body. In 1889, along with the promulgation of the Imperial Constitution, the ordinance concerning the House of Peers was also promulgated. Jointly with the House of Representatives, the House of Peers constituted the Imperial Diet. The House of Representatives was made up of members elected by the people and showed the influence of political parties. As opposed to the House of Representatives, the House of Peers intended to maintain absolute imperialism as advocated by the clan government and was based on the peerage system which was established in 1884 as a bulwark of the throne. The House of Peers was organized by adding imperial nominees and representatives of the highest taxpayers to the peerage members. It was dissolved after World War II, following the promulgation of the new constitution.

kō 講 (religious associations). Associations or corporations formed for a common religious or financial purpose. Originally the members of these associations gathered to attend lectures and commentaries on Buddhist sutras. From ancient times, these gatherings took place in ENRYAKU-JI temple and in the temples of Nara, but from the middle ages to the early Edo period the associations spread among the masses and increased rapidly. The members were affiliated with a particular temple or shrine and worshiped a certain god or Buddha. The associations extolled the Buddhist doctrine, worshiped at temples and shrines, made vicarious pilgrimages, and provided expenses for temple repairs. To meet temple expenses, the associations used a monthly savings system, and they often functioned as financial associations. Before long, those among the merchants, manufacturers, and innkeepers who belonged to the same faith organized religious associations similar to the *kō*. Very early some *kō,* such as the *tanomoshi-kō* (TANOMOSHI) and the *mujin-kō* (MUJIN), developed into finance associations, but the members invariably gathered on determined days, taking food and drink together. These associations in no small degree fostered a spirit of fraternity. In some rural communities which lack recreational facilities, *kō* meetings still exist as a regular annual event.

koban 小判 (ŌBAN, KOBAN)

kōbu-gattai ron 公武合体論 (theory of amalgamation of civil and military power). A theory according to which the military houses could collaborate with the civil aristocracy. In the late Edo period, when internal and external politics were creating turmoil, the BAKUFU, in order to restore its prestige, tried to cooperate with the imperial court. To quell the feud between the shōgun and the emperor, a royal princess, Kazunomiya (1846–77), was given in marriage to the fourteenth shōgun, Iemochi (1846–66). After the incident outside the Sakashita gate (SAKASHITA-MONGAI NO HEN) influential clans, deploring the *bakufu's* policy, tried to alter it. To overcome the critical situation, the daimyō of Satsuma tried to restore the spiritual authority of the court, but the shogunate was opposed. The Satsuma clan was in favor of overthrowing the shogunate, while the Aizu, Kuwana, and other clans were in favor of supporting it. As a result, the *kōbu-gattai* movement failed.

Kōbun-in 弘文院 (private school of the Wake clan). Private educational institution of the early Heian period. The school was established by Wake no Hirose in compliance with the wish of his father Wake no Kiyomaro (733–99). It was located in the southeast section of the state college (DAIGAKU). It possessed about one thousand volumes of Confucian and Buddhist books and forty *chō* (one *chō* is 2.45 acres) of reclaimed land to meet its expenses. The school was for young men of the Wake clan, but when the Wake family became less influential, the school declined. According to the book *Saigūki,* about 150 years after its establishment—that is, around the year 980—the school was abandoned.

Kōbun-kan 弘文館 (private school of the Hayashi clan). Private school of the Hayashi family, Edo period. The school was the forerunner of the SHŌHEIKŌ, the Confucian college in Edo. It was opened in 1630 in a place in Ueno (Edo) called Shinobugaoka after a plot of land had been given to Hayashi Dōshun (Hayashi Razan, 1583–1657) by Shōgun Iemitsu. The school took its name from the title Kōbun'in, which, in 1663, was granted to Dōshun's son Shunsai (1618–80) by Shōgun Tsunayoshi. In 1664, Shunsai opened a school of history at government expense and began the compilation of HONCHŌ TSUGAN. Scholars of the school also worked at government expense. In 1690, Tsunayoshi moved the Kōbun-kan from Ueno to Yushima and constructed a new building. It became the Shōheikō, which was directly controlled by the shogunate.

Kōbu-shō 工部省 (Department of Industry). The Department of Industry in the early Meiji era. Established in 1870, it supervised the development of mines, the construction of railways, telegraph and telephone system, war plants, and other national undertakings, and encouraged private production. Later the government policy of production changed following the disposal of government plants. Matters involving production shifted to the Department of Agriculture and the Department of Commercial Affairs, and the Kōbu-shō was abolished in 1885.

kōchō-jūnisen 皇朝十二銭 (twelve kinds of coins). The generic term for the twelve kinds of coins cast and used during the Nara and Heian periods. Each coin was round, and in the middle was a square opening. Four characters were inscribed clockwise. The circulation of the coins was limited mainly to the provinces around the capital, and it is believed that only people of nobility used them. The last coin in the list below seems to have been minted up until the early eleventh century.

Name of Coin	Year of Casting
Wadō *kaihō* (or *kaichin*)	708
Mannen *tsūhō*	from 760
Jinkō *kaihō*	from 765
Ryūhei *eihō*	769–817
Fūju *shimpō*	818–34
Shōwa *shōhō*	835–47
Chōnen *taihō*	848–58
Jōeki *shimpō*	859–69
Jōgan *eihō*	870–89
Kampyō *taihō*	890–906
Engi *tsūhō*	907–57
Kengen *taihō*	from 959

kōden 功田 (merit fields). Fields granted during the Nara and Heian periods to those who had rendered distinguished service to the state. The area of land granted differed according to the merit. There were *taikōden,* or fields granted in perpetuity; *jōkōden,* or fields granted for three generations; *chūkōden,* or fields granted for two generations; and *gekōden,* or fields granted to the son of the person in question. In principle the field was granted to meritorious persons regardless of their sex and legitimacy of birth. Because the fields granted were considered almost as private land, the possession of *kōden* led to the creation of manors (estates). There were numerous instances of *kōden* granted to men with distinguished war records, to compilers of penal and administrative codes, to envoys to T'ang China, etc.

kōden 公田 (public fields). Land system in the Nara and Heian periods. *Kōden* means land other than private land. Private land included "mouth-share" fields (KUBUNDEN), the extent of which was based upon the number of members in a household; "rank fields" (IDEN), which were fields given to persons of the fifth rank or higher; "official" fields (SHIKIDEN), also known as *shikibunden,* which were fields given to those who held an official post; and "merit" fields (KŌDEN 功田), which were fields given to those who had rendered distinguished service to the country. Public land was directly administered by the nation and was also called *jōden.* Private land was taxable land, but *kōden* was leased land for which only the land rent referred to as CHISHI was to be sent to the Council of State in autumn. Except for this *chishi,* public fields were tax-free. When the "mouth-share" field of a farmer was insufficient, public fields could be alloted to the holder of a "mouth-share" field. This seems to indicate that the farmers who only possessed *kubunden* were at times hard pressed.

kōdō 香道 (the art of incense). The art of appreciating and distinguishing the scent of burning fragrant wood. Incense was introduced from China together with Buddhism. It was held in high esteem by the Buddhist faith. Usually aloeswood *(jinkō)* was used, but during the Heian period various kinds of incense were blended and burned. A blending of superior quality was made and became fashionable, especially among the aristocracy. At the time of the Northern and Southern dynasties (1336–92), the art of incense was made into a popular game. Players vied with each other in their ability to identify by scent various kinds of incense that were burned. However, *kōdō* was brought to perfection about the end of the Muromachi period, when Sanjōnishi Sanetaka (1455–1537) made it into an art.

Koga kubō 古河公方 (shōgun at Koga), The revolt of the Eikyō era in 1438 (EIKYŌ NO RAN) led to the defeat of Ashikaga Mochiuji (1398–1439). Mochiuji was the last of the Ashikaga family to control the Kantō district. However, his son Shigeuji (1434–97) called himself governor of Kantō (KANTŌ KANREI). Because Shigeuji killed Uesugi Noritada (1454), the Uesugi rose against him, and he fled to Koga in Shimōsa Province (Ibaraki Prefecture) and called himself *Koga kubō*—that is, "shōgun at Koga." The Uesugi clan summoned Maatomo (1435–91), the younger brother of Shōgun Yoshimasa. Masatomo planned an expedition against Shigeuji, but the plan failed and he remained n Horikoshi, Izu Province (Shizuoka Prefecture). Both the *Koga kubō* and the *Horikoshi kubō,* or Masatomo, were killed.

kogaku-ha 古学派 (ancient school of philosophy). A school of Confucianism during the Edo period. Rejecting the later interpretations and dogmatism of Chu Hsi and Wang Yang-ming, this school directly inquired into the original meaning of Confucius and Mencius and imitated the way of the ancient sages. Scholars of this school tried to put into practice the new doctrine as a pattern of life. The school was first known as the *kogigaku-ha* of Yamaga Sokō (1622–85) and Itō Jinsai (1627–1705) and then as the *kobungaku-ha* of Ogyū Sorai (1666–1728). All these scholars had their own particular standpoints, but they all advocated a return to the original texts. Because they stressed practice, some of them, such as Yamaga Sokō, were punished by the BAKUFU; others, however, such as Ogyū Sorai, were in the *bakufu's* service. This revival of the ancient interpretation and new study of the classics profoundly influenced the study of Japanese classical literature and marked an important step in the cultural history of the country.

Kōgisho 公議所 (House of Representatives). A legislative body established in 1869. The members were elected by the clans, and their number amounted to about 270. The government in the early Meiji years derived its administrative power from the allied clans and showed a strong collegial character. Gradually, however, and after the "return of the land and people to the emperor" (HANSEKI-HŌKAN) the government became more autocratic. Already in July of the same year, the Kōgisho was called SHŪGI-IN and was consultative in nature.

Kōgo nenjaku 庚午年籍 (household registers of the year Kōgo). Household registers of the year 670, which confirmed names and titles which had been perpetuated since 415. Registers more than thirty years old could be canceled, but it was decided that registers of the year Kōgo were not to be superseded.

koihō 古医方 (KAMPŌ IGAKU)

Kojiki 古事記. The first historical book on Japan. It comprises three volumes. Emperor Temmu (622–86) ordered the master narrator of ancient traditions, Hieda no Are, to read and memorize all the imperial genealogies and successions as well as all the myths and legends transmitted by the court and clans. On the order of Empress Gemmei (661–721), Ō no Yasumaro (?–723) made a selective record based on Hieda no Are's narration. The work was finished in 712. The first volume deals with the age of the gods; the second includes the events from the time of Emperor Jimmu to that of Emperor Ōjin; the third relates the events from the time of Emperor Nintoku to that of Empress Suiko (554–628). The myths, legends, and songs of *Kojiki* have inspired many literary works.

Kojiki-den 古事記伝 (commentary on KOJIKI). Commentary in forty-eight volumes on *Kojiki* written by Moto-ori Norinaga (1730–1801), who spent half his life on the work. In 1763, at the age of thirty-four, Motoori, encouraged by Kamo no Mabuchi (1697–1769), began the work. In 1798, at the age of sixty-nine, after thirty-five years of painstaking efforts, he completed it. It is a commentary on a classic. At the same time, it is a study of antiquity carried out with all the knowledge available at the time. *Kojiki-den* is an outstanding work in the field of national classics as well as in the whole field of Japanese literature.

Kōkai kaisen 黄海海戦 (naval battles in the Yellow Sea). Modern naval battles. In 1894, during the Sino-Japanese War, the Chinese and Japanese squadrons clashed in the Yellow Sea. Japan was victorious and secured command at sea. In 1904, during the Russo-Japanese War, the Japanese squadron routed the Russian squadron which tried to escape from the Port Arthur blockade. This battle, like the other, is called the battle of the Yellow Sea.

Kōkatō jiken 江華島事件 (the incident at Kanghwa-do). An incident between Korea and Japan in the early Meiji years. In 1875, Japan tried to open diplomatic relations by means of military coercion and sent the gunboat *Un'yō* to the west coast of Korea. The action was of an intimidating nature. The Japanese gunboat was attacked at the island of Kanghwa by Korean coast guns, but the captain of the boat, Inoue Yoshika, returned the fire and occupied the fort. Then the Japanese government sent the envoy Kuroda Kiyotaka (1840–1900) to Korea, and the following year an amity treaty was concluded. Korea had to open the port of Pusan and grant consular jurisdiction. This marked the opening of Korea and the beginning of Japanese inroads into Korean territory.

Kokin-denju 古今伝授 (initiation into the mysteries of *Kokinshū*). Transmission of the secrets concerning KOKIN WAKASHŪ. When *waka* poetry was considered a sacred art, its knowledge was secretly transmitted from master to pupil. This transmission became a custom during the Muromachi period. The mysteries were transmitted from Tō Tsuneyori (1401–91) to Sōgi (1421–1502) and from Sōgi to Sanjōnishi Sanetaka (1455–1537) and Shōhaku (1443–1527). From Sanetaka the initiation was transmitted to the warrior Hosokawa Yūsai (Fujitaka, 1534–1610), and from Shōhaku it was transmitted to the merchant-scholar Manjūya Sōji (1456–1540). In the middle of the Edo period, the contents of the initiation were exposed and proved to be worthless.

Kokin Wakashū 古今和歌集. First anthology of *waka* poems, compiled in 905 on the order of Emperor Daigo (885–930). The compilers were Ki no Tsurayuki (?–946), Ki no Tomonori (845–905), Ōshikōchi no Mitsune, and Mibu no Tadamine (868–965). The anthology consists of twenty volumes and contains about 1,100 poems. It includes the poems since the time of MAN'YŌ-SHŪ. As opposed to *Man'yōshū's* poems, which are in the five-seven meter, many poems of *Kokin Wakashū* are in the seven-five meter. Technical skill in the use of words is striking, pivot words and rhetorical words are profusely used, and pathos is the underlying tone. Though elegance and delicacy are achieved, the interest is perhaps spoiled by the overdeveloped technique, and sometimes the contents sound hollow. The subject matter is limited to flowers and birds, wind, and the moon. This feature clearly reflects the taste of the court nobles. Later anthologies looked on *Kokin Wakashū* as their model. The use of *kana* by skillful poets fostered native literature and encouraged the expression of a native attitude.

Kokkai Kisei-dōmei 国会期成同盟 (Association for the Realization of the National Assembly). Political association of the movement for democratic rights, early Meiji era. The movement for democratic rights, which was the outgrowth of antigovernment pressure, revived the Patriotic Association (AIKOKU-SHA) in 1878. In 1880, a national convention in Ōsaka was attended by 114 representatives of twenty-seven political associations, two metropolises, and twenty-two prefectures, with 87,000 people represented. The Association for the Realization of the National Assembly was organized, and it was decided to send a memorial to the throne for the same purpose. The government took drastic action. Regulations restricting public meetings and prohibiting the amalgamation of local political societies were enacted. But the same year a convention was held in Tōkyō. Representing 130,000 people, the delegates attacked the government and demanded freedom of organizing political parties to use the people's influence to the fullest. In 1881, when an imperial edict ordered the inauguration of the National Assembly, the association was dissolved and its members formed the Liberal Party (1881).

Kokka Sōdōin Hō 国家総動員法 (National Mobilization Law). A law promulgated in 1938. The government was given strong authority to direct manpower and material resources toward national defense. During the Pacific War, this power was used to the extreme. It was the driving force of the wartime system. The law was abolished in 1945.

kokkeibon 滑稽本 (comic books). A kind of novel of the late Edo period describing everyday life and the amusements of the Edo townspeople. The comic books reached their climax during the Bunka (1804–18) and Bunsei (1818–30) eras with such authors as Jippensha Ikku (1765–1831), Shikitei Samba (1776–1822), and others. Later these novels tended to become vulgar and fell into mannerism. One of the last writers of *kokkeibon* was Kanagaki Robun (1828–92).

Kokon Chomonshū 古今著聞集. A collection of stories in twenty volumes published in 1254 by Tachibana Narisue (circa 1250). The collection contains "famous stories of the past and present" *(kokon chomon)* and random information. Each story ends with a moral instruction. The book is closely related to JIKKINSHŌ, which was probably written by the same author.

kokubun-ji 国分寺 (provincial temples). Temples built in each province during the Nara period. In 741, Emperor Shōmu (701–56) issued an edict ordering the erection of provincial temples. The purpose was the realization of ideals expressed in Buddhist sutras, the establishment of local administration by means of religious national unity, and the fostering of local culture and of the union of church and state. Consequently, in each province a temple, a monastery, and a nunnery were erected. The building of so many institutions depleted the national treasury, but the age (Tempyō), as a period in art history, greatly prospered.

kokudaka 石高. The amount of rice harvest estimated in *koku* and the area of a rice field. Sometimes it was simply called *taka*. One *koku* equals 4.96 English bushels. Computing the rate of production per *tan* (one *tan* is 0.245 acres), the fields were divided into four grades: superior, middle, inferior, and low. The production rate per *tan* was divided by one *to* (one *to* is 3.97 gallons), and the result was called *koku-mori*. Usually a rice field of superior quality yielded one *koku* and five *to*. Rice fields of middle and inferior quality yielded two *to* less. The *kokudaka* system spread following the land survey by Hideyoshi and replaced the system referred to as KANDAKA, where the amount of rice production was estimated in currency.

kokuga 国衙 (provincial government office). Provincial government office during the Nara and Heian periods, or the seat of the provincial government office. It was also called *kokufu* and *kokuchō*. The seat of the provincial government office was near the main town in a well-developed and densely populated area. In its neighborhood was the provincial temple (KOKUBUN-JI), and the seat was an education center. Today, many localities still have the name *kokufu*. The best-preserved *kokufu* remains are those of Suō Kokufu, the *kokufu* of Yamaguchi Prefecture, or present-day Bōfu City.

kokugaku 国学. 1) An educational system in ancient Japan. In the capital was the college (DAIGAKU), and in each province was a school for the education of public officials. The sons of rural district administrators (GUNJI) learned the classics *(keigaku)*; the sons of common people learned medicine. Each province had one doctor of Chinese classics and one doctor of medicine. The system

eclined when the penal and administrative code *(ritsuryō)* fell into decay.
2) A school of learning which originated during the middle of the Edo
period. The ancient history of Japan was studied, but on the basis of Japanese
classics. Originally this school was called *wagaku, kōchōgaku, kōkokugaku,* and
odōgaku. From the middle ages, a distorted and dogmatic Buddhist and Con-
ucianist interpretation was given to poetry, KOJIKI, NIHON SHOKI, GENJI MONO-
ATARI, etc. Against this interpretation and against the tendency of com-
nunicating this interpretation secretly, *kokugaku* studied the classics to learn
ne orthodox meaning of the ancient terminology and brought to light the
pirit prevailing in ancient days. Rejecting Confucian virtues, this school
tressed ancient morality which preached Japanese virtues. Pioneers of the
chool were Keichū (1640–1701) and Shimokōbe Chōryū (1624–86). The
chool developed under Kada no Azumamaro (1669–1736), Kamo no Mabu-
hi (1697–1769), and others. It reached its climax under Moto-ori Norinaga
1730–1801). The methodology of the school was taken over by Norinaga's
isciple Ban Nobutomo (1773–1846), but when it further developed under
Iirata Atsutane (1776–1843), it became a fanatic kind of revived Shintō
vhich evolved into the leading political principle of the Meiji Restoration.
he ideology came to a standstill at the impact with European and American
deologies, but, together with Confucianism, *kokugaku* survived for a long time
s the keynote of ultranationalism.

:okuga-ryō 国衙領. The territory administered by the provincial govern-
nent office during the time of the manors. In the latter part of the Heian
eriod, as opposition to the increase of manorial estates developed, the *kokuga-
yō* came into being. These territories made up a unit composed of the land
nder title of ownership—that is, name fields (MYŌDEN). The owners of name
elds (MYŌSHU) were controlled by such provincial officials as *hōji* (village
ead), *gōshi* (the head of a rural community), and GUNJI (rural district ad-
ninistrator). These officials also managed the land under direct control of
he landlord *(tsukuda),* so that actually there was no difference between this
and and a manor, and the provincial government officials were considered
o be managers of manors. During the Kamakura period many of these of-
cials became warriors of the shōgun (GO-KENIN) or stewards (JITŌ). At the
me of the Northern and Southern dynasties, the *kokuga-ryō* amounted to
nly one percent of the whole provincial territory and was often commended
o cloistered emperors or to temples and shrines. In Muromachi days the
okuga-ryō declined as the territory became the property of constables (SHUGO
•AIMYŌ).

Kokumin Chōyō Rei 国民徴用令 (National Service Draft Law). In 1939,
he National Service Draft Law was promulgated. Together with the wage-
ontrol ordinance and the law preventing workers' migration it meant the
nobilization of people for the factories and the throwing of the total national

manpower into military production. The law was abolished at the end o the Pacific War.

Kokumin no Tomo 国民の友. A nationalist magazine of Meiji times. In 1887 Tokutomi Sohō (1863–1957) organized the MIN'YŪ-SHA association and pub lished *Kokumin no Tomo*. The magazine was meritorious in various fields, as i commented on politics and new literature, introduced foreign culture sucl as literature, organized the Min'yū-sha school, and encouraged young writers Opposed to the ultranationalist magazine *Nihonjin,* it advocated democracy But the ideological background of the day being nationalistic, *Kokumin n Tomo* advocated war and expansionism at the time of the Sino-Japanese Wa (1894–95). It was discontinued in 1898.

Kokumin-tō 国民党 (the Kuomintang). A Chinese political party. The Re form Society called Hsing-chung Hui, organized in 1892 in Macao by Su₁ Wen, and the Revolutionary League known as Hsinhai Koming (SHINGA KAKUMEI), which went into action in Hankow and Wuchang and which over threw the Ch'ing Dynasty, developed into the Kuomintang Party after th₁ establishment of the Chinese Republic. The Kuomintang Party was dissolve₁ by Yüan Shih-k'ai (in Japanese, En Sei-gai). In 1918, Sun Wen formall₁ organized the Kuomintang and in 1923, impressed by the successful Russia₁ revolution, called Russian advisers of the Communist school to his assistance the chief of whom was the astute revolutionary Michael Borodin. From thi time, Chiang Kai-shek subjected the Communists to pressure. Following th₁ incident of Sian in 1936, the Kuomintang and the Communists collaborate₁ and formed a common front against the Japanese invaders. However, with th₁ fall of Chiang Kai-shek after the war, the Kuomintang lost its influence, an₁ the Communists established political power.

kokuritsu ginkō 国立銀行 (national banks). Chartered banks in the earl₁ Meiji years, established from 1872 in Tōkyō and other places. They wer₁ created because the financial situation required banks authorized to issu₁ convertible notes. Though commerce and industry developed, the govern ment issued only inconvertible paper money. To unify the country's currenc₁ and to replace the inconvertible paper money with national bank notes re deemable in gold and silver, the Japanese national bank law was passed i₁ 1872. Later, when the upper feudal classes were required to exchange thei₁ annual hereditary pensions for government bonds, thus adding to the publi₁ debt, the national banks helped also to redress this debt. In 1882, a centra₁ bank, the Bank of Japan, was established. From this time until 1899, the char tered national banks organized themselves and became commercial banks.

Kokusai Remmei 国際連盟 (the League of Nations). An international or ganization established after World War I. Proposed by President Wilson i₁ order to secure world peace and international cooperation, this organization was provided for in the Treaty of Versailles and established in 1920. There were more than fifty member nations. England, France, Japan, and Italy were permanent member nations, but, because the United States failed to participate, the league was weakened. In 1931, when Japan invaded Manchuria, the league failed to take action and to apply sanctions. In 1933, Japan as well as Nazi Germany withdrew from the league, and in 1934 Italy followed suit. Being powerless, the League of Nations collapsed and, after gradual reductions in staff and services, dissolved itself in 1946.

Kokusai Rengō 国際連合 (the United Nations). An international organization established after World War II. The idea, which had already been expressed in the wartime Atlantic Charter, materialized after the war. In 1945, the United Nations was established in San Francisco, and fifty member nations participated. It corresponds to the League of Nations but is more powerful because both Soviet Russia and the United States are members, and the organization is strengthened by international economic cooperation. Besides, to settle disputes, the major nations, which are permanent members of the Security Council, can make use of the veto power. Participation by Japan was vetoed in 1952 and 1955. Finally, in December 1956, Japan became a member and took its first step on the postwar international stage.

Kokusan kaisho 国産会所 (the production office). A clan office governing the production and sale of products in a fief, Edo period. It was also called *sambutsu kaisho* and *bussan kaisho,* and the officers were called *sambutsu-kata* and *bussan-kata.* After the middle of the Edo period, in order to redress the financial policy of the clans, this office encouraged the production of essential merchandise, hoping to secure the profits of the monopoly of this merchandise and the cooperation of wealthy townspeople. The office offered raw materials, lent money, improved production methods, and examined the manufactured goods. It also set up branch offices in various places within the fief, even in cities such as Kyōto, Ōsaka, Edo, etc.

Kokushi 国司 (provincial administrators). Provincial administrators during the Nara and Heian periods. According to the penal and administrative code, local administration included provinces and smaller districts or *gun.* The provincial office communicated to the people the orders of the central government and had them carried out. Officials were the provincial governor *(kami),* the vice-governor *(suke),* magistrates *(jō),* secretaries *(sakan),* and clerks *(shijō).* Usually they proceeded to their posts from Kyōto. The term of office was six years, and "official land" *(shikibunden)* was granted. Official functions included the supervision of shrines and almost all the functions of the Council of State (DAJŌKAN). With the collapse of the ancient regime and when central authority began to wane, the *kokushi* institution

changed. An office in the absence of the governor *(rusu-dokoro)* was establishe‹
when the "system of the governor residing in the capital" or *yōnin-sei* (YŌNIN
was introduced. After the Kamakura period, this *rusu-dokoro* also lost its mean
ing, and the *kokushi* became a mere name. However, the appellation con
tinued to exist until the Meiji Restoration.

kokusui-shugi 国粋主義 (ultranationalism). The prevailing ideology in th‹
middle of the Meiji era. A reaction set in against the excessive Europeaniza
tion encouraged by the international club ROKUMEI-KAN, and conservativ‹
feeling became stronger. In 1886, the Kōdō-kai, a society for the encourage
ment of moral training, was founded by Nishimura Shigeki (1828–1902), an‹
the SEIKYŌ-SHA or Society for Political Education was founded by Miyak‹
Setsurei (1860–1945). About 1897, ultranationalism became the keynote ‹
the Japanese expansionist policy and resulted in racial prejudice and a‹
attitude of self-sufficiency.

komeba 米場 (rice exchange markets). Rice exchange places at the end ‹
the Muromachi period. The *komeba* of Kyōto was well known. Currenc‹
economy developed, and taxes were paid in money. Rice was transported b‹
professional rice merchants, and exchange markets exclusively for rice, th‹
komeba, were established.

Kome Kubō 米公方 (the "Rice Shōgun"). This epithet was applied to th‹
eighth shōgun, Tokugawa Yoshimune (1684–1751). By means of the Kyōh‹
Reform (KYŌHŌ NO KAIKAKU), Yoshimune tried to adjust the price of rice an‹
to increase rice production, efforts which earned him the nickname "Ric‹
Shōgun."

kome sōdō 米騒動 (rice riots of 1918). Riots of 1918, which occurre‹
simultaneously throughout the country. As a result of World War I, Japa
nese capitalism grew conspicuously but not for the benefit of the peopl‹
Newly rich people appeared in succession, but, because of low wages and hig‹
prices, the life of the common people was miserable. The price of rice wa‹
raised out of all proportion. One *shō* (3.18 pints) of rice, which in prewar da‹
cost twelve cents, cost fifty cents in July 1918. On August 3, 1918, the wiv‹
of fishermen of Namerikawa in Toyama Prefecture held a demonstration d‹
manding a reduction of prices. When this incident appeared in the newspaper‹
the riot spread throughout the country. By about the fifteenth of Septembe‹
1,350,000 rioters had attacked rice stores all over the country, and troops wer‹
mobilized to quell the revolt. This caused the resignation of the cabinet ‹
Terauchi, and a new cabinet was formed with the help of the Association ‹
Political Friends (SEIYŪ-KAI). It was the first party cabinet. The incide‹
occurred almost spontaneously, but it was the beginning of labor and soci‹
movements at home as well as abroad.

kōmon 黄門 (court secretary). The name of an office originating in ancient China when the Imperial Gate was styled Huangmen—in Japanese, Kōmon. In Japan *kōmon* became the Chinese-style name for *chūnagon* or court secretary. In particular, the warlord Tokugawa Mitsukuni (1628–1700) was commonly called *Mito kōmon* or court secretary, heir of the Mito family.

komononari 小物成 (miscellaneous taxes). The generic term for miscellaneous taxes during the Edo period. These taxes were imposed when the farmers used "fields and mountains, rivers and seas" and derived profit from this use. As opposed to the usual taxes, which were called *mononari,* miscellaneous taxes were called *komononari.* They included the tax on the use of unreclaimed land, the yearly tax on the use of mountains, the tax on the rice produce of mountain fields, taxes on fishing income, taxes on tea, taxes on woods, etc. The amount to be paid differed from place to place, but the rich variety of taxes increased every year. In some places a difference was made between *jō-komononari,* which were fixed taxes collected yearly and noted on the records of the community, and the *uki-komononari* (also *chiri-komononari*), which were undetermined taxes.

kondei 健児 (militia). The militia which replaced the system of military detachments (GUNDAN) during the period of the penal and administrative code (646–1185). In 792, all the military forces of the country were abolished. Exception was made of detachments in the provinces Mutsu, Dewa, Sado, and the provinces under the administration of Dazaifu. Young men from the families of district governors (GUNJI) made up the militia and had to guard the national treasury, etc. They were exempted from corvée provided they had been on military duty for sixty days in a year. To prevent slackening of military preparedness, plots of tax-free land known as *kondei-den* were provided to support the militiamen, who, as a rule, were well taken care of. But as they had much time to spare and as their military training was neglected, the militia was disbanded at the middle of the Heian period.

kondenchi-kei shōen 墾田地系荘園 (reclaimed-land manors). Great estates during the late Nara period belonging to Buddhist monasteries and the aristocracy and resulting especially from the acquisition of reclaimed land. Besides the arbitrary appropriation by private persons of unreclaimed arable land, the domains were the result of various processes such as the granting of land by the emperor, the commendation of land by local territorial magnates, the enclosure of public land (KŌDEN), etc. The creation of such estates took place in the provinces around the capital and in the neighboring provinces. The management was generally carried out by the owners, who used their own tools, and by smaller tenant farmers (HANDEN NŌMIN). Territorial magnates functioned as local managers—that is, they were *shōchō* or administrators of tax-free manors (SHŌJI). They had years of experience and managed the estates with a firm hand but were subservient toward the main Buddhist temples and the aristocracy. The economic basis of the national structure under the system of the penal and administrative code (RITSURYŌ-SEI) suffered a hard blow when reclaimed-land manors became numerous and when it became a general practice to appropriate "office land" (SHIKIDEN), or land granted to officials, and "rank land" (IDEN). Another reason for economic collapse was the extent to which wasteland was reclaimed and the influx of land into the tax-free manors of officials. Financial bankruptcy of the imperial household necessarily led to the conferring of land on the emperor (CHOKUSHI-DEN) and to the reservation of tracts of land for the use of the imperial household or of dignitaries with rank *(kanden)*, as well as to the publicly managed field *(kueiden)*, the taxes of which were intended to help the provincial government (KOKUGA). This system of land tenure collapsed in the ninth century, but in the home provinces estates subsisted, though on a relatively smaller scale. The most powerful owner of private estates was Tōdai-ji temple, which in its more prosperous days is believed to have possessed an area of 3,460 *chōbu* (one *chōbu* equals 2.45 acres). All these manors are referred to as the manors of the initial period, or the period of the sudden rise of manorial estates.

konden-shiyū rei 墾田私有令 (reclaimed land ownership law). A law promulgated in 743 for the encouragement of reclaiming land. After the Taika Reform (646), the allotted land *(handen)* system demanded an increase of land, but the penal and administrative code in principle did not recognize private ownership in perpetuity. Consequently the cultivation of wasteland made no progress. However, in 723, the government issued the law known as SANZE-ISSHIN NO HŌ, through which newly reclaimed land became private property for three generations. Again in 743 perpetual ownership was recognized for court nobles, public officials, and common people. However, various conditions had to be fulfilled before the law could be applied, so that ownership was restricted. As a result, reclaimed land increased, but noblemen and monasteries tended to integrate it into their domains.

Kongōbu-ji 金剛峯寺. Central monastery of Kōya-san in Wakayama Prefecture and the headquarters of the Shingon sect of Buddhism. The origin of the monastery may be traced back to the year 816, when Kūkai (774–835) opened an instruction hall for the practice of meditation. First the main instruction hall was the Tō-ji of Kyōto, but from the middle of the Heian period, when Kūkai's religion was founded, Kōya-san gained in importance. Kōya-san educated many illustrious Buddhist priests and remained for a long time the center of the Shingon sect. Regents and advisers to the emperor as well as members of the imperial family became converts, and large manorial estates were offered to the monastery. At the end of the Heian period, practitioners of *nembutsu* asceticism, referred to as *Kōya-hijiri,* came from all parts of the country and gathered at Kōya-san. During the Sengoku period (close of the fifteenth to close of the sixteenth century), Kōya-san became very strong. With the powerful cooperation of its believers, it offered resistance to Nobunaga and Hideyoshi. Kōya-san stores such masterpieces as the paintings *Aka Fudō, Kōbō Daishi Eden, Nijūgo Bosatsu Raigōzu,* etc., as well as sculptural works and classical and ancient books. The structures Daimon, Kondō, and Mieidō are national treasures.

Konjaku Monogatari 今昔物語. A collection of tales in thirty-one volumes, late Heian period. Author and date of completion are unknown. About one thousand tales are divided into three parts—tales of India, tales of China, and tales of Japan. Each story begins with the words *ima wa mukashi*—that is, "once upon a time." Buddhist tales occupy a large part of the collection. Secular stories of Japan vividly describe the life of the common people. They are written in mixed Japanese-Chinese style and constitute rich material for knowledge of the ideas, sentiments, and customs at the end of the Heian era. As the stories make use of colloquial style, they are valuable for the study of the history of the native language.

Konjiki Yasha 金色夜叉. A literary work of the Meiji era. It is the best novel by Ozaki Kōyō (1867–1903) and is widely known. It appeared as a serial in *Yomiuri Shimbun,* but Ozaki died before he could complete the work.

Kōryū-ji 広隆寺. A temple associated with Shōtoku Taishi (573–621) and the oldest temple in Yamashiro Province. It is also called Hachioka-dera and is located in Hachioka, Uzumasa, Ukyō-ku, Kyōto. It seems that Hata no Kawakatsu, in gratitude for a Buddhist statue received from Shōtoku Taishi, built this temple in 622 for the prince. It flourished as the central temple of the Hata family. It was destroyed twice by fire but each time reconstructed. It stores many Buddhist masterpieces. Most famous is the statue Miroku Bosatsu Hanka Zō, which was made during the late Asuka period (552–645) or the Hakuhō period (645–710).

koseki 戸籍 (household registers). Household registers in ancient Japan, intended to control the allotment of land. With the Taika Reform (646), the law imposed the drawing up of population registers. The registers were actually compiled the same year, but the word *koseki* had already appeared in the *Chronicles of Emperor Sujin* (fifth century). From the year 646, household registers were to be compiled every six years, and this practice was continued until the early Heian period. The registers had to contain the total number of household members, their family relationship, the total area of land received, official ranks and positions, age, sickness, etc. But in early Heian times, in order to evade conscripted labor, a large number of women were included in the registers, and false registers began to appear.

kōshi 貢士 (Lower House officials in 1868). Legislative officials during the early Meiji era. In 1868, the bicameral assembly with an Upper House and a Lower House was established. *Kōshi* were the members of the Lower House. They were samurai appointed by the clan lord and represented the clan. Their term of office was not determined. Depending on their talent, these members could be summoned by the Council of State to serve the court. In May of the same year, the name *kōshi* was abolished, and the members of the Lower House served in the newly established public offices.

kōshin-kō 庚申講 (gatherings on the night of *kōshin*). Gatherings based on the belief that on the night of *kanoe-saru* (day of the monkey) the three insects called *sanshichū* (which live in the human body and know man's secret evil) stealthily leave the body of a sleeping person and ascend to heaven, where they report that particular person's crimes. The person dies. Following this Taoist belief, some people sit up all night, talking together or holding a banquet. This is called *kōshin-machi* or *kōshin-kō*. In some places people believe that from the character *saru* 申 a relation is born with the mountain god Sannō who used a *saru* (monkey) as a messenger. By association with the god Sarudahiko, *saru* was also believed to be something like Dōsojin, the guardian deity of travelers. But the characteristic feature of these gatherings is that, even today, though the deity is worshiped as the god of wealth or of agriculture, people worship by sitting up all night. According to popular belief, on the day of the monkey, men should keep away from women and abstain from marrying. There are places where the *kōshin-kō* have developed into financing agencies or serve as general social gatherings for rural communities (Kō).

Koshi-tsū 古史通. Historical study in four volumes of the age of the gods written by Arai Hakuseki (1657–1725). For this study Hakuseki consulted not only NIHON SHOKI but also KOJIKI, *Kujiki, Kogoshūi,* etc. He advocated that "the period of the gods" must be understood in the light of philology and was inclined toward a logical interpretation of mythological tales. He included many passages of *Kujihongi (Kujiki).* Though at times he simply took some myths for actual phenomena, as a rule his method of scrutinizing myths proves that he was far in advance of his time.

Kōshitsu Tempan 皇室典範 (the Imperial Household Law). Fundamental law laying down all matters concerning the imperial household. It was promulgated in 1889 together with the Imperial Constitution. These fundamental rules were supreme and added authority to the *tennō* system. With postwar changes, many rules have been amended.

kōshōgaku 考証学 (methodology of historical research). A school of Confucianism inaugurated during the middle of the Edo period. The school was influenced by Ch'ing China but also represented the positivist spirit which encouraged the study of the Chinese classics. Pioneers were Yamanoi Kanae (Yamanoi Konron, 1680–1728) and Yoshida Kōton (1745–98), who compared the Chinese classics with the original manuscripts. The school developed under Izawa Ranken (1776–1829), Kariya Ekisai (1775–1835), and Yashiro Hirokata (1758–1841). It studied not only the classics but also stone inscriptions, ideographs, phonology, and bibliography and applied its findings to history and geography. Many scholars of Japanese classics used the same methodology, for instance Tanikawa Kotosuga (1707–76), Ban Nobutomo (1773–1846), Ueda Akinari (1734–1809), and Iida Takesato (1827–1900). This scientific approach formed the basis of the acceptance of Western positivism during the Meiji era.

kōshoku tsuihō 公職追放 (purge from public service). Postwar occupational policy. In January 1946, General MacArthur promulgated purge directives excluding from public service all war collaborators. The purged included 1) those who took an active part in militarism and aggressive policy, 2) all ultranationalists and terrorist patriots as well as the members of their organizations, 3) all those who played an important role in the Imperial Rule Assistance Association, the Imperial Rule Assistance Political Rule Association, and the Japan Political Association. The purged included also those who used violence against antimilitarists and those who by speeches and action promoted militarism. When peace was to be concluded with Japan, the Supreme Commander for the Allied Powers put the Japanese government in charge of the purge.

Kōshū budō 甲州葡萄 (Kōshū grapes). Grapes grown in the northeastern mountain district of the Kōfu basin, Yamanashi Prefecture. According to tradition, Kōshū grapes were presented to Minamoto no Yoritomo (1148–99). Takeda Shingen (1521–73) encouraged the culture. This suggests that the Kōshū vine culture is centuries old. It is believed that grapevine trellises were already used in the Eiraku era (1558–70). The vine culture developed during the Edo period as various improvements were made. At the time of the restoration, Kōshū vineyards occupied an area of 200 *chōbu* (one *chōbu* equals 2.45 acres). During the Meiji era, European varieties were imported. Though the grapes were sometimes blighted, remedies as well as improvement of vine breeding were studied. In 1901, the Association of Kōshū Vine Culture was established. Later the amount of production increased as modern iron-wire trellises came into use and transportation facilities were improved. From about 1887, grape wine was made. Today Kōshū's production equals 80 percent of the national output.

Kōtai-ō hi 好太王碑 (memorial stone of King Kōtai). Large memorial stone discovered near the site of an early Kōkuri (a kingdom of Korea) stronghold on the upper waters of the Yalu River. The stone commemorates the distinguished services of King Kōtai or Kōkaido-ō, who was king of Kōkuri, enthroned in 391. The stone is now in T'ungkou, Liaoning Province, China. It mentions that Japan, as early as 391 (some say the year 414), invaded Korea. A valuable historical document, the text gives a faithful account of the social conditions of North Korea and of Korean-Japanese relations in ancient times.

kouta 小唄 (little songs). Generic term for folk songs or ballads. Beginning with the Muromachi period, these songs became popular. The words of many such songs have been collected in KANGINSHŪ. During the Momoyama period, songs known as RYŪTATSU-BUSHI (AZUCHI-MOMOYAMA BUNKA) were written, most of them extolling freedom from care. *Ryūtatsu-bushi,* sung to the accompaniment of the *shamisen,* became fashionable during the Edo period.

Kōzan-ji 高山寺 (Kōzan-ji temple). A Buddhist temple in Togano-o, Kyōto. The Buddhist priest Myōe (1173–1232) lived in Kōzan-ji. The temple became well known in the early Kamakura period, when it served as the instruction hall for the revival of the Kegon sect of Buddhism. The temple stores many treasures such as the painting CHŌJŪ GIGA ascribed to Toba Sōjō (1053–1140).

Kōzengokoku-ron 興禅護国論. A work in three volumes about the Rinzai doctrine written by Eisai (1141–1215), the founder of the Rinzai sect of Buddhism. It was completed in 1198. Eisai brought the Rinzai doctrine from Sung China and steadily spread the new religion. Envious of this success, the traditional sect of Enryaku-ji appealed to the court and tried to prohibit Eisai's preaching. Eisai therefore published this book, in which he explains the origin of Rinzai and the reasons why the religion is necessary for the nation, thus refuting the charges of traditional Buddhism.

kubunden 口分田 (mouth-share fields). The share of allotted field received by each farmer under the land-allotment system. The area of allotted field was two *tan* (one *tan* equals 0.245 acres) for each male of at least six years of age (whether he be a public service man, an official serf, or a slave working for the government); two-thirds of that amount for a female; one-third of that amount for the class of unfree people known as KENIN. The allotment was valid for six years and was revised every six years. The mouth-share field of an official serf and of slaves working for the government was tax-free. It was not permissible to sell or buy the share or to pawn or inherit it. The right to till the field was granted for only one generation. In case of death or desertion, the field was confiscated under official regulations.

Kudara Kannon 百済観音 (the statue of Kudara Kannon). A colored statue of Kanzeon Bosatsu carved in camphor wood during the Asuka period (552–

645). The statue is owned by the Kondō of Hōryū-ji. Its height is 209 centimeters. In this impressive work, the feeling of dignity is strengthened by the skillful carving of the shallow, regular curves of the drapery. The unusually tall figure gives a sense of security and reveals the unique technical skill of the artist. Its lotus pedestal and halo are the original ones. This precious masterpiece represents Asuka sculpture at its best.

kudatama 管玉 (tubular jewels). A personal ornament in olden times. *Kudatama* of both the Yayoi period (about 350 B.C. to A.D. 250) and of the period of the sepulchral mounds have been found. As the name explains, they were tubular jewels which, together with the curved jewels known as MAGATAMA, were used as necklaces or as wrist ornaments. Those of the Yayoi period are of finer workmanship than those of the mound period. They are also smaller and more numerous. Usually they were made of jasper.

kugatachi 盟神深湯 (the boiling-water ordeal). A test in primitive society to judge innocence or guilt. It was interpreted as a divine sentence. The suspect had to take pebbles or mud out of boiling water, to hold a red-hot axe in the palm of his hand, or to put his hand in a jar containing serpents. If hurt, he was pronounced guilty. The chapter "Ingyōki" of the NIHON SHOKI gives examples of this ordeal by boiling water. During the middle ages and the Edo period, the same method was used. It was called *yugishō,* and the suspect had to put his hand in boiling water. It was also used to settle disagreements such as border disputes among rural communities.

kugutsu 傀儡子 (puppets). Puppets used in shows during the Heian period and also the puppet players themselves. Puppet shows flourished from the latter part of the Heian period, when puppet players performed on the roadside at relay stations. They made the wooden puppets dance and displayed their swordsmanship and archery. In the middle ages, puppetry was the specialty of one class of people of Nishinomiya, Hyōgo Prefecture. From the Hirota-sha of Nishinomiya, it spread to Awaji and Tokushima. Later it was called *Awaji-ayatsuri.* At first only one man manipulated the puppets, but later many people were involved. Finally, puppet shows were linked up with JŌRURI ballads and were given in theaters, from which development the celebrated Bunraku theater emerged.

Kuji-kata O-sadamegaki 公事方御定書 (law code). A code of law compiled during the middle Edo period by the councilors of the shōgun (RŌJŪ) and by the three magistrates (EDO-MACHI BUGYŌ) on the orders of Tokugawa Yoshimune, the eighth shōgun. The first part includes eighty-one articles on various laws and ordinances; the second includes 103 articles on criminal law. This second part is also called O-sadamegaki Hyakkajō and constitutes the judicial norm of the day. The code was only for the information of the judges of the Supreme Court (Hyōjōsho) and the three magistrates, and only the prohibition clause was made public.

Kumano mōde 熊野詣 (Kumano pilgrimages). Pilgrimages to the three shrines of Kumano *(Kumano sanzan)* in Wakayama Prefecture. In the latter Heian period, the four cloistered emperors Shirakawa, Toba, Goshirakawa, and Gotoba made pilgrimages to the shrines at great expense. Pilgrimages of court nobles were also frequent. During the middle ages, the shrines became the main center of mountaineering asceticism (SHUGENDŌ). Warriors and common people made pilgrimages in increasing numbers, and the *o-shi* (who guided the pilgrims and gave them shelter) and *sendatsu* (guides) became very active. Kumano religious associations known as *Kumano-kō* were organized.

Kumaso 熊襲 (the Kumaso tribe). Ancient barbarian tribe that lived in southern Kyūshū and sometimes resisted the Yamato forces. According to KOJIKI and NIHON SHOKI, there were revolts of the Kumaso, and the court attempted to suppress the tribe. In the Asuka and Nara periods, the Hayato made their appearance in southern Kyūshū. It is thought that the Kumaso were related to the Hayato, and one theory holds that the Hayato and Kumaso were the same tribe which until the fourth or fifth century was called Kumaso. When its power was broken by Yamato Takeru no Mikoto and his son Emperor Chūai, the tribe was called Hayato. The Hayato were later used as gate guards in the imperial palace.

kumi-gashira 組頭 (assistant headmen of villages). Officials of rural communities during the Edo period. They assisted the village headman, the name master (MYŌSHU), and the general manager (KIMOIRI). There were two or three, sometimes even five or six, *kumi-gashira* in each village. They were chosen from among the village population. Depending on the village, they were known as *kumiai-gashira,* TOSHIYORI, and OSA-BYAKUSHŌ.

kumon 公文 (official documents). Documents of government offices during and after the Heian period; also the office which was in charge of the documents. The office was also called KUMONJO. From the middle of the Heian period, the name *kumon* was also given to official documents concerning temples and shrines, the household offices of regents and councilors and great noblemen, the manorial estates, and yearly taxes. The office in charge was the Kumonjo. Minamoto no Yoritomo (1148–99) established a Kumonjo in which he kept official documents concerning political administration. He considered it a place for deliberation and decisions. Before long, it became the office where important government affairs were discussed, and the name was changed to MANDOKORO, or Administrative Board of the central government.

Kumonjo 公文所 (Administrative Board). The Administrative Board of the central government of the KAMAKURA BAKUFU. It was established during the Heian period as the executive body of the rule of cloistered emperors (IN NO CHŌ) and noblemen, and for temples and shrines. In 1148, Minamoto no Yoritomo (1148–99) established a secretariat for general administration called Kumonjo. He appointed the *bettō* (director of the SAMURAI-DOKORO) Ōe no Hiromoto (1148–1225) chief secretary of the Kumonjo. Later the name Kumonjo was changed to MANDOKORO.

Kunai-shō 宮内省 (Department of the Imperial Household). 1) One of the eight ministries during the Nara and Heian periods. It was the Ministry of the Imperial Household and was originally called Miyanouchi Tsukasa. The Kunai-shō administered the registers of members of the imperial family, the supply and upkeep of clothing, the receipts of tax rice from the imperial rice lands *(kugoden),* the receipts of provincial tributes other than the prescribed taxes, etc. 2) A government office in charge of the affairs of the imperial household. It was established in 1869. As under the penal and administrative code system, this Kunai-shō was controlled by the Council of State (DAJŌKAN). The organization and official title corresponded to those of the Nara and Heian periods, but later the Kunai-shō underwent various reforms. It is presently known as the Kunai-chō 宮内庁.

kuni-ikki 国一揆 (provincial uprisings). Uprisings of name masters (MYŌ-SHU), local gentry (JI-SAMURAI), etc. These men were also known as *kokujin* (owners long settled and locally influential) and *kunishū.* Most famous is the uprising in Yamashiro Province in 1485–86. The *kokujin* resisted the forces of the constable Hatakeyama and thus achieved a measure of self-government. Well known too was the opposition between local gentry and great landowner constables (SHUGO DAIMYŌ). Because quite a number of peasants took part in the action of the *kokujin,* the uprisings became alarmingly powerful. Later, when their power was broken, the landowner constables vanished.

Kuni-kyō 恭仁京. The name of a capital in ancient Japan. There are various views as to the location of this capital. Probably the place was today's town of Kizu in Kyōto Prefecture. During the revolt of Fujiwara no Hirotsugu (?–740), Emperor Shōmu ordered the courtier Tachibana no Moroe (684–757) to construct Kuni-kyō on the banks of Izumi River (740). In 741, the capital was transferred, but the construction of the city made no progress. After the construction of the palace Ōmi-Shigaraki, the emperor discontinued the construction of Kuni-kyō. The transfer of the capital to Kuni-kyō was connected with the violent struggle between the Fujiwara and the Tachibana families.

kuni no miyatsuko 国造 (local chieftains). Local chieftains before the Taika Reform (646). Their origin lies in the development of an agricultural economy.

From the third to the fourth century, primitive society, which was loosely organized in various parts of the country, was gradually bound by subordinate relationship to the powerful Yamato clan. The Yamato court made the former chieftains govern their earlier territories. These chieftains were called *kuni no miyatsuko*. They were replaced at the time of the Taika Reform, when the ablest among these local nobles were made rural district administrators (GUN-JI), but the local authority of the *kuni no miyatsuko* was still in evidence. The name continued to exist, though the *kuni no miyatsuko* became wardens of local shrines. Later, they were absorbed into the organization of the manors.

kuniyaku 国役 (provincial taxes). Taxes imposed on the provinces. They were imposed during the Heian period to meet the deficit of the court's treasury resulting from the increase of manors and the repair of the imperial palace, dikes, riverbanks, and roads. The KAMAKURA BAKUFU followed this example and charged the provinces with corvées and payment of taxes in currency. During the Tokugawa period, payment in money was imposed to repair dikes and to improve rivers, to meet the travel expenses of Korean envoys and of participants in the Buddhist memorial services at Nikkō, to pay the building expenses for the imperial palace, etc. The taxes imposed on artisans in Edo and its outskirts were also called *kuniyaku*. Gradually *kuniyaku* were imposed simultaneously with taxes in money, and some were to be paid only in money.

Kuramae-fū 蔵前風 (FUDASASHI)

kuramono 蔵物 (storehouse deposits). The products accumulated by the clans in the storehouse of Ōsaka, Edo period. Though there were various products such as sugar, paper, indigo dyes, matting, etc., the most important was rice, which was then called *kuramai*. This rice was distinguished from that sold by merchants, which was referred to as *nayamai*. To administer the accounts and transactions, officials from among the clansmen were appointed, but from about the middle of the seventeenth century the administration was taken over by merchants. These merchants were called KURAMOTO. Many *kuramoto* were at the same time moneylenders (KAKEYA).

kuramoto 蔵元 (storehouse officials). Officials in charge of the accounts and pledges of moneylenders in the storehouses during the Edo period. Initially the offices were controlled by daimyō retainers, but later they were in the hands of wealthy moneylenders and merchants. These *kuramoto* also took custody of the proceeds from the pledges deposited in the storehouses and took charge of the finances of the daimyō. As they lent money at a usurious rate of interest, they amassed fortunes.

Kuratsukuri no Tori 鞍作鳥. Sculptor of Buddhist images, Asuka period

(552–645). He is the first known sculptor of Buddhist images in the history of Japan. He was the son of Kuratsukuri no Tasuna, who greatly contributed to the spread of Buddhism in Japan. He was also the descendant of Chinese who became naturalized Japanese. Much favored by the court, he was granted the rank of *taijin* (KAN'I JŪNIKAI NO SEI). One of his masterpieces, which is kept in the Kondō of Hōryū-ji, is the Shaka Nyorai, or Shaka Sanzon, made in 623. The influence of the art of the Chinese Northern Wei dynasty is visible, but the work also shows the particular features of Tori's style.

kurayaku 倉役 (pawnshop tax). Taxes imposed by the MUROMACHI BAKUFU on the wealth of moneylenders of the pawnshops known as DOSŌ or *tsuchi-kura*. The taxes were also referred to as *dosō-yaku* and were imposed to meet the financial deficit of the *bakufu*. In turn, the *bakufu* protected the pawnshops and money markets. As a result, the *dosō* flourished, but warriors and farmers who had to borrow money from them were reduced to destitution.

kura-yashiki 蔵屋敷 (transaction offices). Offices in Ōsaka, Edo, etc. for the handling of provincial products of daimyō, temples and shrines, etc., Edo period. The offices of Ōsaka were of great importance because this city enjoyed convenient water transportation and was linked with the Tosa and Edo canals. About the middle of the nineteenth century, there were 124 *kura-yashiki* in Ōsaka. The officials were the ordinary *kurayakunin* or their deputies, KURAMOTO, moneylenders (KAKEYA), or order takers called *goyōkiki*, etc. *Kurayakunin* were clan officials. Lower officials from deputies down were merchants. The *kura-yashiki* played an important role in meeting the clans' financial deficit, but the merchants gradually assumed the real power.

Kuroudo-dokoro 蔵人所 (Bureau of Archivists). An extralegal office established in 810 for the custody of confidential papers in the imperial palace. At the time of the Kusuko affair (KUSUKO NO RAN), Emperor Saga ordered the courtier Fujiwara no Fuyutsugu (775–826) and Kose no Notari (748–816) to take care of the secret matters of the court. This was the origin of the Kuroudo-dokoro. Its function was of the highest importance, as the officers had knowledge of the court's secrets, issued imperial decrees, informed the throne of memorials, and participated in the emperor's everyday routine affairs. The Kuroudo-dokoro had more prestige than the other official bureaus. Its nature and the extent of its authority underwent changes, but the office continued to exist until the Meiji Restoration.

kusemai 曲舞 (recitative dance). A dance of the middle ages performed to the accompaniment of the beating of a drum and with a simple recitative. It is also simply called *mai*. It derives from the medieval female dancers in white robes, known as *shirabyōshi*, and seems to have been performed with the SARUGAKU at the end of the Kamakura period. Kan'ami (1334–85) made his Nō (NŌGAKU) plays popular by incorporating elements of *kusemai*. Today's Nō songs, as far as their recitative part is concerned, are influenced by *kusemai*. The actors of *kusemai* formed an association like those of Sarugaku, and they often performed to raise funds for pious purposes. The dance *kōwaka-mai,* inaugurated by Momonoi Kōwakamaru (1403–80), was much favored by Nobunaga and Ieyasu. It was a representative *kusemai* dance.

kussō 屈葬 (crouched inhumation). A way of burying in primitive society which was also known as *sonsō*. The legs were bent at the joints of the knees and the hips. Often corpses were buried in very shallow earth, and sometimes the head was covered with an earthen vessel, and a stone was placed on the chest. This method of burying was also in use in neolithic Europe. Crouched inhumation exists even today in less civilized societies.

Kusuko no ran 薬子の乱 (the plot of Kusuko). Court lady Fujiwara no Kusuko (?–810), with the help of her elder brother Nakanari (774–810), plotted to have ex-Emperor Heizei (774–824) resume the throne so that she might be empress and to move the capital from HEIJŌ-KYŌ to Heian. She thereby caused the suicide of Heizei's younger brother, Prince Iyo, whom she had falsely accused. Emperor Heizei, who had ceded the throne, moved to Heijō-kyō, but Kusuko, linking Heian with her former prestige, planned to re-enthrone Heizei and to change the place of the capital. Her plans were frustrated, and in 810 Emperor Saga (786–842) crushed Kusuko and her fellow conspirators. Kusuko committed suicide, and Nakanari was put to death.

Kutani-yaki 九谷焼 (Kutani ware). Porcelain produced in Kanazawa City and in the districts of Enuma and Nomi. Important industrial art of Ishikawa Prefecture. In the early seventeenth century, Maeda Toshiharu (1617–60), the founder of the Daishōji clan, encouraged industrial production in general, but the origin of Kutani porcelain is not known. The technique was perhaps introduced from Hizen or from Ming China. During the Genroku era (1688–1703), or from the end of the seventeenth century, production was temporarily discontinued, but in 1806 the ceramist Aoki Mokubei (1767–1833) was invited from Kyōto at the request of the town council of Kanazawa. Aoki opened a ceramic kiln at Kasugayama (the Kasugayama pottery) in Kanazawa, and Kutani ware, which became known as Minzan-yaki, again flourished. At about the same time Wakasugi-yaki was manufactured in the Nomi district and included articles of practical utility. Then the Yoshidaya kiln was opened on the old site of Kutani. When it was moved to Yamashiro, its name was changed to the Miyamotoya pottery. The ceramist Iidaya Hachirō-emon (1804–52) of the Miyamotoya pottery originated gold and scarlet painting on pottery. This style of painting became the characteristic feature of Kutani porcelain.

Kuwana 桑名. A city in the northeast of Ise Province (Mie Prefecture). Facing the bay of Ise, it was from olden times an important port of navigation and developed into an industrial center. In 1520, it became a free city with a self-governing body. It was called Jūrakunotsu. During the Edo period, it was known as the castle town of the Kuwana clan. Being a post station on the Tōkaidō highway, it flourished as a distributing center for timber and rice.

kuwa-yoboro 钁丁 (plowmen). Able-bodied men (*yoboro* 丁) requisitioned in olden times to plow the land of the imperial estates (MIYAKE). When the *kuwa-yoboro* belonged to relatively wealthy families as farm hands, they were referred to as *ta-be*.

kyaku 格 (administrative regulations). Legislation of the Nara and Heian periods. Among the penal codes *(ritsu)* and administrative codes *(ryō)* established after the Taika Reform (646), many were modeled after those of T'ang China but without having assimilated that legislation. Society changed, and already in the early Nara period several laws were out of touch with the actual situation. The miscellaneous body of regulations known as *kyaku* overcame these legislative deficiencies and corrected shortcomings. To become operative, the *kyaku* were promulgated when called for. The Kōnin, Jōgan, and Engi *kyaku* were arranged and compiled in the early Heian period. They were edited in thirty volumes, fifteen of which are extant. The work is called RUIJŪ SANDAI-KYAKU and is classified according to subject. It is the main source of our knowledge concerning the *kyaku* and the political changes during the Nara and Heian periods.

Kyōbu-shō 教部省 (Board of Religious Instruction). A body designed to spread the national cult in early Meiji years. After the restoration, the influence of revived Shintō was strongly felt. In 1872, the government established the Board of Religious Instruction for the purpose of uniting Shintō, Buddhism, and other religions, and of carrying out the movement for ethical education. Strict control exercised by the government over the ideology and religious thought of the people failed to bring practical results as far as freedom of religion and the struggle among religious bodies were concerned. Consequently, the board was dissolved in 1877.

Kyōgen 狂言 (farcical pieces). A kind of farcical performance. The comical and mimetic dances known as SARUGAKU, after they had incorporated elements of *yūgen* (mysterious beauty), rose to the level of Nō plays (NŌGAKU). Kyōgen were farcical pieces and were often performed together with Nō dramas. The characters included daimyō as well as merchants and farmers. The performance was realistic, and the dialogue used was in the colloquial language of the day. Superiors were satirized, and the Kyōgen were popular. Whereas Nō performances were for the nobility, Kyōgen performances were for the common people. Today the Kyōgen serve as interludes between the Nō plays in a standard program.

Kyōgyōshinshō 教行信証. The main work of Shinran (1173–1262), considered to be the fundamental canon of the JŌDO SHIN-SHŪ religion. It explains salvation through the mercy of Amida Buddha (*tariki-hongan* 他力本願) as professed by Shinran. The work is believed to have been completed in 1247. It consists of two volumes.

kyōha Shintō 教派神道 (denominational Shintō). Thirteen Shintō sects officially recognized as religions in 1945 before the end of the Pacific War. They are Shintō Dai-kyō, Kurozumi-kyō, Shūsei-ha, Taisha-kyō, Fusō-kyō, Jikkō-kyō, Taisei-kyō, Shinshū-kyō, Mitake-kyō, Shinri-kyō, Misogi-kyō, Konkō-kyō, and Tenri-kyō. Among these sects some are old ones such as Fusō-kyō, which originated during the period of civil war (SENGOKU JIDAI) when Hasegawa Kakugyō (1541–1646) founded the associations of Shintō training through austerities (these associations were known as *Fuji-kō*), and Kurozumi-kyō, which began during the Bunka era (1804–18). Tenri-kyō and Konkō-kyō are still flourishing. Usually the sects have a founder, scriptures, and religious communities or churches. As opposed to Shrine Shintō, Shintō sects did not receive national protection. They were based on personal religious experience and developed as peculiar popular religions. After the Pacific War, taking advantage of the social upheaval, many dubious new sects made their appearance but were not officially recognized.

Kyōhō no kaikaku 享保の改革 (reform of the Kyōhō era). A reform carried out by the eighth Tokugawa shōgun, Yoshimune (1684–1751), about the middle of the Edo period. The purpose was to re-establish feudal control, which had suffered by the rapid development of a currency economy since the Genroku era (1688–1704). This development resulted in the weakening of government finances, the extravagance as well as destitution of the warriors, the growing influence of merchants, the impoverishment of rural communities, and frequent peasants' uprisings. Rejecting Arai Hakuseki's civil administration theory, Yoshimune decided that everything should be restored to the condition of Ieyasu's earlier administrative system. Consequently, he introduced numerous measures of frugality, made the earlier taxes heavier, adopted a system of taxes known as AGEMAI, fostered development of newly reclaimed rice fields and production industry, enacted the code KUJI-KATA O-SADAMEGAKI, and encouraged the spread of education through temple schools (TERAKOYA). For the purpose of learning public opinion, he inaugurated a system of complaint boxes (MEYASU-BAKO). Being progressive, Yoshimune relaxed the interdiction upon Western learning, thus permitting the development of *rangaku* (YŌGAKU). The re-establishment of control was fairly successful, and Yoshimune was considered the wise ruler of the restoration. However, the reform, which served as a model for the later Kansei and Tempō reforms, had limitations. The masses grew more and more opposed to the feudal system, and riots broke out in Edo as well as in other places. When crops failed, the riots became more violent.

Kyōiku Chokugo 教育勅語 (Imperial Rescript on Education). An imperial rescript promulgated in 1890. It stressed nationalism and fostered ultranationalism as a reaction against Europeanization. A modern system of school education having been set up, more serious consideration was given to feudal moral education. Since the rescript was an expression of traditional Confucian morality, loyalty and filial piety were stressed. Aimed at the strengthening of tennoism, this national education policy, which was based on the feudal system, was sacred and for fifty years constituted the essence of the spiritual life of the nation. It was abolished by the National Diet in 1948.

Kyōiku Kihonhō 教育基本法 (Fundamental Law on Education). Postwar legislation on education. Enacted in 1947 during the first National Diet, it replaced the Imperial Rescript on Education (KYŌIKU CHOKUGO). Based on the fundamental principles of democracy and pacifism, the new law fosters equal educational opportunities and social education.

kyōka 狂歌 (comic *waka* poems). Popular literary art which flourished during the Edo period and was patterned along the lines of *tanka* poetry. It was an outgrowth of the work of haiku (HAIKAI) poets during the late Muromachi period and reached its climax in the second half of the eighteenth century. The poems, containing witticisms *(share)* and jokes *(odoke),* satirized the society of the time and provided a means for oppressed townspeople to give vent to their dissatisfaction. Representative authors were Yomo no Akara (Ōta Nampo, 1749–1823), Yadoya no Meshimori (Ishikawa Masamochi, 1743–1830), Hamabe no Kurohito (1717–90), Chie no Naishi (1744–1807), and Shikatsube no Magao (1753–1829).

Kyokutō Iin-kai 極東委員会 (Far Eastern Commission). An organ for the occupation policy of postwar Japan. The Far Eastern Commission was created on December 27, 1945, and was actually organized on February 26, 1946. The foreign ministers of the United States, the United Kingdom, and the U.S.S.R. participated in its creation. Based on the Potsdam Declaration and the instrument of surrender, the Far Eastern Commission was the supreme authority of Allied policy formulation. It was composed of representatives of the eleven powers at war with Japan, and its headquarters was in Washington. Decisions of policy were made by the Supreme Commander for the Allied Powers through the government of the United States.

Kyokutō Kokusai Gunji Saiban 極東国際軍事裁判 (International Military

Tribunal for the Far East). Postwar tribunal for war crimes. After Japan's surrender, the Allied Powers, aiming at the extermination of the Japanese military clique and authorized by the Potsdam Declaration, tried the war criminals. The court which tried the Class A criminals was called the Tōkyō Tribunal. It was similar to the Nuremberg Tribunal for the German Class A war criminals. On the order of Supreme Commander MacArthur, the tribunal was composed of representatives of the eleven nations at war with Japan, including the United States, the United Kingdom, Soviet Russia, China, France, and Australia. Charges of crimes against peace and humanity, murder, and atrocities were entered against the criminals. The hearings began in May 1946, the sentences were passed in November 1948, and the executions took place in December 1948. The presiding judge was Sir William Webb, an Australian, and the chief public procurator was Joseph B. Keenan, an American. Among the accused were Tōjō Hideki, Hirota Kōki, and Hiranuma Kiichirō.

kyōshiki 京職 (metropolitan office). The original reading of the characters 京職 is *misato no tsukasa*. Under the penal and administrative code system, this office was divided into the left city office *(sakyōshiki)* and the right city office *(ukyōshiki)*. Each office took charge of registers of houses, labor and taxes, land and dwellings, suits, trade, roads, etc. In NIHON SHOKI the name *sau-kyō-shiki* is mentioned, but the date of the establishment of the office is uncertain. According to the Taihō Code (promulgated in 702), the organization of the metropolitan office was already completed. But when the KEBIISHI made their appearance, the authority of the *kyōshiki* was taken over by the *kebiishi*, and the metropolitan office became a mere name.

Kyōto shoshidai 京都所司代 (BAKUFU representative in Kyōto). The name of an office of the EDO BAKUFU. The word indicates a representative and was borrowed from *shoshi,* which was an office of the MUROMACHI BAKUFU. This representative protected the imperial household but also supervised the court nobles and the daimyō of the western provinces and controlled the *bakufu* officials who served in the capital. After the battle of Sekigahara, Okudaira Nobumasa (1555–1615), Itakura Katsushige (1545–1624), and his son Shige-mune (1586–1656) were appointed *bakufu* representatives in Kyōto. For generations the daimyō hereditarily held this position and were made councilors to the shōgun (RŌJŪ). In 1862, when the office to safeguard Kyōto (KYŌTO SHUGO-SHOKU) was created, the *Kyōto shoshidai* fell under the jurisdiction of this office.

Kyōto shugo-shoku 京都守護職 (office to safeguard Kyōto). The office of military commissioner of Kyōto at the end of the Edo period. Following the antiforeign movement, the situation in Kyōto had become critical. By 1862, the office to safeguard Kyōto had temporarily been created, and its authority even superseded that of the office of governor of Kyōto or the office of the BAKUFU representative in Kyōto (KYŌTO SHOSHIDAI). It was the duty of the officials to guard the imperial household and to keep control over the free samurai. The group of RŌNIN skilled in military arts and known as SHINSEN-GUMI belonged to the office to safeguard Kyōto. The lord of Aizu, Matsudaira Katamori (1836–93), appointed to this office, was temporarily replaced by the lord of Fukui, Matsudaira Yoshinaga (1829–90).

Kyūkakoku Jōyaku 九ヶ国条約 (the Nine-Power Treaty). International agreement concluded during the Taishō era. In 1922, the agreement was concluded in Washington between the United States, Belgium, Great Britain, China, France, Italy, Japan, Holland, and Portugal. Four principles concerning China were adopted: independence of China, unification of the Chinese government, equal opportunity, and the refraining from creating special interests harmful to other countries. Following this agreement, Japan withdrew from the Shantung Peninsula.

kyūrigaku 究理学. The name given to Western astronomy and physics during the Edo period. In this sense, the word first appeared in 1792 in a work translated by Motoki Yoshihide and entitled *Taiyō Kyūri Ryōkai-setsu*. The work *Kyūritsū* by Hoashi Banri (1778–1852) is a compilation of physical knowledge. At the end of the Edo period, some scholars such as Sakuma Shōzan (1811–64) studied *kyūrigaku*. The word *kyūri* is borrowed from Chu Hsi Confucianism.

Kyūshū tandai 九州探題 (commissioner of Kyūshū). An office established by the Kamakura and Muromachi BAKUFU for the administration of Kyūshū. The Hōjō clan created this office for protection against the Mongol invasions and for control of household retainers. The office was abolished during the Kemmu Restoration. Likewise, the MUROMACHI BAKUFU established the office of commissioner of Hakata and controlled the clans of Kyūshū. This office was opposed to those who sided with the Southern dynasty. Later it declined and was finally abolished by Hideyoshi.

L

London Kaigi ロンドン会議 (the London Conference). Third disarmament conference following World War I. It was held in London in 1930. Japan's chief delegate was Wakatsuki Reijirō (1866–1949). The second disarmament conference had taken place in Geneva. The London Conference debated the limitation of the number of cruisers. The United States, Britain, and Japan agreed on a ten-ten-seven ratio.

Luzon (RUSON)

M

mabiki 間引. Abortion and infanticide. The word, which means "the thinning of a row of plants," was especially used during the Edo period. *Mabiki* was practiced because impoverishment made it impossible for the peasants to support children. Other terms were *modosu* and *kaesu,* which mean "to send back." In some places female infants were "sent to gather sagebrush" *(yomogitsumi ni yaru),* and male infants were "sent to the mountain to play" *(yama e asobi ni yaru).* The BAKUFU as well as the clans and the intellectual class denounced the practice, but the root of the evil was the unbearable exploitation of the farmers by feudal rulers, and the evil itself could not be eradicated. It is thought that *mabiki* is the reason why the population did not increase during the Edo period.

machi bugyō 町奉行 (municipal administrators). The officials in charge of town administration during the Edo period. The administration office of Edo was the most important, though town administrators were also appointed in Ōsaka, Shizuoka, Nara, Nikkō, and Nagasaki. The *machi bugyō* was one of the three magistrates, the other two being the BAKUFU finance administrator (KANJŌ BUGYŌ) and the administrator of temples and shrines (JISHA BUGYŌ).

machi yakunin 町役人 (self-government town officials). Officials conducting the self-government of the townspeople during the Edo period. The officials were elected from among the townspeople, and the self-government was under strict surveillance of the municipal administrator (MACHI BUGYŌ). The authority of these officials was limited, as was that of the village officials (MURA YAKUNIN). The officials were either elders *(machi-doshiyori),* name masters *(machi-myōshu),* or those who alternately for one month attended to the business of the merchants *(tsuki-gyōji).*

magatama 勾玉 (curved jewels). Ornaments of prehistoric Japan. They are made of a great variety of materials, such as jade, jasper, etc. They are curved in various degrees, and each one has a hole in one end. In the early Yayoi period (the Yayoi period extends from about 350 B.C. to A.D. 250) it became the custom to make *magatama* of jade.

makie 蒔絵 (gold lacquer). Gold-decorated lacquer ware. Like mother-of-pearl *(raden)* work, *makie* is a technique peculiar to Japan which spread overseas. A rough sketch was first made in the wet lacquer, and gold dust was sprinkled on. After drying, the piece was polished. There are various kinds of *makie,* such as *hira-makie,* in which the sketch is very lightly drawn; *taka-makie* or gold lacquer in relief, in which mixed lacquer is used so as to mark out the design; and *heijin,* in which the surface is scraped until the gold dust appears.

The technique was known from the early Heian period but was greatly improved during the Kamakura and Muromachi periods and reached its climax during the Momoyama period. The *makie* of the Edo period became an exquisite art, one of its pioneers being Hon'ami Kōetsu (1558–1637). After Hon'ami, *makie* became stereotyped, but the art was revived during the Meiji period and is still flourishing today.

Makura no Sōshi 枕草子. Collection of essays written by Sei Shōnagon (circa 1000) and completed after 1020. The contents are divided into miscellaneous descriptions, a diary, and stray notes. The sensitive observation, acute perception, and keen wit of the authoress are apparent everywhere. The work is linked with the aristocratic class and shows only contempt for the lower classes or common people. It is a classic and is valuable because the authoress herself, attracted to the aesthetic aspect of court life, vividly describes court society in a period of degeneration.

mameita-gin 豆板銀 (silver currency). Silver currency of the Edo period. It was a currency by weight. Depending on its form, it was called *kotsubu-gin* and *kodama-gin*. Its weight was from one to ten *momme* (one *momme* equals 3.75 grams). It was used as a supplementary coin to the larger CHŌGIN.

Mandokoro 政所 (Administrative Board of the central government). An office during the Heian period for the household administration of princes and nobles. During the Kamakura period, Minamoto no Yoritomo (1148–99) set up the KUMONJO for the administration of the general affairs of the BAKUFU. In 1191, Yoritomo became the military ruler of the nation, and the Kumonjo was changed to Mandokoro. The first director of the Administrative Board *(bettō)* was Ōe no Hiromoto (1148–1225), who was succeeded by Hōjō Tokimasa (1138–1215), and thereafter the office was held by the members of the Hōjō family. A Mandokoro for the administration of the general affairs of state was also established by the MUROMACHI BAKUFU, but it did not have the same importance as that of the Kamakura period.

Manju-ji 万寿寺. A temple in Kyōto of the Rinzai sect of Buddhism. In 1097, the cloistered emperor Shirakawa (1053–1129) built the Rokujō Midō. In 1258, the temple was called Manju Zen-ji. After the Namboku period (1336–92) it became the fifth of the Kyōto Five Monasteries (Kyōto GOZAN). Now it is the main building *(tatchū)* of Tōfuku-ji in Kyōto.

Manshū jihen 満州事変 (the Manchurian incident). An aggressive war during the Shōwa era. Following the world crisis of 1929, the great powers strengthened their bloc economy. The Japanese overseas market collapsed, and only China was left as the last potential market. At the same time China tried hard to recover her sovereign rights, and a conflict, due to the stiffening Japanese attitude toward Manchuria, was inevitable. The anti-Japanese movement grew in violence, and the Japanese militarists planned a settlement by force. On September 18, 1931, on the pretext that the Chinese had blown up the Manchurian railway at Liut'iaokou, the Japanese began military operations. The following year, the Shanghai incident (SHANGHAI JIHEN) took place. Japan occupied the whole of Manchuria and established it as the state of MANSHŪ-KOKU. Owing to economic antagonism between the United States and Great Britain and Soviet Russia's being in the process of building up her economy, the Western powers confined themselves to launching a protest based on moral justice. The temporary success of the Manchurian incident worsened Japanese difficulties at home, for the war spirit was waning and internationally Japan stood alone. Furthermore, anti-Japanese feeling was at its peak. All this led to the strengthening of Japanese fascism and to the Sino-Japanese and Pacific wars.

Manshūkoku 満州国 (Manchoukuo). A so-called independent state created out of Manchuria by the Japanese militarists during the Shōwa era. When the Manchurian incident (MANSHŪ JIHEN) took place, Japanese army circles established under their own control an independent government for the northeastern provinces. In 1932, they summoned the provincial governors of these four provinces and declared the establishment of an independent state. They set up the last emperor of the Ch'ing dynasty, P'u-i (in Japanese, Fugi), as ruler of the so-called Manchurian empire. Japan had affixed her seal to the Manchuria-Japan protocol, recognizing the independence of Manchoukuo, but the general in command of the Kwantung army was also ambassador to Manchuria and controlled all matters. The entire administrative work was carried out by Japanese nationals, and independence existed only in name. It was decided that the Japanese army should be stationed permanently in Manchuria and that the country should become a war plant of the Japanese military clique. The main interests were the development of the Manchurian railway, the Central Bank of Manchuria, and Manchurian heavy industry. Furthermore, to help solve home problems, one million Japanese nationals were persuaded to emigrate to Manchuria. Japanese monopoly of rice, cotton, etc. resulted in the destitution of Chinese farmers. The Concordia Association, known as Kyōwa-kai (in Chinese, Hsieh-ho Hui), controlled the life of the people. All newspapers and information were controlled by the Association for Public Information (Kōhō Kyōkai). Manchoukuo was a product of the aggressive policy of the Japanese militarists. It ceased to exist with the surrender of Japan in 1945.

Man'yō Daishōki 万葉代匠記. A commentary on MAN'YŌSHŪ in fifty-four volumes written by the Buddhist priest Keichū (1640–1701). The great work was begun in 1683 in compliance with the request of Tokugawa Mitsukuni (1628–1700), the founder of the Mito clan. In 1690, the second revision was completed. Later Keichū added several supplements. His commentary is based on scientific studies and is original. It not only marks an epoch in the study of the *Man'yōshū* but also is a pioneer work in the field of the study of the classics.

Man'yōshū 万葉集. An anthology of poems in twenty volumes, Nara period. It contains about 4,500 poems and is classified into 265 long epic songs, 4,000 *tanka* (thirty-one-syllable verse), sixty-two poems in the 5-7-7 5-7-7 form known as SEDŌKA, and one poem in the 5-7-5 7-7-7 form known as *busso-kuseki*. The names of the compilers and the year of completion of the anthology are not known. Of all the poems represented in the anthology, those of Ōtomo no Yakamochi (?–785) are found in the greatest number. It is believed that the anthology was completed around 759 and that subsequent improvements were made. The poets belong to all classes of society from the Asuka (552–645) to the late Nara period (710–84). The authors of about half of the poems are not known. The places which are extolled in the poetry are mainly the home provinces, but other parts of the country are also represented. The literature of popular songs orally transmitted developed into a literature of individual writings, and many poems of the *Man'yōshū* illustrate this literary development. The name *Man'yōshū* (Collection of Ten Thousand Leaves) implies that the anthology is to be transmitted to countless generations.

mappō-shisō 末法思想 (the doctrine of the latter period of the law). The idea that Buddha's teaching (law) would degenerate. It was particularly strong during the eleventh and twelfth centuries. According to Buddhism, the law goes through three periods. The first period is that of the right law or *shōbō*, during which, after Buddha's death, teaching, practice, and realization carried out according to the doctrine will result in the fruit of enlightenment *(shōka)*. The second period is that of the semblance of the law or *zōbō*, in which only teaching and exterior manifestations exist, but without ascetic practices or fruit of enlightenment. The third period is that of the end of the law or *mappō*, in which only the doctrine remains. There are many views concerning the duration of the three periods. In China, during the Sui (589–618) and T'ang (618–906) dynasties, many people felt that their own time accorded with the *mappō* time. In Japan, it was generally thought that two thousand years after the death of Buddha, or 1051, corresponded with the latter period of the law. This belief resulted not only from numerical calculation but also from the actual circumstances, which corresponded with the Buddhist description of conditions during the latter days. From the middle to the end of the Heian period, the bonzes were degenerate, and, following the Hōgen insurrection (HŌGEN NO RAN), political confusion grew. Besides, famine and many natural calamities of the time seemed to fit the description. Salvation from a world of despair and instability, from grief and anxiety, was promised by the Jōdo religion (JŌDO-SHŪ), which preached the invocation of the name of Amida *(nembutsu)* and rebirth in Amida's paradise.

Maria Kannon マリア観音. Statues of the Blessed Virgin revered by the Christians during the Edo period. To escape from severe inspection by the BAKUFU, statues and images of the Blessed Virgin were made in the form of a Kannon. Some of these images represented Kannon holding a child in her arms.

Maria Luz jiken マリヤルーズ事件 (incident of the *Maria Luz*). An incident which took place in the early Meiji years and resulted in the freeing of Chinese coolies. In 1872, a vessel from Peru, the *Maria Luz,* with 225 Chinese coolies on board who had been bought from traffickers of Ch'ing China, anchored in Yokohama harbor. Many coolies, unable to bear the maltreatment, escaped and asked for help from an English warship. The English minister to Japan appealed to the Japanese foreign minister. The result was that the Japanese authorities freed all the coolies and sent them back to China. But, excepting the British consul, all other consuls protested against Japan because the regulations of the concessions had been disregarded, and Peru demanded indemnification for damages. Japan requested the arbitration of the Russian tsar. In 1875, Japan's contention was sanctioned, and the matter was dropped. But Japan keenly felt the weakness of the treaties. An indirect result of the incident was that, for humane reasons, many licensed prostitutes in Japan were set free.

Masukagami 増鏡. A historical work in seventeen volumes of the Namboku period (1336–92). Of uncertain authorship, it is generally attributed to Nijō Yoshimoto (1320–88). The work belongs to the *kagami* class and describes in particular the Jōkyū uprising (JŌKYŪ NO HEN) and the Genkō uprising (GENKŌ NO HEN). It relates chronologically the events from the birth of Emperor Gotoba in 1180 to the return to Kyōto of Emperor Godaigo in 1333. It also describes the opposition between the shogunate and the imperial court. It deplores the gradual disregard for the imperial court and court nobles. Unlike works in the mixed Sino-Japanese style which was then in use, *Masukagami* uses a pseudo-classical style. The work recalls the old days and resembles the writings of courtiers.

Matsumae bugyō 松前奉行 (administrator of Matsumae). One of the magistrates of the faraway provinces during the late Edo period. As a result of Russian pressure, the BAKUFU decided to directly control eastern Hokkaidō. In 1802, the post of administrator of Ezo was established. It was later called *Hakodate bugyō.* In 1807, the territory of the Matsumae clan, western Hokkaidō, was placed under government administration, and an administrative office *(bugyōsho)* was established in Matsumae. Though the office was later abolished, it was again created following the conclusion of the Kanagawa Treaty (KANAGAWA JŌYAKU), and Ezo once more fell under direct government control. In 1864, a *bugyōsho* was established on the site of the Goryōkaku in Hakodate City (HAKODATE).

Meiji Ishin 明治維新 (the Meiji Restoration). A political revolution which resulted in the abolition of the EDO BAKUFU and the establishment of a new form of government. It marked a step toward civil administration in a united country. Various causes brought about the reform. Production based on the capitalist system was already budding in rural communities, and the southwestern clans had already adopted this new system of production industry. On the international scene, capitalist Europe and the United States pressed Japan to become a peaceful market for their own commercial products. Absolutism, considered to be the highest form of feudalism, had been tried by the Tokugawa clan, but, following the misrule of the *bakufu* and the intensification of the loyalist movement, the reins of government were restored to the emperor. The government of the *bakufu* ceased to exist, the imperial court became the center of the new administration, and the leading authority was in the hands of the Satsuma and Chōshū clans. The battles won at Toba and Fushimi in 1868 by the Satsuma and Chōshū clans enabled the new government to rule over the territory of the Tokugawa clan. The new government was a clan government headed by the great western clans of Satsuma, Chōshū, Hizen, and Tosa and aimed at imperial absolutism. It carried out a policy of industrial enterprise and of free national production and brought about the abolition of the clans and establishment of prefectures. It announced freedom of dealing in and securing real estate, freedom of vocational choice and of betrothal (irrespective of social rank), and tried to do away with all feudal remnants. It dissolved the military class by granting it hereditary stipends (CHITSUROKU SHOBUN) and enforced military service, which marked the end of the ex-military class. However, a remnant of feudalism was the landlord system, which burdened the farmers with obligations resulting from tax revision. The emancipation of farmers was not carried through. A semifeudal influence was still strongly felt in the capitalist development and the polity of modern Japan.

Meiroku-sha 明六社 (Meiji Six Society). A cultural organization in the early Meiji years and the first Japanese learned society. It was established in 1873 upon the advice of Mori Arinori (1847–89), who had just returned from the United States. Leading men of letters such as Tsuda Mamichi, Katō Hiroyuki, Nishi Amane, Fukuzawa Yukichi, Nakamura Keiu, Kanda Naibu, and Mitsukuri Rinshō encouraged Western studies and enlightened the people through lectures and by issuing the journal *Meiroku Zasshi*.

Meitoku no ran 明徳の乱 (the Meitoku revolt). A revolt started by the warrior Yamana Ujikiyo (?–1391) during the Muromachi period. The MURO-MACHI BAKUFU made a poor showing under the pressure of constables who had become great landowners (SHUGO DAIMYŌ). Shōgun Ashikaga Yoshimitsu (1358–1408), with the help of his deputy Hosokawa Yoriyuki (1329–92), decided to subdue the constables. Yamana was concurrently constable of eleven provinces and controlled one-sixth of the whole country. He was therefore called *rokubun-no-ichi dono*. He disregarded the *bakufu's* orders and revolted but was put down by Yoshimitsu in 1391. In 1399, Yoshimitsu defeated Ōuchi Yoshihiro (1355–99) in what is known as the Ōei revolt (ŌEI NO RAN).

metsuke 目付 (censors). Name of officials during the Edo period. They already existed in the early Muromachi period. As the name explains, the *metsuke* were spies and furnished secret information. But during the Edo period they were agents of the shōgun's councilors (RŌJŪ). The head of censors (*ōmetsuke*) was in charge of the surveillance of the vassals' conduct. The *metsuke* wielded great authority, as they informed the junior elders (WAKA-DOSHIYORI) on the conduct of the bannermen (HATAMOTO) and household retainers (GO-KENIN).

meyasu-bako 目安箱 (complaint boxes). Complaint boxes put up by the eighth shōgun, Tokugawa Yoshimune (1684–1751), in order to collect direct petitions and to obtain opinions concerning his political policies. The boxes were affixed in front of the Supreme Court (Hyōjōsho) on the second, eleventh, and twenty-first of each month. The complaints of the RŌNIN Yamashita Kōnai have remained famous because they delivered an attack on the evils of the times.

Mikkyō 密教 (Esoteric Buddhism). A sect of Buddhism in India, China, and Japan. The sutras on which the sect was based were the Dainichi and the Kongōchō. Mikkyō has the characteristic features of magic and of symbolic religions and has taken in heterodox elements. It is believed that it adopted talismanic devices in order to appeal to the people. During the ninth century, Kūkai (774–835), upon his return from China, spread the doctrine in Japan. Occult practices were further stressed by Enchin (814–91) and Ennin (794–868). The religion was called Tō-mitsu in contrast to Taimitsu, which was Tendai Esoteric Buddhism as explained by the Hiei-zan monastery. In a larger sense, Mikkyō includes all religions which do not explain the occult meanings of their doctrine and ceremony.

miko 巫子 (shrine virgins). Virgins in the service of a shrine. Originally they were mediums who communicated divine messages. From ancient times, people strongly believed that the gods communicated their intentions through the mouths of human beings. Those who were believed to be the mediums between the gods and men were the *miko*. According to tradition, such persons as Himiko, Toyosukiire-hime, Yamato-hime, Empress Jingū, and Tamayori-hime were mediums.

mikoshiro 御子代 (MINASHIRO)

Mimana 任那. From the fourth to the sixth century, Mimana was a Japanese colony in South Korea. From about the third century the territory was composed of loosely knit groups. From the middle of the fourth century, it served as a base for Yamato raids on other parts of Korea. Later it was invaded by Kudara (in Korean, Paekche) and Shiragi (in Korean, Silla), and in 562 it ceased to exist.

Minami-Manshū Tetsudō Kabushiki-gaisha 南満州鉄道株式会社 (the South Manchurian Railway Company). A company which served Japan's national policy and was the center of its control over Manchuria. It was also called Mantetsu. Japan, upon her victory over Russia in 1905, assumed control of Manchuria, and her rights over the eastern Chinese railways were recognized. In 1906, an imperial rescript established the Mantetsu. Two hundred million yen, of which half was supplied by the government and half by the citizens, was invested in the new enterprise. In addition, the company also managed the coal mining industry, mines, and transportation. Until 1937, it had administrative authority over engineering works, education, and hygiene. It leased the territory along the railway. With the help of MITSUI and MITSUBISHI it enlarged its enterprises, and at the time of the Manchurian incident (MANSHŪ JIHEN) it possessed a capital of 440 million yen. South Manchuria was transformed into a powerful and modern industrial area. Japan's imperialist economy maintained South Manchuria as a source of raw materials and commercial commodities. It was an overseas enterprise in which Japan had invested the greatest capital and was an important national undertaking both economically and militarily.

minashiro, mikoshiro 御名代・御子代 (namesake groups, succession groups). The namesake groups were units, either families or corporations, created to transmit to posterity the names of emperors, empresses, or princes. The succession groups were units created to transmit to posterity the name of the emperor who had no children, or the name of his dwelling place. In this case the word "guild" *(be)* was suffixed to the name of the emperor or the emperor's dwelling place. The namesake group differed somewhat from the succession group. Such groups as Mibu-be, Tajihi-be, Fujiwara-be, and Anaho-be belonged not to the imperial family but to local chieftains (KUNI NO MIYATSUKO). The taxes they paid were to be transmitted to the imperial household. Corporations such as Hinokumatoneri-be, Shiragayugei-be, and Kashiwade-be were made to serve the imperial court. The namesake and succession groups were abolished by the Taika Reform in 646.

minato-machi 港町 (port towns). Trading centers established in ports during the middle ages. Under the manorial system, warehouses were set up in ports in order to take charge of the commodities which were to be shipped to manorial magnates *(honsho* or *ryōke)*. Those who supervised the shipping were known as TOIMARU. Before long the *toimaru* ceased to serve a particular lord but managed the yearly rice taxes of several manorial estates and took charge of sales. As a result, flourishing trade centers developed in various ports where boatmen, sailors, and traders gathered. Such places as Obama, TSURU-GA, Mikuni, ONOMICHI, etc. developed as transportation centers of yearly rice taxes. Harbor towns which developed through taking charge of manorial taxes were ŌMINATO, ŌTSU, and Sakamoto. They were outports of manorial landlords. Intermediate ports were HYŌGO and SAKAI on the Inland Sea and HAKATA in Kyūshū. They all prospered.

Minobu-san 身延山 (Mount Minobu). The name of a mountain in Yamanashi Prefecture and headquarters (Kuon-ji temple) of the Nichiren sect of Buddhism. Nichiren (1222–82) was banished to Sado. When he was pardoned in 1274, he secluded himself on Mount Minobu. With the help of local farmers he built the Kuon-ji temple and made it into a seminary. Many warriors such as Takeda Shingen (1521–73) protected Mount Minobu.

Mino-gami 美濃紙 (Mino paper). A kind of Japanese paper manufactured in Mino Province (Gifu Prefecture). The origin of the paper is old, for it was already known in the Nara period. The Heian government established papermaking centers. During the Muromachi period, the paper guild organized by the merchants of Gōshū (Shiga Prefecture) secured monopoly rights for Kyōto, and the paper market of Ōyada in Gifu Prefecture prospered. Handwork was replaced by machines during the Taishō era. Mino-gami is mostly used for brush-written letters and documents, as well as for paper sliding doors and windows.

Minsei-tō 民政党 (the Democratic Party). A political party of the Taishō and Shōwa eras. Upon its organization in 1927, Hamaguchi Osachi (1870–1931) was made its president. During the Taishō era, the main component of the Minsei-tō was the KENSEI-KAI or Constitutional Association. Later the two great political parties, the Political Friends Association (SEIYŪ-KAI) and the Minsei-tō, were opposed to each other. Following the incident of May 15, 1932 (GO-ICHIGO JIKEN), the Democratic Party was oppressed by the military authorities. In 1940, it was dissolved and integrated into the Imperial Rule Assistance Association (TAISEI YOKUSAN-KAI). As opposed to the Political Friends Association, which exerted its influence mainly among farmers, the Democratic Party was supported by the urban middle class, but its party program was relatively progressive. The party was on intimate terms with the MITSUBISHI concern.

minsen-giin setsuritsu kempaku 民選議院設立建白 (memorial for the establishment of a democratic parliament). A memorial of the early Meiji years for the establishment of a parliamentary government. Following the settlement of the issue on war with Korea, many councilors retired. Four among them, Itagaki Taisuke, Gotō Shōjirō, Etō Shimpei, and Soejima Taneomi, in cooperation with Komuro Shinobu, sent a memorial to the government (January 1874) and at the same time established the Patriotic Public Party (AIKOKU KŌTŌ). This was meant to curb the political monopoly of the Satsuma and Chōshū clans. It was also an effort to have the ex-military class, the wealthy farmers, and merchants, who had contributed to the restoration, extend their franchise. Though it appealed to the upper classes, the movement aggravated the political demands of the common people, provoked arguments for and against newspapers and magazines, and intensified the turmoil concerning the establishment of a parliament, which spread throughout the country.

Min'yaku Yakuge 民約訳解. The name of a book published during the early Meiji years. The book is Rousseau's *Contrat Social,* which was translated into Chinese (later into Japanese), annotated by Nakae Chōmin (1847–1901), and published in 1882. The book was a theoretical endorsement of the movement for popular rights.

Min'yū-sha 民友社 (the Democratic Friends Society). A literary society of the Meiji era. Established simultaneously with the launching of the magazine *Kokumin no Tomo* by Tokutomi Sohō (1863–1957), it became popular in 1890 when the first edition of *Kokumin Shimbun* saw the light. Many men of letters joined the society. Their school, which deeply influenced the democratic movements, was called Min'yūsha-ha.

Mito-gaku 水戸学 (Mito school of historians). A school of the Edo period, the main activity of which was the compilation of history by the Mito clan. In the initial period, the school started with the compilation of DAI NIHONSHI under the guidance of Tokugawa Mitsukuni (1628–1700). Adding the concept of reverence for the gods and respect for the emperor as advocated by Yamazaki Ansai (1618–82) to the moral obligations of Chu Hsi's Confucianism, the school also reflected its spirit in *Hōken Taiki,* a history of medieval Japan written by Kuriyama Sempō (1671–1706), and in *Chūkō Kangen,* also a history of the middle ages, written by Miyake Kanran (1674–1718). The main figure of the second period was Tokugawa Nariaki (1800–60). Research was now stimulated by troubles both within and without, especially by those of the Tempō era (1830–44). This research, however, was not limited to looking back at the past. Historical research centered around morality and politics and developed into a political movement for "reverence to the emperor and expulsion of foreigners." It influenced the restoration of the imperial house.

Nariaki founded the clan school Kōdō-kan and expressed his views concerning the aim of the school in *Kōdōkanki,* in which he extols the everlasting growth of a country based on Confucianism and the perfection of a moral state. This was the spirit of the school in its ultimate period. Works written in this vein are *Shōmeiron* by Fujita Yūkoku (1774–1826), *Shinron* by Aizawa Seishisai (1782–1863), and *Kōdōkan Kijutsugi* and *Kaitenshishi* by Fujita Tōko (1806–55). But the ideas of the Mito school were put forward from the standpoint of feudal rulers serving the BAKUFU and lost their significance about 1860, when opinions concerning loyalism and antiforeign policy were divided. Even Nariaki and Seishisai changed their ideas in their later years and favored the opening of the country.

Mitsubishi 三菱. A modern ZAIBATSU or financial concern. Together with MITSUI, the mighty Mitsubishi supported Japan, industrially and politically, to the end of the Pacific War. As opposed to Mitsui, which grew through commerce and by lending money at a high rate of interest, Mitsubishi developed through the enterprise of clan bureaucrats of country samurai origin who became businessmen with political affiliations and then monopolistic capitalists. Iwasaki Yatarō (1834–85) was in charge of the finances of the Tosa clan but, after the restoration, established the Tsukumo trading company and, borrowing the clan's ships, started a transportation business. In 1873, he changed the name of the company to Mitsubishi Shōkai. In 1874, the company used military ships and contributed to the conquest of Formosa. From 1885, it secured the protection of the government. Affiliated transportation companies merged into the Nippon Yūsen Kaisha (NIPPON YŪSEN KABUSHIKI-GAISHA). The company, enjoying the privilege of disposing of mines, shipyards, etc. at a low price, developed mining, banking, and railways. In 1928, there were ninety-two firms, including Mitsubishi Joint Stock and the firms belonging to the Iwasaki family. Furthermore, the company was directly concerned in twenty-seven associations. Its nominal capital amounted to 930 million yen, the invested capital being 590 million yen.

Mitsubishi Kisen Kaisha 三菱汽船会社 (Mitsubishi Steamship Company). Maritime transportation company of the early Meiji era. The origin was the private enterprise of Iwasaki Yatarō's (1834–85) Tsukumo 九十九 company for the ships of the Tosa clan (1871). The name was changed to Mitsubishi in 1873. In 1885, with the amalgamation of associated transportation companies, it became Nippon Yūsen Kaisha.

Mitsui 三井. A modern ZAIBATSU or financial concern. It started during the Edo period with commercial transactions and making loans at a high rate of interest. It was the greatest *zaibatsu* to support the country industrially and politically until the end of the Pacific War. The firm originated in the seventeenth century when Mitsui Takatoshi managed a brewery in Matsuzaka in

Ise Province and a pawnshop and rice-lending shop under the name of ECHIGO-YA. Takatoshi's son, also named Takatoshi, set up a chain of dry-goods stores in Edo and branch offices as well as exchange shops in Kyōto and Ōsaka. In 1691, he was appointed purveyor to the BAKUFU. He became banker for both the imperial household and the *bakufu*. After the restoration the company was linked with bureaucrats, political parties, and military circles, under whose protection it monopolized financial business, production matters, warehouses, mines, various kinds of industrial departments, transportation and communication, etc. In 1928, the Mitsui business included six companies in direct line with unlimited partnership, twelve subsidiary companies, and sixteen affiliated companies. The total number of companies was 130 and the nominal capital 1,690 million yen, with an invested capital of 1,170 million yen.

Mitsui Ginkō 三井銀行 (Mitsui Bank). In the early Meiji era and under the control of the government, financial agencies were set up, but civilian application was ruled out, and the request of the Mitsui Company to set up a bank was turned down (1871). The government put its trust in the issuing of convertible notes. In 1876, with the revision of the banking regulations, the Mitsui Bank was first established. It became the center of the MITSUI financial concern.

miyake 屯倉 (storehouses). Granaries for storing rice from the Yamato court's domains. Later the meaning of the word included also the farmers of these domains and the domains themselves *(mita)*. Those who controlled the *miyake* were called *denryō* and *tokuryō*. The farmers of the imperial domains were usually called *ta-be*. From the end of the fourth century, the Yamato court established imperial granaries all over the country. They were abolished with the Taika Reform in 646.

miya-za 宮座. Guilds for religious celebrations organized by the alleged descendants of a tutelary deity. The center of the organization was the tutelary shrine. Various associations were organized according to the age of the members and their social position. The guild which included all the members was called *mura-za,* and a guild with a limited number of members was known as *kabu-za.* On shrine festival days, either the Shintō priest *(kannushi)* or the person in charge of the religious functions *(tōya)* led the activities and performed the various religious rites. The custom flourished in medieval Japan, especially in the home provinces.

mizu-chō 御図帳・水帳 (KENCHI-CHŌ)

Mizukagami 水鏡. Historical romance in three volumes of the late Heian and early Kamakura periods. The work is attributed to Nakayama Tadachika (1131–95). It relates in chronological order the events of the reigns of fifty-four emperors from Jimmu Tennō to Nimmyō, or until 850. It also relates events prior to those mentioned in ōKAGAMI. It is one of the "Four Kagami" or *Shikyō,* the others being *Ōkagami,* IMAKAGAMI, and MASUKAGAMI. As far as literary style and history are concerned, the most outstanding of these works is *Ōkagami.*

mizunomi 水呑. Farmers of the Edo period who owned no farmland. Sometimes the term was also applied to poor farmers who possessed only a small tract of land. They were referred to as *mizunomi-byakushō,* were not even mentioned in land-surveying registers, and served independent farmers (HOM-BYAKUSHŌ). They earned an income by tenancy or by work other than farming. Their social standing was lower than that of independent farmers, and they were more despised. The government tried to check the number of *mizunomi,* but, as a result of trade development, many independent farmers fell to the rank of *mizunomi.* It is noteworthy that at the same time not a few *mizunomi* became independent farmers.

mōdo 問人 (serfs). Serfs of the middle ages and the Edo period. The *mōdo* were serfs of the owners of land in their own name (MYŌSHU) and of independent farmers (HOMBYAKUSHŌ), and their social rank was lower. But they had more freedom than the slave farmers (NAGO) and the dependent farmers known as GENIN. They gradually shook off their shackles and became independent, self-supporting farmers.

momikushi 問民苦使. An extralegal body consisting of messengers sent to all provinces in order to gain information about the complaints of the people. In 758, when the penal and administrative code system was about to collapse, the government, in order to relieve the people from suffering and anxiety resulting from unbearable taxation and from the revolt of Tachibana no Naramaro (circa 750), dispatched these messengers to the home provinces and the regions of the seven districts (SHICHIDŌ).

Monchūjo 問注所 (the Judicial Board). A government office of the Kamakura and Muromachi BAKUFU. It was established by Minamoto no Yoritomo (1148–99) in order to inquire into vassals' disputes. Yoritomo summoned the warrior Miyoshi Yasunobu (1140–1221) from Kyōto and appointed him chief of the Judicial Board. The Muromachi *bakufu* likewise established a Monchūjo. This, however, was less important than that of the Kamakura regime.

Mononobe uji 物部氏 (the Mononobe clan). A powerful family of ancient Japan. From early times the clan's stronghold was the Shiki district in the east of the Yamato plains. The clan worshiped its common deity, Iso no Kami, on Mount Miwayama. The rank (KABANE) of the Mononobe was that of MURAJI or chieftain. Being the leader (TOMO NO MIYATSUKO) of the guild of armorers *(mono no be)*, the clan was a military one by heredity. It spread its influence to the plains of Kawachi and in the sixth century overthrew the Heguri and Ōtomo clans. Under the reign of Emperor Keitai (450–531), when Arakahi (?–536) became chief of chieftains (Ō-MURAJI) and defeated the rebellious Iwai (IWAI NO HANRAN), the clan became powerful. From the middle of the sixth century the clan wielded political power and fought the Soga clan. The feud between Mononobe no Okoshi and Soga no Iname was resumed by their respective sons, Mononobe no Moriya and Soga no Umako (?–626). Toward the end of the sixth century, Moriya opposed the adoption of Buddhism, which had been introduced from China, but was destroyed by the pro-Buddhist Soga clan. Later only two branch families, Enoi no Muraji and Isonokami no Muraji, survived. Both lived in Yamato.

monzen-machi 門前町 (temple town). A cluster of shops, etc. in front of temples and shrines. From the end of the middle ages, people frequently made pilgrimages to temples and shrines. On the approach to the shrines many shops and inns were built for the use of pilgrims; even markets made their appearance. As the crowds grew denser, temple or shrine groups were formed. Most representative were those of Nara, Uji-Yamada, and Sakamoto. Many guides for pilgrims *(o-shi)* lived in Uji-Yamada, especially when pilgrimages to Ise were frequent. They offered prayers and provided lodging.

Mōri uji 毛利氏 (Mōri family). A family of warriors which, from the middle ages, flourished in the Chūgoku district. Its influence spread with Motonari (1497–1571). Motonari's forces fought the warrior Sue Harukata (?–1555) and defeated him at Itsukushima (1555). They also destroyed Ōuchi Yoshinaga (?–1557) and forced Amako Yoshihisa (?–1610) of the San'in district to surrender. Motonari subdued the whole Chūgoku district. His grandson Terumoto (1553–1625) was one of the most trusted of Hideyoshi's lieutenants. During the battle of Sekigahara, he sided with the western forces but was defeated. All of his territories except the two provinces of Suō and Nagato (Yamaguchi Prefecture) were confiscated. At the end of the Edo period and in the early Meiji era, the Mōri clan (Chōshū clan), together with the Satsuma, Tosa, and Hizen clans, played an important role in the formation of modern Japan.

mujin 無尽 (mutual financing associations). Financial associations for mutual relief. Those who belonged to the associations gathered at fixed periods, and shares for mutual aid were paid in installments. The beneficiaries were determined through drawing of lots or submission of a tender, and money was advanced in regular allotments. The system was introduced during the Kamakura period. During the Muromachi period, there were numerous associations in temples and in pawnshops known as DOSŌ. The mutual financing associations known as TANOMOSHI were also popular. As opposed to the *mujin,* the *tanomoshi* did not charge interest or require guarantees. Later, when the *tanomoshi* also began to charge interest and require guarantees, they were often confused with *mujin.*

munabetsu-sen 棟別銭 (house tax). A kind of tax imposed during the Muromachi period. When the BAKUFU could no longer impose taxes on constables (SHUGO) and stewards (JITŌ), it imposed a house tax on the common people. This tax corresponded to TANSEN, a tax imposed on arable land. It was an important revenue for the *bakufu.* Later, the great landlords followed suit and imposed the same tax on their subordinates, reducing the people to destitution. New forms of taxation appeared with the development of trade and with the growing mercantile character of the new towns.

muraji 連 (clan leader). One of the titles (KABANE) in ancient Japan. The word derives from *mure aruji,* which means "leader of a group" and is equivalent to the word *shuchō.* It originally indicated those who in various ways served the court. Later the title came to indicate the distinction between higher and lower ranks. *Muraji* and *omi* (chieftain) were august titles before the reform of titles by Emperor Temmu (622–86). The head of all the clan leaders was styled Ō-MURAJI. Together with the chief of chieftains (Ō-OMI), he took part in state affairs. Examples are Ōtomo no Muraji, Mononobe no Muraji, Nakatomi no Muraji, and Haji no Muraji.

Murasaki Shikibu Nikki 紫式部日記. A journal written by Murasaki Shikibu during the Heian period. When Murasaki was in the service of Jōtō Mon'in Akiko (Shōshi, or Fujiwara no Akiko; 988–1074), she described, from the viewpoint of a court lady, the official affairs and ceremonies of the court, including even those attending childbirth. The leading theme of the book is the disharmony between the life of the authoress and the life at court. Murasaki's critical mind and keen introspection are revealed against this background.

mura yakunin 村役人 (village administrators). The officials who, during the Edo period, controlled a village or what is now called *aza,* a village section. They were also called *murakata yakunin* and JIKATA. Usually one or two name masters (*nanushi* or MYŌSHU)—in the Kansai district many *myōshu* were called *shōya,* and in the Tōhoku and Hokuriku districts they were called KIMOIRI—and two or three or sometimes four or five KUMI-GASHIRA took part in the management of the affairs of the village. Sometimes representatives from among the farmers also took part in the administration. They were called *murakata san'yaku* or *jikata san'yaku.* According to the district, a *daishōya,* or *warimoto,* administered a *kumi,* or *gō,* by bringing together several villages. It was their duty to collect the yearly taxes, to control the water for irrigation, to give technical farming instruction, to protect the farmers, and to maintain order. Usually the *mura yakunin* were elected from among the farmers who possessed much land and who were referred to as *ōtakamochi*. There were also cases of elections of the independent farmers (HOMBYAKUSHŌ) by votes called *irefuda*.

Murō-ji 室生寺. A temple erected during the early Heian period in Uda district, Nara Prefecture. It is believed that it was built (778–93) by the Buddhist priest Kenkei (705–94) of Kōfuku-ji. Originally the temple followed the Hossō religion, but during the Edo period it adopted the Shingon faith. It was inaugurated by En no Ozunu (circa 700; the name is also read En no Ozuno and En no Shōkaku) and restored by Kōbō Daishi (774–835). The Kondō and Gojūnotō are buildings of the early Heian period, and they are the only ninth-century structures still extant. A seated statue of Shaka Nyorai, also of the early Heian period, is a representative work of the Kōnin art period (794–894).

Muromachi bakufu 室町幕府 (the Muromachi military government). Military government established in Muromachi, Kyōto, by the Ashikaga clan. After the Kemmu Restoration (KEMMU NO CHŪKŌ), Ashikaga Takauji (1308–58), in order to subdue the rebellious Hōjō Tokiyuki (?–1353), marched on Kamakura and defeated Tokiyuki. Violating the new Kemmu regulations, he also defeated Nitta Yoshisada (1301–38). In 1336, he created the Northern dynasty in Kyōto with Kōmyō (1321–80) as emperor. In 1338, he became generalissimo and inaugurated his military government. During the administration of the third shōgun, Yoshimitsu (1358–1408), the Northern and Southern courts were reunited (1392). The Muromachi military regime was established in 1368. It resembled that of the Kamakura period. The supreme head was the shōgun. Under him was the governor general (KANREI), similar to the regent (SHIKKEN) of the Kamakura shogunate. The position of *kanrei* was held alternately by the Shiba, Hatakeyama, and Hosokawa, who all belonged to the same Ashikaga clan. Under the governor was the Administrative Board (MANDOKORO), the Judicial Board (MONCHŪJO), the members of the Supreme Court (HYŌJŌ-SHŪ) and the assistant members (HIKITSUKE-SHŪ), and the Disciplinary Board (SAMURAI-DOKORO). Most important was the Samurai-dokoro. The position of minister of the Disciplinary Board *(shoshi)* was alternately held by members of the Akamatsu, Yamana, Kyōgoku, and Isshiki families. Together with the three families who held the position of governor, they were collectively called *sankan-shishoku*. As to the local government organization, there was a governor general of the Kantō district called KANTŌ KANREI, in Kamakura, and a commissioner of Kyūshū (KYŪSHŪ TANDAI) in Hakata. The combined political power of the great landowner constables (SHUGO DAIMYŌ) was strongly felt, and the shōgun's authority was often ignored by the constables. The economic policy of the Muromachi *bakufu* was unstable. The Kakitsu revolt (KAKITSU NO HEN) in 1441 and continuous opposition of the great landowner constables led to the civil war of the Ōnin-Bummei era (1467–87) and to the period of civil war (SENGOKU JIDAI). The *bakufu* lost its prestige. In 1573, the fifteenth shōgun, Yoshiaki (1537–97), was ousted by Nobunaga's forces. This marked the fall of the Muromachi *bakufu*, which had been inaugurated 235 years earlier by Ashikaga Takauji.

museifu-shugi 無政府主義 (anarchism). A political theory introduced in 1907 by Kōtoku Shūsui (1871–1911). It was influential until the end of the Taishō era.

musha-dokoro 武者所. During the period of cloister government (INSEI), the *musha-dokoro* was the place where guards were stationed to keep order among warriors who were to protect the sovereign and his palace. At the time of ex-Emperor Shirakawa (1053–1129) there were palace guards called *hokumen no bushi,* and at the time of ex-Emperor Gotoba (1180–1239) there were those called *saimen no bushi.* Some of these guards served in the *musha-dokoro.* The Kemmu Restoration also established a *musha-dokoro.* The commander *(tōnin)* was Nitta Yoshisada (1301–38), who guarded Kyōto and controlled the warriors.

Myōchin 明珍. A family of metal craftsmen who specialized in the making of armor. The technique developed after the Kamakura period. According to the requirements of the time, many families specialized in armor. The most famous of these was the Myōchin family, which survived until the Edo period.

myōden 名田 (name fields). Fields whose owner's deed was in the name of the original occupant, known as the MYŌSHŪ. The origin of the name fields dates back to the year 743, when, in order to protect property rights, the fields were named after those who brought wasteland under cultivation. This served as official recognition of perpetual property rights for those who reclaimed wasteland. With the development of manorial estates, the name fields became an important factor in the organization of manors. Those of the manorial estates were subject to some specific taxes but were exempt from all others. The owner of a name field levied from the farmers land rent known as CHISHI and additional rents known as *kachishi.* The *chishi* went to the feudal lord, the additional rents to the owner of the name field. During the Kamakura period, constables (JITŌ) were appointed, and the burden of the name field owners became heavier. But the *myōshu* somehow managed to resist the greedy constables as well as the manorial magnates and to establish themselves on firm ground and maintain their rights. Sometimes several *myōden* united and enjoyed an associate administration.

myōga-kin 冥加金 (a miscellaneous tax). One of the Edo miscellaneous taxes. Originally, all sorts of trade were licensed by the BAKUFU or the various clans.

But because trade was protected, an offering of rice or money was requested. The tax was considered a contribution, but before long it became a real tax imposed on trade and of the same nature as the taxes imposed on industry, fisheries, and transportation (UNJŌ). Some *myōga-kin* were imposed on those who operated breweries or oil presses; others were imposed on licensed trade associations (KABU-NAKAMA).

myōhōdō 明法道. One of the branches of learning taught at the state school of higher learning or Daigaku-ryō (DAIGAKU). Under the penal and administrative code system, *myōhōdō* (or *myōbōdō*) corresponded to law and was a course of study which investigated every legal form (SHIKI) of the penal and administrative code as opposed to history, or *kidendō,* and Confucian classics, or MYŌKYŌDŌ, which were limited to the books of China. It involved the study of Japanese administrative and civil codes *(ryō)* and penal codes *(ritsu).*

Myōjō-ha 明星派. A literary school of the Meiji era. The school flourished following the publication of a magazine of poetry called *Myōjō,* edited in 1897 by Yosano Tekkan (1873–1935). During its transition period from neo-lyricism to symbolism, poetry flourished under the stimulus of Suzukida Ryūkin, Kambara Ariaki, and Takamura Kōtarō, and *tanka* (thirty-one-syllable verse) under Tekkan, Tekkan's wife Akiko, and Kubota Utsubo. The salient feature of the school was romanticism.

myōkyōdō 明経道. One of the courses of study at the state school of higher learning or Daigaku-ryō (DAIGAKU) under the penal and administrative code system. *Myōkyōdō* (also *myōgyōdō*) corresponds to the Confucian classics and was the study of the meaning concealed in the classics. The classics are *Shūeki, Shōsho, Mōshi, Saden, Sanrai, Rongo,* and *Kōkyō.*

myōshu 名主 (owner of a name field). Owners of land on a manor in their own name (MYŌDEN) from the Heian to the Muromachi period. To protect the name fields, the *myōshu* entrusted them to influential aristocrats or to great monasteries. Being units of the manorial make-up, the name fields were exempt from taxes and protected by the territorial magnates. *Myōshu* included small landowners, feudal lords, warriors, bonzes, and merchants. The more influential among them were appointed administrators of the manor (SHŌKAN), direct retainers of the shōgun (GO-KENIN), land stewards (JITŌ), constables (SHUGO), etc. During the Kamakura period, when the farmers were organized, some rights such as the *myōshū's* position and profits *(myōshu-shiki)* were firmly established, and the *myōshu* came to be known as the owner of these rights. During the Muromachi period, the word *myōshu* came to mean not only influential farmers but also territorial magnates, monasteries, the aristocracy, etc.

N

Nagasaki 長崎. A harbor city in northwestern Kyūshū. From about the Temmon era (1532–55) Nagasaki became the feudal domain of the Ōmura clan. After the Portuguese had landed, it flourished as a trading port. During the Tenshō era (1573–92) Hideyoshi learned that Nagasaki had become a center of Christianity *(Yaso Kyōkai)*. Trying to exterminate the new religion, he appointed a commissioner of Nagasaki (NAGASAKI BUGYŌ). Nagasaki was then controlled by the central authorities. During the Kan'ei era (1624–44), when the country was isolated, only Nagasaki remained open to foreign trade and developed as a town with an exotic touch. In 1859, Nagasaki, together with Yokohama and Sapporo, became a treaty port and again flourished. During World War II, on August 9, 1945, part of the city was destroyed by an atomic bomb.

Nagasaki bugyō 長崎奉行 (commissioner of Nagasaki). One of the commissioners in remote provinces during the Edo period. He resided in Nagasaki and controlled the trade with China and the Dutch. He also kept an eye on all overseas movements. The commissioner was first appointed by Hideyoshi, but the Tokugawa regime followed the same policy. Originally, the office of commissioner was for obviously commercial reasons, but when the country was closed the main duties of the commissioner consisted of controlling the Nagasaki judicature and police as well as the office called *Nagasaki kaisho,* which was in charge of trade with China and Holland. At the end of the Edo period, the office of commissioner was concerned with the defense of Nagasaki against foreign raiders.

Nagashino no tatakai 長篠の戦 (the battle of Nagashino). When Ieyasu attacked the forces of Takeda Katsuyori (1546–82) at Nagashino Castle in Mikawa Province (Aichi Prefecture), he met strong resistance and called for help from Nobunaga. The combined forces of Ieyasu and Nobunaga besieged Takeda in 1575. The ensuing battle is known as the battle of Nagashino. Nobunaga used foot soldiers with firearms (ASHIGARU) and brought a crushing defeat to Takeda. The courage and strategy of the Takeda forces were of no avail against firearms, which were used for the first time. This marked a transition from individual to collective battle. When Katsuyori was defeated, he returned to Kai Province (Yamanashi Prefecture), where he temporarily remained inactive. Ieyasu subdued Suruga and Tōtōmi provinces (both in Shizuoka Prefecture) and accelerated the unification of the nation begun by Nobunaga.

nago 名子 (farmer-slaves). A kind of farmer-slave. *Na* means the farm and *ko* the one who furnishes labor. During the middle ages, the *nago* belonged to the *nanushi,* or the owner of land in his own name, and was subjected to slave labor. According to the district, different words were used for *nago,* such as *kehō,* BUNZUKE, HIKAN, *fudai, kokata, kanjin,* and the degree of dependence also differed. For food, clothing, and housing, the *nago* were dependent on the landowner, and some took instructions from their master. *Nago* of the Edo period were, as a rule, lower in status than other farmers.

Nakoku (Na no Kuni) 奴国. The name for North Kyūshū as mentioned in the chapter "Tung I Chuan" in the book *Hou Han Shu* (in Japanese, *Gokansho* or GOKANJO) and in the chapter "Wo Jen Chuan" in the Wei Chronicles or *Wei Chih* (in Japanese, *Gishi*). Later the place was called Na no Agata and Nanotsu and was a locality in the vicinity of Hakata. Conjecturing from Chinese sources, Na no Kuni was probably a territory in northern Kyūshū ruled by a powerful tribal chieftain during the first, second, or third century. In 57, a gold seal was sent by the emperor of Han to the king of Wa no Kuni through a Japanese envoy. The gold seal discovered in Shiganoshima in the bay of Hakata at the end of the Edo period (in 1784) is alleged to be the one in question (KAN NO WA NO NA NO KOKUŌ NO KIN'IN).

Namamugi jiken 生麦事件 (the incident at Namamugi Village). The incident of 1862 in which one British subject was killed and two others wounded. Forcing their way through the procession of Lord Shimazu Hisamitsu (1817–87) of the Satsuma clan at Namamugi in Musashi Province, the British were attacked by retainers of Hisamitsu. Britain asked for indemnity for the families of the victims, but as the BAKUFU's answer was not satisfactory, seven British warships attacked Kagoshima (1863), the capital of Satsuma. The Satsuma clan (Shimazu) engaged in battle with the warships *(Satsu-Ei sensō)* but later paid 70,000 *ryō* indemnity.

namban byōbu 南蛮屏風 (folding screens picturing foreigners). Painted folding screens which depict foreigners (NAMBANJIN) in Japan during the early Edo period. European civilization having been introduced to Japan, the subject matter of some paintings was foreigners and foreign manners, and the *namban* folding screens came into being. The paintings were genre pictures representing foreigners, foreign vessels, Christian churches, and world maps. They were made from the end of the sixteenth to the beginning of the seventeenth century, but their popularity declined after the policy of national isolation came into force.

Namban-ji 南蛮寺 (Catholic church). A Catholic church built in Kyōto during the Azuchi-Momoyama period (1573–1600). At first a gathering place was bought in 1560 by Father Vilela. When it deteriorated, Father Organtino built the Namban-ji in 1576 with the help of the faithful and the support of Nobunaga. Hideyoshi placed a ban on the Catholic religion and destroyed the church in 1588. A fan painting representing the Namban-ji is still extant.

nambanjin 南蛮人 (foreigners). Europeans who came to Japan from the end of the Muromachi period. In 1543, the first Portuguese arrived at Tanegashima, and in 1584 the first Spaniards made their appearance at the port of HIRADO in Hizen Province (Nagasaki Prefecture). From this time the Europeans were called *nambanjin* or southern barbarians, and their ships were called NAMBANSEN.

nambansen 南蛮船 (foreign vessels). European ships which entered Japanese waters at the end of the middle ages, especially Portuguese and Spanish ships. The foreigners (NAMBANJIN) spread the Catholic faith and promoted trade *(namban bōeki)*. Foreign vessels are depicted on some *namban* folding screens (NAMBAN BYŌBU).

Nambokuchō no nairan 南北朝の内乱 (the internal strife between the Northern and Southern dynasties, 1336–92). With the decline of the Kamakura shogunate, more warriors became dissatisfied with the Hōjō clan. Emperor Godaigo (1288–1339), plotting with the courtier Hino Toshimoto (?– 1332) and others, tried to overthrow the shogunate but failed. This historical event is referred to as SHŌCHŪ NO HEN. Shōchū was the name of the era 1324– 26. Later, another attempt to overthrow the BAKUFU was made with the help of Kusunoki Masashige (1294–1336), but the plot was detected and the emperor was banished to Oki. This event is known as GENKŌ NO HEN, Genkō being the name of the era 1331–34. In 1333, following the revolt of Ashikaga Takauji (1305–58) and Nitta Yoshisada (1301–38), the Kamakura shogunate was destroyed and the Kemmu Restoration inaugurated (KEMMU NO CHŪKŌ). However, the shortcomings of the new administration were manifold. Furthermore, the demands of the warriors could not be met, and finally Takauji betrayed the emperor. Marching on Kyōto from the eastern provinces, Takauji was temporarily defeated. He retired to Kyūshū, where he gathered forces. Destroying Masashige at Minatogawa (in Kōbe City), he again marched on Kyōto, where he enthroned Emperor Kōmyō (1321– 80). Kōmyō was of the Jimyōin line (JIMYŌIN-TŌ). Therefore, Emperor Godaigo left Kyōto in 1336 and proceeded to Yoshino, where he established a rival court. This Yoshino court is known as the Southern dynasty, the Kyōto court as the Northern dynasty. Takauji established his shogunate in the Northern dynasty. The internal strife between the two dynasties lasted fifty-seven years. When the Southern court began to decline, its political power was mostly confined to the Yoshino district. In 1392, Ashikaga Yoshimitsu (1358– 1408) of the Muromachi shogunate planned to reunite the two courts, and Emperor Gokameyama (1350–1424) of the Southern dynasty abdicated in favor of Emperor Gokomatsu (1377–1433) of the Northern court, bringing about the unity of the two lines of emperors. This civil strife caused opposition between powerful constables (SHUGO) trying to establish feudal power and those trying to revive the ancient regime and to re-establish imperial rule.

Noteworthy in this period is the influence of the farmers, who demanded more freedom and a voice in political affairs.

Nansō Satomi Hakkenden 南総里見八犬伝. A didactic work (YOMIHON) in 98 parts and 106 volumes, written by Takizawa Bakin (1767–1848). It took the author twenty-eight years, from 1814 to 1841, to complete the work. The historical background is the rise and decline of the Satomi family of Kazusa (Chiba Prefecture), especially of Satomi Yoshizane (1417–88), during the period of civil war (SENGOKU JIDAI). The work describes the doings of eight heroes, each of whom has a noble dog as his ancestor. Each dog symbolizes a virtue—benevolence, righteousness, decorum, wisdom, loyalty, sincerity, filial piety, and submissiveness. The saga has been compared with the Chinese *Shui Hu Chuan* (in Japanese, *Suikoden*) because of its magnificent composition and its beautiful sentences in the 7-5 meter. It was the climax of the popular novel. The work stresses the warrior's virtues and Confucian moral values and seeks to "encourage virtue and chastise vice" *(kanzen-chōaku)*.

Nanto Hokurei 南都北嶺. Originally Nanto meant the "southern capital" or Nara, in contrast to Kyōto. But the word also indicates Kōfuku-ji temple. Hokurei means either Hiei-zan or ENRYAKU-JI temple. From the middle of the Heian period, monk-soldiers of various temples engaged in many battles and made direct appeals by force (GŌSO). This was particularly the case with the monk-soldiers of Kōfuku-ji and Enryaku-ji. For this reason the names of both temples are combined to signify these two religious strongholds.

Nanto rokushū 南都六宗 (the six Buddhist sects of Nara). The six sects of Buddhism during the Nara period. They were SANRON-SHŪ, Jōjitsu-shū, HOS-SŌ-SHŪ, Kusha-shū, KEGON-SHŪ, and Risshū. Until the early Nara period, Buddhism was more a learning than a faith, but during the reign of Emperor Shōmu (701–56) it became a genuine religion, and the six sects, each one with its own particular doctrine, came into being. All these sects were of Chinese origin, but they were transplanted to Japanese soil with little change.

Nanto shichi-daiji 南都七大寺 (the seven temples of the southern capital). The generic term for the seven greater temples in the vicinity of Nara. The temples are TŌDAI-JI, Kōfuku-ji, Gangō-ji, Daian-ji, YAKUSHI-JI, Saidai-ji, and HŌRYŪ-JI. During the Nara and Heian periods, they were the center of the "six sects" (NANTO ROKUSHŪ), and during the eleventh century pilgrimages to the seven temples were popular. From the time of the Kamakura shogunate, their influence declined. Each temple stores numerous treasures.

nanushi 名主 (MURA YAKUNIN)

Nanzen-ji 南禅寺. Central monastery of the Nanzen-ji sect of Rinzai Buddhism. In 1293, the detached palace of ex-Emperor Kameyama (1249–1305) was made into a temple, and the founder of this Nanzen-ji was Fumon (1212–91). Later Nanzen-ji became one of the Five Monasteries of Kyōto (Kyōto GOZAN). It flourished after 1386, when it became the leading monastery of the Kyōto Gozan.

Negoro-dera 根来寺. The central monastery in Negoro (Wakayama Prefecture) of the Shingi Shingon-shū. At the end of the Heian period, Kakuban (1095–1143) built the Dempō-in temple. After a quarrel with the priests of Kōya-san, he went to the mountains and in 1130 built his temple in Negoro. During the late Muromachi period, the monk-soldiers of this temple became influential. They acted in concert with the Hongan-ji and resisted Nobunaga. Siding with Ieyasu, the Negoro-dera monk-soldiers fought against Hideyoshi in the battles of Komaki and Nagakute in the Negoro uprisings *(Negoro-ikki)*. In 1585, Hideyoshi burned down most of the temple buildings.

nembutsu odori 念仏踊. Religious dances to the accompaniment of bells and drums, spread by Kūya (903–72) and Ippen (1239–89). During the dance, the name of Buddha was invoked and Buddhist hymns were sung. From the latter part of the Kamakura period, pilgrimages of the priests of the JI-SHŪ sect spread the practice throughout the country. During the sixteenth and seventeenth centuries, the religious dances became secular and were also performed in the OKUNI KABUKI.

Nembutsu-shū 念仏宗. A sect of Buddhism, spread by Kūya (903–72) at the end of the Heian period, which later developed into JŌDO-SHŪ, JŌDO SHIN-SHŪ, and JI-SHŪ. Invocation of the name of Amida and the hope of being reborn in paradise are the main features of the faith.

nengu 年貢 (land tax). Yearly land tax imposed by the Kamakura shogunate. During the Muromachi period, taxes were sometimes paid in rice *(bummai)* or in currency *(bunsen)*. During the Edo period, part of the miscellaneous taxes called KOMONONARI were also known as *nengu,* and there were such yearly taxes as *yama-nengu, cha-nengu,* etc. The word *nengu* was further used to indicate the farm rent *(kosakuryō)*. After the restoration, the words *chiso* and *sozei* were commonly used, and *nengu* meant only the farm rent.

nenki-bōkō 年季奉公 (apprenticeship). A system of long-term employees. Apprentices of a commercial house, of craftsmen, etc. were engaged during a fixed period. They performed miscellaneous duties in the commercial or industrial field and also domestic duties. They were made familiar with trade or initiated into manufacturing techniques. In the early Edo period, the term of employment was determined by the shogunate, but this rule was abolished in the Genroku era (1688–1704). Apprentices who worked for a

craftsman were bound for about ten years before becoming craftsmen themselves, and those who worked for a tradesman were employed for twenty years
before becoming tradesmen or secretaries. At the expiration of the term,
the apprentice was set up in business and became independent. Later this
practice was changed, and in modern times it has declined.

Nichi-Bei Anzen-hoshō Jōyaku 日米安全保障条約 (the Japanese-American
Security Treaty). Postwar international pact. The peace treaty with Japan was
concluded on September 8, 1951, and came into effect on April 28, 1952. For
the defense of Japan, the stationing of American forces in Japan was recognized, but foreign bases on Japanese soil gave rise to many problems.

Nichi-Bei kaidan 日米会談 (Japanese-American negotiations). Diplomatic
negotiations during the Shōwa era. In March and April 1941, Admiral Nomura Kichisaburō and the envoy Kurusu Saburō met with President Roosevelt
and Secretary of State Cordell Hull to discuss means of averting war. Though
the Tripartite Pact between Japan, Germany, and Italy had come into effect,
the Konoe cabinet continued its efforts to avoid a Japanese-American conflict. Japan hoped for the continued neutrality of the United States and Russia
because of her inferior navy potential and because she relied on the United
States and England for financial stability. Japan proposed a meeting in the
Pacific between President Roosevelt and Prime Minister Konoe as a means of
resolving the issues, but the opposition of the Japanese Army interrupted the
negotiations. Konoe had to resign two months before Japan's entry into
World War II.

Nichi-Bei Washin Jōyaku 日米和親条約 (KANAGAWA JŌYAKU)

Nichi-Doku-I Sangoku Dōmei 日独伊三国同盟 (Tripartite Pact). Tripartite
Pact concluded in September 1940 between Germany, Italy, and Japan. It
strengthened the Anti-Comintern Pact concluded between the same countries
in November 1936. The leading position of the individual parties for the establishment of a new order was mutually respected. Japan committed herself to
come to the aid of the other parties if they were attacked by a power not
involved in the European war or in the Sino-Japanese conflict, other than the
Soviet Union. The pact was effective for ten years. It was mainly directed
against England and the United States, the principal enemies in Japanese
eyes. It also sharpened the conflict between the Axis and the Allied Powers
and finally led to World War II.

Nichi-Ei Dōmei 日英同盟 (Anglo-Japanese Alliance). An alliance between
England and Japan, early twentieth century. After the Sino-Japanese War
(1894–95), the Far East witnessed a struggle for colonies by the imperialist
powers. Opposing the great powers, Japan aimed at reaching maturity as a

modern state. But as a young capitalist nation Japan experienced major difficulties in trying to maintain her independence. She therefore looked for alliances with foreign countries. Britain, which was opposed to Russian expansionism, wanted to conclude an alliance with Japan, especially since Japan had shown her real strength in North China. Though there was a pro-Russian as well as a pro-British faction in Japan, the pro-British faction dominated, and the Anglo-Japanese Alliance was concluded in 1902. Both parties committed themselves to remain neutral if either of the two were attacked by a third power and to join the attacked party if either one were attacked by various powers simultaneously. After three years the alliance was strengthened when it became an offensive-defensive alliance. After the end of the Russo-Japanese War in 1905, both parties, Japan and England, became enemies of Germany, and during World War I Japan sided with the Allied Forces. The Anglo-Japanese Alliance was dissolved at the Washington Conference in 1921, and Japan thereafter adopted a rival attitude towards Britain.

Nichi-Futsu Gunji Kyōtei 日仏軍事協定 (Franco-Japanese Military Pact). A pact concluded in 1940 between France and Japan. In the Sino-Japanese conflict, England and France adopted a countermeasure against the blockade of the Chinese coast by Japanese naval forces and sent supplies to China (K'unming) via Burma and Indochina. Meanwhile Japan had been pressing forward in Indochina. On August 30, 1940, a preliminary agreement was reached with France as a basis for further discussions. On September 22, three days after the issuance of a Japanese ultimatum, the French colonial authorities agreed to the Japanese use of three airports in Indochina and to the transit of Japanese forces for operations in China. England and France stopped sending supplies to China.

Nichi-Ro Sensō 日露戦争 (Russo-Japanese War, 1904–5). The war with Russia during the Meiji era. Struggle for supremacy between the two powers led to the war. After the Sino-Japanese War (1894–95), Russia persuaded France and Germany to join her in inducing Japan to return the Liaotung Peninsula to China. In return for this "favor" to China, Russia was granted a lease on Port Arthur (in Japanese, Ryojun) and Dairen, where she made strongholds for her southward expansion. She extended her influence as far as Korea. Japan, which had established a market in Korea, came into conflict with Russia. When the Russian plans were clear, Japan hurriedly concluded the Anglo-Japanese Alliance (1902). Then she attempted to settle the issues with Russia. However, Russia continued to reinforce her military potential and planned to invade Manchuria. This caused the war, the issue of which was in favor of Japan. The main battlefields were P'yongyang (in Japanese, Heijō), Liaoyang, Port Arthur, and Mukden. The sea battles took place in the Yellow Sea, Ulsan (in Japanese, Urusan) on the coast of Korea, and the Japan Sea. Before Russia intended to conclude hostilities, the revolutionary movement in Russia intensified. In late summer, 1905, through the good offices of the United States, and in compliance with the request of the American president Theodore Roosevelt, the plenipotentiary Komura Jutarō and the Russian prime minister Sergei Witte met in Portsmouth, New Hampshire, and concluded a peace treaty. Russia recognized Japan's supremacy in Korea, and Japan replaced Russia in Manchuria. Southern Sakhalin became an integral part of the Japanese empire. After the war, Japan's industry greatly expanded, and the exploitation of Korea and Manchuria established Japan's capitalistic economy on firm ground. It is worth noting that before and during the Russo-Japanese War a strong anti-militaristic attitude was adopted by the Communist Katayama Sen, the poetess Yosano Akiko, and newspapers such as HEIMIN SHIMBUN.

Nihon Eitai-gura 日本永代蔵. One of the realistic novels (UKIYO-ZŌSHI) written by Saikaku (1642–93) and published in 1688. It is a work in six volumes, each volume consisting of five chapters. The author describes the townspeople who have become rich and the ways of accumulating money as well as those of losing it. The work displays a vivid psychological insight into the frame of mind of the merchants during the Edo period.

Nihon-fu 日本府 (government office in Mimana). The government office established in MIMANA, a Japanese enclave on the southern tip of Korea during the Yamato period. The beginnings of the Japanese administration in South Korea are not well known, but they probably date from the fourth century, when the states of Kudara and Shiragi were firmly established. Mimana was placed under Japanese protection. The Japanese court administered Mimana through the Nihon-fu, and the Japanese governor general called *dazai* or *kokushi* resided permanently in Mimana. However, in 520, Mimana was annexed by Kudara, and the Nihon-fu moved to Anra (or Ara). It was abolished in 562.

Nihon Gaishi 日本外史. A historical book written in Chinese by Rai San'yō (1780–1832). Begun in 1802, it was completed in 1826. The following year it was presented to Prime Minister Matsudaira Sadanobu (1758–1829) and then published. The work describes the rise and fall of the Minamoto and Taira warriors' families. Based on Confucian morality, it contributed much to fostering reverence for the imperial family. It also influenced the historical outlook during the early Meiji Restoration.

Nihongi 日本紀. (NIHON SHOKI)

Nihonjin 日本人. A nationalist periodical of the Meiji era. It was launched in 1888 by the Society for Political Education (SEIKYŌ-SHA) under the leadership of Miyake Setsurei (1860–1945). The nationalist spirit as displayed in the periodical grew after the Sino-Japanese War (1894–95), and from 1901 it became tinged with socialism. Along with the magazine KOKUMIN NO TOMO, published by the Democratic Friends Society (MIN'YŪ-SHA), *Nihonjin* fostered the nationalist tendency which had begun to take shape as early as 1887.

Nihonkoku Kempō 日本国憲法 (Japanese Constitution). The new postwar constitution. In August 1945, when Japan accepted the Potsdam Declaration, a new constitution became necessary. In October 1945, the Supreme Commander for the Allied Powers gave instructions for a new constitution based on liberal principles. A constitution was drafted under direction of the Far Eastern Commission. It was promulgated on November 3, 1946, and became effective on May 3, 1947. This new constitution guarantees fundamental civil rights. It also renounces war. Sovereignty is vested in the people. It calls for a parliamentary system, local self-government, and an independent judiciary. A democratic government was established in accordance with the freely expressed will of the people. Equal rights for men and women are guaranteed, and a modification of the family system is effected. Some shortcomings of the new constitution have since come to light.

Nihon-machi 日本町 (Japanese quarters in southern Asia). Japanese communities in southern Asia during the sixteenth and seventeenth centuries. They are also called *Nihonjin-machi*. From the end of the sixteenth century, as a result of the overseas trade, especially of the trade of the red-seal vessels (SHUIN-SEN), Japanese sailed to the Philippines, South Vietnam, Cambodia, and Siam and established permanent quarters in various towns. They had a self-governing system under the leadership of a chief, participated in trade, and even exercised military influence in domestic politics, as in Siam. In fact, the Japanese community in Siam under the leadership of Yamada Nagamasa, who was very active in Ayuthia, was well known. Such Japanese quarters included Tourane in Cochinchina (present-day Da Nang in Vietnam), Manila in the Philippine Islands, Ayuthia in Siam (present-day Ayutthaya in Thailand), and Udon in Cambodia. After the seventeenth century, as a result of the isolation policy of Japan, no Japanese nationals were allowed to leave the country. Trade diminished, and the settlers in the *Nihon-machi* gradually died out.

Nihon Ryōiki 日本霊異記. Abbreviation of *Nihonkoku Gempō Zen'aku Ryōiki*. A collection of stories in three volumes, written in Chinese and containing Buddhist narratives of the Nara period. It is thought to have been compiled in 820 by the Buddhist priest Keikai. It is the oldest collection of Buddhist stories. Material from former books such as *Meihōki* and *Hannya-genki* was used, as well as contemporary popular events. The narratives describe past and present strange events and teach that good will be rewarded and evil punished. The life of contemporary people is accurately described. Many of the narratives have been used in *Sambō Ekotoba,* KONJAKU MONOGATARI, UJISHŪI MONOGATARI, etc.

Nihon Shoki 日本書紀. The oldest official history of Japan, compiled in thirty volumes during the Nara period (in 720) by Prince Toneri (?–735), with the cooperation of Ō no Yasumaro (?–723) and others. It relates events from the age of the gods to the reign of Empress Jitō (645–702). It is written in Chinese and includes the genealogy of the imperial line, myths, and legends as well as traditional tales. After the Taika Reform (646), the establishment of a nation with a central authority called for the compilation of a particular history after the model of the Chinese histories. The work is a valuable source for the study of the history of ancient Japan. It is also known as *Nihongi.*

ni-ichi suto 二・一スト (the strike of February 1, 1947). Postwar labor development. As part of the democratization of the country, labor unions were organized, and as a result of inflation and the food shortage the labor struggle grew more intense. In January 1947, the Federation of Labor, industrial organizations, and labor unions mobilized four million members and demanded an increase in wages, industrial reorganization, and a democratic popular government. It was decided that government office workers should strike on February first. However, General MacArthur intervened openly and prohibited the strike, which, it was feared, would disrupt the national economy. From this time, and in order to combat communism, the Supreme Commander for the Allied Powers felt constrained to restrict the freedom of action accorded earlier to labor organizations.

Nijōgawara no rakugaki 二条河原の落書 (scribbling on the walls at Nijō-gawara). Scribbling in "contemporary style" (IMAYŌ) expressing popular dissatisfaction with the new Kemmu policy (KEMMU NO CHŪKŌ). The scribbling began with the words "night raids, robbery, and forged imperial orders, that is what prevails in the capital today" (*konogoro Kyōto ni hayaru mono, youchi, gōtō, nise-rinshi* 此頃京都にはやるもの夜討強盗にせ綸旨). The scribbling was in the *nagauta* form. After the overthrow of the Kamakura shogunate, the Kemmu Restoration (1334–36) was made possible through the combined efforts of nobles, powerful temples and shrines, and influential warriors. But the satirical gibes had appeared already in 1335, making fun of the political situation, of society, of customs and manners, and of the misrule of the new administration. They also criticized the chaotic situation.

Nijūikkajō Yōkyū 二十一ヶ条要求 (the Twenty-one Demands). Twenty-one demands addressed by Japan to China in 1915. Japan had joined the European and American expansionist movement in China. During World War I, the Western powers were prevented from directing their attention toward China. Taking advantage of the situation, Japan aimed at realizing her ambitions. Joining the war in 1914, Japan placed German-held Shantung Province under military occupation. The following year, Japan thrust her demands before the Chinese government. They included the extension to ninety-nine years of the lease of Port Arthur and Dairen, the recognition by China of Japan's sovereign rights in South Manchuria and in the eastern part of Inner Mongolia, the transformation into a Sino-Japanese company of the Chinese mining company Hanyehp'ing, the transfer to Japan of rights conceded to the Germans in Shantung Province, and prohibition against the cession of Chinese ports to any third power. Some demands were first rejected by China and then amended. Following a Japanese ultimatum (May 7, 1915), China granted all the demands except group five, and the agreement was signed in Peking on May 25, 1915. Though territorial integrity was respected, the demands virtually made China a vassal. Japan consolidated her economic and political position. At the same time anti-Japanese feelings in China grew worse until they reached a climax in the student demonstration of May 4, 1919.

nijūshi-kumi don'ya 二十四組問屋 (twenty-four forwarding agencies). Forwarding agencies in Ōsaka for shipments bound for Edo. With the increase of transportation between Ōsaka and Edo, forwarding agencies for all kinds of shipments organized themselves into companies. Securing a monopoly, they relied on *higaki* cargo vessels (KAISEN and HIGAKI-KAISEN) for transportation. In Edo, ten companies took care of the receipt of shipments.

Nika-kai 二科会. An art society of the Taishō and Shōwa eras. Opposed to the traditional attitude of the Education Ministry's art exhibition (Bunten), a group of Western-style artists withdrew from Bunten and formed a non-government art society in 1914. To the present day, the members of Nika-kai follow new Western tendencies and are considered avant-garde artists.

Nikka jihen 日華事変 (the Sino-Japanese incident, 1937–45). Japanese aggressive war in China. After the occupation of Manchuria, Japan planned to invade North China. In 1935, Chinese students in Peking launched an anti-Japanese movement, and the following year the Kuomintang Party joined the Communist Party in Sian to form a common anti-Japanese front. On July 7, 1937, at a place called Lukouch'iao in the suburbs of Peking, die-hards of the Japanese Kwantung army challenged the Chinese to fight. An undeclared local war followed, which, however, became an all-out one. After the fall of Nanking, the Chinese government moved first to Wuhan, then to Ch'ungch'ing, fiercely resisting to the end. Prime Minister Konoe refused to deal with the Chinese national government and announced the establishment of a new order in East Asia. A friendly solution was out of the question. In 1939, Wang Chao-ming (Wang Ching-wei) fled from Ch'ungch'ing and, following Japanese instructions, formed the Nanking government. Chinese resistance remained as strong as before. To find a solution, and to maintain her military and economic power, Japan invaded Southeast Asia, thus causing a conflict with the United States and Britain. With the outbreak of the Pacific War, Japan's war potential began to weaken, and the Chinese armies took the offensive. On August 15, 1945, Japan accepted unconditional surrender. The war with China, which had lasted eight years, came to an end.

ni-niroku jiken 二・二六事件 (the incident of February 26, 1936). The army rebellion of February 26–29, 1936, in Tokyo. Young unit officers of Konoe's first division, leading a squad, occupied the prime minister's official residence and the War Office, assassinated ex-Finance Minister Takahashi Korekiyo (1854–1936), ex-Premier Saitō Makoto (1858–1936), who was lord keeper of the privy seal, and General Watanabe Jōtarō (1874–1936), who was inspector general of military education. They also seriously wounded Suzuki Kantarō (1867–1948), the grand chamberlain. The army executives tried to give an explanation but failed, and it was decided to quell the military revolt by military means. In response to appeals broadcast by radio, the rebels surrendered, and the riot was subdued. Fifteen officers and several civilian accomplices were executed. Like the revolt of May 15, 1932 (GO-ICHIGO JIKEN), it was an attempt to rebuild the nation by direct action, to reform society, and to actualize the so-called Shōwa restoration. The upper-class politicians and the political parties were already intimidated by militarist fascism. They were no longer able to prevent politics from becoming fascist and Japan from becoming still more militaristic. The incident marked the establishment of a despotic control system.

ninjōbon 人情本. The generic term for a kind of novel of the Edo period. The novels were also known as *chūbon* because they were of medium size, between the YOMIHON or didactic novels and the SHAREBON or gay-quarter novelettes. The *ninjōbon* also included KOKKEIBON. They were artistically illustrated and became popular at the time of the Bunsei era (1818–30). They derive their name from the subject matter, which was the love affairs of townsmen. Whereas the *sharebon* describe loves of passion, the *ninjōbon* deal with love in general. The most representative author was Tamenaga Shunsui (1790–1842), who wrote *Shunshoku Umegoyomi* and *Shunshoku Tatsumi-no-sono*.

ninsoku yoseba 人足寄場 (gathering place for coolies). Gathering place for workmen which formed part of the social policy of Matsudaira Sadanobu (1758–1829) of 1790. Those who had committed a minor offense and had served their sentence were received at the workers' haven in Ishikawajima (in Edo), where they were engaged in handicrafts, such as carpentry, joinery, the making of lacquer ware, etc. Some were rice cleaners or were engaged in public works. All received a reasonable salary. The purpose was to settle them in an honest career.

Nippon Ginkō 日本銀行 (the Bank of Japan). In October 1882, a central bank, the Bank of Japan, was established. Prior to this, in 1872, as a result of the liberalization of the national-bank regulations, numerous new national banks had been established. Between 1876 and 1880, 148 new national banks, all authorized to issue inconvertible paper money, were established. Finance Minister Matsukata Masayoshi (1835–1924) introduced the paper-money system and took the financial situation in hand (1881). In 1882, he established a central bank, the Bank of Japan, which issued convertible bank notes and retired the national-bank notes. National banks were gradually converted into ordinary banks. The last national bank was abolished in 1899.

Nippon Kaika Shōshi 日本開化小史. (*Short History of Japanese Civilization*) A book published in 1877 by the economist and historian Taguchi Ukichi (1855–1905) and patterned after H. T. Buckle's *History of Civilization in England* in two volumes written during the period 1857–61. It was the first Japanese book on the history of Japanese civilization.

Nippon Kōgyō Ginkō 日本興業銀行 (the Industrial Bank of Japan). Following the Sino-Japanese War of 1894–95, Japan concluded with China the Treaty of Shimonoseki, which provided that China pay Japan a war indemnity amounting to 360 million yen. This enabled Japan to expand her industry. By the end of the nineteenth century, Japan had stabilized her money structure by the adoption of the gold standard and by the retirement of practically all the government paper money and national-bank notes. The government's view that the peculiar conditions of Japanese development required banks of a specialized nature in addition to the ordinary banks led in 1900 to the establishment of the Industrial Bank. Its loan funds were obtained by the sale of debentures and by stocks. It also tried to import foreign capital. The bank flourished especially after the Russo-Japanese War (1904–5) and extended its sphere of influence as far as Korea. In time of depression, the bank loaned relief funds.

Nippon Kyōsan-tō 日本共産党 (the Japanese Communist Party). A political party organized by the working class in 1922. The monopolistic tendencies of capitalism after World War I and the powerful impact of the Russian Revolution led to the beginning of a revolutionary movement in Japan. The Japanese branch of the Comintern took shape. Despite some internal difficulties, it pursued its activities against the emperor system and against the mighty trusts known as ZAIBATSU. It also threatened the ruling class. On March 15, 1928, and April 16, 1929, the government subjected the party to hard pressure and suppressed the Labor-Farmer Party and the General Council of Labor Unions. After Japan's defeat in World War II, the Communist Party became a legal party. Top leaders were Tokuda Kyūichi, Shiga Yoshio, and Nozaka Sanzō. The party made great strides, and its membership amounted to several million. In 1950, an order from General MacArthur banished the party from public office, but from 1955 the party tried to keep in line with the law.

Nippon Rōdō-Nōmin-tō 日本労働農民党 (the Japan Labor-Farmer Party). A political party of the Taishō era. Organized in 1926, it split into the Social Democratic Party (SHAKAI MINSHŪ-TŌ), the Japan Labor-Farmer Party (Nippon Rōnō-tō), and the Labor-Farmer Party, known as Rōdō Nōmin-tō.

Nippon Rōdō Sōdōmei 日本労働総同盟 (the Japanese Federation of Labor). One of the earliest organizations in the movement for labor associations. It grew out of the Friendship Association (YŪAI-KAI) established in 1912 by the pioneer of labor unionism Suzuki Bunji (1885–1946). In 1921, the Friendship Association reorganized itself on modern trade-union lines, taking the name of the Japanese Federation of Labor. The federation first advocated cooperation of capital and labor, but the members of the labor associations showed dissatisfaction. Between 1922 and 1923 a definite distinction was made between left-wing and right-wing labor leaders. The struggle between the two classes of executive leaders became more acute, but the right wing took the lead. The withdrawal from the Federation of Labor by the National Council of Japan Labor Unions (1926), the League of Labor Unions (1926), and the National League of Labor Unions (1929) caused the disintegration of the left wing. After the opening of hostilities with China, many right-wing labor leaders espoused the doctrines of ultranationalism, either from conviction or from expediency. They joined the Association for Service to the State Through Industry (DAI NIPPON SANGYŌ HŌKOKU-KAI, usually abbreviated to Sampō). The Federation of Labor was disbanded in 1940 but was revived in 1946.

Nippon Shakai-tō (Meiji) 日本社会党 (明治) (the Socialist Party during the Meiji era). A political party established by Sakai Toshihiko (1870–1933) in 1906. As a result of the development of capitalism after the Sino-Japanese War (1894–95), the friction between labor and capital became more acute, and proletarian parties were formed. Pioneers of the Socialist Party were Kinoshita Naoe (1869–1937), Abe Iso-o (1865–1949), Katayama Sen (1859–1933), and Kōtoku Shūsui (1871–1911). Prime Minister Saionji Kimmochi (1849–1940), of liberalist views, Sakai Toshihiko, and others organized the Socialist Party, which advocated popular suffrage. The party took the lead in the issue of a fare increase for the Tokyo municipal electric railway and was ordered to dissolve in 1908.

Nippon Shakai-tō (sengo) 日本社会党 (戦後) (postwar Socialist Party). The old Socialist Party was re-established after Japan's defeat in 1945. In the general elections of 1947, it became the leading party. When Socialists and Democrats merged, the Socialist Katayama Tetsu (1887–   ) became prime minister. Right-wing and left-wing Socialists broke up in 1951 but were reunited in 1955. In October 1959, Nishio Suehiro withdrew from the Socialist Party and, in January 1960, launched the Democratic Socialist Party.

Nippon Tetsudō-gaisha 日本鉄道会社 (the Japan Railway Company). A private railway company organized in 1882. Plans were made to build a railroad connecting Tōkyō with Aomori. The line, which was the first privately owned railway, was opened in 1891. It was followed by privately owned railways in various parts of the country.

Nippon Yūsen Kabushiki-gaisha 日本郵船株式会社 (the Japan Shipping Company). One of two early major shipping companies. It was established in 1885. In 1871, Iwasaki Yatarō (1834–85) organized the MITSUBISHI Company and concentrated on maritime shipping. At the time of Saigō Takamori's rebellion in 1877, Iwasaki handled military transport. The company, which had secured ships from the government, flourished under government protection. In the competition with American and English shipping companies for coastal service, Iwasaki's company was victorious and secured the monopoly of all coastal service. In 1882, the government, in an effort to break Mitsubishi's monopoly, succeeded in merging various contending companies. The combined company became the Japan Shipping Company and grew especially strong in time of war. The Japan Shipping Company and the Ōsaka Merchant Shipping Company were the two major transportation companies. Their strong development resulted from the government policy of protecting capitalist undertakings. The Japan Shipping Company was the foundation of the Mitsubishi ZAIBATSU.

nise-e 似絵 (portrait painting). Portrait painting in YAMATO-E style. It was the fashion from the close of the Heian to the close of the Kamakura period. Realism and interest in individual personality led to the development of portrait painting. Painters such as Fujiwara no Takanobu (1142–1205) and his son Nobuzane (1176–?) were skilled in portraiture. Portraits of Minamoto no Yoritomo and of Taira no Shigemori preserved in JINGO-JI temple are ascribed to Takanobu. Another representative portrait, that of Emperor Gotoba preserved in Minase Shrine (Minase-jingū), is attributed to Nobuzane. Later the portraits lost their vividness. Along with the ascendancy of Zen Buddhism at the end of the Kamakura period, the painting of illustrious Zen priests flourished. These paintings were referred to as *chinzō*.

Nishijin-ori 西陣織 (Nishijin brocade). Silk fabrics manufactured at Nishijin, Kyōto. The name Nishijin is taken from the place where the warrior Yamana Mochitoyo (1404–73) encamped during the Ōnin Civil War. From early times Kyōto was the center of the weaving industry. Those who served the court in the weavers' office (ORIBE NO TSUKASA) organized a "guild of upper servants" known as *ō-toneri no za*. After the Ōnin Civil War, manufacture of silk fabrics began at Nishijin. Under the stimulus of Hideyoshi, the products improved with the import of Chinese weaving techniques. Twill, damask, and satin were made. Nishijin fabrics are known for their elaborateness and refined taste. Almost all the high-class warriors of the Edo period wore Nishijin clothing. During the Kamakura and Muromachi periods, and from the middle of the Edo period, Nishijin was rivaled by such weaving-industry centers as KIRYŪ, Isesaki, Nagahama, etc. After the Meiji Restoration, Western machines were introduced, but a small hand-weaving business is still being carried on, and the domestic industry system has survived to the present day.

nishiki-e 錦絵 (UKIYO-E)

Nisshin Sensō 日清戦争 (the Sino-Japanese War of 1894–95). The war of 1894–95 between Japan and China. It left a decisive mark on the capitalist expansion of both countries. Since the Kanghwa-do (in Japanese, Kōkatō) incident of 1875, Japan had made many inroads into Korea. But China contended that Korea was within the Chinese sphere of influence. This situation resulted in a scramble for power, not only in the political field but mainly in the economic field. The cotton-cloth market in Korea, which from about 1892 had been favoring Japan, began to favor China. This was a setback keenly felt by Japanese industrial circles, which had started upon large-scale industrial production. The efforts of Li Hung-chang (in Japanese, Ri Kō-shō) to modernize China were partially successful, as Korean diplomatic circles as well as foreign countries recognized China's supremacy over Japan. It was Li's aim that Korea should follow the Chinese, not the Japanese, example. Subject to pressure, Japan wanted to protect her cotton industry. Antigovernment uprisings in Korea provided the occasion for the Japanese invasion. Taking advantage of the Tōgaku Party rebellion in 1894 (TŌGAKU-TŌ NO RAN), Japan sent an army to Korea. The Japanese forces clashed with Chinese troops also sent to Korea. The clash developed into a war. The Japanese forces were victorious in P'yongyang (in Japanese, Heijō), the Yellow Sea, Dairen, Port Arthur, and Weihaiwei (in Japanese, Ikaiei). China surrendered. A peace treaty was signed at Shimonoseki by the Japanese plenipotentiary, Itō Hirobumi, and the Chinese plenipotentiary, Li Hung-chang. China recognized Korea's independence, ceded the Liaotung Peninsula and Formosa to Japan, and paid an indemnity of 200 million taels or 38 million pounds (360 million yen). Russia, Germany, and France, pretending that Japanese possession of Liaotung menaced China's integrity, forced Japan to relinquish this territory. Being unable to combat this intervention, Japan complied. China's weakness had become obvious, and Western powers acquired leaseholds and military bases in China.

Nisso Chūritsu Jōyaku 日ソ中立条約 (the Soviet-Japanese Nonaggression Pact). A pact concluded in 1941 between Japan and Soviet Russia. The term of validity of the pact was five years. The two parties pledged to maintain friendly relations, not to violate each other's territorial integrity, and to remain neutral if either one of the two parties was at war. The Konoe cabinet tried to draw Soviet Russia into the Tripartite Alliance and to readjust Japanese-American diplomatic relations. Though friendly relations with Soviet Russia were strained by Germany's attack on Russia two months later, the pact offered favorable conditions to the Japanese army, which planned to extend its influence to Southeast Asia. The pact was violated by Soviet Russia when this country joined the war against Japan on August 9, 1945.

nōchi kaikaku 農地改革 (agrarian reform). Part of the postwar democratization policy. In December 1945, the Supreme Commander for the Allied Powers ordered that an agrarian reform based on the principles of the Potsdam Declaration should be carried out as a major step towards democratization. The reform removed all parasitic landowners, broke the feudal structure of the farmer communities, and aimed at raising agrarian production. First, the government enacted the agricultural land adjustment law and attempted an initial agrarian reform. But the Allied Council for Japan pointed out that there were some shortcomings in the reform. The law concerning special measures for the establishment of owner farmers (1946) and the amended agricultural land adjustment law resulted in a second reform in November 1947. Noncultivating resident landowners were allowed to possess not more than one *chōbu* (2.45 acres) of arable land. Cultivating resident landowners were allowed to possess not more than three *chōbu*. The surplus of arable land was purchased by the government and sold, by priority, to former tenant farmers. The right of cultivation of tenant farmers was guaranteed, and it was decided that farm rent would amount to 25 percent of the harvest in cash payment. The Agricultural Land Commission was responsible for the enforcement of the law. As a result, the percentage of tenant farmers dropped from a prewar 46 percent to 10 percent, and the number of owner farmers was doubled. But some landowners, being engaged in lumbering, transportation, finance, and other businesses, still exert a semifeudal authority. Japanese agriculture is becoming more and more directly subordinate to the overall capitalist economy.

Nōgaku 能楽 (Nō drama). A kind of lyric drama brought to perfection during the Muromachi period. The initial mimetic dances, which were performed in religious ceremonies and Buddhist memorial services during the Kamakura period, developed into Nōgaku. Kan'ami (1334–85) and his son Zeami (1363–1443) brought the Nō to perfection. They had left the Yūsaki-za in Yamato Province, where SARUGAKU was performed, and enjoyed the protection of Shōgun Ashikaga Yoshimitsu (1358–1408). They took in the strong points of DENGAKU and aimed at "mysterious beauty" *(yūgen-bi)*. Under their leadership, Nō became a refined art. With the schools known as Kanze, Hōshō, Komparu, and Kongō, Nō flourished during the Muromachi period, especially in the four theaters of Yamato (YAMATO-SHIZA). Not only professional actors but also amateurs performed. During the Edo period, Nōgaku, having become the ceremonial drama of the upper-class warriors, lost its elegance and popularity. Today Nōgaku is divided into five schools. The song of the Nō is called YŌKYOKU. Some librettos describe contemporary social conditions, others teach Buddhist tenets. The subject matter is drawn from classical works as well as from tradition.

Nōgyō Zensho 農業全書. A book on agriculture in ten volumes completed in 1696 by the agriculturist Miyazaki Yasusada (1623–97). The author consulted Chinese books on agriculture. He toured all the provinces and gathered firsthand information. He himself cultivated land for many years. He gives a full account of the soil, fertilizer, cultivation, crops, and 150 sorts of farm products. The book contributed greatly to the improvement of agriculture, and Tokugawa Mitsukuni and Kaibara Ekiken praised it. In 1721, the most important parts of the work were brought together in *Nōgyō Zensho Yakugen* by Suyama Don'ō (Suyama Totsuan, 1657–1732). This latter work became a manual of agriculture.

Nomonhan jiken ノモンハン事件 (the incident at Nomonhan). The fighting between Japanese and Soviet forces which began at the end of May and was not terminated until September 1939 at Nomonhan (or Nom-un-han) on the border between Manchuria and Outer Mongolia. Since the Manchurian incident, both forces had been battling each other on the Manchurian-Soviet frontier. Japan was determined to hold the northwestern Manchurian border. Under the pretext that troops of Outer Mongolia had violated Manchurian territory, the combined Manchurian-Japanese forces launched an attack and were severely beaten by the Russians commanded by Zhukov.

Nova Hispania ノバ・イスパニア (Nueva España). The name of Mexico under Spanish domination. In 1521, Mexico became Spanish territory and was called Nueva España. In 1571, Spain occupied Manila. The all-important route linking Mexico with Manila led to relations with Japan, and Ieyasu was on friendly footing with the foreign navigators. When, in 1609, a Spanish ship drifted to Chiba Prefecture, the Kyōto trader Tanaka Katsusuke followed the ship back to the Philippines. In 1613, the warlord Date Masamune (1565–1636) sent one of his retainers, Hasekura Tsunenaga, to Rome via Mexico. Relations were broken off when Christianity was banned.

nuhi 奴婢 (slaves). The lowest class of "unfree people" *(semmin)* during the Nara period. *Nuhi* were divided into two categories: the official public serfs *(kan'yū no kunuhi)* and private slaves *(shi-nuhi)*. Official serfs were under the control of the Imperial Household Department. They included criminals who had been deprived of their civil rights. They were chiefly engaged in cultivating the imperial lands and in miscellaneous corvées. They received the same area of allotted land as the free people *(ryōmin)* and were exempt from both the land tax (so) and the produce tax (CHŌ). Private slaves were less free. They were merely valuable property of the master and received only one-third of the area allotted to free people. Slaves were the main working force of the nobility, territorial magnates, temples, and shrines. After the Nara period, they tended to disappear and were abolished by the Engi-kyaku in 909. The Engi-kyaku is a compilation of amended regulations.

Nutari no ki 淳足柵 (the stockade of Nutari). One of the palisades or forts built against the Ainu during the Nara period. The palisades were bases of operation against the aborigines. According to tradition, the Ainu were subdued by the Yamato court from the time of the fifth century, but the subjugation continued after the Taika Reform, when the national structure was consolidated. At strategic places stockades were erected. The local inhabitants were encouraged to settle, either freely or by force, in these frontier areas and to become a sort of colonial militia. The Ainu who submitted were given clothing and food and were allowed to live on the spot. In 647, a fort was erected in Nutari, in the vicinity of Niigata. It was removed in 712 when the place was made into a rural district, or *gun*.

Ōbaku-shū 黄檗宗 (Ōbaku branch of Zen Buddhism). A branch of Zen Buddhism introduced into Japan during the seventeenth century. It was founded by the Chinese priest Ingen (1592–1673), who was a naturalized Japanese. Ōbaku (in Chinese, Huang Po) is the name of the mountain in China where Ingen studied Buddhism. Invited by Shōgun Ietsuna (1641–80), Ingen arrived at Nagasaki in 1654 and, in 1660, established Mampuku-ji temple in Uji near Kyōto. Ōbaku makes use of the Amida Sutra, which is the main scripture of Amidism. The sect greatly contributed to the study of the Chinese classics.

ōban, koban 大判・小判 (Japanese gold coins). Gold currency. In 1588, Hideyoshi minted elliptic gold coins known as Tenshō *ōban* and *koban*. In 1601, the Edo shogunate inaugurated a "gold guild" (KINZA) and minted the Keichō *ōban* and *koban*. They were often recast during the Genroku (1688–1704) and Kyōhō (1716–36) eras. The weight of an *ōban* was about 40 *momme* (one *momme* equals 3.75 grams); the weight of a *koban* was about 4.7 *momme*. The *koban* was for daily use, but the *ōban* was used only when etiquette demanded.

ōban-yaku 大番役 (the great watch). One of the warriors' duties during the middle ages. Warriors had to serve in the capital for fixed periods in rotation for the protection of the court. The origin was the military guard (EJI) in ancient Japan. The Kamakura shogunate imposed the service on provincial warriors (GO-KENIN). It was the duty of the constable to recruit men for this service and to assume their leadership.

obito 首. One of the titles (KABANE) in ancient Japan. The title was conferred on many TOMO NO MIYATSUKO who were the heads of the guilds and who lived in the capital. From 681, those honored with this title received the title MURAJI (group chief). In 685, when the eight titles (YAKUSA NO KABANE) were determined, the title *obito* was officially abolished, though it was still used by many people.

Odawara 小田原. City in Kanagawa Prefecture. From 1495, when the warlord Hōjō Sōun (1432–1519) founded the powerful Hōjō family in Odawara, the city flourished as the center of the Kantō district. Merchants of various provinces gathered in Odawara, which became the castle town of the Hōjō clan. Like YAMAGUCHI, under the administration of the Ōuchi family, Odawara also became a center of local culture during the Sengoku period (1490–1573). In 1590, Hideyoshi attacked the Hōjō in Odawara, and the castle surrendered after more than three months of resistance.

Odawara seibatsu 小田原征伐 (the subjugation of Odawara). The battle of Hideyoshi against the Hōjō clan in 1590. In subduing the Hōjō in their castle at Odawara, Hideyoshi did not launch a frontal attack but besieged the castle for one hundred days and forced them to surrender. Meanwhile, there were long discussions in the castle between Hōjō Ujinao (1562–91) and his confidants as to what course of action to follow. The negotiations brought no result and were needlessly protracted. They are the origin of the expression *Odawara hyōjō,* which came to mean "endless negotiations." After Hōjō's surrender, Hideyoshi subdued the Kantō and Tōhoku districts and finally united the country.

Ōei no gaikō 応永の外寇 (foreign invasion of the Ōei era). The Korean invasion of Tsushima Island in 1419. From the time of the Kamakura period, Japan followed an expansionist policy. Furthermore, during the Namboku period (1336–92) Japanese pirates, known as WAKŌ, ravaged the Korean coastal region. As the kingdom of Kōrai was almost ruined by pirates, Korea decided to retaliate. General Yi Song-gye (in Japanese Ri Sei-kei) of Kōrai tried to repel the Japanese pirates. He inaugurated the Yi (Ri) dynasty in 1392 and demanded that Japan suppress the pirates. As the pirates continued to harass Korea, Korean troops invaded Tsushima to uproot the pirates' stronghold. This action was called *Ōei no gaikō.* From this time, harmonious diplomatic relations were resumed with Japan, and trade regulations were set up. Japanese vessels sailing to Korea needed tallies (KANGŌFU) to be identified. However, repeated disputes between the Sō clan (SŌ UJI) of Tsushima and Korea resulted in the decline of trade in the sixteenth century.

Ōei no ran 応永の乱 (civil strife of the Ōei era). Revolt of the warrior Ōuchi Yoshihiro (1355–99) against the Ashikaga shogunate. During the Muromachi period, the shogunate was unable to control the powerful constable landowners (SHUGO DAIMYŌ). In an effort to destroy the constable daimyō, Shōgun Ashikaga Yoshimitsu (1358–1408) eliminated Yamana Ujikiyo (?–1391) in what is known as the Meitoku revolt (MEITOKU NO RAN). He also tried to subdue Ōuchi Yoshihiro, who was constable of six provinces. Learning about Yoshimitsu's plan, Yoshihiro plotted with Ashikaga Mitsukane (1377–1409), the governor of Kantō, and fought Shōgun Yoshimitsu at Sakai. Yoshimitsu, with the help of Hatakeyama and Shiba, defeated Yoshihiro in 1399. The incident had far-reaching effects, as it consolidated the shogunate's authority over the constable daimyō and strengthened the Muromachi shogunate.

Ogasawara Shotō 小笠原諸島 (the Bonin Islands). The islands are thought to have been discovered by Ogasawara Sadayori (?–1625) in 1593. The Edo shogunate tried to develop the islands but failed. In 1875, the Meiji government declared the islands Japanese territory, developed communications, and established a strategic base. After the Pacific War, the Bonins were placed under American administration, and in 1951, at the Japanese peace conference, they were put under a United States trusteeship. The natives launched a return-to-Japan movement.

ōgosho 大御所. A retired shōgun. Originally, the word meant the father of a shōgun and was sometimes used to indicate a prince or a distinguished court noble. Tokugawa Ieyasu and Ienari were called *ōgosho*. The period of Ienari's reign—that is, the Bunka-Bunsei era (1804–30)—is called the Ōgosho period. The reason is that Ienari's style of life was known for its luxury and that the people cherished the memory of those extravagant days.

Ōhara Shakai Mondai Kenkyūsho 大原社会問題研究所 (The Ōhara Social Problems Research Institute). A research institute for social problems founded in 1919 in Ōsaka by Ōhara Magosaburō (1880–1943). The institute is known for its outstanding merit in prewar days.

Oie-ryū 御家流 (the Oie style of calligraphy). A school of calligraphy initiated during the Namboku period (1336–92) by Prince Son'en Hosshinnō (Hōshinnō, 1298–1356). It is also called Shōren'in-ryū because the prince, who was a Buddhist priest, lived in Shōren-in temple. When the style of calligraphy referred to as Sesonji-ryū, originated by Fujiwara no Yukinari (972–1027), had lost its vigor, Oie-ryū became popular. During the Edo period, all official documents, clan documents, and notice boards were written in this style. The style was taught at the temple schools (TERAKOYA) and spread over the country. Gradually, it lost its art and became formalized. After the Meiji Restoration, Oie-ryū declined.

Ōjōyōshū 往生要集. A Buddhist book written in 984 by Eshin Sōzu (Genshin, 942–1017). Classifying more than 160 commentaries on Buddhist scriptures *(kyōron)* into ten categories, Eshin wrote the book with special emphasis on rebirth in Amida's paradise. The book did much to encourage the invocation of Buddha's name known as *nembutsu*. It also helped spread the Jōdo faith (JŌDO-SHŪ) among nobles like Fujiwara no Michinaga (966–1027), who called on Amida on his deathbed, and gradually influenced Hōnen's (1133–1212) *nembutsu* religion. From the end of the Heian period, many pictures of the ten Buddhist worlds illustrated the ten categories as explained by Eshin. His book was also greatly admired in Sung China.

Ōkagami 大鏡. A historical work in eight volumes written during the late Heian period at the end of the eleventh century. It is one of the "Four Kagami" or *Shikyō* and is also known as *Yotsugi no Monogatari*. The author and the year of publication are not known. The book is written in the form of a dialogue between an old man called Ōyake no Yotsugi and Natsuyama no Shigeki. Centering around the glories of Fujiwara no Michinaga (966–1027), it describes in *kana* writing and in biographical style the zenith of prosperity of the Fujiwara leaders from 850 to 1025 and covers the same story as EIGA MONOGATARI, although in more critical fashion.

Okehazama no tatakai 桶狭間の戦 (the battle at Okehazama). The battle fought in 1560 between Nobunaga and the warrior Imagawa Yoshimoto (1519–60). Imagawa, who ruled Suruga, Tōtōmi (Shizuoka Prefecture), and Mikawa (Aichi Prefecture), also planned to take Kyōto. To attack Nobunaga, Imagawa invaded Owari (Aichi Prefecture) in 1560, but Nobunaga, taking advantage of a rainstorm, made a surprise attack and killed Imagawa. This and other battles led to the unification of the country.

Oki 隠岐. An island in the Japan Sea, Shimane Prefecture. From ancient times, Oki served as a place of exile. It was the banishment place in 1221 of ex-Emperor Gotoba after the Jōkyū revolt (JŌKYŪ NO HEN) and of Emperor Godaigo after the Genkō revolt (GENKŌ NO HEN).

Okuni Kabuki 阿国歌舞伎. The beginnings of KABUKI are obscure. According to tradition, the origin of Okuni Kabuki seems to be the *nembutsu* dances (NEMBUTSU ODORI) performed in Kyōto in the early seventeenth century by an IZUMO TAISHA shrine virgin (MIKO) known as Okuni. Sensual performance seems to have been the main interest of the acting groups. Okuni's dances, as well as JŌRURI, led to the development of eighteenth- and nineteenth-century Kabuki.

Oku no Hosomichi 奥の細道. A poetic account of a trip to North Honshū by the haiku poet Matsuo Bashō (1644–94). On March 27, 1689, Bashō set out from Edo with his disciple Kawai Sora. Traveling to Nikkō, Matsushima, and Hiraizumi, he passed through Niigata, Kanazawa, and Ōgaki. On September 6, a new shrine was to be dedicated at Ise, and, with the purpose of worshiping there, Bashō sailed to Ise. *Oku no Hosomichi* is an account of this seven-month trip that covered 2,400 kilometers. In this work Bashō greatly improved his haiku (HAIKAI), and his *haibun* (prose containing haiku poems) deeply influenced Japanese literature.

ōkura 大蔵 (Yamato court-property storehouse). One of the storehouses holding the property of the Yamato court. There were three *kura:* the IMI-KURA or storehouse which contained the objects for Shintō ceremonies, the *uchitsukura* or storehouse which contained the presents brought to Japan by envoys of Sankan (Korea), and the *ōkura*. They were collectively called SANZŌ. The *imikura* and *uchitsukura* existed from ancient times. The *ōkura* was established in order to cope with a considerable amount of goods in taxes which had accumulated. After the Taika Reform (646), the *imikura* and *uchitsukura* lost their independence. The *ōkura* became one of the eight ministries of state, namely, the Ministry of the Treasury or Ōkura-shō.

ōmetsuke 大目付 (the head of censors). An office of the Edo shogunate. The number of officials was first limited to four, then to five. They were chosen from among the high-class bannermen (HATAMOTO) and were under the administration of the councilors of the shōgun or RŌJŪ. In peacetime, their duties resolved themselves into surveillance of the conduct of vassals and various officials.

Ōminato 大湊. 1) A port town in Mie Prefecture. It flourished from ancient times, as it was the oldest port of Ise Bay. It was also a port for Ise Shrine and was known during the middle ages for the self-government of the townspeople and their autonomous organizations known as EGŌSHŪ. During the Edo period, Ōminato fell under the municipal administration of Yamada. Its shipyard flourished, but, because of its unfavorable geographic location, it was outstripped by Toba. 2) A port town in Aomori Prefecture, on the southern coast of Shimokita Peninsula. Its importance was recognized from the time of the Meiji Restoration. From 1900, it flourished as a naval station.

Ōmi Ryō 近江令 (the Ōmi Code). The first recorded Japanese legislation, in twenty-one volumes codified during the early Nara period. It reflected the spirit of the constitutional government after the Taika Reform (646) and was codified following an imperial edict through the efforts of Fujiwara no Kamatari (614–69). The promulgation by Emperor Tenchi (621–71) from his palace at Ōtsu in Ōmi Province took place in 668. The text is not extant, but probably the enactments were modeled after those of the Chenkuan era (627–49) of the Chinese T'ang dynasty and inspired the ASUKA NO KIYOMI-GAHARA RYŌ, which was a revision of the Ōmi ryō under Emperor Temmu (622–686), and the Taihō Code (TAIHŌ RITSURYŌ) of 702.

Ōmi shōnin 近江商人 (merchants of Ōmi). Corporations of merchants whose home territory was Ōmi (Shiga Prefecture). From ancient times, communications were favorable and trade flourished in the district east of Lake Biwa. Merchants began to organize themselves. They consolidated their position during the middle ages. Crossing mountains and seas, they engaged in itinerant trade. During the Edo period, trade expanded rapidly. Headquarters were places such as Hachiman, Hino, and Gokashō, and the merchants expanded their itinerant trade all over the country. Some of them settled down, contributing to local industrial production or engaging in the money-lending business. Others were meritorious for aiding the development of Hokkaidō. The solidarity of local tradesmen and their tenacious commercial codes have remained famous.

ō-muraji 大連 (grand group chief). The name of officials in ancient Japan and one of the titles (KABANE). The office was the highest in the Yamato court. The *ō-muraji* was the leader of the group chiefs and was ranked with the ō-OMI or leader of all the clan chieftains. Influential MURAJI were members of the Mononobe and Ōtomo clans. With the decline of these two clans during the sixth century, the office of *ō-muraji* was discontinued, and the power shifted to the *ō-omi* of the Soga clan.

onchi 恩地 (reward fields). Fields awarded by masters to their vassals during the middle ages. It was the custom that the shogunate and daimyō granted fields to their retainers and followers as a reward for their distinguished services. These fields were also referred to as *onshō-chi* and *onkyū-chi*. In principle, pawning as well as buying and selling of these fields was prohibited, but the ancient custom of transmission by heredity still prevailed.

Ōnin no Ran 応仁の乱 (the Ōnin Civil War). The civil war in and around Kyōto which lasted for eleven years, from 1467 through 1477. The shōgun of the MUROMACHI BAKUFU, Ashikaga Yoshimasa (1434–90), led a luxurious life and neglected his duties. When his power was on the decline, his prime minister, Hosokawa Katsumoto (1430–73), fought Yamana Mochitoyo (1404–73), and a scramble for power followed. At the same time, quarrels involving Yoshimasa's successor broke out, and both the Hatakeyama and the Shiba

families were torn by dissension. The situation was aggravated when Katsumoto gave his support to both Hatakeyama Masaie and Shiba Yoshitoshi,
while Mochitoyo supported the other faction, namely, Hatakeyama Yoshinari
and Shiba Yoshikado. Other warlords supported or opposed the antagonists,
and the conflict spread. Katsumoto defended Emperor Tsuchimikado and
Yoshimasa; Mochitoyo supported Yoshimasa's younger brother, Yoshimi.
The *bakufu's* chief vassals and warriors were divided into two antagonistic
groups, and they fought each other for eleven years. The outcome of the civil
strife was that Kyōto was reduced to ashes. After the Ōnin War, the scene
of the battle shifted to the provinces, where the constables fought for their
autonomy and for the increase of their respective fiefs. This period is known
as the period of civil war (SENGOKU JIDAI) and lasted from 1490 to 1573.
The manor system collapsed, and the establishment of a feudal society based
on territorial fiefs of great landlords was accelerated.

Onjō-ji 園城寺. The main temple of the Jimon branch (JIMON-SHŪ) of Tendai
Buddhism. The temple, which is also known as Mii-dera, is in Ōtsu. The
Jimon branch was opposed to Hiei-zan's ENRYAKU-JI, which was called SAM-
MON. It was once thought that Onjō-ji was founded in 687, but actually its
founder was Enchin (814–91), who restored the temple in 859. Later Enchin
came into conflict with the disciples of Ennin (794–864) of Enryaku-ji. The
conflict caused the division into Jimon and Sammon. Onjō-ji was burned
down several times when struggles for power with Enryaku-ji occurred. In
1180, it was burned down by the warrior Mochihito-ō (1151–80), who attempted to destroy the power of the Taira. The temple was also laid waste
in other fires caused by warfare.

Onna Daigaku 女大学. A book on women's education written during the
Edo period and published in 1729. The book, which was widely used, is
ascribed to Kaibara Ekiken (1650–1714). More probably it was written by a
later scholar who made use of Kaibara's *Wazoku Dōji-kun*. The work is based
on the Confucian *sanjū shichikyo* or the threefold submission of women and
the seven reasons for divorce by men. It deals largely with the duties of
women, especially of housewives. The position of women in feudal society
was low.

Ono-gumi 小野組 (the Ono trade corporation). A ZAIBATSU concern which
flourished from the Edo period to the early years of the Meiji era. The
association, which during the Genroku era (1688–1704) established its headquarters in Kyōto, was formed by Ōmi merchants (ŌMI SHŌNIN). The members
of the association were merchants who had secured the official monopoly for
transactions in imported raw silk *(itowappu)*. Later they engaged in the
moneylending business. In the early Meiji years, together with Mitsui-gumi
and Shimoda-gumi, Ono-gumi was commissioned as the office in charge of

government finances known as *kawase-kata*. The bank jointly established by Ono and Mitsui was the First National Bank. From 1871, the Ono-gumi also engaged in silk manufacturing, but in 1875 the business declined and, failing to obtain government help, went bankrupt.

Onomichi 尾道. A harbor city in southeast Hiroshima Prefecture. The place has been known from ancient times and was extolled in MAN'YŌSHŪ as a "jewel bay" *(tama no ura)*. It flourished as a port for Ōtashō in Bingo Province. During the Muromachi period, it was one of the ports for shipment to Ming China. Onomichi suffered from the isolation policy of the Edo administration but entered another flourishing period during the Kambun era (1661–73) when the western roundabout sea route was opened. The city was closely connected with the industry and finance of the Asano clan, and its prosperity and decay influenced the clan's financial policy.

onshō-kata 恩賞方 (office of awards). An office of the Kemmu Restoration. After the Genkō uprising in 1331 (GENKŌ NO HEN) this office was established in 1334 by Emperor Godaigo in order to investigate the claims of those who had contributed to the success of the loyal cause and to give them rewards. But as it exercised no real authority, it did not produce the expected results. Before long the *onshō-kata* was abolished.

on'yōdō 陰陽道 (the way of *yin* and *yang*). A Chinese philosophic doctrine according to which two opposing principles, the active and the regressive, produce all phenomena by their operation upon the five elements. It degenerated into a kind of pseudo-science like fortunetelling. The belief is also called *on'yō-gogyō* and was introduced into Japan via Kudara during the Asuka period (552–645). In Heian times, the study of *on'yōdō* grew, and in one of the departments of state there was a bureau, the On'yōryō, devoted to it. Doctors of *on'yōdō (on'yō hakase)* were appointed, and they taught astronomy, calendar making, and arithmetic. Outstanding scholars of the Heian period were Kamo no Tadayuki and his son Yasunori (?–977) and Abe no Seimei (?–1005). Kamo taught calendar making, and Abe taught astronomy. The Kamo and Abe were hereditary authorities in their respective fields. According to *on'yōdō,* interaction of the ten calendar signs *(jikkan)* and the twelve horary signs *(jūnishi)* determines fortune and misfortune, prosperity and adversity. Divination greatly influenced everyday life. Examples are the avoiding of going in an inauspicious direction *(kata-gatae)* by the Heian aristocracy and confinement to one's house on unlucky days *(monoimi)*.

ō-omi 大臣 (leader of the clan chieftains). The name of officials in ancient Japan and one of the titles (KABANE). The leader of all the clan chieftains was the highest officer in the Yamato court and was the great minister. Heguri no Madori (?–498), who was the grandson of the warrior Takenouchi no Sukune

(?–367), and members of the Soga, Katsuragi, and Kose families were successively appointed *ō-omi*. The Soga held the position for several generations. At the time of Soga no Umako (?–626), the Mononobe were exterminated, and the grand group chiefs (ō-MURAJI), territorial administrative officers of high rank, were abolished. As a result, the office of *ō-omi* was exclusively held by the Soga. At the time of the Taika Reform (646), the *ō-omi* ceded their office to the ministers of the left and of the right and to the *naishin,* who were higher in rank than these ministers.

ōrai-mono 往来物 (text and reference books). Popular text and reference books which played an important part in general education from the end of the Heian to the beginning of the Meiji period. Formerly, education centered around composition based on the epistolary style, but the textbooks gradually came to contain more practical knowledge. In due time, the *ōrai-mono* were used in elementary school and in the so-called temple schools (TERAKOYA) because they offered general information on various subjects.

Oranda fūsetsu-gaki 阿蘭陀風説書 (Western information). Information concerning the West furnished by the Dutch ships during the Edo period. Every time the *capitao* (*kapitan* in Japanese) of a Dutch ship entered Nagasaki, he brought a report on the situation in the West. A Dutch interpreter translated the report into Japanese, and the information was sent to the BAKUFU. After the ban on Christianity, information centered around Portugal and Spain. Later the reports concerned Europe in general, India, and China. Only the *bakufu* authorities were authorized to read the report, but, indirectly at least, the information thus gathered accelerated the growth of Dutch (Western) learning.

oribe no tsukasa 織部司 (the weaving office). One of the five offices of the Ministry of the Treasury (Ōkura-shō) during the Nara and Heian periods. The office was in charge of the weaving of patterned cloth, gauze, cotton, and pongee and of dyeing.

ōryōshi 押領使 (police commissioner). An extralegal emergency body which continued into the feudal period as a means of keeping order in the country. For the maintenance of peace, police commissioners or high sheriffs were chosen from among provincial and rural administrative district officials. They had to be proficient in military arts. Some were also chosen from among wealthy families and were in charge of police duties in peacetime as well as in wartime. They were also in charge of military affairs. The first *ōryōshi* was appointed at the time of the subjugation of the Ainu in 878. He was Fujiwara no Hidesato. Soldiers were recruited for the position of *ōryōshi,* and usually they controlled a whole province. During the Kamakura period, however, the duties of *ōryōshi* were turned over to constables and land stewards.

osa-byakushō (**otona-byakushō**) 長百姓 (influential farmers). Rich farmers in the rural communities of the Edo period. They were influential and controlled the villages. They were also called *takamochi-byakushō* and were assimilated with the independent farmers (HOMBYAKUSHŌ). Probably there was a relation between these farmers and the name masters (MYŌSHU) of the middle ages who were the managers of guilds for religious celebrations (MIYA-ZA) and formed the nucleus of self-governing bodies. The *osa-byakushō* of the Edo period were ranked with the village administrators (MURA YAKUNIN). Some of them represented the whole rural community and became official village administrators or *mura yakunin*.

Ōsaka 大阪. The main commercial and industrial city in the Kansai district. Its position at the mouth of the Yodogawa river is of significance. In ancient times, Ōsaka was called Naniwa. Importance was attached to the place because it was a port for the Yamato court and a port of trade with China. It has been the seat of the central government, and the Shitennō-ji temple was built there. In the middle ages, it was called both Osaka 小坂 and Ōsaka 大坂, and, in 1496, when the ISHIYAMA HONGAN-JI temple was erected, a temple town (MONZEN-MACHI) developed. In 1583, Hideyoshi built Ōsaka Castle, and, after he had summoned the merchants of Sakai and Hirano, a castle town (JŌKA-MACHI) came into being. Ōsaka's dominant economic position was established. Many merchants' houses, however, were burnt down during the winter and summer campaigns of Ieyasu's siege of Ōsaka Castle in 1614 and 1615 (ŌSAKA NO JIN). Then Ōsaka fell under the direct administration of the Edo shogunate, and a supervisor of the Kinki district living in Ōsaka *(jōdai)* and a municipal administrator (MACHI BUGYŌ) were appointed. They were the mainstays of the Kansai district. Ōsaka flourished because of its industry and economy. After the Yodogawa river was improved, the city became a distribution center. Clan offices for transactions in provincial products (KURA-YASHIKI) and money-exchange business houses lined the streets in the neighborhood of Nakanoshima. Not only wholesale firms but also special markets developed. Some of them were the rice market of Dōjima, the vegetable market of Temma, and the fish market of Zakoba. Before long, Ōsaka became the financial center of the whole country. The townspeople not only dominated the rulers with their resources; they also greatly influenced culture, especially during the Genroku era (1688–1704), when the characteristic Ōsaka culture developed. The city further improved with the economic modernization of the Meiji era. The Ōsaka Stock Exchange and the Ōsaka Mint were established, and the place became a modern industrial city. Repeated harbor improvements helped modernization and trade expansion.

Ōsaka jiken 大阪事件 (the Ōsaka incident). An incident caused by the Korean reform movement launched by the left-wing Liberal Party. The movement for democratic rights had lost the support of both leaders and people because of oppressive as well as conciliatory measures taken by the government. In 1884, the Liberal Party was dissolved, and the Progressive Party was at a low ebb. At the same time, the Korean political reform aggravated Sino-Japanese relations. Ōi Kentarō (1843–1922) of the former left-wing Liberal Party tried to curtail Chinese interference in Korea. He threw his support over to the pro-Japanese Independence Party (Dokuritsu-tō) and planned to overthrow the pro-Chinese Conservative Party (JIDAI-TŌ) and achieve Korean freedom and equality. Taking advantage of the tense international relations, he tried to revive the democratic movement. He had the support of Itagaki Taisuke and Gotō Shōjirō. Itō Hirobumi, who sided with the Korean Independence Party, caused the Kōshin rebellion *(Kōshin no ran)* of 1884. The Independence Party was crushed by Chinese forces, which placed the Jidai-tō in power. The Treaty of Tientsin (TENSHIN JŌYAKU) between China and Japan was concluded. In 1885, Ōi Kentarō, who had overthrown the Jidai-tō, planned to sail to Korea. When he was making arrangements to leave Ōsaka, his plans were disclosed, and Ōi was imprisoned for six years.

Ōsaka-jō 大阪城 (Ōsaka Castle). In 1583, Hideyoshi, with the compulsory help of the daimyō of all the provinces, built Ōsaka Castle on the site where ISHIYAMA HONGAN-JI temple once stood. The circumference of the castle was three *ri* (one *ri* equals 3.93 kilometers) and eight *chō* (one *chō* equals 109 meters). The construction was a model of Momoyama castle architecture. In 1615, the castle was destroyed by fire during the Ōsaka campaigns (ŌSAKA NO JIN). Hideyoshi ordered the townspeople of Sakai and Hirano to move to his castle town and the lords to build their mansions there. The municipal area was kept in proper shape and was made the center of Hideyoshi's administrative power. It was the starting point of Ōsaka's growth.

Ōsaka Kaigi 大阪会議 (Ōsaka Conference). A conference in the early Meiji years aimed at strengthening the government. After the discussions concerning the argument for war with Korea, the central administration was weakened, and Kido Takayoshi (1833–77), who opposed the plan to invade Korea, retired from public office. Ōkubo Toshimichi (1831–78), who was at the head of government affairs, tried to reinstate Kido because the rupture among leading statesmen of the restoration menaced the government. Itō Hirobumi and Inoue Kaoru of the Chōshū clan persuaded Ōkubo to reach some sort of compromise with Itagaki and Kido, and a conference was held in Ōsaka (1875). Ōkubo, Kido, Itagaki, and others pledged themselves to cooperate in the establishment of a constitutional government structure.

Ōsaka no jin 大阪の陣 (the Ōsaka campaigns). Ieyasu's campaigns against the Toyotomi. For some time past, Ieyasu had exerted pressure upon Toyotomi Hideyori (1593–1615), but the situation had worsened since the affair of the bell inscription at the Hōkō-ji temple. Hōkō-ji was built by Hideyoshi in 1586. Destroyed by an earthquake in 1596, it was rebuilt by Hideyori in 1612, and a huge bell was added. In the inscription on the bell were the characters *kokka ankō,* of which the second and last formed the name "Ieyasu." Ieyasu, who was looking for a pretext to subdue the Toyotomi, ordered the removal of the characters. In November 1614, Ieyasu besieged Hideyori in Ōsaka Castle. Hideyori had summoned the daimyō, but they did not answer. Mainly relying on RŌNIN, Hideyori resisted bravely. Peace proposals by Ieyasu were accepted. This campaign is called the winter campaign of Ōsaka *(Ōsaka fuyu no jin).* In 1615, Hideyori again raised soldiers. The occasion was the violation by Ieyasu of the peace terms, which included the filling of the castle's outer moat only. The inner moat had been filled too, and the outer ramparts had been pulled down. In May, the siege was resumed. The outcome was victory for the forces of Ieyasu. Hideyori and his mother Yodogimi committed suicide, thus extinguishing the Toyotomi family. The castle fell in the same month, and Ieyasu became the undisputed ruler of Japan. This campaign is known as the summer campaign of Ōsaka *(Ōsaka natsu no jin).* The campaigns are also known as *Keichō to Genna no eki* or the campaigns of the Keichō (1596–1615) and Genna (1615–24) eras.

Ōsaka Shōsen Kaisha 大阪商船会社 (Ōsaka Mercantile Shipping Company). A maritime transportation company. Through the efforts of Ōsaka and other prefectures, the Inland Sea route was opened in 1884. In 1887, the sea route extended as far as Korea and China. From about 1912, the company became the second major Japanese shipping company, next to the Japan Shipping Company (NIPPON YŪSEN KABUSHIKI-GAISHA). Ōsaka Shōsen Kaisha ships now sail the seven seas.

ōsei fukko 王政復古 (the restoration of imperial rule). The overthrow of the shogunate and the restoration of imperial rule. On October 14, 1867, the fifteenth shōgun, Tokugawa Yoshinobu (1827–1913), restored administrative authority to Emperor Meiji. The structure of the new administration was not determined at once, and no arrangements had been made in regard to the Tokugawa. On December 9 of the same year, the regency (SESSHŌ), the office of chief councilor to the emperor (KAMPAKU), that of generalissimo *(seii-taishōgun),* and the shogunate representative in Kyōto (KYŌTO SHOSHIDAI) were abolished. A declaration announced the creation of three new offices: the Presidency (SŌSAI), the office of Senior Council of State (GIJŌ), and that of Junior Council of State (SAN'YO). This declaration is known as *ōsei fukko no dai-gōrei.*

Ōshū tandai 奥州探題 (commissioner of Mutsu). An office of the MUROMACHI BAKUFU. Around the year 1335, Ashikaga Takauji (1305–58), in a first attempt to subdue the Mutsu district, dispatched the warrior Ishidō Yoshifusa to fight Kitabatake of the Southern dynasty. In 1338, a commissioner was appointed for Ōshū (Mutsu) and another for Ushū (Uzen or Yamagata Prefecture and Ugo or Akita Prefecture). From the fifteenth century, both offices declined.

osso 越訴 (appeals). During the Kamakura and Muromachi periods, when a suitor was dissatisfied with the first trial and when the president of the auxiliary deliberative assembly or *hikitsuke-tōnin* (HIKITSUKE-SHŪ) did not accept the complaint, the suitor could appeal to the commissioner of appeals *(osso bugyō)*. This appeal was called *osso*. During the Edo period, some farmers, without following the procedures, filed action against local administrators, accusing them of injustice. This procedure was also called *osso*. There were many instances of such suits against corrupt deputies or DAIKAN. Usually, though the requests were complied with, the accuser was severely punished.

otogi-zōshi お伽草子 (books of fairy tales). The generic term for short novels which were popular from the middle of the Muromachi period to the early Edo period. The authors are unknown. The contents comprise mysterious and legendary stories or tales of the origin of gods and Buddhas. Stories in which birds and beasts, insects and fishes, trees and plants play an active part also appear. Construction and style are inartistic. The description of the life of nobles is attractive, and the stories have a religious and moral tendency. They reveal the consciousness of the people and were eagerly read and very popular in their time. During the Edo period, they evolved into storybooks written in *kana* and known as *kana-zōshi* and into realistic novels called UKIYO-ZŌSHI. They further led to the portrayals of bourgeois life by Ihara Saikaku (1642–93). *Otogi-zōshi* such as *Hachikazuki-hime* and *Issun-bōshi* are famous and are read even today.

Ōtomo uji 大伴氏 (the Ōtomo clan). A wealthy family in ancient Japan. Members of the clan were awarded the title (KABANE) MURAJI or clan leader. Later the title was changed to *sukune* (one of the eight classes of nobles created by Emperor Temmu). The Ōtomo were in charge of the guard of the Yamato court and of military affairs. According to *Nihon Shoki,* during the reign of Emperor Yūryaku, Ōtomo no Muroya was made leader of all clan chiefs (Ō-MURAJI) or territorial administrative officer. Muroya's grandson Ōtomo no Kanamura (circa 500) crushed Heguri no Madori (?–498), who had usurped the court's authority. Thus the Ōtomo secured supremacy. Later the MONO-NOBE UJI flourished. Kanamura's grandson Ōtomo no Fukehi (?–683) made himself meritorious in the Jinshin civil war of 672 (JINSHIN NO RAN), and the Ōtomo were reinstated. The Nara period produced the *waka* poets Ōtomo no Tabito (662–731) and Ōtomo no Yakamochi (?–785). In 866, the whole clan was exterminated by the Fujiwara in the Ōtemmon incident *(Ōtemmon no hen)*.

otona 乙名 (group leader). The leader of a corporation or of a group. The heads of the religious guilds known as MIYA-ZA, of rural communities, etc. were called TOSHIYORI and also *otona*. (See also KARŌ.)

Ōtsu 大津. The chief city of Shiga Prefecture. From ancient times, Ōtsu was a place of significance on the shore of Lake Biwa. In the north of present-day Ōtsu was located the palace of Emperor Tenchi (621–71). The city was also known as the site of Mii-dera temple (ONJŌ-JI) and as a gateway to Kyōto. After the end of the middle ages, when communications around the lake had improved, Ōtsu flourished because it handled the transport of rice and other commodities from the Hokuriku district. During the Edo period, a castle was built at Zeze in the south of Ōtsu. The town prospered as a post station and shopping center. After the restoration it became the center of the prefecture, and in 1888 a municipal administration was established.

Ōtsu-e 大津絵 (Ōtsu pictures). Popular sketches made during the Edo period in the vicinity of Ōtsu and Fushimi. They were also called *oiwake-e* and were sold mainly to travelers. Though the colors were unrefined, people liked their rustic beauty. Originally, they were Buddhist pictures, but later profane subjects were dealt with. Favorite subjects were *fuji-musume, yarimochi-yakko, hyōtan-namazu, oni no nembutsu, taka-jō, Tsurigane Benkei*, etc. The originator of the sketches was a man named Taira. The so-called *Ōtsu-e bushi* were unconventional songs composed about the sketches. Some sketches were used as charms against thunder, fire, theft, etc.

Ōuchi uji 大内氏 (the Ōuchi clan). A powerful family of the Chūgoku district which flourished during the Kamakura and Muromachi periods. In the fourteenth century, the family moved to Yamaguchi, a strategic place with good communications. There making their stronghold, the Ōuchi engaged in trade with China and Korea and consolidated their position. Though Ōuchi Yoshihiro (1355–99) was killed in the civil strife of the Ōei era (ŌEI NO RAN), the family continued to flourish and even spread its authority to the neighboring provinces. Some of its members were constables of several provinces and were themselves powerful constable landowners (SHUGO DAIMYŌ). The center of their activities was Suō and Nagato provinces (Yamaguchi Prefecture). Introducing Chinese culture, they also absorbed the culture of Kyōto court nobles. This resulted in a peculiar Yamaguchi culture. Their castle town of Yamaguchi was called the "western capital." In 1551, however, Ōuchi Yoshitaka (1507–51) was killed by an old retainer, Sue Harukata, and Yoshitaka's son Yoshinaga (?–1575) was killed in 1575 by Mōri Motonari (1497–1571). This marked the end of the Ōuchi family.

The code of regulations of the Ōuchi family contains the laws and ordinances from 1459 to 1495. Some of the regulations concern taxes, trade, communications, and currency. The code throws light upon contemporary society and upon economic conditions within the territories of the Ōuchi magnates.

Ōwada no tomari 大輪田泊 (port of Ōwada). The name of an ancient harbor facing Ōsaka Bay. It was located in the western part of present-day Kōbe. The name Ōwada seems to be an old one, and the port was probably already in operation before the Nara period. During the Nara period, Ōwada became one of the five official ports along the coast of Harima and Settsu provinces. Another of these five ports was Kawajiri, which is a port for present-day Ōsaka. The harbor has been improved several times, but under the rule of Taira no Kiyomori (1118–81) large-scale construction works were undertaken, and Ōwada prospered as a port of trade with Sung China. After the middle ages, the name Ōwada was changed to HYŌGO. Especially during the Muromachi period, the port became a landing place for vessels trading with Ming China and ships carrying envoys there. After the civil war of the Ōei era (ŌEI NO RAN) the port was surpassed by that of SAKAI, which flourished as the port for Ōsaka.

Owari no kuni gunji hyakushō-ra gebumi 尾張国郡司百姓等解文 (appeal of rural district administrators and farmers of Owari Province). During the reign of Emperor Ichijō (980–1011), rural district administrators (GUNJI) and farmers appealed to the Council of State (DAJŌKAN) for the removal from office of the tyrannic Fujiwara no Motonaga. The appeal included thirty-one accusations. It is a valuable historical document, for it shows the corruption of local administrators (who were known as *zuryō*) after the middle of the Heian period, the oppressive sway of some rulers, and the wretched conditions of the farmers.

oyakata, kokata 親方・子方. Persons who were related as parent and child but without blood relationship. The custom is an old one, but in the Edo period it spread to the four social classes: warriors, farmers, artisans, and merchants. The relationship was also customary among craftsmen after the expiration of their term of apprenticeship. Even today the custom has largely survived, and such relationships exist among civil engineering and building contractors, among gamblers and street traders, and the like as vestiges of the old practice.

P

Phaeton-gō jiken フェートン号事件 (the H.M.S. *Phaeton* incident). The incident of the English frigate H.M.S. *Phaeton,* which in 1808 illegally sailed into Nagasaki. Taking advantage of the European situation (the Napoleonic wars), England attacked the overseas territories of France. In 1808, the frigate *Phaeton,* flying a Dutch flag, invaded Deshima, where it anchored for two days before leaving. Because the incident occurred during the period of national isolation, the magistrate of Nagasaki, Matsudaira Yasuhide (1761–1808), took full responsibility for it and committed suicide.

Portsmouth Jōyaku ポーツマス条約 (the Treaty of Portsmouth). The peace treaty concluded in 1905 between Japan and Russia. Russia was defeated, and Japan was unable, financially or militarily, to continue the war. Following the advice of Roosevelt, the president of the United States, both countries concluded a peace treaty at Portsmouth, New Hampshire. Russia recognized Japan's political, economic, and military supremacy in Korea; Russian forces had to withdraw from Manchuria; Russia ceded to Japan her extraterritorial rights in Port Arthur and Dairen; the South Manchurian Railway was ceded to Japan; South Sakhalin became Japanese territory; Russia recognized Japan's fishing rights; etc. The Japanese envoy plenipotentiary was Komura Jutarō, and the Russian envoy plenipotentiary was Sergei Witte (NICHI-RO SENSŌ).

Potsdam Sengen ポツダム宣言 (the Potsdam Declaration). Joint declaration of the Allied terms for Japan's surrender. The declaration was made by the presidents of the United States and China and the prime minister of the United Kingdom on July 26, 1945, at a meeting in Potsdam, Germany. After the Cairo Declaration (1943), the Allies held a conference of the Big Three in Crimea (1945), and a secret pact, which included Russia's participation in the war, was concluded at Yalta. The German surrender came earlier than was expected, and the Big Three, with a representative of the Chinese government, held a conference at Potsdam. Postwar reconstruction of Europe was discussed, and the joint declaration by the United States, the United Kingdom, and China offered Japan a chance to capitulate. The unconditional surrender included the following terms: Japan would never again menace world peace and security; the occupation forces would withdraw after all objectives were achieved; the terms of the Cairo conference would be implemented, and Japanese territory would be limited to the four main islands; Japan would be demobilized and demilitarized; war criminals would be punished; freedom would be established and human rights would be respected. Soviet Russia participated in the declaration. On August 10, the first formal Japanese offer of surrender was made through the intermediary of the Swiss government. On August 14, Japan accepted the Allied terms, and the instrument of surrender was signed on September 2.

puroretariya bungaku undō プロレタリヤ文学運動 (the proletarian literary movement). A literary movement of the Taishō and Shōwa eras. The movement followed the development of the Marxist movement after World War I. It began in 1921 when the magazine *Tane Maku Hito* was launched. It further displayed its activities in the magazines *Bungei Sensen, Senki, NAPF,* etc. Though suffering oppressive measures, the movement produced distinguished authors and works. Representative works are *Taiyō no Nai Machi* by Tokunaga Sunao (1899–   ), *Kani Kōsen* and *Tō-seikatsusha* by Kobayashi Takiji (1903–33), *Umi ni Ikuru Hitobito* by Hayama Yoshiki (1894–1945),

Tetsu no Hanashi by Nakano Shigeharu (1902–   ), etc. Postwar proletarian literature flourished as a democratic literary movement. The leading magazines were *Shin Nihon Bungaku* and *Jimmin Bungaku*. In 1955, the latter changed its name to *Seikatsu to Bungaku*.

R

rakuchū rakugai byōbu 洛中洛外屏風. Popular screen paintings of the Momoyama period (1573–1600). The paintings represent scenic spots and famous places in and around Kyōto, with people thronging the streets. The finest of these paintings are believed to be those of Kanō Eitoku (1543–90). A characteristic feature of the paintings of this epoch was the minute depiction of the life of the common people.

rakuichi-rakuza 楽市・楽座 (abolition of market taxes and guilds). Abolition of the privileges of markets and guilds. The activities of merchants of the middle ages were confined, for they had to pay taxes in all market places as well as business taxes. They were also prevented from freely conducting business because the guilds of the commercial and industrial world had secured all monopolies. With the development of a trade economy, merchants tried to abolish all the privileges and monopolies of the trading centers. The war barons *(sengoku daimyō)* brought the merchants together in their respective castle towns. In order to develop these towns and to increase the wealth of their fiefs, these barons abolished all trade limitations imposed by the commercial world. It was their policy that the merchants should freely frequent markets and sell their commodities. The immunity from market taxes and the abolition of guilds was called *rakuichi-rakuza*. Nobunaga and Hideyoshi extended this policy to the whole country. It resulted in the abolition of commercial and industrial privileges of territorial magnates such as nobles and shrines and temples.

Rakurō-gun 楽浪郡 (the Lo-lang commandery). One of the four *gun* or large commanderies set up in ancient Korea by the Chinese Han emperor Wu Ti. In 108 B.C., Wu Ti destroyed the state of Choson, founded in 190 B.C. by the Chinese Wei Man. Choson had been a flourishing state, with P'yongyang as its capital. Wu Ti set up four commanderies, which were all under his direct control. The other three commanderies failed to survive, but Lo-lang (in Korean, Nangnang) lasted until A.D. 313, when it was destroyed by the Koreans of Kōkuri. The Lo-lang commandery covered the basin of the Daidōkō (in Korean, Taedong) river, and the administrative office was on the bank of the river in P'yongyang. The commandery was a prosperous outpost of Chinese civilization and spread its cultural influence over the neighboring tribes as well as over Japan's primitive society. In recent times, archaeological surveys have been conducted, and many cultural remains of the Han period have been discovered.

rangaku 蘭学 (YŌGAKU)

Rangaku Kaitei 蘭学階梯. *An Introduction to Dutch Learning,* written by Ōtsuki Gentaku (1757–1827) and published in two volumes in 1788. The first volume relates the development of *rangaku* from the earliest Dutch-Japanese relations to the time when it began to flourish. It stresses the usefulness of *rangaku.* The second volume explains the meaning of some Dutch words. As an introduction to Dutch learning, it greatly helped Japanese scholars and was instrumental in further spreading *rangaku* in Japan.

renga 連歌 (linked verse). A literary genre which flourished during the Kamakura and Muromachi periods. The thirty-one-syllable *waka* poem is divided into two hemistichs. One poet of the party would write the first hemistich; others would add the second. In the beginning the game was popular only at court and among the higher society of the BAKUFU; later it spread among the common people. During the Namboku period (1336–92), Nijō Yoshimoto (1320–88) compiled the *renga* anthology TSUKUBASHŪ, in which he laid down the rules for composing *renga.* He made *renga* into an art. Before long, it became an independent literary art, surpassing even *waka,* which had become formalized. After Yoshimoto, other *renga* poets such as Sōgi (1421–1502) and Shōhaku (1443–1527) were called *renga-shi* or masters of *renga.* It was the golden age of *renga.* Those who were able to compose this kind of poem were considered highly educated. When the rules for composing *renga* became more complicated, the poems, like *waka* poems, lost their freedom of expression and became rigid. Yamazaki Sōkan (1465–1553) reformed *renga* and originated *haikai renga.* During the Edo period, *renga* poetry was replaced by haiku poetry.

Rengōgun Shireibu 連合軍司令部 (general headquarters of the Allied Powers). The organ for occupation policy in postwar Japan. In August 1945, the government of the United States established the Supreme Command of the Allied Powers. General Douglas McArthur was appointed Supreme Commander for the Allied Powers (SCAP) by the president of the United States. Occupation policies were formulated by the Far Eastern Commission or by the United States government, but the sole executive authority was SCAP. Decisions of policy were implemented through the Japanese government.

rensho 連署 (assistant regent). An office created by the KAMAKURA BAKUFU. In 1224, Regent Hōjō Yasutoki (1183–1242) appointed his uncle Tokifusa (1175–1240) *rensho* or "co-signer." Tokifusa ably shared with Yasutoki the responsibility of leadership. The office was monopolized by the Hōjō family. Many *rensho* became regents.

renza-hō 連坐法 (joint responsibility). A doctrine according to which several people were punished for the offense of one criminal. The principle was that of collective responsibility. Members of one family or relatives were thus punished for the offense of one individual, this being called *enza,* but the word *renza* includes many other cases. In primitive society, solidarity was very strong, and joint liability of all the members of one tribe was generally admitted. With the development of society, relations within a family group weakened, but joint responsibility was recognized by those living in one territory. One example is the custom during the late Muromachi period of punishing all the members of the self-governing villages or groups of villages known as *gō.* In the Edo period, when the neighborhood associations were organized, all the neighbors were responsible for the the offense of one. The origin of the neighborhood system may be traced back to the *goho-seido* of ancient times, when five families were made into one group, the whole group being responsible for each offense.

Rikkokushi 六国史. Six historical books compiled by imperial order during the Nara and Heian periods. They are NIHON SHOKI, *Shoku Nihongi, Nihon Kōki, Shoku Nihon Kōki, Nihon Montoku Tennō Jitsuroku,* and *Nihon Sandai Jitsuroku.* Following Chinese examples, the *Rikkokushi* relate events in chronological order and are written in Chinese. The subject matter of each book is ancient history, beginning with the age of the gods. The works also describe the characteristic features of the early Japanese nation and the world of the nobility.

Rinzai-shū 臨済宗. A denomination of the Zen sect of Buddhism. A Chinese Buddhist priest founded the sect in China. In 1191, Eisai (1141–1215) returned to Japan from Sung China and founded the sect in Japan. He was protected by the emperor and the nobility, and, because Rinzai tenets appealed to the military temperament, his faith was favorably received by the Kamakura warriors. Rankei Dōryū (1213–78) and Mugaku Sogen (1226–80) came to Japan, and among other distinguished monks Enji Ben'en (1202–80) was meritorious in spreading Rinzai. The sect developed during the Namboku period (1336–92) under the encouragement of Musō Soseki (1275–1351). During the Muromachi period, the sect enjoyed the patronage of the BAKUFU and of upper-class warriors. The Five Zen Monasteries (GOZAN) of Kyōto and of Kamakura represented the height of Rinzai prosperity. From the Kamakura to the Muromachi period, many famous temples were built. Among them are KENNIN-JI, KENCHŌ-JI, TŌFUKU-JI, ENKAKU-JI, NANZEN-JI, Daitoku-ji, Myōshin-ji, TENRYŪ-JI, and Shōkoku-ji.

Risshi-sha 立志社 (Self-Help Society). Political association of the early Meiji era. Founded in 1874 in Tosa Province by Itagaki Taisuke, the association was opposed to clan government. Risshi-sha was a merging of the Patriotic Public Party (AIKOKU KŌTŌ) and the Kainangi-sha association. Initially membership was confined to samurai who had to rely upon their own efforts, but later the association's movement for civil rights spread throughout the country. The association revived the Patriotic Association (AIKOKU-SHA), which held a convention in Ōsaka and was later absorbed into the Liberal Party.

ritsuryō-sei 律令制 (*ritsuryō* political structure). The Nara and Heian political structure as based on the penal code *(ritsu)* and the civil and administrative code *(ryō)* after the Taika Reform (646), also known as *ritsuryō taisei*. Imperial rule conformed to this structure, and the codes were enforced throughout the country. But from the middle of the Heian period, the land-allotment (HANDEN NŌMIN) system deteriorated and began to be replaced by the manorial system, and thus the *ritsuryō* political structure lost its significance.

rōdō sampō 労働三法 (three labor laws). Postwar labor legislation. In March 1946, the Trade Union Law was enforced, and the right of organization and collective bargaining was guaranteed. As the legislation aimed at promoting the labor class, it resulted in a great strengthening of the labor unions. In September 1946, the Labor Relations Adjustment Law was promulgated, and the right of collective bargaining and striking was confirmed. In March 1947, the Labor Standards Law was enacted. Compulsory labor was prohibited; intermediary exploitation was abolished; labor was limited to eight hours a day and forty-eight hours a week; and discriminatory treatment, midnight labor of women, and child labor were prohibited.

rōjū 老中 (councilors to the shōgun). Officials of the EDO BAKUFU. Their number was limited to four or five. They alternately served for one month and were under the direct jurisdiction of the shōgun. They assisted the shōgun in matters of national policy and worked in a bureau within the Edo castle limits, this bureau being known as *goyōbeya*. Their name, which means "elders," derives from that of the *toshiyori*. Because they co-signed the shōgun's official documents, they were called *kahan no retsu* or "those who affix their seal." In principle, the *rōjū* were elected from among the hereditary daimyō with fiefs of at least 25,000 *koku*. In wartime, they commanded soldiers of the various daimyō and, as a rule, had to go to the front.

rokkasen 六歌仙 (the six master poets). The most distinguished poets of the early Heian period. They were Arihara no Narihira (825–80), Sōjō Henshō (816–90), Ono no Komachi (circa 860), Fun'ya no Yasuhide (?–877), Ōtomo no Kuronushi (circa 890), and Kisen Hōshi (circa 950). Flawless technique, which characterizes Heian poetry, was the common feature of these poets. Their skill was used in dealing with sentimental subjects, whereas later poets dealt with more intellectual subject matter.

Rokōkyō 芦溝橋 (Lukouch'iao). Name of a place in China. On July 7, 1937, a clash occurred at Lukouch'iao, on the edge of Peking, between Chinese troops and Japanese soldiers. This minor incident was utilized by the Japanese army to rush reinforcements into Hopei Province. The incident led to the Sino-Japanese conflict.

Rokuhara tandai 六波羅探題 (commissioner of Kyōto). The name of an office established by the KAMAKURA BAKUFU. At the time of the civil war of the Jōkyū era (JŌKYŪ NO HEN), Hōjō Yasutoki (1183–1242) and Tokifusa (1175–1240), commanding *bakufu* troops, marched on Kyōto. When the war was over, troops were stationed at Rokuhara on the southeastern outskirts of Kyōto, and a commissioner (inspector general) was appointed. The *tandai* was a deputy of the shōgun. It was his duty to oversee the court and to make decisions in administrative matters for West Japan (west of Mikawa Province). Thus the Hōjō exerted close military control over Kyōto. The office was monopolized by the Hōjō, who held supreme power during the Kamakura period, but was abolished during the civil strife of the Genkō era (GENKŌ NO HEN) by Ashikaga Takauji (1305–58).

Rokumeikan 鹿鳴館. An international club opened in 1883 for the Westernization of Japan. Modernization, especially in the field of industry, was begun in the first year of Meiji and gradually spread to other fields such as politics, economy, and culture. The government tried to amend the unequal treaties, and, as a means of displaying Western social habits, an international club was opened in the new building Rokumeikan. This policy of exhibiting and praising Western customs was severely criticized by ultranationalists.

rokusai-ichi 六斎市 (the six-days-a-month market). Markets held six days a month. Originally, markets were held at indefinite times and often on temple and shrine festival days. During the Muromachi period, markets opened on definite days and more frequently. The six-days-a-month markets became very popular all over the country. The paper market of Ōyada in Mino Province (Gifu Prefecture) was most famous for its trade in Mino paper (MINO-GAMI).

rōmanshugi ローマン主義 (romanticism). Literary current during the Meiji era. It was a twofold current, one phase being romanticism, the other neoromanticism. The romantic movement of Kitamura Tōkoku's (1868–94) BUNGAKUKAI led to a golden age of poetic literature. From the early twentieth century this influence spread to novels and gave rise to the works of Izumi Kyōka (1873–1939), Higuchi Ichiyō (1872–96), Kunikida Doppo (1871–1939), and Tokutomi Roka (1868–1927). At the same time, the new-style poetry laid the foundation for popular poetry stimulated by Shimazaki Tōson's (1872–1943) collection *Wakanashū* and resulted in the literary activities of the school called MYŌJŌ-HA. From the late Meiji to the early Taishō era, Nagai Kafū (1897–1959), Tanizaki Jun'ichirō (1886–1965), and Ogawa Mimei (1882–1961), along with the literary trend known as *Mita bungaku* of Keiō Gijuku, were part of a neo-romantic literary movement.

rōnin 浪人 (牢人) (masterless samurai). In ancient times *rōnin* were those who deserted their territory and moved to another province, where they became vagrants. One of the reasons was the exorbitant taxes which forced farmers to abandon their fields. From the middle ages to the Edo period, *rōnin* were masterless warriors who had lost their fiefs. The word was written 牢人. Their number was particularly great after the battles of Sekigahara and Ōsaka. Often they became extremely troublesome and disturbed public peace. After Iemitsu's death, they were gradually absorbed by the townspeople or the farmer class. Many of the Edo *rōnin* became teachers at the temple schools (TERAKOYA); others made themselves meritorious as scholars or artists.

Roshiya ロシヤ (Russia). During the second half of the sixteenth century, the Russians advanced into Siberia. After the establishment of an absolute monarchy by Czar Peter the Great, administration of Siberia progressed, and by the beginning of the eighteenth century, Russia's influence extended as far as Kamchatka and the Kurile Islands. At the end of this century, Japan learned from the Dutch about Russian expansionism toward the south. At this time, the *Report on Kamchatka* (AKA-EZO FŪSETSU-KŌ) was published, and during the Tanuma age—that is, the age of Lord Tanuma Okitsugu (1719–88)—land surveys were conducted in Kamchatka. In 1792, the Russian naval officer Laxman returned some shipwrecked Japanese and asked for trade but was refused. Likewise, in 1804, Count Muraviev, the governor-general of Siberia, promoted Russia's Far Eastern policy and reached Sakhalin. In 1853, Putiatin arrived at Nagasaki for trade negotiations. He discussed the boundaries of the Kuriles and Sakhalin. As a result, the Russo-Japanese Friendship Treaty and the Russo-Japanese Commerce and Navigation Treaty were concluded, and both countries entered into diplomatic relations. The boundary discussions were taken over by the Meiji government. A conclusion was reached in 1875 when the Kuriles-Sakhalin Exchange Treaty was signed. Taking advantage of imperialist rivalry between Western powers, Russian Far Eastern policy became more outspoken, and, following the construction of the Siberian railroad, Russia became more interested in Manchuria and Korea. The Triple Intervention (SANGOKU KANSHŌ) took place, the Russo-Chinese Bank was established, and a Russo-Chinese secret treaty was concluded. After 1890, Russia's attitude toward Korea became an issue. In 1898, extraterritorial rights in Port Arthur and Dairen were secured, and, upon construction of the Eastern Chinese Railway, Russian management of Manchuria took shape. The Boxer Rebellion in 1900 gave Russia a chance to occupy the whole of Manchuria. However, the Anglo-Japanese Alliance helped Japan to prepare herself against Russian expansion. In 1903, when peace negotiations failed, the Russo-Japanese War (1904–5) could no longer be averted. In 1905, the Portsmouth Treaty (PORTSMOUTH JŌYAKU) was concluded. International tension brought Japan and Russia closer together. The

Russo-Japanese pacts of 1907, 1910, and 1912, as well as the fishery agreement of 1907, were concluded, and the Russian sphere of influence in East Asia was recognized. In 1917, during World War I, the Russian Revolution took place. During the period 1918–22, a Japanese expedition was in Siberia, where the Nikolaievsk incident, in which 700 Japanese were killed, occurred. At the time of the Manchurian incident, Russo-Japanese relations again became tense, and many clashes occurred on the Russian frontier. In 1941, during World War II, a Russo-Japanese neutrality pact was signed, and Japan launched upon the Pacific War. In 1945, following the Potsdam Declaration, Russia declared war on Japan and occupied Manchuria, Korea, southern Sakhalin, and the Kuriles. After the war, in 1956, Moscow took steps to restore diplomatic relations.

rōtō 郎党 (vassals of warriors). The vassals of warriors during the Heian and Kamakura periods. Some vassals had blood relationship with warriors (IE NO KO). The *rōtō* had none. Usually they lived in rural communities. In wartime, they joined the warrior corps and departed for the front.

Ruijū Sandai-kyaku 類聚三代格. A compilation of amending rules and regulations made during the Heian period. Author and year of compilation are not known. The work includes three compilations of amending rules: Kōnin-kyaku (820), Jōgan-kyaku (869), and Engi-kyaku (909). It is classified according to subject matter. The work is an important historical document for knowledge of legislative systems up to early Heian times.

Ruson 呂宋 (Luzon). The main island of the northern group of the Philippine Islands. In 1571, the Spaniards occupied Manila, on Luzon, but before this time Japan had communications with Luzon. Japanese trade with Ming China was discontinued owing to the Ming isolation policy. In order to buy Chinese commercial articles, Japan had to deal with Chinese merchants in Manila. Through Manila, Sino-Japanese trade relations flourished. Hideyoshi sent envoys to Luzon and demanded tribute. As a result of the ban on Christianity and of the withdrawal of the Spaniards from Japan, Japanese relations with Luzon were severed. In the early Edo period friendly relations were resumed, and red-seal ships (SHUIN-SEN) sailed to Luzon. The Japanese quarter (NIHON-MACHI) in Manila developed. However, because Luzon was a stronghold of Christianity and because Japan had banned Christianity, all relations with Luzon were cut off in 1624. The Spanish-American War in 1900 resulted in the occupation of Luzon by the United States.

Russia (ROSHIYA)

ryōgae 両替 (brokers). Brokerships and also brokers of the Edo period. Originally the word meant the exchange of gold and silver coins and of other money and also the money exchanger. When trade developed, these brokers took up the side business of managing deposit loans, etc. and of controlling finances. Once in charge of the BAKUFU finances, they made a fortune and lent money at high interest. The wealthiest among them were centered in Ōsaka, Edo, and Kyōto. The *jūnin-ryōgae* and *honryōgae,* both of Ōsaka, were most powerful.

ryōge no kan 令外の官 (extralegal offices). Extralegal offices under the penal and administrative code system (RITSURYŌ-SEI). They included offices which existed prior to the Taihō laws (701) but which were not included in these laws. Usually they were offices set up after the compilation of the Taihō laws and were meant to supplement the government organization. Such were the offices of audit officers (KAGEYUSHI), of police commissioners (KEBIISHI), and of the Bureau of Archivists (KURAUDO-DOKORO).

ryōko 陵戸 (tomb serfs). A type of slave *(semmin)* in ancient Japan. They were also called *shuko* and *ryōshu*. They were tomb serfs or wardens of imperial mausoleums. It was their duty to maintain the tombs and the land attached thereto. They were exempt from other corvées. Though they ranked first among the slave people, they were not allowed to marry free people *(ryōmin)*. Because in ancient times criminals were in charge of imperial mausoleums and because death was held in abhorrence, tomb serfs were chosen from among the slaves.

Ryō no Gige 令義解. A commentary on the civil and administrative code *(ryō)* in ten volumes. Because of the diversity of conflicting interpretations of the *ryō,* the compilation of *Ryō no Gige* was undertaken in 833 by Kiyohara no Natsuno (782–837), Minabuchi no Hirosada (776–833), Fujiwara no Tsunetsugu (796–840), Sugawara no Kiyokimi (770–842), Ono no Takamura (802–52), and seven other scholars. The purpose was to give an authoritative version of the *ryō*. Almost the whole text may still be read today.

Ryō no Shūge 令集解. A commentary on the civil and administrative code *(ryō)* in thirty volumes. Following the publication of the earlier RYŌ NO GIGE, most of the conflicting interpretations of the *ryō* were abandoned. The doctor of law Koremune Naomoto (circa 880) compiled *Ryō no Shuge* in the Engi era (901–922). The work is classified into more than twenty categories of regulations. Only twenty-five volumes are extant. They are an invaluable source of information for the study of ancient law.

ryōtō tetsuritsu 両統迭立 (alternating succession by emperors of two lines). The two lines of succession to the throne were the Jimyōin line of Emperor Gofukakusa (JIMYŌIN-TŌ) and the Daikakuji line of Emperor Kameyama (DAIKAKUJI-TŌ). After the civil war of the Jōkyū era (JŌKYŪ NO HEN), the KA-

MAKURA BAKUFU oppressed the court and even interfered with the succession to the throne. After the death of ex-Emperor Gosaga (1220–72), the *bakufu* opposed ex-Emperor Gofukakusa and instituted the cloister government of ex-Emperor Kameyama. A conflict followed, but the *bakufu* tried to reconcile both by making the son of Emperor Gofukakusa (Emperor Fushimi) the crown prince of Emperor Gouda (the son of Emperor Kameyama). As quarrels occurred between the two lines, the *bakufu* used its influence to decide matters. The situation became more complicated when quarrels concerning succession to the imperial estates and disputes among the factions of court nobles broke out. The *bakufu* suggested alternating succession after the reign of Gofushimi of the Jimyōin line and Gonijō of the Daikakuji line. The purpose was to effect a compromise between the two lines. However, the efforts of the *bakufu* failed, and, after the attempt by Godaigo to overthrow the Kamakura shogunate, the alternate succession led to the establishment of the Northern and Southern dynasties.

Ryōunshū 凌雲集. An anthology of poems in Chinese compiled in 814 at the order of Emperor Saga (786–842) by the courtier Ono no Minemori (778–830), the court scholar Sugawara no Kiyokimi (770–842), Isayama Fumitsugu, and others. Instead of five-syllable lines, which had fallen into disuse, seven-syllable lines are used after the T'ang model. The anthology includes ninety-three poems by twenty-three authors.

Ryūjōkō 柳条溝 (Liut'iaokou). Name of a place in Manchuria. On September 18, 1931, the Japanese Kwantung army, stationed in Manchuria, found a pretext for attacking Chinese troops in Mukden in the blowing up of the Japanese railway at Liut'iaokou, on the outskirts of that city. The explosion was interpreted as a hostile attack by the troops of Chang Hsüeh-liang. As a result, all strategic points in Manchuria were immediately occupied by the Japanese Kwantung army. This event marked the beginning of the Manchurian incident (MANSHŪ JIHEN).

Ryūkyū 琉球 (the Ryūkyū Islands). A chain of fifty-five islands in the West Pacific between Japan and Formosa. Because of hard living conditions, people at all times have emigrated from there. Politically the islands have been under Japanese and Chinese domination. From ancient times, there were relations with Japan, but from the time of the Muromachi period (1333–1573) communications became particularly frequent. From the end of the fourteenth century, when Japanese trade with Ming China, Korea, Siam, and the South Seas expanded, the Ryūkyū Islands flourished because they were the main trade entrepôt. During the fifteenth century, the unification of the main islands took place, and Miyako, Ishigaki, and Amami Ōshima came under Japanese rule. The Ryūkyū kingdom was then at the height of its prosperity. Relations with the MUROMACHI BAKUFU were frequent. After the

Ōnin Civil War (1467–77), visits of Ryūkyū envoys to Kyōto were discontinued, but trade was undertaken with merchants of Sakai. In the sixteenth century, the number of Ryūkyū ships in Japanese waters decreased as visits to the islands of Japanese, Chinese, and Portuguese ships increased. From the Sengoku period (1490–1573), the Shimazu clan of South Kyūshū established some control over the islands and claimed to have special trade relations with the Ryūkyūs. Hideyoshi ordered the islands to pay tribute, and when he planned his Korean invasion he used Shimazu as intermediary. In 1609, the Shimazu clan, under the pretext that the Ryūkyū Islands had failed to send envoys, conquered the islands. They annexed the northern islands and made the kings their vassals. The annexed part came under the political administration of Shimazu's commissioner. As a result of the visit of Commodore Perry to Japan, the Ryūkyū Islands concluded a treaty with the United States (1854) and later with France and Holland. In 1871, following the abolition of clans and the establishment of prefectures, the Ryūkyū Islands were placed under the jurisdiction of Kagoshima Prefecture. The following year, King Shōtai of the islands was made head of the Ryūkyū fief. In 1874, when some inhabitants of the islands were killed by aborigines of Formosa, a Chinese territory, Japan sent a punitive force under Saigō Tsugumichi (1843–1902) and occupied part of Formosa. China tacitly renounced suzerainty over the Ryūkyū Islands, and relations between the two declined. In 1879, the Ryūkyū fief was abolished and Okinawa Prefecture established. The royal line was discontinued, and King Shōtai was raised to the Japanese peerage. Following the Treaty of San Francisco on September 8, 1951, the islands were placed under the administration of the United States, but Japan still holds latent sovereignty. The people of the Ryūkyū Islands are very similar to the Japanese people as far as race, language, customs, and culture are concerned.

ryūtatsu-bushi 隆達節. A kind of ditty which was popular during the early Edo period. The ditties were originated in Sakai by the Nichiren bonze Ryūtatsu and were based on KANGINSHŪ and other song anthologies. They suited the public taste, which ran particularly to songs and ballads, and they greatly influenced later songs and dances. The tunes of the songs have not been transmitted, but almost a hundred texts have been preserved. The ditties were sung to the beating of fans *(ōgi-byōshi)* and hand drums and the music of flutes called *shakuhachi*. The *shamisen* was not used.

Ryūzōji uji 竜造寺氏 (the Ryūzōji family). War barons *(sengoku daimyō)* of Hizen Province (Saga Prefecture) in Kyūshū. Being retainers of the shōgun and land stewards (JITŌ) during the Kamakura period, they were very influential. From the middle of the sixteenth century, the war barons possessed the whole territory of Hizen. After their defeat by the Shimazu clan, their power rapidly declined, and their position was taken over by the Nabeshima, former vassals of the Ryūzōji clan.

S

Sado kinginzan 佐渡金銀山 (Sado gold and silver mine). A gold and silver mine in Aikawa-machi, Sado Island, Niigata Prefecture. It was discovered in 1601, but the area seems to have yielded gold dust and silver from earlier times. The development of the mine began in 1603, when the BAKUFU ordered Ōkubo Nagayasu (1545–1613), the magistrate of gold mines, to exploit it. In the early seventeenth century, it reached the height of its prosperity and was the main source of the *bakufu's* gold and silver coins. In the middle of the Meiji era, the mine was transferred to the Mitsubishi Company. In 1952, exploitation was discontinued.

Saga no ran 佐賀の乱 (the Saga rebellion). A revolt of samurai during the early Meiji era. Dissatisfied warriors of Saga were opposed to the policy of the new government and urged an unbending attitude toward Korea. The dissident movement was led by the statesman Etō Shimpei (1835–74), who had resigned from the Council of State following the argument for war with Korea. The rebellion was soon quelled.

saibara 催馬楽. Popular tunes originally sung by farmers while driving their horses. Later, songs of the nobility, popular during feasts and banquets. From the Nara period, *saibara* denoted songs of the Kinki, Chūgoku, and Hokuriku districts. They were often sung at the Kyōto court to the accompaniment of wind and string instruments. *Saibara* became graceful and elegant music, known as *gagaku* or ceremonial court music, but dances were not performed. During the early Heian period, an office called *ōutadokoro* was in charge of the ceremonial music performed at annual festivals *(sekkai)* of the court. At the end of the tenth century, two kinds of *saibara* flourished, those in the Fujiwara style and those in the Minamoto style. They included about sixty tunes. As to the origin of the word *saibara,* opinions differ. According to one opinion, the word derives from *saibari* 前張, the songs prior to *kagura* (miscellaneous songs of the court and shrine music and dance). Another opinion is that the word derives from the word for the songs of pack-horse drivers who brought the provincial taxes to the court.

saifu 割符 (bill of exchange). Bill of exchange during the middle ages. With the development of commerce and industry, bills of exchange were used for transmitting to the lord the yearly taxes of the manors. When money or rice was to be paid at distant places, accounts were settled by means of bills of exchange. In towns or at transportation centers, exchange shops called *kaezeni-ya* (KAEZENI) and exchange brokers known as *saifu-ya* took charge of exchange business. Most of these brokers were wealthy merchants or wine dealers (SA-KAYA) who lent money at a high rate of interest. *Saifu* has no relation with *itowappu* (ONO-GUMI and SAKOKU).

Saigoku Risshi-hen 西国立志編. Translation into Japanese by Nakamura Masanao (1832–91) of Smiles's *Self-Help*. It was published in 1871 and was enthusiastically welcomed for its introduction of Western knowledge.

saikeikoku jōkan 最恵国条款 (most-favored-nation clause). A clause of an an international pact. It was included in the Five Nations Treaties of 1858. It provided for consular jurisdiction and for a fixed customs tariff at very low rates. These provisions led to an outburst of antiforeign sentiment. Japan exerted all her efforts to obtain a revision of the unequal treaties. The revision was obtained in 1897. However, Japan forced Korea and China to include a similar clause in their treaties with Japan.

Saikō Saibansho 最高裁判所 (the Supreme Court). A postwar organ of law. When Japan's new constitution was promulgated, independent judicial power was guaranteed and was based on the separation of the three powers: administrative, legislative, and judiciary. The Supreme Court was established. Its function is to examine cases involving the interpretation of the constitution and to judge appeals. The government appoints fifteen judges, who must be approved by the people.

Sainan jihen 済南事変 (the Tsinan incident). A clash which occurred in 1927 between Japanese and Chinese soldiers in Tsinan, Shantung Province. In their march to subdue the military cliques in North China, the Chinese revolutionary troops reached Shantung Province. Premier Tanaka Giichi (1863–1929), alleging that he had to protect Japanese nationals, sent an expedition to Shantung. The two forces clashed in Tsinan, the Japanese occupied the city, and the northern march of the Chinese troops was temporarily discontinued. The following year, a settlement was reached at Nanking, and the Japanese troops withdrew. This incident produced a deep gulf between the Chinese government and Japan.

Sakai 堺. Industrial port in Ōsaka Prefecture. During the Muromachi period (1333–1573) it flourished as a center of commerce for the trading vessels with official Chinese tallies (KANGŌFU) and as a place through which Christianity and Western civilization entered the country. Sakai became a self-governing town. Autocratic organizations (EGŌSHŪ) and wealthy merchants took charge of the town's administration. The town had a moat on three sides and was prepared against enemy attacks. It opposed the unification of the country by Nobunaga but had to surrender. When Hideyoshi expanded his castle town at Ōsaka, Sakai's prosperity declined.

Sakai bōseki-jo 堺紡績所 (Sakai spinning mill). A government-operated model factory of the early Meiji era. It was founded in 1867 according to the wishes of the warrior Shimazu Nariakira (1809–58) and was established as a branch factory of the Kagoshima spinning mill in 1870. In 1878, it became privately administered.

sakan 主典 (clerks). An office under the penal and administrative code system (RITSURYŌ-SEI). Under this system, the officers of each ministry were divided into four main categories. They were the principals *(kami)*, the assistants *(suke)*, the secretaries *(jō)*, and the clerks *(sakan)*. These four categories were collectively called *shitōkan*. The clerks were in charge of official business, drafted documents, and kept archives.

Sakashita-mongai no hen 坂下門外の変 (the incident outside the Sakashita Gate). The wounding of Minister Andō Nobumasa (1819–71) by antiforeign elements. After Ii Naosuke's assassination in 1860, Andō tried to bring about the union of the shogunate and the court through the marriage of Princess Kazu to Shōgun Iemochi. But loyalists and antiforeign ex-retainers of the Mito clan ambushed and wounded Andō on January 5, 1862, outside the Sakashita Gate of Edo Castle. Andō was forced to resign. The growing weakness of the shogunate became more and more apparent.

sakaya 酒屋 (sakè brewers). Sakè brewers of the Muromachi period (1333–1573). They were notorious because they lent money at a high rate of interest. In the early fifteenth century, there were more than three hundred sakè brewers in Kyōto. The MUROMACHI BAKUFU imposed taxes on the brewers as well as on pawnshops (DOSŌ) and, in return, protected them. As a result, pawnbrokers and brewers flourished.

sakimori 防人 (soldiers for the defense of western Japan). Soldiers assigned to defend the western and especially the northern coast of Kyūshū in ancient Japan. Originally, the word *sakimori* meant the "guards of a cape" (*sakimori* 崎守). Prior to the Taika Reform of 646, these guards were also called *ezomori* and *shimamori*. After the Taika Reform, the guards were organized according to a new system. Soldiers were enrolled from all provinces and had to serve alternately for three years. There were garrisons in Iki, Tsushima, and Tsukushi Province, all under the supervision of DAZAIFU. In particular, soldiers from the eastern provinces were enrolled. This resulted in an impoverishment of agriculture in those provinces. Furthermore, troubles arose because supplies had to be offered by the provinces through which the soldiers passed on their way to the west. The *sakimori* enrolled from the eastern provinces were abolished in 757 and replaced by soldiers from Saikai (Kyūshū) and Shikoku. Many poems describing the grief of the families who had to send a member to the west are preserved in the MAN'YŌSHŪ.

sakoku 鎖国 (national isolation). In the initial stage, the isolation policy was a policy of limitation of foreign trade adopted by the EDO BAKUFU. In 1635,

Japanese were prohibited from leaving the country, and a Japanese living abroad was not allowed to re-enter Japan. In 1639, foreigners were forbidden to enter Japan. An exception was made for Dutch and Chinese traders. Foreign trade was put under strict surveillance. This measure was meant to carry through the ban on Christianity. The main import article was raw silk. Therefore the *bakufu* and only those merchants who had secured the official silk monopoly *(itowappu)* enjoyed the profits of the trade. There are various opinions concerning the merits and demerits of the isolation policy. As it was, it resulted in the consolidation of Japanese feudal society, but at the same time it created a wide gap between the West and Japan in matters of material civilization.

sakunin 作人 (farmers). A class of farmers of the manorial system. They cultivated a small plot of land within the manor and paid the yearly taxes to the landlord or cultivated part of the name field (MYŌDEN) of the powerful name masters (MYŌSHU) and paid tenancy rent *(kajiko)*. Provided they paid the rice taxes, the *sakunin* had the right of cultivation. After the Kamakura period, the nature of the name fields changed. The *sakunin* employed others to cultivate the fields and collected rents. Some of these farmers became name masters.

Sakurada-mongai no hen 桜田門外の変 (the incident outside the Sakurada Gate). The incident in which Prime Minister Ii Naosuke (1815–60) was murdered by ex-retainers of the Mito clan. On March 24, 1860, masterless samurai of the Mito and Satsuma clans were waiting for Ii, who was about to enter Edo Castle. In reprisal for the mass imprisonment and execution of the Ansei era (ANSEI NO TAIGOKU), they assassinated Ii outside the Sakurada Gate of the castle. This incident showed the weakness of the BAKUFU.

Sammon, Jimon 山門・寺門. Sammon indicates the temple ENRYAKU-JI; Jimon, the temple ONJŌ-JI. From ancient times to the end of the middle ages, there was always strong opposition between the two. The opposition often resulted in clashes between the monk-soldiers of both temples.

sampitsu 三筆 (the three master calligraphers of the early Heian period). The three eminent calligraphers of the early Heian period were Kūkai (774–835), Emperor Saga (786–842), and Tachibana no Hayanari (?–842). From a study of their autographs, it appears that only corroborative writings of Tachibana are lacking. The common feature of the calligraphers of this period is a vigorous Chinese style, there being almost no trace of Japanese calligraphy (SANSEKI).

Samurai-dokoro 侍所 (Disciplinary Board). An office of the central government organization of the Kamakura and Muromachi periods. The Samurai-dokoro was already rudimentarily established in the Heian period and supervised the lives of the feudal nobility and gentry. In 1180, Minamoto no Yoritomo (1148–99) established the Samurai-dokoro in Kamakura and made Wada Yoshimori (1147–1213) its director or *bettō*. This office was in charge of military and police affairs. The office of director was later monopolized by the Hōjō. Likewise, the MUROMACHI BAKUFU established the Samurai-dokoro, the director of which was called *shoshi*. The office of *shoshi* was successively given to the Yamana, Isshiki, Kyōgoku, and Akamatsu. These four *shoshi* were collectively called SHI-SHIKI. Only the rank of governor general (KANREI) was higher. It was the *shoshi's* duty to encourage soldiers and advise commanders, to guard Kyōto, and to attend to trials of the military. The *shoshi* was concurrently administrator of Yamashiro Province.

San Francisco Kōwa Kaigi サン・フランシスコ講和会議 (peace conference at San Francisco). Postwar international conference. It was held in September 1951 in San Francisco. Chief delegates of fifty-two countries, including Japan, accepted the invitation of the United States and of Great Britain. A peace treaty with Japan was concluded, although it was not signed by Red China or the Soviet Union.

Sangi-in 参議院 (House of Councilors). One of the three houses in the postwar National Diet. It was established in 1947, following the first general elections. Councilors are elected from the national constituency and from the prefectural constituencies. Their term of office is six years, but after three years half of their number are re-elected. The House of Representatives has about the same legislative power. But compared with the House of Representatives, the House of Councilors has a marked professional representation system.

Sangoku Bōkyō Kyōtei 三国防共協定 (the Tripartite Anti-Comintern Pact). A pact concluded between Japan, Germany, and Italy. In 1936, Japan and Germany concluded an anti-Comintern pact, which was joined by Italy the following year. Italy, after the example of Japan and Germany, announced her withdrawal from the League of Nations. This resulted in the opposition between totalitarianism and communism. A German-Italian cultural agreement and a Japanese-German cultural agreement were concluded. This was followed by a tripartite military alliance. At the same time, American and British economic and political antagonism was strongly felt. The whole situation led to World War II.

Sangoku Kanshō 三国干渉 (the Triple Intervention). A diplomatic issue in the middle of the Meiji era. In 1895, as a result of the Sino-Japanese War, China had ceded the Liaotung Peninsula to Japan. Russia persuaded France and Germany to join her in forcing Japan to relinquish this territory, because it jeopardized the integrity of Chinese territory. Confronted by Russia's Far

Eastern policy and the imperialist designs of France, Germany, and England, Japan was forced to return the peninsula to China. After this bitter experience, Japan's hostile feeling toward Russia was inflamed. Japan decided to develop armed forces sufficiently strong to challenge any enemy. The Triple Intervention led to the Russo-Japanese War of 1904–5.

Sangyō Kakumei 産業革命 (the Industrial Revolution). The revolution in which machine production replaced manual and home labor. It first took shape in England in the eighteenth century and found its way into Europe from the end of the eighteenth through the early nineteenth century. In Japan, machines were introduced after the Meiji Restoration. At the time of the Russo-Japanese War (1904–5), light industry and steam power marked the initial revolution. From the Russo-Japanese War to World War I, the revolution made further progress, and electric power was used for heavy industry.

Sankan seibatsu 三韓征伐 (conquest of the three Korean states). The record of the reign of Empress Jingū in *Nihon Shoki* mentions *Shiragi seibatsu* or the conquest of Silla. This in turn became *Sankan seibatsu*. The word "Sankan" means Kōrai (in Korean, Koryo), Kudara (in Korean, Paekche), and Shiragi (in Korean, Silla). But more correct is the fact that the Sankan were three states which existed earlier, namely Bakan (in Korean, Mahan), a section which occupied the northwestern part of the peninsula; Benkan (in Korean, Pyonhan) on the central stretch of the south coast, or in the southeastern corner; and Shinkan (in Korean, Chinhan) in southeast or central Korea. The alleged conquest of the three Korean states lacks historical foundation.

Sankashū 三家集. A two-volume collection of verse written in the early Kamakura period by the *waka* poet Saigyō (1118–90). Saigyō spent his life traveling and extolled serenity of mind in life's journey. As a lyrical poet, he occupies a unique place among the poets of his day.

sankin kōtai 参勤交代 (alternate attendance). Alternate attendance of vassals at the EDO BAKUFU. Previously there had been cases of alternate attendance, but in 1635 the third shōgun, Iemitsu, established the system in the Laws for the Military Houses (BUKE SHO-HATTO). Each important daimyō was compelled to spend several months yearly at Edo and to leave his wife and family behind when he returned to his fief. As a result, the fief's debts piled up, and the daimyō became impoverished. On the other hand, alternate attendance made Edo and other towns prosperous, developed communications, and contributed to currency circulation.

Sankyō-gisho 三経義疏. The oldest commentary on Buddhist scriptures. It includes one volume on the Shōman Sutra, three volumes on the Yuima Sutra, and four volumes on the Hokke (Lotus) Sutra. It is believed that Shōtoku

Taishi (573–621) is the author. The commentaries of a learned Chinese scholar of the period of the Northern and Southern dynasties (420–589) were consulted, but the author made a selection, faithfully rendering the meaning of the original sutras. It is an important work as far as the early history of Buddhism in Japan is concerned.

Sanron-shū 三論宗 (the Sanron sect of Buddhism). One of the six Buddhist sects of the Nara period (NANTO ROKUSHŪ). It was founded in Japan in 625 by the Korean monk Ekan. Like the Jōjitsu sect (Jōjitsu-shū), Sanron is an idealistic philosophy, emphasizing the unreality of worldly phenomena. This sect split into three schools: those of the Gangō-ji temple, the Daian-ji temple, and the Tōnan-in.

sanseki 三蹟 (the three master calligraphers of the middle Heian period). The three most distinguished calligraphers of the middle Heian period were Ono no Tōfū (Michikaze, 894–964), Fujiwara no Sukemasa (944–98), and Fujiwara no Yukinari (972–1027). Calligraphy of the early Heian period was characterized by the Chinese style of writing (SAMPITSU), but calligraphy of the middle Heian period became more Japanese. The common feature of the *sanseki* is that, taking Ō Gi-shi (in Chinese, Wang Hsi-chih; 321–79) as their model, they did not blindly imitate Chinese calligraphy but instead turned it into an elegant Japanese style.

Santō mondai 山東問題 (the Shantung problem). International issue during the Taishō era. When World War I began, Japanese troops invaded the Shantung Peninsula. After occupying Tsingtao, Japan presented her Twenty-one Demands (NIJŪIKKAJō YōKYū). When the United States and Great Britain protested, the number of demands was reduced to thirteen. Japan wanted to take over former German holdings in Shantung and forced China to comply with the demands. To secure the holdings, Japan entered into diplomatic relations with the Allied Powers but could not avoid clashing with the open-door policy of the United States and therefore concluded the Ishii-Lansing Treaty of 1917 (ISHII-LANSING KYŌTEI). The peace conference of Paris confirmed to Japan the possession of the former German properties in Shantung. China declined to sign the Treaty of Versailles, and a nation-wide boycott against Japanese goods was begun. In 1927, the revolutionary troops, in their advance north, clashed with Japanese troops in Tsinan (SAINAN JIHEN), and a Japanese expedition was sent to Shantung. Japanese intrusion and aggressive policy in China were evident.

Santō shuppei 山東出兵 (the Shantung expeditions). Japanese aggression in China. Chinese nationalist troops, in their advance north, entered Shantung Province. In 1927, Premier Tanaka Giichi (1863–1929), under the pretext of protecting Japanese nationals, sent three expeditions to China, causing the

Tsinan incident (SAINAN JIHEN) and preventing the unification of China by the nationalist government.

San'yo 参与 (Junior Council of State). A government office of the early Meiji era. In 1867, when imperial rule was restored, previous government offices were abolished, and three new offices were created. They were the Presidency (SŌSAI), the Senior Council of State (GIJŌ), and the Junior Council of State. They underwent changes the following year and were abolished in 1869.

sanze-isshin no hō 三世一身法. Legislation of the Nara government aimed at encouraging cultivation of wasteland. It was enacted in 723. The land-allotment system after the Taika Reform (646) conflicted with the lack of arable fields. Furthermore, the penal and administrative code system (RITSURYŌ-SEI) considered arable land as public property, thus harming cultivation of wasteland. Therefore the government recognized private ownership of wasteland newly cultivated for three generations and, for one generation, ownership of wasteland formerly cultivated. Later the government recognized ownership in perpetuity.

sanzō 三蔵 (the three storehouses). The three storehouses of the Yamato court. They were the IMIKURA, the *uchitsukura,* and the ŌKURA. The *imikura* stored the supplies of the court; the *uchitsukura* stored tributes from the three Korean states (Sankan) and government property; and the *ōkura,* which was established about the middle of the fifth century, stored the provincial taxes. The superintendent of the three storehouses was Soga no Machi, and the accounting officials were members of the Hata family (HATA UJI). The records were held by the *Yamato no aya uji* and the *Kawachi no fumi uji* (KAWACHI NO AYA UJI). It is believed that the development of three independent storehouses shows the economic growth of the Yamato court as well as the influence of Chinese immigrants.

Sapporo Nōgakkō 札幌農学校 (the Sapporo School of Agriculture). A school established in 1872 by the commissioner of colonization of Hokkaidō. In 1876, William Clark was appointed vice-director of the school. Along with agricultural education, modern thought based on Christian spirituality characterized the school. Eminent men such as Nitobe Inazō (1862–1933) and Arishima Takeo (1878–1923) were graduates of the school. These men contributed to the development of modern Japanese thought.

Sarugaku 猿楽 (mimetic dances). Performances which were popular from the Nara to the end of the Kamakura period. Initially, they were a sort of mimetic dance performed at court. Later they were performed at religious ceremonies of shrines and temples. From earlier times, there existed associations of Sarugaku performers. They built theaters in Ōmi and Yamato during the middle ages. When shrines and temples became the main place of performance, Sarugaku took on a dramatic form and developed into NŌGAKU. Thus in an early stage, Nōgaku was a variation of Sarugaku performed in a more artistic way. The comic element of Sarugaku developed into the farcical interludes known as KYŌGEN.

Sasame-yuki 細雪. A literary work of the Shōwa era. It is a long novel written by Tanizaki Jun'ichirō (1886–1965), who began the work in 1943 and completed it in 1948. It has been translated into English by Edward Seidensticker as *The Makioka Sisters*.

sashidashi 指出 (reports). Reports on the area of arable land and on yearly taxes under the rule of Oda Nobunaga and Toyotomi Hideyoshi. When Nobunaga conquered new territory, he asked the feudal lords and the nominal owners to submit these reports. Except in urgent cases, a land survey went along with the submitting of the reports. Especially when mere reports proved to be unsatisfactory, land surveying was strictly enforced.

sato-osa 里長 (village headman). In ancient Japan and under the penal and administrative code system (RITSURYŌ-SEI), the *sato-osa* was the head of a rural community. He formed the last step in local administration. It was his duty to control the population within the village, to promote agriculture and mulberry plantations, to investigate violations, and to urge the people to participate in the corvées. His cruelty is described by the poet Yamanoue no Okura (660–733) in the fifth volume of the MAN'YŌSHŪ: *"Shimoto toru sato-osa ga koe wa neyado made kitachi yobahinu"* 楚取る里長が声は寝屋処まで来立ち呼ばひぬ (with whip in hand the headman comes to our sleeping place and growls).

Satsu-Ei sensō 薩英戦争 (NAMAMUGI JIKEN)

sedōka 旋頭歌. A form of Japanese *waka* poem composed of six lines divided into two groups of 5-7-7 syllables each. This form already appears among the songs of the KOJIKI and the NIHON SHOKI, but there are relatively many (sixty-two) *sedōka* in the MAN'YŌSHŪ. Many balladlike *sedōka* by unknown authors are found in various volumes. The form as it appeared in the early *Man'yō* age tended to disappear quickly. It is believed that originally *sedōka* were dialogues or popular songs. It is therefore natural that they tended to disappear when the folk-song *waka* developed into *waka* with an individual character.

seiji shōsetsu 政治小説 (political novels). Novels which describe the ideals of democratic freedom during the early Meiji era. Some writers tried to interpret the political ideals of the democratic movement in plain language. The novels lack literary value, but their social influence was not to be underestimated. Such works as KEIKOKU BIDAN and KAJIN NO KIGU had a resounding success.

seikan ron 征韓論 (argument for war with Korea). The argument for the invasion of Korea, as advocated by Saigō Takamori (1827–77) during the early Meiji era. The antiforeign and loyalist ideology of the late Edo period was adopted by the Meiji government along with the slogan "wealth and military strength" *(fukoku-kyōhei)* and an aggressive policy toward China and Korea. By maintaining her isolation policy, Korea intensified friction with Japan. In 1873, the argument for invasion of Korea became a hot issue, and the cabinet nearly decided in favor of war. Having lost their feudal privileges, the warriors were dissatisfied and launched an antigovernment movement. By engaging in an overseas war, the government intended to soothe the warriors' discontent. But as Iwakura, Ōkubo, and Kido, who had just returned from an inspection tour in Europe and the United States, opposed the government plan, which they considered to be premature, pro-war leaders such as Saigō, Itagaki, Etō, Soejima, and Gotō resigned. Dissatisfied warriors took advantage of the weakened cabinet and started rebellions. Successive rebellions in Saga (SAGA NO RAN) and Hagi (HAGI NO RAN) were accompanied by the Shimpūren revolt (SHIMPŪREN) and the Seinan War (SEINAN SENSŌ).

Seikyō-sha 政教社 (Society for Political Education). Ultranationalist society of the middle Meiji era, established in 1888 by Shiga Shigetaka (1863–1927). Shiga edited the magazine NIHONJIN.

Seinan Sensō 西南戦争 (Seinan War). A warriors' rebellion led by Saigō Takamori (1827–77). After the restoration, the modernization policy adopted by the government resulted in the loss of feudal privileges by the warriors. The warriors' feeling of discontent gradually worsened, and in 1874 revolts occurred. Such were the Saga revolt (SAGA NO RAN), the Shimpūren revolt (SHIMPŪREN), the Akitsuki revolt, and the Hagi revolt (HAGI NO RAN). The Seinan War, which was the last and worst warriors' revolt, was led by Saigō Takamori, who relied on his samurai. Saigō, who had advocated war with Korea and had been defeated in 1873 (SEIKAN RON), opened a private school in his native Kagoshima for the education of the sons of samurai. At that time, the prefectural administration of Kagoshima was conducted by the Saigō faction, which harbored strong antigovernment feeling. This hostile sentiment was intensified when the government adopted countermeasures. Saigō's troops entered Kumamoto but did not besiege the castle. They fought fiercely at Yamaga, Tabaruzaka, and Kichijigoe, but when their stronghold Kagoshima was attacked by government troops, Saigō's forces had to withdraw. Finally, Saigō committed suicide at Shiroyama. Meanwhile, by reducing land taxes, the government succeeded in appeasing the opposition and, obtaining the support of wealthy merchants, avoided a financial crisis.

Seitaisho 政体書 (Statement of the Forms of Government). A statement of the organization of the new government following the Meiji Restoration. The document was issued in April 1868 and is based on the Five-Point Charter Oath (GO-KAJŌ NO SEIMON). It sets forth the principle that all authority is in the hands of the Council of State (DAJŌKAN) and specifically refers to the separation of administrative, legislative, and judicial powers. It was a significant statement for its time, but its provisions were not carried out.

Seitō-sha 青踏社. A women's organization of the late Meiji and Taishō eras. The movement for emancipation of women followed the Russo-Japanese War (1904–5) and was organized into an association in 1911 by the authoress Hiratsuka Raichō (1886–), who published the association's organ called *Seitō*. Initially, the organization intended to develop women's literature, but the members broke away from tradition and were known as "the new women." They advocated the abolition of the family system and were severely criticized by the traditionalists. In 1916, publication of the magazine was discontinued. Seitō-sha members, however, continued their activities in the field of literature and social improvement.

Seiyō Kibun 西洋紀聞. A book written by Arai Hakuseki (1657–1725) following the questioning of the Italian secular priest Sidotti, who had smuggled himself into Japan in 1706 by disembarking on the coast of Yakushima in Ōsumi Province (Kagoshima Prefecture). The book makes it clear that the Japanese have but a shallow knowledge of the West, that Western scientific knowledge is far ahead, and that it is a mistake to ban and fear Christianity. As the BAKUFU was opposed to these views, the book was not circulated. *Seiyō Kibun* was of great significance, for it was an introduction to Western things and a forerunner of the introduction of YŌGAKU or Western learning.

Seiyū-kai 政友会 (Association of Political Friends). Political association and party organized in 1900 by Itō Hirobumi (1841–1909), who felt that it would be impossible to stabilize the political situation only by relying on the court and clan government. Saionji Kimmochi (1849–1940), who formed many cabinets, succeeded Itō as president of the party. The party reached its climax during the Taishō period, following the movement for the defense of constitutionalism, when Hara Takashi (1856–1921) became president of the Seiyū-kai and was appointed prime minister. Later a conflict arose between the two major parties, the Seiyū-kai and the Minsei-tō or Democratic Party. The Seiyū-kai was oppressed by militarists after the incident of May 15, 1932, when Premier Inukai Tsuyoshi (1855–1932) was assassinated by young officers. Finally, the association was dissolved in 1940 and integrated into the Imperial Rule Assistance Association (TAISEI YOKUSAN-KAI). As compared with the Democratic Party, the Seiyū-kai was rather directed toward the propertied class and had certain connections with the MITSUI concern.

sekai kyōkō 世界恐慌 (the world depression). The depression which began in 1929 in the United States and spread to the whole world. It reached Japan in 1930. From 1930 to 1931, prices and stocks dropped 60–70 percent. This was followed by restriction of output, curtailing of operation, a heavy fall in farm production, and a restriction by the United States on silk importation. All this resulted in impoverishment. To effect a break, the government adopted a policy of austerity, and the Bank of Japan as well as the Industrial Bank of Japan released capital, by which action, however, only big finance profited. The powerful ZAIBATSU formed a cartel, and economic measures were followed by extremely severe deflation, causing the destitution of medium and small enterprises, labor, and farmers.

Seken Munezan'yō 世間胸算用. A literary work of the middle Edo period. It is a realistic novel (UKIYO-ZŌSHI) written by Ihara Saikaku (1642–93) and published in 1692. It offers valuable sidelights on the economic life of the townspeople. Together with NIHON EITAI-GURA, *Saikaku Oki-miyage,* and *Saikaku Oridome,* it is considered as a representative work revealing the life of the townspeople.

Sekigahara no tatakai 関ケ原の戦 (the battle of Sekigahara). The battle fought in 1600 between Ieyasu and Ishida Mitsunari (1563–1600). After Hideyoshi's death, Ieyasu, as one of the five ministers (TAIRŌ), assumed control of Japan. But Mitsunari, who favored Hideyoshi's son and heir Hideyori, planned to remove Ieyasu. He raised an army and fought against Ieyasu's forces in Sekigahara, Mino Province (Gifu Prefecture). Ieyasu gained a decisive victory. Mitsunari was beheaded, and the daimyō who had sided with him were either banished or deprived of their domains. Ieyasu became the undisputed ruler of Japan.

sekisen 関銭 (barrier tax). Traffic taxes collected during the middle ages. From the middle of the Kamakura period, crossings were set up in harbors, at important communication centers, and at river banks. Barriers were recklessly established during the Muromachi period. Because they caused great damage to communication, commerce, and industry, they were abolished by Nobunaga and Hideyoshi.

sekisho 関所 (checking stations). Checking stations established at important land and sea communication centers for the inspection of individuals and articles. About the middle of the Heian period, ancient checking stations which had been set up for military purposes had deteriorated. In the Muromachi period, in order to make up for the deficits of manor production, manorial lords established barriers at various places and imposed taxes in the form of money or commodities. But these barriers greatly harmed the development of communications and the economy, and they were abolished by Nobunaga and

Hideyoshi. As a result, commercial commodities and communications greatly improved. During the Edo period, the BAKUFU adopted a policy of setting up checking stations for the control of traffic and for keeping an eye on warriors. The *bakufu* aimed at maintaining national peace and stability. The checking stations of Hakone and Imagire, both on the Tōkaidō, were of the greatest importance for the safeguarding of Edo.

sekkan seiji 摂関政治 (political system of regents and chief councilors to the emperor). A political system based on the office of regency (SESSHŌ) and the office of state represented by the chief councilor to the emperor (KAMPAKU). The office was created by the Fujiwara toward the end of the ninth century. Fujiwara no Yoshifusa (804–72) was the first regent and was appointed in 858. The first *kampaku* was Mototsune (836–91), who was appointed in 887. The regency reached its climax under Michinaga (966–1027) and Yorimichi (992–1074). Following the collapse of the penal and administrative code system and the development of the manorial estates, the national economy changed fundamentally, and the regency was the concrete expression of this change. Furthermore, it meant the negation of the ancient imperial system. However, with the inauguration of the emperors' cloistered government in 1086, the regency and *kampaku* system lost its significance.

semba-koki 千歯こき. A thresher adopted in the later part of the Edo period. Before this time, rice was rubbed by hand, drawn between two bamboo poles or iron bars, or otherwise threshed with primitive implements. From about 1700, the thresher was adopted first for wheat and then for rice. Four legs were fixed on a block, a number of bamboo needles were attached in a row to a crossbar, and the ears of rice plants were threshed. Bamboo needles were later replaced by iron ones. This kind of thresher was used until the Taishō era, when a treading pedal came into use. The *semba-koki* increased threshing efficiency, especially on busy harvest days. Women workers were no longer required and were thus deprived of this work. For this reason the *semba-koki* were called *goke-daoshi* or "widow killers."

semmen koshakyō 扇面古写経 (sutras on painted fans). Sutras written on paper fans and adorned with paintings. They were appreciated by court nobles of the middle and late Heian period. The Lotus Sutra *(Hokke-kyō)* was written on paper fans which were delicately painted. Some of the fans are preserved in Shitennō-ji temple, the Tōkyō National Museum, the Hōryū-ji, the private collection of the Kuhara family, etc. The paintings do not describe the meaning of the sutra but are mainly devoted to the life of children. The gorgeous pictorial style is believed to be that of the Fujiwara period, but such fans from other periods are extant.

Semmyō-reki 宣明暦 (the Semmyō calendar). The calendar used from 862 to 1684. Made in 822 by the Chinese Jo Kō (in Chinese, Hsü Ang), it found its way to Japan in 859. Three years later it was adopted following the order of Emperor Seiwa (850–80). The calendar became obsolete, but no means of revising it were found, and it remained in use until 1684, when the Jōkyō calendar (JŌKYŌ KOYOMI) was prepared by Yasui Santetsu (Shibukawa Shunkai, 1639–1715).

Senchaku Hongan-nembutsushū 選択本願念仏集. The canon of Jōdo Buddhism (JŌDO-SHŪ) as laid down by the founder Hōnen (1133–1212). It is believed to have been written in 1198. The work includes the essence of Hōnen's belief, namely that by abandoning all superfluous practices and by merely repeatedly invoking the name of Amida Buddha one can attain rebirth in paradise.

Sengoku jidai 戦国時代 (the period of civil war). This is the period which followed close upon the Ōnin Civil War (ŌNIN NO RAN) and lasted for a century—that is, until the unification of the country by Hideyoshi. The MURO-MACHI BAKUFU, which represented only the political power of constable land-owners (SHUGO DAIMYŌ), had collapsed. The same constable landowners now grouped the wealthy farmers, who had formed the nucleus of the peasants' uprisings, into bodies of retainers, intending to bolster the defenses of their respective possessions, and jealously maintained sectional authority in the various provinces. They fought against each other for supremacy. The main civil-war barons (DAIMYŌ) were the Date of Mutsu (Aomori Prefecture), the Hōjō of Sagami (Kanagawa Prefecture), the Uesugi of Echigo (Niigata Prefecture), the Takeda of Kai (Yamanashi Prefecture), the Imagawa of Suruga (Shizuoka Prefecture), the Asakura of Echizen (Fukui Prefecture), the Ōuchi of the Chūgoku district (who were replaced by the Mōri), the Chōsokabe in Shikoku, and the Ōtomo and Shimazu in Kyūshū. It was the ambition of most civil-war barons to dominate the country, but only Nobunaga of Owari (Aichi Prefecture) was successful. After Nobunaga's death, Hideyoshi completed the unification of the country.

Senju seijūsho 千住製絨所. A woolen textile factory established by the government in 1876. In addition, the government began the manufacture of woolen cloth and military uniforms. In 1888, the factory became a clothing depot for the army.

senryū 川柳. A kind of witty epigrammatic verse of the middle Edo period. About the middle of the eighteenth century, the poetic game called *maeku-zuke* was very popular. The final fourteen syllables were written first as a kind of hint, and then the preceding seventeen (5-7-5) syllables were composed by any number of people. Among its best judges was Karai Senryū (1718–90), and since he was known as the selector of the best *maeku-zuke* the *senryū* came to be named for him. Like haiku, *senryū* is composed of seventeen syllables (5-7-5), but the usual seasonal theme *(kidai)* of haiku, as well as "fill-in" words such as *kana,* etc., called *kireji,* is lacking. The usual themes of *senryū* are satirical and comic descriptions of daily trifles and follies of society. In 1765, Karai Senryū published *Haifū Yanagidaru.* This was the first selection of many, the last being published in 1833. The whole collection comprises 167 volumes. Later, this kind of verse reflected the degeneration of the times, and *senryū* itself degenerated into the satirical verse called *kyōku.* Several volumes of *senryū* have been translated into English by R. H. Blyth.

Senshūji-ha 専修寺派 (Takada branch of the Shin-shū sect). A branch of the Shin-shū sect of Buddhism. It is also called Shin-shū Takada-ha. Shinran was temporarily exiled to Echigo (Niigata Prefecture), but from Echigo he spread his faith in Takada, Shimotsuke Province (Tochigi Prefecture), and the new branch developed in this locality. The Kyōto Hongan-ji and the Senshū-ji branches are the most influential of Shin-shū. Shin'e (1434–1512), the tenth chief priest of Senshū-ji, simultaneously with Rennyo (1415–99) of the Hongan-ji branch, spread his tenets in the Hokuriku and Kinki districts and, fulfilling the wish of his believers, moved the Senshū-ji temple from Shimotsuke to Isshinden in Ise Province (Mie Prefecture).

Sesonji-ryū 世尊寺流 (the Sesonji style of calligraphy). The style of calligraphy originated by Fujiwara no Yukinari (972–1027). The cursive style of writing which he perfected became the popular style during the late Heian and early Kamakura periods. During the Namboku period (1336–92) Prince Son'en Hosshinnō (1298–1356), departing from the Sesonji style, evolved the style of calligraphy called OIE-RYŪ or Shōren'in-ryū.

sesshō 摂政 (regent or regency). The office or officer in control of state affairs in place of an underage emperor. When an emperor or empress was enthroned before reaching maturity, the administrative affairs of state were conducted by a regent who was at the same time prime minister. At one time Empress Regent Jingū reigned instead of Emperor Ōjin, and members of the imperial family often took the affairs of state in hand. But in 858, during the reign of Emperor Seiwa (850–80), Fujiwara no Yoshifusa (804–72) was made regent. From this time, the Fujiwara, in order to consolidate their position, monopolized the regency and were the real power behind the throne. During the Kamakura period, Hōjō Tokiyori (1227–63) divided the Fujiwara clan into five families: Konoe, Kujō, Nijō, Ichijō, and Takatsukasa. These families were collectively called GO-SEKKE. The power of the Fujiwara was weakened. The regency was abolished in 1868, but in 1889 the regency system was determined according to the imperial house law.

Seto-yaki 瀬戸焼 (Seto pottery). Pottery made in Seto, in the northwestern part of Owari Province (Aichi Prefecture). In 1227, the ceramist Katō Kage-masa (1168–1249) introduced the art from Sung China and built a kiln in Seto. During the Edo period, ceramics formed the main industry of the Owari clan. The industry flourished under the patronage of the shogunate. Along with Kyūshū's ARITA-YAKI, Seto-yaki is one of the most famous types of Japanese pottery.

sewamono 世話物 (realistic dramas). Dramas (and novels) of the Edo period in which contemporary people are realistically depicted in their social environment. *Sewamono* are contrasted with historical novels or plays called *jidaimono,* which describe historical characters.

Shakai Heiken-ron 社会平権論. Translation into Japanese of Herbert Spencer's *Social Statics.* The work was translated in 1881 by Matsushima Tsuyoshi. It greatly influenced the movement for democratic rights and for establishing a national assembly.

Shakai-Minshu-tō 社会民主党 (Social Democratic Party). The first socialist political party. Organized in 1901 by Abe Iso-o, Katayama Sen, and Kōtoku Shūsui, it was promptly dissolved by Itō Hirobumi. Because the party's manifesto, based on socialism and democracy, was published in the newspapers, its ideals were known by the people at large.

Shakai-Minshū-tō 社会民衆党 (Social People's Party). A people's party organized in 1926 by Abe Iso-o (1865–1949) and others. It was based on labor federation. In 1932, it merged with the National Federation of Laborers and Farmers and became the Great Socialist People's Party (Shakai-Taishū-tō). During World War II, it aligned itself with government policy, but in 1940 it was dissolved following Konoe's movement for a new national structure.

shamanizumu シャーマニズム (shamanism). A primitive religion embracing a belief in controlling spirits. The belief holds that shamans are the only mediums who can influence spirits. The religion spread in northeastern Siberia among Siberian tribes, the Buriats, Turks, Mongols, and Manchus. Japanese primitive Shintō originated in shamanism. Shamanism developed from a faith in spirits and in a dualism based on good and evil. Its cosmology includes the three worlds of heaven, earth, and the underworld. Shamans function as priests, sorcerers, exorcists, and soothsayers. Among farmers, shamans are sometimes called on to recite prayers for rain.

shamisen 三味線 (samisen). A three-stringed musical instrument. It was popular among the townspeople of the Edo period. About the middle of the sixteenth century, the *shamisen* was brought to Japan from the Ryūkyū Islands by Japanese merchants and was enjoyed in town houses and gay quarters.

There is a rich variety of *shamisen* types. The instrument is used as an accompaniment to *nagauta* (epic songs) and JŌRURI (puppet ballads).

Shanghai jihen 上海事変 (the Shanghai incident). The incident in which Japanese troops clashed with Chinese troops in the vicinity of Shanghai. Since the Manchu incident, the anti-Japanese movement of the Chinese people had become more intense. Taking advantage of the assassination of a Japanese Buddhist priest in Shanghai, the Japanese government in 1931, in spite of its declared nonaggression policy, dispatched troops to Shanghai. Landing forces clashed with the Chinese Nineteenth Route Army. When the Japanese sent reinforcements, American-Japanese relations worsened. A cease-fire agreement was reached, but anti-Japanese sentiment among the Chinese people had reached its peak. The incident eventually led to the Sino-Japanese war.

sharebon 洒落本 (witty novelettes). Humorous novelettes which were popular from the late eighteenth to the early nineteenth century. The small books were mainly filled with witticisms and "knowledge of a man-about-town," known as *tsū*. The works deal mostly with life in the pleasure quarters and, in conversational form, describe the conduct of the characters. Writers of *sharebon* include Shoku Sanjin (or Ōta Nampo, 1749–1823), Santō Kyōden (1761–1816), Shikitei Samba (1776–1822), and Jippensha Ikku (1765–1831).

Shasekishū 沙石集. Representative collection of Buddhist narratives written in 1283 by the Rinzai Buddhist priest Mujū (or Dōkyō Ichien, 1226–1312). The narratives are written in a popular, colloquial, and easy-to-read style. Stress is laid on Buddhist mercy, and the work recommends invoking the name of Buddha in order to obtain rebirth in paradise. The work also offers valuable material about the life of contemporary people.

Shiba uji 斯波氏 (Shiba family). One of the three families of deputies of the shōgun (KANREI) during the Muromachi period. With the Hosokawa and the Hatakeyama, the Shiba were very powerful, but the inheritance quarrels of the Shiba family led to the Ōnin Civil War (ŌNIN NO RAN, 1467–77). The stronghold of the Shiba was Owari (Aichi Prefecture). Oda family members were their deputy constables *(shugo-dai)*.

Shiberia shuppei シベリア出兵 (expedition to Siberia). A military expedition during the Taishō era. In November 1917, communist power established by the Russian Revolution oppressed antirevolutionary movements in the country. Various powers, however, tried to oppose the Russian Revolution by military means aimed at overthrowing the communist regime. Japan was advised to adopt the same attitude and to prepare to occupy part of Siberia. In 1918, when Britain and the United States proposed to rescue Czechoslovak troops in Russia, Japan promptly mobilized a large force and occupied part of eastern Siberia. But following the Nikolaievsk incident (ROSHIYA), which is referred to as *Ni-Kō jiken,* and denunciation by various countries, Japan withdrew her forces in 1922.

shichi-daiji 七大寺 (NANTO SHICHI-DAIJI)

shichidō 七道 (the seven districts). The seven administrative sections which existed from ancient times. They were Tōkaidō, Tōsandō, Hokurikudō, Nankaidō, San'yōdō, San'indō, and Saikaidō. Before the Taika Reform the districts were but vaguely defined, but after the reform clear-cut boundary lines were established.

shidō-sen 祠堂銭 (donations for the upkeep of Buddhist temples). A *shidō* is a Buddhist monastery temple where memorial rites are performed in honor of ancestors. Money offered to these temples is called *shidō-sen* or *shidō-kin.* From the Muromachi period, the custom existed of lending money in advance at a low interest. Regulations for returning the money were very strict.

Shigaraki no Miya 信楽宮. The imperial palace in Ōmi Province after Emperor Shōmu (701–56) moved the capital in 742. It was also called Kōga no Miya after the name of the county in Shiga Prefecture where the palace was located. Before 744 the emperor moved his capital to KUNI-KYŌ, Shigaraki-kyō, and Naniwa-kyō. But the construction of Shigaraki-kyō was discontinued owing to financial difficulties and the lack of recruited farmers. Following the advice of officials of the Council of State and of Buddhist monasteries, the emperor returned to HEIJŌ-KYŌ in 744.

shigi kempō 私擬憲法 (privately discussed constitutions). The drafts for a constitution in the early Meiji era. In 1880–81, following a violent campaign for popular rights, the emperor issued a rescript which declared that a parliament would be established in 1890. Thereupon, the drafting of a new constitution was discussed everywhere. Not only the Senate (GENRŌ-IN) and the members of the ruling group but also public-spirited men among the common people tried to make several drafts. These drafts by the common people are collectively called *shigi kempō.*

Shiji Tsugan 資治通鑑 *(Tzu Chih T'ung Chien).* Historical work compiled in China during the Sung dynasty (960–1279). The compiler was a scholar and politician of the Northern Sung named Shiba Kō (in Chinese, Ssu-ma Kuang, 1019–86). The work covers, in chronological order, the period from near the end of the fifth century B.C. to the close of the Five Dynasties (907–1124), a period of 1,362 years. The larger history comprises 294 volumes and is supplemented with thirty volumes of tables and thirty volumes of "discussion of doubtful points" (*kōi* 考異). It is a model of history in chronological form which greatly influenced Japanese historians. The title *Shiji Tsugan* means "a mirror (or example) 鑑 which, going through 通 successive generations, contributes 資 to politics 治."

Shijō-ha 四条派 (Shijō school of painting). The name of a school of painting, the founder of which was Matsumura Goshun (1752–1811). The characteristic feature is a blending of Maruyama Ōkyo's (1733–95) realism and the style of Yosa Buson's (1716–83) literary paintings called *bunjin-ga*.

shiki 式 (administrative regulations). The *shiki* (forms, ceremonies, and rituals), together with the KYAKU (administrative and executive procedure), formed the legal system during the Nara and Heian periods. The *shiki* were detailed enforcement regulations which supplemented the *ryō* (administrative code) by describing the functions of departments of state and the duties of officials. Like the *kyaku*, which were detailed regulations supplementing the *ritsu* (penal code), the *shiki* were compiled and adjusted in successive ages. Such adjustments were the Kōnin-shiki, Jōgan-shiki, and ENGI-SHIKI. Only the Engi-shiki is completely extant. It offers important material for the study of politics based on the penal and administrative code (*ritsuryō*).

shikiden 職田 (land of government officials). During the Nara and Heian periods, plots of arable land were given to officials according to their office. These plots were called *shikiden* or *shikibunden*. From the ministers of the Council of State down to the rural district administrators (GUNJI), all received *shikiden* as salary. In principle, these plots were tax-free (FUYUSO-DEN) except those of the rural district administrators. *Shikiden* were offered as soon as the office was assumed and were confiscated upon release from office or at the death of the official. From the middle of the Heian period, when offices were held hereditarily, *shikiden* became private property.

Shiki no agata-nushi 磯城県主 (local official of Shiki). The local official or estate master (AGATA-NUSHI) of Shiki no Agata in Yamato Province during the pre-Taika period. Shiki no Agata was located in the neighborhood of the former Miwa-mura in Shiki County, Nara Prefecture. About the third century, the imperial clan had its stronghold in Takaichi and Katsuragi in the southwestern part of the Nara valley. Subduing the surrounding tribes, it gradually made its authority felt in Yamato. At this time, the ancestors of the local official of Shiki no Agata, together with the ancestors of the local officials of Kasuga no Agata and of Toichi no Agata, were incorporated in the imperial territory and formed a sort of corporation of tribes which centered around the imperial family. Later the estate master of Shiki no Agata was on friendly terms with the imperial family. Shiki and five other estates (*agata*) formed the "six imperial estates of Japan" (*Wakoku mutsu no mi-agata*). They were under the direct administration of the imperial household and for a long time were a source of revenue for the imperial family.

shikken 執権 (regent or regency). An office of the KAMAKURA BAKUFU. The regent assisted the shōgun in matters of administration. Aided by the assistant regent (RENSHO), the members of the Deliberative Assembly (HYŌJŌ-SHŪ), and the assistant members (HIKITSUKE-SHŪ), he conducted the affairs of the *bakufu*. The Hōjō monopolized the office of regent, and, as they held the actual power, the office of shōgun became a mere name.

Shimabara no ran 島原の乱 (the Shimabara insurrection of 1637–38). A rebellion in which Christians were implicated. It was caused by the misrule of the lord of the Shimabara clan, Matsukura Shigemasa, who was an atrocious persecutor of the Christians. Farmers, RŌNIN, and Christians of Shimabara revolted. Their leader was Masuda Shirō, also known as Amakusa Shirō. The BAKUFU dispatched Itakura Shigemasa, but the Christians, who were concentrated in the abandoned castle Hara-no-jō (Hara-no-shiro), offered fierce resistance. Itakura was killed, and the new commander, Matsudaira Nobutsuna, started a hunger blockade. Finally, the castle was captured and the rebellion savagely suppressed. The insurrection was among the immediate causes of Japan's cessation of intercourse with the outside world. It resulted in still more cruel persecution of the Christians.

Shimada-gumi 島田組 (the Shimada Trade Corporation). An early-Meiji trading firm with political affiliations. During the Edo period, the house of Shimada was one of the *jūnin-gumi* or "ten wealthy merchants of Ōsaka" in charge of the finances of the BAKUFU and the daimyō. After the restoration, the Shimada-gumi helped with the finances of the new administration and contributed large sums of money. Together with the Mitsui and Ono corporations, it operated a money-exchange business. In 1874, the Shimada-gumi went bankrupt.

Shimazu uji 島津氏 (the Shimazu clan). A wealthy family which from the middle ages wielded power in South Kyūshū. From the sixteenth century, the family made a fortune trading with Ming China and the Ryūkyū Islands. When Francis Xavier reached Kagoshima, Shimazu Takahisa (1514–71) permitted him to preach Christianity. From the Sengoku period (1490–1573), the Shimazu oppressed the Ōtomo and succeeded in controlling almost the whole of Kyūshū. When they submitted to Hideyoshi, their territory was limited to Satsuma and Ōsumi (Kagoshima Prefecture), and the southern half of Hyūga (Miyazaki Prefecture). At the end of the Edo period, the Shimazu introduced Western civilization and developed industry in their clan. Owing to their military and financial strength, they were able to direct the political situation at the end of the Edo period. Outstanding were Nariakira

(1809–58) and his younger brother Hisamitsu (1817–87). Hisamitsu was one of the motivating spirits of the early Meiji government.

shimbunshi jōrei 新聞紙条令 (the press law). An ordinance for the control of newspapers and magazines which caused great trouble to the government. In 1875, opposing the growing movement for popular rights, the government, in order to keep control of public opinion, enforced the press law together with the law against slander and the publication law. But political parties were established, and they published their party organs. At the same time, the movement for popular rights became more violent. In 1883, the government amended the former laws. This amendment resulted in the disappearance of smaller newspapers but also in the circulation of secret publications.

shimbutsu-bunri 神仏分離 (separation of Shintō from Buddhism). A religious policy of the early Meiji administration. The national scholars of the loyalist school of thought headed the movement for revived Shintō and for the return to old ways. They were strongly opposed to the fusion of Shintō and Buddhism of feudal days and aimed at making Shintō an independent and national religion. In 1868, the new policy as formulated in the "unity of church and state" *(saisei-itchi)* actually separated Shintō from Buddhism. The imperial household rejected Buddhist practices, and the habit of imperial princes becoming Buddhist priests was abolished. Meanwhile, some Buddhist temples and statues were destroyed in what is known as HAIBUTSU-KISHAKU, and Buddhism suffered a severe blow. In 1872, the government organized both Shintō and Buddhism under the control of the Bureau of Religious Instruction (Kyōbu-shō), which was the organ of popular education. However, the government did not obtain the expected results.

shimin-byōdō 四民平等 (equality of the four classes of people). One of the reforms of the early Meiji era. The Meiji Restoration abolished the feudal system of social classes which divided the people into the four classes of warrior, farmer, artisan, and merchant. The new government aimed at establishing a modern and united nation. The feudal classes were changed in 1869 into three ranks. These were the nobility (KAZOKU), the ex-military *(shizoku)*, and the common people *(heimin)*. In 1871, the government abolished the *eta* caste and the pariahs called *hinin* and amalgamated them with the common people. In the same year, the government acknowledged freedom of enterprise. In 1873, a conscription law was promulgated. In 1876, the decree abolishing the wearing of swords was issued, and the warriors were deprived of their feudal privileges and social rank.

Shimoda 下田. A harbor city on the southeastern edge of Izu Peninsula in Shizuoka Prefecture. Shimoda has no hinterland, but its location and topography made it an important place for maritime transportation. In 1616, a commissioner of Shimoda was appointed and a guard station was set up in the bay. During the Edo period, the *higaki* (HIGAKI-KAISEN) and the *taru* (TARU-KAISEN) cargo vessels, as well as the vessels from the northeastern provinces, called at Shimoda, and the harbor flourished. Shimoda was the residence of Townsend Harris, first United States consul in Japan. Following the Treaty of Kanagawa in 1859, the ports of Shimoda and Hakodate were opened to American vessels (KANAGAWA JŌYAKU). Shimoda gradually lost its significance. It is now a mere fishing port and sightseeing area.

Shimonoseki jiken 下関事件 (incident at Shimonoseki). The clash between the Chōshū clan and foreign vessels of four nationalities. In 1863, the Chōshū clan started hostilities by firing upon an American vessel in the Straits of Shimonoseki. A French vessel and a Dutch warship were also attacked. In 1864, a joint expedition from the American, British, French, and Dutch navies attacked Shimonoseki and removed the guns. The Chōshū clan thereupon gave way and established friendly relations with the foreigners. The incident showed the futility of the antiforeign policy and led to the complete opening of the country.

Shimonoseki Jōyaku 下関条約 (the Treaty of Shimonoseki). A treaty concluded in 1895 between China and Japan following the end of the Sino-Japanese War. The plenipotentiaries were Japan's Itō Hirobumi and China's Li Hung-chang (in Japanese, Ri Kō-shō). The treaty was humiliating to China, as she was forced to acknowledge the independence of Korea (thereby renouncing her traditional sovereignty); to cede Formosa, the Pescadores, and the Liaotung Peninsula to Japan; to pay an indemnity amounting to 200 million taels (360 million yen or 38 million pounds); to give Japan the privilege of most favored nation; and to open the ports of Shashih, Ch'ungch'ing, Suchow, and K'angchow. Meanwhile, the Triple Intervention (SANGOKU KANSHŌ) forced Japan to renounce her claims to the Liaotung Peninsula in return for an additional indemnity from China.

shimpan 親藩 (related clans). Collateral descendants of Tokugawa shōguns who did not themselves become shōguns. They included Owari (Nagoya), Kii (Wakayama), and Mito (northeast of Edo), collectively called the "three houses" *(go-sanke)*, and the Echizen and Aizu clans, etc. Tayasu, Hitotsubashi, and Shimizu (three sons of the eighth and ninth shōguns) were called the "three lords" *(go-sankyō)*. They had no autonomous estates but ranked next to the "three houses" and received handsome stipends. One of their duties was to provide a shōgun if the ruling shōgun had no heir. This was also one of the duties of the "three houses."

shimpo jitō 新補地頭 (newly appointed stewards). After the civil war of the Jōkyū era (JŌKYŪ NO HEN), the Hōjō confiscated about three thousand manors from nobles and warriors who had sided with ex-Emperor Gotoba. They then appointed stewards from among the retainer warriors who had sided with the BAKUFU and had been meritorious in war. These warrior stewards were called *shimpo jitō* or newly appointed stewards. The shares of former stewards appointed after Yoritomo's time differed from place to place, but the *shimpo* stewards received one *chō* (2.45 acres) per eleven *chō*, and as a rule they shared the collected taxes with the landlords. The appointment of new stewards was a favor bestowed by the Hōjō and strengthened their authority. It resulted in an increase of power of the warriors and a weakening of the power of nobles whose estates were encroached upon.

Shimpūren 神風連 (the Divine Wind League). A society formed by the Kumamoto clan. It was violently opposed to the government's policy of abolishing Japanese customs and encouraging Western ideas. It was also called Keishin-tō. The league fought for national isolation and for a policy based on Shintō tenets. The head of the league, Ōtaguro Tomo-o, bitterly criticized the government order of 1876 prohibiting the wearing of swords, attacked the imperial garrison of Kumamoto, killed its commander, and then attacked the Kumamoto prefectural office, assassinating the governor.

shinden kaihatsu 新田開発 (cultivation of newly reclaimed rice fields). Cultivation of newly reclaimed rice fields during the Edo period. In ancient times, cultivating wasteland was called *konden*. Today it is called *kaikon*. About the Kyōhō era (1716–36), land was reclaimed all over the country. Feudal lords whose finances were at an ebb encouraged cultivation of wasteland in order to increase their yearly taxes. But this policy resulted in a decrease of grassland and of irrigation water, and this in turn devastated the former rice fields and paradoxically caused floods. Sometimes, also, land was reclaimed upon the advice of deputies (DAIKAN) or simply because of farmers' contracts. Then merchants invested huge sums and exploited large tracts of land. They planted tobacco and cotton, which were highly profitable, and became great landowners. After a period of tax-free exploitation, a regular tax was imposed, but as a rule this tax was lower than that for the original rice fields. Since there was no limit to the acreage of land cultivated, the merchant-landowners made enormous profits.

shinden-zukuri 寝殿造 (*shinden* style of architecture). A type of dwelling for the small aristocratic society of the Heian period. In the center of the dwelling was an oblong building facing the south and called the *shinden*. On either side of it, to the front, were other buildings opening on the east and west and sometimes also a building to the north of it. In front was a pond. All these buildings were spacious apartments connected by corridors. The eastern and western apartments in front of the *shinden* were called *tai-no-ya*. In front of the *tai-no-ya* and connected by corridors were two *tsuridono*. The *tsuridono* were pavilions over the pond and derived their name from the fact that they were intended as places from which one could fish with a rod. This type of dwelling flourished during the Fujiwara period (894–1185). There are no original *shinden*-style dwellings left in Japan today, but the Seiryōden of the Kyōto Imperial Palace, which was restored during the Edo period, shows traces of *shinden-zukuri*.

Shingai Kakumei 辛亥革命 (Shingai Revolution). The Chinese Revolution. In 1911 there had been unrest, particularly in Szechwan, over a foreign loan to finance railways in South, Central, and West China, and over greater centralization of railway administration under Peking. By the end of September 1911, an active revolt had arisen in Szechwan. First, troops in Wuch'ang revolted, then the rebellion spread to various places and finally throughout the country. This resulted in the overthrow of the Ch'ing dynasty and the establishment of the Chinese Republic, of which Sun Wen (Sun Yat-sen, 1866–1925) was elected president. The revolution is called "Shingai" because of the interpretation of the year 1911 according to the sexagenary cycle *kanshi* (SHIN'I).

shingaku 心学 (popular ethics). A moral education movement launched in 1729 by Ishida Baigan (1685–1744). Confucianism was the main basis of the ethics, but Buddhist and Shintoist elements were incorporated. Moral education was explained for the common people in easy terms and simple sentences. Many parables enriched the teaching. Later the teaching became dogmatic and stereotyped and lost its popularity. Teachers of popular ethics included Tejima Toan (1718–86), Nakazawa Dōji (1725–1803), Shibata Kyūō (1783–1839), and Yaguchi Raiō (1782–1858).

Shingon-shū 真言宗 (the Shingon sect of Buddhism). A sect of Buddhism founded in Japan by Kūkai (774–835) in the early Heian period. It is also known as Shingon Mikkyō (Esoteric Shingon) and Tō-mitsu in contrast to Tai-mitsu, which is the Tendai religion. The most representative sect of Esoteric Buddhism, it preaches a pantheistic mysticism according to which the universe embodies the immanent spirit Dainichi. While in China, Kūkai received instruction from the Buddhist priest Keika and, after returning to Japan in 806, published *Jūjūshinron*. Criticizing other religions, he propagated his own views. He chose Kōya-san as his meditation center. He was granted the Tō-ji in Kyōto, which he made into a seminary aimed at preserving peace. At the end of the ninth century, the Buddhist priest Yakushin (826–906) founded the branch Hirozawa-ryū, also known as Ninna-ji, and the priest Shōbō (831–909) founded the branch Ono-ryū, also known as DAIGO-JI. Members of the Fujiwara family were converted to the Ono branch of Shingon Buddhism. In the early twelfth century, the Buddhist priest Kakuban (1095–1143) started the Shingi-Shingon sect.

shin'i 讖緯 (divination). In ancient times it was believed that man's destiny and even the rise and decline of a country could be deduced from the sexagenary cycle called *kanshi* 干支. This divination was practiced in ancient China, where it was believed that there existed ten movements of the sun, or calendar signs called *jikkan,* and twelve meetings of sun and moon, or twelve horary signs called *jūni-shi.* To this was added the ideology of the five natural elements or *go-gyō* and the way of *yin* and *yang,* or the active and regressive principles called ON'YŌDŌ. All natural and human phenomena were explained, and even future events were predicted. For instance, the combination *tsuchinoe* 戊 and *uma* 午 (collectively *bogo* 戊午) was the omen for a year of renovation, and the combination *kanoto* 辛 and *tori* 酉, or *shin'yū* 辛酉, was the omen for a year of reform. Political history was based on the same principle, and historical events were explained accordingly. This kind of divination was introduced into Japan together with Buddhist principles. The book *Jimmu-ki* records that Emperor Jimmu destroyed his enemy Nagasunehiko and inaugurated a holy era in the year *bogo,* and that he was enthroned in the palace of Kashiwabara in the year *shin'yū.* The computation of the year 660 B.C. as the year of Emperor Jimmu's enthronement was also made according to the principle of *shin'i* divination.

Shin Kokin Wakashū 新古今和歌集. An anthology of *waka* poems compiled by imperial order in the early Kamakura period. At the order of ex-Emperor Gotoba (1180–1239), Fujiwara no Sadaie (1162–1242) and Ietaka (1158–1237) compiled the anthology, which was completed in 1205. The work comprises twenty volumes with a total of 1,988 poems. Besides poems of the compilers themselves, poems of Saigyō (1118–90), Jien (1145–1225), Fujiwara no Yoshitsune (1169–1206), Fujiwara no Toshinari (1113–1204), and others were included. The graceful style and technique are known as *Shin Kokin-chō.*

shinsen-gumi 新撰組. An inspection corps established in Kyōto against the maneuvers of the antishogunate faction. In 1862, the BAKUFU assembled the swordsmen and samurai of the Kantō district and dispatched them to Kyōto. Later, part of the corps was withdrawn and sent to Edo. The troops chosen to be left behind were called *shinsen-gumi.* They were under the control of the commissioner of Kyōto, and their commander was Kondō Isami. Bloodshed frequently occurred, such as during the Ikedaya riot and during the search for and oppression of loyalists. After the battles of Toba and Fushimi, the corps returned to Edo and was disbanded.

Shinsen Tsukubashū 新撰菟玖波集. An anthology of linked-verse poems (RENGA) of the Muromachi period. The compilation, which comprises twenty volumes, was made by Sōgi (1421–1502) and was completed in 1495. Together with the *renga* anthology TSUKUBASHŪ compiled by Nijō Yoshimoto (1320–88),

Shirakaba • 261

this work is of great importance for the study of the history of *renga*. It includes poems by Sōgi, Shinkei (1399–1475), Sōchō (1448–1532), and others.

Shinshichō 新思潮. A literary magazine of the late Meiji and Taishō eras. It was launched by Tanizaki Jun'ichirō, Osanai Kaoru, Watsuji Tetsurō, and others. The third and fourth editions of *Shinshichō* inaugurated the neo-realism of the Taishō era.

shintai-shi 新体詩 (new-style poetry). The new-style poetry created in 1882 by Toyama Masaichi (1848–1900), Inoue Tetsujirō (1855–1944), and Yatabe Ryōkichi (1851–99). The poems were in 7-5-syllable meter and in the literary style. Yamada Bimyō (1868–1910) followed with poetry in the colloquial style, and Kitamura Tōkoku (1868–94) wrote *Hōrai-kyoku*. After the Sino-Japanese War (1894–95), Yosano Tekkan (1873–1935) published the anthology *Tōzai-namboku,* and Miyazaki Koshoshi (1864–1922) wrote lyrical poems in the new style. Finally, Shimazaki Tōson (1872–1943) established the position of the new-style poetry with the publication of his *Wakanashū*.

shi-nuhi 私奴婢 (private slaves). One class of unfree people *(semmin)* under the penal and administrative code system (RITSURYŌ-SEI). *Semmin* were divided into four classes of official serfs (KANKO), tomb serfs (RYŌKO), domestic serfs (KENIN), and slaves (NUHI). There were public *(ku-nuhi)* and private slaves *(shi-nuhi)*. Private slaves were lower in position than public ones. They belonged to their master as valuable property and were inherited, donated, or sold. They were allotted one-third of the area allotted to the free people and were exempt from taxes. They could marry only a member of their own class. Most of them were in the service of nobles, wealthy families, temples, and shrines. After the Nara period, they were gradually assimilated into the lower-class farmer group.

Shin'yō Wakashū 新葉和歌集. An anthology of *waka* poems in twenty volumes compiled by imperial order in the Southern-dynasty period. The collection, compiled in 1381 by the son of Emperor Godaigo, Prince Munenaga (?–1385), includes poems written by Emperor Godaigo (1288–1339), members of the imperial household, and nobles of the Southern dynasty. The poems vividly describe events during the Namboku civil strife. In contrast with conventional poetry, they are fresh and deeply emotional.

Shirakaba 白樺. The name of a literary magazine of the late Meiji and Taishō eras which was launched by young people who graduated from the Peers' School. Defending an idealistic and humanistic standpoint, the magazine was opposed to the naturalist literature of the late Meiji era and infused freshness into the literary world. It was launched in 1910 and was discontinued in 1923 following the Kantō earthquake.

shisei-seido 氏姓制度 (system of clan titles). A system in ancient Japan according to which titles (KABANE) were conferred on aristocratic clans in order to define their social rank. Prior to the Taika Reform in 646, the heads of aristocratic clans were in the service of the court. They directed clan members and guild people *(be no tami)*. The word *uji* was used to indicate an aristocratic family line, and a title *(kabane)* was used to indicate the social rank, such as head of a great family *(omi)*, chieftain of a divine clan (MURAJI), local chieftain *(atae)*, and chief of a corporation (OBITO). Many titles were conferred by the court. The system further developed into that of government officials *(kanshi)*. Clans adopted the name of functions existing in the system of clan titles and often of the place where they lived. When the difference of social rank between clans or within clans widened, the titles originally used to indicate the heads of social groups came to indicate the higher and lower ranks within the aristocratic society.

shi-shiki 四職 (four chiefs of the Muromachi SAMURAI-DOKORO). The four chiefs of the Disciplinary Board (Samurai-dokoro) of the Muromachi central government organization. The MUROMACHI BAKUFU, following the example of the KAMAKURA BAKUFU, established a Disciplinary Board, the chief of which was called *shoshi*. The four chiefs were successively Akamatsu, Isshiki, Yamana, and Kyōgoku. They were collectively called *shi-shiki*. Their duties consisted of supervising the samurai, guarding Kyōto, etc.

shitaji-chūbun 下地中分 (division of the manor into halves). A Kamakura custom consisting of dividing a manor into two parts which were then managed independently. Quarrels followed when stewards did not comply with the orders of landlords or failed to pay taxes. To solve the quarrels between landlords and stewards, this measure was adopted. The occasion which led to the quarrels was the existence of a dual controlling authority, that of the estate master and that of the steward. The only means of settling matters was to divide the estate into two parts. Many estates were thus divided from the middle of the Kamakura period. The result was an increase in the power of the stewards, who also controlled the name masters (MYŌSHU) within the manor. Division of estates led to degeneration of the manor system.

Shitennō-ji 四天王寺. A monastery built during the Asuka period (552–645). Located in the Tennō-ji district of Ōsaka City, it was formerly called Arahaka-dera. Shōtoku Taishi built the monastery in accordance with descriptions found in the *Konkōmyō-kyō* sutra. Shitennō-ji was erected in 587 or 593. The Nandaimon, Chūmon, Gojūnotō, Kondō, and Kōdō stand in a row and present a typical example of the "Tennō-ji style." The Hiden-in, Seyaku-in, and Ryōbyō-in allegedly were built by Prince Shōtoku himself. For a long time, the monastery belonged to the Tendai sect of Buddhism but is now independent and teaches Shōtoku's faith, known as Shōtoku-shū.

shizenshugi 自然主義 (naturalism). Literary and artistic tendency during the latter part of the Meiji era. About the time of the Sino-Japanese War (1894–95), Zola's naturalism was introduced to Japan, and from the time of the Russo-Japanese War (1904–5) it flourished for about ten years. Works which represent this tendency are *Futon* by Tayama Katai (1871–1930) and *Hakai* by Shimazaki Tōson (1872–1943).

shizoku jusan 士族授産 (employment for ex-samurai). An economic relief policy in the early Meiji era. Ex-warriors who had lost their occupation following the Meiji Restoration were ordered in 1876 to restore their hereditary stipends to the government. They were then granted hereditary pension bonds. This resulted in the destitution of the majority of lower-rank ex-warriors. The government encouraged exploitation of wasteland and made an advance in money in view of the ex-warriors' finding employment. But as this policy failed to bring forth results, most ex-samurai were ruined.

shizoku no shōhō 士族の商法 (business enterprise of ex-samurai). An aspect of life during the early Meiji era. Ex-samurai who after the Meiji Restoration had lost their hereditary stipends engaged in farming, trade, and industry with an employment loan received from the government. Most of them, lacking necessary knowledge, failed in business. This inexperienced way of conducting affairs is called *shizoku no shōhō,* which might be rendered as "an amateurish venture."

Shōbōgenzō 正法眼蔵. The main work, in ninety-five volumes, of Dōgen (1200–53), the founder of Sōtō sect of Zen Buddhism. The author collected all of his teachings during his travels from 1231 to 1253. Renouncing wealth and fame and opposing luxurious Buddhist buildings, Dōgen stressed the importance of ascetic practices. The *Shōbōgenzō,* which is the main scripture of the Sōtō sect, is an expression of his ideology.

Shobutsu Ruisan 庶物類纂. A work on botany in a thousand volumes published during the Edo period. Inō Jakusui (1655–1715), who was in the service of Lord Maeda of Kanazawa, began the compilation of this monumental work but died before it was completed. Shōgun Yoshimune, regretting that the work was unfinished, asked Niwa Seihaku (1699–1752) to bring it to completion. It took the compilers twenty years to finish the work. The compilation was begun in 1711.

Shōchū no hen 正中の変 (the incident of the Shōchū era). The incident in which Emperor Godaigo (1288–1339) tried to overthrow the KAMAKURA BAKUFU. Dissatisfied because of the *bakufu's* interference with the succession to the imperial throne, the emperor tried to regain power. Together with Hino Toshimoto (?–1332), Hino Suketomo (?–1332), Toki Yorikane (?–1324), and others, he plotted the overthrow of the shogunate and rallied dissatisfied warriors. But in 1324 the plot was discovered. Suketomo was banished to Sado, and Toshimoto was arrested. In 1331, the emperor's plan was temporarily successful and, after the Genkō incident (GENKŌ NO HEN), the Kemmu Restoration was inaugurated (KEMMU NO CHŪKŌ).

shōen 荘園 (manors). The generic term used to indicate estates in the possession of temples and shrines and of the aristocracy from the Nara to the Muromachi period. The previous land-allotment system had collapsed at the close of the Nara period. Allotment land being limited, wasteland was cultivated, giving rise to the formation of manors. The first manors were called "wasteland manors." Originally the word *shō* meant a warehouse; later the ground around the warehouse was included. After the end of the Heian period, there was an increase in the *dento* class, which was made up of farmers who commended their plots of land to landlords or influential families so as to obtain their protection. Likewise, the MYŌSHU class, or owners of land registered in their own name, was on the increase. However, the size of manors grew out of proportion and threatened the foundation of the penal and administrative system, so that adjustment regulations had to be enforced (SHŌEN-SEIRI REI). Some regulations, such as those of 902 and of the cloistered-government period, were successful, though the number of manors grew steadily. Manor personnel consisted of farmers and controllers of manor affairs. Among the farmers, some commended their plots to powerful landlords and families; others were name masters who owned their plots and managed them personally. The landless farmers were mere producers. Having paid their yearly taxes to the nominal or real owner, manor personnel received a share of the profits. There were the controller's share, name master's share, and plain farmer's share. With the establishment of the KAMAKURA BAKUFU, a severe blow was struck at the manor structure. Although in many cases the *bakufu* confirmed the fiefs of the shōgun's warriors, it secured the power of appointing and dismissing stewards, thereby considerably weakening the authority of the landlord. Endless quarrels resulted concerning whether the stewards were to control the whole estate or whether it was to be divided into two parts, each one managed independently. These developments changed the nature of the manors. From the end of the Kamakura period through Namboku times (1336–92), a currency economy grew, and the farmers' class reached maturity. Stewards promised to pay a fixed tax, irrespective of good or bad crops, in return for securing the management of the whole estate. Money was lent at a high rate of interest, and a farmers' movement for the reduction of yearly taxes became more violent. Villages became self-governing bodies, opening the way to the self-governing rural system of the Edo period (GŌSON-SEI) and the collapse of the manor system, which ended with the Ōnin Civil War (1467–77).

shōen-seiri rei 荘園整理令 (manor-adjustment regulations). After the middle of the Heian period, in order to restore national and local economy, newly created and illegal manors were readjusted. In 902, Emperor Daigo abolished the manors without valid land certificates because they hindered state affairs. Other adjustment regulations were issued in 984, 1045, and 1055 but failed to bring results because of the constant increase of domains of the Fujiwara, who monopolized the office of regent and of adviser to the emperor. New regulations were issued in 1068, the year which followed the enthronement of Emperor Gosanjō. The manors created after 1045 and those which existed prior to 1045 but which lacked valid documents were to be abolished. To enforce the regulations, a special bureau for SHŌEN certificates was established. It held jurisdiction over manors of regents, which hitherto had escaped the adjustment regulations. Subsequently, regulations were often issued, but it proved to be extremely difficult to have them enforced.

shōfū 正風 (the right style). The style of haiku as established during the Edo period by Matsuo Bashō (1644–94). It is also called *shōfū* 蕉風 or "the style of Bashō." Rejecting traditional comical and playful elements, Bashō emphasized serenity and elegant simplicity.

Shōgakuin 奨学院 (private school of the Arihara family). A private school of the Arihara clan during the Heian period. It was established in 881 by Arihara no Yukihira (818–93) and was located north of Sanjō-bōmon and west of Mibu in Kyōto. Initially, the school derived its revenue from manors. Before long it was called Nansō, being located in the southern section of the DAIGAKU. Beginning in 963, the Shōgakuin received a yearly stipend from the state. This was also the case with the KANGAKUIN or private school of the Fujiwara. The director of the Shōgakuin, who held the title *bettō,* was the highest court noble of the Minamoto family. Later, the title *bettō* was given to Ashikaga Yoshimitsu (1358–1408), and directorship became an honorific post of the shōguns.

Shōgitai 彰義隊 (the Shōgitai fighting squad). A fighting squad entrenched in Ueno, Edo, at the time of the Boshin Civil War (BOSHIN SEN'EKI). In 1868, Shōgun Yoshinobu (1827–1913) was defeated in the battles of Toba and Fushimi and, returning to Edo, pledged allegiance to the emperor. The forces which had subdued the east entered Edo, but resisting shogunate retainers organized the Shōgitai squad, which was entrenched in Ueno. Yoshinobu ordered the squad to disband, but the order was not heeded. Thereupon Yoshinobu withdrew to Mito and ordered the eastern expeditionary force to attack and crush the Shōgitai.

Shōheikō 昌平校 (the shogunate's Confucian college). The Edo shogunate school. In 1691, the fifth shōgun, Tsunayoshi (1646–1709), built the Taiseiden in Yushima, Edo, and moved the Kōbun-in, built by Hayashi Razan

(1583–1657), to the same place. He then called the whole complex Seidō and the locality Shōheizaka. Hayashi Hōkō (1644–1732) was appointed rector of the shogunate's Confucian college with the title of *daigaku no kami*. The office of rector of the college was always held by a member of the Hayashi family. The main education of the school centered around Chu Hsi Confucianism. With the prohibition of heterodox learning (KANSEI IGAKU NO KIN) the school became a government school for the education of government officials. Free research, however, was lacking, and the school uncompromisingly adhered to Confucian tenets. It began to decline at the end of the Edo period. After the Meiji Restoration, the government tried to revive the school and called it the Shōhei Gakkō. It became the forerunner of Tōkyō University.

shōhekiga 障壁画 (screen and wall paintings). Decorative paintings on walls and sliding doors. Those of the Momoyama period are most famous. A few specimens are still to be admired in Daitoku-ji, Daikaku-ji, and Chishaku-in, three temples in Kyōto. Representative painters are Kanō Eitoku (1543–90) and Sanraku (1559–1635), Kaihō Yūshō (1533–1615), and Hasegawa Tōhaku (1539–1610). The common feature is magnificence of style and the lavish use of gold leaf.

shōhōshi 商法司 (the office of trade). A government office for the control of trade, established in 1868 and abolished in 1869 when it was replaced by the office called TSŪSHŌSHI. The government ushered in a period of intensive modernization of trade finances, promulgated the "Outline of the Commercial Law Code" *(Shōhō-taii)*, abolished the feudal privileged associations, established the Shōhō-kaisho, and provided the merchants with commodity exchanges facilitating trade. The reorganization of the government office followed the furtherance of national trade and industry and led to the consolidation of trade.

shoin-zukuri 書院造 ("living apartment" style). A style of architecture for "living apartments" from the middle of the Muromachi period. It is a compromise between the *shoin* of temples and the mansions of Kamakura warriors (BUKE-ZUKURI). The houses were provided with a porch *(genkan)*, an alcove (tokonoma), shelves adjoining the alcove *(chigai-dana)*, etc. The rooms were separated by sliding doors or screens, straw mats were spread, and a study for reading was built. The Tōgudō of Ginkaku-ji is a representative *shoin-zukuri* building. The custom of embellishing the tokonoma with flowers is related to *shoin-zukuri*, which influenced the art of flower arrangement. Scroll pictures in alcoves and paintings in India ink (SUIBOKU-GA) on sliding doors are a product of *shoin-zukuri*, which is considered to be the forerunner of the modern Japanese dwelling.

shōkan 荘官 (manor officials). The generic term for officials of a manor. It includes the officials of the estate's MANDOKORO and KUMONJO, the officials of the estate's AZUKARI-DOKORO, and the GESU. The *azukari-dokoro* was set up at the close of the Heian period for the purpose of controlling movements within the manor. It was created because the landlord wanted to control the doings in the manor personally. Officials of the *azukari-dokoro* kept an eye on all personnel from the *gesu* down. Many of the officials were the confidants of the landlord. The officials called *gesu* controlled the yearly taxes and kept order in the manor. They were elected from among local influential landowners. Each manor official received as his share a plot of tax-free land called *kyūden* or a plot for which the estate master provided seeds and farming tools (TSUKUDA). The farming of these plots was done by the servants of the people living in the manor. From the Kamakura period on, when the BAKUFU appointed stewards to the manors, quarrels occurred between the *azukari-dokoro* officials and the stewards. A settlement could only be reached by dividing the manor into two parts (SHITAJI-CHŪBUN) and by means of the *jitō-uke,* through which the stewards controlled the whole estate in return for a fixed amount of yearly taxes irrespective of rich or poor harvest. Gradually the management by *shōkan* was taken over by the UKEDOKORO. These officials undertook the levying of taxes, and the real power of manor management fell into their hands.

Shōka-sonjuku 松下村塾. A private school of the Edo period founded in 1856 in Hagi, Yamaguchi Prefecture, by Yoshida Shōin (1831–59). Shōin's uncle, Tamaki Bunnoshin, succeeded to the ownership of the school. During the two and a half years of its existence, the school shaped such talented persons as Takasugi Shinsaku (1838–67), Kusaka Genzui (1839–64), Itō Hirobumi (1841–1909), Shinagawa Yajirō (1843–1900), and others. They all devoted themselves to the interests of the country at the close of the Edo period.

Shokkō Giyū-kai 職工義勇会 (Volunteer Association of Workmen). An association for promoting the labor movement during the Meiji era, organized in 1897 by Jō Sentarō and others. It was the first organized movement for labor unions. The same year, an association was formed for the realization of the plans of labor unions, and a group of laborers was organized.

shokusan kōgyō 殖産興業 (production industry). 1) Edo period. From the middle of the Edo period, countermeasures to cope with the currency economy were devised by feudal landlords, who were exploited by the rising class of merchants. Until then, the finances of the estate master were derived from the levying of yearly rice taxes. When the growth and exploitation of commodity economy resulted in the impoverishment of farmers, the landlords, in order to secure their income, planned to restore the economy of rural communities. They appointed new officials and, receiving assistance and guidance from wealthy merchants, urged the farmers to produce marketable commodities. Textiles of the Yonezawa clan and wax and ginseng of the Aizu clan became popular commodities throughout the country. But the subsequent monopoly policy of the landlords threw the farmers into destitution. The ensuing Tempō reforms (TEMPŌ NO KAIKAKU) resulted in the adoption of the mercantile system for all clans.

2) Meiji period. In the early Meiji era, the government tried to modernize the economy, adopting European and American systems and techniques. Along with the war industry, private factory production was encouraged. The main organs for production industry were the Department of Industry (KŌBU-SHŌ), which was established in 1870, and government-controlled model enterprises. The Department of Industry placed under government management mines, shipyards, railways, the telegraph system, machine industry, and technical industry and established the Tomioka model filature factory (1870), the Senju woolen textile factory (SENJU SEIJŪSHO, 1876), the Aichi cotton mill, and the Hiroshima cotton mill (1878). In 1881, these factories were transferred to private companies and produced private capital. Another phase of production industry was the exploitation of Hokkaidō under the supervision of the commission of colonization.

Shōmyō-ji 称名寺. 1) A monastery of the Shingonritsu sect of Buddhism, built in 1269 in Kanazawa, Sagami Province (in present-day Yokohama), by Hōjō Sanetoki (1224–76). The founder of the monastery was the Buddhist priest Shinkai. In the precincts of the monastery, Sanetoki established the celebrated Kanazawa Library (KANAZAWA BUNKO), in which he collected Chinese and Japanese books. 2) A temple in Nara. During the Muromachi period, the Buddhist priest Shukō (1422–1502), after leaving the temple, formulated tea-drinking manners and customs and made tea drinking into a ceremonial art.

shōrui awaremi no rei 生類憐の令 (decrees of pity for living beings). Decrees issued by the fifth Tokugawa shōgun, Tsunayoshi (1646–1709), prohibiting the killing of animals. Tsunayoshi, after the death of his heir apparent, Tokumatsu, had no other descendants. Complying with the advice of the Buddhist priest Ryūkō (1649–1724) of the Goji-in temple, at which Tsunayoshi's mother Keishōin (1624–1705) was a fervent worshiper, Tsunayoshi often issued decrees prohibiting the killing of animals. Because he was born in the year of the dog (*inu* 戌), he particularly took pity upon dogs. His reign was at first benevolent, for he improved the situation in prisons, took care of unclaimed sick persons, prohibited the abandonment of children, etc. But gradually he went from one extreme to another. He built doghouses in Ōkubo, Yotsuya, Nakano, and other places, kept thousands of stray dogs, and prescribed detailed rules prohibiting the killing of living beings, such as birds and fishes, cats and mice. As any violation was severely punished, many people were arrested. According to his will, the regulations were to last a hundred generations. His successor, Ienobu (1662–1712), abolished them at once.

Shōsetsu Shinzui 小説神髄. Literary criticism on the art of the novel, published in 1885 by Tsubouchi Shōyō (1859–1935). Rejecting literature with a moral purpose, the author advocated realism.

shoshidai 所司代 (deputy of the SAMURAI-DOKORO). 1) Muromachi period. The deputy of the Samurai-dokoro. In the latter part of the fourteenth century, the office of deputy of the Samurai-dokoro was inaugurated by the head of the Samurai-dokoro, Sasaki Takauji (or Dōyo, 1306–1372), who entrusted his warrior Yoshida Genkaku with the affairs of that department. The office of deputy was discontinued in the latter part of the fifteenth century. During the Sengoku period (1490–1573), Miyoshi Chōkei (1523–64) was called deputy in spite of the fact that the Samurai-dokoro had no chief. 2) Edo period. The office of deputy of the shōgun in Kyōto, in charge of the supervision of the imperial palace.

Shōshi-kai 尚歯会. An association of students of Western learning *(rangaku)* during the Edo period. It was formed by Watanabe Kazan (1793–1841), Takano Chōei (1804–50), and others. Members of the association were Ozeki San'ei (1788–1840) of the BAKUFU's astronomy office, Suzuki Shunzan (1801–46) of the Tahara clan, and others. The members were later oppressed by the *bakufu* because of the Siebold affair (in which the Dutch scholar Siebold was given forbidden information by his disciples). The event is referred to as "the oppression of scholars of Dutch learning" (BANSHA NO GOKU).

Shōsō-in 正倉院. A treasure repository in the precincts of Nara's Tōdai-ji which stores cultural objects from the reign of Emperor Shōmu (701–56). The treasury is divided into northern, middle, and southern storehouses and is built in the style known as *azekura-zukuri*. In 756, on the forty-ninth day after the death of Emperor Shōmu, Empress Kōmyō, praying for the repose of the emperor's soul, stored in this treasury all the relics and daily utensils of the deceased emperor. They have reached the present day unimpaired. Other valuable cultural objects are also stored in the Shōsō-in. The contents throw some light on the life of the contemporary nobility and are invaluable material for knowledge of ancient culture and cultural relations with Korea and China.

Shōwa no hen 承和の変 (the incident of the Shōwa era). Political disturbance in the early Heian period (842). The Shōwa era lasted from 834 to 848. Emperor Nimmyō (810–50), though Prince Michiyasu was his own son, proclaimed as heir apparent Prince Tsunesada, the son of ex-Emperor Junna (786–840). Crown Prince Tsunesada, however, had no authority. Fujiwara no Yoshifusa (804–72), the uncle of Prince Tsunesada's mother, and Tachibana no Ujigimi (783–847) took charge of state affairs. After the death of ex-Emperor Junna in 840 and that of ex-Emperor Saga (786–842) in 842,

Ban no Kowamine, Tachibana no Hayanari, and others, obeying the orders of Crown Prince Tsunesada, planned to raise soldiers in the eastern provinces and to rebel. The plot was discovered, and the rebels were exiled. Tsunesada was dethroned, and Prince Michiyasu was made crown prince. Political opponents, in particular the Ban family, were defeated. The incident is believed to have been due to the machinations of the Fujiwara, who wanted to establish their own political power.

shōya 庄屋 (MURA YAKUNIN)

Shugeishuchi-in 綜芸種智院. A private school established in 828 in Kujō, Kyōto, by Kūkai (774–835) for the education of people of all classes. Buddhism was mainly taught, but Confucian principles were not neglected. In 840, the place became the property of Tō-ji temple, and the private school was closed.

shugendō 修験道 (mountaineer asceticism). A form of mountaineer asceticism inaugurated in the early middle ages. Ascetic practices were performed in the mountains, where religious experiences were believed to be particularly forceful. Centers of these practices were the mountain range Ōmine and Mount Kimbusen in Yamato Province (Nara Prefecture), Kumano in Kii Province (Wakayama Prefecture), and other "sacred mountains" *(reisan)*. The ascetics climbed the mountains and practiced austerities. The priests who practiced acts of self-discipline were called *yamabushi*. Later the practice spread to the common people.

Shūgi-in 集議院. A parliamentary body in the early Meiji era through which the Council of State exercised its powers. In 1868, the House of Representatives (KŌGISHO) was established, and the following year it was renamed as Shūgi-in. After the abolition of the clans and the establishment of prefectures, the office came under the jurisdiction of the Ministry of the Left (Sa-in).

Shūgi-in 衆議院 (House of Representatives). A legislative organ. In 1889, the constitution was promulgated and the Imperial Diet established. The Imperial Diet consisted of the House of Peers and the House of Representatives. The following year, general elections of members of the House of Representatives took place for the first time, and the Imperial Diet was inaugurated. It was abolished after the Pacific War when a new constitution was promulgated. Under the new constitution, the National Diet includes the House of Councilors, or Upper House, and the House of Representatives, or Lower House. Members of both houses are publicly elected. In the postwar Diet, the House of Representatives occupies the dominant position.

shugo 守護 (constables). The name of an office of warriors in the middle ages.

Aiming at the chastisement of Minamoto no Yoshitsune (1159–89) and at the suppression of rebellions, Minamoto no Yoritomo (1148–99) appointed constables as well as stewards (JITŌ) in all provinces. His own warriors (GO-KENIN) were appointed constables. It was their function to keep an eye on the activities of the court, to investigate and pass judgment on treason and other crimes, etc. Later, the constables took charge of general administration within the provinces. From the middle Kamakura period, they controlled even provincial stewards and warriors and were bound by a master-servant relationship to the shōgun. They made their authority felt in the manors and consolidated their own influence. After the Namboku period (1336–92), the Ashikaga established the MUROMACHI BAKUFU. Ashikaga Takauji (1305–58) derived his support from the constables. When the authority of the *bakufu* was declining, the constables administered the provinces, further strengthening their position. Establishing their supremacy in the manors, they became SHUGO DAIMYŌ, or constable daimyō, at times ruling over several provinces simultaneously.

shugo daimyō 守護大名 (constable daimyō). As time went by, the constables appointed in all provinces by the KAMAKURA BAKUFU lost their original function. During the Muromachi period (1333–1573) they became feudal lords ruling over a whole province and even over several provinces. They were called "great landowners" (daimyō). Initially, influential warriors of the Kamakura period were appointed constables. But, carrying out their duties, they extended their influence to the whole province and penetrated into manorial estates. They became more ambitious after the Namboku period (1336–92). Controlling the provincial warriors, they secured for themselves the yearly taxes of the manors *(shugo-uke)* and then administered the manorial estates. Enlarging their estates, they reduced the authority of the provincial governors (KOKUSHI). During the Muromachi period, they further consolidated their position, becoming constables of several provinces and mighty landowners (daimyō). Yamana Ujikiyo (?–1391) was known as *rokubun-no-ichi dono,* or "the ruler of one-sixth of Japan," because he ruled over eleven provinces. The MUROMACHI BAKUFU was the combined political power of these *shugo daimyō.* The three deputies of the shōgun *(san-kanrei)* and the four chiefs of the SAMURAI-DOKORO (SHI-SHIKI) were powerful constables. They included the Hosokawa, who ruled over ten provinces, and the Ōuchi, with six provinces. The Sengoku period (1490–1573) followed the Ōnin Civil War (1467–77), and deputy constables strengthened their position by oppressing the constable daimyō and becoming in turn estate masters. The power of the constable daimyō declined, and deputy constables were known as *sengoku daimyō* or civil-war barons. An example is Oda Nobunaga, who himself came from a family of deputy constables. In the early Edo period, with the exception of Shimazu of Satsuma Province, all constable daimyō were removed and replaced by deputy constables.

shuin-jō 朱印状 (red-seal license). A document on which a seal was printed with cinnabar seal ink. After the Sengoku period (1490–1573), warriors who conducted state affairs used the red-seal license, but it was particularly used for administrative documents by Oda Nobunaga, Toyotomi Hideyoshi, and Tokugawa Ieyasu. During the Edo period, it was widely used. Trade vessels authorized to sail overseas carried the red-seal license and were called red-seal vessels (SHUIN-SEN). A plot of land, ownership of which had been certified, was referred to as "red-seal land" *(shuin-chi)*.

shuin-sen 朱印船 (red-seal vessels). From the sixteenth to the earlier part of the seventeenth century, trade vessels were given a license for foreign trade. The document carried an official red seal, and the vessels were called *shuin-sen*. The license legalized trade vessels and distinguished them from pirate vessels. Red-seal vessels enjoyed various facilities in foreign countries. The licensing system resulted from the centralized authoritarian rule and political power of Nobunaga and Hideyoshi and that of the BAKUFU clans. It was an outgrowth of the developing economy. From 1604 to 1636 (from 1636 all vessels were prohibited to leave territorial waters), more than 300 red-seal vessels crossed the seas. The main traders utilizing red-seal vessels were daimyō such as Shimazu and wealthy merchants such as Suminokuu Ryōi (1554–1614), Chaya Shirojirō (1542–96), and Sueyoshi Magozaemon (1570–1617). Trade vessels sailed to Luzon, Annam, Cambodia, Siam, etc. Japanese merchants emigrated to those countries, where they founded Japanese quarters referred to as NIHON-MACHI. Export articles were silver, copper, and general merchandise. Import articles were raw silk, silk fabrics, and products of China and the South Seas. The trade greatly influenced the Japanese economy. When the national isolation policy (SAKOKU) of the Tokugawa government prohibited trade vessels to leave Japanese waters, the system of red-seal vessels was abolished.

shūkai jōrei 集会条例 (public-meetings ordinance). Early Meiji regulations concerning movements for popular rights. The regulations were issued in 1880, were amended several times, and were in force until 1890. They were concerned with public meetings and associations. The ordinance restricted public meetings and prohibited the organization of political associations. Political organizations being banned, political activities came to a standstill. This law, the press law (SHUPPAN JŌREI), and the newspaper law (SHIMBUNSHI JŌREI) were collectively called "the three evil laws."

shukōgyō 手工業 (handicrafts). Small industries using manual tools for the manufacture of commodities. The producers were semi-slaves belonging to the court, the nobility, and temples and shrines and also farmers who simultaneously engaged in farming and manufacturing. Production made to order developed into market production, and manufacturing developed into mechanical mass production. But handicraft trade still exists, maintained as it is by the apprentice system.

shūmon-aratame nimbetsu-chō 宗門改人別帳 (census register for religious investigation). A kind of census register in use during the Edo period, aimed at the extermination of Christianity. Every Japanese had to become a member of a Buddhist sect, and every family was ordered to register at a Buddhist family temple *(danna-dera)*. Information about each individual family was recorded, including the name and date of birth of the head, the members, and the servants. The register was confirmed by town officials or village officials and sent to the religious investigation office *(shūmon-aratame yaku)*.

Shunkei-nuri 春慶塗 (Shunkei lacquer ware). A kind of lacquer ware believed to have been manufactured at the end of the fourteenth century by the lacquer artist Shunkei of Sakai. During the seventeenth century, the daimyō of Hida (Gifu Prefecture), Kanamori Sōwa (1584–1656), who was a tea-ceremony master, ordered his lacquer artists to manufacture Shunkei lacquer ware. From the middle of the Edo period, this particular lacquer ware was manufactured in several places and distributed all over the country.

Shun'yō-kai 春陽会 (Shun'yō Art Association). An art association of the Taishō and Shōwa eras. It was founded in 1922 by painters in Western style after they had left the Japan Academy of Art. The following year, the association held its first exhibition. It was followed by several others.

shuppan jōrei 出版条例 (press regulations). Early Meiji regulations for the control of publications. In 1875, the movement for popular rights reached a peak. In order to control expressions of public opinion, the press law was ruthlessly enforced, and many editors were thrown into prison. The law corresponded with the law against slander (ZAMBŌ-RITSU) and the law for the control of newspapers (SHIMBUNSHI JŌREI).

Shushi-gaku 朱子学 (Chu Hsi Confucianism). A system of Confucian thought elaborated by the Chinese scholar Chu Hsi (in Japanese, Shu Ki; 1130–1200). Also known as SŌGAKU, it was introduced during the Kamakura period. During Namboku times (1336–92) it influenced the "relations of sovereign and subjects" *(taigi-meibun)*. During the Muromachi period (1333–1573) it was recommended by the Zen priests of the GOZAN and, after the Ōnin Civil War (1467–77), spread throughout the country. It was beneficial to the civil-war barons *(sengoku daimyō)* as it helped them in the administration of their domains. During the Edo period, Shushi-gaku broke with Buddhism and reached the climax of its influence. It became the theoretical foundation for feudal society and the guiding principle for feudal morality. The BAKUFU supported it and made it into the official doctrine. In general, the clans followed suit. As society further developed, Shushi-gaku lost some of its prestige. With the prohibition of heterodox learning during the Kansei era (1789–1801), Shushi-gaku again obtained official support but eventually became a hollow system. Suika Shintō, which was started by Yamazaki Ansai (1618–82), stressed moral obligation and spread among the masses. At the close of the Edo period, it became the ideological background of the anti-foreign loyalist movement.

so 租 (the rice tax). A tax system in ancient Japan. It was a land tax paid in rice. Before the Taika Reform in 646, it amounted to fifteen sheaves per fifty *shiro* (50 *shiro* is equal to one *tan* or 0.245 acres). After the Taika Reform, one *tan* was made equal to a plot of thirty *ho* (one *ho* equals 1.82 meters) long and twelve *ho* wide, and the rice tax amounted to twenty-two sheaves per *tan*. This tax was imposed on allotment land (KUBUNDEN). Part of the rice tax was sent to the central government, but the larger part was stored in the granaries of the provincial government office (KOKUGA). Until the middle Heian period, and along with the rise and decline of the penal and administrative code system, rice taxes underwent changes but were always at a lower rate than the labor tax (YŌ) and the produce tax (CHŌ).

soba-yōnin 側用人 (grand chamberlain). An office of the EDO BAKUFU. Established in 1681, it was not a standing office. The grand chamberlain was in close association with the shōgun and communicated the shōgun's orders to the elders (RŌJŪ) and the elders' reports to the shōgun. The office increased in power, and such *soba-yōnin* as Yanagisawa Yoshiyasu (1658–1714) and Tanuma Okitsugu (1719–88) exerted influence upon the shōgun. On the whole, government officials were of high descent, and the selection of fit persons for high functions was a difficult task. Selection of grand chamberlains, however, was relatively easy, and men of merit were given a chance to fill the office.

Sōgaku 宋学 (Sung learning). A school of Confucianism inaugurated during the Chinese Sung dynasty and perfected by the scholar Chu Hsi (1130–1200) of the Southern Sung dynasty. It spread to Japan during the Kamakura period and greatly animated the learning of those days. Its advocacy of "reverence for the emperor and expulsion of the usurper" was the backbone of Emperor Godaigo's movement for the overthrow of the BAKUFU. During the Edo period, it was referred to as SHUSHI-GAKU. Encouraged by the shogunate, it flourished widely.

Soga Monogatari 曾我物語. A tale in twelve volumes describing the vendetta of the Soga brothers. The Soga brothers were Sukenari (1172–93) and Tokimune (1174–93). After their father was killed by Kudō Suketsune (?–1193), the brothers killed Suketsune in 1193. The author of the work and the year of completion are not known, but it was written during the Nambuku period (1336–92) and was a popular work. The vendetta as described in the work is celebrated in many Nō and Kabuki dramas.

Soga uji 蘇我氏 (the Soga clan). A powerful family of ancient Japan. Takeno-uchi no Sukune is believed to have been one of its ancestors. Taking into their service the AYABITO, the Soga controlled these naturalized Japanese and thus increased their power. They had an influential hand in court finances and were the opponents of the Mononobe clan. The conflict concerning Buddhism led Soga no Umako to assassinate Mononobe no Moriya (?–587). Under the reign of Soga no Emishi (?–645) and Iruka (?–645), the Soga consolidated their authority but were exterminated about the time of the Taika Reform (646).

sōhei 僧兵 (monk-soldiers). The origin of the monk-soldier was the result of the need for defense of temple manors against aggression. Monk-soldiers existed as early as Heian times. They were composed of lower-class monks, temple servants, and soldiers of temple manors. Sometimes temples feuded with each other, or monk-soldiers marched on Kyōto carrying a portable shrine *(mikoshi)* and a sacred tree *(shimboku)* and made an appeal by force to the throne (GŌSO). The monk-soldiers of Kōfuku-ji in Nara and those of ENRYAKU-JI on Mount Hiei were called, respectively, the monk-soldiers of Nanto (Nara) and of Hokurei (Mount Hiei). Their fanaticism was notorious. They were powerful all through the middle ages but were exterminated by Nobunaga and Hideyoshi.

sonnō-ron 尊王論 (reverence for the emperor). Advocacy of imperial rule at the end of the Edo period. It was the outgrowth of the study of Confucianism, the national classics, and national history. Takenouchi Shikibu (1712–67), who had been punished for spreading his views among Kyōto court nobles, is considered to have been the forerunner of the royalist movement. At the end of the Edo period, it became a powerful political movement which was linked with that of exclusion of foreigners (JŌI-RON) and formed the ideological basis of absolutism.

sōryō 惣領. During the middle ages, the *sōryō* was a superior kinsman who claimed administrative rights over the land of vassals (IE NO KO and RŌTŌ) and their kinsmen. He divided the lands and the patrimony among the vassals' kinsmen and exercised control. The administrative structure of the *sōryō* system formed the substance of the Kamakura corporations of warriors (BUSHIDAN), which were in a master-servant relationship with the shōgun (GO-KENIN). Later, when the kinsmen became more independent, the system of divided patrimony was abandoned, and the rule of undivided inheritance, to which the head of the clan succeeded, was adopted.

Sōsai 総裁 (President of the Council). An office of the early Meiji era. In 1867, the order restoring the imperial regime was issued, and previous offices were abolished. Three new offices, the Presidency (sōsaɪ), the Senior Council of State (the Upper House of the Deliberative Chamber, ɢɪjō), and the Junior Council of State (the Lower House of the Deliberative Chamber, sanʼyo), were created. They were abolished the following year.

sōsen 宋銭 (Sung currency). Copper currency minted in China during the Sung dynasty (960–1279). In Japan no currency was minted after the minting of the twelve types of coins which were used during the Nara and Heian periods (kōchō-jūnisen). From the end of the Heian through the Kamakura period, Sung currency imported through trade with Sung China was used. It spread particularly during the thirteenth century and helped the development of markets and of toɪmaru. *Toimaru* were the forerunners of present-day wholesale dealers. As currency economy infiltrated rural communities, it determined national economy to a large extent.

sōson 惣村. The organization into bodies by self-governing farmers. Though the organization had already taken shape in the home provinces during the late Kamakura period, it grew in importance during the civil strife of the Namboku period (1136–92). The farmers' solidarity was strengthened by sharing the use of firewood, irrigation water, and fertilizer and by reducing yearly taxes. Even fields were jointly exploited (ɪrɪaɪ). The group leader (otona) and the head of the rural community (toshɪyorɪ) were chosen from among the owners of name fields (myōshu). It was the leader's duty to organize meetings, fix regulations, and pass judgments. In their opposition to landlords and warriors, these bodies fomented the agrarian uprisings (do-ɪkkɪ). Powerful *myōshu,* however, formed the nucleus of these organized communities and, gaining more power, eventually oppressed the *sōson.*

Sōtō-shū 曹洞宗 (Sōtō sect of Zen Buddhism). The Sōtō, like the Rinzai, is a sect of Zen Buddhism. Dōgen (1200–53) introduced the sect from Sung China. He declined all honors and favors offered by Hōjō Tokiyori (1227–63) and went to live at the eɪheɪ-jɪ in Fukui Prefecture, where he educated his disciples. As opposed to Rinzai, which flourished in political centers such as Kamakura and Kyōto, Sōtō spread among local farmers and warriors.

Sō uji 宗氏 (Sō family). The lords of Tsushima. From the Muromachi period, the family was subjected to foreign invasions, such as the Korean invasion during the Ōei era (1394–1428). Later, friendly relations with Korea were restored. As far as Japanese trade with Korea was concerned, Tsushima occupied an important position. The Sō clan played the role of intermediary between Japan and Korea.

sue-be (suetsukuri-be) 陶部 (potters' guild). Hereditary guild. People belonging to this guild *(be no tami)* in the time of ancient tombs (250–552) were the property of the nobility. The skill of these craftsmen was transmitted from generation to generation. They specialized in the manufacture of earthen vessels. They were immigrants and naturalized Japanese. Initially, earthen vessels were made by members of the *haji-be* guild according to the primitive techniques of Yayoi potters. For the manufacture of ceramic ware, *sue-be* potters used kilns the temperature of which was raised to about 1,000°. *Sue-be* potters were far superior to *haji-be* potters.

Sugihara-gami 杉原紙 (Sugihara paper). A kind of paper produced in Sugihara Village, Harima Province (Hyōgo Prefecture). The paper was used for documents and the like by Kamakura warriors. During the Namboku period (1336–92) it came into wide use among the nobility and temples and shrines. From the end of the middle ages, the paper was manufactured in several places.

suiboku-ga 水墨画 (India-ink painting). A kind of painting done during the Muromachi period (1333–1573). No colors were used, as the paintings were done in tonalities of black ink. In China, the art developed from the Sung dynasty (960–1279). It was introduced into Japan by Kamakura Zen monks. Some of these monks painted as a hobby. Kaō (?–1345) and others are well known. In the Muromachi period, distinguished monk-painters appeared. The foundations of Muromachi *suiboku-ga* were laid by Minchō (1352–1431) and Josetsu. The art reached its climax under Shūbun and Sesshū (1420–1506). Sesshū was unequaled. He departed from Chinese models, and his paintings of nature appealed to the Japanese taste. From about this time, instead of Zen monks, some descendants of warriors' families became noted painters. Such were Kanō Masanobu (1454–90) and his son Motonobu (1476–1559). Uniting the techniques of *suiboku-ga* and of YAMATO-E, they began the Kanō school. In the Edo period, *suiboku-ga* became formalized.

Suika Shintō 垂加神道 (Suika Shintoism). A school of Shintoism based on Confucianism and inaugurated during the Edo period by the Yamazaki Ansai (1618–82). The teaching of Ansai was based on a monistic universe. He stressed the duties of master and servant and the importance of modesty. His doctrine influenced the later loyalist movement. It developed along with Tachibana Shintō, originated by Tamaki Masahide (?–1736), and Bōnangen Shintō as propagated by Wakabayashi Kyōsai (1679–1733).

suiko 出挙 (loans). Loans in ancient Japan. Public and private goods were loaned and interest charged. Especially seed rice was loaned. Actually, the purpose was to help destitute farmers, but during the eighth century, when public finances were in trouble, farmers were forced to borrow. Tax rates were 50 percent to be paid by those who borrowed public goods and 100 percent by those who borrowed private goods. The first victims of this system were the farmers. After the Wadō-Yōrō era (708–23), the government repeatedly planned to reduce the taxes or to exempt borrowers from taxes, but in practice nothing changed. *Suiko* was practiced by temples and shrines, provincial governors (KOKUSHI), wealthy farmers, and others.

sukegō 助郷 (supply villages). Self-governing villages (GŌSON-SEI) in the neighborhood of post stations on which was imposed the corvée of replenishing a deficiency of horses and servants in the post stations. The system was enforced from about 1635. In 1694, it was prescribed that two men and two horses per hundred *koku* of income had to be provided. Around 1780, some villages were supplying 300 to 400 men. Permanent supply villages were known as *jō-sukegō;* temporary supply villages were referred to as *dai-sukegō*. It was a heavy burden on the farmers, who often resorted to uprisings in protest. Later, money was exacted instead of horses and men, but this measure oppressed the farmers economically. *Sukegō* were abolished in the Meiji era.

Sumitomo 住友. A financial combine (ZAIBATSU). During the Edo period the Sumitomo owned the Besshi copper mine (BESSHI DŌZAN). Initially, in 1623, they sold copperware in an establishment called the Izumiya. Later, they operated exchange shops. The Sumitomo were active as storehouse officials (KURAMOTO), monetary agents (KAKEYA), and brokers for bannermen (FUDASASHI). At the close of the Edo period, their power waned, and at the time of the Meiji Restoration they were in financial trouble. With the modernization of the Besshi copper mine, the Sumitomo became active in the financial world of the Kansai district. The Sumitomo *zaibatsu* is ranked third, following MITSUI and MITSUBISHI.

Sūmitsu-in 枢密院 (the Privy Council). A legal political body but one separate from the parliamentary government. It was a standing advisory committee created in 1888 for the purpose of advising the emperor on matters of high policy. It had to approve Itō Hirobumi's draft of a constitution before the constitution could be promulgated. Membership was denied to those who took part in the movement for popular rights. Among its members were powerful clansmen who, in the presence of the emperor, discussed the draft of a constitution. The draft was then promulgated as the Imperial Constitution. This so-called advisory body exercised decisive political influence in both domestic and foreign affairs. It was imbued with absolutist ideas and controlled the Deliberative Assembly and the Cabinet. Both the Privy Council and the Imperial Constitution were abolished after the Pacific War.

Sumiyoshi-ha 住吉派 (Sumiyoshi school of painting in Japanese style). A school of YAMATO-E painters who had parted from the Tosa school (TOSA-HA). During the early Edo period, Sumiyoshi Jokei (1599–1670) left the Tosa school and was opposed to the Kanō school (KANŌ-HA). Together with his son Gukei (1631–1705), he became a shogunate official master painter and founded the Sumiyoshi school. The school, however, did not flourish. Celebrated works which were jointly painted by Jokei and Gukei are *Tōnomine Engi* and *Tōshōgū Engi*.

Sumpu 駿府. The ancient name of present-day Shizuoka City. After the Namboku period (1336–92) the Imagawa family controlled the territory, in which it built a castle town. Later, Sumpu passed into the hands of the Takeda family. In 1607, Ieyasu made it into his retreat and built a castle there. He controlled the town, which was an important communication center on the Tōkaidō highway. Sumpu flourished as the center of the local administration and industry.

T

tadokoro 田荘 (private land). Private land owned by wealthy families before the Taika Reform (646). In the center of the property was a villa, and the land was mainly reclaimed land which had been cultivated. The administration and structure of these domains resembled those of the Yamato court domains called MIYAKE. The only difference was that the administration was not carried out by the imperial household. When the domain became so large that the magnate could no longer administer it, part of the domain was leased. *Tadokoro* were abolished by the Taika Reform because they promoted class differences. They did not completely vanish, however, and under the penal and administrative code system remains of the former *tadokoro* system were found in the early manors.

Taga-jō 多賀城 (Taga fort). A frontier post in the northeastern district, established during the Nara period for operations against rebellious aborigines. Remains of the fort still exist in the town of Tagajō, Miyagi Prefecture. According to one opinion, the fort was built by the warrior Ōno Azumahito (?–742), but this is questionable. The central government was much harassed by Ainu uprisings in the first decade of the eighth century. The fort of Taga was built, and a heavy garrison was stationed to hold the Ainu in check. In 802, the Japanese were able to push the frontier as far north as Izawa in Iwate Prefecture (IZAWA-JŌ), where headquarters were established. Later, the fort of Taga became the seat of the local government of Mutsu until the Muromachi period.

Tāheru Anatomia ターヘル・アナトミア (*Tabulae Anatomicae:* KAITAI SHINSHO)

Taiheiki 太平記. Military saga in forty volumes written during the Muromachi period and completed in 1370 or 1371. It is believed that the author is the scholar Kojima Hōshi (?–1374), but the work was compiled and corrected by several authors. It describes in grandiose style and with many details the course of events in the fifty years when Japan was divided into the Northern and Southern dynasties, from the time when Emperor Godaigo was enthroned (1318) to the year in which Ashikaga Yoshimitsu (1358–1408) was proclaimed shōgun (1368). *Taiheiki* and HEIKE MONOGATARI are considered the two masterpieces of military-romance literature. The style of *Taiheiki* is not as fluent as that of *Heike Monogatari,* but the warriors' activities in the various provinces are more vividly described. Later, professional *Taiheiki* storytellers appeared and made the work known throughout the country.

Taihō Ritsuryō 大宝律令 (the Taihō Code). Penal and administrative laws of the early Nara period compiled in 701 by Prince Osakabe (?–705), Fujiwara no Fuhito (659–720), Awata no Mahito (?–719), and others. The code was promulgated in 702. It was a revision, based on the legal system of the Chinese T'ang dynasty, of previous legislation which was known as Kiyomigahara Ryō (ASUKA KIYOMIGAHARA RYŌ). The Taihō Code included six volumes of penal laws *(ritsu)* and eleven volumes of administrative laws *(ryō).* The code is not extant, but a revision was made in 718 which is known as the Yōrō Code (YŌRŌ RITSURYŌ). There are no essential differences between the two codes, but each article has been slightly amended. The Taihō Code was enforced until the latter part of the Nara period.

Taika no Kaishin 大化の改新 (the Taika Reform). An ancient political reform inaugurated in 646. In 645, Nakanoōe no Ōji (626–71), together with Nakatomi no Kamatari (614–69) and others, destroyed the mighty Soga clan (SOGA UJI). After the defeat of the Soga clan, and upon the enthronement of Emperor Kōtoku (596–654) in 645, a new era was inaugurated. It was called "Taika" or "great reform." The following year the reform edict *(kaishin no shō)* was proclaimed, and the political reform carried out. Article one deprives the local magnates of their domains and serfs. Article two establishes the authority of the central government in the provinces where provincial administrators (KOKUSHI) and rural district administrators (GUNJI) are appointed. Article three orders the drawing up of registers of population and specifies the units of allotment area of land. Article four introduces a new system of taxes: the land tax paid in rice (SO), the labor tax (YŌ), and the produce tax (CHŌ). The imperial household is the absolute ruler, the former powerful clans are given official posts or ranks and emoluments according to their standing, and a system of land allotment, by which arable fields are distributed among farmers, is worked out.

taikō 太閤 A title used by a retired KAMPAKU after he had ceded his post to his son. Best known is the title *taikō* conferred on Hideyoshi, who was called *hō-taikō.* Hideyoshi's land survey was referred to as *taikō-kenchi,* and biographies of Hideyoshi are known as *taikō-ki.*

Tai-Nichi Kōwa Jōyaku 対日講和条約 (the Peace Treaty with Japan). A postwar international pact. As early as March 1947, General MacArthur stated that the time had come for the Allied Powers to consider a peace treaty for Japan. In 1950, when John Foster Dulles assumed office of adviser to the State Department, Japanese relations with other countries were restored, and a peace treaty with all countries, except Russia, was discussed. A violent dispute was launched when the Liberal Party advocated a separate peace treaty and the Democrats argued for an overall peace treaty. On September 8, 1951, a peace treaty between Japan and forty-eight other countries was concluded in San Francisco. Soviet Russia opposed and declined to sign the treaty. India, Burma, and China did not participate. At the same time, the American-Japanese security pact was concluded. This was followed by a peace treaty with Formosa and India in 1952 and by resumption of diplomatic relations with Russia in 1956.

Tai-Nichi Rijikai 対日理事会 (the Allied Council for Japan). An Allied council for Japan set up in Tōkyō for the formulation and execution of occupational policies. The council included representatives of the United States, Britain, Soviet Russia, and China. These four participants made recommendations on the formulation of occupation policies to their respective governments and to the Far Eastern Commission in Washington. The Allied Council became active in April 1946.

tairō 大老 (the great elders). The highest office in the Edo shogunate. Its origin is to be found in the "five great elders" of the Momoyama period (1573–1614). The office became a reality in 1638 with the appointment of Doi Toshikatsu (1573–1644) and Sakai Tadakatsu (1587–1662). *Tairō* were placed over elders (RŌJŪ), but the post was filled only in times of emergency. The *tairō* were in a sense prime ministers and functioned as arbitrators between elders and shōgun. They were chosen from among hereditary daimyō *(fudai)* with an income of at least 100,000 *koku* such as Doi, Sakai, Hotta, and Ii. Ii Naosuke (1815–60) broke with custom when he did not occupy the top seat among the elders. Instead, he assumed general control of the elders and attended to government affairs. After Ii's death, the office of *tairō* lost its importance.

Taisei Yokusan-kai 大政翼賛会 (the Imperial Rule Assistance Association). A fascist organization aimed at the prolongation of the Sino-Japanese incident. It was formed in 1940, and its first president was Konoe Ayamaro

(1891–1945). After the incident of February 26, 1936 (NI-NIROKU JIKEN), the military clique took the lead. With the promulgation of the national general mobilization law in 1938, the new political parties became active, but in 1940 the Socialist Popular Party (Shatai-tō or Shakai Taishū-tō), the Political Friends Association (SEIYŪ-KAI), and the Democratic Party (MINSEI-TŌ) were abolished, and the Imperial Rule Assistance Association, under the motto "fulfilment of the duties of the people to the throne" *(shindō-jissen),* started its activities. It aimed at totalitarian organization of national politics, economy, and culture. It was dissolved after Japan's surrender.

Takada jiken 高田事件 (incident at Takada). An incident caused by the intensification of the movement for popular rights. In 1883, a youth of Takada in Niigata Prefecture plotted the overthrow of the government and the assassination of high officials. The plot was discovered, and members of the Liberal Party of the Hokuriku district were thrown into prison.

takadoko jūkyo 高床住居 (aboveground houses). A kind of house in ancient Japan. Its origin is traced back to the Yayoi period (about 350 B.C. to A.D. 250), when the Japanese lived in half-underground pit houses known as TATE-ANA JŪKYO. The *takadoko* is thought to have been a granary. In the time of the ancient tombs, houses were more elaborate, dwellings of wealthy families being built in the style referred to as *irimoya-zukuri*. An extra building was added in the form of a theater box. Sketches on ancient mirrors and earthen figures (HANIWA) in the form of houses reveal that *takadoko* were relatively small storehouses without windows. The SHŌSŌ-IN, which was built later, and other structures in *azekura* style *(azekura-zukuri)* evolved from the ancient *takadoko* dwellings.

takatsuki 高杯. Earthen vessel for serving food. It was first made during the Yayoi period (about 350 B.C. to A.D. 250), when vessels of various shapes were made. During the ancient-tombs period, the *takatsuki* took on more complicated forms. One type of *takatsuki* was called *komochi-takatsuki*.

Takeda uji 武田氏 (the Takeda clan). A wealthy clan of Kai (Yamanashi Prefecture) during the middle ages. Members of the clan were civil-war barons *(sengoku daimyō)*. Descended from the Seiwa branch of the Minamoto family, the Takeda became powerful in the Kamakura period and consolidated their strength under Takeda Shingen (1521–73). Shingen sent troops to conquer Shinano (Nagano Prefecture). He became lord of Shinano and fought against Uesugi Kenshin (1530–78) in Echigo (Niigata Prefecture). Contemplating the unification of the country, Shingen planned to march on Kyōto, but he became ill and died before his plan could materialize. His son Katsuyori (1546–82) was destroyed by the combined forces of Nobunaga and Ieyasu. This marked the end of the Takeda clan.

Takekurabe たけくらべ. A novel of the middle Meiji era. It was written in 1895 by Higuchi Ichiyō (1872–96). *Takekurabe, Nigorie,* and *Jūsan'ya* are representative works of the authoress.

Taketori Monogatari 竹取物語. A tale of the early Heian period. As far as author and date of completion are concerned, opinions differ. An old bamboo gatherer, splitting a section of bamboo, finds a tiny girl in it. The little girl grows quickly and becomes a beautiful princess. Five courtiers and the emperor himself fall in love with the princess, but their courtships all end in failure. In the end, the princess, in reality a divinity, returns to her heavenly dwelling. The story is based on contemporary legends and fairy tales. A strong romantic and descriptive style is apparent, as well as some witticism. The work is written in the Japanese syllabary. Other *monogatari* of the Heian time are UTSUBO MONOGATARI and *Ochikubo Monogatari*.

Takikawa jiken 滝川事件 (the Takikawa affair). An incident of the early Shōwa era which resulted in the suppression of academic freedom. In 1933, Takikawa Yukitoki (1891–1962), professor of Kyōto University, was released from office following the publication of his *Keihō Tokuhon,* which was banned by the government. Violent protests were launched by professors and students who fought for academic freedom. But freedom of learning, thought, and speech were even more actively suppressed by fascist militarism.

Tamamushi no Zushi 玉虫厨子 (the Tamamushi Shrine). A miniature shrine preserved in the Hōryū-ji monastery. A representative work of applied art and a relic of the Asuka period (552–645), it is composed of the shrine itself and its pedestal. Under the metal mountings in openwork, which are adorned with tiny pillars, beams, and braces, were arranged side by side the wing sheaths of the beetle known as "jewel insect" *(tamamushi),* but these have almost completely exfoliated. On the four sides of the pedestal are lacquer paintings illustrating episodes from the life of Buddha in various incarnations, one of them picturing the tale of how he gave his body to feed hungry tigers. The work is of great value for the study of Asuka temple architecture and painting techniques.

tamatsukuri-be 玉作部 (the jewelers' guild). A guild in ancient Japan, the members of which worked for the nobility and manufactured personal ornaments such as bracelets, curved jewels (MAGATAMA), tubular jewels (KUDA-TAMA), and smaller jewels *(kodama)*. Many of these jewels were also made during the Jōmon period (about 3000 B.C. to 350 B.C.). Jewelry of superior quality was made up to the first half of the period of the ancient tombs (250–552). At this time, the jewelers' guild was established. Later, material was of inferior quality and manufacture less skillful. The TOMO NO MIYATSUKO were the leaders of the industrial group of jewelers. The name *tamatsukuri* has been transmitted to present-day places such as Tamatsukuri in Ōsaka and in Shimane Prefecture, because in those places grindstones for jewels or semiprocessed precious stones were discovered.

tanagari 店借 (house tenancy). The renting of town houses during the Edo period. The tenant was called *tanagari-bito* and *kariya-bito*. To obtain a contract it was necessary to provide a guarantee for a tenant *(tanauke-nin)*, to countersign the tenancy document *(tanauke-jō)*, to transfer the document to the owner of the house or his representative *(yamori)*, and to send it to the town officials. Socially, a tenant occupied a lower rank than a householder or a landowner.

Tanegashima 種子島. The name of an island in Kagoshima Prefecture. The first Europeans to land in Japan were three Portuguese who arrived at Tanegashima in 1543. The lord of the island, Tanegashima Tokitaka (1528–79) bought two rifles from the Portuguese and studied their mechanism. There was a great demand on the part of the civil-war barons *(sengoku daimyō)* for the rifles, which came to be manufactured in the country. The rifle itself was called *tanegashima*. It came into use throughout the country and greatly influenced military strategy and the building of castles. It played a role in the unification of the country. In the battle of Nagashino (NAGASHINO NO TATA-KAI), the forces of Nobunaga, which used the rifle, destroyed the forces of Takeda Katsuyori, which still relied on ancient strategy. After the introduction of the gun, Portuguese merchant vessels came to Japan in great numbers. Six years later, in 1549, Francis Xavier arrived in Kagoshima and introduced Christianity.

Tannishō 歎異抄. A book published by Shinran's disciples. After the death of their master, the disciples of Shinran (1173–1262) deplored *(tan* 歎) and criticized the heterodox *(i* 異) teaching which had begun to spread. They collected Shinran's last injunctions and published them. The book represents the essence of Shinran's ideology. More than his KYŌGYŌSHINSHŌ, *Tannishō* stresses the possibility of salvation even for the wicked.

tanomoshi 頼母子 (financial associations). A kind of financial system which existed from ancient times. The word *tanomoshi* derives from *tanomu* 頼む (to request). The purpose of the *tanomoshi* was to help those who formed the associations known as KŌ and who were in financial trouble. Initially, no interest was charged, but from the middle ages security was put up and interest was generally charged. A promoter *(oya)* was appointed, assemblies were held for definite periods, and a determined amount of rice was contributed. One member of the association was indicated by lot to receive a loan in money. The system was especially prevalent during the Edo period. There were all kinds of associations, from those for temple and shrine pilgrimages *(shaji-sankei kō)* and commodity purchasing *(buppin-kōnyū kō)* to those organized to adjust debts. The common gathering for food and drink by the members fostered the spirit of fraternity. Some associations were given to gambling, though gambling was strictly forbidden. After the restoration, *tanomoshi* declined as banking facilities developed, but in some rural communities the custom still exists.

tansen 段銭 (land tax). A kind of tax of the middle ages. It was originally the imperial court and the government which imposed tax on arable land, but they did it only periodically and as occasion demanded. From the Muromachi period, the tax became an important source of revenue, and constables and stewards, temples and shrines imposed the tax. In quite a few cases, the tax was collected regularly and even more than once a year. When money was collected, the tax was called *tansen;* when rice was collected, it was called *tammai.*

taru-kaisen 樽回船 (*taru* cargo vessels). A marine transportation business of the Edo period which began operating following support obtained from wine dealers of Nishinomiya, Nada, and other places. The main cargo from Ōsaka to Edo was barrels of wine, but other products from the neighborhood of Nishinomiya were also shipped. *Taru-kaisen* competed with HIGAKI-KAISEN.

tateana jūkyo 竪穴住居 (half-underground pit dwellings). A kind of dwelling in primitive Japan and in early ancient Japan. The main feature of the dwelling was the placement of the floor below ground level. The dwellings were scattered all over Hokkaidō and the northeastern area of Honshū. A number of dwellings discovered in 1926 in a shell mound on Mount Ubayama in Chiba Prefecture have a floor surface 50 centimeters below ground level and a diameter of 6 to 7 meters. Four to six pillar holes, with a diameter of 30–45 centimeters each, are disposed at an equal distance from each other. All around the floor is a ditch for drainage. It is believed that the floor was dug deep in the ground for protection against cold. The remains of these dwellings offer valuable data for the study of the family structure in primitive society.

tato 田堵 (landowners). Small landowners of the Heian period. Initially, *tato* meant the actual field; later the word, which is also written 田頭 and is often pronounced *dento,* came to mean the people who actually cultivated the field. Until the middle of the Heian period, the *tato* had no management rights, but as he lived on the spot he actually managed the field. Furthermore, as he was the occupant, he attached his name to it and finally secured possession of the plot as a name field (MYŌDEN). Consolidating their position, the *tato* became the forerunners of the Kamakura name masters (MYŌSHU).

tawara-mono 俵物 (marine products). Marine products exported from

Nagasaki. From the middle of the Edo period, when copper output was on the decline, marine products replaced copper as exchange commodities for articles imported to Nagasaki. The marine products were parched sea cucumbers *(iri-namako)*, dried abalone *(hoshi-awabi)*, and shark fins *(fuka no hire)*. Unlike sea tangle *(kombu)*, dried cuttlefish *(surume)*, agar-agar *(tengusa)*, etc., they were packed in straw bags and consequently called *tawara-mono*. For the purchase of *tawara-mono*, an agency was set up in Nagasaki on a contract basis, but the results were not satisfactory, and, beginning in 1785, stocks were obtained directly from the producing centers.

Teikin Ōrai 庭訓往来. A handbook which was the moral code for the masses for many generations and was extensively read from the time of the early Muromachi period. The work is believed to have been written by the Buddhist priest Gen'e (1269–1350). *Teikin* means "home teaching," and *ōrai* means "a correspondence manual." The style and ideas of *Teikin Ōrai* gave rise to the later text and reference books called ŌRAI-MONO, which all contained moral instruction.

Teimon-ha 貞門派 (the Teimon school). A school of haiku poetry (HAIKAI) founded by Matsunaga Teitoku (1571–1653). The Teimon school is known as the school of the old style *(kofū)* as opposed to the new style of the later Danrin school. It flourished until the start of the Danrin school (DANRIN-FŪ).

Teisei-tō 帝政党 (the Teisei political party). A political party of the early Meiji era. As the movement for popular rights approached its climax, the government committed itself to the establishment of a national assembly. In conjunction with this pledge, the Liberal Party and the Progressive Party were organized. But, as a countermeasure, the government first gave its support to Fukuchi Gen'ichirō (1841–1906), who established the Teisei-tō (1882). A paper war was waged between the parties, but in 1883 the Teisei-tō, in compliance with the wish of the government, was dissolved.

Tempō no kaikaku 天保の改革 (reforms of the Tempō era). Reforms carried out in 1841 by Mizuno Tadakuni (1794–1851), the shōgun's chief minister. Tadakuni considered the reforms of the Kyōhō (1716–36) and Kansei (1784–1801) eras as model reforms. He enforced official discipline, prohibited luxury, attempted to reform public morals, abolished the trading corporations (KABU-NAKAMA), and encouraged the literary and military arts. The economic reforms were too sweeping and caused a depression. They also caused antagonistic feelings because commodity prices failed to decrease. In particular, the daimyō were opposed when the BAKUFU, planning an increase in revenue, forced them and the bannermen who had domains near Edo and Ōsaka to exchange them for less productive land elsewhere. The purpose of the *agechi-rei*, or ordinance concerning the cession of private domains to the *bakufu*, was to consolidate the *bakufu* domains scattered all over the country. Around Edo and Ōsaka, an area of 39.30 square kilometers thus had to be ceded. Tadakuni was dismissed from office in 1843, and his reforms crumbled within two and a half years. The powerful southwestern clans, in particular the Satsuma and Chōshū clans, were more successful in their clan-policy reforms.

Tenchū-gumi 天誅組 (the Tenchū force). A loyalist organization which conspired to overthrow the EDO BAKUFU. On March 13, 1863, when an imperial decree announced the emperor's journey to Yamato, Yoshimura Toratarō of Tosa, Fujimoto Tesseki of Bizen, and Matsumoto Keidō of Mikawa, following their leader the ex-chamberlain Nakayama Tadamitsu, conspired and planned to raise a volunteer corps for the imperial cause. The Tenchū-gumi was led to Gojō in Yamato, where it attacked the deputy's office. However, the plot miscarried when Emperor Kōmei (1831–66) suddenly called off his Yamato visit (August 18, 1863). The volunteer corps was attacked by soldiers of several clans. Gathering the country samurai of Totsugawa-gō, the corps accepted battle but was soon wiped out.

Tendai-shū 天台宗 (Tendai sect of Buddhism). A sect of Buddhism founded in Japan by Saichō (767–822) in the early Heian period. In China, during the Sui dynasty (589–618), Tendai was founded by Chih I and Hui Ssu, and the religion took its name from a mountain in Chekiang called T'ien T'ai, to which Chih I retired. In 804, Saichō introduced the sect from China and added the Esoteric doctrine (MIKKYŌ) and precepts. Ennin (794–864) and Enchin (814–91) further developed the Esoteric aspects of the doctrine. The doctrine greatly differed from Chinese Tendai. The sect's main scripture is the Lotus Sutra *(Hokke-kyō)*. All the new religions of the Kamakura period originated in Tendai. The main temple of Tendai is ENRYAKU-JI on Mount Hiei in Kyōto.

Tengyō no ran 天慶の乱 (revolt of the Tengyō era). The Tengyō era lasted from 938 to 947. This revolt in the Kantō district was led by Taira no Masakado (?–940) and resulted from the internal strife of the Taira clan, which had extended its grip to the eastern provinces. Masakado, who killed his uncle Kunika, supported Fujiwara no Kuroaki, who was banished by the provincial governor. He also revolted against the provincial government office (KOKU-GA) and was successful for a while. However, the country's security was threatened when Fujiwara no Sumitomo (?–941) rebelled at the same time (939). In 940, Taira no Sadamori and Fujiwara no Hidesato joined forces and destroyed Masakado.

tenjiku-yō 天竺様 *(tenjiku* style of architecture). A style of architecture used during the Kamakura period. It was introduced from Sung China by the Buddhist priest Chōgen and adopted for the restoration of Tōdai-ji monastery.

The techniques of *tenjiku-yō* were plain and bold, but the style itself soon vanished. An example of *tenjiku* architecture is the Nandaimon of Tōdai-ji, Nara.

Tenjukoku Shuchō 天寿国繍帳 (embroidery picturing the Buddhist paradise). Fragments of embroidery of the Asuka period (552–645), preserved in the Chūgū-ji temple of Hōryū-ji. They are two pieces of embroidered hangings made in 622 after the death of Prince Shōtoku (573–621) by court ladies-in-waiting *(uneme)* by order of Shōtoku's consort, Tachibana no Ōiratsume. They represent the Buddhist paradise *(tenjukoku)* and are often referred to as the Tenjukoku Mandara. Originally there was an inscription of four hundred characters embroidered on the tapestry, but only twenty-four are left. The complete text, however, is quoted in the book *Jōgū Shōtoku Taishi Hōō Teisetsu.* This book mentions the purpose of the making of the embroidery as well as the names of the designers. The tapestry cloth is made of gauze, silk damask, and plain silk, each element showing a different method of stitching. The color scheme is beautiful, and the work is a representative piece of contemporary applied art.

tennō-kikansetsu 天皇機関説 (emperor-as-an-organ theory). A constitutional theory of the Taishō and Shōwa eras advocated in 1935 by the liberalists and severely criticized by the nationalists. Opposing Hozumi Yatsuka's (1860–1912) theory of the constitution, which was founded on emperor worship, Minobe Tatsukichi (1873–1948) held that the real sovereign power rested with the people, while the emperor was only an organ of the state.

Tenryū-ji 天竜寺. The main temple of the Tenryū-ji branch of Rinzai Buddhism and one of the Kyōto Five Monasteries (GOZAN). In 1339, when Emperor Godaigo (1288–1339) died in Yoshino, Ashikaga Takauji (1305–58) built this temple in order to offer prayers for the repose of the soul of the deceased emperor. Takauji appointed the Buddhist priest Musō Soseki (1275–1351) founder of the temple (1340). To provide the necessary funds for the completion of the temple, Takauji, on Soseki's advice, resumed relations with China, which had been broken off following the Mongol invasions. Ships were sent to China for trade, and the accruing profits were spent on the building of the temple. The ships were called TENRYŪJI-BUNE. The temple was completed in 1343. The garden of the temple, representative of Muromachi garden architecture, was made by Soseki, who was a noted garden designer.

Tenryūji-bune 天竜寺船 (Tenryū-ji ships). Trade vessels which sailed to Yüan China during the Namboku period (1336–92). In order to pray for the repose of the soul of Emperor Godaigo (1288–1339), Ashikaga Takauji (1305–58) planned to build TENRYŪ-JI temple. As funds were insufficient, Takauji, following the advice of Soseki, sent trade vessels to China. He promised to protect the trade provided that 5,000 *kan* (one *kan* equals ten *sen*) be paid in tax upon the return to Japan of each trading vessel.

Tenshin Jōyaku 天津条約 (the Treaty of Tientsin). A diplomatic treaty concluded in the early Meiji era between China and Japan. In 1885, after the Korean Kōshin uprising *(Kōshin no hen),* the Chinese plenipotentiary Li Hung-chang and the Japanese plenipotentiary Itō Hirobumi negotiated in Tientsin. China and Japan each agreed to withdraw its troops from Korea, to abolish the system of military instructors, and not to send troops again to Korea without notifying each other. The treaty meant the renunciation of China's suzerainty over the peninsula and the equal status of Japan and China toward Korea. It led to the Sino-Japanese War of 1894–95. (See also TŌGAKU-TŌ NO RAN.)

Tenshō ken'ō shisetsu 天正遣欧使節 (Japanese envoys to Europe in the Tenshō era). These were envoys sent to Europe by the daimyō of Kyūshū during the Tenshō era (1573-92). Three Catholic daimyō of Kyūshū, Ōtomo Sōrin (1530–87), Arima Harunobu (1567–1612), and Ōmura Sumitada (1533–87), sent the Japanese nobles Itō Yoshikata (Itō Mancio, 1572–98), and Chijiwa Seizaemon (Don Miguel) as envoys to the pope of Rome and the king of Spain. Joined by two companions, they left Nagasaki in 1582. In 1585, they were received in audience by Pope Gregory XIII. The pope and the Romans treated them courteously and accorded them Roman citizenship. They returned to Nagasaki in 1590 after having observed European culture and introduced Japanese culture in western Europe, thus greatly contributing to mutual understanding.

tenshukaku 天守閣 (castle towers). Towers or keeps of castles during the Edo period. The origin of the towers is not known, but they invariably occupied the highest spot within the castle compound. They were provided with several superstructures. Previously, the towers seem to have been used as living quarters for castle lords, but during the Edo period they served as observation platforms, command towers, and final strongholds of defense during an attack. In peacetime, a second citadel, called *ni-no-maru,* was the living place of the lord, and the castle itself was a mere ornamental building which displayed the lord's might.

teppō no denrai 鉄砲の伝来 (introduction of the gun: TANEGASHIMA)

Teradaya sōdō 寺田屋騒動 (the Teradaya riot). A violent incident at Fushimi, Kyōto, during the late Edo period. On April 23, 1862, a radical group under Shimazu Hisamitsu (1817–87), the lord of Satsuma, disagreeing with the lord's efforts to reconcile the court and the shogunate, met in Fushimi at an inn called Teradaya and planned to raise soldiers to overthrow the

BAKUFU. Hisamitsu sent his men to persuade the plotters to abandon their plan. As the conspirators refused to change their minds, fighting ensued. Arima Shinshichi and seven of his henchmen were killed. Others were arrested and condemned to death.

terakoya 寺子屋 (temple schools). Temple schools for the primary education of the common people during the middle ages and the Edo period. Initially, part of the temple was made into a classroom, and a bonze was appointed instructor. The schools were especially popular during the Edo period. Not only bonzes, but Shintō priests, physicians, and even RŌNIN were made teachers. The subjects taught were penmanship, reading, abacus, etc. The books used were the usual text and reference books known as ŌRAI-MONO. The teaching, which was adapted to the actual needs of the pupils, may be said to have been pragmatic. The course of study lasted from three to five years, and children were enrolled at the age of eight or nine. In the early Meiji era, grammar schools were established, but the *terakoya* still survived for a time.

terauke-seido 寺請制度 (temple certificate system). A system of the Edo shogunate according to which people had to prove that they were not Christians. It was a means of eradicating Christianity, since every individual, irrespective of his social rank or profession, had to belong to the family temple *(danna-dera)* and to possess a temple certificate. A census register was also kept. For marriage, travel, moving one's residence, and other purposes, the temple certificate was as necessary as the identification card.

tō 党 (corporations of warriors). A kind of warriors' corporation (BUSHIDAN) during the middle ages (Kamakura and Muromachi periods). Various Kamakura warriors' groups were organized into *tō*. Most warriors who only possessed a relatively small plot of land were united territorially or by blood relationship. Warriors who organized themselves in this way were imbued with a strong individual spirit of independence. However, during the Muromachi period, the *tō* collapsed under the powerful sway of the daimyō.

Toba-Fushimi no tatakai 鳥羽・伏見の戦 (the battles of Toba-Fushimi). The battles fought in January 1868 between soldiers of the Satsuma and Chōshū clans and shogunate forces. After the shōgun Tokugawa Yoshinobu (1827–1913) had withdrawn his forces from Kyōto to Ōsaka, the Satsuma and Chōshū clans tried to destroy remnants of the shogunate forces and to complete the Meiji Restoration. They urged Yoshinobu to resign. The angry shogunate clans, trying to repulse the enemy forces, marched on Kyōto. They clashed with Satsuma and Chōshū forces in Toba and Fushimi (south of Kyōto) but were defeated, and in May 1868 Yoshinobu was deposed.

Tōdai-ji 東大寺. A monastery of the Kegon sect of Buddhism, established during the Nara period in Nara. It is one of the "seven larger monasteries of Nara " (NANTO SHICHI-DAIJI). Emperor Shōmu (701–56), who was a devout Buddhist, ordered the erection of Tōdai-ji as head temple of all provincial temples (KOKUBUN-JI). It took seven years—from 745 to 752—to build the temple. It was destroyed twice by fire caused by warfare but was rebuilt each time and is still standing today. In ancient times and during the middle ages, the temple acquired numerous manors in the provinces around the capital. During the Edo period, it was granted an income of 3,300 *koku* by the shogunate. When Tōdai-ji was being built, the statue of the Great Buddha and many other Buddhist images were made. A number of these, including the Great Buddha itself (although several times damaged and imperfectly repaired), are still to be seen. Also surviving from the original Tōdai-ji is the main hall of the Hokkedō.

Tōfuku-ji 東福寺. The central monastery of the Tōfuku-ji branch of the Rinzai sect of Buddhism. It is located in Higashiyama-ku, Kyōto, and is one of the Kyōto Five Monasteries or Kyōto GOZAN. In 1236, Kujō Michiie (1193–1252), adviser to the emperor, made a vow to build the temple, which was completed in 1255. Enji, or Ben'en (1202–80), became the founder of the temple in 1243.

Tōgaku-tō no ran 東学党の乱 (the revolt of the Tonghak sect). A revolt in Korea during the Meiji era. The Tonghak sect (in Japanese, Tōgaku-tō), a religious group of South Korea, intensified its opposition to Confucianism, the national religion. The government took steps and suppressed the Tōgaku-tō. This gave rise to a popular revolt (1894) against the government's maladministration. The government, with the help of Chinese forces, quelled the revolt, but Japan, alleging violation of the Tientsin Treaty, according to which China had agreed not to send troops to Korea without notifying Japan (TENSHIN JŌYAKU), started the Sino-Japanese War.

Toichi no agata-nushi 十市県主 (estate master of Toichi). The local chieftain of Toichi no Agata in Yamato Province, pre-Taika period. Toichi was a large estate in pre-Taika days and became a rural district *(gun)* around the time of the Taika Reform (646). The place was in the neighborhood of today's Miminashi, Kashihara City, Nara Prefecture.

toimaru 問丸 (shipment agents). Transportation service in harbors during the middle ages was taken care of by *toimaru*. They were also referred to as *toi*. First, they were in charge of shipments and handling of produce of the manors and of the freight yards. These freight yards, set up in harbors, were called *tsuya*. *Toimaru* were under the authority of the lord of the manor but had about the same authority as manor officials. When communications developed, the circulation of manor products increased. *Toimaru* attached to one manorial estate also took charge of the shipment of the produce of other manors and offered their services for the shipment of special commodities. During the Muromachi period, *toimaru* served in such harbors as Obama, Tsuruga, Hyōgo, Yodo, Ōtsu, etc. Gradually they not only offered their services for selling the yearly rice taxes, but also for the transaction of all commercial articles, and amassed a huge capital. In every town where commodities were collected and distributed on a large scale, some *toimaru* were busy. Local merchants took advantage of the facilities thus offered and aspired to become wholesale traders. During the Edo period, they became *toiya,* or wholesale dealers.

Toi no nyūkō 刀伊の入寇 (invasion of the Jürched). The Toi belonged to a Tungusic tribe known in Chinese as "Juchen," or "Nüchen," and usually referred to as Jürched. The tribe raided North Kyūshū during the middle of the Heian period. The Jürched founded the Chin dynasty in North China, which lasted from 1115 to 1234. They were first heard of in Manchuria, west of the Yalu River (in Japanese, Ōryokkō), where they formed a small tribe. Before long, they invaded Koryo, or Korea, and, from the early eleventh century, their pirates infested the waters from the east coast of Korea to Ullung (Dagelet) Island (in Japanese, Utsuryō-tō). In 1019, the Jürched left the south coast of Koryo in fifty ships, raided Iki Island and Tsushima Island, and plundered the shore of Hakata Bay. The chief of Dazaifu in Kyūshū, Fujiwara no Takaie (974–1044), sent a report to the throne, led imperial troops, and repulsed the Jürched pirates. Then the pirates raided the shores of Hizen Province (Nagasaki Prefecture). They were defeated and retreated to the east coast of Korea, where they were crushed by the Koryo forces. Later, when envoys from Koryo repatriated two hundred Japanese nationals who had been taken captive by the raiders, Japan learned for the first time that the pirates were Jürched or, in the language of Koryo, Toi.

toiya-sei kanai-kōgyō 問屋制家内工業 (home industry as organized by wholesale dealers). A system of industrial production which spread during the latter part of the Edo period. Wholesale dealers provided the townspeople and farmers with raw material and had them make the finished goods. Some wholesale dealers *(toiya)* advanced funds and tools. Merchants became capitalists. Small producers were dependent upon the *toiya* and actually became wage laborers, a position to which the system confined them. The textile industry developed early under the *toiya* system, but the system was applied to other forms of industry as well. It may be considered as a preliminary stage finally leading to full-scale manufacture.

Tō-ji 東寺. The headquarters of the Tō-ji branch of the Kogi Shingon sect of Buddhism. The temple is also called Kyōōgokoku-ji. When the Heian capital was being built, the Tō-ji was erected east of the Rashōmon gate in order to obtain the protection of the place. In 823, Kūkai (774–835) was granted the Tō-ji, which became a monastery of the Shingon sect. After Kūkai's death, the temple deteriorated because of lack of funds. From the end of the Heian period, as far as religious education and life were concerned, the Tō-ji was surpassed by Kōya-san, but it still stores many cultural treasures. The paintings *Tō-ji Jūni-ten Zu* and the landscape screens known as *senzui byōbu* are among the most famous of these.

Tōkan Kikō 東関紀行. A travelogue in one volume written during the Kamakura period. The author and date of publication are not known. It was probably published a few years later than KAIDŌKI (circa 1223). The author left Kyōto in 1242, stayed two months in Kamakura, and returned to Kyōto. The book describes the journey in mixed Japanese-Chinese style.

Tokubetsu Kōtō Keisatsu 特別高等警察 (Special Secret Service Police). Police corps established at the end of the Meiji era in order to maintain control over the socialist movement. It was commonly known as Tokkō. From the beginning of the Shōwa era, it not only controlled communist agitation but also suppressed freedom of thought and speech all through the Pacific War. It was abolished in 1945 by the general headquarters of the Allied Powers.

to-kumi don'ya 十組問屋 (the ten forwarding agencies). Large forwarding agencies of Edo. Those of Ōsaka were known as the "twenty-four forwarding agencies" (NIJŪSHI-KUMI DON'YA). During the Edo period, Ōsaka was the center of collection and distribution of commodities, but the largest consumption area was Edo. Therefore, from the Jōkyō-Genroku eras (1684–1704), transport agencies organized companies in both places, monopolizing freight transport and receipt of commodities. As a result of the reform of 1841, they were temporarily abolished but soon resumed business, which then lasted until the early Meiji era.

tokusei-ikki 徳政一揆 (the moratorium uprisings). Agrarian revolts during the Muromachi period calling for the issuing of an "act of grace" (*tokusei* or virtuous administration), by which loans would be canceled and sale of land voided. The usury of the moneylenders (DOSŌ) was unbearable to the farmers, who had to pawn their land. In addition, the farmers were pressed by heavy taxes and lost their tracts of land. They rose in revolt against the moneylenders and unjust landlords and demanded an act of grace from the shogunate. The first large-scale uprising occurred in 1428. It spread from Ōmi to the provinces around the capital. Pawnbrokers and sakè brewers were raided everywhere. The shogunate capitulated and promulgated an act of grace. But, as most of the leaders of the revolts were middle-class landowners of the *ji-samurai* type, or rural gentry, they became retainers of the civil-war barons, or *sengoku daimyō* (DAIMYŌ), and their interests obviously differed from those of the lower-class farmers. As a result, the solidarity of the peasants who had revolted crumbled, and the uprisings themselves became ineffective.

tokusei-rei 徳政令 (moratorium decrees). Acts issued during the middle ages which amounted to the cancellation of debts. In 1297, the Kamakura shogunate issued an act of grace because the shogunate retainers (GO-KENIN), who had had to pawn or sell their land to pawnbrokers or moneylenders, were in a state of destitution. The land was then gratuitously returned to the former owners. But it now became difficult for impoverished retainers to borrow any more money, since moneylenders were naturally reluctant to make further loans, and consequently the decree was rescinded the following year. During the Muromachi period, destitute farmers who had lost their land as a result of the usury of the moneylenders rose in revolt (TOKUSEI-IKKI) and demanded an act of grace from the BAKUFU. The act was often granted.

Tokushi Yoron 読史余論. Historical book in three volumes written by Arai Hakuseki (1657–1725). The book comprises lectures on Japanese history given in the presence of Shōgun Ienobu (1662–1712). The first volume discusses the changes that occurred during nine historical periods and the general trend up to the time when political power shifted to the military class. The second volume describes the events from the rise of the warrior class to the establishment of the military administration. The third volume discusses the rise and fall of the warrior class from the establishment of the MUROMACHI BAKUFU to that of the EDO BAKUFU. As opposed to previous historical works, which imitated the style and ideology of Chinese historical books, Hakuseki's work has a wide command of the historical scene. For the study of Japanese history the work is extremely valuable.

Tōkyō Bijutsu Gakkō 東京美術学校 (Tōkyō School of Fine Arts). A modern school for the education of students of fine arts. In the early Meiji era, the Kōbu Bijutsu Gakkō was temporarily set up, but in 1887 the Tōkyō School of Fine Arts was founded. It became the main institution for the education of art students.

Tōkyō Daigaku 東京大学 (Tōkyō University). A modern national university. In 1877, the Tōkyō Kaisei Gakkō and the Tōkyō Igakkō, or the Tōkyō School of Medicine, merged and became Tōkyō University. Later, when Kōbu Daigakkō was added, Tōkyō University became the Imperial University (Teikoku Daigaku) and a legitimate university. As the highest institution for the education of government officials and technicians, Tōkyō University occupies an important position.

Tōkyō sento 東京遷都 (transfer of the capital to Tōkyō). The capital was transferred at the time of the Meiji Restoration in 1868. At the restoration of the imperial rule, some Japanese were in favor of Ōsaka as the site of the new capital. Because of the necessity of controlling the Kantō district, Edo was chosen. In July 1868, the name Edo was changed to that of Tōkyō. In September of the same year, Emperor Meiji left Kyōto and reached Tōkyō the following month. Tōkyō became the capital of Japan, and the emperor has since resided there.

Tomioka Seishi Kōjō 富岡製糸工場 (the Tomioka Silk Mill). A government-operated factory of the early Meiji era. In 1870, in order to improve the quality of raw silk for exportation, a model silk mill was built in Tomioka, Gumma Prefecture. Shibusawa Eiichi (1840–1931) invited French engineers to Japan for the construction of the mill and the installation of machinery. The mill was completed in 1872. It was instrumental in spreading the manufacture of spun silk and educated many young people who later became instructors. The factory girls of Tomioka were known all over the country. Later, the mill was taken over by the Mitsui concern.

tomo-be 品部 (guilds). Guilds engaged in the production of industrial products and artifacts for the court under the penal and administrative code system (RITSURYŌ-SEI). *Tomo-be* is another name for the generic term *be no tami* or guild people. At the time of the Taika Reform (646), the system of guild people was abolished. Only specially skilled workers were included in the penal and administrative code system and were called *tomo-be* and *zakko* (BE). These corporations of skilled workers were formerly attached to the imperial family, but under the new law they belonged to government departments. Examples of *tomo-be* were the paper guild *(kami-be)* belonging to the bureau of books and drawings *(zusho-ryō)* of the Department of Central Affairs (Nakatsukasa-shō), the guild of musicians *(gaku-be)* of the bureau of music *(uta-ryō)* of the Department of Civil Administration (Jibu-shō), and the brewers' guild *(saka-be)* of the imperial wine office *(miki no tsukasa)* of the Imperial Household Department (KUNAI-SHŌ).

Under the penal and administrative code system, the *tomo-be* members were exempt from the produce tax (CHŌ) and from miscellaneous corvées (ZATSUYŌ). Though they belonged to the class of free people *(ryōmin)*, they were despised as base (unfree) people *(semmin)*. *Tomo-be* and *zakko* belonged to the rankless class of *zōshiki* or artisans. The *tomo-be* system was abolished in 759.

tomo no miyatsuko 伴造 (hereditary leaders of guilds). The leader of pre-Taika guild people *(be no tami)* directly engaged in court service. He controlled the manufacturing of commodities for the court by the guild people. The office was hereditary, and the titles (KABANE) of the leader were most frequently MURAJI and *miyatsuko*. There was no blood relationship between the *tomo no* *miyatsuko* and the guild people. After the Taika Reform (646), part of the *tomo no miyatsuko* as well as part of the guild people were included in the government setup of the penal and administrative code (BE). They were employed in the departments of ministries dealing with public affairs (*tsukasa* and *ryō*).

tōmotsu 唐物 (imported articles). In ancient Japan and during the middle ages (Kamakura and Muromachi periods), imported articles were called *karamono*. During the Edo period, imported articles such as medicines, silk, textiles, etc. were called *tōmotsu*. During the Meiji era, muslin, woolen goods, and other Western textiles were also called *tōmotsu*.

tondenhei-seido 屯田兵制度 (colonial-troops system). Colonial-troops system of the early Meiji era when Hokkaidō was being developed. Colonial troops, which already existed at the end of the shogunate period, were reorganized in 1874 through the efforts of Kuroda Kiyotaka (1840–1900), vice-governor of the development board of Hokkaidō. Colonial troops existed until 1904. The original purpose of the organization of colonial troops was to relieve warriors who had become destitute following the hereditary-stipend measure (CHITSU-ROKU SHOBUN), but the troops also helped the local inhabitants and defended the territory (HOKKAIDŌ KAITAKU-SHI). The *tondenhei* were instrumental in developing Hokkaidō through improvement of the soil and betterment of agricultural production.

tone 刀禰 (rural leaders). Rural leaders during the Heian, Kamakura, and Muromachi periods. Originally, they represented those who guaranteed transactions in land. Under the manorial system, the *tone* were manor officials. They were influential farmers settled in a rural community and had a strong desire to establish self-governing villages (GŌSON-SEI).

Toro iseki 登呂遺跡 (remains in Toro). Remains of the Yayoi period (about 350 B.C. to A.D. 250) discovered in 1943 in Toro on the outskirts of Shizuoka City. The area, which is divided into a dwelling zone and a zone of ridges between rice fields, covers 100,000 *tsubo* (one *tsubo* equals 3.95 square yards or 3.31 square meters). Remains of Yayoi rural communities, of wooden articles, and of ridges between rice fields accurately portray the state of primitive agriculture.

Tosa-ha 土佐派 (Tosa school of painting). A school of painting started in the Muromachi period. It followed the orthodox tradition of Yamato painting (YAMATO-E). It was founded by Tosa Mitsunobu (1434–1525) and flourished under the rule of Shōgun Ashikaga Yoshimasa (1434–90). In the early Edo period, it was surpassed by the Kanō school (KANŌ-HA), but its reputation was restored by Tosa Mitsuoki (1617–91).

Tōsei Shosei-katagi 当世書生気質. A novel of the early Meiji era. In 1885, Tsubouchi Shōyō (1859–1935), who advocated realism, wrote SHŌSETSU SHIN-ZUI. *Tōsei Shosei-katagi,* also written in 1885, concerned college life in Tōkyō.

toshiyori 年寄 (rural community leaders). The leaders of a rural community. They were also called OTONA. From ancient times, elderly people with knowledge and experience were esteemed by the farmers. However, knowledge and experience did not necessarily belong only to the elderly, and the more important people of the rural community, irrespective of age, were called *toshiyori*. They were the administrative, religious, and economic leaders. The same situation prevailed in towns, and during the Edo period offices such as *mura-doshiyori* and *machi-doshiyori* existed. The *mura-doshiyori* assisted the *nanushi* or village administrators (MURA YAKUNIN) and the *shōya*. They attended to the affairs of the village. Office names of the Edo period, such as TAIRŌ (chief minister), RŌJŪ (councilor of the shōgun), KARŌ (minister of a daimyō), and *naka-doshiyori* (assistant councilor of the shōgun), are derived from office names in rural society.

Tōshōdai-ji 唐招提寺. The central temple of the Ritsu sect of Buddhism, located in Gojō, Nara City. It was founded in 759 by the T'ang Chinese Buddhist priest Ganjin (688–763) and was the first training center for the monks of the sect. Up to early Heian times, the temple flourished, as it was granted land by the court. Later it declined. The Tōshōdai-ji houses many valuable Buddhist images representative of the Tempyō art period (710–94) and is the best existing example of Tempyō architecture. It is a highly valued specimen in the history of ancient art.

Tōshō-gū 東照宮. The famous mausoleum of Tokugawa Ieyasu (1542–1616) in Nikkō, Tochigi Prefecture. It was built in 1617 in accordance with the will of Ieyasu. The main building *(shaden)* was enlarged between 1634 and 1636 by Iemitsu (1604–51) in the elaborate architectural style of the times. Many of the buildings, such as the Yōmei-mon, strive for magnificence, but there is a feeling of exaggerated showiness about the architecture and its complicated surface decoration.

tōsui-ken 統帥権 (the prerogative of supreme command). Authority of the militarists in modern times. The army circles were invested with this authority by the army staff in 1878. In 1886, when the naval general staff became a separate organization, the authority of the army and that of the navy became independent. Under the Meiji Constitution, the prerogative of supreme command was recognized as a power of the sovereign. Together with "the right of direct appeal to the throne by military authorities" (IAKU JŌSŌKEN), it formed the autonomy of military power from Meiji times and led to the strengthening of military fascism during the Shōwa era.

totei-seido 徒弟制度 (apprentice system). A system according to which apprentices were admitted by the master in order to learn industrial production and handicraft techniques. The system was in general use during the Edo period. The term of apprenticeship was about ten years. During this period, apprentices were trained in various techniques, were allowed no salary, and rendered miscellaneous services in the house of the master. When the term expired, they were recognized as full-fledged craftsmen. Even after the Meiji Restoration, the tradition was cherished, though somewhat altered to suit different occupations. After World War II, the custom was discontinued.

Tōyō Jiyū Shimbun 東洋自由新聞. A newspaper of the early Meiji period. It was launched in 1881. The president of the newspaper company was Saionji Kimmochi (1849–1940), and the editor in chief was Nakae Chōmin (1847–1901). The newspaper advocated Western democracy based on French ideology. The government feared its influence and its socialist tendencies, and an imperial order banned its publication.

tozama daimyō 外様大名 (outside lords). The name existed from the Kamakura period, but from about the time of the battle of Sekigahara (1600) the word *tozama* was used to indicate the daimyō who had no hereditary tie with the Tokugawa. Such were Maeda, Date, Mōri, Shimazu, etc. Their stipend was generally high. Many of the *tozama daimyō* lived far from the capital.

tsuibushi 追捕使 (constables). Constables of the penal and administrative code period (646–1185). They were appointed to arrest plotters and robbers. Many of them were elected from among provincial administrators (KOKUSHI) or rural district administrators (GUNJI). They had to be skilled in the military arts. *Tsuibushi* are already mentioned in the records of 932, and in 956 their office became a permanent one. Minamoto no Yoritomo (1148–99) appointed *tsuibushi* in all the provinces he conquered. The duties of the *tsuibushi* were the same as those of the later constables known as *shugo*. After the Kenkyū era (1190–99), the constables (now called *sō-tsuibushi*) were empowered to make arrests within the compounds of temples and shrines and on manors.

Tsukiji Shō-gekijō 築地小劇場 (the Tsukiji Little Theater). A dramatic troupe of the Taishō and Shōwa eras. In 1924, Osanai Kaoru (1881–1928) and Hijikata Yoshi (1898–1959) organized the troupe for experimental theatrical performances. This helped spread the new theater movement, and many small dramatic troupes came into being. Performances of translated plays were very popular. The Tsukiji troupe split after Osanai's death, and Hijikata organized a new Tsukiji theatrical troupe. In 1930, the Tsukiji Shō-gekijō was dissolved.

Tsukubashū 菟玖波集. A twenty-volume anthology of linked verse (RENGA) of the Namboku period (1336–92) compiled by the courtier Nijō Yoshimoto (1320–88) and Guzai (also pronounced Gusai or Guzei). It was the first anthology of linked verse and was collected by imperial command in 1357. Sōgi's (1421–1502) SHINSEN TSUKUBASHŪ and Yamazaki Sōkan's (1465–1553) *Inu Tsukubashū* were inspired by *Tsukubashū*.

tsukuda 佃 (land under direct administration of the landlord). Land directly administered by the landlord under the manor system. The meaning of *tsukuda* is *tsukurida* 作り田 or "land under cultivation." The landlord provided the farmers with tools and food and had them cultivate the land, but the whole crop belonged to the landlord. Some land stewards (JITŌ) used the same system and had the slave farmers (GENIN) cultivate the farmland. Other land stewards let out land on loan to the MYŌSHU and common farmers and levied the yearly taxes on them. In the farming season, *myōshu* and common farmers were forced to cultivate the *tsukuda*. During the Muromachi period, farmers became more independent, and the direct management of *tsukuda* declined.

Tsurezuregusa 徒然草. A collection of essays written by Yoshida Kenkō (1283–1350) during the Namboku period (1336–92). Kenkō incorporates in this volume the taste of the Heian nobility and the Buddhist feeling of evanescence, as well as the ideology of Lao Tzu and Chuang Tzu. The work, a masterpiece of essay literature, is ranked in the same class as MAKURA NO SŌSHI.

Tsuruga 敦賀. An important port in the Hokuriku district in Fukui Prefecture. In olden times it was called "Tsunuga." Contacts with the Gulf of Pechili (in Japanese, Bokkaiwan) during the Nara period were made from Tsuruga. During the middle ages, Tsuruga was an important place linking Kyōto with the northern provinces. Shipment agents (TOIMARU) made ENRYAKU-JI their base of operations. They took care of the shipment of manor products, and under them the harbor of Tsuruga flourished.

Tsurugaoka Hachiman-gū 鶴岡八幡宮. The name of a shrine in Kamakura. It is also known as "Kamakura Hachiman." It is the shrine where the clan god of the Minamoto family was worshiped. Minamoto no Yoshitsune's (1159–89) mistress Shizuka-gozen, after being taken captive by Minamoto no Yoritomo (1148–99), performed dances in front of the shrine. It was also in front of this shrine that the third Kamakura shōgun, Minamoto no Sanetomo (1192–1219), was assassinated by his nephew Kugyō (1201–19). Kugyō was the grandson of Minamoto no Yoritomo.

tsūshōshi 通商司 (trade office). A public office for trade established in the early Meiji era. In 1869, the office was set up for foreign trade in all open ports. In the same year, the trade office called SHŌHŌSHI disappeared when it merged with the *tsūshōshi*. From this time on, the *tsūshōshi* handled all domestic trade. It was abolished in 1871.

U

ubusuna-gami 産土神 (the tutelary deity). The original meaning of the word *ubusuna-gami* is "the god of the place of one's birth," but from the Edo period the name was used to indicate the clan god or the local deity. As protégés of the tutelary deity, people who were born in a village that worshiped the same *ubusuna-gami* were referred to as *ujiko*.

uchi-kowashi 打毀し (rioting). Food riots. During the Edo period, desperate townspeople rioted because poor harvests and famine caused a rise in prices of daily commodities. Large crowds of suffering townspeople attacked wealthy merchants, rice dealers, and sakè brewers, raided their shops and houses, and looted food and other possessions. Sometimes riots occurred in smaller towns and the rioters joined the farmers' uprisings. A typical example was the riot of 1733 in Edo. It was followed by three riots during the Temmei era (1781–89). The raid of 1787, at the end of a long famine (1782–86), spread from Edo to Kyōto, Ōsaka, Fushimi, and several other places. Likewise, the riot of the Tempō era (1830–44) spread to various places. The largest uprising was the one led by Ōshio Heihachirō (1796–1837) in 1837. In 1866, when the downfall of the shogunate was near, riots occurred in Edo and in the western provinces. They exposed the weakness of the shogunate and precipitated its collapse.

uchitsu-omi 内臣 (minister of the interior). An office of the imperial court in ancient Japan. The minister of the interior attended to the personal affairs of the sovereign, to the interior of the palace, and to important matters of administration. The office was above that of the ministers of the left and of the right *(saudaijin)*. At the time of the the Taika Reform (646), Nakatomi no Kamatari (614–69) was appointed minister of the interior, but after his death the chancellor of the Council of State *(dajō-daijin)*, holding the office of administrator, succeeded to this function. During the Nara period, the function of *naidaijin,* or *naishin,* was about the same as that of minister of the right or of the left, thus differing from that of the *uchitsu-omi.*

Uesugi uji 上杉氏 (the Uesugi family). An illustrious family of warriors. The Uesugi had their origin in the Kamakura period. Uesugi Noriaki (1306–68) served Ashikaga Takauji (1305–58) with great merit. He was appointed deputy *(shitsuji)* of the governor general of the Kantō district (KANTŌ KANREI). Becoming more powerful, the Uesugi feuded with the Ōgigayatsu, Yamanouchi, and other families. Uesugi Norizane (?–1466) turned against Ashikaga Mochiuji (1398–1439), the governor general of the Kantō district, in what is known as the Eikyō revolt (EIKYŌ NO RAN). The prestige of the rising Hōjō was threatened by the Uesugi. Uesugi Norimasa (1523–79) waged a losing battle with Hōjō Ujiyasu (1515–71). He then sought shelter with Nagao Kagetora (1530–78) of Echigo (Niigata Prefecture). Nagao succeeded Uesugi Norimasa as the head of the Uesugi family and changed his name to Uesugi Kenshin. His adopted son Kagekatsu (1555–1623) and Kagekatsu's descendants were the lords of Yonezawa in Dewa (Yamagata Prefecture). During the Edo period, the Uesugi were leading figures among the outside lords (TOZAMA DAIMYŌ). Uesugi Yōzan (Harunori, 1756–1822) was held in high esteem because he was a benevolent lord and wise administrator.

Ugetsu Monogatari 雨月物語. A literary work of the middle Edo period. The author is Ueda Akinari (1734–1809). It is the greatest masterpiece of the class of literature known as YOMIHON, or storybooks. The work was completed in 1768 and published in 1776. It is a collection of nine weird stories. The subject matter is borrowed from Japanese and Chinese classical works but is given substance by the author's knowledge and taste. The work is unique because of the excellent plotting and the graceful style. It profoundly influenced later writers of *yomihon*.

Uji-cha 宇治茶 (Uji tea). Uji is a town on the southern outskirts of Kyōto. It has always been cherished for its picturesque scenery and its celebrated temple, the BYŌDŌ-IN. The terraces around Uji are well suited for the cultivation of tea, and the town has been a tea-producing center since the Kamakura period. When the tea ceremony was introduced in the fifteenth century, Uji tea acquired fame. Its production was patronized by Nobunaga and Hideyoshi. During the Edo period, tea manufacturers were given the honor of being called *go-chashi*. They produced tea for the BAKUFU, the court, and the landlords and were placed under the control of the Kambayashi family. The *go-chashi* yearly presented the authorities with a certain amount of tea, for which they were rewarded, and their livelihood was guaranteed. In principle, this gift tea could not be sold on the market. After the Meiji Restoration, the *go-chashi* lost their privileges. At the same time, less privileged and often oppressed tea manufacturers started a revival movement. They were successful owing to the development of the method of preparing refined green tea. This green tea of superior quality was known as *gyokuro*. Export of Uji tea is behind that of Shizuoka tea, but Uji remains the traditional production center of superior tea for domestic consumption.

ujigami 氏神 (clan god). Clan god, guardian god, or tutelary local deity. Sometimes a god of one clan was adopted by a related clan. For instance, Amenokoyane no Mikoto was the deity of the Fujiwara family and was worshiped at the KASUGA-JINJA. Actually this deity was the alleged ancestor of the Nakatomi family, but Emperor Tenchi (626–71) gave the surname Fuji-wara to Nakatomi no Kamatari (614–69), the ancestor of the Fujiwara family. In ancient times it was an important duty to worship the clan god. Many warriors' corporations (BUSHIDAN) of the middle ages (Kamakura and Muromachi periods) adopted as their own clan god the god worshiped by landlords or a local guardian deity.

Ujishūi Monogatari 宇治拾遺物語. A literary work in fifteen volumes of the early Kamakura period. It belongs to the class of legendary tales. The author is unknown, but the work was published about the year 1215. In construction and content, the tales resemble those of KONJAKU MONOGATARI. The narratives are interwoven with Buddhist ideology. It is an outstanding collection of stories, and the literary merit of the work is highly prized. It also offers valuable information concerning contemporary society.

Uji-Yamada 宇治山田. A city in the southern part of Mie Prefecture. Amaterasu Ōmikami, the legendary ancestor of the imperial family, is worshiped in the Kō Daijingū shrine (or *naikū*) of Uji, and Toyoke Ōmikami, the god of the harvest, is worshiped in the Toyoke Daijingū (or *gekū*) of Yamada. From ancient times, Uji-Yamada was called "Shinto" (capital of the gods). As many pilgrims visited the shrines, shrine towns (MONZEN-MACHI) flourished. Previously, the shrines were granted estates for their subsistence, but during the Edo period a Yamada commissioner *(Yamada bugyō)* was appointed for their protection and reconstruction. In 1955, Uji-Yamada became Ise City.

Ukedokoro 請所. Another reading is *ukesho*. An office of the manor system during the Kamakura and Muromachi periods. The office was held by stewards (JITŌ), constables (SHUGO), or influential farmers who agreed to pay the owner of the manor a fixed amount of yearly taxes in return for the control and administration of the whole manor. Depending on the person who was entrusted with this control, the agreement was called *jitō-uke, shugo-uke,* or HYAKUSHŌ-UKE. In a manor thus controlled, entry was forbidden to other officials in the service of the owner. From the Namboku period (1336–92) the number of constables controlling manors increased considerably. Gradually the manors became the property of the constables, who administered the territory as well as the profits (ICHIEN CHIGYŌ). The situation led to the system of whole provinces being controlled and administered by constables *(shugo-ryōkoku-sei)*.

Ukigumo 浮雲. A literary work of the Meiji era, published in 1877. It was Futabatei Shimei's (1864–1909) first novel, the starting point of realism in modern Japanese literature, and the first novel to use a colloquial style. *Ukigumo* (translated as *The Floating Cloud*) is also the name of a post-World War II novel by Hayashi Fumiko.

Ukiyo-buro 浮世風呂. A masterpiece of realism and humor written in the late Edo period by Shikitei Samba (1776–1822). Using a bathhouse as the scene of the story, the author describes in a realistic and humorous way the life of unconventional and ignorant townspeople. The scene of the novel *Ukiyo-doko* by the same author is laid in a hairdresser's shop. The two works are Shikitei's best-known novels.

ukiyo-e 浮世絵 (genre paintings). Genre paintings and prints of the Edo period. Influenced by *genre* paintings of the Momoyama period (1573–1614), Hishikawa Moronobu (1618–94) developed the Edo *ukiyo-e*. During and after the Genroku era (1688–1704), the subject matter of the paintings was the gay life of the townspeople. As prints were made from wood blocks, the *ukiyo-e* were produced in large numbers and became very popular. Initially the prints were monochromes, but they developed into beautiful multicolored woodblock prints referred to as *nishiki-e*. The main artists of *ukiyo-e* were the painters of actors, Torii Kiyonobu (1664–1729) and Tōshūsai Sharaku (circa 1790); the painters of beautiful women, Suzuki Harunobu (1725–70), Kitagawa Utamaro (1753–1806), and Torii Kiyonaga (1752–1815); and the landscape painters, Katsushika Hokusai (1760–1849) and Andō Hiroshige (1797–1858).

ukiyo-zōshi 浮世草子 (genre literature). A class of novels of the middle Edo period, especially popular in the Kamigata or Kansai district. First, the books dealt with the life in the gay quarters and were called *kōshoku-mono;* later, they included samurai romances *(buke-mono),* "idle talk" novels *(zatsuwa-mono),* novels about townspeople *(chōnin-mono),* etc. The representative author of *ukiyo-zōshi* is Ihara Saikaku (1642–93).

unjō 運上 (miscellaneous tax). One of the Edo-period miscellaneous taxes. During the middle ages, when government property was shipped to Kyōto, taxes were to be paid to the government. The *unjō* tax derived from this custom. Occupations such as trade, industry, fishery, hunting, transportation, etc. were taxable. *Unjō* was a kind of license fee and was of the same nature as the miscellaneous tax called *myōga* (MYŌGA-KIN).

Untei 芸亭. A library founded during the late Nara period by the poet Isonokami no Yakatsugu (729–81), who converted his residence into a temple which he called Ashuku-ji. In one corner of the temple precincts, he built the library called Geten-no-in (*geten* means books other than Buddhist sutras), and opened it to the public. It is said to have been the first public library in Japan. Yakatsugu invited the most distinguished scholar of the time, Kaya no Toyotoshi (751–815), for the purpose of having him make an extended study of the books in the collection. From the ideological standpoint of the union of Confucianism and Buddhism, Yakatsugu aimed at mastering the true nature of Buddhism. The library flourished until about the Enryaku era (782–806) and fell into disuse from about the Tenchō era (824–34).

Uraga 浦賀. A harbor at the entrance of Tōkyō Bay at the southeastern extremity of the Miura Peninsula, Kanagawa Prefecture. From the middle ages (Kamakura and Muromachi periods), Uraga was an important port for maritime transportation. During the Edo period, a commissioner *(bugyō)* was appointed to Uraga. The place is well known as the harbor where Commodore Perry landed in 1853 and 1854 to negotiate the opening of relations between the United States and Japan.

uta-awase 歌合 (poetry tournament). A literary pastime consisting of dividing participating poets into two groups and requiring each poet to recite an original *waka* poem. A judge *(hanja)* would then compare the qualities of the reciters and their poems and decide the winning group. The game was most popular from the middle Heian to the early Kamakura period. It declined after the Muromachi period.

Utsubo Monogatari 宇津保物語. A tale in twenty volumes written between the years 970 and 990. The author is thought to have been either the poet Minamoto no Shitagō (911–83) or the poet Fujiwara no Tametoki (about the end of the tenth century). Tametoki was the father of Murasaki Shikibu (978–1016). The central character of the first part of *Utsubo Monogatari* is Nakatada. The moral excellence of music is extolled. The second part describes a courtship in the imperial palace. The characteristic features of the work are strong realism and vivid descriptions. The work deeply impressed later *monogatari* writers.

V

Versailles Jōyaku ヴェルサイユ条約 (the Treaty of Versailles). The treaty concluded after World War I, in 1919, between the Allied Powers and Germany. The Versailles Peace Conference, which was held by the major powers in the same year, and at which Japan sat as one of these powers, was based on the Fourteen Points formulated by President Wilson of the United States. It stressed self-determination of peoples. The conference solved the question of former German possessions. The Japanese delegation to the Versailles Peace Conference was headed by Saionji Kimmochi (1849–1940). Succession to Japan of the German rights in the Chinese Shantung district and the Japanese claim to Western Pacific islands north of the equator were recognized. This stirred Chinese anger and was the immediate cause of the Chinese incident of May 4, 1919 *(go-shi undō)*. Because of the arrangement with regard to Japan's rights in Shantung the treaty was not signed by China, nor was it ratified by the United States, and the matter was carried over to the Washington Conference of 1921–22. Although Japan became a member of the League of Nations, which was created by the Treaty of Versailles, she withdrew from it in 1933 after her conquest of Manchuria.

W

Wadō-kaihō 和銅開珎 (Wadō coins). The earliest Japanese silver and copper coins, minted during the Nara period. According to one report, the coins were cast in 708 (the first year of the Wadō era), but another holds that they were cast earlier. There exists also a discrepancy as to the reading *kaihō,* since some scholars believe that the correct reading is *kaichin.* The government at this time issued the regulation *chikusen-joi,* which means "to confer a rank in reward for saving money." The purpose was to encourage the use of coins.

waka-doshiyori 若年寄 (junior elders or assistant councilors of the shōgun). This is the name of an office of the EDO BAKUFU. The office was below that of RŌJŪ, or councilor of the shōgun. It was also known as *rokunin-shū* (six-man group) because, in 1633, six people were appointed *waka-doshiyori.* Ordinarily, three or four junior elders were elected from among the hereditary-vassalage daimyō *(fudai daimyō).* The function of the *waka-doshiyori,* who were alternated every month, was to supervise the bannermen (HATAMOTO) and to receive information from the censors (METSUKE). Later many *waka-doshiyori* became *rōjū.*

wake 別 (chief). One of the ancient titles (KABANE). Etymologically, the word probably means "head" or "chief." It has been thought that the title was conferred on a member of the imperial household after he had become a mere local official, but this is uncertain. It was a relatively ancient title, for it had already been abolished at the time of the change of titles under the reign of Emperor Temmu (622–86) (YAKUSA NO KABANE).

waki-ōkan 脇往還 (side roads). The roads other than the five highways of the Edo period. They were also known as *waki-kaidō.* Ise-ji, Mino-ji, Chūgoku-ji, Nagasaki-ji, and other roads carried a great deal of traffic on account of the alternate attendance of daimyō (SANKIN KŌTAI). The roads were already in use before Edo became the center of traffic. They were under the direct control not of the BAKUFU but of the finance administrator (KANJŌ BUGYŌ) and the commissioner of temples and shrines (JISHA BUGYŌ).

wakō 倭寇 (Japanese pirates). The general term given by the Chinese to the Japanese pirates who, from the fourteenth to the sixteenth century, raided the Korean and Chinese coasts. "Wa" is the ancient Chinese appellation for

Japan. From the end of the Kamakura period, pirates of the Inland Sea and merchants frequently sailed to the Chinese continent. As a result of trade disputes, the Japanese often raided the Chinese coast. One cause of the destruction of the Korean kingdom of Koryo (in Japanese, Kōrai) was the activities of Japanese pirates. General Yi Song-gye, who accomplished the downfall of Koryo and established the Yi dynasty, had earlier distinguished himself by repulsing the pirates. Ming China as well as Korea sent envoys to Japan demanding the suppression of piracy. Shōgun Ashikaga Yoshimitsu (1358–1408) succeeded in controlling the pirates and sent envoys to Ming China (KEMMINSHI) asking for trading privileges. The pirates were temporarily subdued, but about the middle of the sixteenth century, when the BAKUFU began to lose its control, they resumed their activities. When the Ming dynasty adopted an isolation policy, dissatisfied Chinese traders became pirates and were joined by Japanese pirates, whom they called *wakō*. The *wakō* were finally wiped out by Hideyoshi.

Wamyō Ruijushō 倭名類聚抄. The oldest classified Chinese-Japanese dictionary. It is sometimes called *Wamyōshō*. The dictionary was compiled by the *waka* poet Minamoto no Shitagō (911–83) by order of the daughter of Emperor Daigo (885–930). The work, completed about the year 935, is divided into 24 parts and 128 classes. Each Chinese word is followed by its pronunciation, meaning, and Japanese reading. From ancient times, there existed written copies in ten and in twenty volumes. The dictionary contains rich material for the study of ancient culture and language. The twenty-volume copies carry entries concerning provinces and rural districts, government offices, and yearly events. As this information is a later addition, the material should be used with caution.

Waōbu 倭王武 (Emperor Yūryaku). Appellation of Emperor Yūryaku (418–79) as mentioned in the Chinese standard histories. The memorial presented in 478 to Shun Ti (an emperor of the Liu Sung, one of the Six Dynasties, 220–589) by Waōbu is well known. It is mentioned in a commentary on Wakoku (Japan) in the *History of the Liu Sung Dynasty* (the Southern dynasty). Yūryaku's policy as formulated in the memorial was a mere continuation of a policy adopted from Emperor Nintoku (313–99). It consisted of trying to maintain Japanese control over the colony of MIMANA in the Korean state of Kōkuri and of trying to subdue Shiragi (in Korea) with the approval of the emperor of China. Yūryaku's plan was not endorsed by local farmers, who had to shoulder the burden of the Korean expeditions. Farmers and mighty clans such as the Kibi launched a movement against the court. Though the nation was suffering greatly, the emperor still planned to broaden the national structure. He set up independently the "three storehouses" (SANZŌ): the IMIKURA or palace storehouse, the *uchitsukura* or storehouse of personal belongings of the imperial household, and the ŌKURA or national treasury. He also established new departments. Japanese chronicles vividly portray Yūryaku as committing unspeakable atrocities, but the stories are probably fabricated.

wasan 和算 (Japanese mathematics). The Chinese system of mathematics had been introduced into Japan in early times, but during the Edo period (about 1600) Mōri Kambei (Mōri Shigeyoshi), who had studied in Ming China, and Mōri's pupil Yoshida Mitsuyoshi (1592–1672), who in 1641 published *Jinkōki*, rendered great service to Japan by spreading the knowledge of mathematics. The science was further developed by Shibukawa Shunkai (1639–1715) and Seki Takakazu (1642–1708). Seki was the founder of the Seki school of mathematics and discovered new mathematical principles. The Seki school declined after Western mathematics was introduced. Only the abacus has survived.

Waseda Daigaku 早稲田大学 (Waseda University). A private university in Tōkyō. The nucleus was Tōkyō College (Tōkyō Semmon Gakkō), established in 1882 by Ōkuma Shigenobu (1838–1922). Waseda University contributed greatly to the development of literary and political activities and to the solution of social problems.

Washington Kaigi ワシントン会議 (the Washington Conference). First international disarmament conference, held in Washington from 1921 to 1922. The chief Japanese delegate was Katō Tomosaburō (1861–1923). England, the United States, Japan, France, and Italy agreed to reduce their naval armaments to the ratio of 5:5:3:1.67:1.67. The agreement was kept for ten years. The Four-Power Agreement (YONKAKOKU JŌYAKU) was concluded for the security of the Pacific and the Nine-Power Treaty (KYŪKAKOKU JŌYAKU) for the solution of Chinese problems.

wayo 和与 (mutual understanding). Disputes between the owner of a manorial estate and land stewards (JITŌ) were not settled by a BAKUFU trial, but by mutual understanding. However, the stewards often did not fulfill the conditions of mutual consent and invaded the manor. The situation contributed to the decline of the manorial system.

Y

yabusame 流鏑馬 (equestrian archery). Shooting from horseback practiced during the Kamakura period. The arrows were shot while riding on a running horse. *Yabusame* already existed in the Heian period but became popular when the Kamakura warriors practiced it for the sake of mastering martial arts.

Yahata Seitetsu-sho 八幡製鉄所 (the Yahata Iron Works). A government-managed iron foundry established in 1897. It was the largest iron and steel factory of the nation and developed greatly during the Russo-Japanese War and World War I. In 1933, it became a private enterprise and adopted the name Japan Iron Manufacture (Nippon Seitetsu).

yakusa no kabane 八色の姓 (the eight titles). The official titles created in 684 by Emperor Temmu (622–86). They were *mahito, asomi, sukune, imiki, michinoshi, omi,* MURAJI, and INAGI. After the Jinshin civil war (JINSHIN NO RAN), the Yamato court expanded its political control and despotism. The creation of official titles had the same purpose. Ancient wealthy clans and clans which had sided with the court during the Jinshin revolt were granted titles lower than court titles. The highest of the titles, *mahito,* was conferred only on relatives of the emperor.

Yakushi-ji 薬師寺 (Yakushi Temple). One of the seven major temples of Nara (NANTO SHICHI-DAIJI) and the headquarters of the Hossō sect (HOSSŌ-SHŪ) of Buddhism. According to tradition, the temple was built in 680 by Emperor Temmu (622–86). With the transfer of the capital HEIJŌ-KYŌ, the temple was also moved. It has been laid waste several times by fires and earthquakes. The three-storied Tōtō is a representative structure of the Hakuhō cultural period (645–710).

Yalta Kaidan ヤルタ会談 (the Yalta Conference). During World War II (February 1945), Roosevelt, Churchill, and Stalin met in Yalta, a Crimean Republic seaport on the Black Sea. Plans were made for peace after the German surrender, and a secret arrangement was made to force Japan to cede the Kurile Islands and the southern part of Sakhalin to Soviet Russia.

Yamaguchi 山口. The capital of Yamaguchi Prefecture and, in earlier times, the flourishing castle town of the Ōuchi family (ŌUCHI UJI). The Ōuchi family made Yamaguchi into its stronghold and engaged in foreign trade with Ming China and Korea. Ōuchi ships had an identification mark issued by the Chinese authorities (KANGŌFU). The family derived huge profits from the overseas trade, and Yamaguchi flourished to the extent that it was called the "western capital" as opposed to Kyōto, the "eastern capital." Francis Xavier lived for a while in Yamaguchi and propagated Christianity there.

Yamatai-koku 邪馬台国 (the Yamatai kingdom). In the Chinese chronicles of the Wei dynasty (220–65) known as *Wei Chih Wo Jen Chuan,* Yamatai-koku is mentioned as being a powerful kingdom of the third century which controlled more than thirty territories. The woman ruler was Himiko, a queen who had devoted herself to magic. This Yamatai-koku had repeated intercourse with Korea and Wei China. It has not yet been established whether

Yamatai-koku was in Yamato (as the *Yamato-setsu* or "Yamato opinion" holds) or in Kyūshū (as the *Kyūshū-setsu* or "Kyūshū opinion" holds).

Yamato-e 大和絵 (Yamato painting). As opposed to *Kara-e* or Chinese-style painting, the *Yamato-e* is a style of painting which originated and developed in Japan. From the end of the ninth century, the *Yamato-e,* which mainly depicted scenery and customs, developed as a national style. About the early Kamakura period, the style and subject of the paintings changed. From the end of this period to the Muromachi period, the *Kara-e* school flourished. Following that, the Tosa school (TOSA-HA), which was opposed to *Kara-e,* restored the traditional *Yamato-e.* It was popular during the early Muromachi period but was surpassed by the Kanō school (KANŌ-HA) of Chinese style *(kanga).* Though the Tosa school became temporarily inactive, it was revived during the Edo period and flourished together with the Sumiyoshi school (SUMIYOSHI-HA). The *Yamato-e* style is mainly represented by the Tosa and Sumiyoshi schools.

Yamato no Aya no Atae 東漢直. The name given to the descendants of Achiki, who, during the fourth century, under the reign of Emperor Ōjin (circa 270–310), became a naturalized Japanese. According to tradition, Achiki came to Japan as a good-will envoy from the king of Kudara and became a naturalized Japanese. The son of Emperor Ōjin, Prince Uji no Waki-iratsuko, studied the sutras under Achiki, who invited the scholar Wani from Kudara. Achiki's descendants made their headquarters in Takechi County, Yamato Province, and were active in the economic and cultural fields. The *Yamato no aya uji* (AYABITO) belonged to the guild of scribes *(fubito-be)* and wrote chronicles at the court. Their title (KABANE) was *atae* (also pronounced *atai*). As Achiki's descendants became politically more influential, one of them, Yamato no Aya no Atai Tsuka, ranking with the territorial administrator (Ō-MURAJI) Ōtomo no Muroya, became a deeply trusted aide of Emperor Yūryaku (418–79).

Yamato-shiza 大和四座 (four theatrical troupes of Yamato). Theatrical troupes or schools of the Kamakura and Muromachi periods. During the Muromachi period, Kan'ami (1334–85) and his son Zeami (1363–1443), incorporating the best elements of SARUGAKU, a form of mimetic dance, and DENGAKU, the prototype of Nō (NŌGAKU), made Nō into a refined art. The four Yamato theatrical troupes excelled in the performance of Sarugaku and Nō and were patronized by the Kōfuku-ji. They were the Tobi, Yūsaki, Sakado, and Emmai troupes. Later they changed their names. The Tobi became Hōshō, the Yūsaki became Kanze, the Sakado became Kongō, and the Emmai became Komparu. Kan'ami and Zeami of the Kanze troupe were patronized by Shōgun Ashikaga Yoshimitsu (1358–1408), and Nō performances greatly improved. During the Edo period, Nō music became the official ceremonial music *(shikigaku)* of the warriors. A new school, the Kita school (Kita-ryū), founded by Kita Shichidayū (1582–1653), was added, and Nō was performed by five schools. Today's Nō has its origin in those schools.

Yayoi-shiki doki 弥生式土器 (Yayoi-type pottery). Pottery of primitive Japan. At the end of the rope-pattern period (JŌMON-SHIKI DOKI), a new culture was introduced from China, and agriculture made rapid progress. The new Yayoi pottery replaced the Jōmon pottery. The color of the new pottery was reddish brown, and its patterns were simple. As compared with the Jōmon pottery, Yayoi pottery shows less freedom of design, but its forms vary according to the use of the pottery. Technically, Yayoi pottery is superior. According to their form, Yayoi-type vessels belong to an early, middle, or late period. The Yayoi period lasted from about 350 B.C. to A.D. 250.

yō 庸 (labor tax payable in produce). One of the taxes in ancient Japan. The actual *yō* corvée, which consisted of ten days of labor a year, was payable in produce such as cloth, silk, rice, etc. The taxable males included those from twenty-one to sixty years of age *(shōchō)* and partly incapacitated men *(jichō)*. In 712, the tax became payable in currency (WADŌ-KAIHŌ). The labor tax, as well as the produce tax (CHŌ) and the miscellaneous corvées (ZATSUYŌ), was a heavy burden for the cultivators. It precipitated the collapse of the penal and administrative code system (RITSURYŌ-SEI).

Yodo 淀. A town situated in the center of the Yamashiro basin in Yamashiro Province (Kyōto Prefecture). It was the point of confluence of the Kamo, Katsura, Uji, and Kizu rivers. In ancient times, Yodo flourished because it was the place of disembarkment for tax rice from the manors. The rice came from several provinces and had to be shipped to Kyōto via Yodo. Trade vessels from the western provinces made transactions with their marine products and rice in Yodo, and shipment agents (TOIMARU) became prosperous. From the middle of the Muromachi period, as the fish market of Yodo developed, the town became a wholesale fish market. When Hideyoshi built his castle in Fushimi, Yodo tended to decline. In the Edo period, it became the castle town of the Inaba family. It was the stronghold of licensed vessels *(kasho-bune* or *kaso-bune)* which traveled from Kyōto to Ōsaka via Yodo. But, becoming the outport for Kyōto, the place lost its importance.

yōgaku 洋学 (Western learning). The study of Western sciences and Western countries during the Edo period. The study, which was also referred to as *namban-gaku,* was begun at the close of the Muromachi period. From the middle of the Edo period, Japanese scholars became more critical. *Rangaku,* or Dutch or Western learning, was encouraged by Shōgun Yoshimune (1684–1751). Western natural sciences were eagerly studied and deeply influenced discussions concerning the opening of the country and coastal defense at the end of the Tokugawa shogunate. The Siebold affair (Siebold was expelled from Japan because he obtained classified information from his pupils) and the oppression of scholars of Dutch learning (BANSHA NO GOKU) hurt the pioneers of *yōgaku*. However, the painstaking efforts of *rangakusha* (scholars of Western learning) led to the all-out introduction of Western civilization after the opening of ports.

yokoana-shiki sekishitsu 横穴式石室 (cave tombs). A form of tomb in ancient Japan which was rapidly adopted from the early sixth century. An excavation was made into the side of a hill or mountain and lined with stone, a single stone slab serving as the ceiling, and a stone coffin was placed inside. This method of burial was of Chinese origin. It replaced the "pit tombs" or *tateana-shiki sekishitsu*.

Yokosuka Zōsen-jo 横須賀造船所 (the Yokosuka Dockyard). A modern military industrial establishment. In 1864, the Tokugawa BAKUFU, with the aid of foreign engineers, opened an iron foundry. In 1868, the foundry became a government-operated naval dockyard.

yōkyoku 謡曲 (Nō librettos). The librettos of Nō dramas. The subject matter for a libretto was taken from ancient classical literature, described contemporary social conditions, or was imbued with Buddhist ideology. The diction was poetical, the atmosphere grave. The Nō libretto contrasts sharply with the farcical KYŌGEN libretto. Many librettos were written from the Muromachi to the Edo period. About 230 are extant. Those written by Kan'ami (1334–85) and his son Zeami (1363–1443) are the most numerous and the most beautiful. During the Muromachi period, four theatrical troupes or schools performed Nō (YAMATO-SHIZA). They were the Kanze, Hōshō, Komparu, and Kongō. During the Edo period, a new school, the Kita school (Kita-ryū), was added.

Yōmei-gaku 陽明学 (Wang Yang-ming Confucianism). Confucianism as advocated by Wang Yang-ming (in Japanese, Ō Yō-mei; 1472–1529) of the Chinese Ming dynasty. In Japan, the Confucianism of Wang Yang-ming, as well as that of Chu Hsi (in Japanese, Shu Ki; 1130–1200), was studied from the middle ages. Buddhist priests of the Five Zen Monasteries (GOZAN) led the study. Yōmei-gaku was made an independent branch of learning during the Edo period by Nakae Tōju (1608–48). Among Tōju's followers was Kumazawa Banzan (1619–91). After that, Yōmei-gaku was in official disfavor, and it languished. At the middle of the Edo period, it was revived under the stimulus of Miwa Shissai (1669–1744). Ōshio Heihachirō (1796–1837), remembered for his bravery in resisting the shogunate (UCHI-KOWASHI), belonged to the Miwa school of Confucianism.

yomihon 読本 (storybooks). A kind of novel of the Edo period. The word *yomihon* (books to read) is used in contrast to works of illustration only. In the early Edo period, many of these books were translations or adaptations of Chinese meditative novels. They were particularly popular in the Kamigata or Kansai district. The representative *yomihon* is Ueda Akinari's (1734–1809) UGETSU MONOGATARI. During the late Edo period, idealistic works extolling chivalry were numerous and popular, especially in Edo. Another representative work is Takizawa Bakin's (1767–1848) NANSŌ SATOMI HAKKENDEN.

yōnin 遙任 (administration by proxy). Under the penal and administrative code system (RITSURYŌ-SEI), the provincial administrator (KOKUSHI) had to attend to his official duties in the territory under his jurisdiction. But the official remained in Kyōto and had his duties performed by others *(kugai),* such as *mokudai,* etc. The practice was known as *yōju.* The seat of the provincial government office (KOKUGA) of the absent *kokushi* was called *rusu-dokoro.* The practice of *yōnin* had already existed during the Nara period but became quite common in the middle of the Heian period, especially when regents (SESSHŌ) and advisers to the emperor (KAMPAKU) attended to the affairs of state. As a result, local administration became confused.

Yonkakoku Jōyaku 四ケ国条約 (the Four-Power Treaty). In 1921, at the time of the Nine-Power Treaty (KYŪKAKOKU JŌYAKU), a treaty was concluded between Japan, England, the United States, and France. The treaty required the four powers to respect each other's possessions in the Pacific, stressed respect of rights in mandated territories, and disposed of various related problems. In cases of violation of established rights by other powers, the matter would be decided by negotiation. At the same time, the Anglo-Japanese Alliance of 1902 (NICHI-EI DŌMEI) was abolished.

Yōrō Ritsuryō 養老律令 (the Yōrō Code of Laws). A code of laws compiled during the Nara period. The code consists of twelve chapters of penal laws *(ritsu)* and thirty chapters of administrative laws *(ryō).* In compliance with the order of Empress Genshō (680–748), the code was compiled in 718 (second year of the Yōrō era) by Fujiwara no Fuhito (659–720). The Yōrō Code is a revision of the Taihō Code (TAIHŌ RITSURYŌ) and, up to the Meiji era, was considered fundamental law by the court.

Yoshida Shintō 吉田神道 (Yoshida Shintoism). This Shintō doctrine is also referred to as "Yuiitsu Shintō." In the middle of the Muromachi period, Yoshida Kanetomo (1435–1511) began to preach this form of Shintoism. Opposing the older doctrine based on the theory that Shintō gods were only manifestations of Buddhas and Bodhisattvas (HONCHI-SUIJAKU), Yoshida held that Shintoism was the foundation not only of Buddhism but also of Confucianism.

Yūai-kai 友愛会 (the Friendship Association). A socialist organization. The Yūai-kai was organized by Suzuki Bunji (1885–1946) in 1912. Suzuki, impressed by Christian humanism, aimed at raising the living standards of working people. He was strongly in favor of labor-capital cooperation. In 1919, his Yūai-kai became the General Labor Organization, and its name was changed to Nihon Sōdōmei Yūai-kai.

yūbin-seido 郵便制度 (postal system). Before the Taika Reform in 646, the relay-station system (EKI-SEI) was already in use. News was transmitted by means of relay horses *(temma)*. From about the Kamakura period, postmen (HIKYAKU) appeared, and during the Edo period both relay horses and postmen were used. Soon after the Meiji Restoration, an administrator of postal service *(ekitei-shi)* was appointed. Through the services of Maejima Hisoka (1835–1919), the government-managed postal service was organized. From 1871, postal letters and postage stamps were introduced on the Tōkaidō, and from there the modern postal system spread throughout the country. In 1877, Japan joined the International Postal Union. Foreign mail service and parcel-post service were introduced. The government post office underwent various modifications, but since 1947 the Ministry of Communications has been separated into the Ministry of Postal Services and the Ministry of Telecommunications.

yui 結 (joint labor). Joint interchange of labor. The word derives from *musubu* 結ぶ (to tie), and its origin is old. Sometimes the word was used for joint corvées of families with large tracts of land to cultivate, but usually it indicated the mutual help of small farmers. The planting of rice seedlings and the harvesting of the rice crop were called *yui,* but so were the roofing of houses and even women's hairdressing. In principle, *yui,* which was not rewarded, was done by relatives or members of the same clan, but other forms of *yui* existed as well. As the economy became more complex and specialized, *yui* declined. Fishing communities employed a form of cooperative production known as *moyai* in which many boats sailed out together for the common haul.

Yumedono 夢殿. A central hall in the eastern part of Hōryū-ji temple, situated in the town of Ikaruga, Nara Prefecture. The temple is built on the site of Prince Shōtoku's (573–621) palace called IKARUGA NO MIYA. Later, in 739, on the ruins of the palace, the monks of Hōryū-ji built the Yumedono, which is an octagonal hall. The main object of worship there is a statue of GUZE KANNON. The name Yumedono was given to the hall at a later time.

yūsoku-kojitsu 有職故実 (court and military practices and usages). From the Heian period, court politics, ceremonies, etc. became formalized custom. A knowledge of tradition concerning ancient court and military practices was therefore necessary. The poet Fujiwara no Kintō (966–1041) and the scholar

Ōe no Masafusa (1041–1111), who were well versed in ancient court practices and ceremonies, published books on the subject. When the influence of court nobles declined, ancient customs and manners were considered a thing of the past and divorced from actual life. From the Muromachi period, only military customs and manners were studied by the BAKUFU.

Z

za 座 (guilds). Craft or trade associations organized during the middle ages (Kamakura and Muromachi periods). The beginnings of the guilds go back to the late Heian period, but during the Muromachi period, when trade and economy had considerably developed, guilds became a dominant feature of the economy, especially in the provinces around the capital. Usually, guilds had their strongholds in the precincts of a temple or a shrine and placed themselves under the patronage of some powerful person. Instead of paying taxes and rendering services, they enjoyed many privileges. Among these privileges were the monopoly of stocking and selling goods, exemption from barrier taxes, tolls, market taxes, etc. The baldachin carriers' guild *(shifu-gayochō-za)* in the service of the court, the cotton clothiers' guild of the Gion Shrine *(Gion-sha no men-za)*, the yeast brewers' guild of the Kitano Shrine *(Kitano-jinja no kōji-za)*, etc. were well known. In Nara and vicinity, more than eighty guilds belonged to the Kōfuku-ji. They specialized in the production or transport of certain goods such as paper, vegetable oils, sakè, malt, *konnyaku* (a paste made from the starch of the devil's-tongue root), gelidium jelly *(tokoroten)*, etc. But when commodities increased and the economy expanded, the guilds' privileges hindered the development of free industry. Furthermore, the authority of such patrons as nobles, temples, and shrines began to decline. Nobunaga and Hideyoshi abolished market taxes and guilds (RAKUICHI-RAKUZA). Trade guilds, like ecclesiastical institutions, were deprived of their liberties. In addition to the trade guilds, troupes of dancers and musicians were organized into guilds, including those of SARUGAKU, NŌ-GAKU, and the YAMATO-SHIZA. There were also such guilds as the MIYA-ZA and the guilds of workers in the GINZA mints.

zaibatsu 財閥 (big financial combines). A form of enterprise. After the Meiji Restoration, Japanese combines were organized under the patronage of the government. They conducted financial business and managed military and other basic industries. In wartime and at a time of financial crisis, they invariably provided the necessary capital. Having special relations with the government, the *zaibatsu* turned an important segment of industry, the basis of which was war industry, into a business with political affiliations. Family partnership, based on a solid master-servant relationship as it existed in the feudal family system, was a dominant feature of the *zaibatsu*. After World War

II, the *zaibatsu* were dissolved by the Allied Powers, but they obviously tended to revive. According to their origin and development, the *zaibatsu* can be divided into four groups: 1) MITSUI and SUMITOMO, which developed from feudal commercial and industrial capital and from the lending of money at high interest; 2) MITSUBISHI, Shibusawa, and Yasuda, which, after the Meiji Restoration, controlled commerce and industry with monopolistic capital; 3) Ōkura and Furukawa, which, at the time of the Russo-Japanese War and World War I, enlarged their possessions on a speculative venture and acquired monopolistic capital; and 4) Nakajima, Noguchi, Ayukawa, and others, which, from the start of the Manchurian incident to the end of the Pacific War, exploited war industry and in a short time increased their holdings.

zaibatsu kaitai 財閥解体 (dissolution of the big financial combines). An administrative policy adopted by the Allied Powers after World War II. In November 1945, the Allied Powers issued an order to dissolve the ZAIBATSU. Consequently, the Japanese government established the Holding Company Liquidation Commission and dissolved the joint-stock corporations. Following the purge from public service, the former *zaibatsu* owners and directors of firms were removed and all monopolistic institutions dissolved. But in recent times the *zaibatsu* have shown signs of reviving.

zaigō-gunjin-kai 在郷軍人会 (association of reservists). A modern military organization. In 1910, the army united all local associations of reservists and established the Imperial Association of Reservists (Teikoku Zaigō-Gunjin-Kai), which was joined by the navy in 1914. The association was not a mere training center for ex-servicemen. Veteran soldiers were mobilized for militaristic propaganda and took an active part in the movement for "clarification of the fundamental concept of national polity" *(kokutai-meichō)*.

zambō-ritsu 讒謗律 (speech-control ordinance). A speech-control ordinance of the early Meiji era. It was promulgated in 1875 and aimed at suppressing the movement for democratic rights. Many editors of newspapers and magazines were thrown into prison, and the press law (SHIMBUNSHI JŌREI) was enforced. At the same time freedom of speech was controlled.

zampatsu-dattō rei 斬髪脱刀令 (ordinance prohibiting topknots and sword wearing). A policy of the early Meiji years. In 1871, the government promulgated the ordinance prohibiting topknots and sword wearing. The law was intended to abolish feudal social ranks and to promote Western customs.

zasso ketsudansho 雑訴決断所 (court of miscellaneous claims). A tribunal set up during the Kemmu Restoration (KEMMU NO CHŪKŌ). At the time of the Kemmu Restoration, Emperor Godaigo (1288–1339) established the office for important lawsuits called KIROKUSHO and the office for various claims or *zasso ketsudansho*. This latter office dealt with minor suits in connection with fiefs. When Ashikaga Takauji (1305–58) revolted, the tribunal, which had lasted only two years, was abolished.

zatsuyō 雑徭 (miscellaneous corvées). In ancient Japan, under the penal and administrative code system (RITSURYŌ-SEI), *zatsuyō* was the generic term for corvées other than the actual labor tax or YŌ. The maximum corvée tax, sixty days a year, was required from males between twenty-one and sixty years of age *(shōchō)*; half the amount from males between sixty and sixty-five or partly incapacitated males *(jichō)*; and one quarter from males between seventeen and twenty-one *(chūnan)*. According to the need, the corvées consisted of repairing dikes, constructing roads, building government temples, and bringing new land under cultivation. As a rule, corvées, including the labor tax *(yō)*, were imposed for about a hundred days a year. But the right of imposing corvées was abused by provincial governors (KOKUSHI) and rural district administrators (GUNJI). The government tried repeatedly to reduce the time of the corvées and to limit the corvée duties to the *shōchō*. From 734, miscellaneous corvée taxes were payable in currency. They were called *yō-bunsen, yōbun,* or *yōsen*.

zempō-kōen fun 前方後円墳 (burial mound). A distinctively Japanese form of burial mound. The mound is composed of a square and a circular part. This particular form of burial mound originated in the provinces around the capital (KINAI), was rapidly adopted in other parts of the country, and was used until the end of the ancient-tombs period. In the initial period (from the third to the fourth century), the mounds were made on the top of a mountain or a hill. The circular front was large, and the square rear was long, low, and flat. Examples are the burial mounds of Emperors Sujin and Keikō. In the main period (fifth century), the mounds were made on level ground. Both the front and the rear were large. Examples are the burial mounds of Emperors Ōjin and Nintoku. In the final period, the square front surpassed the circular rear in size, but the total size was smaller than that of previous mounds. Examples are the burial mounds of Emperors Seinei (444–84) and Bidatsu (538–85).

Zen-kunen no Eki 前九年の役 (the Early Nine Years War). The war of 1051–62 fought during the middle of the Heian period in Mutsu Province (Aomori Prefecture). The military commander in chief of the province, Abe no Yoritoki (?–1057), disregarded the orders of the provincial governor (KOKU-SHI). The court ordered Minamoto no Yoriyoshi (988–1075) and his son Yoshiie (1039–1106) to subdue Abe. At times the fighting was bitter. Abe was killed in 1057, but his son Abe no Sadatō (1019–62) resumed the battle. Yoriyoshi obtained the help of fresh troops from Dewa (Yamagata and Akita prefectures). These troops were sent by the governor, who was a member of the KIYOHARA family. Sadatō capitulated in 1062 at the Kuriyagawa stockade, and peace was restored. This marked the beginning of the Minamoto ascendancy in the eastern provinces.

Zen-shū 禅宗 (Zen sect of Buddhism). A sect of Buddhism. Zen Buddhism was introduced into China about the sixth century and reached Japan during the Kamakura period. Eisai (1141–1215) introduced Rinzai Zen, and Dōgen (1200–53) propagated Sōtō Zen. Zen was particularly popular among the warrior society and deeply influenced learning, philosophy, literature, and the arts.

zentaishugi 全体主義 (totalitarianism). A political philosophy of the Shōwa era. Disregarding personal liberty, each individual was to serve the state. Based on a totalitarian ideology, fascist dictatorship developed during the early Shōwa era. The Japanese army and the ultranationalists, following an aggressive policy, considered Japan in a state of national defense. Clinging to a totalitarian theory, they opposed political parties as well as the government policy. They condemned both liberalism and socialism, held that nationalism was the only national polity, and rejected international cooperation. Their theories led to the establishment of a militaristic organization by dictators who tried to justify their aggressive policy.

Zōhei-kyoku 造幣局 (the Mint Bureau). A government office for minting coins. In 1868, the government, trying to put public finances on solid ground and to safeguard a capitalistic economy, decided to mint new coins. It established a mint bureau in Ōsaka. The following year, an order was issued to mint new coins. The mint was completed in 1870, and new money was coined.

APPENDICES

1. Pre-Meiji Provinces and Modern Prefectures

Province		Prefecture	
Aki	安芸	Hiroshima	広島
Awa	安房	Chiba	千葉
Awa	阿波	Tokushima	徳島
Awaji	淡路	Ōsaka	大阪
Bingo	備後	Hiroshima	広島
Bitchū	備中	Okayama	岡山
Bizen	備前	Okayama	岡山
Bungo	豊後	Ōita	大分
Buzen	豊前	Fukuoka	福岡
		Ōita	大分
Chikugo	筑後	Fukuoka	福岡
Chikuzen	筑前	Fukuoka	福岡
Echigo	越後	Niigata	新潟
Echizen	越前	Fukui	福井
Etchū	越中	Toyama	富山
Harima	播磨	Hyōgo	兵庫
Hida	飛驒	Gifu	岐阜
Higo	肥後	Kumamoto	熊本
Hitachi	常陸	Ibaraki	茨城
Hizen	肥前	Saga	佐賀
		Nagasaki	長崎
Hōki	伯耆	Tottori	鳥取
Hyūga	日向	Miyazaki	宮崎
Iga	伊賀	Mie	三重
Iki	壱岐	Nagasaki	長崎
Inaba	因幡	Tottori	鳥取
Ise	伊勢	Mie	三重
Iwaki	磐城	Fukushima	福島
		Miyagi	宮城
Iwami	石見	Shimane	島根
Iwashiro	岩代	Fukushima	福島
Iyo	伊予	Ehime	愛媛
Izu	伊豆	Shizuoka	静岡
Izumi	和泉	Ōsaka	大阪
Izumo	出雲	Shimane	島根
Kaga	加賀	Ishikawa	石川
Kai	甲斐	Yamanashi	山梨
Kawachi	河内	Ōsaka	大阪
Kazusa	上総	Chiba	千葉
Kii	紀伊	Wakayama	和歌山
		Mie	三重
Kōzuke	上野	Gumma	群馬
Mikawa	三河	Aichi	愛知
Mimasaka	美作	Okayama	岡山
Mino	美濃	Gifu	岐阜
Musashi	武蔵	Saitama	埼玉
		Tōkyō	東京
		Kanagawa	神奈川
Mutsu	陸奥	Aomori	青森
		Iwate	岩手
		Akita	秋田
Nagato	長門	Yamaguchi	山口
Noto	能登	Ishikawa	石川
Oki	隠岐	Shimane	島根
Ōmi	近江	Shiga	滋賀
Ōsumi	大隅	Kagoshima	鹿児島
Owari	尾張	Aichi	愛知
Rikuchū	陸中	Iwate	岩手
Rikuzen	陸前	Miyagi	宮城
		Iwate	岩手
Sado	佐渡	Niigata	新潟
Sagami	相模	Kanagawa	神奈川
Sanuki	讃岐	Kagawa	香川
Satsuma	薩摩	Kagoshima	鹿児島
Settsu	摂津	Ōsaka	大阪
		Hyōgo	兵庫
Shima	志摩	Mie	三重
Shimōsa	下総	Chiba	千葉
		Ibaraki	茨城

Shimotsuke	下野	Tochigi	栃木	Tosa	土佐	Kōchi	高知
Shinano	信濃	Nagano	長野	Tōtōmi	遠江	Shizuoka	静岡
Suō	周防	Yamaguchi	山口	Tsushima	対島	Nagasaki	長崎
Suruga	駿河	Shizuoka	静岡	Ugo	羽後	Akita	秋田
Tajima	但馬	Hyōgo	兵庫	Uzen	羽前	Yamagata	山形
Tamba	丹波	Kyōto	京都	Wakasa	若狹	Fukui	福井
		Hyōgo	兵庫	Yamashiro	山城	Kyōto	京都
Tango	丹後	Kyōto	京都	Yamato	大和	Nara	奈良

2. Japanese Era Names and Dates

(N.D. refers to the Northern Dynasty)

An'ei	安永	1772–81	Chōshō	長承	1132–35
Angen	安元	1175–77	Chōtoku	長徳	995–99
Anna	安和	968–70	Chōwa	長和	1012–17
Ansei	安政	1854–60	Daidō	大同	806–10
Antei	安貞	1227–29	Daiei	大永	1521–28
Bummei	文明	1469–87	Daiji	大治	1126–31
Bumpō	文保	1317–19	Eichō	永長	1096–97
Bunchū	文中	1372–75	Eien	永延	987–89
Bun'ei	文永	1264–75	Eihō	永保	1081–84
Bunji	文治	1185–90	Eiji	永治	1141–42
Bunka	文化	1804–18	Eikan	永親	983–85
Bunki	文亀	1501–4	Eikyō	永享	1429–41
Bunkyū	文久	1861–64	Eikyū	永久	1113–18
Bunna (N.D.) 文和		1352–56	Eiman	永万	1165–66
Bunnan	文安	1444–49	Einin	永仁	1293–99
Bun'ō	文応	1260–61	Eiryaku	永暦	1160–61
Bunroku	文禄	1592–96	Eiroku	永禄	1558–70
Bunryaku	文暦	1234–35	Eishō	永承	1046–53
Bunsei	文政	1818–30	Eishō	永正	1504–21
Bunshō	文正	1466–67	Eiso	永祚	989–90
Chōgen	長元	1028–37	Eitoku (N.D.) 永徳		1381–84
Chōhō	長保	999–1004	Eiwa (N.D.) 永和		1375–79
Chōji	長治	1104–6	Embun (N.D.) 延文		1356–61
Chōkan	長寛	1163–65	Empō	延宝	1673–81
Chōkyō	長享	1487–89	Enchō	延長	923–31
Chōkyū	長久	1040–44	Engen	延元	1336–40
Chōroku	長禄	1457–60	Engi	延喜	901–23
Chōryaku	長暦	1037–40	Enkyō	延慶	1308–11

Enkyō 延享	1744–48
Enkyū 延久	1069–74
En'ō 延応	1239–40
Enryaku 延暦	782–806
Entoku 延徳	1489–92
Gembun 元文	1736–41
Genchū 元中	1384–92
Gen'ei 元永	1118–20
Genji 元治	1864–65
Genkei 元慶	877–85
Genki 元亀	1570–73
Genkō 元亨	1321–24
Genkō 元弘	1331–34
Genkyū 元久	1204–6
Genna 元和	1615–24
Gennin 元仁	1224–25
Gen'ō 元応	1319–21
Genroku 元禄	1688–1704
Genryaku 元暦	1184–85
Gentoku 元徳	1329–31
Hakuchi 白雉	650–55
Heiji 平治	1159–60
Hōan 保安	1120–24
Hōei 宝永	1704–11
Hōen 保延	1135–41
Hōgen 保元	1156–59
Hōji 宝治	1247–49
Hōki 宝亀	770–81
Hōreki (Hōryaku) 宝暦	1751–64
Hōtoku 宝徳	1449–52
Jian 治安	1021–24
Jingo-keiun 神護景雲	767–70
Jinki 神亀	724–29
Jiryaku 治暦	1065–69
Jishō 治承	1177–81
Jōei 貞永	1232–33
Jōgan 貞観	859–77
Jōgen 承元	1207–11
Jōgen 貞元	976–78
Jōhō 承保	1074–77
Jōji (N.D.) 貞治	1362–68
Jōkyō 貞享	1684–88
Jōkyū 承久	1219–22
Jōō 承応	1652–55

Jōō 貞応	1222–24
Jōtoku 承徳	1097–99
Jōwa (N.D.) 貞和	1345–50
Juei 寿永	1182–84
Kaei 嘉永	1848–54
Kagen 嘉元	1303–6
Kahō 嘉保	1094–96
Kakei (N.D.) 嘉慶	1387–89
Kakitsu 嘉吉	1441–44
Kambun 寛文	1661–73
Kampō 寛保	1741–44
Kampyō 寛平	889–98
Kan'ei 寛永	1624–44
Kan'en 寛延	1748–51
Kangen 寛元	1243–47
Kanji 寛治	1087–94
Kanki 寛喜	1229–32
Kankō 寛弘	1004–12
Kanna 寛和	985–87
Kannin 寛仁	1017–21
Kan'ō (N.D.) 観応	1350–52
Kansei 寛政	1789–1801
Kanshō 寛正	1460–66
Kantoku 寛徳	1044–46
Kaō 嘉応	1169–71
Karoku 嘉禄	1225–27
Karyaku 嘉暦	1326–29
Kashō (Kajō) 嘉承	1106–8
Kashō (Kajō) 嘉祥	848–51
Katei 嘉禎	1235–38
Keian 慶安	1648–52
Keichō 慶長	1596–1615
Keiō 慶応	1865–68
Keiun 慶雲	704–8
Kemmu 建武	1334–36
Kempō 建保	1213–19
Kenchō 建長	1249–56
Ken'ei 建永	1206–7
Kengen 乾元	1302–3
Kenji 建治	1275–78
Kenkyū 建久	1190–99
Kennin 建仁	1201–4
Kenryaku 建暦	1211–13
Kentoku 建徳	1370–72

Kōan 弘安	1278–88	
Kōan (N.D.) 康安	1361–62	
Kōchō 弘長	1261–64	
Kōei (N.D.) 康永	1342–45	
Kōgen 康元	1256–57	
Kōhei 康平	1058–65	
Kōhō 康保	964–68	
Kōji 康治	1142–44	
Kōji 弘治	1555–58	
Kōka 弘化	1844–48	
Kōkoku 興国	1340–46	
Kōnin 弘仁	810–24	
Kōō (N.D.) 弘応	1389–90	
Kōryaku (N.D.) 康暦	1379–81	
Kōshō 康正	1455–57	
Kōwa 康和	1099–1104	
Kōwa 弘和	1381–84	
Kyōhō 享保	1716–36	
Kyōroku 享禄	1528–32	
Kyōtoku 享徳	1452–55	
Kyōwa 享和	1801–4	
Kyūan 久安	1145–51	
Kyūju 久寿	1154–56	
Man'en 万延	1860–61	
Manji 万治	1658–61	
Manju 万寿	1024–28	
Meiji 明治	1868–1912	
Meiō 明応	1492–1501	
Meireki 明暦	1655–58	
Meitoku (N.D. till 1392) 明徳	1390–94	
Meiwa 明和	1764–72	
Nimpei 仁平	1151–54	
Nin'an 仁安	1166–69	
Ninji 仁治	1240–43	
Ninju 仁寿	851–54	
Ninna 仁和	885–89	
Ōan (N.D.) 応安	1368–75	
Ōchō 応長	1311–12	
Ōei 応永	1394–1428	
Ōhō 応保	1161–63	
Ōnin 応仁	1467–69	
Ōtoku 応徳	1084–87	
Ōwa 応和	961–64	
Reiki 霊亀	715–17	
Ryakunin 暦仁	1238–39	
Ryakuō (N.D.) 暦応	1338–42	
Saikō 斉衡	854–57	
Shitoku (N.D.) 至徳	1384–87	
Shōan 承安	1171–75	
Shōan 正安	1299–1302	
Shōchō 正長	1428–29	
Shōchū 正中	1324–26	
Shōgen 正元	1259–60	
Shōhei 承平	931–38	
Shōhei 正平	1346–70	
Shōhō 正保	1644–48	
Shōji 正治	1199–1201	
Shōka 正嘉	1257–59	
Shōkei (N.D.) 正慶	1332–33	
Shōō 正応	1288–93	
Shōryaku 正暦	990–95	
Shōryaku 承暦	1077–81	
Shōtai 昌泰	898–901	
Shōtoku 正徳	1711–16	
Shōwa 正和	1312–17	
Shōwa 承和	834–48	
Shōwa 昭和	1926–	
Shuchō 朱鳥	686–701	
Taihō 大宝	701–4	
Taika 大化	645–50	
Taishō 大正	1912–26	
Tembun (Temmon) 天文	1532–55	
Temmei 天明	1781–89	
Tempō 天保	1830–44	
Tempuku 天福	1233–44	
Tempyō 天平	729–49	
Tempyō-hōji 天平宝字	757–65	
Tempyō-jingo 天平神護	765–67	
Tempyō-kampō 天平感宝	749	
Tempyō-shōhō 天平勝宝	749–57	
Ten'an (Tennan) 天安	857–59	
Tenchō 天長	824–34	
Ten'ei 天永	1110–13	
Ten'en 天延	973–76	
Tengen 天元	978–83	

Tengi 天喜	1053–58	
Tengyō 天慶	938–47	
Tenji 天治	1124–26	
Tenju 天授	1375–81	
Tenna 天和	1681–84	
Tennin 天仁	1108–10	
Ten'ō 天応	781–82	
Tenroku 天禄	970–73	
Tenryaku 天暦	947–57	

Tenshō 天承	1131–32
Tenshō 天正	1573–92
Tentoku 天徳	957–61
Ten'yō 天養	1144–45
Tokuji 徳治	1306–8
Wadō 和銅	708–15
Yōrō 養老	717–24
Yōwa 養和	1181–82

SUBJECT INDEX

This index lists all the important terms appearing in the main text. In general, terms which are not dictionary entries are followed by their kanji, but the kanji for the entries themselves are not repeated from the main text. Page references in italic type indicate dictionary entries. Since a number of terms appear with great frequency throughout the book, only substantive references are given for these. The listing, like that of the main text, is in strict dictionary order, irrespective of the number of words involved in any given term.

A

Abe Iso-o 安部磯雄, 205, 251
Abe no Hirafu　阿倍比羅夫, 49
Abe no Nakamaro 阿倍仲麿, 137
Abe no Sadatō 安倍貞任, 316
Abe no Seimei 安倍晴明, 217
Abe no Yoritoki 安倍頼時, 316
Abutsu Ni 阿仏尼, 99
Achiki 阿直岐, 16, 309
achiki no fuhito 阿直岐史, 50
Achi no Omi 阿知使主, 16
agata-nushi, 11, 128, 254
agechi-rei 上地令, 286
agehama-shiki 揚浜式, 47
agemai, 11, 170
Agura-nabe, 11
Aikawa-machi 相川町, 236
Aikoku Kōtō, 11, 12, 183, 228
Aikoku-sha, 12, 151, 229
Aizawa Seishisai 会沢正志斎, 184
Aizu 会津 clan, 146, 257, 267; battle against, 20, 73
Aka-Ezo Fūsetsu-kō, 12, 231
Aka Fudō 赤不動, 159
akahata jiken 赤旗事件, 34
akahon 赤本, 138
Akamatsu 赤松, head of Samurai-dokoro, 189, 240, 262
Akamatsu 赤松 family
　Mitsusuke 満祐, 118

Norimura 則村, 57
　Sadamura 貞村, 118
Akasaka 赤坂 fortress, 57
Akechi Mitsuhide 明智光秀, 87
Akitsuki 秋月 revolt, 245
Akō 赤穂 salt manufacturing, 47
akunin-shōki 悪人正機, 107
Amako Yoshihisa 尼子義久, 187
Amakusa-bon Heike Monogatari 天草本 平家物語, 142
Amakusa Shirō 天草四郎, 255
Amami Ōshima 奄美大島, 234
Amaterasu Ōmikami 天照大神, 302
Amenohobi no Mikoto 天穂日命, 99
Amenokoyane no Mikoto 天児屋根命, 128, 301
Amida Nyorai 阿弥陀如来, 86
Amida 阿弥陀 Sutra, 210
Amidism, 48
amimoto-amiko, 12
Anaho-be 孔王部, 181
Andō Hiroshige 安藤広重, 303
Andō Nobumasa 安藤信正, 238
Anglo-Japanese Alliance, *see* Nichi-Ei Dōmei
Ankoku-ji, *12*
Anna no hen, 13
Anra 安羅, 199　　　　　　　　　「26
Ansei gokakoku jōyaku 安政五ヶ国条約,
Ansei no kari-jōyaku, 13, 26, 90, 115
Ansei no taigoku, 13

325

Anshan 鞍山, 13
An Ti 安帝, Chinese emperor, 63
Antoku 安徳, emperor, 50
Anzan seitetsu-jo, 13
aohon 青本, 138
Aoki Mokubei 青木木米, 168
Aoki Shūzō 青木周蔵, 110
Ara 安羅, 199
Arahaka-dera 荒陵寺, 262 ⌈246, 294
Arai Hakuseki 新井白石, 160, 170,
Arakida Moritake 荒木田守武, 71
Araragi-ha, *14*
Arihara 在原 family, 265
  Narihira 業平, 97, 229
  Yukihira 行平, 265
Arima Harunobu 有馬晴信, 289
Arima Shinshichi 有馬新七, 290
Arimatsu-shibori, *14*
Arishima Takeo 有島武郎, 243
Arita-yaki, *14, 251*
Asaka Tampaku 安積澹泊, 36
Asakura Toshikage Jūshichi Kajō
  朝倉敏景十七箇条, 23
Asakura 朝倉 war barons, 249
Asakura Yoshikage 朝倉義景, 128
Asano Nagamasa 浅野長政, 61
ashigaru, 14, 192
Ashikaga 足利 family, *15,* 93
  Masatomo 政知, 148
  Mitsukane 満兼, 212
  Mochiuji 持氏, 45, 126, 148, 301
  Motouji 基氏, 126
  Shigeuji 成氏, 118, 148
  Takauji 尊氏, 17, 35, 57, 76, 101,
    126, 133, 189, 194, 221, 230,
    271, 288, 316
  Yoshiaki 義昭, 15, 190
  Yoshikane 義兼, 109
  Yoshikatsu 義勝, 118 ⌈215
  Yoshimasa 義政, 15, 59, 79, 145,
  Yoshimi 義視, 88, 216
  Yoshimitsu 義満, 15, 45, 66, 67,
    133, 135, 140, 145, 180, 194,
    208, 212, 265, 306, 309

Yoshimochi 義持, 45, 133
Yoshinori 義教, 15, 45, 118, 133
Yoshitane 義稙, 55
Yoshiteru 義輝, 126
Yoshizumi 義純, 76
Ashikaga Gakkō, *14*
Ashikaga *uji, 15,* 93
Ashio dōzan, 15
Ashuku-ji 阿閦寺, 303
asomi 朝臣, 308
Asuka 飛鳥, 50
Asuka-dera 飛鳥寺, 85 ⌈280
Asuka Kiyomigahara Ryō, *15,* 215,
Asuka no Kiyomihara no Miya 飛鳥
  浄御原宮, 102
atai (atae) 直, 11, 262, 309
Awaji-ayatsuri 淡路操, 163 ⌈128
Awataguchi Yoshimitsu 粟田口吉光,
Awata no Mahito 粟田真人, 137,
  280
ayabito, 15, 34, 50, 77, 94, 129, 275,
Ayukawa 鮎川 *zaibatsu,* 315 ⌊309
Ayuthia (Ayutthaya), 200
aza 字, 188
azechi 按察使, 111
azekura-zukuri 校倉造, 269, 282
Azuchi, *16*
Azuchi-jō 安土城, 16
Azuchi-Momoyama bunka, 16
azukari-dokoro, 17, 91, 267
Azuma Kagami, 17

B

Baba Kochō 馬場孤蝶, 21
Bakan (Mahan) 馬韓, 241
Bakin, *see* Takizawa Bakin
bakufu, 17
bakuhan taisei, 18 ⌈47
Ban Dainagon Ekotoba 伴大納言絵詞,
Ban Nobutomo 伴信友, 153, 161
Ban no Kowamine 伴健岑, 270
Bansha no goku, 18, 269, 311
Bansho Torishirabesho, *18,* 116

bantō, *18*

banzai sōjō jiken 万歳騒擾事件, 31

bashaku, *19,* 41

bashaku-ikki 馬借一揆, 19

Bashō, *see* Matsuo Bashō

be, *19,* 135, 181, *295, 296*

beisatsu 米札, 75

Ben'en 弁円, 291

Benkan (Pyon-han) 弁韓, 241

be no tami 部民, *19,* 118, 135, 262, *277, 295*

Besshi dōzan, *19,* 278

bettō 別当: chief secretary of an ex-emperor's court, 95; chief of Samurai-dokoro, 119, 165, 175, 240; director of Shōgaku-in, 265

Bidatsu 敏達, emperor, 316

biwa hōshi, *20,* 69, 78

Bojutsu seihen 戊戌政変, 85

Boki Ekotoba 慕帰絵詞, 47 「299

Bokkaiwan 渤海湾 (Pechili Gulf),

bōko, *20,* 63

Bōnangen Shintō 望楠軒神道, 277

Bon odori, 26

Bōnotsu 坊津, 72

Borodin, Michael, 154

Boshin Sen'eki, *20,* 75, 138, 265

bugyōnin 奉行人, 93

bugyōsho 奉行所, 72, 178

buke-mono 武家物, 303

Buke Sho-Hatto, *20,* 36, 241

buke-zukuri, *20,* 266

bummai 分米, 196

bummei kaika, 21

Bummeiron no Gairyaku, 21

bunchi-seigen rei, 21

Bun'ei no eki 文永の役, 57

Bungakukai (Bungakkai), *21,* 230

Bungei Kyōkai, *22,* 55

Bungei Sensen 文芸戦線, 225

bunjin-ga 文人画, 254

Bunka-Bunsei jidai, 22

Bunka Shūreishū, *22,* 131

bunkoku, *22, 23*

bunkoku-hō, 23

Bunroku-Keichō no eki, *23,* 31

bunsen 分銭, 121, 196

Bunten 文展, 202

buntsuke, *see* bunzuke

bunzuke, *24,* 134, 193

bunzuke hyakushō 分付百姓, 24

buppin-kōnyū kō 物品購入講, 284

bushidan, *24,* 275, 290, 302

Buson, *see* Yosa Buson

bussan kaisho 物産会所, 155

bussan-kata 物産方, 155

bussokuseki 仏足石, 177

buyaku 夫役, 80, 86

Byakuren-kyō 白蓮教, 85

Byōdō-in, *24,* 81, 301

C

Cairo Sengen, *24*

Cambodia, *see* Kamboja

cha-nengu 茶年貢, 196

Ch'ang-an 長安, 77

Chang Hsüeh-liang 張学良, 234

Changkufeng 張鼓峰, 30

cha-no-yu, *25*

Chaya Shirojirō 茶屋四郎次郎, 272

Ch'en Shou 陳寿, 60

chi 智 (rank), 122

Chiang Kai-shek 蔣介石, *25,* 154

Chian-iji Hō, *25*

Chichibu jiken, *26,* 105

Chie no Naishi 智恵内子, 171

Ch'ien-tzu-wen 千字文, 129

chigai hōken, *26*

chigyō, *26,* 90

chigyōkoku-sei, *26*

chigyō-tori 知行取, 26

chihanji, *27,* 76

Chihaya 千早 fortress, 57

Chih I 智顗, 287

Chihōkan-kaigi 地方官会議, 58

Chijiwa Seizaemon (Don Miguel) 千々石清左衛門, 289 「門, 110

Chikamatsu Monzaemon 近松門左衛

chikusen-joi 畜銭叙位, 305

chimbata, 27

chin 賃 (tenancy rent), 27

Chin 晋 (Chinese dynasty, 265–420), 60

Chin 金 (Chinese dynasty, 1115–1234), 292

Ch'in 秦 (Chinese dynasty, 255–206 B.C.), 77

Chinhan 辰韓, 241

chinjufu 鎮守府, 99

chinjufu-shōgun 鎮守府将軍, 81

chinso, 27

Chinzei bugyō, 27, 119

Chinzei tandai 鎮西探題, 119

chinzō 頂相, 206

Chion-in, *28,* 107

chiri-komononari 散小物成, 157

chishi, 28, 113, 148, 190

chishisen, 28

chiso 地租, 196

chiso kaisei, 28

chitsuroku shobun, 28, 179, 296

chō (tax), *29,* 63, 68, 101, 210, 280

chō 町 (square measure), 91, 144, 146, 258

chōbu 町歩, 103, 158, 208

Chōgen 重源, 287

chōgin, 29, 175

chōhei rei, 29

Chōjū Giga, 29, 47, 162

Chōkohō jiken, 30

Chokugen 直言, 79

chokushahō 直煮法, 47

chokushi-den, 30, 53, 158

Chōnen *taihō* 長年大宝, 147

chōnin-mono 町人物, 303

Chōsen *(kindai), 30*

Chōsen *(kodai), 31*

Chōsen (Ri-shi), *31*

Chōsen sōtoku-fu, 32

chōshi, 32

Chōshū seibatsu, 32, 138

Chōsokabe 長曾我部 family, *32*

   Morichika 盛親, 32

   Motochika 元親, 32

Chōsokabe Motochika Hyakkajō 長曾我部元親百箇条, 23, 32

Chōsokabe *uji, 32*

Chōsokabe 長曾我部 war barons, 249

Choson 朝鮮, 226

Chūai 仲哀, emperor, 164

Chuang Tzu 荘子, 115, 299

chūbon 中本, 203

Chūgoku-ji 中国路, 305

Chūgū-ji 中宮寺, 288

Chu Hsi 朱熹, 111, 117, 124, 125, 149, 183, 273, 311

chūkōden 中功田, 148

Chūkō Kangen 中興鑑言, 183

chūnagon 中納言, 157

chūnan 中男, 29, 316

Ch'ungch'ing 重慶, 202, 257

Churchill, Winston, 25, 308

Chūson-ji, *33,* 81

Chu Tan-ch'i 朱丹渓, 120

Clark, William, 243

Confucius, 149

Contrat Social, 183

D

Dagelet Island, *see* Utsuryō-tō

Daian-ji 大安寺, 195, 242

dai-daikan 大代官, 35

Daidairi 大内裏, 77, 78

Daidō Danketsu undō, 33 226

Daidōkō 大同江 (Taedong River),

Daigaku, *33,* 146, 152, 191

Daigaku Nankō 大学南校, 115

daigaku no kami 大学頭, 266

daigaku rei, 34

Daigaku-ryō 大学寮, 33, 54, 191

Daigaku Tōkō 大学東校, 115

daigeki 大外記, 145

Daigo 醍醐, emperor, 34, 47, 151

Daigo-ji 醍醐寺, *34,* 111, 259

daigyaku jiken, 34

Daiichi Ginkō, *34*

Daiinkun 大院君, 30

Daikakuji-tō, 35, 57, 65, 101, 233
daikan, 35, 66, 68, 222, 258
Dai Kankoku 大韓国, 30, 32
daikansho 代官所, 99
Daikoku Jōze 大黒常是, 60
daimyō, 35, 65, 83, 104, 249, 294
daimyō-hikyaku 大名飛脚, 80
daimyō ryōgoku-sei 大名領国制, 41
dainagon 大納言, 38
Dainichi Nyorai 大日如来, 86, 259
Dainichi 大日 Sutra, 180
Dai Nihonshi, 36, 183
Dai Nippon Sangyō Hōkoku-kai, 36
Dai Nippon Teikoku Kempō, 37
Dairen 大連, 198, 202, 207, 225, 231
Daishōji 大聖寺 family, 168
daishōya 大庄屋, 188
dai-sukegō 代助郷, 278
Dai Tō-A Kyōeiken, 37
Daitoku-ji 大徳寺, 112, 228
Daizōkyō, 38
dajō-daijin 太政大臣, 38, 300
Dajōkan, 38, 125, 131, 155, 224;
  in Meiji times, 58, 61, 165, 246
dajōkan-satsu, 38
dakkatsu kanshitsu 脱活乾漆, 51
Da Nang (Tourane), 200
danjōdai 弾正台, 130
danna-dera 檀那寺, 273, 290
Dannoura, 39
Danrin-fū, 39
Danrin 談林 school, 39, 286
Danrin Toppyaku-in 談(壇)林十百韻, 39
Dan Takuma 団琢磨, 61, 137
Date Masamune 伊達正宗, 209
Date *tozama daimyō,* 298
Date war barons, 249
dazai 太宰, 199
Dazaifu, 39, 72, 142, 238
debata 出機, 27
dembata eidai baibai kinshi rei, 39
Dempō-in 伝法院, 196
denchō 田調, 29
Dengaku, 40, 209, 309

Dengaku Nō 田楽能, 40
denryō 田領, 185
Denshū-kan 伝習館, 75
dento (tato) 田塔, 74, 264, 285
Deshima, 40, 81
dōchū bugyō 道中奉行, 62
Dodge, Joseph M., 132
Dōgen 道元, 45, 48, 263, 276, 317
dogū, 40
dōhoko, 40, 42
doi, 41
do-ikki, 41, 55, 276
Doi Toshikatsu 土井利勝, 281
Dōjima 堂島, 42, 219
Dōjima kome ichiba, 42
dōken, 40
Dokuritsu-tō 独立党, 100, 220
Dōkyō Ichien 道鏡一円, 252
domin 土民, 41
Dōshin 道琛, 73
Dōshisha, 42
Dōshō 道昭, 89
dosō, 41, 42, 127, 167, 187, 238, 293
Dōsojin 道祖神, 160
dosō-yaku 土倉役, 167
dōtaku, 40, 42
dōza, 42
Dulles, John Foster, 281
Dutch learning, see *rangaku*

E

eboshi, 43
eboshi-ko 烏帽子子, 43
eboshi-oya 烏帽子親, 43
Echigoya, 43, 185
Echizen shimpan 越前親藩, 257
Edo *bakufu,* 17, 43
Edo Halma 江戸ハルマ, 76
Edo-machi bugyō, 44, 123
efu, 44, 46
egōshū, 44, 214, 237
eidaka, 44, 122
Eiga Monogatari, 45, 213

Eihei-ji, *45,* 276
Eikyō no ran, 45, 126, 148, 300
eiraku-sen 永楽銭, 45, 122
Eiraku tsūhō, 45, 122
Eisai 栄西, 25, 48, 135, 162, 228, 317
eji, 46, 68, 211
Ekan 慧灌, 242
ekiba-temma, 46
ekiden 駅田, 53
ekiko 駅戸, 46
Ekikyō 易経, 64
eki-sei, 46, 313
ekitei-shi 駅逓司, 313
emakimono, 46, 56
Emishi 蝦夷, 49
Emmai 円満井, 309
emman 円満, 48
emon 衛門, 44
emon-fu 衛門府, 46, 130
empon, 47
Enchin 円珍, 180, 216, 287
endenhō, 47
Engaku-ji, *see* Enkaku-ji
Engi-kyaku 延喜格, 169, 210, 232
Engi-shiki, *47,* 254
Engi *tsūhō* 延喜通宝, 147
engyō 円教, 48
Enichi 恵日, 120
Enji Ben'en 円爾弁円, 228
Enkaku-ji, *48,* 66, 106, 127, 135, 228
En-Mitsu-Zen-Kai 円密禅戒, 48
Enni 円爾, 291
Ennin 円仁, 106, 180, 216, 287
En no Ozunu (En no Ozuno, En no Shōkaku) 役小角, 189
Enoi no Muraji 榎井連, 187
Enomoto Takeaki 榎本武揚, 73
Enryaku-ji, *48,* 50, 65, 79, 146, 195, 216, 239, 275, 287
En Sei-gai 袁世凱, 154
enza 縁坐, 23, 130, 228
erizeni, 48
erizeni rei 撰銭令, 49
Eshin Sōzu 恵心僧都, 106, 213

Etō Shimpei 江藤新平, 11, 183, 236,
Exclusion Act (U.S., 1924), 71 ⌊245
Ezo, *49,* 83, 98, 99
ezo-mori 夷守, 238

F

Fan Yeh 范曄, 62
Formosa, 207
fubito, see *fuhito*
fubito-be 史部, 19, 309
fudai 譜代, 36, 193, 281, 305
fudasashi, 49, 141, 278
fudoki, 49
fueki-ryō 賦役令, 29
Fugi (Ch'ing emperor) 溥儀, 176
fuhito, 50
Fuji-kō 富士講, 170
Fujimoto Tesseki 藤本鉄石, 287
fuji-musume 藤娘, 223
fujin-sansei ken, 50
Fujita Tōko 藤田東湖, 184
Fujita Yūkoku 藤田幽谷, 184
Fujiwara-be 藤原部, 181
Fujiwara 藤原 family, 120, 302
  Akiko 彰子, 188
  Fuhito 不比等, 280, 312
  Fuyutsugu 冬嗣, 22, 122, 167
  Hidehira 秀衡, 81
  Hidesato 秀郷, 218, 287
  Hirotsugu 広嗣, 165
  Ietaka 家隆, 260
  Kamatari 鎌足, 215
  Kaneie 兼家, 114
  Kintō 公任, 313
  Kiyohira 清衡, 33
  Korefusa 伊房, 56
  Kuroaki 玄明, 287
  Kusuko 薬子, 168   ⌈248
  Michinaga 道長, 24, 45, 129, 213
  Michinori 通憲, 78   ⌈114
  Michitsuna no Haha 道綱の母,
  Motohira 基衡, 81
  Motonaga 元命, 224

Mototsune 基経, 120, 248
Motozane 基実, 64
Nakanari 仲成, 168
Nobuyori 信頼, 78
Nobuzane 信実, 206
Sadaie 定家, 260
Saneyori 実頼, 13
Sukemasa 佐理, 242
Sumitomo 純友, 287
Tadahira 忠平, 47
Tadamichi 忠通, 64, 82
Takaie 隆家, 292
Takanobu 隆信, 102, 206
Takayoshi 隆能, 56
Tametoki 為時, 304
Tokihira 時平, 47
Toshinari 俊成, 260
Tsunetsugu 常嗣, 233
Yasuhira 康衡, 81
Yorimichi 頼通, 24, 248
Yorinaga 頼長, 82
Yoshifusa 良房, 111, 248, 250, 269
Yoshitsune 良経, 260
Yukinari 行成, 212, 242, 250
Fujiwara-kyō, 50
Fūju shimpō 富寿神宝, 147
fuko (fugo) 封戸, 101
fukoku-kyōhei 富国強兵, 245
Fukuchi Gen'ichirō 福地源一郎, 286
Fukuhara, 50, 77, 89
Fukūkenjaku Kannon Zō, 51
Fukuoka Kōtei 福岡孝弟, 62
Fukuoka Sukemune 福岡助宗, 128
Fukushima jiken 51, 92, 105, 112
fuku-shōgun 副将軍, 68
Fukuzawa Yukichi 福沢諭吉, 21, 54,
    104, 116, 132, 179
fumie, 51, 142
fumihito 文人, 50
fumi no imiki 文忌寸, 129
fumi no obito 文首, 129
Fumon 普門, 196
Funai, 51
fune no fuhito 船史, 50

fune no osa 船長, 50
fune no tsukasa 船長, 50
Fun'ya no Yasuhide 文屋康秀, 229
funyū 不入, 144
furōnin, 51, 74   ⌈95
Furukawa Ichibei 古河市兵衛, 15,
Furukawa 古河 zaibatsu, 315
Fusen Jōyaku, 52
Fushimi 伏見, battle of, 265
Fushimi 伏見, emperor, 234
Fushimi-jō, 52   ⌈52
Fushimi-Momoyama-jō 伏見桃山城,
Fushun 撫順, 13
Fusō-kyō 扶桑教, 170
Futabatei Shimei 二葉亭四迷, 302
futomani, 52
Futon 蒲団, 263
futsū-senkyo undō, 52
fuyu 不輸, 144
fuyufunyū-ken, 53, 144
fuyu no jin 冬の陣, 221
fuyuso-den, 30, 53, 254

G

gagaku 雅楽, 236
gaikokusen uchiharai rei, 53, 108
Gakkan-in, 54
Gakkō 月光 (Bodhisattva), 51
gakkō rei, 54
gaku-be 楽戸, 295
Gakumon no Susume, 54
gakusei happu, 54
Gakushū-kan 学習館, 75
Gangō-ji 元興寺, 85, 195, 242
Ganjin 鑑真, 297
Gankō-ji, see Gangō-ji
Garakuta Bunko, 55, 137
geba-fuda 下馬札, 55
geba shōgun, 55
Geijutsu-za, 55
gekōden 下功田, 148
gekokujō, 55, 80
gekū 外宮, 302

Gembō 玄昉, 89, 137

Gemmei 元明, empress, 149

Gempei Seisuiki, 55, 69

Genchi 源智, 28

Gen'e 玄恵, 286

Geneva Conference (1927), 67

Genghis Khan, 57

genin, 56, 103, 186, 299

Genji Monogatari, 45, 56, 97, 153

Genji Monogatari Emaki, 47, 56

Genji no hen 元治の変, 73

Genkō (Mongol invasions), *57*

Genkō no hen (Genkō no ran), 57, 133, 138, 178, 194, 213, 217, 230, 264

Genkō Shakusho, 57

Genkū 源空, 48

Genna-ryō 元和令, 20

gen-Nihonjin, 58

genrō 元老, 74

Genrōin, *58,* 253

Genroku bunka, 58

Genroku jidai, 58

Genshin 源信, 106, 213

Genshō 元正, empress, 85, 312

Gentlemen's Agreement, 71

gesu, 58, 91, 144, 267

geten, 外典 303

Geten-no-in 外典の院, 303

gi 義 (rank), 122

gidayū-bushi, 義太夫節, 110

Gidō Shūshin 義堂周信, 67, 145

Gijō, 59, 221, 243, 276

Gijō-kan, 59

Gikeiki, 59, 69

gimu-kyōiku seido, 59

ginfukinin 銀吹人, 60

Ginkaku, *59,* 79

Ginkaku-ji 銀閣寺, 266

ginsatsu 銀札, 75

ginza, 60, 314

Gion-sha no men-za 祇園社の綿座, 314

Gishi 魏志, 60, 193

Gishi Wajin Den, 60, 63

gisō, 60

Giwa-dan (I Ho T'uan) 義和団, 85

gō 郷 (village), 63, 188, 228

Gobō no Keiji, *61*

go-bugyō, 61

Godaigo 後醍醐, emperor, 35, 57, 133, 142, 194, 213, 217, 234, 261, 263, 288, 315

Godai Kokūzō 五大虚空蔵, 102

Godai Tomoatsu 五代友厚, 84, 104

Gofukakusa 後深草, emperor, 35, 101, 233

Gofushimi 後伏見, emperor, 234

go-gyō 五行, 260

Gohōjō 後北条 (Odawara Hōjō), 83

goho-seido 五保制度, 228

go-ichigo jiken, 61, 182, 203

Goji-in 護持院, 268

Gojō Yorimoto 五条頼元, 143

go-kaidō, 61

Go-kajō no Seimon, 59, 61, *62,* 246

Gokameyama 後亀山, emperor, 194

Gokanjo, 59, 62, 193

Gokanjo Waden 後漢書倭伝, 62

Gokansho, see *Gokanjo*

goke-daoshi 後家倒, 248

go-kenin, 49, *63,* 76, 93, 141, 153, 180, 191, 212, 271, 275, 294

goki-shichidō 五畿七道, 139

gōko, 63, 74 ⌈194

Gokomatsu 後小松, emperor, 35, 36,

gokyō hakase, 64

gomomme-gin 五匁銀, 29

Gomurakami 後村上, emperor, 102

Gonijō 後二条, emperor, 234

gonin-gumi, 64, 66

Goryōkaku 五陵 (稜) 郭, 72, 179

Gosaga 後嵯峨, emperor, 234

Gosanjō 後三条, emperor, 95, 143, 265

go-sanke 御三家, 257

go-sankyō 御三卿, 257

Go-sannen no Eki, *64,* 81

Goseibai Shikimoku 御成敗式目, 107

go-sekke, 64, 250

gōshi 郷司 (village head), 153
gōshi (village samurai), 65
Goshirakawa 後白河, emperor, 50, 82, 94, 95, 164
go-shi undō 五・四運動, 304
Goshun, *see* Matsumura Goshun
gōso, 65, 79, 102, 128, 195, 275
gōson 郷村, 65
gōson-sei, 65, 264, 296
go-tairō, 66
Gotoba 後鳥羽, emperor, 95, 103, 109, 164, 190, 206, 213, 258, 260
Gotō Kichigorō 後藤吉五郎, 60
Gotō Mitsutsugu 後藤光次, 60
Gotō Shōjirō 後藤象二郎, 11, 33, 74, 183, 245
Gottan Funei 兀庵普寧, 106
Gouda 後宇多, emperor, 234
goyōbeya 御用部屋, 229
goyōkiki 御用聞, 167
Goyōzei 後陽成, emperor, 87, 112
Gozan, 48, 66, 106, 109, 135, 228, 273, 288, 291, 311
Gozan-ban, 66
Gozan-bungaku, 67, 145
Gukanshō, 67, 102
gumbi shukushō, 67
Gumma jiken, 67, 105
gun 郡, 155
gundai, 35, 66, 68, 86
gundan, 68, 157
gunji, 68, 153, 166, 244, 254, 280, 298, 316
gunkimono, 59, 69, 78
gunki-monogatari, 軍記物語, 78
Gunsho-ruijū, 69
Gunzan (Kunsan) 群山, 73
Guzai (Gusai) 救済, 299
Guze Kannon, 69, 86, 88, 313
Guzei, *see* Guzai
Gyōbu-shō, 38, 70, 130
gyokuro 玉露, 301
Gyōnen 凝然, 131
Gyōshin 行信, 92

H

habaka 波波迦, 52
Hachijō 八条 family
Toshihito 智仁, 129
Toshitada 智忠, 129
Hachikazuki-hime 鉢かずき姫, 222
Hachiman-gū 八幡宮, 102
Hachimanjin 八幡神, 86
Hachioka-dera 蜂岡寺, 159
Hagi no ran, 70, 245
haibun 俳文, 213
haibutsu kishaku, 70, 256
Haifū Yanagidaru 俳風柳樽, 250
haihan-chiken, 70
haikai, 71
haikai renga 俳諧連歌, 227
hai-Nichi undō, 71
Hai Sei-sei 裴世清, 137
haji-be 土師部, 277
Haji no Muraji 土師連, 188
Hakai 破戒, 263
Hakata, 72, 182
Hakodate, 72; battle of, 121, 179
Hakodate bugyō 函館奉行, 178
Hakone 箱根, 248
Hakuba-kai, 73
Hakuhō 白鳳 culture, 50, 308
Hakusonkō (Hakusukinoe) no tatakai, 73
Halma, François, 76
Hamabe no Kurohito 浜辺黒人, 171
Hamaguchi Osachi 浜口雄幸, 52, 67, 140, 182
Hamaguri-gomon no hen, 32, 73
hambatsu, 73
Hanawa Hokinoichi 塙保己一, 69
handen 班田, 158
handen nōmin, 27, 30, 74, 157, 229
hangaku, 74
hanishi no muraji 土師連, 75
haniwa, 75, 282
hanja 判者, 304
hankandai 判官代, 95
hankō, 74

Hannya-genki 般若験記, 200
hansai, see *hanzei*
hansatsu, 38, *75*
hanseki-hōkan, 70, *75,* 149
Han Shan-tʻung 韓山童, 85
Han Wu Ti 漢武帝, 226
Hanyehpʻing 漢冶萍, 202
hanzei, 76, 91
Hara-no-jō (Hara-no-shiro) 原城, 255
Hara Takashi 原敬, 74, 246
Haruma Wage, 76
Harunobu, *see* Suzuki Harunobu
Hasegawa Kakugyō 長谷川角行, 170
Hasegawa Tōhaku 長谷川等伯, 266
Hasekura Tsunenaga 支倉常長, 209
Hata-be 秦部, 77
Hata 秦 family, *77, 94,* 243
　　Kawakatsu 河勝, 77, 159
　　Sakenokimi 酒公, 77　　　　「252
Hatakeyama 畠山 family, 15, *76,* 124,
　　Masaie 正家, 216
　　Masanaga 正長, 76
　　Shigetada 重忠, 76
　　Yoshinari 義就, 76, 216
　　Yoshinobu 義宣, 84　　　　　「252
Hatakeyama 畠山 *kanrei,* 124, 189,
Hatakeyama *uji, 76*
hatamoto, 49, *63, 76,* 123, 125, 138,
　　141, 180, 214, 305
Hatano Yoshishige 波多野義重, 45
Hata *uji,* 77
Hatoyama Ichirō 鳩山一郎, 106
hayabito 隼人, 131
Hayama Yoshiki 葉山嘉樹, 225
Hayashi 林 family, 87
　　Baidō 梅桐, 87
　　Hōkō 鳳岡, 87, 266　　　「147, 265
　　Razan 羅山 (Dōshun 道春), 87,
　　Shunsai 春斎, 87, 147
Hayashi Shihei 林子平, 12, 115, 125
Hayato (Hayabito) 隼人 tribe, 164
Heguri 平群 clan, 187　　　　　「222
Heguri no Madori 平群真鳥, 217,

Heian-kyō, *77,* 122
Heiji Monogatari, 69, 77　　　　　「47
Heiji Monogatari Ekotoba 平治物語絵詞,
heijin 平塵 *(makie),* 174
Heiji no ran, 77　　　　　　　「207, 226
Heijō (Pʻyongyang) 平壤, 23, 198,
Heijō-kyō, 50, *78,* 85, 128, 168, 253,
Heike biwa 平家琵琶, 20　　　　　⌊308
Heike Monogatari, 20, 56, 69, *78,* 280
heikyoku 平曲, 20
heimin 平民, 256
Heimin-sha, *78*
Heimin Shimbun, 78, 199
Heizei 平成, emperor, 98, 168
Hiden-in 悲田院, 262
Hideyoshi, *see* Toyotomi Hideyoshi
Hieda no Are 稗田阿礼, 149
Hie-jinja, 65, *79*
higaki-kaisen, 79, 116, 202, 257, 285
Higashi Hongan-ji 東本願寺, 87
Higashiyama bunka, 79, 145
hi go-kenin 非御家人, 63　　　　「283
Higuchi Ichiyō 樋口一葉, 22, 230,
Hijikata Yoshi 土方与志, 298
hikan, 80, 193
Hikari 光, 79
Hikaru Genji 光源氏, 56
hikitsuke-shū, 80, 119, 189, 222, 255
hikitsuke-tōnin 引付頭人, 222
hikyaku, 80, 129, 313
Himegami 比売神, 128
Himiko 卑弥呼, 181, 308
hinin 非人, 256　　　　　「*Uta), 80*
Hinkyū-mondō Ka (Hinkyū-mondō no
Hino 日野 family
　　Suketomo 資朝, 57, 263
　　Toshimoto 俊基, 57, 194, 263
Hinokumatoneri-be 檜前舎人部, 181
Hirado, 72, *80*
Hiraizumi, 33, *81*
hira-makie 平蒔絵, 174
Hirano Kuniomi 平野国臣, 93
Hiranuma Kiichirō 平沼騏一郎, 172
Hirata Atsutane 平田篤胤, 153

Hirata Tokuboku 平田禿木, 21
Hiratsuka Raichō 平塚雷鳥, 246
Hiroshige, *see* Andō Hiroshige
Hirota Kōki 広田弘毅, 172
Hirozawa-ryū 広沢流, 259
Hishikawa Moronobu 菱川師宣, 303
History of Civilization in England, 204
hitogaeshi, 81
Hiunkaku, *81,* 112
Hizen 肥前 clan, 73
ho 歩 (linear measure), 274
hoan jōrei, 33, 53, 82
hoantai 保安隊, 100
Hoashi Banri 帆足万里, 173
hōe 法会, 106
Hōgen Monogatari, 69, 77, *82*
Hōgen no ran, 82, 177
hōji 保司, 153
Hōjō 北条 family, *83*
  Morotoki 師時, 106
  Munemasa 宗政, 106
  Sanetoki 実時, 121, 268
  Sōun 早雲, 83, 211
  Takatoki 高時, 83
  Tokifusa 時房, 227, 230
  Tokimasa 時政, 76, 83, 175
  Tokimune 時宗, 48, 57, 119
  Tokiyori 時頼, 80, 134, 250, 276
  Tokiyuki 時行, 189
  Ujinao 氏直, 211
  Ujiyasu 氏康, 126, 301   ⌈230
  Yasutoki 泰時, 90, 107, 119, 227,
Hōjōki, 82
Hōjō *uji:* family of Kamakura, 44,
  83, 227, 255; family of Odawara,
Hōjō 北条 war barons, 249 ⌊*83,* 211
hōken shakai seido, 83
Hōken Taiki 保建大記, 183
Hokkaidō kaitaku-shi, 83, 296
*Hokkaidō kaitaku-shi kambutsu-haraisage
  jiken, 84,* 104, 116
Hokke-ikki, 84   ⌈241, 248, 287
Hokke-kyō 法華経 (Lotus Sutra), 84,
Hokke-shū, *84,* 97

hōkō 奉公, 63
Hōkō-ji (in Asuka), *85*
Hōkō-ji 方広寺 (in Kyōto), 221
hokumen no bushi 北面の武士, 95, 190
Hokurei 北嶺 (Enryaku-ji), 275
Hokurikudō 北陸道, 253
Hokusai, *see* Katsushika Hokusai
Hoku-Shin jihen, 85
hombyakushō, 85, 186, 189, 219
Homma Ken'ichirō 本間憲一郎, 61
hompa-shiki chōhō, 86
Hon'ami Kōetsu 本阿弥光悦, 175
honchi-suijaku, 36, 97, 312
Honchō Hennen-roku 本朝編年録, 87
Honchō Tsugan, 87, 147
Honda Toshiaki 本田利明, 12   ⌈249
Hōnen 法然, 28, 48, 106, 107, 213,
Hōnen Shōnin Gyōjō Ekotoba 法然上人
Hongan-ji, *87, 92*   ⌊行状絵詞, 47
Hongan-ji 本願寺 branch of Shin-shū
hongi 本紀, 36   ⌊sect, 250
Honnō-ji no hen, 87
honryō-ando, 63, 88
honryōgae 本両替, 233
honsho 本所, 89, 91, 144, 182
honsō-gaku, 88
Hōōdō 鳳凰堂, 24
Hōrai-kyoku 蓬萊曲, 261
Horikoshi kubō 堀越公方, 149
hori no uchi 堀内, 41
Hōryū-ji, *88,* 195   ⌈king, 73
Hōshō (Pung Chang) 豊璋, Korean
Hōshō 宝生 Nō school, 209, 309, 311
Hosokawa 細川 family, 15, *88*
  Katsumoto 勝元, 76, 88, 215
  Masamoto 政元, 55
  Tadaoki 忠興, 88
  Tadatoshi 忠利, 89
  Yoriyuki 頼之, 180   ⌈150
  Yūsai (Fujitaka) 幽斎 (藤孝), 88,
Hosokawa 細川 *kanrei,* 124, 189
Hosokawa *uji, 88,* 271
Hossō-shū, 88, *89,* 131, 195, 308
hō-taikō 豊太閤, 281

Hotta Masatoshi 堀田正俊, 281 「193

Hou Han Shu (Gokanjo), 60, *62*, 124,

Hozumi Yatsuka 穂積八束, 288

Hsieh-ho Hui 協合会, 176

Hsing-chung Hui 興中会, 154

Hsinhai Koming 辛亥革命, 154

Hsü Ang 徐昂, 249

Hsüan-tsang 玄奘, 89

Huangmen 黄門, 157

Hui Ssu 慧思, 287

Hull, Cordell, 197

hyakushō-dai 百姓代, 86, 100

hyakushō-ikki, 41, *89*

hyakushō-uke, *89*, 302

hyō 表 (tables in *Dai Nihonshi*), 36

Hyōbu-shō 兵部省, 38

Hyōgo, *89*, 182, 244, 292

Hyōjōsho 評定所, 44, 164, 180

Hyōjō-shū, 80, *90*, 119, 189, 255

hyōrō-mai, 90

hyōtan-namazu 瓢箪鯰, 223

I

iaku jōsō-ken, *90*, 297

ichien chigyō, 26, *90*, 302

Ichijō 一条, emperor, 224

Ichijō 一条 (Fujiwara branch family), 64, 250

Ichikawa Sadanji 市川左団次, 104

ichizoku 一族, 24

iden, *91*, 148, 158

Ido-kokuō no in 委奴国王の印, 124

ie no ko, 24, *91*, 232, 275

Ieyasu, *see* Tokugawa Ieyasu

ifu 位封, 101   「247, 303

Ihara Saikaku 井原西鶴, 39, 199, 222,

Iida jiken, *91*, 105

Iida Takesato 飯田竹郷, 161 「門, 168

Iidaya Hachirōemon 飯田屋八郎右衛

Ii Naosuke 井伊直弼, 13, 238, 239,

Ikaiei (Weihaiwei), *92*   ⌊281

Ikaruga-dera 斑鳩寺, 92

Ikaruga no Miya, *92*, 313

ikebana 生花, 114

Ikedaya 池田屋 riot, 260

Ikenobō Senkei 池坊専慶, 80, 114

Iki-jima 壱岐島, 57, 142, 238, 292

ikkō-ikki, 84, *92*, 107, 121

Ikkō-shū, 84, *92*, 97, 101, 107, 142

ikoku keigoban, *92*

Ikuno ginzan, *93*

Ikuno no hen, *93*

Imagawa 今川 family, 15, *93*, 279

    Sadayo 貞世, 93

    Yoshimoto 義元, 93, 213

Imagawa-ke Kana-mokuroku 今川家

Imagawa *uji*, 93   ⌊仮名目録, 23

Imagawa 今川 war barons, 249

Imagire 今切, 248

Imakagami, *93*, 186

Imari-yaki 伊万里焼, 14

imayō, *94*, 201

imayō-awase 今様合, 94

Imibe (Imbe) 忌部 clan, 94

imiki 忌寸, 308

imikura, *94*, 214, 243, 306

Imna 任那, 31

imoji, *94*

in 院, 95

Inaba 稲葉 family, 310

inagi, *94*, 308

Inamura Sampaku 稲村三伯, 76

Ina Tadatsugu 伊奈忠次, 68

Ingen 隠元, 210

"Ingyōki" 允恭紀, 163

Innai ginzan, *94*

Innai Ginzan Ki 院内銀山記, 94

in no chō, *95*, 165

in no tsukasa, *95*

Inode 猪手 family, 63

Inō Jakusui 稲生若水, 88, 263   「137

Inoue Junnosuke 井上準之助, 61,

Inoue Kaoru 井上馨, 33, 110, 220

Inoue Kowashi 井上毅, 37, 75, 110

Inoue Nisshō 井上日昭, 137

Inoue Tetsujirō 井上哲次郎, 261

Inoue Yoshika 井上良馨, 150

insei, 27, *95*, 190
inshi, *95*
Inukai Tsuyoshi 犬養毅, 61, 116, ⌈136, 246
Inu Kubō, *95*
inu-ou-mono, *96*, 127
Inu Tsukubashū 犬菟玖波集, 299
inzen, *96*
Ippen 一遍, 103, 196
Ippen Shōnin Eden 一遍上人絵伝, 47
ippon 一品, 91
irefuda 入れ札, 189
iriai, *96*, 276
irihama 入浜, 47
irimoya-zukuri 入母屋造, 282
Isayama Fumitsugu 勇山文継, 234
Ise Heishi, *96*
Ise-ji 伊勢路, 305
Ise Monogatari, 56, *97*
Ise Nagauji 伊勢長氏, 83
Ise-shi 伊勢市, 302
Ise Shintō, *97*
Ishida Baigan 石田梅巌, 259
Ishida Mitsunari 石田三成, 61, 247
Ishidō Yoshifusa 石塔義房, 221
Ishigaki-jima 石垣島, 234
Ishii Kikujirō 石井菊次郎, 97
Ishii-Lansing Kyōtei, *97*, 242
Ishikawa Masamochi 石川雅望, 171
Ishiyama-dera Engi 石山寺縁起, 47
Ishiyama Hongan-ji, 87, 92, *97*, 101, ⌊219, 220
Isoho Monogatari, *98*, 142
Iso no Kami 石上, 186
Isonokami no Muraji 石上連, 187
Isonokami no Yakatsugu 石上宅嗣, 303
Isoppu Monogatari イソップ物語, 142
Issaikyō 一切経, 38
isse-ichigen, *98* ⌈189, 240, 262
Isshiki 一色, head of Samurai-dokoro, ⌊
Issun-bōshi 一寸法師, 222
Itagaki Taisuke 板垣退助, 11, 12, 74, 104, 105, 136, 183, 220, 228, 245
Itakura 板倉 family
   Katsushige 勝重, 103, 172

Shigemasa 重昌, 255
Shigemune 重宗, 172
Itō Hirobumi 伊藤博文, 30, 33, 37, 82, 135, 207, 220, 246, 251, 257, ⌊267, 289
Itō Jinsai 伊藤仁斎, 149
Itō Mancio 伊東満所, 289
Itō Miyoji 伊東巳代治, 37
Itō Sachio 伊藤左千夫, 14
itowappu 糸割符, 216, 236, 239 ⌈cio
Itō Yoshikata 伊東義賢, *see* Itō Man-
Iwafune no ki, 98
Iwai no hanran, *98*, 187
Iwainushi no Mikoto 伊波比主命, 128
Iwakura Tomomi 岩倉具視, 110, ⌊245
Iwami ginzan, 98
Iwasaki Yatarō 岩崎弥太郎, 184, ⌊206
Iyo 伊予, prince, 168
Izawa-jō, *99*, 279
Izawa Ranken 伊沢蘭軒, 161
Izayoi Nikki, *99*, 115
Izumi Kyōka 泉鏡花, 230
Izumiya 泉屋 (Sumitomo), 19, 278
Izumo no Okuni, *99*
Izumo Taisha, 16, *99*, 213

J

Jagatara-bumi, 99
Jibu-shō 治部省, 38, 295
jichō 次丁, 29, 310, 316
jidaimono 時代物, 251
Jidai-tō, *100*, 220
jiden 寺田, 53
Jidō-fukushi Hō, *100*
Jidō Kenshō 児童憲章, 100
jieitai, *100*
Jien 慈円, 67, 260
jiin hatto, *100*
jikata, *100*, 188
jikata-san'yaku 地方三役, *100*, 188
jikata-yakunin 地方役人, 100
jikifu, *101*
jikiso 直訴, see *hyakushō-ikki*
jikkan 十干, 217, 260

Jikkinshō, 101, 152
Jikkō-kyō 実行教, 170
Jimmin Bungaku 人民文学, 226
Jimmu 神武, emperor, 87, 150, 260
Jimmuki 神武紀, 260
Jimon-shū 時門宗, 216
Jimyōin-tō, 35, 65, *101,* 194, 233
jin 仁 (rank), 122
jinai-machi, 98, 101
Jingikan 神祇官, 38
Jingo-ji, *101,* 206
Jingo no hen 壬午の変, 100   ⌈250
Jingū 神功, empress, 36, 181, 241,
jingū-ji 神宮寺, 86
Jinkai-shū 塵芥集, 23
jinkō 沈香, 148
Jinkō *kaiho* 神功開宝, 147
Jinkōki 塵却記, 307
jinnin, 102, 128
Jinnō Shōtōki, 102
Jinshin no ran, 102, 222, 308
Jinshin 壬辰 wars, 31
jinushi tezukuri, 102   ⌈252
Jippensha Ikku 十返舎一九, 138, 151,
ji-samurai 地侍, 41, 165, 293
jisha bugyō, 103, 123, 174, 305
Jishō-ji 慈照寺, 59
Ji-shū, 92, *103,* 196
Jishū-kan 時習館, 75
Jisshū Enden 十州塩田, 47
jitō, 17, 24, 59, 63, 90, *103,* 119, 153,
   188, 190, 191, 235, 271, 299, 302,
Jitō 持統, empress, 50, 201   ⌊307
jitō-dai 地頭代, 35
jitō-uke 地頭請, 267, 302
Jitsugokyō, 104
Jiyū Gekijō, *104*
jiyū minken undō, 104
Jiyū no Ri, 105
Jiyū-tō, 104, *105*
jō 条 (avenue), 78
jō 掾 (magistrate), 155
jō 判官 (secretary), 238
Jōchi-ji, 66, *106*

Jōchō 定朝, 24
jōdai 城代, 219
jōden 乗田, 148
Jōdo-kyō, 106
Jōdo Shin-shū, 87, 92, *107,* 170, 196
Jōdo-shū, 28, 48, 103, 106, *107,* 131,
   178, 196, 213, 249
Jōei Shikimoku, 23, *107,* 119
Jōeki *shimpō* 饒益神宝, 147
Jōgan *eihō* 貞観永宝, 147
Jōgan-kyaku 貞観格, 169, 232
Jōgan-shiki 貞観式, 48, 254
jōgō, 107
Jōgū Shōtoku Taishi Hōō Teisetsu 上宮
   聖徳太子法王帝説, 288
Jōgyō-zammai 常行三昧, 106   ⌈54
jōi kekkō no dai-gōrei 攘夷決行の大号令,
jōi-ron, 108, 275
Jōjitsu-shū 成実宗, 195, 242
jōka-machi, 108, 134, 219
Jō Kō 徐昂, 249
jōkōden 上功田, 148
jō-komononari 定小物成, 157
Jōkyō-koyomi (Jōkyō-reki), 108, 249
Jōkyū no hen (Jōkyū no ran), 95, *107,*
   109, 119, 178, 213, 230, 233, 257
jōmen hō, 109, 132
Jōmon-shiki doki, 109, 310
Jōmyō-ji, 66, *109*
jōroku 定六, 80
jōruri, 16, *110,* 120, 163, 214, 252
Jō Sentarō 城泉太郎, 267
Josetsu 如拙, 145, 277
jō-sukegō 定助郷, 278   ⌈188
Jōtō Mon'in Akiko 上東門院彰子,
Jōwa no hen, see *Shōwa no hen*
jōyaku kaisei, 110
Juchen 女真, 292
Jufuku-ji 寿福寺, 66
jū-ichii 従一位, 91
Jūjūshinron 十住心論, 259
jukō, 111
Jukyō, 111
jūnin-gumi 十人組, 64, 255

jūnin-ryōgae 十人両替, 233
jūnishi 十二支, 217, 260
Junna 淳和, emperor, 98, 131, 269
junsatsu-shi, 111
Jurakudai, 82, *111*
Jūrakunotsu 十楽の津, 169
Jürched 女真, 292
jusangō 准三后, 111
jusangū 准三宮, 111
jūsan'ya 十三夜, 283
Jūshichijō no Kempō, *112*　　　┌116
Jūtei Kaitai Shinsho 重訂解体新書,

K

kabane, 11, 50, *112,* 123, 188, 211,
　　215, 217, 262, 295, 305
Kabayama jiken, 105, *112*
Kabuki, 16, *112,* 120, 141, 275
kabu-nakama, 49, *113,* 139, 191, 286
kabu-za 株座, 185
kachishi 加地子, 190
kachōmai, 113
Kada no Azumamaro 荷田春満, 153
Kadensho, 113
kadō, 113
kaemai, 114, 129
kaesu 返す, 174
kaezeni, 114, 129
kaezeni-ya 替銭屋, 114, 236
kafuchō-sei, 53, *114,* 130
kagami-tsukuri-be 鏡作部, 19
Kaga 加賀 uprisings, 92, 121
Kagerō Nikki, 114
kageyushi, 115, 233
kagura 神楽, 236
kahan no retsu 加判の列, 229
kahō 家法, 23　　　　・　　　┌216
Kaibara Ekiken 貝原益軒, 88, 209,
kaichin 開珎, 305
Kaichōon, 115
Kaidōki, 115, 293
Kaifūsō, 115
Kaihō Yūshō 海北友松, 266

kaikō, 115
kaikoku, 115
Kaikoku Heidan, 115, 125
kaikon 開墾, 258
Kainangi-sha 海南義社, 228
kairitsu 戒律, 48
Kaisei Gakkō, *115*
Kaiseijo, 18, 115, *116*
kaisen, 116, 202
Kaisen Shikimoku 回船式目, 116
Kaishin no shō 改新の詔, 280
Kaishin-tō, 105, *116*
kaisōsen 回送船, 116
Kaitai Shinsho, 116
Kaitenshishi 回天詩史, 184
Kaitoku-dō, *116*
Kai-tsūshō Kō, 117
kaizuka, 117
kaji, 117
kaji-kitō 加持祈禱, 106
kajiko 加地子, 239
Kajin no Kigū, 117, 245
kakeya, 117, 166, 167, 278
kakibe, 118
Kakitsu no hen, 118, 189　　　　┌47
Kako Genzai Inga-kyō 過去現在因果経,
Kakuban 覚鑁, 196, 259
Kakunyo 覚如, 87
Kakushin-ni 覚信尼, 87
Kamakura, *118*
Kamakura *bakufu,* 17, *118*
Kamakura Gozan 鎌倉五山, 48, 118
Kamukura Hachiman 鎌倉八幡, 299
Kamakura ōban-yaku 鎌倉大番役, 93
Kambara Ariaki 蒲原有明, 191
Kambayashi 上林 family, 301
Kamboja, *119*
Kamchatka, 231
kamekan, 119
kame-ura 亀卜, 52　　　　┌196, 233
Kameyama 亀山, emperor, 35, 101,
kami 長官 (principal ministry officer),
　　238
kami 守 (provincial governor), 155

kami-be 紙戸, 295

Kamigata 上方, 58, 303

Kamiya Jutei 神谷寿亭, 98 ⌈98

Kammu 桓武, emperor, 68, 77, 96,

Kammu Heishi 桓武平氏, 97

Kamo no Chōmei 鴨長明, 82 ⌈153

Kamo no Mabuchi 賀茂真淵, 150,

Kamo no Tadayuki 賀茂忠行, 217

Kamo no Yasunori 賀茂保憲, 217

kampaku, 13, 38, 52, 64, *120*, 221,

kampō igaku, 120 ⌊248, 281, 312

Kampyō *taihō* 寛平大宝, 147

Kanadehon Chūshingura, 120

Kanagaki Robun 仮名垣魯文, 11, 151

Kanagawa, *121*

Kanagawa Jōyaku, 72, *121,* 179, 257

Kan'ami 観阿弥, 113, 145, 167, 208,
   309, 311

Kanamori Sōwa 金森宗和, 273

Kanazawa, *121*

Kanazawa Bunko *121, 268*

kana-zōshi 仮名草子, 222

kandaka, 44, *121,* 134, 152

Kanda Naibu 神田乃武, 179

kanden 官田, 53, 158

kandō 勘当, 130

Kan'ei *tsūhō, 122*

Kaneko Kentarō 金子堅太郎, 37

Kanenaga 懐良, prince, 133, 138

kanga 漢画, 124, 309

Kangakuin, *122,* 265

K'angchow 抗州, 257

Kanginshū, 122, 162, 235

kangōfu, 122, 133, 212, 237, 308

K'ang Yu-wei 康有為, 85

kan'i jūnikai no sei, 122, 167

Kani Kōsen 蟹工船, 225

kanji 官寺, 66

kanjin 間人, 193

Kanjin Dengaku 勧進田楽, 40

kanjō bugyō, 43, 68, *123,* 174, 305

kanko, 123, 261

Kankō Ammō 漢高安茂, 64 ⌈分田, 53

kanko-kannuhi kubunden 官戸官奴婢口

Kankoku heigō, 123

Kan no Wa no Na no kokuō no kin'in,

kannushi 神主, 185 ⌊124

kanoe-saru 庚申, 160

Kanō 狩野 family
   Eitoku 永徳, 16, 124, 226, 266
   Masanobu 正信, 124, 277
   Motonobu 元信, 124, 277
   Sanraku 山楽, 16, 124, 266
   Tan'yū 探幽, 124

Kanō-ha, *124,* 279, 296, 309

kanrei, 55, 88, *124,* 189, 240, 252

Kansei igaku no kin, 124, 125, 266

Kansei no Kaikaku, 22, 77, *125*

kanshi 干支 (sexagenary cycle), 259,

kanshi 官司 (officials), 262 ⌊260

kanshitsu-zukuri 乾漆造, 51

kanshōfu-shō, 53, *125*

Kantō dai-shinsai, 125

Kantō Go-bunkoku 関東御分国, 27

Kantō kanrei, 119, *126,* 148, 189, 300

kan'yū no kunuhi 官有の公奴婢, 210

kan'yūchi-iriai 官有地入会, 96

kanzei jishuken, 126

kanzen-chōaku 勧善懲悪, 195

Kanze 観世 Nō school, 209, 309, 311

Kanzeon Bosatsu 観世音菩薩: Guze
   Kannon, 69; Kudara Kannon, 162

Kaō 可翁, 277

Kaoru Kimi 薫公, 56

Kara-e 唐絵, 309

Karafuto, *126* ⌈126

Karafuto-Chishima Kōkan Jōyaku,

Karai Senryū 柄井川柳, 250

Karak, 31 ⌈Jurakudai, 112

Karamon 唐門: at Fushimi-jō, 52; at

karamono 唐物, 296

Kara-yō, 48, *127,* 140

karei 家令, 132

kariya-bito 借家人, 284

Kariya Ekisai 狩谷棭斎, 161

karō, 127, 297

karoku, 127

kasagake, 127

Kasagi-yama 笠置山, *57*
kashiage, 127
Kashiwabara 橿原 palace, 260
Kashiwade-be 膳部, 181
kasho-bune (kaso-bune) 過書船, 310
Kasuga Gongen Reigenki 春日権現霊験
Kasuga-jinja, 65, *128,* 301   ⌐記, 47
Kasuga no Agata 春日県, 254
Kasuga no agata-nushi, 128
Kasuganochō 春日野町, 127
Kasuga-yama 春日山, 168
Kasuga-zukuri 春日造, 127
kata-gatae 方違, 217
katana-gari, 128, 134
katana-kaji, 128
Kataoka Kenkichi 片岡健吉, 104
Katayama Sen 片山潜, 199, 205,
Katayama Tetsu 片山哲, 205   ⌐251
Katō Hiroyuki 加藤弘之, 179
Katō Kagemasa 加藤景正, 251
katoku, 128
Katō Takaaki 加藤高明, 135, 136
Katō Tomosaburō 加藤友三郎, 307
Katsura 桂, prince, 129
Katsuragawa Hoshū 桂川甫周, 116
Katsuragi 葛城, 254
Katsuragi 葛城 family, 218
Katsura Rikyū, *129*
Katsura Tarō 桂太郎, 34, 135, 136
Katsushika Hokusai 葛飾北斎, 303
katte-kata 勝手方, 123
Kawachi no aya 西文, 94
Kawachi no aya uji (Kawachi no fumi uji), 16, *129,* 243
Kawachi no fubito-be 西史部, 16
Kawai Sora 河合曾良, 213
Kawajiri 川尻, 224
kawase, 114, 129
kawase-kata 為替方, 217
kawashi カワシ, 129
Kaya, 31
Kaya no Toyotoshi 賀陽豊年, 303
kazoku (nobility), *130,* 256
kazoku seido, 130

Kazunomiya 和宮, 146, 238
kebiishi, 44, 70, *130,* 172, 233
kebiishi-chō 検非違使庁, 130
Keenan, Joseph B., 172
Kegon-shū, 85, *130,* 195, 290
kehō 家抱, 193
Keian no o-furegaki, 131
keibitai 警備隊, 100
keichō, 131   ⌐221
Keichō to Genna no eki 慶長と元和の役,
Keichū 契沖, 153, 176
keigaku 経学, 152
Keihō-kan 刑法官, 70
Keihō Tokuhon 刑法読本, 283
Keika 恵果, 259
Keikai 景戒, 200
Keikō 景行, emperor, 316
Keikoku Bidan, 117, *131,* 245
Keikokushū, 22, *131*
Keiō Gijuku, *132,* 230
keishi, 132
Keishin-tō 敬神党, 258
Keishōin 桂昌院, 268
Keitai 継体, emperor, 98, 187
keizai-antei kyū-gensoku, 132
Kellogg-Briand Pact, 52, 67
kemi hō, 109, *132*
kemminshi, 133, 306
Kemmu no Chūkō, 35, 55, 57, *133,* 142, 189, 190, 194, 217, 264, 315
kenchi, 134
kenchi-chō, 134
Kenchō-ji, 48, 66, 118, *134,* 228
Kengen *taihō* 乾元大宝, 147
kenin, 135, 162, 261
Kenkei 賢璟, 189
kenkei 券契, 143
Kenkō, *see* Yoshida Kenkō
Kennin-ji, 66, *135,* 228
Kennyo 顕如, 87
Kensei-kai, 116, *135,* 136, 182
Kensei-tō, *135*
kensei-yōgo undō, 136
kentōshi, 136

Ken'yū-sha, 55, *137*

kenzuishi, 137

kesa-dasuki 袈裟襷, 42

kessho 闕所, 42

Ketsumei-dan jiken, 137

Khubilai, 57

ki 柵 (palisade), 49

Kibi 吉備 clan, 306

Kibi no Mabi 吉備真備, 137

kiboku 亀卜, 52

kibyōshi, 138

Kichijigoe 吉次越, 245

kidai 季題, 250

kiden 紀伝, 32

kidendō 紀伝道, 191 「220, 245

Kido Takayoshi 木戸孝允, 70, 74, 75,

kien-rei, 138

kiheitai, 32, 138

Kii 紀伊 clan, 257

kikō 奇口, 63

Kikuchi Takemitsu 菊池武光, 138

Kikuchi *uji, 138*

Kimbusen 金峯山, 270

kimi 君 (title), 11

Kim Il-sung (Kin Jissei) 金日成, 31

Kimmei 欽明, emperor, 50

Kimmon no hen 禁門の変, 73

kimoiri, 100, *139,* 164, 188

Kinai, 46, *139,* 316

kin-aratame yaku 金改役, 60

Kinchū narabi-ni Kuge Sho-Hatto, 139

kinhon'i-sei, 139

Kin Jissei, *see* Kim Il-sung

kin-kaikin, 139

Kinkaishū, 140

Kinkaku, 59, *140* 「生栄花夢, 138

Kinkin Sensei Eiga no Yume 金々先

Kinkō 錦江 (Kum River), 73

Kinoshita Naoe 木下尚江, 205

Ki no Tomonori 紀友則, 150

Ki no Tsurayuki 紀貫之, 150

kinsatsu 金札, 38, 75

kinseki-heiyō bunka, 140

kin'yū kinkyū-sochi rei, 140

kin'yū kyōkō, 141

kinza, 60, 210, 314

kireji 切字, 250

Kiri Hitoha, 141

kirimai, 26, *141*

kirimai-tori 切米取, 26

Kirishitan-ban, 141

Kirishitan-shū, *142*

Kirishitan yashiki キリシタン屋敷, 51

kiroku, 142

kirokusho, 133, *142,* 143, 315

kiroku shōen kenkeisho, 142, 143

Kiryū, *143,* 207

Kisen Hōshi 喜撰法師, 229

kishinchi-kei shōen, 143

Kishitsu Fukushin 鬼室福信, 73

kishōmon, 142, *144*

Kishū mikan, 144

Kitabatake Akinobu 北畠顕信, 221

Kitabatake Chikafusa 北畠親房, 102, 111

Kitagawa Utamaro 喜多川歌麿, 303

Kitaminato 北湊, 145 「261

Kitamura Tōkoku 北村透谷, 21, 230,

Kitano-jinja no kōji-za 北野神社の麹座,

Kita Nō school, *see* Kita-ryū 」314

Kitano Tenjin Engi 北野天神縁起, 47

Kita-ryū 喜多流, 310, 311

Kita Shichidayū 喜多七太夫, 310

Kitayama bunka, 140, *145*

Kiyohara 清原 family, *145,* 317

    Iehira 家衡, 64

    Natsuno 夏野, 145, 233

    Sanehira 真衡, 64

    Takehira 武衡, 64

    Takenori 武則, 145

    Yorinori 頼業, 145

Kiyohara *uji, 145* 「gahara Ryō

Kiyomigahara Ryō, *see* Asuka Kiyomi-

Kiyonaga, *see* Torii Kiyonaga

Kiyonobu, *see* Torii Kiyonobu

Kiyoura Keigo 清浦奎吾, 136

Kizoku-in, *145*

Kizu 木津, 19, 165

Kizuki Taisha 杵築大社, 99
ko 戸, 63
kō, 146, 160, 284
Kōan no eki 弘安の役, 57
koban (kobang), 60, *146*
kobang, see *koban*
Kobayashi Issa 小林一茶, 71
Kobayashi Takiji 小林多喜二, 225
Kōben 高弁, 131
Kōbō Daishi 弘法大師, 189
Kōbō Daishi Eden 弘法大師絵伝, 159
Kobori Enshū 小堀遠州, 129   ⌐294
Kōbu Bijutsu Gakkō 工部美術学校,
Kōbu Daigakkō 工部大学校, 294
kōbu-gattai ron, 146
Kōbun 弘文, emperor, 102
kobungaku-ha 古文学派, 149
Kōbun-in 弘文院: of Edo period, 265;
    of Heian period, *146*
Kōbun-kan, *147*
Kōbu-shō, 95, *147, 268*
kōchōgaku 皇朝学, 153
kōchō-jūnisen, 147, 276
Kō Daijingū 皇大神宮, 302
kodama 小玉, 283
kodama-gin 小玉銀, 175
kōden (merit field), *147*
kōden (public field), *148,* 157
kōdō, 148
kodōgaku 古道学, 153
Kōdō-kai 弘道会, 156   ⌐184
Kōdō-kan 弘道館 (Mito, Saga), 75,
Kōdō-kan 講道館 (Takamatsu), 75
Kōdōkanki 弘道館記, 184
Kōdōkan Kijutsugi 弘道館記述義, 184
Kōfu 甲府, 161
kōfu 功封, 101
Kōfuku-anzen-sha 幸福安全社, 11
Kōfuku-ji 興福寺, 65, 128, 195, 275,
Koga 古河, 118   ⌐309, 314
Koga kubō, 118, *148*
kogaku-ha, 149
Kōga no Miya 甲賀宮, 253
kogigaku-ha 古義学派, 149

Kogi Shingon 古義真言, 292
Kōgisho, *149,* 270
Kōgo nenjaku, 149
Kogoshūi 古語拾遺, 160
Koguryo 高句麗, 16, 31
Kōhō Kyōkai 広報協会, 176
koihō, see *kampō igaku*
Koikawa Harumachi 恋川春町, 138
Kojiki, 149, 150, 152, 160, 164, 244
Kojiki-den, 150
Kojima Hōshi 小島法師, 280
Kōjō-kan 興譲館, 75
Kōkaido-ō 広開土王, 162
Kōkai kaisen, 150
kokata 子方, 193
Kōkatō jiken, 150, 207
Koken Shiren 虎関師錬, 57, 67
Kokin-denju, 150
Kokin Wakashū, 150, *151*
kokka ankō 国家安康, 221
Kokkai Kisei-dōmei, *151*
Kokka Sōdōin Hō, *151*
kokkeibon, 151, 203
Kōkō 光孝, emperor, 36, 120
kōkokugaku 皇国学, 153
Kokon Chomonshū, 152
kokubun-ji, 152, 291
kokuchō 国庁, 152
kokudaka, 112, 133, 134, *152*
kokufu 国府, 152
kokuga, 152, 158, 274, 287, 312
kokugaku, 152
kokuga-ryō, 153
kokujin 国人, 165
Kokumin Chōyō Rei, *153*
Kokumin no Tomo, 154, 183, 200
Kokumin Shimbun 国民新聞, 183
Kokumin-tō, 136, *154*
koku-mori 石盛, 152
Kōkuri 高句麗, 16, 31, 226, 306
kokuritsu ginkō, 154
Kokusai Remmei, *154*
Kokusai Rengō, *155*
kokusan kaisho, 155

kokushi 国司 (governor general of Mimana), 199

kokushi (provincial administrator), 69, 143, *155,* 271, 278

kokusui-shugi, 156

kokutai-meichō 国体明徴, 315

Kōkyō 孝経, 191

komaichō 戸毎調, 29

Komaki 小牧, battle of, 196

komeba, 156

Kome Kubō, 156

Kōmei 孝明, emperor, 93, 287

kome sōdō, 34, *156*

komochi-takatsuki 子持高杯, 282

kōmon, 157

komononari, 157 ⌈309, 311

Komparu 今春 (金春) Nō school, 209,

Komparu Zenchiku 金春禅竹, 79

Komura Jutarō 小村寿太郎, 111, 199, 225

Komuro Shinobu 小室信夫, 183

Kōmyō 光明, emperor, 101, 189, 194

Kōmyō 光明, empress, 269

kondei, 157

kondei-den 健児田, 157

konden 墾田, 258

kondenchi-kei shōen, 157

konden-shiyū rei, 158

Kondō Isami 近藤勇, 260

Kongōbu-ji, *158*

Kongōchō 金剛頂 Sutra, 180

Kongō 金剛 Nō school, 209, 309, 311

Kongō Rikishi 金剛力士, 51

Kong Yang, *see* Kyōjō

Kōnin 弘仁 art period, 189

Kōnin-kyaku 弘仁格, 169, 232

Kōnin-shiki 弘仁式, 48, 254

Konjaku Monogatari, 159, 201, 302

Konji-in 金地院, 100, 103

Konjikidō 金色堂 at Chūson-ji, 33

Konjiki Yasha, 159

Konkō-kyō 金光教, 170

Konkōmyō-kyō 金光明経, 262

konnyaku 蒟蒻, 314

Konoe 近衛 (Fujiwara branch family), 64, 250

Konoe Ayamaro 近衛文麿, 197, 202, 281

Kōno Hironaka 河野広中, 12, 51, 104

Kōnoike Zen'emon 鴻池善右衛門, 118

Kōrai 高麗, 31, 57, 211, 241, 292, 306

Koremune Naomoto 惟宗直本, 233

Koryo, *see* Kōrai

kōryō 公領, 90

Kōryū-ji, 77, *159*

kosakuryō 小作料, 196

Kose 巨勢 family, 218

koseki, 131, *159*

Kose no Notari 巨勢野足, 167

kōshi (officials), *160*

kōshin-kō, 160

kōshin-machi 庚申待, 160 ⌈220, 289

Kōshin no ran (hen) 甲申の乱 (変), 100,

Koshi-tsū, 160

Kōshitsu Tempan, *160*

kōshōgaku, 160

kōshoku-mono 好色物, 303

kōshoku tsuihō, 161

Kōshū budō, 161

Kōshūkaidō 甲州街道, 62

kōso 貢租, 74

Kōtai 好太, king, 161

Kōtai-ō hi, 161

Kōtoku 孝徳, emperor, 280

Kōtoku Shūsui 幸徳秋水, 34, 78, 190,

kotsubu-gin 小粒銀, 175 ⌊205, 251

kouta, 122, *162*

kōwaka-mai 幸若舞, 168

Kōya-hijiri 高野聖, 158

Kōya-san 高野山, 158, 259, 293

Kōzan-ji, 30, *162*

Kōzengokoku-ron, 162

kōzoku 皇族, 130

Kuang Hsü 光緒, 85

Kuang Wu Ti 光武帝, 63

Kubota Utsubo 窪田空穂, 191

kubunden, 27, 123, 148, *162,* 274

Kudara 百済, 16, 31, 73, 129, 181, 199, 241, 309
Kudara Kannon, 88, *162*
kudatama, 163, 283
Kudō Heisuke 工藤平助, 12
Kudō Suketsune 工藤祐経, 274
kueiden 公営田, 158
kugai 公廨, 312
kugaiden 公廨田, 53
kugatachi, 163
kugoden 供御田, 165
kugutsu, 163
Kugyō 公暁, 299
Kuhara 久原 family, 248
Kujihongi 旧事本紀, 160
kuji-kata 公事方, 123
Kuji-kata O-sadamegaki, *163,* 170
Kujiki 旧事紀, 160   「64, 250
Kujō 九条 (Fujiwara branch family),
Kujō Kanezane 九条兼実, 64
Kujō Michiie 九条道家, 291
Kūkai 空海, 101, 132, 137, 158, 180, 239, 259, 270, 293
Kumano 熊野 (mountain), 270
Kumano-kō 熊野講, 164
Kumano mōde, 164
Kumano sanzan 熊野三山, 164
Kumaso, *164*
Kumazawa Banzan 熊沢蕃山, 311
Kume Keiichirō 久米桂一郎, 73
kumi 組, 188
kumiai-gashira 組合頭, 100, 164
kumi-gashira, 86, 100, *164,* 188
kumon, 164 「*164,* 175; of estate, 267
Kumonjo: of Kamakura *bakufu,* 119,
Kum River, *see* Kinkō
Kunai-chō, *see* Kunai-shō
Kunai-shō, *165,* 295
kuni-ikki, 165
Kunikida Doppo 国木田独歩, 230
Kuni-kyō, *165, 253*
kuni no miyatsuko, 11, 68, 99, *165,* 181
kunishū 国衆, 165
kuniyaku, 166

K'unming 昆明, 198
Kunsan, *see* Gunzan
ku-nuhi 公奴婢, 261
Kuon-ji 久遠寺, 182
kura bugyō 蔵奉行, 141
Kuramae 蔵前, 49, 141
Kuramae-fū 蔵前風, 49
kuramai 蔵米, 166
kuramai-tori 蔵米取, 26, 141
kuramono, 166
kuramoto, 166, 167, 278   「蔵人, 130
kurando (kurabito, kuraudo, kuroudo)
Kuratsukuri no Tasuna 鞍作多須奈,
Kuratsukuri no Tori, *166*   └167
Kuraudo-dokoro, *see* Kuroudo-dokoro
kurayaku, 167
kurayakunin 蔵役人, 167
kura-yashiki, 118, *167,* 219
Kurile Islands, 126, 232, 308
Kuriyagawa 厨川, 317
Kuriyama Sempō 栗山潜峰, 183
Kuroda 黒田 family, 72   「296
Kuroda Kiyotaka 黒田清隆, 83, 150,
Kuroda Kiyoteru 黒田清輝, 73
kurohon 黒本, 138
Kuroudo-dokoro, 38, *167,* 233
Kurozumi-kyō 黒住教, 170
Kurusu Saburō 来栖三郎, 197
Kusaka Gensui 久坂玄瑞, 267
kusazōshi 草双紙, 138
kusemai, 167
Kusha-shū 倶舎宗, 89, 195
kussō, 168
Kusuko no ran, 167, 168
Kusunoki Masashige 楠木正成, 57,
Kutani-yaki, 168   └133, 143, 194
Kuwana, *169*
Kuwana 桑名 clan, 73, 146
Kuwana-Sekigahara 桑名関ヶ原, 109
kuwa-yoboro, 169
Kūya 空也, 106, 196
Kuze Kannon 救世観音, 69
Kwantung Army, 176, 202, 234
kyaku, 169, 254

Kyōbu-shō, *169,* 256
Kyōgen, *169,* 244, 311
Kyōgoku 京極 family, 189, 240, 262
Kyōgōshinshō, 170, 284
kyōha Shintō, 170
Kyōhō no kaikaku, 156, *170*
Kyōiku Chokugo, *171*
Kyōiku Kihonhō, *171*
kyōiku rei 教育令, 55
Kyōjō (Kong Yang) 恭讓, Korean king, 31
kyōka, 171
kyōku 狂句, 250
Kyokutō Iin-kai, *171*
Kyokutō Kokusai Gunji Saiban, *171*
Kyōnyo 教如, 87
Kyōōgokoku-ji 教王護国寺, 292
kyōron 経論, 213
kyōshiki, 130, *172*
Kyōto Gozan 京都五山, 175, 196, 291
Kyōto ōban-yaku 京都大番役, 93
Kyōto shoshidai, 172, 173, 221
Kyōto shugo-shoku, 119, *172*
Kyōwa-kai 協和会, 176
kyūden 給田, 267
Kyūkakoku Jōyaku, *173,* 307, 312
kyūri 究理 (study of natural laws), 173
kyūri 久離 (severance of relations), 130
kyūrigaku, 173
Kyūritsū 究理通, 173
Kyūshū tandai, 27, 93, *138, 173,* 189
Kyūshū-setsu 九州説, 309

L

Lansing, Robert, 97
Lao Tzu 老子, 115, 299
Laxman, Adam, 231
League of Nations, 154, 305
Lee Sung-man 李承晩 (Syngman Rhee), 31
Liaoning 遼寧, 162
Liaotung 遼東 Peninsula, 198, 207, 240
Liaoyang 遼陽, 198
Li-Chu 李朱 medicinal art, 120

Li Hung-chang (Ri Kō-shō), 李鴻章, 207, 257, 289
Li Tung-t'an 李東坦, 120
Liu Sung 劉宗, 306 234
Liut'iaokou (Ryūjōkō) 柳条溝, 176, 16, 226
Lo-lang (Nangnang, Rakurō) 楽浪, London Kaigi, 137, *173,*
Lotus Sutra, see *Hokke-kyō* 229
Lukouch'iao (Rokōkyō) 芦溝橋, 202,
Lun Yü 論語, 129
Luzon, *see* Ruson

M

mabiki, 174 201, 205, 227, 281
MacArthur, Douglas, 132, 161, 172,
machibikyaku 町飛脚, 80
machi bugyō, 174, 219
machi-doshiyori 町年寄, 174, 297
machi-kata 町方, 100
machi-myōshu 町名主, 174
machi yakunin, 139, *174*
Maebara Issei 前原一誠, 70
Maeda 前田 family
  Toshiharu 利治, 168
  Toshiie 利家, 66, 121
Maeda Gen'i 前田玄以, 61
Maeda 前田 *tozama daimyō,* 298
Maejima Hisoka 前島密, 116, 313
maeku-zuke 前句付, 249
Maeno Ryōtaku 前野良沢, 116
magatama, 163, *174,* 283
Mahan, *see* Bakan
mahito 真人, 308
mai 舞, 161
makie, 174
Makura no Sōshi, 175, 299
mameita-gin, 29, *175*
Mamiya Rinzō 間宮林蔵, 126
Mampuku-ji 万福寺, 210
Manase Dōzan 曲真瀬道三, 120
Manchōhō 万朝報, 78
mandara 曼陀羅, 84 267
Mandokoro, 165, *175,* 189; of estate,

Manila, 200, 209
Manju-ji, 66, *175*
Manjūya Sōji 饅頭屋宗二, 150
Manju Zen-ji 万寿禅寺, 175
Mannen *tsūhō* 万年通宝, 147
Mansai 満済, 111
Manshū jihen, 72, 139, *175,* 176, 181, ⌐234, 315
Manshūkoku, *176*
Mantetsu 満鉄, 181
man'yo 万世, 177
man'yo 万葉, 177
Man'yō Daishōki, 176 ⌐238, 244
Man'yōshū, 80, 115, 140, 151, *177,*
mappō-jokuse 末法濁世, 106
mappō-shisō, 177
Maria Kannon, *178*
Maria Luz jiken, 178
Maruyama Ōkyo 円山応挙, 254
Masaoka Shiki 正岡子規, 14, 71
Masuda Nagamori 増田長盛, 61
Masuda Shirō 益田四郎, 255
Masukagami, 178, 186
Matsudaira 松平 family
　Katamori 容保, 73, 173
　Nobutsuna 信綱, 255 ⌐203
　Sadanobu 定信, 22, 125, 138, 199,
　Yasuhide 康英, 224
　Yoshinaga 慶永, 173
Matsui Sumako 松井須磨子, 22, 55
Matsukata Masayoshi 松方正義, 204
Matsukura Shigemasa 松倉重政, 255
Matsumae bugyō, 178
Matsumae 松前 family, 72, 126
Matsumae-machi 松前町, 72
Matsumoto Keidō 松本圭堂, 287
Matsumura Goshun 松村呉春, 254
Matsunaga Hisahide 松永久秀, 55
Matsunaga Teitoku 松永貞徳, 39, 71, 286
Matsuo Bashō 松尾芭蕉, 71, 213, 265
Matsushima Tsuyoshi 松島剛, 251
Matsuura 松浦 family, 81
Meihōki 冥報記, 200
Meiji 明治, emperor, 295

Meiji Ishin, *179*
Meirin-dō 明倫堂, 75
Meirin-kan 明倫館, 75
Meiroku-sha, *179*
Meiroku Zasshi 明六雑誌, 179
Meitoku no ran, 179, 212
Mencius, 149
metsuke, 180, 305
Mexico, 209
meyasu-bako, 170, *180*
Mibu-be 壬生部, 181
Mibu no Tadamine 壬生忠岑, 151
michinoshi 道師, 308
Michiyasu 道康, prince, 269
Mii-dera 三井寺, 216, 233
miki no tsukasa 造酒司, 295
Mikkyō, 48, *180,* 287
miko, 180, 213
mikoshi 御輿, 275
mikoshiro, 19, *181*
Mill, John Stuart, 105
Mimana, 31, 98, *181,* 199, 306
Mimbu-shō 民部省, 125 ⌐233
Minabuchi no Hirosada 南淵弘貞,
Minami-Manshū Tetsudō Kabushiki-
Minamoto 源 family ⌐gaisha, *181*
　Sanetomo 実朝, 109, 119, 140, 299
　Shitagō 順, 304, 306
　Takaakira 高明, 13
　Tametomo 為朝, 82
　Tameyoshi 為義, 82
　Tōru 融, 24
　Yoriie 頼家, 119
　Yorimasa 頼政, 50
　Yoritomo 頼朝, 17, 27, 64, 81, 90, 102, 103, 118, 164, 175, 186, 206, 240, 271, 298, 299
　Yoriyoshi 頼義, 316
　Yoshiie 義家, 15, 64, 316
　Yoshitomo 義朝, 77
　Yoshitsune 義経, 59, 69, 81, 90, 103, 271, 299
Minase-jingū 水無頼神宮, 206
minashiro, 19, *181*

Minatogawa 湊川, 194

minato-machi, 182

Minchō 明兆, 145, 277

Minobe Tatsukichi 美濃部達吉, 288

Minobu-san, 84, *182*

Mino-gami, *182, 230*

Mino-ji 美濃路, 305 ⌈282

Minsei-tō, 116, 135, 137, *182,* 246,

minsen-giin setsuritsu kempaku, 183

Minshu Jiyū-tō 民主自由党, 106

Min'yaku Yakuge, 183

Min'yū-sha, 154, *183,* 200

Min'yūsha-ha 民友社派, 102

Minzan-yaki 民山焼, 168

Miroku Bosatsu Hanka Zō 弥勒菩薩
半跏像, 159

misato no tsukasa 京職, 172 ⌈112

Mishima Michitsune 三島通庸, 51,

Misogi-kyō 禊教, 170

mita 屯田, 185

Mita bungaku 三田文学, 230

Mitake-kyō 御岳教, 170 ⌈*sanke,* 257

Mito 水戸 clan, 238, 239; and *go-*
Mito kōmon 水戸黄門, 157

Mito-gaku, 108, *183*

Mitsubishi 三菱 Company, 93, 135,
181, *184,* 206, 236, 278, 315

Mitsubishi Kisen Kaisha, *184*

Mitsubishi Shōkai 三菱商会, 184

Mitsui 三井 Company 137, 181, *184,*
185, 216, 255, 278, 315

Mitsui Dry Goods Stores, 43

Mitsui 三井 family
Takatoshi 高俊, 184
Takatoshi (Hachirōemon), 高利
(八郎右衛門) 43, 185

Mitsui Ginkō, *185*

Mitsukuri Rinshō 箕作麟祥, 179

Miwa 三輪 school of Confucianism,
Miwa Shissai 三輪執斎, 311 ⌊311

miyake, 50, 169, *185,* 279

Miyake Kanran 三宅観瀾, 183

Miyake Sekian 三宅石庵, 116

Miyake Setsurei 三宅雪嶺, 156, 199

Miyako-jima 宮古島, 234

Miyamotoya 宮本屋 pottery, 168

Miyanouchi Tsukasa 宮内司, 165

miyatsuko 造, 295

miya-za, 185, 219, 223, 314

Miyazaki Koshoshi 宮崎湖処子, 261

Miyazaki Yasusada 宮崎安貞, 209

Miyoshi Chōkei 三好長慶, 55, 269

Miyoshi Shōraku 三好松洛, 120

Miyoshi Yasunobu 三善康信, 186

mizu-chō 水帳 (御図帳), 134

Mizukagami, 185

mizunomi, 85, *186* ⌈186

mizunomi-byakushō 水呑百姓, 85, 86,

Mizuno Tadakuni 水野忠邦, 81, 113,

Mochihito-ō 以仁王, 216 ⌊286

mōdo, 186

modosu 戻す, 174

Mogami Tokunai 最上徳内, 126

mokudai 目代, 312

momikushi, 186

momme 匁, 175, 210

Mommu 文武, emperor, 50, 98

Momonoi Kōwakamaru 桃井幸若丸,

Momoyama-jō 桃山城, 52, 220 ⌊168

mon 文 (coin), 122

Monchūjo, 119, *186,* 189

Mongaku 文覚, 102

monjō 文章, 33

monjō hakase 文章博士, 145

monoimi 物忌み, 217

mononari 物成, 157 ⌈218, 222

Mononobe 物部 family, *186,* 215,
Arakahi (Arakabi) 麁鹿火, 98, 187
Moriya 守屋, 187, 275
Muraji 連, 188
Okoshi 尾輿, 187

Mononobe *uji, 186*

monzeki 門跡, 139

monzen-machi, 101, *187,* 219, 302

Mori Arinori 森有礼, 54, 179

Mōri 毛利 family, *187*
Motonari 元就, 187, 223
Terumoto 輝元, 66, 87, 187

Mōri Kambei (Shigeyoshi) 毛利勘兵衛 (重能), 307
Morinaga 護良, prince, 57, 133
Mōri 毛利 *tozama daimyō*, 298
Mōri *uji*, 187
Mōri 毛利 war barons, 249
Moronobu, *see* Hishikawa Moronobu
Morrison (ship), 18
Mōshi 毛詩, 191
Motoki Yoshihide 本木良英, 173
Moto-ori Norinaga 本居宣長, 150, 153
moyai (fishery cooperative), 313
Mugaku Sogen 無学祖元, 48, 228
mujin, 187
mujin-kō 無尽講, 146
Mujū 無住, 252
Mukden, 198
Muko 武庫, 89
munabetsu-sen, 188
Munenaga 宗良, prince, 261
mu-ninen uchiharai rei 無二念打払令, 53
mura-doshiyori 村年寄, 297 ⌈ 295, 308
muraji, 11, 112, 186, *188*, 211, 215, 262,
Murakami 村上, emperor, 34
murakata san'yaku 村方三役, 188
murakata yakunin 村方役人, 188
Murasaki Shikibu 紫式部, 56, 188,
Murasaki Shikibu Nikki, 188 ⌊304
Muraviev, count, 231 ⌈297
mura yakunin, 86, 139, 174, *188*, 219,
Murayama Sōbei 村山宗兵衛, 94
mura-za 村座, 185
mure-aruji 群主, 188
Murō-ji, *189*
Muromachi *bakufu*, 17, *189*
museifu-shugi, 190
musha-dokoro, 133, *190*
Musō Soseki 夢窓疎石, 12, 228, 288
Mutsu 陸奥 (Fujiwara branch family),
Mutsu Munemitsu 陸奥宗光, 110 ⌊33
Mutsu rusu-shoku 陸奥留守職, 119
myōbō 明法, 33
Myōchin, *190*
myōden, 35, 153, *190*, 191, 239, 285

Myōe 明恵, 131, 162
myōga 冥加, 303
myōga-kin, 113, *190*, 303
myōgyō 明経, 33
myōhōdō, 191
Myōjō 明星, 191
Myōjō-ha, 191
myōkyōdō (myōgyōdō), 191
Myōshin-ji 妙心寺, 228
myōshu, 56, 74, 127, 143, 190, *191*, 264, 285, 299
myōshu-shiki 名主職, 191

N

Nabeshima 鍋島 clan, 235
Nabeshima Naoshige 鍋島直茂, 14
Nada 灘, 285
Nagai Kafū 永井荷風, 230
Nagakute 長久手, battle of, 196
Nagao Kagetora 長尾景虎, 301
Nagaoka-kyō 長岡京, 77
Nagasaki, *192*
Nagasaki bugyō, 192
Nagasaki-ji 長崎路, 305
Nagasaki kaisho 長崎会所, 192
Nagashino no tatakai, 14, 192, 284
Nagasunehiko 長髄彦, 260
Nagatsuka Masaie 長束正家, 61
nagauta 長唄, 252
nageire 投入れ, 114
nago, 65, 80, 186, *192*
naidaijin 内大臣, 300
naikū 内宮, 302
naishin 内臣, 218, 300
naka-doshiyori 中年寄, 297 ⌈298
Nakae Chōmin 中江兆民, 104, 183,
Nakae Tōju 中江藤樹, 311
Nakagawa Jun'an 中川淳庵, 116
Nakai Chikuzan 中井竹山, 117
Nakajima 中島 Company, 315 ⌈179
Nakamura Keiu 中村敬宇, 104, 105,
Nakamura Masanao 中村正直, 237
Nakanoōe no Ōji 中大兄皇子, 280

Nakano Shigeharu 中野重治, 226
Nakasendō 中山道, 62
Nakatomi-be 中臣部, 19
Nakatomi 中臣 clan, 102, 302
Nakatomi no Kamatari, 中臣鎌足, 280, 300, 302
Nakatomi no Muraji 中臣連, 188
Nakatsukasa-shō 中務省, 38, 295
Nakayama Shin 中山信, 69
Nakayama Tadachika 中山忠親, 185
Nakayama Tadamitsu 中山忠光, 287
Nakazawa Dōji 中沢道二, 259
Nakoku, *193*
Namamugi jiken, 193
namban bōeki 南蛮貿易, 194
namban bunka 南蛮文化, 17
namban byōbu, 193, 194
namban-gaku 南蛮学, 310
Namban-ji, *193*
nambanjin, 193, *194*
nambansen, 194
Nambokuchō 南北朝, 134
Nambokuchō no nairan, 194
Namerikawa 滑川, 156
Namiki Senryū 並木千柳, 120
Namiki Sōsuke 並木宗輔, 120
nami-sen 波 (浪) 銭, 122
Nammon 南門 of Tōdai-ji, 288
Namu Amida Butsu 南無阿弥陀仏, 107
namu myōhō renge-kyō 南無妙法華経, Nangnang, *see* Lo-lang ⌊84
Naniwa 浪速 (難波), 219
Naniwa-kyō 難波京, 253
Nankaidō 南海道, 253
Na no Agata 儺県, 193
Na no Kuni, *193*
Nanotsu 那津, 193
Nansō 南曹, 265
Nansō Satomi Hakkenden, 195, 312
Nanto 南都, 195, 275
Nanto Hokurei, *195,* 275
Nanto rokushū, 89, 131, *195,* 242
Nanto shichi-daiji, 85, 88, *195,* 291, 308

nanushi (myōshu), 86, 188, 192, 297
Nanzen-ji, 66, *195,* 228
NAPF ナップ (magazine), 225
Narumi 鳴海, 14
natsu no jin 夏の陣, 221
Nawa Nagatoshi 名和長年, 143
nayamai 納屋米, 166
Negoro-dera, *196*
Negoro-ikki 根来一揆, 196
nembutsu 念仏, 16, 28, 48, 103, 106, 158, 178, 213
nembutsu-hijiri 念仏聖, 106
nembutsu-odori, 16, 99, *196,* 213
Nembutsu-shū, *196*
nengu, 196
Nenjū Gyōji Emaki 年中行事絵巻, 47
nenki-bōkō, 196
nennyo 年預, 95
Netherlands East India Company, 40
Nichi-Bei Anzen-hoshō Jōyaku, *197*
Nichi-Bei kaidan, 197 「gawa Jōyaku
Nichi-Bei Washin Jōyaku, *see* Kana-
Nichi-Doku-I Sangoku Dōmei, *197*
Nichi-Ei Dōmei, 85, *197,* 231, 312
Nichi-Futsu Gunji Kyōtei, *198*
Nichiren 日蓮, 48, 84, 182
Nichiren-shū 日蓮宗, 48, 84, 182
Nichi-Ro Sensō, 111, *198,* 225
Nigorie にごりえ, 283
nihon 二品, 91
Nihon Eitai-gura, 199, 247
Nihon-fu, *199*
Nihon Gaishi, 199
Nihongi 日本紀, see *Nihon Shoki*
Nihonjin (magazine), 154, *199,* 245
Nihon Kōki 日本後紀, 228
Nihonkoku Gempō Zen'aku Ryōiki 日本
国現報善悪霊異記, 200
Nihonkoku Kempō, *200*
Nihon-machi, 119, *200,* 232, 272
Nihon Montoku Tennō Jitsuroku 日本文
徳天皇実録, 228
Nihon Ryōiki, 200 「228
Nihon Sandai Jitsuroku 日本三代実録,

Nihon Shoki, 64, 77, 153, 160, 163, 164, 172, *201,* 222, 228, 241, 244

Nihon Sōdōmei Yūai-kai 日本総同盟

ni-ichi suto, 201 └友愛会, 313

Niihama 新居浜 port, 19

Niijima Jō 新島襄, 42 └64, 250

Nijō 二条 (Fujiwara branch family), *Nijōgawara no rakugaki, 201*

Nijō Yoshimoto 二条良基, 145, 178, 227, 260, 299 └迎図, 159

Nijūgo Bosatsu Raigōzu 二十五菩薩来

Nijūikkajō Yōkyū, 72, *201,* 242

nijūshi-kumi don'ya, 79, *202,* 293

nijūshi-kumi Edo-zumi-doiya 二十四組江

Nika-kai, *202* └戸積問屋, 79

Nikka jihen, 202

Nikkō 日光, 297

Nikkō 日光 (Bodhisattva), 51

Nikkōkaidō 日光街道, 62 └incident

Ni-Kō jiken 尼港事件, *see* Nikolaevsk

Nikolaevsk incident, 232, 253

Nimmyō 仁明, emperor, 186, 269

ni-niroku jiken, 203, 282

ninjōbon, 203

Ninkō 仁孝, emperor, 58

Ninna-ji 仁和寺, 259

ni-no-maru 二の丸, 289

ninsoku yoseba, 203

Nintoku 仁徳, emperor, 150, 306, 316

Nippon Ginkō, *204*

Nippon Kaika Shōshi, 204

Nippon Kōgyō Ginkō, *204*

Nippon Kyōsan-tō, *204*

Nippon Rōdō-Nōmin-tō, *205*

Nippon Rōdō Sōdōmei, *205*

Nippon Rōnō-tō 日本労農党, 205

Nippon Seitetsu 日本製鉄, 308

Nippon Shakai-tō, *205*

Nippon Tetsudō-gaisha, *206*

Nippon Yūsen Kabushiki-gaisha, 184,

nise-e, 206 └*206,* 221

Nishi Amane 西周, 179

Nishi Hongan-ji 西本願寺, 81, 112

Nishijin 西陣, 143

Nishijin-ori, *206*

Nishikawa Joken 西川如見, 117

nishiki-e 錦絵, 303

Nishimura Shigeki 西村茂樹, 156

Nishiyama Sōin 西山宗因, 39, 71

nishu-gin 二朱銀, 29

Nisshin 日親, 85

Nisshin-kan 日新館, 75

Nisshin Sensō, 207

Nisso Chūritsu Jōyaku, *208*

Nitchi-kan 日知館, 75

Nitobe Inazō 新渡戸稲造, 243

Nitta Yoshisada 新田義貞, 57, 83, 133, 189, 190, 194

Niwa Seihaku 丹羽正伯, 263

Nō, *see* Nōgaku

Nobunaga, *see* Oda Nobunaga

nōchi kaikaku, 208

Nōgaku (Nō), 40, 79, 113, 168, 169, *208,* 244, 275, 309, 311, 314

Noguchi 野口 Company, 315

Nōgyō Zensho, 209 └209

Nōgyō Zensho Yakugen 農業全書約言,

Nomi no Sukune 野見宿禰, 75

Nomonhan jiken, 209

Nomura Kichisaburō 野村吉三郎, 197

Nova Hispania, *209*

Nozaka Sanzō 野坂参三, 204

Nüchen 女真, 292

nuhi, 135, *209,* 261

Nutari no ki, 210

O

Ōama no Ōji 大海人皇子, 102

Ōbaku-shū, *210*

Obama 小浜 port, 182, 292

ōban (obang), 60, 210

ōban 大番, 63

obang, see first *ōban* above

ōban-yaku, 211

ōban-za 大判座, 60

obito, 11, 129, *211,* 262

o-chashi 御茶師, 301

Ochikubo Monogatari 落窪物語, 283

Oda 小田 (castle town), 102

Oda 織田 deputy constables, 252

Oda Nobunaga 織田信長, 16, 87, 92, 192, 213, 249, 272

Odawara, *211*

Odawara hyōjō 小田原評定, 211

Odawara seibatsu, 211

odoke 諧謔, 171

Ōei no gaikō, 211

Ōei no ran, 180, *212,* 223, 224

Ōe no Hiromoto 大江広元, 165, 212

Ōe no Masafusa 大江匡房, 314

Ogasawara Sadayori 小笠原貞頼, 212

Ogasawara Shotō, 18, *212*

Ogawa Mimei 小川未明, 230

ōgi-byōshi 扇拍子, 235

Ōgigayatsu 扇谷 family, 300

Ō Gi-shi (Wang Hsi-chih) 王羲之, *ōgosho, 212* ⌊242

Ogyū Sorai 荻生徂徠, 149

Ōhara Magosaburō 大原孫三郎, 212

Ōhara Shakai Mondai Kenkyūsho, *212*

Ōi Kentarō 大井憲太郎, 105, 220

Oie-ryū, *212,* 250

Ōita 大分, 51

oiwake-e 追分絵, 223

Ōjin 応神, emperor, 16, 77, 129, 150, *Ōjōyōshū,* 106, *213* ⌊250, 309, 316

Ōkagami 大鏡, 93, 186, *213*

Ōkawa Shūmei 大川周明, 61

Okazaki Masamune 岡崎正宗, 128

Okehazama 桶狭間, 93

Okehazama no tatakai, 213

Oki, 57, 133, 194, *213*

Ōkubo Nagayasu 大久保長安, 236

Ōkubo Toshimichi 大久保利通, 70, 74, 75, 220, 245

Okudaira Nobumasa 奥平信昌, 172

Ōkuma Shigenobu 大隈重信, 22, 75, 84, 104, 110, 116, 136, 307 ⌈*213*

Okuni Kabuki, 16, 99, 112, 196,

Ōkuninushi no Mikoto 大国主神, 99

Oku no Hosomichi, 214

ōkura (Yamato court storehouses), 94, *214,* 243, 306

Ōkura 大倉 Company, 315

Ōkura-shō 大蔵省, 38, 214, 218

Ōkyo, *see* Maruyama Ōkyo

ōmetsuke, 180, *214*

omi 臣, 112, 188, 262

Ōminato, 182, *214*

Ōmine 大峯, 270

Ōmi no Kenu 近江毛野, 98

Ōmi no Mifune 淡海三船, 115

Ōmi Ryō, 15, *214*

Ōmi-Shigaraki 近江紫香楽, 165

Ōmi shōnin, 215, 216

omoya 母屋, 21

Ōmura 大村 clan, 192 ⌈309

ō-muraji, 112, 187, 188, *215,* 218, 222,

Ōmura Masujirō 大村益次郎, 29

Ōmura Sumitada 大村純忠, 289

onchi, 88, *215*

on hakase 音博士, 33 ⌈*215,* 249, 252

Ōnin no Ran, 14, 15, 22, 76, 88,

oni no nembutsu 鬼念仏, 223

Onjō-ji, *216,* 223, 239

onkyū-chi 恩給地, 215

Onna Daigaku, 130, *216*

Onna Kabuki 女歌舞伎, 112

Ōno Azumahito 大野東人, 279

Ono Azusa 小野梓, 116

Ono corporation, *see* Ono-gumi

Ono-gumi, 95, *216,* 236, 255

Onomichi, 182, *217*

Ono no Imoko 小野妹子, 137

Ono no Komachi 小野小町, 229

Ono no Minemori 小野岑守, 234

Ono no Takamura 小野篁, 233 ⌈242

Ono no Tōfū (Michikaze) 小野道風, ⌈259

Ono-ryū 小野流 (Shingon branch),

Ō no Yasumaro 太安万侶, 149, 201

onri-edo 厭離穢土, 106

onshō-chi 恩賞地, 215

onshō-kata, 133, *217*
on'yōdō, *217*, 260
on'yō-gogyō 陰陽五行, *217*
on'yō hakase 陰陽博士, *217*
On'yōryō 陰陽寮, *217*
Ōoka (Echizen no Kami) Tadasuke 大岡（越前守）忠相, 44
ō-oku 大奥, 125
ō-omi 大臣, 112, 188, 215, *217*
Opium War, 54
ōrai-mono, *218*, 286, 290
Oranda fūsetsu-gaki, *218*
Organtino, Father Gnecchi, 193
oribe no tsukasa, 207, *218*
Ōryokkō 鴨緑江 (Yalu River), 292
ōryōshi, 81, *218*
Ō Ryū-ki 王柳貴, 64
osa-byakushō, 164, *219* ⌈条, 163
O-sadamegaki Hyakkajō 御定書百箇
Osada Tadamune 長田忠致, 78
Osafune Nagamitsu 長船長光, 128
Ōsaka, *219* ⌈Ōsaka), 219
Osaka 小坂 (medieval name of
Osakabe 刑部, prince, 280
Ōsaka jiken, *219*
Ōsaka-jō, 220
Ōsaka Kaigi, *220*
Ōsaka no jin, *219*, 220
Ōsaka Shōsen Kaisha, *221*
Osanai Kaoru 小山内薫, 104, 261, 298
ōsei fukko, *221*
ōsei fukko no dai-gōrei 王政復古の大号令, 221
o-shi (pilgrim guides) 御師, 104, 187
Ōshikōchi no Mitsune 凡河内躬恒,
Ō Shin-ji 王辰爾, 50 ⌊151
Ōshio Heihachirō 大塩平八郎, 300,
Ōshūkaidō 奥州街道, 62 ⌊311
Ōshū tandai, *221*
osso, *222*
osso bugyō 越訴奉行, 222
Ōtaguro Tomo-o 太田黒伴雄, 258
ōtakamochi 大高持, 189
Ōta Nampo 太田南畝, 171, 252

Ōtani Hongan-ji 大谷本願寺, 87
Ōtashō 太田庄, *217*
Ōtemmon no hen 応天門の変, 222
otogi-zōshi, 222
Ōtomo-be 大伴部, 19
Ōtomo 大伴 clan of ancient Japan, 118, 187, 215, *222*
  Fukehi 吹負, 222
  Kanamura 金村, 222
  Muroya 室屋, 222, 309
  Tabito 旅人, 222
  Yakamochi 家持, 177, 222 ⌈255
Ōtomo 大友 clan of Bungo, 51, 72,
Ōtomo no Kuronushi 大伴黒主, 229
Ōtomo no Muraji 大伴連, 188
Ōtomo no Ōji 大友皇子, 102
Ōtomo Sōrin 大友宗麟, 51, 289
Ōtomo *uji*, 222
Ōtomo 大友 war barons, 249
otona 老 (chief retainers of manorial lords), 127 ⌈222, 276, 297
otona (rural corporation leaders), 65,
otona-byakushō, *219*
ō-toneri no za 大舎人座, 207
Ōtsu, 19, 182, *223*, 292
Ōtsu-e, *223*
Ōtsu-e bushi 大津絵節, 223 ⌈227
Ōtsuki Gentaku 大槻玄沢, 76, 116,
Ōu 奥羽, 81
Ōuchi 大内 family, *223*, 271, 308
  Yoshihiro 義弘, 180, 212, 223
  Yoshinaga 義長, 187, 223
  Yoshitaka 義隆, 223
Ōuchi *uji*, 223
Ōuchi-uji Hekisho 大内氏壁書, 23
Ōuchi 大内 war barons, 249
ōuta-dokoro 大歌所, 236
Ōwada no Tomari, 89, *224*
Owari 尾張 *(kuni)*, 14
Owari 尾張 clan, and *go-sanke*, 257
Owari-no-kuni gunji hyakushō-ra gebumi,
oya 親 (promoter), 284 ⌊224
Ōyada 大矢田, 182, 230
oyakata-kokata, 224

Oyama 尾山 Castle, 121 ⌈111, 311
Ō Yō-mei (Wang Yang-ming) 王陽明,
Ozaki Kōyō 尾崎紅葉, 55, 137, 159
Ozaki Yukio 尾崎行雄, 116, 136
Ozeki San'ei 小関三英, 18, 269

P

Paekche 百済, 16, 31, 73, 181, 241
Pai Lien Chiao 白蓮教, 85
Pechili Gulf, *see* Bokkaiwan
P'ei Shih-ch'ing 裴世清, 137
Peiyang 北洋 squadron, 92
Perry, Matthew C., 121, 235, 304
Phaeton incident, *224*
Pnom-Penh, 119 ⌈231
Port Arthur, 150, 198, 202, 207, 225,
Portsmouth Treaty, *225*
Potsdam Declaration, 25, 171, 200,
P'u-i 溥儀, 176 ⌊208, *225, 232*
Pung Chang, *see* Hōshō
puroretariya bungaku undō, 225
Pusan 釜山, 35, 150
Putiatin, admiral, 231
P'yongyang 平壌, 23, 198, 207, 226
Pyon-han, *see* Benkan

R

raden 螺鈿, 174
Rai San'yō 頼山陽, 199
Raiki 礼記, 64
rakuchū rakugai byōbu, 226
raku-ichi 楽市, 16
rakuichi-rakuza, 16, 108, *226,* 314
Rakurō (Lo-lang) 楽浪, 16, 226
Rakurō-gun, 226
rangaku 蘭学, 170, 227, 246, 269, 310
Rangaku-juku 蘭学塾, 132
Rangaku Kaitei, 227
rangakusha 蘭学者, 311
Rankei Dōryū 蘭渓道隆, 134, 228
Rashōmon 羅生門, 293
rei 礼, 122

reisan 霊山, 270
Reizei 冷泉, emperor, 13
renga, 71, 145, *227,* 260, 298
renga-shi 連歌師, 227
Rengōgun Shireibu, *227*
Rennyo 蓮如, 87, 92, 97, 107, 250
rensho, 119, *227,* 255
renza-hō, 228
retsuden 列伝, 36
Rhee, Syngman, *see* Lee Sung-man
ri 里 (village), 63
ri 里 (linear measure), 220
rikka (tatebana) 立花, 114
Rikken Dōshi-kai 立憲同志会, 135
Rikkokushi, 45, *228*
Ri Kō-shō, *see* Li Hung-chang
rinshi 綸旨, 96 ⌈*228,* 276, 291, 317
Rinzai-shū, 48, 106, 109, 134, 135,
Ri Sam-pei, *see* Yi Sam-p'yong
Ri Sei-kei, *see* Yi Song-gye
Rishōtō 利生塔, 13
Risshi-sha, 12, 104, 105, *228*
Risshū 律宗, 195, 297
ritsu 律 (penal code), 169, 191, 254,
   280, 312
Ritsu, *see* Risshū
ritsuryō 律令, 26, 28, 30, 33, 153, 254
ritsuryō-sei, 27, 38, 46, 52, 53, 61, 63,
   68, 70, 74, 78, 88, 101, 108, 111,
   158, *229,* 233, 238, 243, 244, 261,
   295, 310, 312, 316
Rōben 良弁, 131
Rōdō Nōmin-tō 労働農民党, 205
rōdō sampō, 229
Roesler, Karl, 37
rōjū, 123, 127, 163, 172, 180, 214,
   229, 274, 281, 297, 305
Rokkaku-dō 六角堂, 114
Rokkaku 六角 family, 23
rokkasen, 229
Rokōkyō, *see* Lukouch'iao
rokubun-no-ichi dono 六分一殿, 180, 271
Rokuhara 六波羅, 57, 109, 133
Rokuhara tandai, 119, *230*

Rokujōgawara 六条河原, 78
Rokujō Midō 六条御堂, 175
Rokumei-kan, 156, *230*
rokunin-shū 六人衆, 305
Rokuon-ji 鹿苑寺, 140
rokusai-ichi, 230
rōmanshugi, 230
Rondon Kaigi, *see* London Kaigi
Rongo 論語, 129, 191
rōnin, 231
Roosevelt, Franklin D., 308
Roosevelt, Theodore, 199, 225
Roshiya (Russia), *231,* 253
rōtō, 24, 91, *231,* 275
Ruijū Sandai-kyaku, 169, *232*
Ruson (Luzon), *232*
Russia, *see* Roshiya
rusu-dokoro 留守所, 156, 312
ryō 令 (administrative code), 169, 191, 254, 280, 312
ryō 寮 (public affairs bureau), 296
Ryōbyō-in 療病院, 262
ryōgae, 114, *232*
ryōgae-ya 両替屋, 130
ryōge 令外, 111, 115
ryōge no kan, 233
Ryōjinhishō 梁塵秘抄, 94
Ryojun 旅順, 198
ryōke 領家, 89, 91, 144, 182, 302
ryōko (tomb serfs), *233,* 261
ryōmin 良民, 118, 123, 135, 210, 233, 295
Ryōnin 良忍, 48
Ryō no Gige, 233
Ryō no Shūge, 233
ryōshu 陵守, 233
ryōtō tetsuritsu, 233
Ryōunshū, 131, *234*
Ryūhei *eihō* 隆平永宝, 147
Ryūjōkō, *see* Liut'iaokou
Ryūkō 隆光, 268
Ryūkyū, *234*
ryūtatsu-bushi, 16, 162, *235*
Ryuzōji *uji,* 72, *235*

S

sachūben 左中弁, 38
sadaiben 左大弁, 38
sadaijin 左大臣, 38
Saden 左伝, 191
Sado kinginzan, 236
saeji 左衛士, 44
saeki-be 佐伯部, 19
Saga 嵯峨, emperor, 22, 54, 98, 130, 167, 168, 234, 239, 269
Saga no ran, 236, 245
Saghalien, *see* Sakhalin
sahyōe 左兵衛, 44
saibara, 236
saibari 前張, 236
Saichō 最澄, 48, 106, 137, 287
Saidai-ji 西大寺, 195
saifu, 114, 129, *236*
saifu-ya 割符屋, 114, 236
Saigoku Risshi-hen, 「104, 206, 245
Saigō Takamori 西郷隆盛, 29, 74,
Saigō Tsugumichi 西郷従道, 235
Saigūki 西宮記, 146
Saigyō 西行, 241, 260
Saikaidō 西海道, 39, 253
saikaishi 西海使, 136
Saikaku Oki-miyage 西鶴置土産, 247
Saikaku Oridome 西鶴織留, 247
saikeikoku jōkan, 237
Saikō Saibansho, *237*
saimen no bushi 西面の武士, 190
Sa-in 左院, 270
Sainan jihen, 237, 242
Saionji Kimmochi 西園寺公望, 34, 136, 205, 246, 298, 304
saisei-itchi 祭政一致, 70, 256
Saitō Makoto 斎藤実, 203
saka-be 酒戸, 295
Sakado 坂戸 (theatrical troupe), 309
Sakai, 182, 235, *237*
Sakai bōseki-jo, 237
Sakai Tadakatsu 酒井忠勝, 281
Sakai Tadakiyo 酒井忠清, 55

Sakai Toshihiko 堺利彦, 78, 205
Sakamoto 坂本, 19, 122, 182, 187
sakan (clerks), *238*
sakan 目 (secretaries), 155
sakani-nushi 酒荷主, 79
Sakanoue no Tamuramaro 坂上田村
　麻呂, 49, 99
Sakashita-mongai no hen, 146, *238*
sakaya, 236, *238*
Sakhalin, 126, 127, 199, 225, 231, ⌈232, 308
sakimori, 68, *238*
sakimori 崎守, 238
sakimori no tsukasa 防人司, 39
sakoku, 238
Sakuma Morimasa 佐久間盛政, 121
Sakuma Shōzan 佐久間象山, 173
sakunin, 239
Sakurada-mon 桜田門, 13
Sakurada-mongai no hen, 239
Sakyō 左京, 77
sakyōshiki 左京職, 172
Sambō Ekotoba 三宝絵詞, 201
Sambō-in 三宝院 of Daigo-ji, 34
sambon 三品, 91
sambutsu kaisho 産物会所, 155
sambutsu-kata 産物方, 155
samisen, see *shamisen*
sammoku-hachibi 三目八臂, 51
Sammon, 216, *239*
sampitsu, 239, 242　　　⌈Hōkoku-kai
Sampō 産報, see Dai Nippon Sangyō
Samurai-dokoro, 119, 165, 189, *239,*
　262, 269; of an estate, 271
san 算, 38
san bugyō 三奉行, 103
sandaichokusai 三大勅祭, 128
Sandai Jitsuroku 三代実録, 36
sando-hikyaku 三度飛脚, 80
San Francisco Kōwa Kaigi, *240*
Sangi 参議, 59
Sangi-in, 240
Sangoku Bōkyō Kyōtei, *240*
Sangoku Kanshō, *240,* 257
Sangokushi 三国志, 60, 63

Sangyō Hōkoku-kai, *see* Dai Nippon
　Sangyō Hōkoku-kai
Sangyō Kakumei, *241*
San'indō 山陰道, 253
Sanjōnishi Sanetaka 三条西実隆, 148,
　150
sanjū-shichikyo 三従七去, 216
sankan 三管 (shōgun's deputies), 124
Sankan 三韓 (ancient Korea), 214,
san kanrei 三管領, 271　　　⌊241, 243
Sankan seibatsu, 241
sankan-shishoku 三管四職, 189
Sankashū, 241
sankin kōtai, 11, 36, 43, *241,* 305
San-kuo Chih 三国志, 60, 63
Sankyō-gisho, 241
Sannō 山王, 160
Sanrai 三礼, 191
Sanron-shū, 131, 195, *242*
sanseki, 242
sanshichū 三尸虫, 160
Santō Kyōden 山東京伝, 138, 252
Santō mondai, 242
Santō shuppei, 242
San'yo, 59, 221, *243,* 276
San'yōdō 山陽道, 253
sanze-isshin no hō, 158, *243*
sanzō, 94, 214, *243,* 306
Sapporo 札幌, 192
Sapporo Nōgakkō, *243*
Sarudahiko 猿田彦, 160　　　⌈309, 314
Sarugaku, 167, 168, 169, 208, *243,*
Sarugaku Nō 猿楽能, 40
Sasaki Takauji (Dōyo) 佐々木高氏
Sasame-yuki, 244　　　⌊(道誉), 269
sashidashi, 244
sashōben 左少弁, 38
satabito 沙汰人, 65, 276
Satake 佐竹 family, 95
Satomi Yoshizane 里見義実, 195
sato-osa, 244
Satsu-Ei sensō, see *Namamugi jiken*
Satsuma 薩摩 clan, 65, 73, 146, 183,
saudaijin 左右大臣, 300　　　⌊239, 290

sau-daishōgeki 左右大少外記, 38

sau-daishōshi 左右大少史, 38

sau-eji-fu 左右衛士府, 46

sau-kebiishi-chō 左右検非違使庁, 130

sau-konoe 左右近衛, 44

sau-kyōshiki 左右京職, 172

sedōka, 177, *244*

Seidō 聖堂, 266

seii-taishōgun 征夷大将軍, 17, 119, 221

seiji shōsetsu, *244*

seikan ron, *245*

Seikatsu to Bungaku 生活と文学, 226

Seike 清家 clan, 145

Seikyō-sha, 156, 199, *245*

Seinan Sensō, 104, *245*

Seinei 清寧, emperor, 316

Seiryōden 清涼殿, 259

Sei Shōnagon 清少納言, 145, 175

Seitaisho, 32, *246*

Seitō 青踏, 246

Seitō-sha, *246*

Seiwa 清和, emperor, 36, 249, 250

Seiwa 清和 (Minamoto branch family), 282

Seiyō Kibun, 246

Seiyū-kai, 61, 136, 156, 182, *246, 282*

sekai kyōkō, *247*

Seken Munezan'yō, *247*

Sekigahara no tatakai, *247*

sekisen, *247*

sekisho, *247*

Seki Takakazu 関孝和, 307

Sekiyō-sha 石陽社, 104

sekkai 節会, 236

sekkan seiji, *248*

sekke-shōgun 摂家将軍, 119

Self-Help (Smiles), 237

semba-koki, *248*

semmen koshakyō, *248*　　　　　　┌295

semmin 賤民, 123, 135, 209, 233, 261,

Semmyō-reki, 108, *248*

sen 銭, 289

Senchaku Hongan-nembutsushū, *249*

sendatsu 先達, 164

sengoku daimyō 戦国大名, 36, 41, 44, 55, 65, 83, 226, 235, 271, 273, 282, 284, 294　　　　┌195, 216, *249*

Sengoku jidai, 23, 55, 142, 170, 190,

Senjimon 千字文, 129

Senju seijūsho, *249*, 268

Senki 戦旗, 225

senkimono 戦記物, 69

Sen no Rikyū 千利休, 25

senryū, *249*

Senshūji-ha, *250*

senzui byōbu 山水屏風, 293

Sesonji-ryū, 212, *250*

sesshō, 13, 64, 221, 248, *250*, 312

Sesshū 雪舟, 79, 277

Seto-yaki, *250*

sewamono, *251*

Seyaku-in 施薬院, 262

shaden 社殿: of Kasuga-jinja, 128; of Tōshō-gū, 297

shaji-sankei kō 社寺参詣講, 284

Shakai Heiken-ron, *251*

Shakai-Minshu-tō, *251*

Shakai-Minshū-tō, 205, *251*　　┌282

Shakai-Taishū-tō 社会大衆党, 251,

Shaka Nyorai: 釈迦如来 at Murō-ji, 189; at Hōryū-ji, 167　　┌88, 167

Shaka Sanzon 釈迦三尊 at Hōryū-ji,

shakuhachi 尺八, 235

shamanizumu, *251*

shamisen (*samisen*) 三味線, 110, *251*

Shanghai jihen, 176, *252*

Sharaku, *see* Tōshūsai Sharaku

share 洒落, 171

sharebon (*sharehon*), 203, *252*

Shariden 舎利殿 at Enkaku-ji, 48

Shasekishū, *252*

Sha-shih 沙市, 257

Shatai-tō 社大党, 282

shi 志 (classified history), 36

Shiba 斯波 family, 15, 124, *252*

Shiba 斯波 *kanrei*, 124, 189

Shiba Kō 司馬光, 253

Shibano Ritsuzan 柴野栗山, 125

Shiba Shirō 柴四郎, 117
Shibata Katsuie 柴田勝家, 128
Shibata Kyūō 柴田鳩翁, 259
Shiba *uji*, 252
Shiba Yoshikado 斯波義廉, 216
Shiba Yoshitoshi 斯波義敏, 216
Shiberia shuppei, 252 ⌈249, 307
Shibukawa Shunkai 渋川春海, 109,
Shibusawa Eiichi 渋沢栄一, 34, 295
Shibusawa *zaibatsu*, 15, 315
shichi-daiji, see *Nanto shichi-daiji*
shichidō, 186, *253*
shidō-kin 祠堂金, 253
shidō-sen, 253
shifu-gayochō-za 四府駕輿丁座, 314
Shiganoshima 志賀島, 124, 193
Shigaraki no Miya, *253*
Shiga Shigetaka 志賀重昂, 245
Shiga Yoshio 志賀義雄, 204
Shigeno Sadanushi 滋野貞主, 131
shigi kempō, 253 ⌈47, 56
Shigisan Engi Emaki 信貴山縁起絵巻,
Shih Chi 史記, 36
Shih Huang Ti 始皇帝, 77
shihon 四品, 91
Shihō-shō 司法省, 70
Shiji Tsugan, 87, 253
shijō 史定, 155
Shijō-ha, *254* ⌈171
Shikatsube no Magao 鹿都部真顔,
shika-ura 鹿卜 (鹿占), 52
shiki (legal forms), 191, *254*
Shiki 磯城, 186
Shikibu-shō 式部省, 38
shikibunden 職分田, 53, 148, 155, 254
shikiden, 53, 68, 148, 158, *254*
shikifu 職封, 101
shikigaku 式楽, 310
Shiki no agata-nushi, 254 ⌈252, 303
Shikitei Samba 式亭三馬, 138, 151,
shikken, 189, *255*
Shikyō 詩経, 64
Shikyō 四鏡, 186, 213
Shimabara no ran, 142, *255*

Shimada-gumi, *255*
Shimada Saburō 島田三郎, 116
shima-mori 島守, 238
Shimamura Hōgetsu 島村抱月, 22, 55
Shimazaki Tōson 島崎藤村, 21, 230,
261, 263
Shimazu 島津 family, 235, *255*, 271
Hisamitsu 久光, 193, 255, 289
Nariakira 斉彬, 237, 255
Takahisa 貴久, 255
Shimazu 島津 *tozama daimyō*, 298
Shimazu *uji*, 255
Shimazu 島津 war barons, 249
shimboku 神木, 65, 128, 275
shimbunshi jōrei, 256, 272, 273, 315
shimbutsu-bunri, 70, *256*
shimbutsu-konkō 神仏混淆, 70
shimbutsu-shūgō 神仏習合, 86
shimin-byōdō, 256
Shimoda, 72, 121, *256*
Shimoda-gumi 下田組, 216
Shimokita-hantō 下北半島, 214
Shimokōbe Chōryū 下河辺長流, 153
Shimonoseki jiken, 32, *257*
Shimonoseki Jōyaku, 204, 207, *257*
shimpan, 36, *257*
shimpo jitō, 103, 109, 113, *257*
Shimpo-tō 進歩党, 116
Shimpūren, 245, *258*
shin 信 (rank), 122
Shinagawa Yajirō 品川弥二郎, 267
Shina-tō 支那党, 100
shinden 神田 (shrine land), 53
shinden kaihatsu, 258
shinden-zukuri, 20, 59, 140, *258*
shindō-jissen 臣道実践, 282
Shin'e 真慧, 250
Shingai Kakumei, 154, *259*
shingaku, 259
Shingen Kahō 信玄家法, 23 ⌈259
Shingi Shingon-shū 新義真言宗, 196,
Shingon Mikkyō 真言密教, 259
Shingonritsu 真言律, 268
Shingon-shū, 101, 158, 189, *259*

shin'i, 259, 260

Shinkai 審海, 268

Shinkan 辰韓, 241

Shinkei 心敬, 261

Shin-kigen 新紀元, 79

Shinki-ron 慎機論, 18

Shin Kokin-chō 新古今調, 260

Shin Kokin Wakashū, 260

Shin Nihon Bungaku 新日本文学, 226

shinnō-shōgun 親王将軍, 119

Shinobugaoka 忍岡, 87, 147

shin'on 新恩, 63   ⌐284

Shinran 親鸞, 48, 92, 107, 170, 250,

Shinri-kyō 神理教, 170

Shinron 新論, 184

shinsai-tegata 震災手形, 141

shinsen-gumi, 173, 260

Shinsen Shōji-roku 新撰姓氏録, 16

Shinsen Tsukubashū, 260, 299

Shinshichō, 261

Shinshō 審祥, 131

Shin-shū 真宗, 48, 92, 107, 131, 250

Shinshū Hongan-ji 真宗本願寺, 87

Shinshū-kyō 神習教, 170

Shinshū Takada-ha 真宗高田派, 250

shintai-shi, 261

Shinto 神都 (Uji-Yamada), 302

Shintō 神道, 153

Shintō Dai-kyō 神道大教, 170

Shintō Gobu-sho 神道五部書, 97

shi-nuhi, 210, 261

Shin'yō Wakashū, 261

shirabyōshi 白拍子, 94, 167

Shiragayugei-be 白髪靱負部, 181

Shiragi 新羅, 31, 73, 89, 181, 199,
   241, 306

Shiragi seibatsu 新羅征伐, 241

shirai no fuhito 白猪史, 50

Shirakaba, 261   ⌐175, 190

Shirakawa 白河, emperor, 95, 164,

shiro 代 (square measure), 274

Shiroyama 城山, 245

shisei-seido, 262

Shishigari Monkin 獅子狩文錦, 88

shi-shiki, 240, 262, 271

shitaji-chūbun, 91, 103, 262, 267

shita-zukasa 下司, 58

Shitennō-ji, 219, 248, 262

shitōkan 四等官, 238

shitsuji 執事, 126, 300

shiyūchi-iriai 私有地入会, 96

shizenshugi, 263

shizoku 士族, 256

shizoku jusan, 263

shizoku no shōhō, 263

Shizuka-gozen 静御前, 299   ⌐156

shō 升 (measure of capacity), 90, 113,

shō 荘 (warehouse), 264

sho 書 (writing), 33

Shōbō 聖宝, 34, 259

shōbō 正法, 177

Shōbōgenzō, 263

Shobutsu Ruisan, 263

shōchō 荘長, 157

shōchō 正丁, 29, 310, 316

Shōchō no do-ikki 正長の土一揆, 41

Shōchū no hen, 57, 133, 194, 263

shōen, 264

shōen-seiri rei, 30, 264

shōfū 蕉風 (Bashō style), 265

shōfū (the right style), 265

Shōfuku-ji 正福寺, 127

Shōgakuin, 265

shōgi 小毅, 68

Shōgitai, 20, 265

shōgun 将軍 (general), 68

Shōhaku 肖柏, 150, 227

Shōhei Gakkō 昌平学校, 266

Shōheikō, 147, 265

Shōheizaka 昌平坂, 266

shōhekiga, 266

Shōhō-kaisho 商法会所, 266

shōhōshi, 266, 299

Shōhō-taii 商法大意, 266

shō-ichii 正一位, 91

shoin 書院, 52, 114, 129

shoin-zukuri, 21, 59, 79, 82, 114, 266

shōji 荘司, 69, 91, 144, 157

shōka 証果 (enlightenment), 177
shōkan, 69, 91, 144, 191, *266,* 302
Shō Kannon 聖観音, 69
Shōka-sonjuku, *267*
Shokkō Giyū-kai, *267*
shōkō-kan 彰考館, 36
Shōkoku-ji 相国寺, 66, 228
Shoku Nihongi 続日本紀, 227
Shoku Nihon Kōki 続日本後紀, 227
Shoku Sanjin 蜀山人, 252
shokusan kōgyō, 267
Shokyō 書経, 64
Shōman 勝鬘 Sutra, 241
Shōmeiron 正名論, 184
Shōmu 聖武, emperor, 152, 165, 195,
   253, 269, 291
Shōmyō-ji, 121, *268*
shōnagon 少納言, 38
Shōren'in-ryū 青蓮院流, 212, 250
shōrui awaremi no rei, 96, *268*
shōryō 小領, 68
Shōsetsu Shinzui, 269, 297
shoshi 所司, 172, 189, 240, 262
shoshidai, 269
Shōshi-kai, 18, *269*
Shōsho 尚書, 191
Shōsō-in, 131, *269, 282*
Shōtai 尚泰, king, 235
shōtoku 小徳, 122
Shōtoku-shū 聖徳宗, 262
Shōtoku Taishi 聖徳太子, 69, 77,
   92, 106, 112, 122, 137, 159, 241,
   ⌐262, 288, 313
Shōwa no hen, 269
Shōwa *shōhō* 承和昌宝, 147
shōya 庄屋, 86, 100, 188, 297
shōzui-saii 祥瑞災異, 98
Shrine Shintō, 170
Shūbun 周文, 145, 277
shuchō 主帖, 68
shuchō 首長, 188
Shūeki 周易, 191
Shugeishuchi-in, *270*
shugendō, 164, *270*
Shūgi-in (former Kōgisho), 149, *270*

Shūgi-in (House of Representatives),
   270   ⌐*270,* 298, 302
shugo, 22, 55, 63, 119, 188, 191, 194,
shugo-dai 守護代, 35, 252
shugo daimyō, 35, 55, 88, 91, 92, 153,
   165, 180, 189, 212, 223, 249, *271*
shugo-ryōkoku-sei 守護領国制, 302
shūgō-Shintō 習合神道, 86
shugo-uke 守護請, 271, 302
Shui Hu Chuan 水滸伝, 195
shuin-chi 朱印地, 272
shuin-jō, 272
shuin-sen, 17, 119, 200, 232, *272*
shujitsu 手実, 131
shūkai jōrei, 272
Shu Ki, *see* Chu Hsi
shuko 守戸 (tomb serfs), 233
Shukō 珠光, 25, 79, 268
shukōgyō, 272
shukueki 宿駅, 62
shukurō 宿老, 127
Shukyū-tō 守旧党, 100
shūmon-aratame nimbetsu-chō, 273
shūmon-aratame yaku 宗門改役, 273
Shunjū 春秋, 64
Shunkei 春慶, 273
Shunkei-nuri, *273*
Shun'oku Myōha 春屋妙葩, 145
Shunshoku Tatsumi-no-sono 春色辰巳園,
   203
Shunshoku Umegoyomi 春色梅暦, 203
Shun Ti 順帝, 306
Shun'yō-kai, *273*
shuppan jōrei, 272, 273
shusei 主政, 68
Shūsei-ha 修正派, 170
Shushi-gaku, *273*
shutendai 主典代, 95
Shūyū-kan 修猷館, 75
Sidotti, Giovanni, 246
Siebold affair, 269, 311   ⌐306
Silla 新羅, 31, 73, 89, 98, 199, 241,
Smiles, Samuel, 237   ⌐*274,* 280
so (land tax in rice), 63, 101, 210,

so 租 (tenancy rent), 27

Soa 祖阿, 133

Sōami 相阿弥, 60

soba-yōnin, 274

Sōchō 宗長, 122, 261　　　「245

Soejima Taneomi 副島種臣, 74, 183,

Soga-be 蘇我部, 19

Soga 蘇我 family, 102, 118, 187, 215, 218, *275*, 280

　Emishi 蝦夷, 275

　Iname 稲目, 187

　Iruka 入鹿, 92, 275

　Machi 満智, 243

　Umako 馬子, 85, 187, 218, 275

Sōgaku, 273, *274*

Soga Monogatari, 69, *274*

Soga Sukenari 曾我祐成, 69, 274

Soga Tokimune 曾我時致, 69, 274

Soga *uji*, 275

Sōgi 宗祇, 150, 227, 261, 299

sōhei, 275

Sōjō Henshō 僧上遍昭, 229　　　「30

Son Byong-hui (Son Hei-ki) 孫秉熙,

sonchū-iriai 村中入会, 96　　　「250

Son'en Hosshinnō 尊円法親王, 212,

Son Hei-ki, *see* Son Byong-hui

sonnō-jōi 尊王攘夷, 13

sonnō-ron, 108, *275*

sonsō 蹲葬, 168

sōryō, 24, *275*

Sōsai, 59, 221, 243, *276*

sōsen (Sung currency), *276*

sōshaban 奏者番, 103

sōson, 276

Sōtō-shū, 45, 48, 263, *276*, 317

sotsu 帥, 39

sō-tsuibushi 総追捕使, 298

Sō *uji*, 212, *276*　　　「二十一箇条, 23

sozei 租税, 196

Spaniards, 194, 232

Spencer, Herbert, 251

Ssu-ma Kuang 司馬光, 253

Stalin, Josef, 308

Suchow 蘇州, 257

Sūden 崇伝, 100, 103

sue-be (suetsukuri-be), *277*

Sue Harukata 陶晴賢, 187, 223

Sueyoshi Magozaemon 末吉孫左衛門, 272

Sugawara no Kiyokimi 菅原清公, 233, 234

Sugawara no Michizane 菅原道真, 137

Sugihara-gami, *277*

Sugita Gempaku 杉田玄白, 116

Sui 隋 (Chinese dynasty), 287

suiboku-ga, 145, 266, *277*

Suika Shintō, 274, *277*

Suiko 推古 empress, 150

suiko (loans), *277*

Suikoden 水滸伝, 195

Suinin 垂仁, emperor, 75

Sujin 崇神, emperor, 159, 316

Sujin-gi 崇神紀, 29, 159

suke 次官 (assistants), 238

suke 介 (vice-governor), 155

sukegō, 278

sukune 宿禰, 222, 308

Suminokuu Ryōi 角食了以, 272

Sumitomo *zaibatsu*, 19, *278*, 315

Sūmitsu-in, *278*

Sumiyoshi Gukei 住吉具慶, 279

Sumiyoshi-ha, *279*, 309

Sumiyoshi Jokei 住吉如慶, 279

Sumpu, *279*

Sun Wen 孫文, 154, 259

Suō Kokufu 周防国府, 152

Sutoku 崇徳, emperor, 82

Suyama Don'ō 陶山鈍翁, 209

Suyama Totsuan 陶山訥庵, 209

Suzaku 朱雀, emperor, 34

Suzaku-ōji 朱雀大路, 77, 78

Suzuki Bunji 鈴木文治, 205, 313

Suzuki Harunobu 鈴木春信, 303

Suzuki Kantarō 鈴木貫太郎, 203

Suzuki Shunzan 鈴木春山, 269

Suzukida Ryūkin 薄田泣菫, 191

T

Tabaruzaka 田原坂, 245
ta-be 田部, 19, 169, 185
Tabulae Anatomicae, 116
Tachibana 橘 family, 54
  Hayanari 逸勢, 239, 270
  Kachiko 嘉智子, 54
  Moroe 諸兄, 165
  Naramaro 奈良麻呂, 186
  Ōiratsume 大郎女, 288
  Ujigimi 氏公, 54, 269
Tachibana Kōzaburō 橘孝三郎, 61
Tachibana Narisue 橘成季, 152
Tachibana Shintō 橘神道, 277
Tachikawa 立川 copper mine, 19
tadokoro, 297
Taedong 大同 River (Daidōkō), 226
Taga-jō, 99, *279*
Taguchi Ukichi 田口卯吉, 204
Tāheru Anatomia, see *Kaitai Shinsho*
taigi 大毅, 68
taigi-meibun 大義名分, 273
Taiheiki, 69, *280*   「*280*, 312
Taihō Ritsuryō, 15, 29, 38, 46, 215,
taijin 大仁, 167
Taika no Kaishin, 46, *280*
taikō, 120, *281*
taikōden 大功田, 148
taikō-kenchi 太閤検地, 134, 281
taikō-ki 太閤記, 281
Tai-mitsu 台密, 180, 259
Tai-Nichi Kōwa Jōyaku, *281*
Tai-Nichi Rijikai, *281*
tai-no-ya 対屋, 258
Taira 平 family, 78
  Kiyomori 清盛, 50, 56, 69, 78, 82,
    89, 90, 103, 224
  Koremori 維盛, 97
  Kunika 国香, 287
  Masakado 将門, 287
  Masako 政子, 110
  Sadamori 貞盛, 287
  Shigemori 重盛, 206

Tadamasa 忠正, 82
tairō, 66, 127, 247, *281*, 297
tairyō 大領, 68
Taisei-den 大成殿, 265
Taisei-kyō 大成教, 170
Taisei Yokusan-kai, 182, 246, *281*
Taisha-kyō 大社教, 170
taisha-zukuri 大社造, 99
taishōgun 大将軍, 68
taitoku 大徳, 122
taitokukan 大徳冠, 123
Taiwan Ginkō 台湾銀行, 141
Taiyō Kyūri Ryōkai-setsu 太陽究理了
  解説, 173   「225
Taiyō no Nai Machi 太陽のない街,
Tajihi-be 蝮部, 181
taka 高, 152
takabata 高機, 143
Takada 高田, 250
Takada jiken, 282
Takada Sanae 高田早苗, 116
takadoko jūkyo, 282
Takahashi Korekiyo 高橋是清, 203
Takaichi 高市, 50, 254
taka-jō 鷹匠, 223
Takakura 高倉, emperor, 50
taka-makie 高蒔絵, 174
Takamochi 高望親王, prince, 96
takamochi-byakushō 高持百姓, 219
Takamura Kōtarō 高村光太郎, 191
Takano Chōei 高野長英, 18, 269
Takasugi Shinsaku 高杉晋作, 32,
  138, 267   「family), 64, 250
Takatsukasa 鷹司 (Fujiwara branch
takatsuki, 282
Takechi-gun 高市郡, 50, 309
Takechi no Agata 高市県, 85
Takeda 武田 family, *282*
  Katsuyori 勝頼, 14, 192, 282, 284
  Shingen 信玄, 161, 182, 282
Takeda Izumo 竹田出雲, 120
Takeda *uji, 282*
Takeda 武田 war barons, 249
Takekurabe, 283

Takemikazuchi no Mikoto 建御賀豆智命, 128

Takemoto Gidayū 竹本義太夫, 110

Takemoto-za 竹本座, 110

Takeno Jōō 武野紹鷗, 25 ⌈217, 275

Takenouchi no Sukune 武内宿禰, 275

Takenouchi Shikibu 竹内式部, 275

Taketori Monogatari, 56, 97, *283*

Takikawa jiken, 283

Takikawa Yukitoki 滝川幸辰, 283

Takizawa Bakin 滝沢馬琴, 195, 312

Tamaki Bunnoshin 玉木文之進, 267

Tamaki Masahide 玉木正英, 277

Tamamushi no Zushi, 88, *283*

tama no ura 多麻宇良 ("jewel bay" of Onomichi), 217

Tamatsukuri 玉造, 284

tamatsukuri-be, 283

Tamayori-hime 玉依姫, 181

Tamenaga Shunsui 為永春水, 203

tammai 段米, 285

tan 段 (反) (square measure), 74, 90, 113, 152, 162, 274

tanagari, 284

tanagari-bito 店借人, 284 ⌈237, 242

Tanaka Giichi 田中義一, 25, 141,

Tanaka Katsusuke 田中勝助, 209

tanasue no mitsugi 手末調, 29

tanauke-jō 店請状, 284

tanauke-nin 店請人, 284

tandai 探題, 109

Tanegashima, 194, *284* ⌈284

Tanegashima Tokitaka 種子島時堯,

Tane Maku Hito 種蒔く人, 225

Tanikawa Kotosuga 谷川士清, 161

Tanizaki Jun'ichirō 谷崎潤一郎, 230,

tanka 短歌, 14, 171 ⌊244, 261

Tannishō, 284

tanomoshi, 187, *284*

tanomoshi-kō 頼母子講, 146

tansen, 188, *285* ⌈125, 231, 274

Tanuma Okitsugu 田沼意次, 43, 113,

Tan Yō-ji 段楊爾, 64

tariki 他力, 107

tariki-hongan 他力本願, 170

taru-kaisen, 79, 116, *285*

Tashiro Sanki 田代三喜, 120

Tashiro Shōi 田代松意, 39

tason-iriai 他村入会, 96

tatchū 塔頭, 175

tateana jūkyo, 282, *285*

tateana-shiki sekishitsu 竪穴式石室, 311

tato (dento), 143, *285*

tawara-mono, 285

Tayama Katai 田山花袋, 22, 263

Teikin-ōrai, 286

Teikoku Daigaku 帝国大学, 294

Teikoku Zaigō-Gunjin-kai 帝国在郷軍人会, 315

Teimon-fū 貞門風, 39

Teimon-ha, 39, *286*

Teisei-tō, 105, *286*

Tejima Toan 手島堵庵, 259

temma 伝馬, 46, 62, 313

Temma 天満, 219

Temmu 天武, emperor, 94, 102, 129, 145, 149, 188, 215, 222, 305, 308

Temmu ryō 天武令, 15

Tempō no kaikaku, 81, 268, *286*

Tempyō 天平 art period, 51, 152, 297 ⌈223, 302

Tenchi 天智, emperor, 36, 102, 215,

Tenchū-gumi, 93, *287*

Tendai-shū, 48, 131, 180, *287*

Tendō-kyō, 30

Tengyō no ran, 287

tenjiku-yō, 287 ⌈288

Tenjukoku Mandara 天寿国曼荼羅,

Tenjukoku Shuchō, *288*

Tenkai 天海, 38

Tenkai-ban 天海版, 38

tennō kikansetsu, 288

Tenri-kyō 天理教, 170

Tenryū-ji, 66, 228, *288*

Tenryūji-bune, 288

Tenshin Jōyaku, 220, *289,* 291

Tenshō ken'ō shisetsu, 289

tenshukaku, 289

teppō no denrai, see Tanegashima
Teradaya sōdō, 289
Terajima Munenori 寺島宗則, 110
terakoya, 170, 213, 218, 231, *290*
Terauchi Masatake 寺内正毅, 156
terauke-seido, 142, *290*
Tetsugen 鉄眼, 38
Tetsugen-ban 鉄眼版, 38
Tetsu no Hanashi 鉄の話, 226
T'ien T'ai 天台, 287
Ting Ju-ch'ang 丁汝昌, 92
to 斗 (measure of capacity), 152
tō (warriors' corporation), 24, *290*
Toba, see *Toba-Fushimi no tatakai*
Toba 鳥羽, emperor, 95, 164
Toba-Fushimi no tatakai, 20, 131, 179,
   265, *290*   ⌈162
Toba Sōjō Kakuyū 鳥羽僧上覚猷, 29,
Tobi 外山 theatrical troupe, 309
Tōdai-ji, 51, 131, 195, 287, *290*
Tōfuku-ji, 57, 66, 175, 228, *291*
Tōgaku-tō no ran, 123, 207, 289, *291*
Togashi Masachika 富樫政親, 92
Tōgudō Dōjinsai 東求堂同仁斎, 60,
Toichi no Agata 十市県, 254   ⌊266
Toichi no agata-nushi, 291
toimaru, 89, 182, 276, *291, 299,* 310
Toi no nyūkō, 292
toiya 問屋, 291
toiya-sei kanai-kōgyō, 292
Tō-ji, 158, 259, 270, *292*
Tō-ji Jūni-ten Zu 東寺十二天図, 293
Tōjō Hideki 東条英樹, 37, 172
Tōkaidō 東海道, 61, 253
Tōkai Sanshi (Shiba Shirō) 東海散士
Tōkan Kikō, 115, *293*   ⌊(柴四郎), 117
Toki Yorikane 土岐頼兼, 263
Tokkō 特高, 293
tokonoma 床間, 114, 266
tokoroten 心太, 314
toku 徳 (rank), 122
Tokubetsu Kōtō Keisatsu, *293*
Tokuda Kyūichi 徳田球一, 204
Tokugawa *bakufu, see* Edo *bakufu*

Tokugawa 徳川 family
  Hidetada 秀忠, 20   ⌈297
  Iemitsu 家光, 20, 131, 142, 241,
  Iemochi 家茂, 32, 146, 238
  Ienari 家斉, 22, 212
  Ienobu 家宣, 268, 294
  Ietsuna 家綱, 55, 210
  Ieyasu 家康, 17, 43, 66, 139, 142,
    192, 212 220, 272, 297
  Mitsukuni 光圀, 36, 157, 176, 183,
  Nariaki 斉昭, 183   ⌊209
  Tokumatsu 徳松, 268   ⌈268
  Tsunayoshi 綱吉, 58, 96, 147, 265,
  Yoshimune 吉宗, 117, 156, 163,
    170, 180, 263, 310   ⌈290
  Yoshinobu 慶喜, 20, 32, 221, 265,
  Yoshitomi 慶福, 13
to-kumi don'ya, 293
Tokunaga Sunao 徳永直, 225
to-kura 土倉, 42
tokuryō 督領, 185
tokusei 徳政, 41
tokusei-ikki, 41, *293,* 294
tokusei-rei, 41, 127, 138, *294*
Tokushi Yoron, 294
Tokutomi Roka 徳富芦花, 230
Tokutomi Sohō 徳富蘇峰, 154, 183
Tōkyō Bijutsu Gakkō, *294*
Tōkyō Daigaku, *294*
Tōkyō Igakkō 東京医学校, 294
Tōkyō Imperial University, 116
Tōkyō Kaisei Gakkō 東京開成学校,
  294   ⌈307
Tōkyō Semmon Gakkō 東京専門学校,
Tōkyō sento, 294
tomeru hyakushō 富める百姓, 74
Tomioka Seishi Kōjō, 268, *295*
Tō-mitsu 東密, 180, 259
tomo-be, 19, *295*
tomo no miyatsuko, 186, 211, 283, *295*
tōmotsu, 296
Tōnan'in 東南院, 242
tondenhei-seido, 83, *296*
tone, 296

Toneri 舎人親王, prince, 145, 201
tōnin 頭人, 190
Tōnomine Engi 多武峰縁起, 279
Torii Kiyonaga 鳥居清長, 303
Torii Kiyonobu 鳥居清信, 303
Torii Yōzō 鳥居耀蔵, 18
torikoshi-mai 取越米, 141
Toro iseki, 296
Tosa-ha, 279, 296, 309
Tosa Mitsunobu 土佐光信, 296
Tosa Mitsuoki 土佐光起, 296
Tōsandō 東山道, 253
Tō-seikatsusha 党生活者, 225
Tōsei Shosei-katagi, 297
toshiyori 年寄 (elders), 127, 229
toshiyori (rural community leaders),
Tōshō-gū, 297   ⌊223, 276, 297
Tōshō-gū Engi 東照宮縁起, 279
Tōshūsai Sharaku 東州斎写楽, 303
tōsui-ken, 90, 297
totei-seido, 298
Tōtō 東塔 at Yakushi-ji, 308
Totsugawa-gō 十津川郷, 287
Tō Tsuneyori 東常縁, 150
Tourane (Da Nang), 200
tōya 頭屋 (religious attendant), 185
Toyama Masaichi 外山正一, 261
Tōyō Jiyū Shimbun, 298
Toyoke Daijingū 豊受大神宮, 302
Toyoke Ōmikami 豊受大神, 302
Toyosukiire-hime 豊鍬入姫, 181
Toyotomi 豊臣 family, 33
    Hidetsugu 秀次, 52, 120
    Hideyori 秀頼, 61, 220, 247
    Hideyoshi 秀吉, 23, 31, 52, 83, 87,
        98, 111, 134, 142, 143, 192, 193,
        196, 249, 272
Tōzai-namboku 東西南北, 261
tozama daimyō, 36, 298, 301
tōzamurai 遠侍, 21
Tripartite Pact, 197, 208
Tsinan incident, see Sainan jihen
tsū 通 (knowledge), 252   ⌈269, 297
Tsubouchi Shōyō 坪内逍遙, 22, 141,

tsuchi-kura 土倉, 42, 167
Tsuchimikado 土御門, emperor, 216
Tsuda Mamichi 津田真道, 179
tsugibikyaku 継飛脚, 80
tsuibushi, 298
tsukasa 司, 296
tsuki-gyōji 月行事, 174
Tsukiji Shō-gekijō, 298
Tsukubashū, 227, 260, 298
tsukuda, 153, 267, 299
Tsukumo 九十九 company, 184
Tsukushi 筑紫, 39, 238
Tsunesada 恒貞, prince, 269
Tsunuga 角鹿, 299
Tsurezuregusa, 299
tsuridono 釣殿, 258
Tsurigane Benkei 釣鐘弁慶, 223
Tsuruga, 182, 292, 299
Tsurugaoka Hachiman-gū, 118, 299
Tsushima 対島, 57, 142, 211, 238,
tsūshōshi, 266, 299   ⌊276, 292
tsuya 津屋, 291
"Tung I Chuan" 東夷伝, 60, 62, 193
T'ungkou 通溝, 162   ⌈Yōkyū
Twenty-one Demands, see Nijūikkajō
Tzu-chih T'ung-chien, see Shiji Tsugan
Tz'u Hsi 慈禧, 85

U

Ubayama 姥山, 285
ubusuna-gami, 300
uchi-kowashi, 300, 311
uchitsukura 内蔵, 94, 214, 243, 306
uchitsu-omi, 300
uchūben 右中弁, 38
Uda 宇太, 77
Uda 宇多, emperor, 45
udaiben 右大弁, 38
udaijin 右大臣, 38
Udon, 200
Ueda Akinari 上田秋成, 161, 301, 312
Ueda Bin 上田敏, 115
ueji 右衛士, 44

Ueki Emori 植木枝盛, 105
Uesugi 上杉 family, *300*
  Harunori 治憲, 301
  Kagekatsu 景勝, 66, 301
  Kenshin 謙信, 126, 282, 301
  Noriaki 憲顕, 126, 300
  Norimasa 憲政, 126, 301
  Noritada 憲忠, 148
  Norizane 憲実, 14, 45, 300
  Yōzan 鷹山, 301
Uesugi *uji, 300*
Uesugi 上杉 war barons, 249
Ugetsu Monogatari, 301, 312
uhyōe 右兵衛, 44
Uji-cha, 301
ujigami, 301
Ujigimi 氏公, 54
Uji jūjō 宇治十帖, 56
ujiko 氏子, 300
Uji no Wakiiratsuko 菟道稚郎子, 309
Ujishūi Monogatari, 201, *302*
Uji-Yamada, 187, *302*
ukedokoro, 103, 267, *302*
ukesho 請所, 302
Ukigumo, 302
uki-komononari 浮小物成, 157
Ukita Hideie 宇喜田秀家, 66
Ukiyo-buro, 303
Ukiyo-doko 浮世床, 303
ukiyo-e, 58, 138, *303*
ukiyo-zōshi, 58, 199, 222, 247, *303*
Ukyō 右京, 77
ukyōshiki 右京職, 172
Ullung Island, *see* Utsuryō-tō
Ulsan (Urusan) 蔚山, 198
umaya 厩 (駅), 21, 46 ⌈225
Umi ni Ikuru Hitobito 海に生くる人々,
uneme 采女, 288
unjō, 191, *303*
Untei library, *303*
Un'yō 雲揚 (gunboat), 150
urabon 盂蘭盆, 20
Uraga, 121, *304*
Urusan, *see* Ulsan

ushōben 右少弁, 38
Ushū 羽州, 222 ⌈94
Usui Shichirōzaemon 薄井七郎左衛門,
Usukeshi (ancient name of Hakodate),
  72
uta-awase, 304
Utaetadasu-tsukasa 刑部省, 70
Utamaro, *see* Kitagawa Utamaro
uta-ryō 雅楽寮, 295
Utsubo Monogatari, 283, 304
Utsuryō-tō 欝陵島 (Dagelet Island,
  Ullung Island), 292
Uzumasa 太秦, 77, 159

V

Versailles Jōyaku, 31, 155, *304*
Vilela, Father Gaspard, 193

W

Wa 委, 60
wabi-cha 佗茶, 25
Wada Yoshimori 和田義盛, 119, 024
Wadō kaihō, 147, *305,* 310
wagaku 和学, 153
wajin 倭人, 60, 62
Wakabayashi Kyōsai 若林強斎, 277
waka-doshiyori, 127, 180, *305*
Wakanashū 若菜集, 230, 261 ⌈113
Wakashu Kabuki 若衆歌舞伎, 112,
Wakasugi-yaki 若杉焼, 168
wake (title), *305* ⌊141, 173
wakei-seijaku 和敬清寂, 25
Wake no Hirose 和気広世, 146 ⌈146
Wake no Kiyomaro 和気清麻呂, 77,
waki-kaidō 脇街道, 305
waki-ōkan, 305
wakō, 211, *305*
Wakoku 倭国, 306 ⌈254
Wakoku mutsu no mi-agata 倭国六御県,
Wamyō Ruijushō, 306
Wamyōshō 倭名抄, 306

Wang Chao-ming 汪兆銘, 202
Wang Ching-wei 汪精衛, 202
Wang Hsi-chih 王羲之, 242
Wang Yang-ming 王陽明, 111, 117,
Wani 王仁, 16, 129, 309 ⌊149, 311
Wa no Kuni 倭国, 193
Wa no Na 倭奴, 124
Waōbu (Emperor Yūryaku), 306
warichi 割地, 86
warimoto 割元, 188
wasan, 307
Waseda Daigaku, 307
Washington Kaigi, 307
Watanabe Jōtarō 渡辺錠太郎, 203
Watanabe Kazan 渡辺崋山, 18, 269
Watarai Shintō 度会神道, 97
Watsuji Tetsurō 和辻哲郎, 261
wayo (mutual understanding), 307
Wa-yō 和様 (Japanese style), 127
Wazoku Dōji-kun 和俗童子訓, 216
Webb, William, 172
Wei Chih 魏志, 60, 193 ⌈308
Wei Chih Wo Jen Chuan 魏志倭人伝,
Weihaiwei, see Ikaiei
Wei Man 衛満, 226
Wilson, Woodrow, 154
Witte, Sergei, 199, 225
"Wo Jen Chuan" 倭人伝, 193, 308
Wuch'ang 武昌, 259
Wuhan 武漢, 202
Wu Ti 武帝, 226

X

Xavier, Francis, 142, 255, 284, 308

Y

yabusame, 127, 307
Yadoya no Meshimori 宿屋飯盛, 171
Yaguchi Raiō 矢口来応, 259
yagura 櫓, 21
Yahata Seitetsu-sho, 308
yakahito 家人, 135

yakusa no kabane, 50, 94, 112, 211,
305, 308
Yakushi-ji, 195, 308
Yakushima 屋久島, 246
Yakushin 益信, 259 ⌈102
Yakushi Nyorai 薬師如来 at Jingo-ji,
Yalta Kaidan, 308
Yalu River, 292
yamabushi 山伏, 270
Yamada Bimyō 山田美妙, 261
Yamada bugyō 山田奉行, 302
Yamada Nagamasa 山田長政, 200
yama e asobi ni yaru 山へ遊びにやる
(infanticide), 174
Yamaga 山鹿, 245
Yamaga Sokō 山鹿素行, 149
Yamagata Aritomo 山県有明, 29, 136
Yamaguchi, 308
Yamana 山名, head of Samurai-
dokoro, 189, 240, 262
Yamana Mochitoyo 山名持豊, 76,
118, 215 ⌈271
Yamana Ujikiyo 山名氏清, 180, 212,
yama-nengu 山年貢, 196 ⌈(崑崙), 161
Yamanoi Kanae (Konron) 山井鼎,
Yamanouchi 山内 family, 300
Yamanoue (Yamanoe) no Okura
山上憶良, 80, 244 ⌈87, 97
Yamashina Hongan-ji 山科本願寺,
Yamashiro no Ōe no Ō 山背大兄王,
Yamashita Kōnai 山下幸内, 180 ⌊92
Yamatai-koku, 60, 308
Yamato-e, 56, 124, 206, 277, 279, 309
Yamato-hime 倭姫, 181
Yamato no aya 東文, 94
Yamato no Aya no Atae, 309
Yamato no Aya no Atai Tsuka
東漢直掬, 309 ⌈129, 243, 309
Yamato no aya uji 東文氏 (東漢氏), 16,
Yamato no fubito-be 東史部, 16, 309
Yamato-setsu 大和説, 309
Yamato-shiza, 209, 309, 311, 314
Yamato Takeru no Mikoto 日本武尊,
49, 164

Yamazaki Ansai 山崎闇斎, 183, 274, 277

Yamazaki Sōkan 山崎宗鑑, 71, 227, ⌊299

yamori 家守, 284

Yanagisawa Yoshiyasu 柳沢吉保, 274

Yano Ryūkei 矢野竜渓, 117, 131

yarimochi-yakko 槍持奴, 223

Yarō Kabuki 野郎歌舞伎, 113

Yashiro Hirokata 屋代弘賢, 69, 161

Yaso Kyōkai 耶蘇教会 192

Yasuda 安田 *zaibatsu,* 315

Yasui Santetsu 安井算哲, 109, 249

Yatabe Ryōkichi 矢田部良吉, 261

Yayoi 弥生 period, 117, 120, 140, 163, 174, 282, 296

Yayoi 弥生 potters, 277

Yayoi-shiki doki, 117, *310* ⌈14

Yi Sam-p'yong (Ri Sam-pei) 李参平,

Yi Song-gye (Ri Sei-kei) 李成桂, 31, 211, 306 ⌈280, *310, 316*

yō (labor tax), 52, 63, 68, 101, 274,

yoboro 丁, 169

yōbun 徭分, 316

yōbunsen 徭分銭, 316

Yodo, 292, *310*

Yodogawa 淀川, 219

Yodogimi 淀君, 221

Yodoya 淀屋, 42

yōeki 徭役, 74, 118

yōgaku, 310

Yōgakusho 洋学所, 18, 116

yōju 遙授, 312

yokoana-shiki sekishitsu, 311

Yokohama 横浜, 192

Yokosuka Zōsen-jo, *311*

yōkyoku, 209, *311*

Yōmei-gaku, *311*

Yōmei-mon 陽明門 at Tōshō-gū, 297

yomihon, 195, 203, 301, *312*

yomogi-tsumi ni yaru 蓬つみにやる (infanticide), 174

Yomo no Akara 四方赤良, 171 ⌈301

Yonezawa 米沢: clan, 267; lords of,

yōnin, 156, *312*

yōnin-sei 遙任制, 156

Yonkakukoku Jōyaku, 307, *312*

Yōrō Ritsuryō, 29, 280, *312*

yoryūdo 寄人, 132, 143

Yosa Buson 与謝蕪村, 71, 254

Yosano Akiko 与謝野晶子, 191, 199

Yosano Tekkan 与謝野鉄幹, 191, 261

yōsen 徭銭, 316

Yoshida Genkaku 吉田源覚, 269

Yoshida Kanetomo 吉田兼倶, 87, *312*

Yoshida Kenkō 吉田兼好, 299

Yoshida Kōton 吉田篁墩, 161

Yoshida Mitsuyoshi 吉田光由, 307

Yoshida Shigeru 吉田茂, 106

Yoshida Shintō, 87, *312*

Yoshida Shōin 吉田松陰, 267

Yoshidaya 吉田屋 kiln, 168

Yoshiharu Shikimoku 義治式目, 23

Yoshimine no Yasuyo 良岑安世, 131

Yoshimura Toratarō 吉村寅太郎, 287

Yoshino 吉野 court, 194

Yoshizaki 吉崎, 87

Yōsho Shirabesho 洋書調所, 18

Yōzei 陽成, emperor, 36

Yūai-kai, 205, *313*

Yüan 元 (Mongol) dynasty, 288

Yüan Shih-k'ai 袁世凱, 154

yūbin-seido, 313

yūgen 幽玄, 169

yūgen-bi 幽玄美, 209

yugishō 湯起請, 163

yugyō no hijiri 遊行聖, 103

yuhazu no mitsugi 弓弭調, 29

yui (joint labor), *313*

Yuiitsu Shintō 唯一神道, 312

Yuima 維摩 Sutra, 241

yūjo 遊女, 94

Yūki-ke Hatto 結城家法度, 23

Yume Monogatari 夢物語, 18

Yumedono, 88, 92, *313*

Yura 由良 clan, 143

Yuri Kimimasa 由利公正, 11, 62

Yūryaku 雄略, emperor, 222, 306, 309

Yūsaki-za 結崎座, 208, 309

Yushima 湯島 in Edo, 147, 265
yūsoku-kojitsu, 313
Yuzuki no Kimi 弓月君, 77
Yūzū Nembutsu 融通念仏, 48

Z

za, 314 「*314*, 315
zaibatsu, 61, 184, 204, 216, 247, 278,
zaibatsu kaitai, 315
Zaichūshō no Nikki 在中将の日記, 97
Zaigo-chūshō nikki 在五中将日記, 97
Zaigo-ga-Monogatari 在五が物語, 97
zaigō-gunjin-kai, 315
zakko 雑戸, 19, 295
Zakoba 雑喉場, 219
zambō-ritsu, 273, *315*
zampatsu-dattō rei, 315
zasso ketsudansho, 133, 142, *315*
zatsuwa-mono 雑話物, 303
zatsuyō, 295, *316*

zazen 坐禅, 45
Zeami 世阿弥, 113, 145, 208, 309, 311
Zekkai Chūshin 絶海中津, 67, 145
zempō-kōen fun, 316
zenisatsu 銭札, 75
zenkō 禅閣, 120
Zen-kunen no Eki, *316*
Zen-shū, 48, 131, *317*
zentaishugi, 317
zetsumyō 絶妙, 48
Zeze 膳所, 223 「209
Zhukov, Grigori Konstantinovich,
zōbō 像法, 177
Zōhei-kyoku, *317*
zōhyō 雑兵, 14
Zoku Gunsho-ruijū 続群書類従, 69
Zola, Emile, 263
Zōshi-kan 造士館, 75
zōshiki 雑色, 295
zuryō 受領, 224
zusho-ryō 図書寮, 295

CHARACTER INDEX

This index, intended for readers of Japanese texts who need to look up the readings of unfamiliar terms, presents the Japanese terms of the main text in kanji. The index follows the order of kanji *in Andrew N. Nelson's* Modern Reader's Japanese-English Character Dictionary— *that is, the order of the 214 radicals for the first (or only)* kanji *of a given term and the order of increasing number of strokes for succeeding* kanji *when there is more than one term in any single* kanji *division. When the succeeding* kanji *have the same number of strokes, the order of the 214 radicals is followed.*

RAD. — 1

一寸法師 Issun-bōshi
一円知行 ichien chigyō
一切経 Issaikyō
一世一元 isse-ichigen
一向一揆 Ikkō-ikki
一向宗 Ikkō-shū
一色 Isshiki
一条 Ichijō (Fujiwara branch)
一条天皇 Ichijō Tennō
一身田 isshinden
一品 ippon
一族 ichizoku
一遍 Ippen
一遍上人絵伝 Ippen Shōnin Eden
一橋 Hitotsubashi
丁 yoboro
丁汝昌 Ting Ju-ch'ang
丁銀 chōgin
兀庵普寧 Gottan Funei
与謝野晶子 Yosano Akiko
与謝野鉄幹 Yosano Tekkan
与謝蕪村 Yosa Buson
万世 man'yo
万年通宝 Mannen tsūhō
万寿寺 Manju-ji
万寿禅寺 Manju Zen-ji
万朝報 Manchōhō

万葉 man'yō
万葉代匠記 Man'yō Daishōki
万葉集 Man'yōshū
万歳騒擾事件 Banzai sōjō jiken
万福寺 Mampuku-ji
三大勅祭 sandaichokusai
三尸虫 sanshichū
三井 Mitsui
三井寺 Mii-dera
三井高利（八郎右衛門）Mitsui Taka-toshi (Hachirōemon)
三井高俊 Mitsui Takatoshi
三井銀行 Mitsui Ginkō
三月堂 Sangatsu-dō
三世一身法 sanze-isshin no hō
三代実録 Sandai Jitsuroku
三田文学 Mita bungaku
三目八臂 sammoku-hachibi
三礼 Sanrai
三好松洛 Miyoshi Shōraku
三好長慶 Miyoshi Chōkei
三宅石庵 Miyake Sekian
三宅雪嶺 Miyake Setsurei
三宅観瀾 Miyake Kanran
三条西実隆 Sanjōnishi Sanetaka
三奉行 san bugyō
三味線 shamisen (samisen)
三国 Mikuni (port town)
三国干渉 Sangoku Kanshō

371

三国防共協定 Sangoku Bōkyō Kyōtei
三国志 Sangokushi (in Chinese, San-kuo Chih)
三宝院 Sambō-in
三宝絵詞 Sambō Ekotoba
三品 sambon
三度飛脚 sando-hikyaku
三島通庸 Mishima Michitsune
三家集 Sankashū
三従七法 sanjū-shichikyo
三浦 Miura
三経義疏 Sankyō-gisho
三菱 Mitsubishi
三菱汽船会社 Mitsubishi Kisen Kai-sha
三菱商会 Mitsubishi Shōkai
三善康信 Miyoshi Yasunobu
三筆 sampitsu
三管 sankan
三管四職 sankan-shishoku
三管領 san kanrei
三蔵 sanzō
三論宗 Sanron-shū
三輪 Miwa
三輪執斎 Miwa Shissai
三蹟 sanseki
三韓 Sankan
三韓征伐 Sankan seibatsu
下人 genin
下北半島 Shimokita-hantō
下司 shita-zukasa (gesu)
下功田 gekōden
下田組 Shimoda-gumi
下地中分 shitaji-chūbun
下河辺長流 Shimokōbe Chōryū
下剋上 gekokujō
下馬札 geba-fuda
下馬将軍 geba shōgun
下関条約 Shimonoseki Jōyaku
下関事件 Shimonoseki jiken
五ヶ条の誓文 Go-kajō no Seimon
五・一五事件 go-ichigo jiken
五人組 gonin-gumi
五大老 go-tairō

五大虚空蔵 Godai Kokūzō
五山 Gozan
五山文学 Gozan-bungaku
五山版 Gozan-ban
五匁銀 gomomme-gin
五代友厚 Godai Tomoatsu
五・四運動 go-shi undō
五行 go-gyō
五条頼元 Gojō Yorimoto
五奉行 go-bugyō
五保制度 goho-seido
五陵 (稜) 郭 Goryōkaku
五経博士 gokyō hakase
五傍の掲示 Gobō no Keiji
五街道 go-kaidō
五摂家 go-sekke
五畿七道 goki-shichidō
天平 Tempyō
天正遣欧使節 Tenshō ken'ō shisetsu
天台 Tendai (in Chinese, T'ien T'ai)
天守閣 tenshukaku
天武天皇 Temmu Tennō
天武令 Temmu ryō
天寿国曼荼羅 Tenjukoku Mandara
天寿国繍帳 Tenjukoku Shuchō
天児屋根命 Amenokoyane no Mikoto
天竺様 tenjiku-yō
天保の改革 Tempō no kaikaku
天津条約 Tenshin Jōyaku
天海 Tenkai
天海版 Tenkai-ban
天皇機関説 tennō kikansetsu
天草本平家物語 Amakusa-bon Heike Monogatari
天草四郎 Amakusa Shirō
天竜寺 Tenryū-ji
天竜寺船 Tenryūji-bune
天理教 Tenri-kyō
天道教 Tendō-kyō
天智天皇 Tenchi Tennō
天満 Temma
天照大神 Amaterasu Ōmikami
天誅組 Tenchū-gumi
天慶の乱 Tengyō no ran

天穂日命 Amenohobi no Mikoto
不入 funyū 「Zō
不空羂索観音像 Fukūkenjaku Kannon
不戦条約 Fusen Jōyaku
不輸 fuyu
不輸不入権 fuyufunyū-ken
不輸租田 fuyuso-den
可翁 Kaō
民山焼 Minzan-yaki
民友社 Min'yū-sha
民友社派 Min'yūsha-ha
民主自由党 Minshu Jiyū-tō
民政党 Minsei-tō
民約訳解 Min'yaku Yakuge
民部省 Mimbu-shō
民選議院設立建白 minsen-giin setsuritsu kempaku
平戸 Hirado
平民 heimin
平民社 Heimin-sha
平民新聞 Heimin Shimbun
平田禿木 Hirata Tokuboku
平田篤胤 Hirata Atsutane
平曲 heikyoku
平安京 Heian-kyō
平国香 Taira no Kunika
平忠正 Taira no Tadamasa
平沼騏一郎 Hiranuma Kiichirō
平治の乱 Heiji no ran
平治物語 Heiji Monogatari
平治物語絵詞 Heiji Monogatari Ekotoba
平重盛 Taira no Shigemori
平貞盛 Taira no Sadamori
平城天皇 Heizei Tennō
平城京 Heijō-kyō
平政子 Taira no Masako
平泉 Hiraizumi
平家物語 Heike Monogatari
平家琵琶 Heike biwa
平将門 Taira no Masakado
平清盛 Taira no Kiyomori
平野国臣 Hirano Kuniomi
平塚雷鳥 Hiratsuka Raichō

平等院 Byōdō-in
平群 Heguri
平群真鳥 Heguri no Madori
平蒔絵 hira-makie
平維盛 Taira no Koremori
平塵 heijin
平壌 Heijō (in Korean, P'yongyang)
正一位 shō-ichii
正丁 shōchō
正中の変 Shōchū no hen
正名論 Shōmeiron
正岡子規 Masaoka Shiki
正法 shōbō
正法眼蔵 Shōbōgenzō
正長の土一揆 Shōchō no do-ikki
正風 shōfū
正倉院 Shōsō-in
正福寺 Shōfuku-ji
百姓一揆 hyakushō-ikki
百姓代 hyakushō-dai
百姓請 hyakushō-uke
百済 Kudara (in Korean, Paekche)
百済観音 Kudara Kannon
両替 ryōgae
両替屋 ryōgae-ya
両統迭立 ryōtō tetsuritsu
吾妻鏡 Azuma Kagami
巫子 miko
盂蘭盆 urabon
函館 Hakodate
函館奉行 Hakodate bugyō
武士団 bushidan
武内宿禰 Takenouchi no Sukune
武田氏 Takeda uji
武田信玄 Takeda Shingen
武田勝頼 Takeda Katsuyori
武者所 musha-dokoro
武帝 Wu Ti
武家造 buke-zukuri
武家物 buke-mono
武家諸法度 Buke Sho-Hatto
武庫 Muko
武野紹鷗 Takeno Jōō
武漢 Wuhan

晋 Chin (Chinese dynasty)
夏の陣 natsu no jin
悪人正機 akunin-shōki

━━━━━━ RAD. | 2 ━━━━━━

中大兄皇子 Nakanoōe no Ōji
中山忠光 Nakayama Tadamitsu
中山忠親 Nakayama Tadachika
中山信 Nakayama Shin
中山道 Nakasendō
中川淳庵 Nakagawa Jun'an
中井竹山 Nakai Chikuzan
中本 chūbon
中功田 chūkōden
中年寄 naka-doshiyori
中江兆民 Nakae Chōmin
中江藤樹 Nakae Tōju
中村正直 Nakamura Masanao
中村敬宇 Nakamura Keiu
中沢道二 Nakazawa Dōji
中男 chūnan
中臣 Nakatomi (clan)
中臣連 Nakatomi no Muraji
中臣部 Nakatomi-be
中臣鎌足 Nakatomi no Kamatari
中国寺 Chūgoku-ji
中島 Nakajima (company)
中宮寺 Chūgū-ji
中納言 chūnagon
中務省 Nakatsukasa-shō
中野重治 Nakano Shigeharu
中尊寺 Chūson-ji
中興鑑言 Chūkō Kangen
内大臣 naidaijin
内臣 uchitsu-omi (naishin)
内宮 naikū
内蔵 uchitsukura
由利公正 Yuri Kimimasa
由良 Yura (clan)
史 fubito (fuhito)
史定 shijō
史記 Shih Chi
史部 fubito-be

甲申の乱 (変) Kōshin no ran (hen)
甲必丹 kapitan (capitao)
甲州街道 Kōshūkaidō
甲州葡萄 Kōshū budō
甲府 Kōfu
甲賀宮 Kōga no Miya
旧事本紀 Kujihongi
旧事紀 Kujiki
世阿弥 Zeami
世界恐慌 sekai kyōkō
世尊寺流 Sesonji-ryū
世間胸算用 Seken Munezan'yō
世話物 sewamono
本木良英 Motoki Yoshihide
本田利明 Honda Toshiaki
本百姓 hombyakushō
本両替 honryōgae
本地垂迹 honchi-suijaku
本阿弥光悦 Hon'ami Kōetsu
本居宣長 Moto-ori Norinaga
本所 honsho
本紀 hongi
本草学 honsō-gaku
本能寺の変 Honnō-ji no hen
本朝通鑑 Honchō Tsugan
本朝編年録 Honchō Hennen-roku
本間憲一郎 Homma Ken'ichirō
本領安堵 honryō-ando
本願寺 Hongan-ji
出版条例 shuppan jōrei
出島 Deshima
出挙 suiko
出雲の阿国 Izumo no Okuni
出雲大社 Izumo Taisha
出機 debata
曲真瀬道三 Manase Dōzan
表 hyō (tables in *Dai Nihon Shi*)
帥 sotsu
幽玄 yūgen
幽玄美 yūgen-bi
師宣 Moronobu (=Hishikawa Moronobu)
鴨長明 Kamo no Chōmei
鴨緑江 Ōryokkō (Yalu River)

━━━━ RAD. ヽ 3 ━━━━

永井荷風 Nagai Kafū
永平寺 Eihei-ji
永享の乱 Eikyō no ran
永高 eidaka
永楽通宝 Eiraku tsūhō
永楽銭 eiraku-sen
半済 hansai (hanzei)
為永春水 Tamenaga Shunsui
為替 kawase
為替方 kawase-kata

━━━━ RAD. ノ 4 ━━━━

九ヶ国条約 Kyūkakoku Jōyaku
九十九 Tsukumo (company)
九州探題 Kyūshū tandai
九州説 Kyūshū-setsu
九条 Kujō
九条兼実 Kujō Kanezane
九条道家 Kujō Michiie
九谷焼 Kutani-yaki
九米桂一郎 Kume Keiichirō
久坂玄瑞 Kusaka Gensui
久原 Kuhara
久遠寺 Kuon-ji
久離 kyūri
千々石清左衛門 Chijiwa Seizaemon
千字文 Senjimon (in Chinese, Ch'ien-
千早 Chihaya   tzu-wen)
千住製絨所 Senju seijūsho
千利休 Sen no Rikyū
千歯こき semba-koki
匁 momme
升 shō
丹羽正伯 Niwa Seihaku
夫役 buyaku
井上日昭 Inoue Nisshō
井上良馨 Inoue Yoshika
井上哲次郎 Inoue Tetsujirō
井上準之助 Inoue Junnosuke
井上毅 Inoue Kowashi
井上馨 Inoue Kaoru

井伊直弼 Ii Naosuke
井原西鶴 Ihara Saikaku
少納言 shōnagon
末吉孫左衛門 Sueyoshi Magozaemon
末法思想 mappō-shisō
末法濁世 mappō-jokuse
夷守 Ezo-mori
朱子学 Shushi-gaku
朱丹渓 Chu Tan-ch'i
朱印地 shuin-chi
朱印状 shuin-jō
朱印船 shuin-sen (shuin-bune)
朱雀大路 Suzaku-ōji
朱雀天皇 Suzaku Tennō
朱熹 Shu Ki (in Chinese, Chu Hsi)
年中行事絵巻 Nenjū Gyōji Emaki
年季奉公 nenki-bōkō
年貢 nengu
年寄 toshiyori
年預 nennyo
寿福寺 Jufuku-ji
承久の変 Jōkyū no hen
承和の変 Shōwa no hen (Jōwa no hen)
承和昌宝 Shōwa shōhō
我楽多文庫 Garakuta Bunko
兵庫 Hyōgo
兵部省 Hyōbu-shō
兵糧米 hyōrō-mai
来栖三郎 Kurusu Saburō
垂仁天皇 Suinin Tennō
垂加神道 Suika Shintō
奉公 hōkō
奉行人 bugyōnin
奉行所 bugyōsho
東大寺 Tōdai-ji
東山文化 Higashiyama bunka
東山道 Tōsandō
東文 Yamato no aya
東文氏 (東漢氏) Yamato no aya uji
東史部 Yamato no fubito-be
東本願寺 Higashi Hongan-ji
東州斎写楽 Tōshūsai Sharaku
東夷伝 Tung I Chuan
東寺 Tō-ji

東寺十二天図 Tō-ji Jūni-ten Zu
東西南北 Tōzai-namboku
東求堂同仁斎 Tōgudō Dōjinsai
東条英機 Tōjō Hideki
東京大学 Tōkyō Daigaku
東京医学校 Tōkyō Igakkō
東京美術学校 Tōkyō Bijutsu Gakkō
東京専門学校 Tōkyō Semmon Gakkō
東京開成学校 Tōkyō Kaisei Gakkō
東京遷都 Tōkyō sento
東学党の乱 Tōgaku-tō no ran
東南院 Tōnan'in
東洋自由新聞 Tōyō Jiyū Shimbun
東海道 Tōkaidō   「Shirō)
東海散士 Tōkai Sanshi (=Shiba
東密 Tō-mitsu
東常縁 Tō Tsuneyori
東塔 Tōtō
東漢直 Yamato no Aya no Atae
東漢直掬 Yamato no Aya no Atai
東照宮 Tōshō-gū   「Tsuka
東福寺 Tōfuku-ji
東関紀行 Tōkan Kikō
卑弥呼 Himiko
乗田 jōden
重訂解体新書 Jūtei Kaitai Shinsho
重源 Chōgen
重慶 Ch'ungch'ing
烏帽子 eboshi
烏帽子子 eboshi-ko
烏帽子親 eboshi-oya
島田三郎 Shimada Saburō
島田組 Shimada-gumi
島守 shima-mori
島村抱月 Shimamura Hōgetsu
島津 Shimazu
島津久光 Shimazu Hisamitsu
島津外様 Shimazu tozama
島津斉彬 Shimazu Nariakira
島津貴久 Shimazu Takahisa
島原の乱 Shimabara no ran
島崎藤村 Shimazaki Tōson
奥の細道 Oku no Hosomichi
奥平信昌 Okudaira Nobumasa

奥州探題 Ōshū tandai
奥州街道 Ōshūkaidō
奥羽 Ōu
厳島 Itsukushima

——————— **RAD. 乙 5** ———————

乙名 otome
七大寺 shichi-daiji
七道 shichidō
屯田 mita
屯田兵制度 tondenhei-seido
屯倉 miyake

——————— **RAD. 亅 6** ———————

事大党 Jidai-tō

——————— **RAD. 二 7** ———————

二の丸 ni-no-maru
二・二六事件 ni-niroku jiken
二十一ヶ条要求 Nijūikkajō Yōkyū
二十五菩薩来迎図 Nijūgo Bosatsu Rai-
gōzu   「zumi-doiya
二十四組江戸積問屋 nijūshi-kumi Edo-
二十四組問屋 nijūshi-kumi don'ya
二朱銀 nishu-gin
二条 Nijō (Fujiwara branch)
二条良基 Nijō Yoshimoto   「gaki
二条河原の落書 Nijōgawara no raku-
二品 nihon
二科会 Nika-kai
二葉亭四迷 Futabatei Shimei
元 Yüan (Mongol dynasty)
元正天皇 Genshō Tennō
元弘の変 Genkō no hen
元老 genrō
元老院 Genrōin
元享釈書 Genkō Shakusho
元明天皇 Gemmei Tennō
元治の変 Genji no hen
元和令 Genna-ryō
元冠 Genkō

元禄文化 Genroku bunka
元禄時代 Genroku jidai
元興寺 Gangō-ji (Gankō-ji)

──── **RAD. 亠 8** ────

六人衆 Rokunin-shū
六分一殿 rokubun-no-ichi dono
六条河原 Rokujōgawara
六条御堂 Rokujō Midō
六角 Rokkaku (family)
六角堂 Rokkaku-dō
六国史 Rikkoku Shi
六波羅 Rokuhara
六波羅探題 Rokuhara tandai
六斎市 rokusai-ichi
六歌仙 rokkasen
市川左団次 Ichikawa Sadanji
主典 sakan
主典代 shutendai
主帖 shuchō
主政 shusei
享保の改革 Kyōhō no kaikaku
京都大番役 Kyōto ōban-yaku
京都五山 Kyōto Gozan
京都守護職 Kyōto shugo-shoku
京都所司代 Kyōto shoshidai
京極 Kyōgoku
京職 misato no tsukasa
京職 kyōshiki
帝国大学 Teikoku Daigaku
帝国在郷軍人会 Teikoku Zaigō-Gun-
帝政党 Teisei-tō   ⌞jin-kai
恋川春町 Koikawa Harumachi
商法大意 Shōhō-taii
商法司 shōhōshi
商法会所 Shōhō-kaisho
棄捐令 kien-rei
甕棺 kamekan

──── **RAD. 人 9** ────

人民文学 Jimmin Bungaku
人返 hitogaeshi

人足寄場 ninsoku yoseba
人情本 ninjōbon
以仁王 Mochihiko-ō
仁 jin (rank)
仁孝天皇 Ninkō Tennō
仁明天皇 Nimmyō Tennō
仁和寺 Ninna-ji
仁徳天皇 Nintoku Tennō
仏足石 bussokuseki
仏殿 Butsuden
今川氏 Imagawa uji
今川貞世 Imagawa Sadayo
今川家仮名目録 Imagawa-ke Kana-
  mokuroku
今川義元 Imagawa Yoshimoto
今切 Imagire
今昔物語 Konjaku Monogatari
今様 imayō
今様合 imayō-awase
今鏡 Imakagami
令 ryō (administrative code)
令外 ryōge
令外の官 ryōge no kan
令集解 Ryō no Shūge
令義解 Ryō no Gige
他力 tariki
他力本願 tariki-hongan
他村入会 tason-iriai
代 shiro
代助郷 dai-sukegō
代官 daikan
代官所 daikansho
伊万里 Imari
伊万里焼 Imari-yaki
伊予 Iyo
伊沢蘭軒 Izawa Ranken
伊東巳代治 Itō Miyoji
伊東満所 Itō Mancio
伊東義賢 Itō Yoshikata
伊奈忠次 Ina Tadatsugu
伊波比主命 Iwainushi no Mikoto
伊達 Date
伊達正宗 Date Masamune
伊曾保物語 Isoho Monogatari

伊勢平氏 Ise Heishi
伊勢市 Ise-shi
伊勢物語 Ise Monogatari
伊勢長氏 Ise Nagauji
伊勢神道 Ise Shintō
伊勢路 Ise-ji
伊藤仁斎 Itō Jinsai
伊藤左千夫 Itō Sachio
伊藤博文 Itō Hirobumi
任那 Mimana (in Korean, Imna)
似絵 nise-e
伏見天皇 Fushimi Tennō
伏見城 Fushimi-jō
伏見戦 Fushimi no tatakai
仲哀天皇 Chūai Tennō
伝法院 Dempō-in
伝馬 temma
伝習館 Denshū-kan
会合衆 egōshū
会沢正志斎 Aizawa Seishisai
会津 Aizu
仮名 kana   「gura
仮名手本忠臣蔵 Kanadehon Chūshin-
仮名垣魯文 Kanagaki Robun
仮名草子 kana-zōshi
全体主義 zentai-shugi
坐禅 zazen
佃 tsukuda
佐久間盛政 Sakuma Morimasa
佐久間象山 Sakuma Shōzan
佐々木高氏 （道誉） Sasaki Takauji
佐竹 Satake   ∟(Dōyo)
佐伯部 saeki-be
佐渡金銀山 Sado kinginzan
佐賀の乱 Saga no ran
伴大納言絵詞 Ban Dainagon Ekotoba
伴信友 Ban Nobutomo
伴造 tomo no miyatsuko
伴健岑 Ban no Kowamine
位田 iden
位封 ifu
住友 Sumitomo
住吉派 Sumiyoshi-ha
作人 sakunin

舎人親王 Toneri Shinnō
舎利殿 Shariden
念仏 nembutsu
念仏宗 Nembutsu-shū
念仏踊 nembutsu-odori
侍所 Samurai-dokoro
佳人の奇遇 Kajin no Kigū
供御田 kugoden
信 shin (rank)
信玄家法 Shingen Kahō
信長 Nobunaga (＝Oda Nobunaga)
信貴山縁起絵巻 Shigisan Engi Emaki
信楽宮 Shigaraki no Miya
保元の乱 Hōgen no ran
保元物語 Hōgen Monogatari
保司 hōji
保安条例 hoan jōrei
保安隊 hoantai
保建大記 Hōken Taiki
俵物 tawara-mono
倭人 wajin   「Jen Chuan)
倭人伝 Wajinden (in Chinese, Wo
倭王武 Waōbu
倭名抄 Wamyōshō
倭名類聚抄 Wamyō Ruijushō
倭国 Wakoku (Wa no Kuni)
倭国六御県 Wakoku mutsu no mi-
倭姫 Yamato-hime   ∟agata
倭寇 wakō
倶舎宗 Kusha-shū
俳文 haibun
俳風柳樽 Haifū Yanagidaru
俳諧 haikai
俳諧連歌 haikai renga
倉役 kurayaku
借上 kashiage
借家人 kariya-bito
修正派 Shūsei-ha
修猷館 Shūyū-kan
修験道 shugendō
側用人 soba-yōnin
健児 kondei
健児田 kondei-den
傀儡子 kugutsu

催馬楽 saibara
傾く kabuku
僧上遍昭 Sōjō Henshō
僧兵 sōhei
像法 zōbō
儒教 Jukyō
儺県 Na no Agata

━━━━━ RAD. 儿 10 ━━━━━

先達 sendatsu
児童福祉法 Jidō-fukushi Hō
児童憲章 Jidō Kenshō

━━━━━ RAD. 入 11 ━━━━━

入れ札 irefuda
入母屋造 irimoya-zukuri
入会 iriai
入浜 irihama

━━━━━ RAD. 八 12 ━━━━━

八色の姓 yakusa no kabane
八条宮智仁 Hachijōnomiya Toshihiko
八条宮智忠 Hachijōnomiya Toshitada
八幡 Hachiman
八幡神 Hachimanjin
八幡宮 Hachiman-gū
八幡製鉄所 Yahata Seitetsu-sho
分付 bunzuke (buntsuke)
分付百姓 bunzuke hyakushō
分地制限令 bunchi-seigen rei
分米 bummai
分国 bunkoku
分国法 bunkoku-hō
分銭 bunsen
公文 kumon
公文所 Kumonjo
公奴婢 ku-nuhi
公田 kōden
公武合体論 kōbu-gattai ron
公事方 kuji-kata
公事方御定書 Kuji-kata O-sadamegaki

公営田 kueiden
公領 kōryō
公廨 kugai
公廨田 kugaiden
公職追放 kōshoku tsuihō
公議所 Kōgisho
典舞 kusemai
並木千柳 Namiki Senryū
並木宗輔 Namiki Sōsuke
盆踊 Bon odori
前九年の役 Zen-kunen no Eki
前方後円墳 zempō-kōen fun
前句付 maeku-zuke
前田 Maeda (tozama)
前田玄以 Maeda Gen'i
前田利治 Maeda Toshiharu
前田利家 Maeda Toshiie
前田密 Maeda Hisoka
前原一誠 Maebara Issei
前張 saibari
前野良沢 Maeno Ryōtaku
益田四郎 Masuda Shirō
益信 Yakushin
兼好 Kenkō 「kyū-mondō no Uta)
貧窮問答歌 Hinkyū-mondō Ka (Hin-
曾我物語 Soga Monogatari
曾我祐成 Soga Sukenari
曾我時致 Soga Tokimune
普門 Fumon
普通選挙運動 futsū-senkyo undō
尊円法親王 Son'en Hosshinnō
尊王論 sonnō-ron
尊王攘夷 sonnō-jōi
慈円 Jien
慈照寺 Jishō-ji
慈禧 Tz'u Hsi
興中会 Hsing-chung Hui
興禅護国論 Kōzengokoku-ron
興福寺 Kōfuku-ji
興譲館 Kōjō-kan

━━━━━ RAD. 冂 13 ━━━━━

円山応挙 Maruyama Ōkyo

円仁 Ennin
円本 empon
円珍 Enchin
円密禅戒 En-Mitsu-Zen-Kai
円教 engyō
円満 emman
円満井 Emmai
円覚寺 Enkaku-ji (Engaku-ji)
円爾 Enni
円爾弁円 Enji Ben'en
同志社 Dōshisha
岡崎正宗 Okazaki Masamune
周文 Shūbun
周防国府 Suō Kokufu
周易 Shūeki

━━━━━ **RAD. 宀 14** ━━━━━

冠位十二階の制 kan'i jūnikai no sei
軍団 gundan
軍記物 gunkimono
軍記物語 gunki-monogatari
軍備縮小 gumbi shukushō
冥加 myōga
冥加金 myōga-kin
冥報記 Meihōki

━━━━━ **RAD. 冫 15** ━━━━━

次丁 Jichō
次官 suke
冷泉天皇 Reizei Tennō
凌雲集 Ryōunshū
准三后 jusangō
准三宮 jusangū
准后 jukō (jugō)
凝然 Gyōnen

━━━━━ **RAD. 几 16** ━━━━━

凡河内躬恒 Ōshikōchi no Mitsune
鳳凰堂 Hōōdō

━━━━━ **RAD. 刀 18** ━━━━━

刀伊の入寇 Toi no nyūkō
刀狩 katana-gari
刀鍛冶 katana-kaji
刀禰 tone
切字 kireji
切米 kirimai
切米取 kirimai-tori
刑法官 Keihō-kan
刑法読本 Keihō Tokuhon
刑部 gyōbu   「kasa)
刑部省 Gyōbu-shō (Utaetadasu-tsu-
刑部親王 Osakabe Shinnō
判官 jō (secretary)
判官代 hankandai
判者 hanja
別 wake
別子銅山 Besshi dōzan
別当 bettō
副島種臣 Soejima Taneomi
副将軍 fuku-shōgun
割元 warimoto
割地 warichi
割符 saifu
割符屋 saifu-ya
劉宗 Liu Sung

━━━━━ **RAD. 力 19** ━━━━━

加地子 kajiko (kajishi, kachishi)
加判の列 kahan no retsu
加波山事件 Kabayama jiken
加持祈禱 kaji-kitō
加賀 Kaga
加徴米 kachōmai
加藤友三郎 Katō Tomosaburō
加藤弘之 Katō Hiroyuki
加藤高明 Katō Takaaki
加藤景正 Katō Kagemasa
助郷 sukegō
労働三法 rōdō sampō
労働農民党 Rōdō Nōmin-tō
勅旨田 chokushi-den

勇山文継 Isayama Fumitsugu
勘合符 kangōfu
勘当 kandō
勘定奉行 kanjō bugyō
勘進田楽 Kanjin Dengaku
勘解由使 kageyushi
勧学院 Kangakuin
勧善懲悪 kanzen-chōaku

──── RAD. 勹 20 ────

勾玉 magatama

──── RAD. 匕 21 ────

北山文化 Kitayama bunka
北条氏 Hōjō uji
北条氏直 Hōjō Ujinao
北条氏康 Hōjō Ujiyasu
北条早雲 Hōjō Sōun
北条宗政 Hōjō Munemasa
北条実時 Hōjō Sanetoki
北条師時 Hōjō Morotoki
北条泰時 Hōjō Yasutoki
北条時行 Hōjō Tokiyuki
北条時宗 Hōjō Tokimune
北条時房 Hōjō Tokifusa
北条時政 Hōjō Tokimasa
北条時頼 Hōjō Tokiyori
北条高時 Hōjō Takatoki
北村透谷 Kitamura Tōkoku
北洋 Peiyang (squadron)
北海道開拓使 Hokkaidō kaitaku-shi
北海道開拓使官物払下事件　Hokkaidō
　kaitaku-shi　kambutsu-haraisage
　jiken
北面の武士 hokumen no bushi
北畠親房 Kitabatake Chikafusa
北畠顕信 Kitabatake Akinobu
北陸道 Hokurikudō
北清事件 Hoku-Shin jiken
北野天神縁起 Kitano Tenjin Engi
北野神社の麹座 Kitano-jinja no kōji-za
北湊 Kitaminato

北嶺 Hokurei

──── RAD. 匚 22 ────

巨勢 Kose
巨勢野足 Kose no Notari

──── RAD. 十 24 ────

十七条憲法 Jūshichijō no Kempō
十二支 jūnishi
十人両替 jūnin-ryōgae
十人組 jūnin-gumi
十三夜 Jūsan'ya
十干 jikkan
十六夜日記 Izayoi Nikki
十市県 Toichi no Agata
十市県主 Toichi no agata-nushi
十州塩田 Jisshū enden
十返舎一九 Jippensha Ikku
十住心論 Jūjūshinron
十津川郷 Totsugawa-gō
十訓抄 Jikkinshō
十組問屋 to-kumi don'ya
十楽の津 Jūrakunotsu
古今伝授 Kokin-denju
古今和歌集 Kokin Wakashū
古今著聞集 Kokon Chomonshū
古文学派 kobungaku-ha
古史通 Koshi-tsū
古医方 koihō
古事記 Kojiki
古事記伝 Kojiki-den
古学派 kogaku-ha
古河 Koga
古河公方 Koga kubō
古河市兵衛 Furukawa Ichibei
古風 kofū
古道学 kodōgaku
古義学派 kogigaku-ha
古義真言 Kogi Shingon
古語拾遺 Kogoshūi
孝明天皇 Kōmei Tennō
孝経 Kōkyō

孝徳天皇 Kōtoku Tennō　　「ho Hui)
協合会 Kyōwa-kai (in Chinese, Hsieh-
直 atai (atae)
直言 Chokugen (newspaper)
直煮法 chokushahō
直訴 jikiso
南北朝 Nambokuchō
南北朝の内乱 Nambokuchō no nairan
南門 Nammon
南海道 Nankaidō
南都 Nanto
南都七大寺 Nanto shichi-daiji
南都六宗 Nanto rokushū
南都北嶺 Nanto Hokurei
南曹 Nansō (Arihara school)
南蛮人 nambanjin
南蛮文化 namban bunka
南蛮寺 Namban-ji
南蛮学 namban-gaku
南蛮屏風 namban byōbu
南蛮船 nambansen
南蛮貿易 namban bōeki　　「kyō
南無妙法蓮華経 namu myōhō renge-
南無阿弥陀仏 Namu Amida Butsu
南淵弘貞 Minabushi no Hirosada
南満州鉄道株式会社　Minami-Manshū
　Tetsudō Kabushiki-gaisha
南禅寺 Nanzen-ji　　　　「ken den
南総里見八犬伝 Nansō Satomi Hak-
真人 mahito
真言宗 Shingon-shū
真言律 Shingonritsu
真言密教 Shingon Mikkyō
真宗 Shin-shū
真宗本願寺 Shinshū Hongan-ji
真宗高田派 Shinshū Takada-ha
真慧 Shin'e
乾元大宝 Kengen taihō
乾漆造 kanshitsu-zukuri
博多 Hakata

RAD. ╞ 25

上方 Kamigata

上功田 jōkōden
上田秋成 Ueda Akinari
上田敏 Ueda Bin
上地令 agechi-rei
上米 agemai
上杉 Uesugi (family)
上杉治憲 Uesugi Harunori
上杉景勝 Uesugi Kagekatsu
上杉憲実 Uesugi Norizane
上杉憲忠 Uesugi Noritada
上杉憲政 Uesugi Norimasa
上杉憲顕 Uesugi Noriaki
上杉謙信 Uesugi Kenshin
上杉鷹山 Uesugi Yōzan
上東門院彰子 Jōtō Mon'in Akiko
上海事変 Shanghai jihen
上宮聖徳太子法王帝説　Jōgū Shōtoku
　Taishi Hōō Teisetsu
貞永式目 Jōei Shikimoku
貞享暦 Jōkyō-reki (Jōkyō-koyomi)
貞門派 Teimon-ha
貞門風 Teimon-fū
貞観永宝 Jōgan eihō
貞観式 Jōgan-shiki
貞観格 Jōgan-kyaku

RAD. ╔ 27

反 tan (square measure)
原日本人 gen-Nihonjin　　　「ra-jō)
原城 Hara-no-jō (Hara-no-shiro, Ha-
原敬 Hara Takashi
厨川 Kuriyagawa
厩 umaya
厭離穢土 onri-edo

RAD. ム 28

允恭紀 Ingyōki
弁円 Ben'en
弁韓 Benkan (in Korean, Pyon-han)
台密 Tai-mitsu
台湾銀行 Taiwan Ginkō
参与 San'yo

参勤交代 sankin kōtai
参議 Sangi
参議院 Sangi-in
能 (能楽) Nō (Nōgaku)

——— RAD. 又 29 ———

友愛会 Yūai-kai
桑名 Kuwana
桑名関ヶ原 Kuwana-Sekigahara

——— RAD. 口 30 ———

口分田 kubunden
司 tsukasa
司法省 Shihō-shō   「Kuang)
司馬光 Shiba Kō (in Chinese, Ssu-ma
右大弁 udaiben
右大臣 udaijin
右中弁 uchūben
右少弁 ushōben
右兵衛 uhyōe
右京 Ukyō
右京職 ukyōshiki
右衛士 ueji
呂宋 Ruson (Luzon)
君 kimi
品川弥二郎 Shinagawa Yajirō
品部 tomo-be
唯一神道 Yuiitsu Shintō
鳴海 Narumi

——— RAD. 囗 31 ———

四ヶ国条約 Yonkakoku Jōyaku
四天王寺 Shitennō-ji
四方赤良 Yomo no Akara
四民平等 shimin-byōdō
四条派 Shijō-ha
四府駕輿丁座 shifu-gayochō-za
四品 shihon
四等官 shitōkan
四職 shi-shiki
四鏡 Shikyō

団琢磨 Dan Takuma
回天詩史 Kaitenshishi
回送船 kaisō-sen
回船 kaisen
回船式目 Kaisen Shikimoku
図書寮 zusho-ryō
国一揆 kuni-ikki
国人 kokujin
国分寺 kokubun-ji
国木田独歩 Kunikida Doppo
国民の友 Kokumin no Tomo
国民党 Kokumin-tō
国民新聞 Kokumin Shimbun
国民徴用令 kokumin chōyō rei
国司 kokushi
国庁 kokuchō
国立銀行 kokuritsu ginkō
国会期成同盟 Kokkai Kisei-dōmei
国体明徴 kokutai-meichō
国役 kuniyaku
国学 kokugaku
国府 kokufu
国造 kuni no miyatsuko
国家安康 kokka ankō
国家総動員法 kokka sōdōin hō
国粋主義 kokusui-shugi
国産会所 kokusan kaisho
国衆 kunishū
国衙 kokuga
国衙領 kokuga-ryō
国際連合 Kokusai Rengō
国際連盟 Kokusai Remmei
園城寺 Onjō-ji

——— RAD. 土 32 ———

土一揆 do-ikki
土井利勝 Doi Toshikatsu
土方与志 Hijikata Yoshi
土民 domin
土佐光信 Tosa Mitsunobu
土佐光起 Tosa Mitsuoki
土佐派 Tosa-ha
土岐頼兼 Toki Yorikane

土居 doi 「Muraji)

土師連 Haji no Muraji (Hanishi no

土師部 haji-be

土倉 dosō, (tsuchi-kura, to-kura)

土倉役 dosō-yaku

土偶 dogū

土御門天皇 Tsuchimikado Tennō

吉田光由 Yoshida Mitsuyoshi

吉田松陰 Yoshida Shōin

吉田茂 Yoshida Shigeru

吉田屋 Yoshidaya

吉田神道 Yoshida Shintō

吉田兼好 Yoshida Kenkō

吉田兼俱 Yoshida Kanetomo

吉田源覚 Yoshida Genkaku

吉田篁墩 Yoshida Kōton

吉次越 Kichijigoe

吉村寅太郎 Yoshimura Toratarō

吉利支丹 (切支丹) 宗 Kirishitan-shū

吉利支丹版 Kirishitan-ban

吉利支丹屋敷 Kirishitan yashiki

吉崎 Yoshizaki

吉野 Yoshino

吉備 Kibi

吉備真備 Kibi no Mabi

寺子屋 terakoya

寺内正毅 Terauchi Masatake

寺内町 jinai-machi

寺田 jiden

寺田屋騒動 Teradaya sōdō

寺社奉行 jisha bugyō

寺院法度 jiin hatto

寺島宗則 Terajima Munenori

寺請制度 terauke-seido

在五が物語 Zaigo-ga-Monogatari

在五中将日記 Zaigo-chūshō Nikki

在中将の日記 Zaichūshō no Nikki

在原行平 Arihara no Yukihira

在原業平 Arihara no Narihira

在郷軍人会 zaigō-gunjin-kai

地子 chishi

地子銭 chishisen

地方 jikata

地方三役 jikata-san'yaku

地方役人 jikata-yakunin

地方官会議 Chihōkan-kaigi

地主手作 jinushi tezukuri

地侍 ji-samurai

地租 chiso

地租改正 chiso-kaisei

地頭 jitō

地頭代 jitō-dai

地頭請 jitō-uke

壱岐島 Iki-jima 「hen

坂下門外の変 Sakashita-mongai no

坂上田村麻呂 Sakanoue no Tamura-

坂戸 Sakado 」maro

坂本 Sakamoto

坊津 Bōnotsu

志 shi (classified history)

志賀重昂 Shiga Shigetaka

志賀島 Shiganoshima

志賀義雄 Shiga Yoshio

坪内逍遙 Tsubouchi Shōyō

幸若舞 kōwaka-mai

辛福安全社 Kōfuku-anzen-sha

辛徳秋水 Kōtoku Shūsui

城下町 jōka-machi

城山 Shiroyama

城代 jōdai

城泉太郎 Jō Sentarō 「Shih-k'ai)

袁世凱 En Seigai (in Chinese, Yüan

埴輪 haniwa

執事 shitsuji

執権 shikken

堺 Sakai

堺利彦 Sakai Toshihiko

堺紡績所 Sakai bōseki-jo

塔頭 tatchū

喜多七太夫 Kita Shichidayū

喜多川歌麿 Kitagawa Utamaro

喜多流 Kita-ryū

喜撰法師 Kisen Hōshi

塙保己一 Hanawa Hokinoichi

塩田法 endenhō

嘉吉の変 Kakitsu no hen

増田長盛 Masuda Nagamori

増鏡 Masukagami

墾田 konden
墾田地系荘園 kondenchi-kei shōen
墾田私有令 konden-shiyū rei
壇の浦 Dannoura

━━━━━ RAD. 士 33 ━━━━━

士族 shizoku
士族の商法 shizoku no shōhō
士族授産 shizoku jusan

━━━━━ RAD. 冬 34 ━━━━━

冬の陣 fuyu no jin
条 jō (avenue)
条約改正 jōyaku kaisei

━━━━━ RAD. 夕 36 ━━━━━

外山 Tobi (theatrical troupe)
外山正一 Toyama Masaichi
外典 Geten
外典の院 Geten-no-in
外国船打払令 gaikokusen-uchiharai rei
外宮 gekū
外様大名 tozama daimyō
多武峰縁起 Tōnomine Engi
多麻宇良 tama no ura (Onomichi)
多賀城 Taga-jō
名子 nago
名主 myōshu (nanushi)
名主職 myōshu-shiki
名田 myōden
名和長年 Nawa Nagatoshi

━━━━━ RAD. 大 37 ━━━━━

大久保利通 Ōkubo Toshimichi
大久保長安 Ōkubo Nagayasu
大川周明 Ōkawa Shūmei
大内氏 Ōuchi uji
大内氏壁書 Ōuchi-uji Hekisho
大内裏 Daidairi
大内義弘 Ōuchi Yoshihiro
大内義長 Ōuchi Yoshinaga
大内義隆 Ōuchi Yoshitaka
大井憲太郎 Ōi Kentarō
大仁 taijin
大化の改新 Taika no Kaishin
大分 Ōita
大友宗麟 Ōtomo Sōrin
大友皇子 Ōtomo no Ōji
大日本史 Dai Nihon Shi 「Kempō
大日本帝国憲法 Dai Nippon Teikoku
大日本産業報国会 Dai Nippon Sangyō
 Hōkoku-kai
大日如来 Dainichi Nyorai
大代官 dai-daikan
大功田 taikōden
大外記 daigeki
大目付 ōmetsuke
大矢田 Ōyada
大同 Daidō (in Korean, Taedong)
大同団結運動 Daidō Danketsu undō
大同江 Daidōkō (Taedong River)
大名 daimyō
大名飛脚 daimyō-hikyaku
大名領国制 daimyō ryōgoku sei
大安寺 Daian-ji
大庄屋 daishōya
大成教 Taisei-kyō
大成殿 Taisei-den
大江広元 Ōe no Hiromoto
大江匡房 Ōe no Masafusa
大老 tairō
大阪 Ōsaka
大阪の陣 Ōsaka no jin
大阪会議 Ōsaka Kaigi
大阪事件 Ōsaka jiken
大阪城 Ōsaka-jō
大阪商船会社 Ōsaka Shōsen Kaisha
大伴氏 Ōtomo uji
大伴吹負 Ōtomo no Fukehi
大伴金村 Ōtomo no Kanamura
大伴室屋 Ōtomo no Muroya
大伴連 Ōtomo no Muraji
大伴家持 Ōtomo no Yakamochi
大伴旅人 Ōtomo no Tabito

大伴部 Ōtomo-be
大伴黒主 Ōtomo no Kuronushi
大判 ōban
大判座 ōban-za
大村 Ōmura (clan)
大村益次郎 Ōmura Masujirō
大村純忠 Ōmura Sumitada
大社造 taisha-zukuri
大社教 Taisha-kyō
大臣 ō-omi
大谷本願寺 Ōtani Hongan-ji
大東亜共栄圏 Dai Tō-A Kyōeiken
大舎人座 ōtoneri-za
大岡（越前守）忠相 Ōoka (Echizen no Kami) Tadasuke
大国主神 Ōkuninushi no Mikoto
大学 Daigaku
大学令 daigaku rei
大学寮 Daigaku-ryō
大宝律令 Taihō Ritsuryō
大和四座 Yamato-shiza
大和説 Yamato-setsu
大和絵 Yamato-e
大逆事件 daigyaku jiken
大政翼賛会 Taisei Yokusan-kai
大津 Ōtsu
大津絵 Ōtsu-e
大津絵節 Ōtsu-e bushi
大海人皇子 Ōama no Ōji
大連 ō-muraji
大連 Dairen
大院君 Daiinkun
大原社会問題研究所 Ōhara Shakai Mondai Kenkyusho
大原孫三郎 Ōhara Magosaburō
大峯 Ōmine
大将軍 taishōgun
大納言 dainagon
大高持 ōtakamochi
大御所 ōgosho
大野東人 Ōno Azumahito
大黒常是 Daikoku Jōze
大隈重信 Ōkuma Shigenobu
大奥 ō-oku

大湊 Ōminato
大覚寺 Daikaku-ji
大覚寺統 Daikakuji-tō
大番 ōban
大番役 ōban-yaku
大塩平八郎 Ōshio Heihachirō
大聖寺 Daishōji (family)
大義名分 taigi-meibun
大徳 taitoku
大徳寺 Daitoku-ji
大徳冠 taitokukan
大歌所 ōuta-dokoro
大領 tairyō
大槻玄沢 Ōtsuki Gentaku
大毅 taigi
大蔵 ōkura
大蔵省 Ōkura-shō
大蔵経 Daizōkyō
大輪田泊 Ōwada no Tomari
大韓国 Dai Kankoku
大鏡 Ōkagami
太平記 Taiheiki
太占 futomani
太田庄 Ōtashō
太田南畝 Ōta Nampo
太田黒伴雄 Ōtaguro Tomo-o
太安万侶 Ō no Yasumaro
太政大臣 dajō-daijin
太政官 Dajōkan
太政官札 dajōkan-satsu
太宰 dazai
太宰府 Dazaifu
太秦 Uzumasa
太陽のない街 Taiyō no Nai Machi
太陽究理了解説 Taiyō Kyūri Ryōkai-setsu
太閤 taikō
太閤記 taikō-ki
太閤検地 taikō-kenchi
奄美大島 Amami Ōshima
奇口 kikō
奇兵隊 kiheitai
契冲 Keichū
奏者番 sōshaban

獎学院 Shōgakuin

───── RAD. 女 38 ─────

女大学 Onna Daigaku
女真 Nüchen (Juchen, Jürched)
女歌舞伎 Onna Kabuki
奴国 Nakoku (Na no Kuni)
奴婢 nuhi
如拙 Josetsu
好太 Kōtai
好太王碑 Kōtai-ō hi
好色物 kōshoku-mono
妙心寺 Myōshin-ji
姓 kabane
始皇帝 Shih Huang Ti
姥山 Ubayama
婦人参政権 fujin-sansei ken

───── RAD. 子 39 ─────

子方 kokata
子持高杯 komochi-takatsuki
孔王部 Anaho-be
学制発布 gakusei happu
学校令 gakkō rei
学習館 Gakushū-kan
学問のすすめ Gakumon no Susume
学館院 Gakkan'in
孫文 Son Bun (in Chinese, Sun Wen)
孫秉熙 Son Hei-ki (in Korean, Son Byong-hui)

───── RAD. 宀 40 ─────

宇太野 Udano
宇多天皇 Uda Tennō
宇治十帖 Uji jūjō
宇治山田 Uji-Yamada
宇治川 Ujigawa
宇治拾遺物語 Ujishūi Monogatari
宇治茶 Uji-cha
宇津保物語 Utsubo Monogatari
宇喜田秀家 Ukita Hideie

字 aza
守 kami
守戸 shuko
守旧党 Shukyū-tō
守護 shugo
守護大名 shugo daimyō
守護代 shugo-dai
守護領国制 shugo-ryōkoku-sei
守護請 shugo-uke
安土 Azuchi
安土城 Azuchi-jō
安土桃山文化 Azuchi-Momoyama 「bunka
安井算哲 Yasui Santetsu
安田 Yasuda
安和の変 Anna no hen
安政の仮条約 Ansei no kari-jōyaku
安政五ヶ国条約 Ansei Gokakoku Jō- 「yaku
安国寺 Ankoku-ji ⌊yaku
安帝 An Ti
安倍貞任 Abe no Sadatō
安倍晴明 Abe no Seimei
安倍頼時 Abe no Yoritoki
安倍磯雄 Abe Iso-o
安愚楽鍋 Agura-nabe
安徳天皇 Antoku Tennō
安積澹泊 Asaka Tampaku
安藤広重 Andō Hiroshige
安藤信正 Andō Nobumasa
安羅 Anra (Ara)
宝生 Hōshō (Nō school)
宗氏 Sō uji
宗良親王 Munenaga Shinnō
宗学 Sōgaku
宗長 Sōchō 「tsu-chō
宗門改人別帳 shūmon-aratame nimbe-
宗門改役 shūmon-aratame yaku
宗祇 Sōgi
宗銭 Sōsen
官戸 kanko 「bunden
官戸宮奴婢口分田 kanko-kannuhi ku-
官司 kanshi
官田 kanden
官寺 kanji
官有の公奴婢 kan'yū no kunuhi

官有地入会 kan'yūchi-iriai
官省符荘 kanshōfu-shō
定小物成 jō-komononari
定六 jōroku
定助郷 jō-sukegō
定免法 jōmen hō
定朝 Jōchō
実行教 Jikkō-kyō
実語教 Jitsugokyō
室生寺 Murō-ji
室町幕府 Muromachi bakufu
宣明暦 Semmyō-reki
宮内司 Miyanouchi Tsukasa
宮内省 Kunai-shō
宮本屋 Miyamotoya
宮古島 Miyako-jima
宮座 miya-za
宮崎安貞 Miyazaki Yasusada
宮崎湖処子 Miyazaki Koshoshi
家の子 ie no ko
家人 yakahito (kenin)
家父長制 kafuchō-sei
家令 karei
家司 keishi
家守 yamori
家老 karō
家抱 kehō
家法 kahō
家族制度 kazoku seido
家禄 karoku
家督 katoku
密教 Mikkyō
宿老 shukurō
宿屋飯盛 Yadoya no Meshimori
宿駅 shukueki
宿禰 sukune
寄人 yoryūdo
寄進地系荘園 kishinchi-kei shōen
富める百姓 tomeru hyakushō
富士講 Fuji-kō
富寿神宝 Fūju Shimpō
富岡製系工場 Tomioka Seishi Kōjō
富国強兵 fukoku-kyōhei
富樫政親 Togashi Masachika

寛平大宝 Kampyō taihō
寛永通宝 Kan'ei tsūhō
寛政の改革 Kansei no Kaikaku
寛政異学の禁 Kansei igaku no kin
寝殿造 shinden-zukuri
寮 ryō (public affairs bureau)
審海 Shinkai
審祥 Shinshō
憲政会 Kensei-kai
憲政党 Kensei-tō
憲政擁護運動 kensei-yōgo undō

——— RAD. 寸 41 ———

封戸 fuko (fugo)
封建社会制度 hōken shakai seido
専修寺派 Senshūji-ha

——— RAD. 小 42 ———

小山内薫 Osanai Kaoru
小川未明 Ogawa Mimei
小玉 kodama
小玉銀 kodama-gin
小田 Oda (castle town)
小田原 Odawara
小田原征伐 Odawara seibatsu
小田原評定 Odawara hyōjō
小作料 kosakuryō
小判 koban
小坂 Osaka
小村寿太郎 Komura Jutarō
小林一茶 Kobayashi Issa
小牧 Komaki
小物成 komononari
小室信夫 Komuro Shinobu
小島法師 Kojima Hōshi
小唄 kouta
小浜 Obama
小堀遠州 Kobori Enshū
小笠原貞頼 Ogasawara Sadayori
小笠原諸島 Ogasawara Shotō
小粒銀 kotsubu-gin
小野 Ono (corporation)
小野小町 Ono no Komachi

小野岑守 Ono no Minemori
小野妹子 Ono no Imoko
小野流 Ono-ryū (Shingon branch)
小野梓 Ono Azusa
小野道風 Ono no Tōfū (Michikaze)
小野篁 Ono no Takamura
小徳 shōtoku
小説神髄 Shōsetsu Shinzui
小関三英 Ozeki San'ei
小領 shōryō
小毅 shōgi
光 Hikari (newspaper)
光孝天皇 Kōkō Tennō
光武帝 Kuang Wu Ti
光明天皇 Kōmyō Tennō
光源氏 Hikaru Genji
光緒 Kuang Hsü
当世書生気質 Tōsei Shosei-katagi
肖柏 Shōhaku
尚泰 Shōtai
尚書 Shōsho
尚歯会 Shōshi-kai
県主 agata-nushi
党 tō (warriors' corporation)
党生活者 Tō-seikatsusha
常行三昧 Jōgyō-zammai
堂島 Dōjima
堂島米市場 Dōjima kome ichiba

━━━━━━ RAD. 尸 44 ━━━━━━

尺八 shakuhachi
尼子義久 Amako Yoshihisa
尼港事件 Ni-Kō jiken
尾山 Oyama
尾崎行雄 Ozaki Yukio
尾崎紅葉 Ozaki Kōyō
尾張 Owari (clan)
尾張国郡司百姓等解文 Owari-no-kuni
  gunji hyakushō-ra gebumi
尾道 Onomichi
屈葬 kussō
屋久島 Yakushima
屋代弘賢 Yashiro Hirokata

━━━━━━ RAD. 山 46 ━━━━━━

山へ遊びにやる yama e asobi ni yaru
山下幸内 Yamashita Kōnai
山上憶良 Yamanoue (Yamanoe) no
山口 Yamaguchi   ⌞Okura
山内 Yamanouchi   ⌐ron)
山井鼎 (崑崙) Yamanoi Kanae (Kon-
山水屏風 senzui byōbu
山王 Sannō
山田奉行 Yamada bugyō
山田長政 Yamada Nagamasa
山田美妙 Yamada Bimyō
山年貢 yama-nengu
山伏 yamabushi
山名 Yamana
山名氏清 Yamana Ujikiyo
山名持豊 Yamana Mochitoyo
山東出兵 Santō shuppei
山東京伝 Santō Kyōden
山東問題 Santō mondai
山門 Sammon
山背大兄王 Yamashiro no Ōe no Ō
山県有朋 Yamagata Aritomo
山科本願寺 Yamashina Hongan-ji
山陰道 San'indō
山崎宗鑑 Yamazaki Sōkan
山崎闇斎 Yamazaki Ansai
山陽道 San'yōdō
山鹿 Yamaga
山鹿素行 Yamaga Sokō
岩倉具視 Iwakura Tomomi
岩崎弥太郎 Iwasaki Yatarō
崇伝 Sūden
崇神天皇 Sujin Tennō
崇神紀 Sujin-gi
崇徳天皇 Sutoku Tennō
嵯峨 Saga
嵯峨天皇 Saga Tennō

━━━━━━ RAD. 川 47 ━━━━━━

川尻 Kawajiri
川柳 senryū

川柳点 senryū-ten
順帝 Shun Ti

——————— RAD. 工 48 ———————

工部大学校 Kōbu Daigakkō
工部省 Kōbu-shō
工部美術学校 Kōbu Bijutsu Gakkō
工藤平助 Kudō Heisuke
工藤祐経 Kudō Suketsune
功田 kōden
功封 kōfu
左大弁 sadaiben
左大臣 sadaijin
左中弁 sachūben
左少弁 sashōben
左右大少史 sau-daishōshi
左右大少外記 sau-daishōgeki
左右大臣 saudaijin
左右近衛 sau-konoe
左右京職 sau-kyōshiki
左右検非違使庁 sau-kebiishi-chō
左右衛士府 sau-eji-fu
左伝 Saden
左兵衛 sahyōe
左京 Sakyō
左京職 sakyō-shiki
左院 Sa-in
左衛士 saeji
貢士 kōshi
貢租 kōso

——————— RAD. 己 49 ———————

忌寸 imiki
忌部 Imbe (Imibe)
改進党 Kaishin-tō
改新の詔 kaishin no shō

——————— RAD. 巾 50 ———————

帆足万里 Hoashi Banri
帷幄上奏権 iaku jōsō-ken

——————— RAD. 干 51 ———————

干支 kanshi

——————— RAD. 幺 52 ———————

畿内 Kinai

——————— RAD. 广 53 ———————

広田弘毅 Hirota Kōki
広田社 Hirota-sha
広沢流 Hirozawa-ryū
広島 Hiroshima
広隆寺 Kōryū-ji
広報協会 Kōhō Kyōkai
広開土王 Kōkaido-ō
庄屋 shōya
床間 tokonoma
応天門の変 Ōtemmon no hen
応仁の乱 Ōnin no Ran
応永の外寇 Ōei no gaikō
応永の乱 Ōei no ran
応神天皇 Ōjin Tennō
応挙 Ōkyo (=Maruyama Ōkyo)
庚午年籍 Kōgo nenjaku
庚申 kanoe-saru
庚申侍 kōshin-machi
庚申講 kōshin-kō
府内 Funai
店借 tanagari
店借人 tanagari-bito
店請人 tanauke-nin
店請状 tanauke-jō
度会神道 Watarai Shintō
庭訓往来 Teikin-ōrai
座 za
唐招提寺 Tōshōdai-ji
唐物 tōmotsu (karamono)
唐門 Karamon
唐絵 Kara-e
唐様 Kara-yō
康有為 K'ang Yu-wei
庸 yō

庶物類纂 Shobutsu Ruisan
廃藩置県 haihan-chiken
慶安の御触書 Keian no o-furegaki
慶応義塾 Keiō Gijuku 「eki
慶長と元和の役 Keichō to Genna no
鷹司 Takatsukasa (Fujiwara branch)
鷹匠 Taka-jō

━━━━━ RAD. 廴 54 ━━━━━

延喜式 Engi-shiki
延喜通宝 Engi tsūhō
延喜格 Engi-kyaku
延暦寺 Enryaku-ji
建仁寺 Kennin-ji
建武中興 Kemmu no Chūkō
建長寺 Kenchō-ji
建御賀豆智命 Takemikazuchi no Mikoto

━━━━━ RAD. 弋 56 ━━━━━

式 shiki
式亭三馬 Shikitei Samba
式楽 shikigaku

━━━━━ RAD. 弓 57 ━━━━━

弓月君 Yuzuki no Kimi
弓弭調 yuhazu no mitsugi
引付衆 hikitsuke-shū
引付頭人 hikitsuke-tōnin
弘仁 Kōnin
弘仁式 Kōnin-shiki
弘仁格 Kōnin-kyaku
弘文天皇 Kōbun Tennō
弘文院 Kōbun-in
弘文館 Kōbun-kan
弘安の役 Kōan no eki
弘法大師 Kōbō Daishi
弘法大師絵伝 Kōbō Daishi Eden
弘道会 Kōdō-kai
弘道館 Kōdō-kan
弘道館記 Kōdōkanki

弘道館記述義 Kōdōkan Kijutsugi
弥生 Yayoi
弥生式 Yayoi-shiki
弥生式土器 Yayoi-shiki doki
弥生時代 Yayoi jidai
弥勒菩薩半跏像 Miroku Bosatsu Hanka
Zō
張学良 Chang Hsüeh-liang
張鼓峰 Chōkohō (in Chinese, Changkufeng)
張鼓峰事件 Chōkohō jiken
強訴 gōso
弾正台 danjōdai

━━━━━ RAD. 彡 59 ━━━━━

彰考館 Shōkō-kan
彰義隊 Shōgitai

━━━━━ RAD. 彳 60 ━━━━━

役小角 En no Ozuno (En no Ozunu,
En no Shōkaku)
征夷大将軍 seii-taishōgun
征韓論 seikan-ron
往生要集 Ōjōyōshū
往来物 ōrai-mono
律 ritsu (penal code)
律令 ritsuryō
律令制 ritsuryō-sei
律宗 Risshū
後二条天皇 Gonijō Tennō
後三年の役 Go-sannen no Eki
後三条天皇 Gosanjō Tennō
後小松天皇 Gokomatsu Tennō
後北条 Gohōjō (Odawara Hōjō)
後白河天皇 Goshirakawa Tennō
後伏見天皇 Gofushimi Tennō
後宇多天皇 Gouda Tennō
後村上天皇 Gomurakami Tennō
後家倒 goke-daoshi
後深草天皇 Gofukakusa Tennō
後陽成天皇 Goyōzei Tennō
後鳥羽天皇 Gotoba Tennō

後亀山天皇 Gokameyama Tennō
後嵯峨天皇 Gosaga Tennō
後漢書 Gokanjo or Gokansho (in Chinese, *Hou Han Shu*)
後漢書倭伝 Gokanjo Waden
後醍醐天皇 Godaigo Tennō
後藤吉五郎 Gotō Kichigorō
後藤光次 Gotō Mitsutsugu
後藤象二郎 Gotō Shōjirō
徐昂 Jo Kō (in Chinese, Hsü Ang)
従一位 jū-ichii
徒弟制度 totei-seido
徒然草 Tsurezuregusa
御三家 go-sanke
御三卿 go-sankyō
御子代 mikoshiro
御用部屋 goyōbeya
御用聞 goyōkiki
御名代 minashiro
御成敗式目 Goseibai Shikimoku
御岳教 Mitake-kyō
御定書百箇条 O-sadamegaki Hyakkajō
御師 o-shi
御家人 go-kenin
御家流 Oie-ryū
御茶師 o-chashi
御輿 mikoshi
徭分 yōbun
徭分銭 yōbunsen
徭役 yōeki
徭銭 yōsen
徳 toku (rank)
徳川吉宗 Tokugawa Yoshimune
徳川光圀 Tokugawa Mitsukuni
徳川秀忠 Tokugawa Hidetada
徳川斉昭 Tokugawa Nariaki
徳川家光 Tokugawa Iemitsu
徳川家茂 Tokugawa Iemochi
徳川家斉 Tokugawa Ienari
徳川家宣 Tokugawa Ienobu
徳川家康 Tokugawa Ieyasu
徳川家綱 Tokugawa Ietsuna
徳川幕府 Tokugawa bakufu
徳川徳松 Tokugawa Tokumatsu

徳川綱吉 Tokugawa Tsunayoshi
徳川慶喜 Tokugawa Yoshinobu
徳川慶福 Tokugawa Yoshitomi
徳永直 Tokunaga Sunao
徳田球一 Tokuda Kyūichi
徳政 tokusei
徳政一揆 tokusei-ikki
徳政令 tokusei-rei
徳富蘆花 Tokutomi Roka
徳富蘇峰 Tokutomi Sohō
徴士 chōshi
徴兵令 chōhei-rei
衛士 eji
衛府 efu
衛門 emon
衛門府 emon-fu
衛満 Wei Man

———— RAD. 心 61 ————

心太 tokoroten
心学 shingaku
心敬 Shinkei
忍岡 Shinobugaoka
恭仁京 Kuni-kyō
恭譲 Kyōjō (in Korean, Kong Yang)
恵心僧都 Eshin Sōzu
恵日 Enichi
恵果 Keika
恒貞親王 Tsunesada Shinnō
恩地 onchi
恩給地 onkyū-chi
恩賞方 onshō-kata
恩賞地 onshō-chi
惣村 sōson
惣領 sōryō
惟宗直本 Koremune Naomoto
愚管抄 Gukanshō
慎機論 Shinki-ron
慧思 Hui Ssu
慧灌 Ekan
懐良親王 Kanenaga Shinnō
懐風藻 Kaifūsō
懐徳堂 Kaitoku-dō

━━━ RAD. 戈 62 ━━━

戊戌政変 Bojutsu seihen
戊辰戦役 Boshin sen'eki
成功 jōgō
成実宗 Jōjitsu-shū
戒律 kairitsu
威海衛 Ikaiei (in Chinese, Weihaiwei)
戦国大名 sengoku daimyō
戦国時代 Sengoku jidai
戦記物 senki-mono
戦旗 Senki (magazine)

━━━ RAD. 戸 63 ━━━

戸 ko
戸毎調 komaichō
戸籍 koseki
戻す modosu (infanticide)
房戸 bōko
所司 shoshi
所司代 shoshidai
扇谷 Ōgigayatsu
扇拍子 ōgi-byōshi
扇面古写経 semmen koshakyō

━━━ RAD. 手 64 ━━━

手工業 shukōgyō
手末調 tanasue no mitsugi
手実 shujitsu
手島堵庵 Tejima Toan
打毀し uchi-kowashi
扶桑教 Fusō-kyō
抗州 K'angchow
投入れ nageire
押領使 ōryōshi
按察使 azechi
持明院統 Jimyōin-tō
持統天皇 Jitō Tennō
指出 sashidashi
堀内 hori no uchi
堀田正俊 Hotta Masatoshi
堀越 Horikoshi

堀越公方 Horikoshi kubō
排仏毀釈 haibutsu-kishaku
排日運動 hai-Nichi undō
探題 tandai
推古天皇 Suiko Tennō
掛屋 kakeya
揚浜式 agehama-shiki
摂政 sesshō
摂家将軍 sekke-shōgun
摂関政治 sekkan-seiji
撰銭 erizeni
撰銭令 erizeni-rei
撫順 Fushun
攘夷決行の大号令 jōi kekkō no daigōrei
攘夷論 jōi-ron

━━━ RAD. 支 65 ━━━

支那党 Shina-tō
支倉常長 Hasekura Tsunenaga

━━━ RAD. 攵 66 ━━━

政友会 Seiyū-kai
政体書 Seitaisho
政所 Mandokoro
政治小説 seiji shōsetsu
政教社 Seikyō-sha
敏達天皇 Bidatsu (Bitatsu) Tennō
救世観音 Kuze Kannon (Guze Kannon)
救済 Guzai (Gusai, Guzei)
教王護国寺 Kyōōgokoku-ji
教如 Kyōnyo
教行信証 Kyōgyōshinshō
教育令 kyōiku rei
教育勅語 Kyōiku Chokugo
教育基本法 Kyōiku Kihonhō
教派神道 Kyōha Shintō
教部省 Kyōbu-shō
敦賀 Tsuruga
敬神党 Keishin-tō
散小物成 chiri-komononari

──────── RAD. 文 67 ────────

文 mon (coin denomination)
文人 fumihito
文人画 bunjin-ga
文化文政時代 Bunka-Bunsei jidai
文永の役 Bun'ei no eki
文忌寸 fumi no imiki
文芸協会 Bungei Kyōkai
文芸戦線 Bungei Sensen
文武天皇 Mommu Tennō
文学界 Bungakukai (Bungakkai)
文明開化 bummei kaika
文明論の概略 Bummeiron no Gairyaku
文屋康秀 Fun'ya no Yasuhide
文首 fumi no obito
文展 Bunten
文華秀麗集 Bunka Shūreishū
文章 monjō
文章博士 monjō-hakase
文禄慶長の役 Bunroku-Keichō no eki
文覚 Mongaku
対日理事会 Tai-Nichi Rijikai
対日講和条約 Tai-Nichi Kōwa Jōyaku
対屋 tai-no-ya
対島 Tsushima

──────── RAD. 斗 68 ────────

斗 to (measure of capacity)

──────── RAD. 斤 69 ────────

斯波氏 Shiba uji
斯波義敏 Shiba Yoshitoshi
斯波義廉 Shiba Yoshikado
新井白石 Arai Hakuseki
新日本文学 Shin Nihon Bungaku
新古今和歌集 Shin Kokin Wakashū
新古今調 Shin Kokin-chō
新田開発 shinden kaihatsu
新田義貞 Nitta Yoshisada
新体詩 shintai-shi
新居浜 Niihama

新思潮 Shinshichō
新紀元 Shin-kigen
新島裏 Niijima Jō
新恩 shin'on
新渡戸稲造 Nitobe Inazō
新葉和歌集 Shin'yō Wakashū
新補地頭 shimpo jitō
新義真言宗 Shingi Shingon-shū
新聞紙条令 shimbunshi jōrei
新撰姓氏録 Shinsen Shōji-roku
新撰組 shinsen-gumi
新撰菟玖波集 Shinsen Tsukubashū
新論 Shinron
新羅 Shiragi (in Korean, Silla)
新羅征伐 Shiragi seibatsu

──────── RAD. 方 70 ────────

方丈記 Hōjōki
方広寺 Hōkō-ji
方違 kata-gatae
施薬院 Seyaku-in
旅順 Ryojun
旋頭歌 sedōka
旗本 hatamoto

──────── RAD. 日 72 ────────

日ソ中立条約 Nisso Chūritsu Jōyaku
日仏軍事協定 Nichi-Futsu Gunji Kyō- ⌊tei
日本人 Nihonjin (magazine)
日本三代実録 Nihon Sandai Jitsuroku
日本文徳天皇実録 Nihon Montoku Tennō Jitsuroku
日本永代蔵 Nihon Eitai-gura
日本外史 Nihon-gaishi
日本共産党 Nippon Kyōsan-tō ⌈tō
日本労働農民党 Nippon Rōdō Nōmin-
日本労働総同盟 Nippon Rōdō Sōdōmei
日本労農党 Nippon Rōnō-tō
日本町 Nihon-machi
日本社会党 Nippon Shakai-tō
日本武尊 Yamato Takeru no Mikoto

日本国現報善悪霊異記　Nihonkoku
　Gempō Zen'aku Ryōiki
日本国憲法 Nihonkoku Kempō
日本府 Nihon-fu
日本後紀 Nihon Kōki
日本紀 Nihongi
日本書記 Nihon Shoki 「bushiki-gaisha
日本郵船株式会社 Nippon Yūsen Ka-
日本開化小史 Nippon Kaika Shōshi
日本鉄道会社 Nippon Tetsudō-gaisha
日本総同盟友愛会　Nihon　Sōdōmei
日本製鉄 Nippon Seitetsu 「Yūai-kai
日本銀行 Nippon Ginkō
日本霊異記 Nihon Ryōiki
日本興業銀行 Nippon Kōgyō Ginkō
日吉神社 Hie-jinja
日光 Nikkō
日光街道 Nikkōkaidō
日米会談 Nichi-Bei kaidan
日米安全保障条約 Nichi-Bei Anzen-ho-
　shō Jōyaku　　　　　　　　「yaku
日米和親条約　Nichi-Bei　Washin　Jō-
日知館 Nitchi-kan
日英同盟 Nichi-Ei Dōmei
日独伊三国同盟 Nichi-Doku-I Sango-
日華事変 Nikka jihen 　　「ku Dōmei
日清戦争 Nisshin Sensō
日野 Hino
日野俊基 Hino Toshimoto
日野資朝 Hino Suketomo
日蓮 Nichiren
日蓮宗 Nichiren-shū
日親 Nisshin
日新館 Nisshin-kan
日露戦争 Nichi-Ro Sensō 「ichi Kajō
早雲寺殿二十一箇条 Sounji-dono Nijū-
早稲田大学 Waseda Daigaku
昌平坂 Shōheizaka
昌平学校 Shōhei Gakkō
昌平校 Shōheikō
昆明 K'unming
易経 Ekikyō
明六社 Meiroku-sha
明六雑誌 Meiroku Zasshi

明兆 Minchō
明治天皇 Meiji Tennō
明治維新 Meiji Ishin
明法 myōbō
明法道 myōhōdō
明星 Myōjō
明星派 Myōjō-ha
明珍 Myōchin
明倫堂 Meirin-dō
明倫館 Meirin-kan
明恵 Myōe
明経 myōgyō
明智光秀 Akechi Mitsuhide
明徳の乱 Meitoku no ran
春日山 Kasugayama
春日県 Kasuga no Agata
春日県主 Kasuga no agata-nushi
春日神社 Kasuga-jinja
春日造 Kasuga-zukuri
春日野町 Kasuganochō
春日権現霊験記 Kasuga Gongen Rei-
　genki　　　　　　　　　　「sono
春色辰巳園 Shunshoku Tatsumi-no-
春色梅暦 Shunshoku Umegoyomi
春屋妙葩 Shun'oku Myōha
春秋 Shunjū
春陽会 Shun'yō-kai
春慶 Shunkei
春慶塗 Shunkei-nuri
時代物 jidaimono
時宗 Ji-shū
時門宗 Jimon-shū
時習館 Jishū-kan
曼陀羅 mandara
曹洞宗 Sōtō-shū
替米 kaemai
替銭 kaezeni
替銭屋 kaezeni-ya
景戒 Keikai
智 chi (rank)
智恵内子 Chie no Naishi
智積院 Chishaku-in
智顗 Chih I
最上徳内 Mogami Tokunai

最恵国条款 saikeikoku jōkan
最高裁判所 Saikō Saibansho
最澄 Saichō

─────── RAD. 月 74 ───────

月光 Gakkō (Bodhisattva)
月行事 tsuki-gyōji

─────── RAD. 木 75 ───────

木下尚江 Kinoshita Naoe
木戸孝允 Kido Takayoshi
木津 Kizu
木津川 Kizugawa
札差 fudasashi
札幌 Sapporo
札幌農学校 Sapporo Nōgakkō
李朱 Li-Chu (medicinal art)
李成桂 Ri Sei-kei (in Korean, Yi
　Song-gye)　　　　　「Sung-man)
李承晩 Ri Shō-ban (in Korean, Lee
李東坦 Li Tung-t'an
李参平 Ri Sam-pei (in Korean, Yi
　Sam-p'yong)　　　「Hung-chang)
李鴻章 Ri Kō-shō (in Chinese, Li
杉田玄白 Sugita Gempaku
杉原紙 Sugihara-gami
村上天皇 Murakami Tennō
村山宗兵衛 Murayama Sōbei
村中入会 sonchū-iriai
村方三役 murakata san'yaku
村方役人 murakata yakunin
村年寄 mura-doshiyori
村役人 mura yakunin
村座 mura-za
杵築大社 Kizuki Taisha
枢密院 Sūmitsu-in
枕草子 Makura no Sōshi
林子平 Hayashi Shihei
林春斎 Hayashi Shunsai
林梅桐 Hayashi Baidō
林道春 Hayashi Dōshun
林鳳岡 Hayashi Hōkō

林羅山 Hayashi Razan
松下村塾 Shōka-sonjuku
松井須磨子 Matsui Sumako
松方正義 Matsukata Masayoshi
松平定信 Matsudaira Sadanobu
松平信綱 Matsudaira Nobutsuna
松平容保 Matsudaira Katamori
松平康英 Matsudaira Yasuhide
松平慶永 Matsudaira Yoshinaga
松本圭堂 Matsumoto Keidō
松永久秀 Matsunaga Hisahide
松永貞徳 Matsunaga Teitoku
松尾芭蕉 Matsuo Bashō
松村呉春 Matsumura Goshun
松前 Matsumae (family)
松前町 Matsumae-machi
松前奉行 Matsumae bugyō
松島剛 Matsushima Tsuyoshi
松倉重政 Matsukura Shigemasa
松浦 Matsuura (family)
板垣退助 Itagaki Taisuke
板倉重宗 Itakura Shigemune
板倉重昌 Itakura Shigemasa
板倉勝重 Itakura Katsushige
柵 ki　　　　　　　　　　「kou)
柳条溝 Ryūjōkō (in Chinese, Liut'iao-
柳沢吉保 Yanagisawa Yoshiyasu
柄井川柳 Karai Senryū
栄西 Eisai
栄華物語 Eiga Monogatari
相川町 Aikawa-machi
相阿弥 Sōami
相国寺 Shōkoku-ji
桐一葉 Kiri Hitoha
桐生 Kiryū
柴四郎 Shiba Shirō
柴田勝家 Shibata Katsuie
柴田鳩翁 Shibata Kyūō
柴野栗山 Shibano Ritsuzan
桂川甫周 Katsuragawa Hoshū
桂太郎 Katsura Tarō
桂昌院 Keishōin
桂宮 Katsuranomiya
桂離宮 Katsura Rikyū